The Works of William James

Editors
Frederick H. Burkhardt, General Editor
Fredson Bowers, Textual Editor
Ignas K. Skrupskelis, Associate Editor

*This edition of the Works of William James
is sponsored by the American Council of
Learned Societies*

Introduction to this volume by
William R. Woodward

William James c. 1894

photograph by Mrs. Montgomery Sears;
courtesy Houghton Library, Harvard University

Essays in Psychology

William James

HARVARD UNIVERSITY PRESS
Cambridge, Massachusetts
and London, England
1983

CENTER FOR
SCHOLARLY EDITIONS
AN APPROVED EDITION
MODERN LANGUAGE
ASSOCIATION OF AMERICA

Library of Congress Cataloging in Publication Data

James, William, 1842–1910.
Essays in psychology.

(The Works of William James)
Includes bibliographical references and index.
1. Psychology—Addresses, essays, lectures. I. Title.
II. Series: James, William, 1842–1910. Works. 1975.
BF149.J34   1983   150   83–8452
ISBN 0–674–26714–1

Foreword

This edition of *Essays in Psychology* brings together all of James's shorter psychological writings for professional and popular journals, with the exception of the articles that he republished in revised but substantially intact form in *The Principles of Psychology* and his articles on psychical research, which will be published in a forthcoming volume of THE WORKS OF WILLIAM JAMES to be devoted entirely to that subject. The twenty-nine pieces consist of essays, letters to editors, an encyclopedia article, and introductions to books by Boris Sidis and Edward L. Thorndike, whose works James admired. They are printed in chronological order, ranging from "Brute and Human Intellect," which was written in 1878, before James set to work on *The Principles of Psychology*, to "On Some Mental Effects of the Earthquake," of 1906.

William R. Woodward, Associate Professor of Psychology at the University of New Hampshire, in his Introduction discusses the sources of James's psychological ideas, how he developed them into a scientific psychology, and how James's view of psychology as a natural science was related to his philosophical and humanistic world-view.

This volume is the eleventh title and the thirteenth volume in THE WORKS OF WILLIAM JAMES. It has been edited in accordance with the editorial policy of the edition as a whole. Briefly stated, that policy employs the principles and techniques of modern textual criticism to provide an authoritative text that represents as closely as possible James's final intentions. The policy is described in detail in the Note on the Editorial Method by Fredson Bowers, Linden Kent Professor of English, Emeritus, at the University of Virginia, the Textual Editor of the WORKS. Professor Bowers also provides a discussion of the texts and their source documents, together with a textual apparatus that will enable scholars to reconstruct the documents used in the editing.

The reference Notes to the text have been prepared by Professor Ignas K. Skrupskelis of the University of South Carolina, who also contributed to the documentation of the publishing history of the essays.

Nine of the essays in this volume are closely related to James's masterpiece, *The Principles of Psychology*, the writing of which occupied him for a period of twelve years. During that time he submitted some of the chapters for publication as separate articles in various journals, chiefly *Mind* and the *Journal of Speculative Philosophy*. Seven of these journal articles were used in their entirety in *Principles*. The nine articles in the present volume, however, were extensively revised before publication in *Principles*, some were divided among several chapters, and some portions were omitted entirely. These articles are included in the present volume in the form in which they appeared in the journals. To aid the reader interested in the changes James made in them for *Principles*, the apparatus provides references to the passages that were used, together with their substantive variants. The articles are listed below in the order of their composition, and the chapters of *Principles* in which the material of the essays was used are given.

"Brute and Human Intellect"	1878	XIII, XXII
"Are We Automata?"	1879	V, IX
"The Spatial Quale"	1879	XX
"The Feeling of Effort"	1880	XXVI
"On Some Omissions of Introspective Psychology"	1884	VII, IX, XII
"What Is an Emotion?"	1884	XXV
"Report of the Committee on Hypnotism"	1886	XXII, XXVII
"What the Will Effects"	1888	XXVI
"The Hidden Self"	1890	VIII, X

Foreword

The editors wish to express their indebtedness to the following institutions and individuals for their help in the preparation of *Essays in Psychology*:

The National Endowment for the Humanities has provided generous grants for the editorial work on this volume, as it has for all the other volumes of this edition of THE WORKS OF WILLIAM JAMES.

The Barra Foundation made a matching grant in support of this and forthcoming volumes of the edition.

Alexander James and Dr. William Bond of the Houghton Library have granted permission to use and reproduce printed and manuscript texts and illustrations in the William James Collection at Harvard University.

The staff members of the Houghton Library Reading Room and of the Reference Room of the Alderman Library of the University of Virginia have given the editors efficient assistance with their research problems.

The University of South Carolina has provided the Associate Editor with research assistance and working space.

The Harvard Medical Library in the Francis A. Countway Library of Medicine provided a letter from James to J. J. Putnam bearing on "Are We Automata?"

The Department of Manuscripts and University Archives of Cornell University made available a postcard from James to Jacob Gould Schurman and two letters from James to E. B. Titchener.

The Bancroft Library of the University of California at Berkeley provided letters from James to George M. Stratton and J. Mark Baldwin.

The Library of Congress furnished a postcard and a note from James to James McKeen Cattell.

The Henry Holt Archives, Princeton University Library, provided a note from James to Henry Holt.

Dr. George F. Farr, Jr., gave friendly advice to the editors throughout his tenure in the Division of Research Grants of the National Endowment for the Humanities.

Audrone Skrupskelis assisted the Associate Editor in bibliographical and reference research.

Christine Guyonneau assisted with the French essay, "Réponse de M. W. James aux remarques de M. Renouvier."

Anne Schlabach Burkhardt helped as an advisor on James's philosophical views.

Charlotte Bowman contributed her services as Administrative Assistant to the General Editor.

The labor of checking, proofreading, and preparing the volume for the printer was carried out with great patience and accuracy by Elizabeth Berkeley, Wilma Bradbeer, Mary Mikalson, and Judith Nelson, under the supervision of Anne McCoy, the Editorial Coordinator of the project.

Frederick H. Burkhardt

Contents

Contents

Introduction

by

William R. Woodward

The essays in this volume, now brought together for the first time, are a unique record of the maturing of William James's psychological thought. Many of the ideas of his earliest essays were reworked in the more comprehensive and systematic work, *The Principles of Psychology*. After 1890 his continuing and developing interests in hypnosis, secondary personalities, language, and "saving sick souls" are prominent in the essays. As a record of the genesis and growth of both James's psychology and philosophy, the essays bring the reader close to his sources, and thereby illuminate his indebtedness to others and his own departures from tradition.[1]

One of these departures is succinctly expressed in the short essay "A Plea for Psychology as a 'Natural Science,'" published in 1892. Composed in reply to a hostile review of *Principles* by George Trumbull Ladd of Yale University,[2] James's essay argues for a radically new approach to explanation in psychology. The proper concern of psychology is with that aspect of our being "which falls

[1] For further background on James's early career, see Ralph Barton Perry, *The Thought and Character of William James* (Boston: Little, Brown, 1935); Sheldon Stern, "William James and the New Psychology," in Paul Buck, ed., *Social Sciences at Harvard: 1860–1920* (Cambridge, Mass.: Harvard University Press, 1965); and James William Anderson, "'The Worst Kind of Melancholy': William James in 1869," *Harvard Library Bulletin*, 30 (1982), 369–386.

[2] George Trumbull Ladd, "Psychology as So-Called 'Natural Science,'" *Philosophical Review*, 1 (1892), 24–53.

wholly within the sphere of natural history"—with those conscious states that are "temporal events," whose causes "lie certainly in large part in the physical world" (*Essays in Psychology*, hereafter *EPs*, p. 272).

Opposing the old division of "rational" (philosophical) and "empirical" psychology (both often practiced by the same inquirer, such as Ladd himself), James advocated a decisive abandonment by psychologists of questions relating to soul, transcendental ego, and mind stuff—questions that he believed should be left to philosophers, whose enterprise was of a different character. Prediction and control of behavior, the analysis and correction of conduct, derived little benefit from the concepts of general philosophy, which tended to be "barren of particular consequences" (*EPs*, p. 274, n. 3). By contrast, philosophers and psychologists had much to learn about the logic of controlled investigation from the practical approaches of biology, medicine, and even psychical research. As Ernest Nagel has clarified this logic for the social sciences in our time, it is essentially an extension of the experiment: one holds constant certain conditions and observes the effect on the phenomenon of varying other ones.[3]

Few readers of James would deny that he also places a heavy reliance upon the description of mental states as they appear in consciousness, a method quite different from controlled investigation. James was equally emphatic on this point in "A Plea for Psychology as a 'Natural Science.'" "Cannot philosophers and biologists both become 'psychologists' on this common basis? Cannot both forego ulterior inquiries, and agree that, provisionally at least, the mental state shall be the ultimate datum so far as 'psychology' cares to go?" (*EPs*, p. 274). There is little doubt that James opposed the reduction of psychological phenomena to biological or philosophical terms. In his advocacy of description as well as explanation, he helped prepare the way for a new discipline,

3 Ernest Nagel, *The Structure of Science* (New York: Harcourt, Brace & World, 1961), pp. 452–455. Since Nagel here credits John Stuart Mill as the "foremost advocate" of applying the logic of the natural sciences to the social sciences, it is important to be aware of James's departure from Mill. In his copy of John Stuart Mill, *A System of Logic* (London: Longmans, Green, Reader & Dyer, 1872), p. 448, James wrote that "Mill treats these [inductive methods] as if they were mainly methods of *discovering* causes. 9 times out of 10 they are used merely for *testing* causes hypothetically conceived."

one which would have a foot not only in the sciences but also in the humanities.[4]

The secondary literature on James does not always preserve this fruitful tension. Much of the James commentary is written from the point of view of either "functional psychology" or "phenomenological psychology." By simply drawing upon insights of both James interpretations here, we may come closer to realizing that James's ability to hold the two approaches in a "productive paradox" was a better paradigm for the significant study of psychology than either would be alone.[5]

Modern psychology, of course, is firmly committed to the assumption that man evolved from simpler orders of life and indeed that mental behavior is to be conceived in evolutionary terms. In Anglo-American thought, the dichotomy between the principles of physiological psychology and mental philosophy, between the study of the body and that of the mind, was very sharp. It was believed that if Darwinian theory were to be accepted, this cleavage would have to be modified and even the human mind and spirit would require interpretation as products of evolutionary forces.[6]

---

[4] Andrew J. Reck, *Introduction to William James: An Essay and Selected Texts* (Bloomington: Indiana University Press, 1967), pp. 85–86, concludes that "a return to James's thought today may serve to bridge the gulf which . . . divides Europe from America, correcting in Europe the excesses of existentialism and in America the excesses of scientism." Evidence that this has begun to occur is found in Don S. Browning, *Pluralism and Personality: William James and Some Contemporary Cultures of Psychology* (Lewisburg, Pa.: Bucknell University Press, 1980), pp. 32–33, 64–86; and Jürgen Habermas, *Knowledge and Human Interests* (London: Heinemann, 1972 [1968], pp. 91–139 (albeit on C. S. Peirce rather than James). See note 42. See especially William J. Gavin, "William James' Philosophy of Science," *The New Scholasticism*, 52 (1978), 413–420.

[5] Gordon W. Allport, "The Productive Paradoxes of William James," *Psychological Review*, 50 (January 1943), 95–120. Allport was one psychologist who seriously tried to sustain this paradox. Cf. Richard P. High and William R. Woodward, "William James and Gordon Allport: Parallels in Their Maturing Conceptions of Self and Personality," in Robert W. Rieber and Kurt Salzinger, eds., *Psychology: Theoretical-Historical Perspectives* (New York: Academic Press, 1980), pp. 57–59.

[6] Frank M. Turner, *Between Science and Religion: The Reaction to Scientific Naturalism in Late Victorian England* (New Haven: Yale University Press, 1974). The continuing interest in mental evolution of sociobiologists in Great Britain and North America is reflected in Robert J. Richards, "Darwin and the Biologizing of Moral Behavior," in William R. Woodward and Mitchell G. Ash, eds., *The Problematic Science: Psychology in Nineteenth-Century Thought* (New York: Praeger, 1982), pp. 43–64. For a Continental critique of this preoccupation with mental instead of

Introduction

The exploration of the theoretical implications of evolution, of the hypotheses of chance variation and natural selection for a broad range of intellectual concerns, was a task informally undertaken in the 1860s and 70s by a small group of scholars living in the vicinity of Harvard. Later called the Metaphysical Club by Charles Sanders Peirce, its members included James, Peirce, Oliver Wendell Holmes, Jr., and several others.

James's first psychological essay, "Brute and Human Intellect," published in 1878, reflects the elaboration of the central tenets of Darwin's theory into a theory of mental development, one of the topics frequently discussed by the Metaphysical Club. In the position that James takes here may be discerned the influence of the three major intellectual traditions that were conjoined in the thinking 'of the Club's members. These were Darwinism, British associationism, and the Kantian philosophy of science. The Kantian influence is generally underestimated in studies of the thought of this group.[7]

In this essay James undertook to define the nature of reasoning, the activity traditionally regarded as distinctively human. Rejecting, as might be expected, any sharp bifurcation of animal and human nature, James acknowledged that the higher animals were probably capable of the same kind of spontaneous reverie and empirical contemplation that occupies much of human thought— trains of images or concrete terms linked by their associations in experience that build habit structures enabling brutes and men to respond appropriately to familiar stimuli. Present signs suggest remote realities. Inference, conscious or unconscious, occurs.[8]

To illustrate the thinking shared by man and brute, James re-

---

sociocultural evolution, see Kurt Danziger, "On the Threshold of the New Psychology: Situating Wundt and James," in Wolfgang G. Bringmann and Ryan D. Tweney, eds., *Wundt Studies* (Toronto: C. J. Hofgrefe, 1980), pp. 363–379.

[7] Bruce Kuklick, *The Rise of American Philosophy: Cambridge, Massachusetts, 1860–1930* (New Haven: Yale University Press, 1977), p. 54, does mention without documenting in detail that "for the club a connection to definite human purposes and conceivable empirical consequences guided all reasoning. . . . Whatever the substantive relations between the Americans and Kant, his *pragmatisch* became the English *pragmatic*, and it did so as an extension of Darwinian ideas."

[8] This account of reasoning sounds superficially like that of the British associationists, whose combination of language, habit, and thought culminated in Herbert Spencer's evolutionism. Cf. Robert M. Young, *Mind, Brain, and Adaptation in the Nineteenth Century* (Oxford: Clarendon Press, 1970). In fact, it was this mechanistic interpretation of mental evolution that James was attacking.

called the story of the man who, upon discovering a boat full of water and mud, gestured—but only half seriously—to his dog that it should fetch the sponge that had been left at the house. The dog, although untrained in that particular act, did bring the sponge, thus exciting the master's admiration and winning James's agreement that the animal's spontaneous observations were indeed remarkable. However, James held that this behavior was merely association by contiguity and that there was no evidence in it of anything other than the coupling of two concrete things, two sense experiences: water-in-boat and sponge.

Had the dog returned with either a dipper or a mop, as a human being might have done, there would have been evidence of a different kind of thought. Such substitutes for the sponge would have meant the presence of the concept of "taking up water" and would have suggested the capacity for *dissociation*.[9] Reasoning is a kind of behavior in which experiences are linked not as mere experiences but through the mediating agency of similar abstractions or partial characters that provide reasons and instruments, and thus both theoretical and practical consequences.[10] Dissociation is the process whereby the human thinker breaks up the concretes of immediate experience and substitutes those similar essences, attributes, or abstractions in ways that solve problems and serve interests. It involves selection from all the richness and complexity of fact of the partial character that is deemed right for the occasion. Whereas association by contiguity and similarity proceeds by characters of which we may not even be aware, dissociation is conscious, conceptual, and intentional.

From an evolutionary point of view, the consequences of the emergence of reason are sweeping. Whereas brute intellect had been confined to instinctive and learned responses to the familiar,

[9] Edward H. Madden, *Chauncey Wright and the Foundations of Pragmatism* (Seattle: University of Washington Press, 1963), pp. 135–137, shows that Wright still used the term "dissociation" in the manner of associationism. He raises but does not answer the question of the sources of James's divergence from Wright; I think the Kantian tradition holds the answer. I am otherwise much indebted to Madden's analysis. Mark R. Schwehn, "Making the World: William James and the Life of the Mind," *Harvard Library Bulletin*, 30 (1982), 437–438, ascribes the cause of James's divergence from Wright to Charles S. Peirce, who, of course, was very knowledgeable about Kant and the Kantians.

[10] Here is the connection to James's later pragmatism. Cf. H. S. Thayer, Introduction, *Pragmatism*, WORKS.

reasoning provided a new form of adaptation by equipping men to cope with change, with what was novel. It was applicable to what had not been experienced, whereas brute thinking was always limited to the directly experienced.

James's conjectures about the explanation of this ability almost ruled out experience as the source. Nor was he persuaded by the Lamarckian or Spencerian hypothesis that acquired habit can become a congenital tendency. "So vast a superstructure is raised upon this principle, both by Mr. Spencer and by others, that the paucity of empirical evidence for it has alike been matter of regret to its adherents, and of triumph to its opponents" (*EPs*, p. 36).

Surprisingly, James leaned more in a Kantian direction, toward an a priori source of cognitive and logical form.[11] He was inclined to look toward our subjective nature, to the organic structure of mind. He concludes,

If the theory be true which assigns to the cerebral hemispheres definite localities in which the various images, motor and sensible, which constitute our thoughts are stored up, then it follows that the great cerebral difference between habitual and reasoned thinking is this: that in the former an entire system of cells vibrating at any one moment discharges in its totality into another entire system, and that the order of the discharges tends to be a constant one in time; whilst in the latter a part of the prior system still keeps vibrating in the midst of the subsequent system, and the order—which part this shall be, and what shall be its concomitants in the subsequent system—has little tendency to fixedness in time (*EPs*, pp. 34–35).

The task of discovering the facts underlying the unstable equilibrium of the human brain upon which the highest forms of reasoning depend is assigned to the physiologist. The pattern of his analysis may be Kantian, but the explanation sought is naturalistic.

The reason for James's preoccupation with Spencer is that the

---

[11] James owned and annotated the major books of German logic by Hermann Lotze, Christian Sigwart, and Wilhelm Wundt; also, of course, W. Stanley Jevons, *Elementary Lessons in Logic: Deductive and Inductive* (London: Macmillan, 1870) and the work of John Stuart Mill (note 3 above). The most profusely annotated is his copy of Hermann Lotze, *Logik: Drei Bücher, vom Denken, vom Untersuchen und vom Erkennen* (Leipzig: S. Hirzel, 1874). In Post-Kantian German logic, as John Passmore has described it, "the starting point of logic, then, is not the idea taken simply as something 'in my mind'—the 'ideal content'—but the idea considered as having a meaning, pointing to a reality." In John Passmore, *A Hundred Years of Philosophy* (Harmondsworth, England: Penguin Books, 1968; orig. pub. 1957), p. 157.

latter had proposed a more explicit theory of mental development *and* mental evolution than Darwin. This theory contained two parts, which James in *Principles* dubbed the "front door" and the "back door" of experience.[12] The front door, as described above by dissociation and selective attention, referred to the acquisition of knowledge during the lifetime of the individual. James agreed with Spencer that acquired habit is more important than instinct, while he insisted that the agent of selection lay in the individual organism as much as in the environment. James sided with Darwin, however, about the "back door" of experience, or the experience of the human race. Here he was referring to the variation and selection of brain and bodily structures during the course of evolutionary time. Reviewing Darwin in 1868, he commended his agnosticism concerning the causes of variation;[13] two decades later, when Weismann suggested that variations have to take place in the germ cell to be hereditary, James was quick to embrace that hypothesis.[14] He was able to do so because, unlike Spencer and the Neo-Lamarckians, he had all along distinguished between the front and back doors of experience.

The second essay, "Are We Automata?", was used in part in the early methodological chapter of *Principles*, "The Automaton Theory," as well as in the more substantive "The Stream of Thought." Its content identifies it, however, as a predecessor of the chapter "Attention."[15]

In it, James's background in medicine as well as in evolutionary biology is evident. He taught comparative anatomy and physiology during the 1870s and was well versed in the contemporary literature of brain physiology.

Research on the central nervous system, primarily of frogs and dogs, was focused upon the reflex basis of behavior and the cerebral localization of mental functions, and it was this research which had become the basis for the automaton theory, a position made famous in 1874 by T. H. Huxley in his essay "On the Hypothesis that

---

12 James, *Principles*, Works, vol. 2, pp. 1222–26.

13 William James, Review of Charles Darwin, *The Variation of Animals and Plants Under Domestication* (New York: Orange Judd, 1868), *North American Review*, 107 (1868), 362–368.

14 James, *Principles*, Works, vol. 2, p. 1278, citing August Weismann, *Essays Upon Heredity*, ed. and trans. E. Poulton et al. (Oxford: Clarendon Press, 1889).

15 James, *Principles*, Works, vol. 1, p. 424.

Animals Are Automata, and Its History."[16] James himself had been more impressed by Shadworth Hodgson's statement of it in 1870 in *The Theory of Practice*.[17]

The claim that in everything outward, human beings as well as all other creatures were nothing but material machines whose feelings were merely collateral products of nervous processes seemed to James an unwarranted extension of the actual findings of brain physiology. In particular, he objected to the strict physiological determinism and to the elimination of teleology.

He observed that value terms such as "self-preservation" and "struggle for survival" still played a role in evolutionary theory. Brain physiologists continued to refer to "useful discharge," "appropriate direction," and "right reaction," all of which presuppose animal goals or ends which serve as criteria.

The obligation of the evolutionist was the recognition that consciousness had in fact evolved and survived. On the assumption that it, like all organs in the animal series, would have a use, investigation of its utility in the natural economy was required. If found, the discovery would overthrow the theory that consciousness is a mere supernumerary, without efficacy.[18]

Proceeding on the Darwinian assumption that all animal life is constantly engaged in reacting to environing circumstances, James asked how the responses of creatures of low brain development compare with those of perfected brain development and answered that the former have predictability, which is lacking in the latter. The latter would seem to live in an environment far more extensive and complicated than the former. The low brain does few things and in doing them perfectly forfeits other uses. The high brain's reactions to minute alterations in the surroundings, whether those immediately present or those signified, are chancy and in unstable equilibrium. If only the physical cerebrum prevailed, James argues, human behavior would be completely random, a lottery game. If, however, consciousness represents the

---

[16] Reprinted in T. H. Huxley, *Collected Essays*, vol. 1, *Method and Results* (London: Macmillan, 1893; rpt. Hildesheim: Olms, 1970), pp. 199–250.

[17] James, *Principles*, WORKS, vol. 1, pp. 133–137.

[18] The a priori and empirical parts of James's Darwinian argument are convincingly distinguished by Robert J. Richards, "The Personal Equation in Science: William James's Psychological and Moral Uses of Darwinian Theory," *Harvard Library Bulletin*, 30 (1982), 406–409. However, Richards seems needlessly to trivialize this argument by ascribing it to "the psychology of individual personality," p. 425.

power of exerting pressure in the direction of survival and if the human organism grows to the modes in which consciousness has trained it, there is great reduction of the rule of chance. The argument for the efficacy of consciousness is an argument that associates the automaton theory with undirected, uncontrolled cerebral activity, which would indeed be disastrous for the human species. In fact, however, James argues that it is precisely because a conscious creature can respond to environing circumstance with awareness of ends and goals, of what will jeopardize or secure them, with choice of means for effecting those aims, that the unstable organic equilibrium created by the perfected brain can be turned to evolutionary advantage. Consciousness is not exclusively reactive, passive, and receptive but active and selective in many ways. The senses are organs of selection, determining what we respond to; attention selects from what sense gives, reinforcing or inhibiting response. Alternative possibilities are weighed, some supported and others rejected. If consciousness were merely epiphenomenal, no explanation would be possible for the control of cerebral activity, which has in fact survived the test of natural selection—thus far.

The assumption of this active and reactive relationship with nature, which figured so prominently in Darwinian theory of behavior, is developed by James and others into the modern conception of the functional relation of response and stimulus.[19] The behavior of a conscious, goal-oriented organism could be described in either physical or psychological terms, depending upon investigative interests. Its environment could provide physical, mental, or cultural stimuli.

There are many anticipations in James of the idea of sign learning in both animals and men and of theories of linguistic behavior, which prepare the way for social behaviorism and its theory of language and social interaction.[20] As man developed his power of abstraction and analysis and linguistic facility so crucial to human learning and social relations, his power over environmental contingencies and the flexibility of his responses could be expected to

19 Cf. Madden, *Chauncey Wright*, pp. 137–142. Although James did not use the terms "stimulus" and "response" systematically, he did establish the logic underlying their use—namely, the specification of the functional conditions of behavior in the environment.

20 William R. Woodward, "The 'Discovery' of Social Behaviorism and Social Learning Theory, 1870–1980," *American Psychologist*, 37 (1982), 396–410.

minimize the vulnerability of cerebral response and to substitute direction toward human ends.

The implications of this line of thought for theories of cognitive development and educational theory are wide-ranging. James recognized different levels of intellectual attainment, brute and human, child and adult, pedestrian and genius. He distinguished between minds that were predominantly intuitive and those predominantly analytic. The latter, in his view, represent the highest stage of development, but it was in the blending of both capacities, as in Plato, that greatness was to be found.

James's functional psychology derived from Darwin, and was, by 1880, critically at odds with the associationist, the Kantian, and the physiological traditions. As we have seen, however, he gave the two factors of variation and natural selection a new twist. Concerning the first, James differed from Darwin in his greater emphasis on the "spontaneity" of behavioral variation. In regard to the second, he ascribed selection to every level of conscious life, so that the organism helps nature along by its choices (*EPs*, p. 53).[21]

Having sketched a methodological program for the explanation of mental development, James turned next to the most hallowed bastion of mental philosophers, the explanation of volition. The title of his essay "The Feeling of Effort," written in 1880, makes clear that he was attacking the received view of voluntary behavior held by Hermann von Helmholtz and Wilhelm Wundt. In order to reconcile volition with the reflex automaton theory, sensory psychologists and physiological psychologists had assumed that the command function over the involuntary nervous system was mediated by the cerebrum and motor nerves. Moreover, evidence from introspection testified to the "force of will," "feeling of innervation," or "feeling of effort" in these outgoing motor nerves. A psychophysical parallelism was invoked by psychologists insofar as they postulated, and introspected, this efferent feeling of movement.

James adopted instead an outspoken interactionist position, in which the interaction could go in either direction. He argued against Helmholtz and Wundt as follows:

[21] These two points are made by Philip P. Wiener, *Evolution and the Founders of Pragmatism* (Cambridge, Mass.: Harvard University Press, 1949), pp. 97–105.

In opposition to this popular view, I maintain that the feeling of *muscular* energy put forth is a complex *afferent* sensation coming from the tense muscles, the strained ligaments, squeezed joints, fixed chest, closed glottis, contracted brow, clenched jaws, etc., etc. That there is over and above this another feeling of effort involved, I do not deny; but this latter is purely moral and has nothing to do with the motor discharge (*EPs*, p. 85).

The passage expresses a dualism in James's scientific psychology that it is important to acknowledge. He himself referred to the above muscular feelings as the "effect-theory," and he ascribed moral feelings to the "cause-theory."[22] We need to relate them here both to his position on evolution and to contemporary psychology.

James emphasized "effected" movements by italics (*EPs*, pp. 93, 95, 101, 102, 123) because of the immense systematic importance of acknowledging the reflex basis of behavior. Unknown environmental or organismic stimuli elicit habitual actions—for example, we notice a pin on the floor, and this triggers a complicated action of picking it up. If a complex action such as this can be conducted spontaneously with no feeling of effort, this becomes an important concession to the automaton theory in the province of feeling and will.

Nevertheless, not all of our actions are the mere effects of stimuli. James emphasized the causal side of will in both his 1880 and 1888 essays reprinted here. From personal experience in wrestling with questions of career and marriage, James knew the importance of committing oneself to a course of action. As a youth, suffering from suicidal depression, he found support for this theory of an efficacious consciousness in the writings of the French philosopher Charles Renouvier. When James later referred to will as a mental relation of ideas, he meant the kind of resolve illustrated by a "still small voice," which, "when the death-bringing consideration comes, looks at its face, consents to its presence, clings to it, affirms it, and holds it fast, in spite of the host of exciting mental images which rise in revolt against it and would expel it from the mind" (*EPs*, p. 227).

Since James's time, his two feelings of effort have become separated and each has been developed into a theory to the exclusion of

---

[22] "The reader will please observe that I am saying all that can *possibly* be said in favor of the effect-theory, since, inclining as I do myself to the cause-theory, I do not want to undervalue the enemy." In *Principles*, Works, vol. 1, pp. 424–425.

the other.[23] Some have emphasized the "effect-theory" alone, as did Edward Thorndike, who formulated his "law of effect" in a textbook that James praised for its "quality of exceeding realism" (*EPs*, pp. 329–330).[24] Others, in the humanistic and existential schools, have stressed variants of what James called the "cause-theory."[25] Not only has each been made into a caricature, but the logic of the variation in an immense repertoire of automatic responses and their selection by an effort of will has been unnecessarily torn asunder. In this way, James inadvertently contributed to a misunderstanding that his "evolutionary epistemology" was designed to avoid.[26]

The evolutionary logic of James's theory of emotions has also been widely misunderstood. Behavioral psychologists often cite the following passage from "What Is an Emotion?" (1884)—a passage that is repeated in the related chapter in *Principles*, "The Emotions": "Common sense says, we lose our fortune, are sorry and weep; we meet a bear, are frightened and run; we are insulted by a rival, are angry and strike. The hypothesis here to be defended says that this order of sequence is incorrect, . . . that the more rational statement is that we feel sorry because we cry, angry because we strike, afraid because we tremble" (*EPs*, p. 170). Out of context, James seemed to early behaviorists to be saying that behavior always precedes experience. In fact, as more recent cognitive psychologists have argued, James was also expressing the view that emotions depend upon one's interpretation of a situation. These two half-truths can be combined by appreciating a more comprehensive explanation in terms of variation and selection.

23 William R. Woodward, "William James's Psychology of Will: Its Revolutionary Impact on American Psychology," in Josef Brozek, ed., *Explorations in the History of Psychology in the United States* (Lewisburg, Pa.: Bucknell University Press, forthcoming).

24 The law of effect broadens hedonism to claim that an action that is followed by "reinforcing" effects will be strengthened (more likely to reoccur) and one followed by "non-reinforcing" effects will be weakened. Cf. John C. Malone, "William James and B. F. Skinner: Behaviorism, Reinforcement, and Interest," *Behaviorism*, 3 (1975), 142–143.

25 E.g., Rollo May, *Love and Will* (New York: W. W. Norton, 1969), p. 219.

26 The emergence of James's evolutionary epistemology is well documented in Robert J. Richards, *Darwin and the Emergence of Evolutionary Theories of Mind and Behavior* (Chicago: University of Chicago Press, forthcoming). It is important, I would caution, to accentuate regress as well as progress in the history of ideas.

This evolutionary explanation requires that physiological arousal be considered a source of variation, and that the subjective response be treated as a selective factor. For example, one's reception by a host may inspire fear or joy, depending upon the circumstances: "What the action itself may be is quite insignificant, so long as I can perceive in it intent or *animus*. *That* is the emotion-arousing perception; and may give rise to as strong bodily convulsions in me, a civilized man experiencing the treatment of an artificial society, as in any savage prisoner of war, learning whether his captors are about to eat him or to make him a member of their tribe" (*EPs*, p. 176). Here bodily reactions depend upon perceived intentions.[27] The variation of our instinctive emotional reactions provides a repertoire for behavioral selection; the variation of our past experience offers a spectrum for cognitive selection. On this Darwinian basis, therefore, James sought a way out of the dilemma created by the contrasting tenets of "reflex possibilities" and "the exclusively mental character of will."

In 1887 James's essay "The Consciousness of Lost Limbs" offered an *experimentum crucis* for his theory of volition and emotion. The paralytic or the amputee had become evidence for the association theory of the British empiricists and the German psychophysicists. According to them, we associate outgoing feelings of movement with incoming sensations; therefore, the amputee should be conscious of lost limbs—the so-called phantom limb phenomenon— because the cerebral feelings of movement are presumably associated with the presence of that limb. James's questionnaire, however, revealed contradictory evidence: "How, then, comes it that there can be any patients who lack the false sense in question? In one hundred and forty of my cases, about fifty lacked it completely" (*EPs*, p. 213). James concluded that such a consciousness of phantom limbs is like the rudimentary organs described by Darwin: "Being functionless, selection has no hold on them, the environment exerts no influence to keep them up" (*EPs*, p. 213). Conversely, consciousness is subject to the environment only insofar as it is functional. Notice that the subject matter of psychology

---

[27] This point is made by Hans Linschoten, *On the Way Toward a Phenomenological Psychology: The Psychology of William James* (Pittsburgh: Duquesne University Press, 1968; orig. pub. in the Netherlands, 1959), p. 216: "This means *that intentionality is based on corporeity*." Cf. pp. 277–284 on emotion as "experience of bodily reactions." However, Linschoten overlooks the evolutionary context.

is now consciousness as organic function; as such, consciousness undergoes variation and selection. The laws of psychology, too, are functional in that they express concurrent relationships between the environment and an organism, expressed in terms of stimulus and response.

James's interpretation of consciousness as functional in the adjustment of the organism to the environment is also an important key to his reworking of the traditional view of representative perception. His 1879 article "The Spatial Quale" leads into this theory of perception, which comprises subtheories about the perception of time, things, and movement. The article was one segment of a manuscript, which eventually appeared in four parts as "The Perception of Space," in *Mind* during 1887. The set of articles then reappeared "with considerable revision" in *Principles*. Taking the several articles together, one might reconstruct a picture of James waging a dual battle against the rationalist deduction of space by the Neo-Hegelians in the *Journal of Speculative Philosophy*, as well as against the empiricist derivation of space in *Mind*. Indeed, he did point out the "psychologist's fallacy" in each case. Moreover, a functional interpretation informed his own doctrine of spatial perception, and this interpretation was drawn from several important (but often neglected) thinkers.

In 1878, the year preceding "The Spatial Quale," James drew up the following outline of his theory of spatial perception for his Lowell Lectures. In it he contrasted the "empiricist" and "intellectualist" views with his own "sensationalist" position:

I. Deny *quale*   Associational empiricists (Mill, Bain?)

II. 1. Intellectualists
   a. complete from first   Kant
   b. not existing at first   Those who insist on
      suggested by non-spatial   spontaneity aspect
      experience   (psych. stimulists)
          Wundt, Lotze

  2. Sensationalists
   a. complete fm. first
      common sense, Hering
      "Nativists" (Müller)
   b. dim at first &
      developed by experience
      Empiricists (Bailey? Stumpf myself)

> The division between a priorists & empiricists may be made
> a cross division. Thus in II.1 we have an empirical & an
> intuitional wing; in its b division the same; in II.2 the same.
> This suggests [material crossed out] that we begin by think-
> ing of a priori & empirical as representing two tendencies
> [rather] than 2 sharply defined things.[28]

The first point to notice is that James classified himself with Samuel Bailey and Carl Stumpf (*EPs*, pp. 80–82).[29] Each was a critic of
his own tradition, the Berkeleyan and the Kantian, respectively.
James's reading notes and his correspondence document the fact
that he drew from each at crucial points in reaching his own theory
of perception.

Bishop Berkeley, followed by John Stuart Mill and Alexander
Bain, contended that the eye is incapable by itself of perceiving
space. It receives mere intensive sensations of light and color. Only
by means of associated tactile and kinesthetic sensations does the
visual sensation acquire spatial features. Bailey had attacked this
"associational empiricist" theory, as James called it, saying that
objects in space are directly given in perception.[30] James's note-
books in 1870 contain thirty pages in which he pitted Bailey's
arguments against Mill's.[31] From this exercise came the empiricist
version of the "psychologist's fallacy"—namely, James contended
that empiricist psychologists erred in imputing sensations and
ideas as building blocks to the percipient's mind, while leaving
out the percipient's qualitative feelings of relation, or *quale*, between them.[32]

As the outline indicates, James was also critical of what he considered the Kantian rationalist tradition. In general this "machine
shop" tradition, as he termed it, posited that mind supplies the
relations between ideas. James criticized the Kantian tradition for

[28] William James's Papers on Psychology, The Lowell and Baltimore Lectures,
1878–79, Houghton Library, Harvard (bMS Am 1092.9 [4395]).

[29] James, *Principles*, WORKS, vol. 2, pp. 911–912.

[30] Samuel Bailey, *A Review of Berkeley's Theory of Vision* (London: Ridgway,
1842).

[31] Perry, *The Thought and Character of William James*, vol. 1, p. 575.

[32] Amedeo Giorgi, "On the Relationship Among the Psychologist's Fallacy, Psy-
chologism and the Phenomenological Reduction," *Journal of Phenomenological
Psychology*, 12 (1981), 75–86. Cf. Richard High, "Shadworth Hodgson and William
James' Formulation of Space Perception: Phenomenology and Perceptual Realism,"
Journal of the History of the Behavioral Sciences, 17 (1981), 466–485.

what may be called the rationalist version of the "psychologist's fallacy." For example, Kant's view of space as an a priori form of intuition seemed to rule out experience as a fundamental factor in the organization of perception. Kantian physiologists had made some concessions to experience by acknowledging "local signs" on the sensory surfaces, whereby the organism learns spatial localization.[33] However, following Carl Stumpf's critique of this tradition, James argued that "space-perception" is not organized in the mind or brain or sensory surfaces but in the experience itself, as given to the percipient.[34]

If Bailey and Stumpf gave James his critical orientation toward the British empiricists and the German rationalists, it was two men conversant with both traditions who led him to his positive formulation. One mentor was Shadworth Hodgson, whose book *Time and Space* maintained that the experience of space is original.[35] James echoed him when he wrote that "this vague original consciousness of a space in which separate positions and directions have not, as yet, been mentally discriminated, deserves . . . the name of sensation quite as much as does the color, 'blue' " (*EPs*, p. 64). The other mentor was Chauncey Wright, who in 1873 had propounded a genetic account of consciousness in which the world of self and spatial objects are discriminated through experience. To these views James again added the functional explanation that the key to our perception is "selective attention" to "local differences" in sensory experience—that is, variation and selection (*EPs*, p. 75).

This novel theory set off a boiling controversy that lasted for at least a dozen years. The next installment was " 'The Psychological Theory of Extension' " which was published in 1889, a reply to an essay of the same title by the editor of *Mind*, George Croom Robertson. Robertson had conceded James's arguments against the empiricist version of the psychologist's fallacy, but he could not bring himself to admit the sensationalist alternative that spatial

[33] Cf. William R. Woodward, "From Association to Gestalt: The Fate of Hermann Lotze's Theory of Spatial Perception, 1846–1920," *Isis*, 69 (1978), 572–582.

[34] The term *Raumvorstellung* (spatial presentation) is important in the title of Carl Stumpf, *Über den psychologischen Ursprung der Raumvorstellung* (Leipzig: Hirzel, 1873). It connotes an immediate organization, which James sometimes tagged "sensationalism" in his own work and which Stumpf's students, Wolfgang Köhler and Kurt Koffka, termed "Gestalt perception."

[35] Shadworth Hodgson, *Time and Space* (London: Longman, Green, Longman, Roberts and Green, 1865). Cf. note 32.

extension requires no association of sight and movement.[36] He cited Thomas Montgomery, F. H. Bradley, James Ward, and Herbert Spencer, all of whom acknowledged the impossibility of deriving extensive sensations from intensive stimuli. James replied that the logic of scientific explanation requires us not only to take certain variables as given in experience, but also to connect them in functional relationships: "Science can never *explain the qualities* of the successive elements, if they show new qualities, appearing then for the first time. It can only name the moment and conditions of their appearance, and its whole problem is to name these aright" (*EPs*, p. 241).

A fine illustration of the power of this pattern of functional explanation is James's empirical test of "the sense of dizziness in deaf-mutes," reported in an essay of 1882: "Imagine a person without even the sense of gravity to guide him, and the 'disorientation' ought to be complete—a sort of bewilderment concerning his relations to his environment in all three dimensions will ensue, to which ordinary life offers absolutely no parallel. Now this case seems realized when a non-dizzy deaf-mute dives under water with his eyes closed" (*EPs*, p. 134). The results of his questionnaire study of 519 deaf mutes confirmed the prediction that impairment of the semicircular canals would result in disturbances in motion and balance, accompanied by dizziness. It was not only the finding itself, but the firm grasp of the relation of predictive laws and their test by observation, which distinguished James's functionalism from the conventional explanation of perception by empiricists and rationalists.

Language has always posed a special problem for theories of cognition. For many centuries, language and logic seemed to distinguish man from animals. Evolutionary and comparative linguistic evidence gradually undermined this view, as the naturalistic case for the continuity of physical and mental development became increasingly strong. As early as 1863, when he was just twenty-one years old, James was already wrestling with this problem in his reading notes to Friedrich Max Müller's *Lectures on the Science of Language*: "Men differ from brutes by speech. This not a physical difference, for many brutes can articulate. It is then caused by

---

[36] George Croom Robertson, "The Psychological Theory of Extension," *Mind*, 13 (1888), 418–424.

a mental diff. If it be true that we differ mentally from b's by the faculty of general conception from this faculty must flow our power of speech. Let us look at the facts given by language."[37] James here accepted the evolutionary assumption of continuity between animal and man; he pointed out, however, that whereas the vocal apparatus is not significantly different, the ability to form general ideas is. By 1878 he had provided a functional account of the difference in the "use" of language; we recognize similar meanings in different objects or events

as soon as the notion of the sign *as such*, apart from any particular import, is born; and it is born by dissociation from the outstanding portions of a number of concrete cases of signification. The "yelp," the "beg," the "rat," differ as to their import—and as to their own physical constitution. They agree only in so far as they have the same *use*—to be signs, to stand for something more important than themselves. The dog whom this similarity could strike would have grasped the sign *per se* as such, and would have become a speaker in the human sense (*EPs*, p. 27).

The key to cognition and language is the principle of similarity, by which humans dissociate the original whole experience into meaningful parts.

The essay "On Some Omissions of Introspective Psychology," written in 1884, took this insight further in a grammatical direction.[38] One so-called omission was the "feeling of relation" that connects thoughts with "verbal skeletons of logical relations"; these feelings give life to such bloodless logical connectives as "naught but," "either one or the other," or even the mere "*intention-to-say-so-and-so*" (*EPs*, pp. 155–156). James believed that the

---

37 William James's Notebook 3, February 4–5, 1863, Houghton Library, Harvard (bMS Am 1092.9 [4497]). Cf. Friedrich Max Müller, *Lectures on the Science of Language* (New York: Scribner's, 1862). A sensitive reassessment of the importance of language in its intentional and contextual aspects is William J. Gavin, "William James on Language," *International Philosophical Quarterly*, 16 (1976), 81–86.

38. Note that James's cognitive theory originated in a methodological critique of introspectionism. As he consolidated his previous insights about consciousness at the Aristotelian Society in 1883 and again at the Transcendentalist Club at Concord in 1884, he came to realize that despite greater lip service paid to introspection in the British school, the German school was also guilty of a similar error. For a perspicacious comparison of the high estimation of introspection in the British philosophical tradition, and the low estimation in the German tradition, see Kurt Danziger, "The History of Introspection Reconsidered," *Journal of the History of the Behavioral Sciences*, 16 (1980), 241–262. James thus occupied an original middle position.

prevailing schools of psychology placed too much emphasis on the "substantive" portions of consciousness, the names of objects including sensations and ideas, and too little emphasis on the "transitive" parts such as verbs and conjunctions.

The continuity between animals and man thus led James to the continuity of consciousness itself. He came to believe that consciousness, as a naturalistic subject matter, had been mishandled insofar as it had been described by analogy to logical, grammatical, or physical elements without due regard to an important methodological distinction. In this connection, James wrote: "Let us now pass to another introspective difficulty and source of fallacy, different from the one hitherto considered, but quite as baleful to psychology. I mean the *confusion between the psychologist's standpoint and the standpoint of the feeling* upon which he is supposed to be making his report" (*EPs*, p. 161). Consciousness comprises fringes of meaning and feelings of tendency, such as are encountered when trying to recall a forgotten name. Thus, when we judge a "sameness-with-something-else" as constituting a general idea, our psychologist's standpoint must not be confused with the object itself: the object is the same, but the same thought about it is never to be had twice.[39]

These two methodological points—that the subject matter of consciousness includes both contents and feelings of relation, and that the reporting must be distinguished from the thinking or feeling of them—became a separate chapter, "The Methods and Snares of Psychology," in *Principles*. The 1890 version was clearer, but it did not emphasize the important new distinction between struc-

[39] It is appropriate to recall at this point John Dewey's contention that in the period 1890 to 1904 James "had thrown over his knowing Thought or Consciousness as a mere echo of a departed soul." See Dewey, "The Vanishing Subject in the Psychology of James," *Journal of Philosophy*, 37 (1940), 589–599. In fact, James accomplished this feat during the 1870s and 1880s. His confidence derived from the fact that he was standing on the shoulders of giants, Hegel, Lotze, and Hodgson, who each converged on a critique of the rationalistic principle of identity underlying subject-predicate logic; but he wanted to do for this principle in psychology what they had done for it in logic and metaphysics. Its conditional character must be recognized. As he noted in the margin of Lotze, *Logik* (Leipzig: Hirzel, 1874), p. 574: "For him, the essential form of rational connection in thought is $S + x = P$ in which x is the condition or ground of S becoming P." The x for psychology was the feeling of relation, of how it feels to him, "of the *wie ihm zu Muthe ist*, as Lotze would say" (*EPs*, p. 150). The inclusion of the conditions under which something is the case became the crux of James's functional view of the logic of controlled inquiry.

ture and function. In 1884 James had written that the conventional distinction between feeling and thought must be replaced by
"two *aspects*, in which all mental facts without exception may be
taken; their structural aspect, as being subjective, and their functional aspect, as being cognitions" (*EPs*, p. 160).

In 1892 James found a way of testing the hypothesis that prior
to language the stream of thought is capable of selecting similar
events to forge a general notion. In the essay "Thought Before
Language: A Deaf-Mute's Recollections," he described how the
deaf-mute Mr. d'Estrella experienced a "conversion to honesty"
upon stealing a gold piece, which was far more valuable than
anything he had previously stolen. He evidently realized that "bad
deeds will end by *tasting* bad" (*EPs*, p. 290), an example of the
principle of similarity. To James, this case showed that a person
deficient in language could nevertheless form general principles
of morality and science.

James was sometimes an ambivalent exponent of psychology as
a natural science, and never more so than in his treatment of language. He treated language largely in terms of individual consciousness, its states and intentions. In contrast, European schools
of language study considered that this method did violence to
language as a cultural phenomenon. To Wilhelm Wundt or Wilhelm Dilthey, for example, meaning was conveyed by the sentence
or the understanding rather than by James's "passing thought."[40]
They held that it was better to respect the integrity of language
as a social phenomenon by approaching it through comparative
linguistics, mythology, religion, law, art, or history than to subject
it to experiment. Yet James's view was close to that of the hermeneutic tradition, in which expressive movements, signs, and
language became the foundation for the human sciences (*Geistes-
wissenschaften*). His successors, including George Herbert Mead,
Charles Morris, and Jean Piaget, attempted to add a social meaning
to James's conception of a science of language, through social
behaviorism, semiotics, and genetic epistemology.[41] Today's lan-

40 William R. Woodward, "Wilhelm Wundt's Program for the New Psychology:
Vicissitudes of Experiment, Theory, and System," in Woodward and Ash, *The
Problematic Science*, pp. 187–191, n. 5; Michael Ermarth, *Wilhelm Dilthey: The
Critique of Historical Reason* (Chicago: University of Chicago Press, 1978), p. 279,
refers to the "constitutive function of language, which cannot be fully explained
(*erklärt*) but only elucidated."

41 On James, Mead, and Piaget, see David L. Miller, "Mead's Theory of Univer-

guage-based schools of "syntactic structures" and "communicative action"[42] indicate the possible convergence of the hermeneutic and functional traditions.

Attention has been called to the fact that James was not entirely consistent in his commitment to a natural scientific approach in psychology. There was another "humanistic" side to his development as a psychologist, reflected in his concern with personality, in his dualistic view of moral as well as an afferent feeling of effort, and in his conception of the signs underlying human linguistic communication. The root of these concerns may be discerned in the influence of that forceful idiosyncratic theologian, Henry James, Senior. When his father died in 1882, William James wrote: "It is singular how I'm learning every day now how the thought of his comment on my experiences has hitherto formed an integral part of my daily consciousness, without my having realized it at all."[43] What was the nature of this comment on his experience? First, Henry James, Senior, was critical of any self-righteous moralism that judged right and wrong from the standpoint of dogma, be it liberal Unitarianism or conservative Anglicanism. One detects echoes of what Henry, Senior, called "spiritual evil" in what William in another context came to call the "psychologist's fallacy," the mistaking of a conceptual framework for the observation in its original richness.

The second fundamental legacy from his father was a naturalistic interpretation of redemption, which was conducive to a humanistic social psychology. His father maintained that "spiritual evil" was overcome through "spiritual creation," a personal renewal achieved by accepting "that great unitary life of God in our nature, which we call society."[44] In his chapter "The Consciousness of

---

sals," in Walter R. Corti, ed., *The Philosophy of George Herbert Mead* (Amriswil, Switzerland: Amriswiler Bücherei, 1973), p. 92; on Peirce, Mead, and Morris, see Peter List, "Mead's Formulation of the Disposition Theory of Meaning," in Corti, *Mead*, pp. 118–121.

42 Noam Chomsky, *Rules and Representations* (Oxford: Basil Blackwell, 1980); Jürgen Habermas, *Theorie des kommunikativen Handelns*, 2 vols. (Frankfurt: Suhrkamp Verlag, 1981). An overview of American and German linguistic traditions is provided by Karl-Otto Apel, *Toward a Transformation of Philosophy*, trans. Glyn Adey and David Frisby (London: Routledge & Kegan Paul, 1980; 1st German ed., 1973).

43 William James to Mrs. Gibbens (early 1883) in Henry James, Jr., ed., *Letters of William James*, vol. 1 (Boston: Atlantic Monthly Press, 1920), p. 222.

44 Frederic Harold Young, *The Philosophy of Henry James, Sr.* (New York: Book-

Self" in *Principles*, William observed that "a man's social Self is the recognition which he gets from his mates. . . . And when it is recognized his contentment passes all bounds."[45] Both father and son insisted upon viewing man as a social being, whose sense of worth depends upon acceptance by others, and whose moral growth comes through self-sacrifice.

We find echoes of these teachings of his father in James's deep interest in exceptional mental states and their relation to personality (and selfhood). Initially James sought to understand change or differences in people by experiment. When hypnotism became popular in the 1880s, for example, James was attracted by the "practical effects" of suggestion on people. In his "Report of the Committee on Hypnotism" for the American Society for Psychical Research, he noted that the subject would remember a line pointed out in a "monotonous ornamental pattern," whereas a normal person would lose the place. He explained that the hypnotic subject "surrenders himself to the general look," which is "lost upon the normal looker-on, bent as he is on concentration, analysis, and emphasis." The memory for patterns in the trance is rote; the memory in the normal state is found "by picking out their 'essential' character." James concluded: "The evolution of man's mind is altogether in the analytic direction" (*EPs*, p. 194).

James criticized his former student G. Stanley Hall for failing to establish an important distinction between the hypnotic and the normal state. In his note "Reaction-Time in the Hypnotic Trance" in 1887, he disputed Hall's finding that a person in a hypnotic trance has a shorter reaction time.[46] James found on the basis of some eight hundred observations that "the opposite was the case"; although he drew no conclusions, he cautioned against "making rash generalizations from few cases" (*EPs*, pp. 202–203). James

---

man Associates, 1951), p. 303, quoting Henry James, Sr., *The Secret of Swedenborg: Being an Elucidation of His Doctrine of the Divine Natural Humanity* (Boston: Fields, Osgood, 1869), p. 145. Henry Samuel Levinson, *The Religious Investigations of William James* (Chapel Hill: University of North Carolina Press, 1981), p. 14, notes that for Henry, Sr., "salvation occurred in society, not in ritual."

45 James, *Principles*, WORKS, vol. 1, pp. 281–282. Cf. William J. Gavin, "Vagueness and Empathy: A Jamesian View," *The Journal of Medicine and Philosophy*, 6 (1981), 45–65.

46 G. Stanley Hall, "Reaction-Time and Attention in the Hypnotic State," *Mind*, 8 (1883), 170–182.

regarded Hall's result as instructive because of what it lacked, a hypothesis which relates variables concurrently, such that a certain behavior is a function of a certain stimulus condition. Furthermore, it bore no explicit relation to a larger theory of mental evolution.

Such a larger theory came to James from a direction other than evolutionary theory. In 1887 Edmund Gurney discovered through automatic writing experiments that a "secondary personality," which sometimes appears under hypnosis, has the ability to perform nonautomatic actions on command. This self is therefore awake, attentive, and capable of competing for consciousness with the "primary personality" (*EPs*, p. 263).

Then, in 1889, Pierre Janet's book *De l'automatisme psychologique* appeared. Janet showed that certain hysterical patients had as many as three distinct personalities. Particularly striking was the fact that their hysterical anesthesias, such as a paralyzed limb or temporary blindness, were dependent upon which personality was in control. James reviewed this book in his essay "The Hidden Self" in 1890, and also cited it extensively in *Principles*. The implications for the traditional doctrine of the association of ideas, not to mention his own doctrine of the stream of consciousness, were manifold: first, there were clearly "breaches in the association of ideas" (*EPs*, p. 255); second, there was a "simultaneous coexistence of the different personages" (*EPs*, p. 258); and third, there was "their possible application to the relief of human misery" (*EPs*, p. 265).

The results of hypnosis and multiple personalities made so great an impression on James that he participated in numerous experimental sessions, read widely, and reported his findings in the Lowell Lectures on "Exceptional Mental States" in 1896.[47] He finally published his voluminous materials in *The Varieties of Religious Experience* in 1902, after delivering them in the Gifford Lectures at Edinburgh in 1901 and 1902.

James never relinquished the naturalistic interpretation of mental life that preoccupied the generation of scholars after Dar-

[47] William James, Lowell Lectures, 8 folders, Houghton Library, Harvard (bMS Am 1092.9). Cf. Eugene Taylor, Jr., "William James on Psychopathology: The 1896 Lowell Lectures on 'Exceptional Mental States,'" *Harvard Library Bulletin*, 30 (1982), 455–479.

win. At the same time, however, he sought to square this naturalism with the doctrine of personal renewal that he had imbibed from his father.[48] His preoccupation with the case of Ansel Bourne, the preacher who became a storekeeper named A. J. Brown and who forgot all the details of his previous life, was published as a note of May 30, 1891, in Richard Hodgson's article "A Case of Double Consciousness" and is entitled "Notes on Ansel Bourne" in the present volume (*EPs*, p. 269).[49] This case study, reported later in *Varieties*, was one in which James himself conducted hypnosis experiments on Bourne to bring out his second personality. In his article "Person and Personality," reprinted here, James briefly set out his notion of the fringes and meanings surrounding our conscious states: "It is clear already that the margins and outskirts of what we take to be our personality extend into unknown regions" (*EPs*, p. 321).

James's definition of personal renewal entailed a relationship to the depths of one's own consciousness, and, as well, of man to nature. In his note "Consciousness Under Nitrous Oxide" (1898), he concluded that "normal human consciousness is only a narrow extract from a great sea of possible human consciousness, of whose limits we know nothing" (*EPs*, p. 322). In 1906 his article "On Some Mental Effects of the Earthquake" described the variety of subjective reactions elicited by this natural calamity, ranging from various superstitious explanations to his own "glee and admiration" (*EPs*, p. 332). We may compare this sense of wonder with his father's awe of "the divine natural humanity"; both emphasized the whole person and the living relation with its natural mysteries. Some would term this an existential or humanistic psychology.[50] Certainly James's psychology exceeded the limits of the conventional theory and experimentation represented by his student Boris Sidis, of whose scientistic diagrams of interacting ideas and their neurophysiological correlates he wrote that he was "not convinced" (*EPs*, p. 326).

48 Eugene Taylor, Jr., "William James and American Pragmatism: The Swedenborgian and Transcendentalist Connection," four lectures given at the Swedenborg Chapel, Cambridge, Mass., between October 25 and November 15, 1981.

49 Richard Hodgson, "III. A Case of Double Consciousness," *Proceedings of the Society for Psychical Research*, 7 (1891), 221–255.

50 Julius Seelye Bixler, "The Existentialists and William James," *The American Scholar*, 29 (1959), 80–90.

In histories of psychology, James's contribution to psychology is often classified as functionalism.[51] It is seldom so classified in histories of philosophy, where his "dualistic" psychology is generally regarded as having been superseded by his mature pragmatism and radical empiricism.[52] This introduction has attempted to bridge these interpretations with a more historical account of the origin of his philosophical thinking about psychological problems. The chronological arrangement of *Essays in Psychology* has lent itself to this task, and tracing the topics discussed in them has helped to separate the contexts and senses of functionalism that emerged during his career. Finally, by comparing James's 1904 critique of the Chicago Functional School with his own evolving position as detailed here, we can sharpen our understanding of what functionalism meant to him and to his successors in psychology, philosophy, and education.

Functionalism refers, as seen in James's review of Ladd, to a pattern of scientific explanation involving order in time, antecedent and consequent conditions. Describing Chicago Functionalism, James wrote: "A situation implies at least two factors, each of which is both an independent variable and a function of the other variable. Call them E (environment) and O (organism) for simplicity's sake."[53] James agreed with Dewey and his students that we must abstract the stimulus conditions from the environment and the response from the organism. But stimulus and response conditions acquire explanatory power for theory and practice only through subsuming them under laws. Explanations for James were functional in that they provided predictions, which in turn offer an opportunity for empirical testing. If a certain law holds, then specifiable "practical effects" can be expected under specified conditions. If the effects of this concurrent relationship do not obtain, the hypothesis must be rejected or revised.

---

[51] Edwin G. Boring, *A History of Experimental Psychology* (New York: Appleton-Century-Crofts, 1950; orig. pub. 1929), p. 515. More recent histories have largely followed Boring's rather superficial account, with one exception: Brian D. Mackenzie, *Behaviourism and the Limits of Scientific Method* (Atlantic Highlands, N.J.: Humanities Press, 1977).

[52] This is the view of Marcus Ford, *William James's Philosophy: A New Perspective* (Amherst: University of Massachusetts Press, 1982).

[53] William James, "The Chicago School," *Psychological Bulletin*, 1 (1904), 2; in *Essays in Philosophy*, WORKS, p. 103.

A second feature of functionalism is the implications it has for truth. His father's spiritual evolutionism, Darwin's natural evolutionism, and his own conviction of the reality of the unseen persuaded James that functional truth "works" through a process in which many investigators are engaged. Each person converges on the nature of reality from a different standpoint. This is the background of his criticism of the Functionalists—that there is "no account of the fact (which I assume the writers to believe in) that different subjects share a common object-world."[54] His emphasis on the psychologist's fallacy in the perception of space shows that he agreed with Dewey on the function of the percipient, not just the scientist, in constructing reality. Reality became for James and his followers, the Functionalists and the Neo-Realists, that which is verifiable through experience. But the collective experience of the individual and the race must lead to a truth that exists independent of the observer. In this respect, James's view of eventual truth as "a common object-world" independent of the observer was closer to Swedenborg's or Baldwin's genetic view of reality.[55]

Third, functionalism has to do with the operation of mind and its role in mental development. In his 1878 essay on reasoning in animals and man, for example, James stated that knowledge is discovered through the individual's selection of the essential attribute in thought and action. In his 1884 essay on introspection, he noted that "this function is the mysterious *plus*, the understood meaning" (*EPs*, p. 159). Reviewing Dewey's *Studies in Logical Theory* in 1904, James still began with the mental operation of individuals: "The predicate is thus essentially hypothetical—the situations to which the use of it leads may have quickly to be reconstructed in turn. In brief, S is a stimulus intellectually irritating; P is an hypothesis in response; SP is a mental action, which normally is destined to lead or pass into action in a wider sense."[56] James reworked the formal logic of post-Kantian philosophers into a Darwinian account of reasoning and language. Building upon James's synthesis of Kantian and Darwinian theories of mind,

54 Ibid., p. 105.

55 Cf. James Mark Baldwin, *A Genetic Theory of Reality* (New York: Putnam's, 1915). See also Armi Varila, *The Swedenborgian Background of William James' Philosophy* (Helsinki: Suomalainen Tiedeakatemia, 1977).

56 *Essays in Philosophy*, WORKS, p. 104.

Introduction

Dewey and Mead brought to it a Hegelian concern with social reality.

A fourth aspect of functionalism is its explanation of the presence of consciousness by its functions. As we have noted, James's conception of feeling following movement reversed the popular notion of "feelings of innervation" held by Helmholtz and Wundt, and his conception of feeling as relation between ideas affirmed Renouvier's primacy of mental resolve. In 1895 Dewey followed James in reinterpreting the reflex arc as a "functional coordination,"[57] and in 1904 James showed his basic agreement by accurately paraphrasing Dewey as follows: "Consciousness is functionally active in readjustment. In perfectly 'adapted' situations, where adjustments are fluent and stereotyped, it exists in minimal degree. Only where there is hesitation, only where past habit will not run, do we find that the situation awakens explicit thought. Thought is thus incidental to change in experience, to conflict between the old and the new."[58] Here James placed the problem of freedom and determinism on the physiological foundation of adjustment and habit, which nevertheless allowed for, and even demanded, existential choice. This fruitful tension was lost when behaviorists developed one side of James's theory of action and existentialists pursued the other.

Fifth, functionalism offered an important epistemological foundation for psychology and philosophy. Rather than moving from dualism toward radical empiricism as Dewey claimed in 1940, James's early theories of perception and cognition reveal the latter position already fully articulated by the 1880s.[59] Then he called it sensationalism. He was critical of the psychologist's fallacy on both sides—on the empirical side for taking the constituents of consciousness for real instead of analytic elements, and on the rational side for ascribing a mind thinking to conscious thoughts. He held that experience is originally a whole, containing substantive and transitive portions, and that it is subsequently analyzed in accordance with a cognitive and linguistic principle of similarity. Too generously, perhaps, James recognized a sympathetic approach

[57] John Dewey, "The Reflex Arc Concept in Psychology," *Psychological Review*, 3 (1896), 357–370.
[58] *Essays in Philosophy*, WORKS, pp. 103–104.
[59] See note 39 above on Dewey, "The Vanishing Subject."

in Chicago Functionalism: "It seems a promising *via media* between the empiricist and transcendentalist tendencies of our time. Like empiricism, it is individualistic and phenomenalistic; it places truth *in rebus*, and not *ante rem*. It resembles transcendentalism, on the other hand, in making value and fact inseparable, and in standing for continuities and purposes in things."[60] Radical empiricism in some sense provided the epistemological basis for functionalism all along, and not just later on as Dewey implied.[61]

A sixth and final characteristic of functionalism, both for James and the psychology that came after him, is its pluralism. Under the sway of his encounter with the variety of altered states and multiple consciousnesses in the 1880s and 1890s, James seems increasingly to have tended toward pluralism.[62] His chapter "The Perception of Reality" in *Principles* explored the seven "subuniverses of reality," from common sense and science to madness and the supernatural. Behind the multiplicity of realities lay every person's "right to believe" and the uniqueness of being "for itself."[63] In contrast to the richness of lived experience, objected James, "Dewey's favorite word is 'situation.'"[64] Psychology and a naturalistic theology of self-renewal were replaced in Dewey by a social view of nature. James felt that something was lost in this view: "There is no cosmology, no positive account of the order of physical fact, as contrasted with mental fact."[65] In broadening ex-

[60] *Essays in Philosophy*, WORKS, pp. 105–106.

[61] Miliç Çapek, "The Reappearance of the Self in the Last Philosophy of William James," *Philosophical Review*, 62 (1953), 526–544.

[62] David E. Leary, "William James, Psychical Research, and the Origins of American Psychology," presentation at the 88th Annual Meeting of the American Psychological Association, Montreal, September 1–5, 1980.

[63] James took the concept of the "right to believe" from Chauncey Wright and Alexander Bain. Cf. Edward Madden, Introduction, *The Will to Believe*, WORKS, pp. xvi-xviii. He found support for his view that personality is reality in Lotze's being "for itself": "Compare Lotze's doctrine that the only meaning we can attach to the notion of a thing as it is 'in itself' is by conceiving it as it is *for* itself; i.e., as a piece of full experience with a private sense of 'pinch' or inner activity of some sort going with it." In William James, *The Varieties of Religious Experience* (London: Longmans, Green, 1902), p. 499n.

[64] *Essays in Philosophy*, WORKS, p. 103.

[65] Ibid., p. 105. Dewey may have taken this charge to heart, as shown by his title two decades later, *Experience and Nature*, in *John Dewey: The Later Works, 1925–1953*, ed. Jo Ann Boydston, vol. 1 (Carbondale: Southern Illinois University Press, 1981). Cf. William J. Gavin, "James' Metaphysics: Language as the House of 'Pure Experience,'" *Man and World*, 12 (1979), 142–159.

perience from individual to social, Dewey had made the functional character of consciousness into a social interaction. Spiritual evolution and natural evolution had given way to social evolution. One may well ask whether this was a loss or a gain in our understanding of the pluralistic confrontation of human beings with nature, including human nature, over historical time.[66]

[66] The preparation of this introduction was supported in part by NIH Grant LM 03492 from the National Library of Medicine and in part by the Alexander von Humboldt-Stiftung. For their generous time and assistance, I am grateful to Elizabeth Berkeley, David E. Leary, Anne McCoy, Edward Madden, Maurice Mandelbaum, Mary Mikalson, Robert J. Richards, Eugene Taylor, Jr., H. S. Thayer, and Duane Whittier.

Essays in Psychology

Brute and Human Intellect

Everyone who has owned a dog must, over and over again, have felt a strange sense of wonder that the animal, being as intelligent as he is, should not be vastly more so. His conditions would be easier to understand if he were either more universally stupid or more generally rational. The quickness with which he learns the signs which indicate that his master is going out, such as putting off slippers and putting on overcoat, seems incompatible with his utter inability to learn that dropping more coal into the grate will make a hotter fire. Accordingly, quite apart from theological and metaphysical prejudice, it is not surprising that men's opinions regarding the mental state of brutes should have oscillated between the two extremes of claiming for them, on the one hand, reasoning powers in no essential respect other than those of man, and, on the other, of denying to them all properly intellectual attributes whatever, and calling their powers of appropriate action the result of "instinct," or, still worse, of mere blind mechanism. Most of us adopt a medium course, and feel as if our domestic pets had real, though peculiarly limited, intellectual powers, and at various times attempts have been made to define exactly what this limitation consists in. It has been said that they were like men dreaming; that they could not form abstract ideas; that they had no proper self-consciousness; that they were incapable of apprehending the notion of a sign as such; that they were incapable of language; and that these incapacities, severally or all together, were sufficient to explain the observed differences. All these statements are, no doubt, true in the main. Everyone in fact feels them to be true when he goes into the midst of his quadrupedal relatives, and yet these formulas hardly clear up the matters much, for they themselves express results, rather than elementary factors in the case. *Why* does not a dog frame abstract ideas? *Why* does he not reflect on his self, or *ego*? And the rest. If we could find the elementary point of divergence in his mental constitution which leads to all these peculiar shortcomings, we should be much better off.

Now, it seems to the writer that to a certain extent we can reduce all the above differences, and others too, to one simpler difference; and, although this last is itself by no means ultimate, still, to have ascertained it will be a real progress as far as it goes, and may put us, moreover, on the track of further definite inquiries. A new question distinctly formulated is always a philosophic gain.

To make clear if possible what this common root is which makes our dog's thoughts seem so different from our own is the object of the present essay. If it dwells chiefly on his thoughts, and little on his passions, emotions, and so forth, it is for obvious reasons: first, the lack of space; and, second, the relative plainness of the latter phenomena. But, to find what difference there is between brute thinking and human thinking, we must begin by forming a clear idea of what human thinking is.

To say that all human thinking is essentially of two kinds— reasoning on the one hand, and narrative, descriptive, contemplative thinking on the other—is to say only what every reader's experience will corroborate. If, further, it be asked what the latter kind of thinking is, everyone will reply that in the main it consists of a procession through the mind of groups of images of concrete things, persons, places, and events, together with the feelings which they awaken, and in an order which, if our attention is guided by some dominant interest, such as recollecting an actual set of facts, or inventing a coherent story, is in the main derived from our actual experience of the order of things in the real outward world. If, on the contrary, there be no presiding interest, but our thoughts merely bud one out of the other according to the caprice of our revery, there may occur very abrupt transitions between one set of images and the next, so that we may juxtapose thoughts whose *things* were never juxtaposed since the world stood. In the case where there is a presiding interest the link by which one thought is made to succeed another is in the main that known to psychologists by the name of "association by contiguity." We are apt to go over the circumstances as they happened or were likely to happen. The thought of a last summer's sunset will call up the vessel's deck from which I saw it, the companions of my voyage, and the arrival into port.

In revery, on the other hand, "association by similarity" is more prominent. A sunset may lead me to think of the letters of the Greek alphabet, and I may at first be quite unable to give the steps by which so incongruous a consequence was suggested to me. When ascertained, however, I may see that I was reminded in succession of the recent attempts to explain nearly all mythology by solar myths, of Hercules' history as such a myth, of Hector's funeral pyre, of Homer, and whether he could write, and then of the Greek alphabet.

Where contiguity predominates we have a dry, prosaic, literal sort of mind; and, on the contrary, where similarity has free play, we are apt to call the person fanciful, poetic, or witty. But both cases agree, the reader will notice, in this: that the thinker passes along from one concrete whole of representation to another. His thought is always of matters taken in their entirety. Having been thinking of one, he finds later that he is thinking of another, to which, as it were, he has been naturally lifted along, he hardly knows how. If an abstract quality figures for a moment in the procession, it arrests the attention but for a moment, and fades into something else; and it is never very abstract. Thus, in thinking of the sun-myths, I may have a gleam of admiration at the *gracefulness* of the primitive human mind, or a moment of disgust at the *narrowness* of modern interpreters. But, in the main, I think less of qualities than of whole things, real or possible, just as I may experience them.

Having mentioned the two kinds of association, let us now pause for a moment before proceeding further, and form a somewhat more distinct notion of the way in which they differ from each other. The law of association by contiguity has been thus stated: "Actions, Sensations, and States of Feeling, occurring together, or in close succession, tend to grow together, or cohere, in such a way that when any of them is afterwards presented to the mind, the others are apt to be brought up in idea."[1]

The same writer has expressed the law of Similarity as follows: "Present Actions, Sensations, Thoughts, or Emotions tend to revive their LIKE among previously occurring states."[2] Let us make schematic diagrams of these two modes of association. Since all logical processes are to-day hypothetically explained as brain processes, by translating ideas into cells and their connections into fibers, the same figures will do for an imaginary representation of what goes on in the brain—each circle being supposed to represent a group of cells united by fibers, whilst the dotted lines are fibers alone.

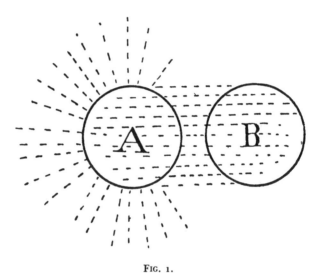

FIG. 1.

Fig. 1 represents association by contiguity; all the elements of the whole A are operative together, and call up all the elements of B together, B having been previously experienced in company with A. In Fig. 2, on the contrary, where association by similarity is represented, most of the elements of A are inactive. The single element, *m*, breaks out from its concert with them—a concert which would naturally have resulted in their combining in the only *united* action possible to them, viz., the arousal of B—and calls up a whole with which *it* alone has contiguous associations, the whole

---

[1] Alexander Bain's *Mental and Moral Science*, London, 1868, p. 85.
[2] *Ibid.*, p. 127.

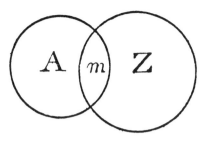

Fig. 2.

Z. But, now, does not a mere glance at the figure show us that A and Z are called similar only because they are in part identical? identical in the character *m*, which vibrates throughout both? This *m*, it is true, may be larger or smaller; but, whichever it is, it cannot, as it exists in Z, fitly be said to be associated with itself as it exists in A. On the contrary, it is one and the same *m* in both. Association properly so called obtains between the residual ingredients of A and Z respectively. Each set of these is associated with the common *m*, and, moreover, associated with it by contiguity pure and simple. All association, therefore, is at bottom association by contiguity—that alone binds two ideas together. What in ordinary parlance is called contiguous association is only the particular case of it in which all the items of a cluster of ideas operate *together* to call up another cluster with which in its totality they were each and all once experienced. What we call "similarity" is only the other special case, in which a *part* of a cluster acts, as we say, on its own hook, and revives another cluster with whose totality *it* alone has been experienced. The two clusters cohere together by respectively cohering by their *residual* characters with *it*. But this cohesion is contiguous. The *m*—the character by which the clusters are identical in the fullest sense of the term—is the common heart of both, and indirectly keeps them together by its contiguity with their several other parts. Contiguity is, then, the only operative bond of association. Identity is no association at all. What is called similarity is a resultant, compounded of both identity and contiguity.

Having thus parenthetically defined our notions of association, let us pass on to reasoned thinking. Wherein does it differ from the contemplative—or, as we may now call it, empirical—thinking, which we have alone considered hitherto? Reason may be, and

5

often is, defined in two ways: Either as the power to understand things by their causes, or as the power, if the notion of an end is given, to find the means of attaining it. That is, reason has a theoretic and a practical sphere. But in their essence the two spheres are one; they involve the same form of process, which is simply that of finding an intermediate representation, m, which will, in a peculiarly evident manner, link together two *data*, A and Z. In the theoretic sphere m is the "reason" for "inferring" Z; in the sphere of action it is the "means" (or the instrument) for "attaining" Z. The immensely superior utility of reasoned to merely habitual thinking lies in this: that by reason we may infer or attain Z, even though Z and A may never have been conjoined in our actual experience. In empirical thinking this would be impossible. To get at Z at all in empirical thought we must already have passed, in some concrete case, from A to it. If in the theoretic sphere that has happened, then when A next recurs it will suggest Z—pass us on to it by a law which we blindly obey, we know not why. Whilst, if the previous experience was in the realm of practice, the notion of the end, Z, coinciding with our actual circumstances, A, will together resuscitate a representation of the manner, x, in which we formerly passed from one to the other.

In reasoned thought, on the other hand, no previous experience is needed of the concrete case we have to deal with. We pass over the bridge, m, whose relations to the terms A and Z we may never have been aware of before. What is m? It is always a partial character (or a combination of such, with their suggestions) embedded in the totality of one or both of our items of thought, which we dissect out and fix our attention upon. Particular cases of reasoning vary enormously in complication. Thus, in theoretic reasoning, Z may from the first be an abstract attribute, and then, probably, the extraction of the partial characters will be performed solely upon A. Vermilion is heavy, for example. Why? Because it contains mercury, and that is heavy. Sometimes, again, A and Z are both concretes, and m unites them by our noticing that it is a common, identical, partial character in both. Thus I may perceive five francs to be equal to four shillings as soon as, in the mass of different suggestions of each, I discern the common character of being equal to a dollar. Equivalence to a dollar is the m here, as mercury was in the previous case. Or, I may be in an inclosure, over the north wall of which someone is calling to me; but I may

6

see no way of getting to him till I observe that in the south wall there is a passage to the street, and that the street will lead me to my friend. Here the *m* is double; first, the inclosure yields the character of a southern exit to the street, and the street, among its other included characters, contains that of leading to the spot I wish to reach.

The accompanying diagrams will symbolize the process in these simple cases. In Fig. 3 the mercury, or the dollar value, involved as an ingredient in A calls up the Z, with which it is equally con-

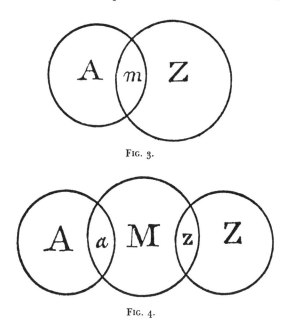

FIG. 3.

FIG. 4.

gruent, and binds it and the A together. In Fig. 4 the southern exit, *a*, is part of the larger whole, M, the street, one of whose other parts is *z*, which is also congruent with Z, the place of my friend.[3]

3 The reader will, of course, observe the difference between these and the ordinary syllogism diagrams of logical treatises. Fig. 3, for example, if taken to symbolize a syllogism, would yield no valid conclusion. The syllogisms of logical treatises differ, however, from the living acts of reasoning, which I am here describing, by this very point: that they are ideally perfect, while our concrete acts of reasoning are almost always liable to error, and to the particular form of error which Fig. 3 makes manifest. Only *so far as we are right* in identifying in our thought the total A and the total Z, with their ingredient, *m*, and in ignoring the outlying portions of the circles, can we reason from one to the other. If either identification be

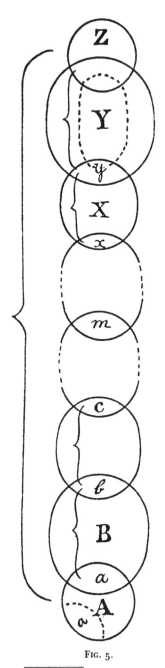

Fig. 5.

The most complicated cases may be symbolized by a mere extension of the last diagram, such as Fig. 5 shows us.

Here the reason or process for passing from A to Z consists of a long series of links, each of which is constructed in the same fashion. A partial character, *a*, embedded in A, will redintegrate (that is, recall) its associates, and among them *b*, which in like manner recalls *c*, and so forth until Z is reached. Or the analysis of Z into *z*, which calls up *y*, and so on, may be simultaneously begun. In that case the two ends of the chain advancing towards each other will meet somewhere in the middle, *m* being a term resulting from both analyses—consequently identical in each. The result is, of course, the same. The whole chain of steps may in a large way be called the "reason," M, why A and B are related to each other as they are; or any partial number of them taken together may become the "means" by which we reach Z from A, if the junction of these terms be a practical problem.

The large bracket, uniting directly A to Z, symbolizes their junction when we know it merely empirically, as when we simply learn that alkalies will cure some cases of dyspepsia, or oxalic acid remove ink-spots. The small brackets represent that in almost every case in which the partial characters, *a* and *b*, *b* and *c*, and so on, suggest each other, it is equally by virtue of an empirical connection of the same sort that they do so. Even when they form two features of the same phenome-

inapt, we have made a blunder. And it is just in this that the difficulty of going right lies. *Which* part of a phenomenon—*which m*—shall we consider its essence in any given case? What concept shall subsume it?

8

non, we are seldom able to say *why* they do so. For instance, we may go on to learn that sodic carbonate calls forth in a dog's stomach a flow of gastric juice, on the one hand, and that some cases of human dyspepsia, on the other hand, seem due to a defect of this flow. Z here, the cured dyspepsia, involves the flow, as a partial character contained in its phenomenal totality. A, the alkaline application, contains it in like manner. It is a character identically in A and Z. But why it exists in A—why soda involves among its innumerable properties that of making gastric juice flow—no one can yet say. It is empirically known, and that is all. Just so if we take the cured dyspepsia. It involves among its other attributes the notion of the food being dissolved. This solution, Z, redintegrates the total notion of a normal digestion, Y, which, among its other partial characters, contains that of an abundance of gastric juice, y. Why y, in the phenomenon Y, should produce Z, we cannot rationally state; or, at least, we can make but a single approximation to a rational statement. Pepsin and acid will dissolve meat, and gastric juice contains both these ingredients. The smaller dotted circle may be taken to represent this additional reason—which, however, itself is merely a new empirical statement. Such empirical laws as these are called "proximate" reasons. The terms which are coupled in them might, for aught we can understand to the contrary, have been coupled in other ways. But in some rare cases we can carry our dissection of characters so far that we find a link or more in the chain formed of a couple of characters whose disjunction we cannot even conceive. Such a couple as this is an axiom, or "ultimate" reason for the phenomenal *data* it binds together. The nature of such ultimate reasons has long been a bone of contention among philosophers. The *a priori* school has asserted that the two characters thus evidently joined—*e.g.*, the characters of straightness and shortness in a line—are at bottom but two aspects of the same character, a primordial synthesis; whilst the empiricists have contended that they are distinct in essence, and that their bond owes its illusory appearance of necessity and evidence merely to the familiarity which great generality has produced in our minds. Into this quarrel we, of course, cannot enter. The *a priorists* would have to modify our diagram, in case the bond $c{\sim}x$ were such an axiom, by making these two segments coalesce into one, as at m. These two letters would then merely represent the two manners in which the fundamental fact, m, looks towards the terms of the main proposition. Action and reaction, having a sensation and knowing it (J. Mill), swiftness and mechanical effectiveness, would be examples of terms united in this way.

This will no doubt have been found by the reader a pretty dry description. We may sum it up by a simple definition: Reasoning is the substitution of parts and their couplings for wholes and their couplings. The utility of the process lies wholly in the fact, that when we have got the parts clearly in our minds, *their* couplings become more obvious, more evident, than were the couplings of the wholes. Later we shall ask why the parts are more obviously connected than the wholes; but here the reader must pause to notice one fact, and that is the absolute necessity that the partial character taken as a reason should be the right one. If in the total called sodic carbonate we do not light upon the ingredient "makes gastric juice flow," but on some other ingredient, such as "effervesces with acids," it will be worse than useless to lead us to the anti-dyspeptic conclusion. In Fig. 5, *a* is the only partial character of A which leads to Z, and *a*, for example, has no connection with it. But if it were required to find the reason for another Z—for instance, why a man who has just taken a spoonful of the carbonate for "acidity" should feel a pressure at the epigastrum—*a* (if it stood for the effervescence) would be the right character to choose. In a word, we may say that the particular part which may be substituted for the whole, and considered its equivalent in an act of reasoning, wholly depends on our purpose, interest, or point of view at the time. No rules can be given for choosing it except that it *must lead to the result,* and to follow this rule is an affair of *genius.* This, which is a matter of the deepest philosophic importance, must merely be noticed here in passing, and not further discussed.

Before leaving the diagrams it may be well again parenthetically to call attention to their resemblance to the diagram by which association by similarity was represented (Fig. 2). There, also, partial characters redintegrated their circumstances, and so passed us on to ideas of new wholes. But there, as a rule, we were not aware of the partial characters *in se.* They operated without separately attracting our notice. In reasoning proper they only operate by attracting our attention; but it is obvious that a man starting from the fact A might evolve the truth Z in either way, by consciously using the right successively embedded characters to deduce Z, or, on the other hand, by merely obeying their influence and at last finding Z suggested to him, he knows not how. Later on we shall see how similar association and reasoning do often coincide in this way in their results.

Let us now, by a few concrete examples, clear up whatever obscurity our abstract account may have left upon the reader's mind. We have to illustrate two points: first, that in every reasoning an extracted character is taken as equivalent to the entire *datum* from which it comes; and, second, that the couplings of the characters thus taken have an extreme degree of evidence. Take the first point first.

Suppose I say, when offered a piece of cloth, "I won't buy that; it looks as if it would fade," meaning merely that something about it suggests the idea of fading to my mind, my judgment, though possibly quite correct, is purely empirical; but, if I can say that into the color enters a certain dye which I know to be chemically unstable, and that *therefore* the color will not last, my judgment is reasoned. The notion of the dye which is one of the ingredients of the cloth is the connecting link between the latter and the notion of fading. So, again, an uneducated man will expect from past experience to see a piece of ice melt if placed near the fire, and the tip of his finger look coarse if he views it through a convex glass. A child may open a refractory door by lifting it bodily on its hinges; or he may know enough to tip sideways a stopped mantel-clock, to make it tick again after winding it up—in each case, because the process "always" has the desired effect—and in none of these cases could the result be anticipated without full previous acquaintance with the entire phenomenon.

It is not reasoned; but a man who should conceive heat as a mode of motion, and liquefaction as identical with increased motion of molecules; who should know that curved surfaces bend light-rays in special ways, and that the apparent size of anything is connected with the amount of the "bend" of its light-rays as they enter the eye; who should perceive that this particular door sags on its *sill*, or should reflect that no clock can tick until its pendulum swing, and that tipping may start the oscillations of a hidden pendulum—such a man would handle all these objects intelligently, even though he had never in his life had any concrete experience of them; and he would do this because the ideas which we have above supposed him to possess mediate in his mind between the phenomena he starts with and the conclusions he draws.

But these ideas or reasons for his conclusions are all mere extracted portions or circumstances singled out from the mass of characters which make up the entire phenomena. The motions which form heat, the bending of the light-waves, are, it is true, excessively recondite ingredients; the hidden pendulum is less so; and the sticking of the door on its sill is hardly so at all. But each and all bear a more evident relation to the consequent idea than did the antecedent in its full totality.

The difficulty is, in each case, to extract from the antecedent phenomenon that particular ingredient which shall have this very evident relation to the consequent. Every phenomenon or so-called "fact" has an infinity of aspects or properties. Even so simple a fact as a line which you trace in the air may be considered in respect to its form, its length, its direction, and its location. When we reach more complex facts, the number of ways in which we may regard them is literally countless. They are perfect well-springs of properties, which are only little by little developed to our knowledge; but each of which may in turn come to be regarded as the essence of the phenomenon or fact in question, while the rest can be for that occasion ignored. Thus a Man is a complex fact. But out of the complexity all that an army commissary need pick out as important for his purposes is his property of eating so many pounds a day; the general, of marching so many miles; the chair-maker, of having such a shape; the orator, of responding to such and such feeling; the theater-manager, of being willing to pay just such a price, and no more, for an evening's amusement. Each of these persons singles out the particular side of the entire man which has a bearing on *his* concerns, and not till this side is distinctly and separately conceived can the proper practical conclusions be drawn. The existence of the separate side or partial aspect which each of these several persons may substitute for the whole complex man in laying his plans is the *reason* for those plans.

These simple examples show sufficiently that our first point is true. Each case of reasoning involves the extraction of a particular partial aspect of the phenomena thought about. Whilst Empirical Thought simply associates the phenomena in their entirety, Reasoned Thought couples them by the conscious use of this extract.

And, now, to prove the second point: Why are the couplings of extracts more evident and obvious than those of entire phenomena?

For two reasons: First, the extracted characters are more general than the concretes, and the connections they may have are, therefore, more familiar to us, as having been more often met in our experience. Think of heat as motion, and whatever is true of motion will be true of heat; but we have had a hundred experiences of motion for every one of heat. Think of the rays passing through this lens as bending towards the perpendicular, and you substitute for the unfamiliar lens the very familiar notion of a particular change in direction of a line, of which notion every day brings us countless examples. The other reason why the relations of the extracted characters are so evident is that their properties are so *few*, compared with the properties of the whole, from which we derived them. In every concrete total the characters and their consequences are so inexhaustibly numerous that we may lose our way among them before noticing the particular consequence it behooves us to draw. But, if we are lucky enough to single out the proper character, we take in, as it were, by a single glance all of its possible consequences. Thus the character of scraping the sill has very few suggestions, prominent among which is the suggestion that the scraping will cease if we raise the door; whilst the entire refractory door suggests an enormous number of notions to the mind.

Take another example. I am sitting in a railroad car, waiting for the train to start. It is winter, and the stove fills the car with pungent smoke. The brakeman enters, and my neighbor asks him to "stop that stove smoking." He replies that it will stop entirely as soon as the car begins to move. "Why so," asks the passenger. "It *always* does," replies the brakeman. It is evident from this "always" that the connection between car moving and smoke stopping was a purely empirical one in the brakeman's mind, bred of habit. But, if the passenger had been an acute reasoner, he, with no experience of what that stove always did, might have anticipated the brakeman's reply, and spared his own question. Had he singled out of all the numerous points involved in a stove's not smoking the one special point of smoke pouring freely out of the stovepipe's mouth, he would, probably, owing to the few associations of that idea, have been immediately reminded of the law that a fluid passes more rapidly out of a pipe's mouth if another fluid be at the same time streaming over that mouth; and then the rapid

13

draught of air over the stove-pipe's mouth, which is one of the points involved in the car's motion, would immediately have occurred to him.

Thus a couple of extracted characters, with a couple of their few and obvious connections, would have formed the reasoned link in the passenger's mind between the concrete phenomena, smoke stopping and car moving, which were only linked as wholes in the brakeman's mind. Such examples may seem trivial, but they contain the essence of the most refined and transcendental theorizing. The reason why physics grows more deductive the more the fundamental properties it assumes are of a mathematical sort, such as molecular mass or wave length, is that the immediate consequences of such a mathematical notion are so few that we can survey them all at once, and promptly pick out the one which concerns us.

To reason, then, we must be able to extract characters, and not *any* characters, but the right characters for our conclusion. If we extract the wrong character, it will not lead to that conclusion. Here, then, is the difficulty: How are characters extracted, and why does it require the advent of a genius in many cases before the fitting character is brought to light? Why does it need a Newton to notice the law of the squares, a Darwin, to notice the survival of the fittest? To answer these questions we must begin a new research, and see how our insight into facts naturally grows.

All our knowledge at first is vague. When we say that a thing is vague, we mean that it has no subdivisions *ab intra*, nor precise limitations *ab extra*, but, still, all the forms of thought may apply to it. It may have unity, reality, externality, extent, and what not —*thinghood*, in a word, but thinghood only as a whole. In this vague way, probably, does the room appear to the babe who first begins to be conscious of it as something other than his moving nurse. It has no subdivisions in his mind, unless, perhaps, the window is able to attract his separate notice. In this vague way, certainly, does every entirely new experience appear to the adult. A library, a museum, a machine-shop, are mere confused wholes to the uninstructed, but the machinist, the antiquary, and the bookworm perhaps hardly notice the whole at all, so eager are they to pounce upon the details. Familiarity has in them bred discrimination. Such vague terms as "grass," "mould," and "meat" do not exist for the botanist or the anatomist. They know too much about grasses, moulds, and muscles. A certain person said to Mr. Kingsley, who was showing him the dissection of a caterpillar, with its exquisite viscera, "Why, I thought it was nothing but skin and squash!" A layman present at a shipwreck, a battle, or a fire is helpless. Discrimination has been so little awakened in him by experience that his consciousness leaves no single point of the complex situation accented and standing out for him to begin to act upon. But the sailor, the fireman, and the general know directly at what point to take up the business. They "see into the situation" —that is, analyze it—with their first glance. Knowledge, then, if it begins thus with vague confusion, is not, as some philosophers say, purely and simply the result of association. To quote Mr. Martineau, in an admirable passage, "It is an utter falsification of the order of nature to speak of sensations grouping themselves to aggregates, and so composing for us the objects of which we think; and the whole language of the theory [of association], in regard to the field of synchronous existences, is a direct inversion of the truth. Experience proceeds and intellect is trained, not by Association, but by *Dissociation*, not by reduction of pluralities of impression to one, but by the opening out of one into many; and a true psychological history must expound itself in analytic rather than synthetic terms."[4]

According to this, any original Whole of experience is an eternal well of ever new and more delicately differenced ingredients, which little by little come to light. A man's reasoning powers may, then, if our previous account of reasoning is correct, be said to be in direct proportion to his ability to break up these wholes and dissociate their ingredients.

How, then, do we come to dissociate the elements of the originally vague syncretism of consciousness? By noticing or attending to them, of course. But what determines which element we shall attend to first? There are two immediate and obvious answers: first, our practical interests; and, second, our æsthetic interests. The dog singles out of any situation its smells, and the horse its sounds, because they may reveal facts of practical moment. The child notices the candle-flame or the window, and ignores the rest of the room, because these objects give him a vivid pleasure. So, the

4 James Martineau: *Essays, Philosophical and Theological*, Boston, 1866, p. 273.

country boy dissociates the blackberry, the chestnut, and the wintergreen, from the vague mass of other shrubs and trees, for their practical uses, and the savage is delighted with the beads, the bits of looking-glass, brought by an exploring vessel, and gives no heed to the features of the vessel itself, which is too much beyond his sphere. These æsthetic and practical interests, then, are the weightiest factors in making particular ingredients stand out in high relief. What they lay their accent on, that we notice; but what they are in themselves, we cannot say. We must content ourselves here with simply accepting them as irreducible ultimate factors in determining the way our knowledge grows.

Now, a creature which has few interests, practical or æsthetic, will dissociate few characters, and will, at best, have limited reasoning powers; whilst one whose interests are very varied will reason much better. Man, by his immensely varied practical wants, and his æsthetic feelings, to which every sense contributes, would, by dint of these alone, be sure to dissociate vastly more characters than any other animal, and, accordingly, we find that the lowest savages reason incomparably better than the highest brutes. But if these were the only operators of dissociation, man's superiority would rest here, and he would remain a savage. We must have recourse to another cause to explain dissociation of characters to which the spur of acute practical or æsthetic interest is lacking, and which we attend to, as we say, merely out of disinterested curiosity. Why are such characters not left slumbering forever? how do we single them out at all? They are singled out by a process which many psychologists have recognized; but none, perhaps, as emphatically as it deserves. This process is so important that we shall perhaps do well to baptize it by a special name, and call it the *Law of dissociation by varying concomitants.* This law would run as follows: "In order that a character, possessing no vivid practical or æsthetic interest be dissociated from a group, it must have been previously experienced in connection with *other* characters than those of that group." As Spencer says, "If the property A occurs here along with the properties B, C, D; there along with C, F, H; and again with E, G, B; . . . it must happen that by multiplication of experiences, the impressions produced by these properties on the organism will be disconnected, and rendered so far independent in the organism as the properties are in the environment.

Whence must eventually result a power to recognize attributes in themselves, apart from particular bodies."[5] As expressed still better by Mr. Martineau, "When a red ivory-ball, seen for the first time, has been withdrawn, it will leave a mental representation of itself, in which all that it simultaneously gave us will indistinguishably co-exist. Let a white ball succeed to it; now, and not before, will an attribute detach itself, and the *color*, by force of contrast, be shaken out into the foreground. Let the white ball be replaced by an egg: and this new difference will bring the *form* into notice from its previous slumber. And thus, that which began by being simply an object, cut out from the surrounding scene, becomes for us first a *red* object, and then a *red round* object; and so on. Instead, therefore, of the qualities, as separately given, subscribing together and adding themselves up to present us with the object as their aggregate, the object is beforehand with them, and from its integrity delivers them out to our knowledge, one by one."[6]

In other words, an absolutely unchanging group of attributes could never be analyzed. If all liquids were transparent, and no non-liquid was transparent, it would be long before we had separate names for liquidity and transparency. If the color blue, for example, were a function of position above the earth's surface, so that the higher a thing was, the bluer it became, one word would serve for blue and high. We have, in truth, a number of sensations whose concomitants are invariably the same. When, for example, we look at a near object, we have two sets of sensations: one, that produced by converging the eye-balls; the other, that which results from accommodating the focus. For every distance of the object these sensations are, in common life, immutably linked. The consequence is that we are wholly unable to separate them from each other in our consciousness, or to separate them as a whole from the particular distance on the part of the object to which they testify. The genius of Helmholtz has shown what a vast number of such unseparated sensations underlie our perceptions. We never think of them except as embedded in the totality of the perception to which they belong. Helmholtz calls them its "unconscious premises." We may, however, bring them separately to our consciousness by an artificial device which consists in nothing but

5 Herbert Spencer: *Psychology*, vol. I, p. 345.
6 James Martineau: *Essays, Philosophical and Theological*, Boston, 1866, pp. 271–272.

varying their concomitants. I may, for example, by prisms cause my eyes to change their convergence when looking at a near object, and I may succeed, at least, in accommodating my focus for the nearness of the object, in spite of the very unusual convergence of the eye-balls. In this case I shall end by becoming aware of the accommodation in itself, and afterwards succeed in reproducing it at will without the prisms.

Why the repetition of the character in combination with different wholes will cause it thus to break up its adhesion with any one of them, and roll out, as it were, alone upon the table of consciousness, must here be left a mystery. Mr. Spencer appears to think that the mere fact of its being repeated more often than any one of its associates will, of itself, give it a degree of intensity equivalent to the accent derived from interest.

This, at first sight, has a plausible sound, but breaks down when examined closely. It is not always the often-repeated character which is first noticed when its concomitants have varied a certain number of times; it is even more likely to be the most novel of all the concomitants which will succeed in arresting our attention. If a boy has seen nothing all his life but sloops and schooners, he will probably never distinctly have singled out in his notion of "sail" the character of being hung lengthwise. When for the first time he sees a square-rigged ship, the opportunity of extracting the lengthwise mode of hanging as a special accident, and of dissociating it from the general notion of sail, is offered. But there are twenty chances to one that that will not be the form of the boy's consciousness. What he *notices* will be the new and exceptional character of being hung crosswise. He will go home and speak of that, and perhaps never consciously formulate what the often-repeated peculiarity consists in. Leaving, then, the question of *how* and *why* the law operates as one of the most interesting questions of psychology, we may content ourselves with simply registering it as empirically true.

So far, then, we have found out two things: *First,* a reasoning animal must easily dissociate and extract characters; *second,* in order to do so, characters must have some peculiar æsthetic or practical interest for him; *third,* or, failing in that, must form variable connections in his experience.

The English writer who has professed to give the most thorough account of the evolution of the mind is Mr. Herbert Spencer, in his *Principles of Psychology*. Perhaps a brief criticism of his theory will be the easiest manner in which fully to clear up what may still seem obscure in our own. Spencer, throughout his work, ignores entirely the reactive spontaneity, both emotional and practical, of the animal. Devoted to his great task of proving that mind from its lowest to its highest forms is a mere product of the environment, he is unwilling, even cursorily, to allude to such notorious facts (which, nevertheless, in *principle* are perfectly consistent with his fundamental idea) as the existence of peculiar idiosyncrasies of interest or selective attention on the part of every sentient being. He regards the creature as absolutely passive clay, upon which "experience" rains down. The clay will be impressed most deeply where the drops fall thickest, and so the final shape of the mind is moulded. Give time enough, and all sentient things must end by assuming an identical mental constitution—for "experience," the sole shaper, is a constant fact, and the order of its items must end by being exactly reflected by the passive mirror which we call the sentient organism. The law of dissociation would work, on this theory, only for the first reason suggested above. That is, in the varied shufflings and rearrangements of characters which natural groups of objects and events afford, the character which objectively recurred the oftenest would be the first one noticed by us; the rest would passively follow in the order of their frequency, as experience presented them; and "experience" here would mean the mere presence of the outward fact to the animal's senses.

How Mr. Spencer came to give so inadequate an account, we shall not here inquire. But every reader will already cry out against his interpretation of the word "experience" as being equivalent to the mere presence of a certain outward order. Millions of items of the outward order are present to my senses which never properly enter into my experience. Why? Because they have no interest for me. My experience is what I agree to attend to. Only those items which I notice shape my mind—without selective interest, experience is an utter chaos. Interest alone gives accent and emphasis, light and shade, background and foreground—intelligible perspective, in a word. It varies in every creature, but without it the consciousness of every creature would be a gray chaotic uniformity, impossible for us even to conceive. If Spencer's account were true, a race of dogs bred for generations, say in the Vatican, would have characters of visual shape, sculptured in marble, presented to their eyes, in every variety of form and combination. The result of this reiterated "experience" would be to make them dissociate and discriminate before long the finest shades of these peculiar characters. In a word, they would infallibly become, if time were given, accomplished *connoisseurs* of sculpture. The reader may judge of the probability of this consummation. Surely an eternity of experience of the statues would leave the dog as inartistic as he was at first, for the lack of an original interest to knit his discriminations onto. Meanwhile the odors at the bases of the pedestals would have organized themselves in the consciousness of this breed of dogs into a system of "correspondences" to which the most hereditary caste of *custodi* would never approximate, merely because to them, as human beings, the dog's interest in those odors would forever be an inscrutable mystery. Mr. Spencer has, then, utterly ignored the glaring fact that subjective interest may, by laying its weighty index-finger on particular items of experience, so accent them as to give to the least frequent associations far more power to shape our forms of thought than the most frequent ones possess.

But, if Mr. Spencer is at fault in his account of those cases where powerful interests do the analytic work, we think he is hardly less so in the cases where powerful interest is absent, and "where the law of dissociation by varying concomitants" has all alone to play into the hands of disinterested curiosity. Mr. Spencer writes as if, under these circumstances, man, before he could single out a character, would have merely to wait until such time as nature should sufficiently have varied the concomitants of that character for him. He would single out the notion quadruped, for example, earlier than the notion vertebrate, because vertebrate coexisted more uniformly than quadruped with the other animal attributes. On page 464 of his first volume he writes as if any character frequently repeated in the outer world will, *ipso facto*, tend to stand out prominently in the mind. An "accumulation of experiences" is by itself sufficient to shake out the embedded character. If this were true, man, to dissociate characters, would be wholly at the mercy of the order of frequency in which they outwardly had been present to him. But the fact is that man is, even in the absence of the stronger interests, in the highest degree independent of this outward order, and has within himself a means of abridging in the most striking manner the slow work of nature. This means is nothing else than our familiar friend, *association by similarity*. But here the plot begins to thicken, and as we are approaching the elementary difference we sought between the mind of man and the mind of brutes we will pause an instant, and, by going back a few steps, advance with all the greater impetus.

What does the reader do who wishes to see in what the precise likeness or difference of two objects lies? He transfers his attention as rapidly as possible, backwards and forwards, from one to the other. The rapid alteration in consciousness shakes out, as it were, the points of difference or agreement, which would have slumbered forever unnoticed if the consciousness of the objects compared had occurred at widely distant periods of time. What does the scientific man do who searches for the reason or law embedded in a phenomenon? He deliberately accumulates all the instances he can find which have any analogy to that phenomenon, and, by simultaneously filling his mind with them all, he frequently succeeds in detaching from the collection the peculiarity which he was unable to formulate in one alone; even though that one had been preceded in his former experience by all of those with which he now at once confronts it. These examples show that the mere general fact of having occurred at some time in one's experience, with varying concomitants, is not by itself a sufficient reason for a character to be dissociated now. We need something more; we need that the varying concomitants should in all their variety be brought into consciousness *at once*. Not till then will the character in question escape from its adhesion to each and all of them, and stand revealed alone. Spencer's account omits this last condition, which will immediately be recognized by the reader as the ground of utility in Mill's famous methods of induction, the "method of Agreement," that of "Difference," of "concomitant variations," etc.

But, now, is it not immediately obvious that this condition is supplied in the organization of every mind in which similar association is largely developed? If the character m in the midst of A will call up C, D, E, and F immediately—these being phenomena which resemble A in possessing m, but which may not have entered for months into the experience of the animal who now experiences A, why, plainly, such association performs the part of the deliberately rapid comparison referred to above, and of the systematic simultaneous consideration of like cases by the scientific investigator. Certainly this is obvious, and no conclusion is left to us but to assert that, after the few most powerful practical and æsthetic interests, our only instrument for dissecting out those special characters of phenomena, which, when once possessed and named, are used as reasons, *is this association by similarity*. Without it, indeed, the deliberate procedure of the scientific man would be impossible; he could never collect his analogous instances. But it operates of itself in highly-gifted minds without any deliberation, spontaneously collecting analogous instances, uniting in a moment what in nature the whole breadth of space and time keeps separate, and so permitting a perception of identical points in the midst of different circumstances, which minds governed wholly by the law of contiguity could never begin to attain.

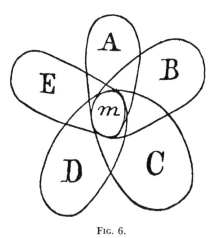

FIG. 6.

Diagram 6 shows this. If *m*, in the present representation A, calls up B, C, D, and E, which are similar to A in possessing it, and calls them up in rapid succession, then *m*, being associated almost simultaneously with such varying concomitants, will "roll out" and attract our separate notice.

If so much is clear to the reader, he will be willing to admit that the mind *in which this mode of association most prevails* will, from its better opportunity of extricating characters, be one most prone to reasoned thinking; whilst, on the other hand, a mind in which we do not detect reasoned thinking will probably be one in which association by contiguity holds almost exclusive sway.

I will try now to show, by taking the best stories I can find of animal sagacity, that the mental process involved may as a rule be perfectly accounted for by mere contiguous association, based on experience. Mr. Darwin, in his *Descent of Man*, instances the Arctic dogs, described by Dr. Hayes, as scattering, when drawing a sledge, as soon as the ice begins to crack. This might be called by some an exercise of reason. The test would be, Would the most intelligent Esquimau dogs that ever lived act so when placed upon ice for the first time together? A band of men from the tropics might do so easily. Recognizing cracking to be a sign of breaking, and seizing immediately the partial character that the point of rupture is the point of greatest strain, and that the massing of weight at a given point concentrates there the strain, a Hindoo might quickly infer that scattering would stop the cracking, and by crying out to his comrades to disperse save the party from immersion. But in the dog's case we need only suppose that they have individually experienced wet skins after cracking, that they have often noticed cracking to begin when they were huddled together, and that they have observed it to cease when they scattered. Naturally, therefore, the sound would redintegrate all these former experiences, including that of scattering, which latter they would promptly renew.

A friend of the writer gave as a proof of the almost human intelligence of his dog that he took him one day down to his boat on the shore, but found the boat full of dirt and water. He remembered that the sponge was up at the house, a third of a mile distant; but, disliking to go back himself, he made various gestures of wiping out the boat and so forth, saying to his terrier, "Sponge, sponge; go fetch the sponge." But he had little expectation of a result, since the dog had never received the slightest training with the boat or the sponge. Nevertheless, off trotted the latter to the house, and, to his owner's great surprise and admiration, brought the sponge in his jaws. Sagacious as this was, it required nothing but ordinary contiguous association of ideas. The terrier was only exceptional in the minuteness of his spontaneous observation. Most terriers would have taken no interest in the boat-cleaning operation, nor noticed what the sponge was for. This terrier, in having picked those details out of the crude mass of boat experience distinctly enough to be reminded of them, was truly enough ahead of his peers on the line which leads to human reason. But his act was not yet an act of reasoning proper. It might fairly have been called so if, unable to find the sponge at the house, he had brought back a dipper or a mop instead. Such a substitution would have shown that, embedded in the very different appearances of these articles, he had been able to discriminate the identical partial attribute of capacity to take up water, and had reflected, "For the present purpose they are identical." This, which the dog did not do, any man but the very stupidest could not fail to do.

If the reader will take the trouble to analyze the best dog and elephant stories he knows, he will find that, in most cases, this simple contiguous calling up of one whole by another is quite sufficient to explain the phenomena. Sometimes, it is true, we have to suppose the recognition of a property or character as such, but it is then a character which the mere practical interest of the animal may have singled out. A dog, noticing his master's hat on its peg, may possibly infer that he has not gone out. Intelligent dogs recognize by the tone of the master's voice whether the latter is angry or not. A dog will perceive whether you have kicked him by accident or by design, and behave accordingly. The character inferred by him, the particular mental state in you, whether represented in his mind by images of further hostile or friendly acts, or in whatever other way, is still a partial character extracted from the totality of your phenomenal being, and is his reason for crouching and skulking, or the reverse. Dogs, moreover, seem to have the feeling of the value of their master's personal property, or at least a particular *interest* in objects their master uses. A dog left with his master's coat will defend it, though never taught to do so. We know of a dog accustomed to swim after sticks in the water, but who always refused to dive for stones. Nevertheless, when a fish-basket, which he had never been trained to carry, but merely knew as his master's, fell overboard from a boat, he immediately dove after it and brought it up. Dogs thus discern, at any rate so far as to be able to act, this partial character of *being valuable*, which lies hidden in certain things. Stories are told of dogs carrying coppers to pastry-cooks to get buns, and it is said that a certain dog, if he gave two coppers, would never leave without two buns. This may have been mere contiguous association, but it is possible that the animal noticed the character of duality, and identified it as the same in the coin and the cake. If so, it is probably the maximum of canine abstract thinking. Another story told to the writer is this: A dog was sent to a lumber-camp to fetch a wedge, with which he was known to be acquainted. After half an hour, not returning, he was sought and found biting and tugging at the handle of an axe which was driven deeply into a stump. The wedge could not be found. The teller of the story thought that the dog must have had a clear perception of the common character of serving to split which was involved in both the instruments, and, from their identity in this respect, inferred their identity for the purposes required.

It cannot be denied that this interpretation is a possible one, but it seems to us to far transcend the limits of ordinary canine abstraction. The property in question was not one which had direct personal interest for the dog, such as that of mere belonging to his master is in the case of the coat or the basket. If the dog in the sponge story had returned to the boat with a dipper, it would have hardly been more remarkable. It seems more probable, therefore, that this wood-cutter's dog had also been accustomed to carry the axe, and now, excited by the vain hunt for the wedge, had discharged his carrying powers upon the former instrument in a sort of confusion—just as a man may pick up a sieve to carry water in, in the excitement of putting out a fire.[7]

Thus, then, the characters extracted by animals are very few, and always related to their immediate interests or emotions. That dissociation by varying concomitants, which in man is based so largely on association by similarity, hardly seems to take place at all in the mind of brutes. One total thought suggests to them another total thought, and they find themselves acting with propriety, they know not why. The great, the fundamental, defect of their minds seems to be the inability of their groups of ideas to break across in unaccustomed places. They are enslaved to routine, to cut and dried thinking, and if the most prosaic of human beings could be transported into his dog's sensorium, he would be appalled at the utter absence of fancy which reigns there. Thoughts will not call up their similars, but only their habitual successors. Sunsets will not suggest heroes' deaths, but only supper-time. This is why man is the only metaphysical animal. To wonder why the universe should be as it is presupposes the notion of its being different, and a brute which never reduces the actual to fluidity by breaking up its literal sequences in his imagination can never

---

[7] This matter of confusion is important and interesting. Since confusion is mistaking the wrong part of the phenomenon for the whole, whilst reasoning is, according to our definition, based on the substitution of the right part for the whole, it might be said that confusion and reasoning were generically the same process. There are, however, other and more subtle considerations which intervene and prevent us from treating the matter further in this place.

form such a notion. He takes the world simply for granted, and never wonders at it at all.

Another well-known *differentia* of man is that he is the only laughing animal. But humor has been defined as the recognition of certain identities in things different. When the man in *Coriolanus* says of that hero that "there is no more mercy in him than there is milk in a male tiger," both the invention of the phrase and its enjoyment by the hearer depend on a peculiarly perplexing power to associate ideas by similarity.

Language is certainly a capital distinction between man and brute. But it may readily be shown how this distinction merely flows from those we have pointed out, easy dissociation of a representation into its ingredients, and association by similarity.

Language is a system of *signs*, different from the things signified, but able to suggest them.

No doubt brutes have a number of such signs. When a dog yelps in front of a door, and his master, understanding his desire, opens it, the dog may, after a certain number of repetitions, get to repeat in cold blood a yelp which was at first the involuntary interjectional expression of strong emotion. The same dog may be taught to "beg" for food, and afterwards come to do so deliberately when hungry. The dog also learns to understand the signs of men, and the word "rat" uttered to a terrier suggests exciting thoughts of the rat-hunt. If the dog had the varied impulse to vocal utterance which some other animals have, he would probably repeat the word "rat" whenever he spontaneously happened to think of a rat-hunt—he no doubt does have it as an auditory image, just as a parrot calls out different words spontaneously from its repertory, and having learned the name of a given dog will utter it on the sight of a different dog. In each of these separate cases the particular sign *may* be consciously noticed by the animal, as distinct from the particular thing signified, and will thus, so far as it goes, be a true manifestation of language. But when we come to man we find a great difference. He has a deliberate intention to apply a sign to everything. The linguistic impulse is with him generalized and systematic. For things hitherto unnoticed or unfelt, he *desires* a sign before he has one. Even though the dog should possess his "yelp" for this thing, his "beg" for that, and his auditory image "rat" for a third, the matter with him rests there. If a fourth thing interests him for which no sign happens already to have been learned, he remains tranquilly without it and goes no further. But the man *postulates* it, its absence irritates him, and he ends by inventing it. This *general purpose* constitutes, I take it, the peculiarity of human speech, and explains its prodigious development.

How, then, does the general purpose arise? As soon as the notion of the sign *as such*, apart from any particular import, is born; and it is born by dissociation from the outstanding portions of a number of concrete cases of signification. The "yelp," the "beg," the "rat," differ as to their import—and as to their own physical constitution. They agree only in so far as they have the same *use*—to be signs, to stand for something more important than themselves. The dog whom this similarity could strike would have grasped the sign *per se* as such, and would have become a speaker in the human sense. But how can the similarity strike him? Not without the juxtaposition of the similars (in virtue of the law we have so often repeated, that in order to be segregated an experience must be repeated with varying concomitants)—not unless the "yelp" of the dog at the moment it occurs *recalls* to him his "beg," by the delicate bond of their subtle similarity of use—not till then can this thought flash through his mind: "Why, yelp and beg, in spite of all their unlikeness, are yet alike in this: that they are actions, signs, which lead to important boons. Other boons, *any* boons, may then be got by other signs!" This reflection made, the gulf is passed. Animals probably never make it, because the bond of similarity is not delicate enough. Each sign is drowned in *its* import, and never awakens other signs and other imports in juxtaposition. The rat-hunt idea is too absorbingly interesting in itself to be interrupted by anything so uncontiguous to it as the "beg for food," or "the door-open yelp," nor in their turn do they awaken the rat-hunt.

In the human child, however, these ruptures of contiguous association are very soon made; far off cases of sign-using arise when we make a sign now; and soon language is launched. The child in each case makes the discovery for himself. No one can help him except by furnishing him with the conditions. But as he is constituted, the conditions will sooner or later shoot together into the result.[8]

---

[8] There are two other conditions of language in the human being, additional to association by similarity, that assist its action, or rather pave the way for it. These are: first, the great natural loquacity; and, second, the great imitativeness of man. The first produces the original reflex interjectional sign; the second (as Bleek has

The exceedingly interesting account which Dr. Howe gives of the education of his various blind-deaf mutes illustrates this point admirably. He began to teach Laura Bridgman by gumming raised letters on various familiar articles. The child was taught by mere contiguity to pick out a certain number of particular articles when made to feel the letters. But this was merely a collection of particular signs out of the mass of which the general purpose of *signification* had not yet been extracted by the child's mind. Dr. Howe compares his situation at this moment to that of one lowering a line to the bottom of the deep sea in which Laura's soul lay, and waiting until she should spontaneously take hold of it and be raised into the light. The moment came, "accompanied by a radiant flash of intelligence and glow of joy"; she seemed suddenly to become aware of the general purpose embedded in the different details of all these signs, and from that moment her education went on with extreme rapidity.

Another of the great capacities in which man has been said to differ fundamentally from the animal is that of possessing self-consciousness or reflective knowledge of himself as a thinker. But this capacity also flows from our criterion—without going into the matter very deeply, we may say that the brute never reflects on himself as a thinker, because he has never clearly dissociated, in the full concrete act of thought, the element of the thing thought

---

well shown) fixes it, stamps it, and ends by multiplying the number of determinate specific signs which are a requisite preliminary to the general conscious purpose of sign-making, which I have called the characteristic human element in language. The way in which imitativeness fixes the meaning of signs is this: When a primeval man has a given emotion, he utters his natural interjection; or when (to avoid supposing that the reflex sounds are exceedingly determinate by nature) a group of such men experience a common emotion, and one takes the lead in the cry, the others cry like him from sympathy or imitativeness. Now, let one of the group hear another, who is in presence of the experience, utter the cry; he, even without the experience, will repeat the cry from pure imitativeness. But, as he repeats the sign, he will be reminded by it of his own former experience. Thus, first, he has the sign with the emotion; then, without it; then, with it again. It is "dissociated by change of concomitants"; he feels it as a separate entity and yet as having a connection with the emotion. Immediately it becomes possible for him to couple it deliberately with the emotion, in cases where the latter would either have provoked no interjectional cry or not the same one. In a word, his mental procedure tends to *fix* this cry on *that* emotion; and when this occurs, in many instances, he is provided with a stock of signs, like the yelp, beg, rat of the dog, each of which suggests a determinate image. On this stock, then, similarity works in the way above explained.

of and the operation by which he thinks it. They remain always fused, conglomerated—just as the interjectional vocal sign of the brute almost invariably merges in his mind with the thing signified, and is not independently attended to *in se*.[9]

Now, the dissociation of these two elements probably occurs first in the child's mind on the occasion of some error or false expectation which would make him experience the shock of difference between merely imagining a thing and getting it. The thought experienced once with the concomitant reality, and then without it or with opposite concomitants, reminds the child of other cases in which the same provoking phenomenon occurred. Thus the general ingredient of error may be dissociated and noticed *per se*, and from the notion of error or wrong thought to that of thought in general, the transition is easy. The brute, no doubt, has plenty of instances of error and disappointment in his life, but the similar shock is in him most likely always swallowed up in the accidents of the actual case. An expectation disappointed may breed dubiety as to the realization of that particular thing when the dog next expects it. But that disappointment, that dubiety, while they are present in the mind, will not call up other cases in which the material details were different, but this feature of possible error was the same. The brute will, therefore, stop short of dissociating the general notion of error *per se*, and *a fortiori* will never attain the conception of Thought itself as such.

We may then, we think, consider it proven that the most characteristic single difference between the human mind and that of brutes lies in this deficiency on the brute's part to associate ideas by similarity—characters, the abstraction of which depends on this sort of association, must in the brute always remain drowned, swamped in the total phenomenon which they help constitute, and never used to reason from. But *other* characters (few and far between) may be singled out by practical interests.

But, now, since nature never makes a jump, it is evident that we should find the lowest men occupying in this respect an intermediate position between the brutes and the highest men, and so we do. Beyond the analogies which their own minds suggest by breaking up the literal sequence of their experience, there is a

---

[9] See an interesting article on the "Evolution of Self-Consciousness" in *Philosophical Discussions*, by Chauncey Wright. New York: Holt & Co., 1877.

whole world of analogies which they can appreciate when imparted
to them by their betters, but which they could never excogitate
alone. This answers the question we asked some time back, why
Darwin and Newton had to be waited for so long. The flash of
similarity between an apple and the moon, between the rivalry for
food in nature and the rivalry for man's approbation, was too
recondite to have occurred to any but exceptional minds. Genius,
then, is identical with the possession of Similar Association to an
extreme degree. Professor Bain, in his admirable work on the *Study
of Character*, says: "This I count the leading fact of genius . . . I
consider it quite impossible to afford any explanation of intellectual originality, except on the supposition of an unusual energy
on this point" (p. 327). He proceeds to show how alike in the arts,
in literature, in practical affairs, and in science, association by similarity is the prime condition of success. But as, according to our
view, there are two stages in reasoned thought, one where similarity
merely *operates* to call up cognate thoughts, and another farther
stage, where the bond of identity between the cognate thoughts is
noticed, so minds of genius may be divided into two main sorts,
those who notice the bond and those who merely obey it. The first
are the abstract reasoners, the men of science, and philosophers—
the analysts, in a word; the latter are the poets, the critics—the
artists, in a word, the men of intuitions. These judge rightly, classify
cases, characterize them by the most striking analogic epithets, but
go no further. At first sight it might seem that the analytic mind
represented simply a higher intellectual stage, and that the intuitive mind represented an arrested stage of intellectual development; but the difference is not so simple as this. Professor Bain has
said that a man's advance to the scientific stage (the stage of noticing and abstracting the bond of association) may often be due to
an *absence* of certain emotional sensibilities. The sense of color,
he says, may no less determine a mind away from science than it
determines it towards painting. There must be a penury in one's
interest in the details of particular forms in order to permit the
forces of the intellect to be concentrated on what is common to
many forms.[10] In other words, supposing a mind fertile in the suggestions of analogies, but, at the same time, keenly interested in
the particulars of each suggested image, that mind would be far

10 Bain: *On the Study of Character*, p. 317.

less apt to single out the particular character which called up the analogy than one whose interests were less generally lively. A certain richness of the æsthetic nature may, therefore, easily keep one in the intuitive stage. All the poets are examples of this. Take Homer: "Ulysses, too, spied round the house to see if any man were still alive and hiding, trying to get away from gloomy death. He found them all fallen in the blood and dirt, and in such number as the fish which the fishermen to the low shore, out of the foaming sea, drag with their meshy nets. These all, sick for the ocean water, are strewn around the sands, while the blazing sun takes their life from them. So there the suitors lay strewn round on one another." Or again: "And as when a Mæonian or a Carian woman stains ivory with purple to be a cheek-piece for horses, and it is kept in the chamber, and many horsemen have prayed to bear it off; but it is kept a treasure for a king, both a trapping for his horse and a glory to the driver—in such wise were thy stout thighs, Menelaos, and legs and fair ankles stained with blood."

A man in whom all the accidents of an analogy rise up as vividly as this, may be excused for not attending to the ground of the analogy. But he need not on that account be deemed intellectually the inferior of a man of drier mind, in whom the ground should not be eclipsed by the general splendor. Rarely are both sorts of intellect, the splendid and the analytic, found in conjunction. Plato among philosophers, and M. Taine, who cannot quote a child's saying without describing the *"voix chantante, étonnée, heureuse"* in which it is uttered, are only exceptions, whose strangeness proves the rule.

An often-quoted writer has said that Shakespeare possessed more *intellectual power* than anyone else that ever lived. If by this he meant the power to pass from given premises to right or congruous conclusions, it is no doubt true. The abrupt transitions in Shakespeare's thought astonish the reader by their unexpectedness no less than they delight him by their fitness. Why, for instance, does the death of Othello so stir the spectator's blood and leave him with a sense of reconcilement? Shakespeare himself could very likely not say why; for his invention, though rational, was not ratiocinative. Wishing the curtain to fall upon a reinstated Othello, that speech about the turbaned Turk suddenly simply flashed across him as the right end of all that went before. The dry critic who comes after can, however, point out the subtle bonds of identity that guided

Shakespeare's pen through that speech to the death of the Moor. Othello is sunk in ignominy, lapsed from his height at the beginning of the play. What better way to rescue him at last from this abasement than to make him for an instant identify himself in memory with the old Othello of better days, and then execute justice on his present disowned body, as he used then to smite all enemies of the State? But Shakespeare, whose mind supplied these means, could probably not have told why they were so effective.

But though this is true, and though it would be absurd in an absolute way to say that a given analytic mind was superior to any intuitional one, yet it is none the less true that the former *represents* the higher stage. Men, taken historically, reason by analogy long before they have learned to reason by abstract characters. We saw some time back how association by similarity and true reasoning were identical in their results. If a philosopher wishes to prove to you why you should do a certain thing, he may do so by using abstract considerations exclusively; a savage will prove the same by reminding you of a similar case in which you notoriously do as he now proposes, and this with no ability to state the *point* in which the cases are similar. In all primitive literature, in all savage oratory, we find persuasion carried on exclusively by parables and similes, and travelers in savage countries readily adopt the native custom. Take, for example, Dr. Livingstone's argument with the negro conjurer. The missionary was trying to dissuade the savage from his fetichistic ways of invoking rain. You see, said he, that, after all your operations, sometimes it rains and sometimes it doesn't, exactly as when you have not operated at all. But, replied the sorcerer, it is just the same with you doctors; you give your remedies, and sometimes the patient gets well and sometimes he dies, just as when you do nothing at all. To that the pious missionary replied, the doctor does his duty, after which God performs the cure if it pleases Him. Well, rejoined the savage, it is just so with me. I do what is necessary to procure rain, after which God sends it or withholds it according to His pleasure.[11]

This is the stage in which proverbial philosophy reigns supreme. "An empty sack can't stand straight" will stand for the reason why a man with debts may lose his honesty; and "a bird in the hand is worth two in the bush" will serve to back up one's exhortations to

[11] Quoted by Renouvier: *Critique Philosophique*, October 19, 1876.

prudence. Or we answer the question: "Why is snow white?" by saying, "For the same reason that soap-suds or whipped eggs are white"—in other words, instead of giving the *reason* for a fact, we give another *example* of the same fact. This offering a similar instance, instead of a reason, has often been criticised as one of the forms of logical depravity in men. But manifestly it is not a perverse act of thought, but only an incomplete one. Furnishing parallel cases is the necessary first step towards abstracting the reason embedded in them all.

As it is with reasons, so it is with words. The first words are probably always names of entire things and entire actions—extensive, coherent groups. A new experience in the primitive man can only be talked about by him in terms of the old experiences which have received names. It reminds him of certain ones from among them, but the *points* in which it agrees with them are neither named nor dissociated. Pure similarity must work before the abstraction which is based upon it. The first words are probably names of entire things and entire actions—extensive, coherent groups. Similarity working before abstraction, which as a rule we have seen to be based upon it, the first adjectives will be total nouns embodying the striking character. The primeval man will say not "the bread is hard," but "the bread is stone"; not "the face is round," but "the face is moon"; not "the fruit is sweet," but "the fruit is sugar-cane." The first words are thus neither particular nor general, but *vaguely* concrete. Just as we speak of an "oval" face, a "velvet" skin, or an "iron" will, without meaning to connote any other attributes of the adjective-noun than those in which it *does* resemble the noun it is used to qualify. After a while certain of these adjectively-used nouns come only to signify the particular quality for whose sake they are oftenest used; the *entire thing* which they originally meant receives another name, and they become true abstract and general terms. Oval, for example, with us suggests *only* shape. The first abstract qualities thus formed are, no doubt, qualities of the same sense, found in different objects—as big, sweet; next, analogies between different senses, as "sharp" of taste, "high" of sound, etc.; then, analogies of motor combinations, or form of relation, as simple, confused, difficult, reciprocal, relative, spontaneous, etc. The extreme degree of subtlety in analogy is reached in such cases, as when we say certain English art critics' writing reminds us of a close room in which pastilles have been burning, or that the mind of certain Frenchmen is like old Roquefort cheese. Here language utterly fails to hit upon the bases of resemblance.

Over an immense department of our thought we are still, all of us, in the savage state. Similarity operates in us, but abstraction has not taken place. We know what the present case is like, we know what it reminds us of, we have an intuition of the right course to take, if it be a practical matter. But analytic thought has made no tracks, and we cannot justify ourselves to others. In ethical, psychological, and æsthetic matters, to give a clear reason for one's judgment is universally recognized as a mark of rare genius. The helplessness of uneducated people to account for their likes and dislikes is often ludicrous. Ask the first Irish girl why she likes this country better or worse than her home, and see how much she can tell you. But if you ask your most educated friend why he prefers Titian to Paul Veronese, you will hardly get more of a reply; and you will probably get absolutely none if you inquire why Beethoven reminds him of Michael Angelo, or how it comes that a mere reclining figure by the latter can suggest all the moral tragedy of life. His thought obeys a *nexus*, but can't name it. And so it is with all those judgments of *experts*, which even though unmotived are so valuable. Saturated with experience of a particular class of materials, an expert intuitively feels whether a newly-reported fact is probable or not, whether a proposed hypothesis is worthless or the reverse. He instinctively knows that, in a novel case, this and not that will be the promising course of action. The well-known story of the old judge advising the new one never to give reasons for his decisions, "the decisions will probably be right, the reasons will surely be wrong," illustrates this. The doctor will feel that the patient is doomed, the dentist will have a premonition that the tooth will break, though neither can articulate a reason for his foreboding. The reason lies embedded, but not yet laid bare, in all the countless previous cases dimly suggested by the actual one, all calling up the same conclusion, which the adept thus finds himself swept on to, he knows not how or why.

A final conclusion remains to be drawn. If the theory be true which assigns to the cerebral hemispheres definite localities in which the various images, motor and sensible, which constitute our thoughts are stored up, then it follows that the great cerebral difference between habitual and reasoned thinking is this: that in the

former an entire system of cells vibrating at any one moment discharges in its totality into another entire system, and that the order
of the discharges tends to be a constant one in time; whilst in the
latter a part of the prior system still keeps vibrating in the midst of
the subsequent system, and the order—which part this shall be,
and what shall be its concomitants in the subsequent system—has
little tendency to fixedness in time. But this physical selection, so
to call it, of one part to vibrate persistently whilst the others rise
and subside, which is the basis of similar association, seems but a
minor degree of that still more urgent and importunate localize-
vibration which we can easiest conceive to underlie the mental fact
of interest, attention, or dissociation. In terms of the brain-process,
then, all these mental facts resolve themselves into a single peculiarity: that of indeterminateness of connection between the different
tracts, and tendency of action to focalize itself, so to speak, in small
localities which vary infinitely at different times, and from which
irradiation may proceed in countless shifting ways. (Compare Diagram 6.) To discover, or (what more befits the present stage of nerve
physiology) to adumbrate by some at least possible guess, on what
chemical or molecular-mechanical fact this instable equilibrium of
the human brain may depend, should be the next task of the physiologist who ponders over the passage from brute to man. Whatever the physical peculiarity in question may be, *it* is the cause
why a man, whose brain has it, reasons so much, whilst his horse,
whose brain lacks it, reasons so little. We have ourselves tried our
best to form some hypothesis, but wholly without success. We bequeath, therefore, the problem to abler hands.

But, meanwhile, this mode of stating the matter suggests a couple of other inferences, with which we may conclude. The first is
brief. If *focalization* of brain activity be the fundamental fact of
reasonable thought, we see why intense interest or concentrated
passion makes us think so much more truly and profoundly. The
persistent *focalization* of motion in certain tracts is the cerebral
fact corresponding to the persistent domination in consciousness
of the important feature of the subject. When not "focalized," we
are scatter-brained; but, when thoroughly impassioned, we never
wander from the point. None but congruous and relevant' images
arise. When roused by indignation or moral enthusiasm, how tren-
chant are our reflections, how smiting are our words. The whole
net-work of petty scruples and bye-considerations which, at ordi-

nary languid times, surrounded the matter like a cobweb, holding back our thought, as Gulliver was pinned to the earth by the myriad Liliputian threads, are dashed through at a blow, and the subject stands with its essential and vital lines revealed.

The last point is relative to Spencer's theory that what was acquired habit in the ancestor may become congenital tendency in the offspring. So vast a superstructure is raised upon this principle, both by Mr. Spencer and by others, that the paucity of empirical evidence for it has alike been matter of regret to its adherents, and of triumph to its opponents. The pointer pup, the birds on desert islands, the young of the tame rabbit, and Brown-Séquard's epileptic guinea-pigs constitute the whole beggarly array of proof. In the human race, where our opportunities for observation are the most complete, we seem to have no evidence whatever which would support the hypothesis, unless it be the probable law that city-bred children are more apt to be near-sighted than country children, and that is not a *mental* law. In the mental world we do not observe that the children of great travelers get their geography lessons with unusual ease, or that a baby whose ancestors have spoken German for thirty generations will, on that account, learn Italian any the less easily from its Italian nurse. But, if the considerations we have been led to are true, they explain perfectly well why this law of Spencer's *should not* be verified in the human race, and why, therefore, in looking for evidence on the subject, we should confine ourselves exclusively to lower animals. In them fixed habit is the essential and characteristic law of nervous action. The brain grows to the exact modes in which it has been exercised, and the inheritance of these modes—then called instincts—would have in it nothing surprising. But in man the negation of all fixed modes is the essential characteristic. He owes his whole preëminence as a reasoner, his whole human quality, we may say, to the facility with which a given mode of thought in him may suddenly be broken up into elements, which re-combine anew. Only at the price of inheriting no settled instinctive tendencies, is he able to settle every novel case by the fresh discovery by his reason of novel principles. He is, *par excellence*, the *educable* animal. If, then, Spencer's law were found exemplified in him, he would, in so far forth, fall short of his human perfections, and, when we survey the human races, we actually do find that those which are most instinctive at the outset are those which, on the whole, are least educated in the end.

An untutored Italian is, to a great extent, a man of the world; he has instinctive perceptions, tendencies to behavior, reactions, in a word, upon his environment, which the untutored German wholly lacks. If the latter be not drilled, he is apt to be a thoroughly loutish personage; but, on the other hand, the mere absence in his brain of definite innate tendencies enables him to advance by the development, through education, of his purely reasoned thinking, into complex regions of consciousness that the Italian probably could never approach.

We observe an identical difference between men as a whole, and women as a whole. A young woman of twenty reacts with intuitive promptitude and security in all the usual circumstances in which she may be placed. Her likes and dislikes are formed; her opinions, to a great extent, the same that they will be through life. Her character is, in fact, finished in its essentials. How inferior to her is a boy of twenty in all these respects. His character is still gelatinous, uncertain what shape to assume, "trying it on" in every direction. Feeling his power, yet ignorant of the manner in which he shall express it, he is, when compared with his sister, a being of no definite contour. But this absence of prompt tendency in his brain to set into particular modes is the very condition which insures that it shall ultimately become so much more efficient than the woman's. The very lack of pre-appointed trains of thought is the condition by which general principles and heads of classification are formed; and the masculine brain deals with new and complex matter indirectly by means of these, in a manner which the feminine method of direct intuition, admirably and rapidly as it performs within its limits, can vainly hope to cope with.

Are We Automata?

Everyone is now acquainted with the Conscious-Automaton-theory to which Prof. Huxley[1] gave such publicity in his Belfast address; which the late Mr. D. A. Spalding punctiliously made the pivot of all his book-notices in *Nature*; which Prof. Clifford fulminated as a dogma essential to salvation in a lecture on "Body and Mind";[2] but which found its earliest and ablest exposition in Mr. Hodgson's magnificent work, *The Theory of Practice*.[3] The theory maintains that in everything outward we are pure material machines. Feeling is a mere collateral product of our nervous processes, unable to react upon them any more than a shadow reacts on the steps of the traveller whom it accompanies. Inert, uninfluential, a simple passenger in the voyage of life, it is allowed to remain on board, but not to touch the helm or handle the rigging.

The theory also maintains that we are in error to suppose that our thoughts awaken each other by inward congruity or rational necessity, that disappointed hopes *cause* sadness, premises conclusions, etc. The feelings are merely juxtaposed in that order without mutual cohesion, because the nerve-processes to which they severally correspond awaken each other in that order.

It may seem strange that this latter part of the theory should be

[1] *Fortnightly Review*, N. S. Vol. XVI, p. 555.
[2] *Ibid.*, p. 714.
[3] Vol. I, pp. 416 ff.

held by writers, who like Prof. Huxley have openly expressed their belief in Hume's doctrine of causality. That doctrine asserts that the causality we seem to find between the terms of a physical chain of events, is an illegitimate outward projection of the inward necessity by which we feel each thought to sprout out of its customary antecedent. Strip the string of necessity from between ideas themselves, and it becomes hard indeed for a Humian to say how the notion of causality ever was born at all.

This, however, is an *argumentum ad hominem* which need not detain us. The theory itself is an inevitable consequence of the extension of the notion of reflex action to the higher nerve-centres. Prof. Huxley starts from a decapitated frog which performs rational-seeming acts although probably it has no consciousness, and passing up to the hemispheres of man concludes that the rationality of their performances can owe nothing to the feelings that coexist with it. This is the inverse of Mr. Lewes's procedure. He starts from the hemispheres, and finding their performances apparently guided by feeling concludes, when he comes to the spinal cord, that feeling though latent must still be there to make it act so rationally. Clearly such arguments as these may mutually eat each other up to all eternity.

The reason why the writers we speak of venture to dogmatize as they do on this subject, seems due to a sort of philosophic faith, bred like most faiths from an æsthetic demand. Mental and physical events are, on all hands, admitted to present the strongest contrast in the entire field of being. The chasm which yawns between them is less easily bridged over by the mind than any interval we know. Why then not call it an absolute chasm? And say not only that the two worlds are different, but that they are independent? This gives us the comfort of all simple and absolute formulas, and it makes each chain homogeneous to our consideration. When talking of nervous tremors and bodily actions, we may feel secure against intrusion from an irrelevant mental world. When, on the other hand, we speak of feelings, we may with equal consistency use terms always of one denomination, and never be annoyed by what Aristotle calls "slipping into another kind." The desire on the part of men educated in laboratories not to have their physical reasonings mixed up with such incommensurable factors as feelings is certainly very strong. Nothing is commoner than to hear them speak of conscious events as something so essentially vague and

39

(1879)

shadowy as even doubtfully to exist at all. I have heard a most intelligent biologist say: "It is high time for scientific men to protest against the recognition of any such thing as consciousness in a scientific investigation." In a word, feeling constitutes the "unscientific" half of existence, and anyone who enjoys calling himself a "scientist" will be too happy to purchase an untrammeled homogeneity of terms in the studies of his predilection, at the slight cost of admitting a dualism which, in the same breath that it allows to mind an independent status of being, banishes it to a limbo of causal inertness, from whence no intrusion or interruption on its part need ever be feared.

But Common Sense also may have its æsthetic demands, and among them may be a craving for unity. The spectacle of an ultimate and inexplicable dualism in the nature of things may be as unsatisfying as the obligation to calculate with heterogeneous terms. Two "aspects," *nemine adspiciente*, seem uncalled for. One may well refuse, until absolutely overpowered by the evidence, to believe that the world contains items which in no wise influence their neighbors; whose existence or non-existence need, so far as the remainder go, be taken into no account. It is a smoother and more harmonious thought to imagine all the items of the world without exception as interlocked in bonds of action and reaction, and forming a single dynamic whole.

And now, who shall decide between such rival æsthetic needs? *A priori* to shrink from a "chasm" between the objects of one's contemplation is as respectable as to dislike heterogeneity in the factors of one's reasoning operations. The truth is, then, that neither æsthetic motives nor ostensible reasons entitle us to decide between the Conscious-Automaton-theory and the theory of Common Sense. Both alike are conceptions of the possible, and for anyone dogmatically to affirm the truth of either is, in the present state of our knowledge, an extremely unscientific procedure.

The question for us then is: Can we get light from any facts hitherto ignored in the discussion? Since the direct evidence of our living feeling is ruled out of court as mendacious, can we find circumstantial evidence which will incline the balance either way, and save us from the dreary strife of prejudice and prepossession?

I think we can, and propose in the remainder of this article to show that this presumptive evidence wholly favors the efficacity of Consciousness. Consciousness, namely, has been slowly evolved in the animal series, and resembles in this all organs that have a use. Since the mere supernumerary depicted by the Conscious-Automaton-theory would be useless, it follows that if we can discover the utility of consciousness we shall overthrow that theory.

Our problem consequently is: Of what use to a nervous system is a superadded consciousness? Can a brain which has it function better than a brain without it? And to answer this question, we must know, first, the natural defects of the brain, and secondly, the peculiar powers of its mental correlate.

Since consciousness is presumably at its minimum in creatures whose nervous system is simple, and at its maximum in the hypertrophied cerebrum of man, the natural inference is that, as an *organe de perfectionnement,* it is most needed where the nervous system is highly evolved; and the form our first question takes is: What are the defects characteristic of highly evolved nervous centres?

If we take the actions of lower animals and the actions of lower ganglia in higher animals, what strikes us most in them is the determinateness with which they respond to a given stimulus. The addition of the cerebral hemispheres immediately introduces a certain incalculableness into the result, and this incalculableness attains its maximum with the relatively enormous brain-convolutions of man. In the beheaded frog the legs twitch as fatally when we touch the skin with acid as do a jumping-jack's when we pull the string. The machinery is as narrow and perfect in the one case as in the other. Even if all the centres above the cord except the cerebral hemispheres are left in place, the machine-like regularity of the animal's response is hardly less striking. He breathes, he swallows, he crawls, he turns over from his back, he moves up or down on his support, he swims and stops at a given moment, he croaks, he leaps forwards two or three times—each and all with almost unerring regularity at my word of command, provided I only be an experienced physiologist and know what ganglia to leave and what particular spur will elicit the action I desire. Thus if I merely remove his hemispheres and tilt my hand down, he will crawl up it but not jump off. If I pinch him under the arm-pits, he will croak once for each pinch; if I throw him into water, he will swim until I touch his hands with a stick, when he will immediately stop. Over a frog with an entire brain, the physiologist has no such power. The signal may be given, but ideas, emotions or

41

caprices will be aroused instead of the fatal motor reply, and whether the animal will leap, croak, sink or swim or swell up without moving, is impossible to predict. In a man's brain the utterly remote and unforeseen courses of action to which a given impression on the senses may give rise, is too notorious to need illustration. Whether we notice it at all depends on our mental preoccupations at the moment. If we do notice it, our action again depends on the "considerations" which it awakens, and these again may depend as much on our transient mood or on our latest experience as on any constant tendencies organized in our nature.

We may thus lay it down as an established fact that the most perfected parts of the brain are those whose actions are least determinate. It is this very vagueness which constitutes their advantage. They allow their possessor to adapt his conduct to the minutest alterations in the environing circumstances, any one of which may be for him a sign, suggesting distant motives more powerful than any present solicitations of sense. Now it seems as if certain mechanical conclusions should be drawn from this state of things. An organ swayed by slight impressions is an organ whose natural state is one of unstable equilibrium. We may imagine the various lines of discharge in the cerebrum to be almost on a par in point of permeability—what discharge a given small impression will produce may be called accidental, in the sense in which we say it is a matter of accident whether a rain-drop falling on a mountain ridge descend the eastern or the western slope. It is in this sense that we may call it a matter of accident whether a woman's first child be a boy or a girl. The ovum is so unstable a body that certain causes too minute for our apprehension may at a certain moment tip it one way or the other. The natural law of an organ constituted after this fashion can be nothing but a law of caprice. I do not see how one could reasonably expect from it any certain pursuance of useful lines of reaction such as the few and fatally determined performances of the lower centres constitute within their narrow sphere. The dilemma in regard to the nervous system seems to be of the following kind. We may construct one which will react infallibly and certainly, but it will then be capable of reacting to very few changes in the environment—it will fail to be adapted to all the rest. We may, on the other hand, construct a nervous system potentially adapted to respond to an infinite variety of minute features in the situation; but its fallibility will then be as great as its elaboration. We can never be sure that its equilibrium will be upset in the appropriate direction. In short, a high brain may do many things, and may do each of them at a very slight hint. But its hair-trigger organization makes of it a happy-go-lucky, hit-or-miss affair. It is as likely to do the crazy as the sane thing at any given moment. A low brain does few things, and in doing them perfectly forfeits all other use. The performances of a high brain are like dice thrown forever on a table. Unless they be loaded, what chance is there that the highest number will turn up oftener than the lowest?

All this is said of the brain as a physical machine pure and simple. Can consciousness increase its efficiency by loading its dice? Such is our next problem.

But before directly attacking it, we must pause a moment to make sure that we clearly apprehend the import of such expressions as *useful discharge, appropriate direction, right reaction,* and the like, which we have been using. They all presuppose some Good, End or Interest to be the animal's. Until this goal of his salvation be posited, we have no criterion by which to estimate the utility of any of his reactions. Now the important thing to notice is that the goal cannot be posited at all so long as we consider the purely physical order of existence. Matter has no ideals. It must be entirely indifferent to the molecules of C, H, N and O, whether they combine in a live body or a dead one. What the present conditions fatally necessitate, that they do with equal infallibility and cheerfulness; whether the result of their action be the perfume of a rose or the odor of carrion, the words of a Renouvier or the crackling of thorns under a pot, it is brought forth with as little reluctance in the one case as in the other. Good involves the notion of less good, necessitates comparison, and for a drop of water either to compare its present state with an absent state or to compare its total self with a drop of wine, would involve a process not commonly thought of as physical. Comparison requires a *tertium quid,* a *locus* —call it what you will—in which the two outward existences may meet on equal terms. This forum is what is known as a consciousness. Even sensations cannot be supposed, simply as such, to be aware of their relations to each other. A succession of feelings is not (as James Mill reiterates) one and the same thing with a feeling of succession, but a wholly different thing. The latter feeling requires a self-transcendency of each item, so that each not only *is* in relation, but knows its relation, to the other. This self-transcendency of data constitutes the conscious form. Where we suppose it to exist we have mind; where mind exists we have it.

You may, it is true, ascribe mind to a physical process. You may allow that the atom engaged in some present energy has a dreamlike consciousness of residual powers and a judgment which says, "Those are better than this." You may make the rain-drop flowing downhill posit an impossible ascent as its highest good. Or you may make the C, H, N and O atoms of my body knowingly to conspire in its construction as the best act of which they are capable. But if you do this, you have abandoned the sphere of purely physical relations.

Thus, then, the words Use, Advantage, Interest, Good, find no application in a world in which no consciousness exists. Things there are neither good nor bad; they simply are or are not. Ideal truth to exist at all requires that a mind also exist which shall deal with it as a judge deals with the law, really creating that which it professes only to declare.

But, granting such a mind, we must furthermore note that the direction of the verdict as to whether A or B be best, is an ultimate, arbitrary expression of feeling, an absolute fiat or decree. What feels good *is* good; if not it is only because it negates some other good which the same power of feeling stamps as a Better.[4]

Thus much, then, is certain, that in venturing to discuss the perfection and uses of the brain at all, we assume at the outset the existence of *someone's* consciousness to make the discussion possible by defining some particular good or interest as the standard by which the brain's excellence shall be measured. Without such measure Bismarck's brain is no better than a suicidal maniac's, for the one works as perfectly as the other to its end. Considered as

---

4 I have treated this matter of teleology being an exclusively conscious function more at length in an article on "Spencer's Definition of Mind" (*Journal of Speculative Philosophy*, Jan., 1878), to which I take the liberty of referring the reader. The fact that each consciousness simply *stakes* its ends and challenges the world thereby, is most conspicuous in the case of what is called Self-love. There the end staked by each mind is peculiar to itself, whilst in respect of other ends many minds may unite in a common position. But in their psychological essence these impersonal ends in no wise differ from self-interest. Abolish the minds to whom they seem good and they have no status; any more than the categorical imperative that perish who may John Smith must wax fat and prosper, has a *ratio existendi* after Smith's peculiar lusts have been annihilated.

mere existence, a festering corpse is as real as a live chancellor, and, for aught physics can say, as desirable. Consciousness in declaring the superiority of either one, simply creates what previous to its fiat had no existence. The judge makes the law while announcing it: if the judge be a maggot, the suicide's brain will be best; if a king, the chancellor's.

The consciousness of Mr. Darwin lays it down as axiomatic that self-preservation or survival is the essential or universal good for all living things. The mechanical processes of "spontaneous variation" and "natural selection" bring about this good by their combined action; but being physical processes they can in no sense be said to intend it. It merely floats off here and there accidentally as one of a thousand other physical results. The followers of Darwin rightly scorn those teleologists who claim that the physical process, as such, of evolution follows an ideal of perfection. But now suppose that not only our Darwinian consciousness, but with even greater energy the consciousness of the creature itself, postulates survival as its *summum bonum*, and by its cognitive faculty recognizes as well as Mr. Darwin which of its actions and functions subserves this good; would not the addition of causal efficacy to this consciousness enable it to furnish forth the means as well as fix the end—make it teleologically a fighter as well as a standard-bearer? Might not, in other words, such a consciousness promote or increase by its function of efficacity the amount of that "usefulness" on the part of the brain which it defines and estimates by its other functions? To answer such a question, we must analyze somewhat closely the peculiarities of the individual consciousness as it phenomenally presents itself to our notice.

If we use the old word category to denote every irreducibly peculiar form of synthesis in which phenomena may be combined and related, we shall certainly have to erect a category of consciousness, or what with Renouvier we may, if we prefer, call a category of personality. This category might be defined as the mode in which data are brought together for *comparison with a view to choice.*[5]

5 Neither 'association' nor 'dissociation' is synthesis of a peculiar kind; they are mere generic modes, and are wholly unfit to serve as *differentiæ* of psychical phenomena in any general philosophical classification. Comparison and choice, on the contrary, are each *sui generis*. Let it not be said that a magnet compares the different filings in a machine-shop to choose the iron filings from the heap. There is no proof that the brass filings appeal to it at all. In comparison, both terms equally appeal to consciousness.

Both these points, comparison and choice, will be found alike omnipresent in the different stages of its activity. The former has always been recognized; the latter less than it deserves.

Many have been the definitions given by psychologists of the essence of consciousness. One of the most acute and emphatic of all is that of Ulrici, who in his *Leib und Seele* and elsewhere exactly reverses the formula of the reigning British school, by calling consciousness a discriminating activity—an *Unterscheidungsvermögen*. But even Ulrici does not pretend that consciousness creates the differences it becomes aware of in its objects. They pre-exist and consciousness only discerns them; so that after all Ulrici's definition amounts to little more than saying that consciousness is a faculty of cognition—a rather barren result. I think we may go farther and add that the powers of cognition, discrimination and comparison which it possesses, exist only for the sake of something beyond themselves, namely, Selection. Whoever studies consciousness, from any point of view whatever, is ultimately brought up against the mystery of *interest* and *selective attention*. There are a great many things which consciousness *is* in a passive and receptive way by its cognitive and registrative powers. But there is one thing which it *does, suâ sponte*, and which seems an original peculiarity of its own; and that is, always to choose out of the manifold experiences present to it at a given time some one for particular accentuation, and to ignore the rest. And I shall now show how, from its simplest to its most complicated forms, it exerts this function with unremitting industry.

To begin at the bottom, even in the infra-conscious region which Mr. Spencer says is the lowest stage of mentality. What are our senses themselves but organs of selection? Out of the infinite chaos of movements, of which physics teaches us that the outer world consists, each sense-organ picks out those which fall within certain limits of velocity. To these it responds, but ignores the rest as completely as if they did not exist. It thus accentuates particular movements in a manner for which objectively there seems no valid ground; for, as Lange says, there is no reason whatever to think that the gap in nature between the highest sound-waves and the lowest heat-waves is an abrupt break like that of our sensations, or that the difference between violet and ultra-violet rays has anything like the objective importance subjectively represented by that between light and darkness. Out of what is in itself an undistinguishable, swarming *continuum*, devoid of distinction or emphasis, our senses make for us, by attending to this motion and ignoring that, a world full of contrasts, of sharp accents, of abrupt changes, in a word, of picturesque light and shade.

If the sensations we receive from a given organ have their causes thus picked out for us by the conformation of the organ's termination, the attention, on the other hand, out of all the sensations yielded, picks out certain ones as worthy of its notice and suppresses all the rest. Helmholtz's immortal work on *Physiological Optics* is little more than a study of those visual sensations of which common men never become aware—blind spots, *muscæ volitantes*, after-images, irradiation, chromatic fringes, marginal changes of color, double images, astigmatism, movements of accommodation and convergence, retinal rivalry, and more besides. We do not even know, as Professor William B. Rogers pointed out, on which of our eyes an image falls, until trained to notice the local sensation. So habitually overlooked is this by most men that one may be blind for years of a single eye and not know it.[6]

Helmholtz says we only use our sensations as *signs*. The sensations from which we avert our attention are those which are valueless as tokens of the presence of objective things. These *things* are called the Objects of perception. But what are *they*? Nothing, as it seems to me, but groups of coherent sensations. This is no place to criticise Helmholtz's treatment of perception, but I may say, in passing, that I think his rather indefinite and oracular statements

---

[6] If one cared to indulge in *a priori* constructions *à la* Spencer, one might easily show how the differentiation of sense-organs arose in the primitive polyp through this reinforcement by a selective attention (supposed efficacious) of particular portions of the feeling yielded by an organ already nascent. The integument of the animal might, for instance, at first be affected both by light-vibrations and by those far below them. But if the former were picked out by the consciousness as most interesting, the nervous movements would soon grow more and more harmonious with them, and more and more out of tune with the rest. An optic nerve and retina would thus result. One might corroborate this reasoning by pointing to what happens in cases of squint. The squinting eye gives double images which are so inconvenient that the mind is forced to abstract its attention from them. This resolute refusal to attend to the sensations of one eye soon makes it totally blind. It would seem, indeed, that the attention positively suppressed the function of the retina, for the presence of cataract which keeps the image from it altogether, results in no such paralysis. I do not insist on this point, partly because such speculation is rather cheap—"all may raise the flowers now, for all have got the seed"—and partly because there seems some reason to doubt whether the usually received explanation of strabismic blindness be correct.

about the part played by the intellect therein have momentarily contributed to retard psychological inquiry. We find the Kantian philosophers everywhere hailing him as the great experimental corroborator of their master's views. They say he has proved the present sensation to have nothing to do with the construction of the Object—that is an original act of the intellect which the sensation merely instigates but does not furnish forth: it contains ultra-sensational elements. All that Helmholtz really *does* prove is, that the so-called Object is constituted of *absent* sensations. What he has not explicitly noticed is, that among these the mind picks out certain particular ones to be more essential and characteristic than the rest. When, for example, on getting a peculiar retinal sensation with two acute and two obtuse angles, I *perceive* a square table-top, which thus contradicts my present image; what is the *squareness* but one out of an infinite number of possible retinal sensations which the same object may yield? From all these the mind, for æsthetic reasons of its own, has singled out this one and chosen to call it the object's essential attribute? Were room here given, I think it might be shown that perception involves nothing beyond association and selection. The antithesis is not, as Helmholtz's admirers would have it, between sensations on the one hand as signs and original intellectual products, materially different from sensations on the other, as Objects. It is between present sensations as signs and certain absent sensations as Objects, these latter being moreover arbitrarily selected out of a large number as being more objective and real than the rest. The real form of the circle is deemed to be the sensation it gives when the line of vision is perpendicular to its centre—all its other sensations are signs of this sensation. The real sound of the cannon is the sensation it makes when the ear is close by. The real color of the brick is the sensation it gives when the eye looks squarely at it from a near point, out of the sunshine and yet not in the gloom; under other circumstances it gives us other color-sensations which are but signs of this—we then see it looks pinker or blacker than it really is. The reader knows no object which he does not represent to himself by preference as in some typical attitude, of some normal size, at some characteristic distance, of some standard tint, etc., etc. But all these essential characteristics, which together form the genuine objectivity of the thing and are contrasted with the subjective sensations we may happen to get from it at a given moment, are themselves sensations pure and simple, susceptible of being fully given at *some* other moment. The spontaneity of the mind does not consist in conjuring up any new non-sensational quality of objectivity. It consists solely in deciding what the particular sensation shall be whose native objectivity shall be held more valid than that of all the rest.[7]

Thus perception involves a twofold choice. Out of all present sensations, we notice mainly such as are significant of absent ones; and out of all the absent associates which these suggest, we again pick out a very few to be the bearers *par excellence* of objective reality. We could have no more exquisite example of the mind's selective industry.

That industry goes on to deal with the objects thus given in perception. A man's Empirical Thought depends on the objects and events he has experienced, but what these shall be is to a large extent determined by his habits of attention. An object may be present to him a thousand times, but if he persistently fails to notice it, it cannot be said to enter into his experience. We are all seeing flies, moths, and beetles by the thousand, but to whom, save an entomologist, do they say anything distinct? On the other hand, an object met only once in a life-time may leave an indelible experience in the memory. Let four men make a tour in Europe. One will bring home only picturesque impressions—costumes and colors, parks and views and works of architecture, pictures and statues. To another all this will be non-existent; and distances and prices, populations and drainage-arrangements, door- and window-fastenings, and other useful statistics will take their place. A third will give a rich account of the theatres, restaurants, and pub-

---

[7] When I say Objects are wholly formed of associated and selected sensations, I hope the reader will not understand me to profess adhesion to the old atomic doctrine of association, so thoroughly riddled of late by Professor Green. The association of sensations of which I speak, presupposes comparison and memory which are functions not given in any one sensation. All I mean is, that these mental functions are already at work in the first beginnings of sensation and that the simplest changes of sensation moreover involve consciousness of all the categories—time, space, number, objectivity, causality. There is not first a passive act of sensation proper, followed by an active production or projection ("inference") of the attributes of objectivity by the mind. These all come to us together with the sensible qualities, and their progress from vagueness to distinctness is the only process psychologists have to explain. What I mean to say in the text is, that this process involves nothing but association and selection, all new production of either material or formal elements being denied.

lic balls, and naught beside; whilst the fourth will perhaps have been so wrapped in his own subjective broodings as to tell little more than a few names of places through which he passed. Each has selected, out of the same mass of presented objects, those which suited his private interest and has made his experience thereby.

If, now, leaving the empirical combination of objects, we ask how the mind proceeds *rationally* to connect them we find selection again to be omnipotent. In an article on "Brute and Human Intellect" in the *Journal of Speculative Philosophy*, July 1878, p. 236 [*ed.*, p. 1], I have tried to show that all Reasoning depends on the ability of the mind to break up the totality of the phenomenon reasoned about into partial factors or elements, and to pick out from among these the particular one which, in our given theoretical or practical emergency, may lead to the proper conclusion. Another predicament will need another conclusion, and require another element to be picked out. The man of genius is he who will always stick-in his bill, as it were, at the right point, and bring it out with the right element—"reason" if the emergency be theoretical, "means" if it be practical—transfixed upon it. Association by similarity I have shown to be an important help to this breaking-up of represented things into their elements. But this association is only the minimum of that same selection of which picking out the right reason is a maximum. I here confine myself to this brief statement, but it may suffice to show that Reasoning is but another form of that selective activity which appears to be the true sphere of mental spontaneity.

If now we pass to the Æsthetic activity of the mind, the application of our law is still more obvious. The artist notoriously selects his items, rejecting all tones, colors, shapes, which do not harmonize with each other and with the main purpose of his work. That unity, harmony, "convergence of characters," as M. Taine calls it, which gives to works of art their superiority over works of nature, is wholly due to *elimination*. Any natural subject will do, if the artist has wit enough to pounce upon some one feature of it as characteristic, and suppress all merely accidental items which do not harmonize with this.

Ascending still higher we reach the plane of Ethics, where choice reigns notoriously supreme. An act has no ethical quality whatever unless it be chosen out of several all equally possible. To sustain the arguments for the good course and keep them ever before

us, to stifle longing for more flowery ways, to keep the foot unflinchingly on the arduous path, these are characteristic ethical energies. But more than these; for these but deal with the means of
compassing interests already felt by the man to be supreme. The
ethical energy *par excellence* has to go farther and choose which
interest out of several equally coercive shall become supreme. The
issue here is of the utmost pregnancy, for it decides a man's entire
career. When he debates, Shall I commit this crime? choose that
profession? accept that office, or marry this fortune?—his choice
really lies between one of several equally possible future *Selves*.
What his entire empirical *Ego* shall become, is fixed by the conduct of this moment. Schopenhauer, who enforces his determinism
by the argument that with a given fixed character only one reaction
is possible under given circumstances, forgets that, in these critical
ethical moments, what consciously *seems* to be in question is the
very complexion of the character. The problem with the man is
less what act he shall now choose to do, than what kind of a being
he shall now resolve to become.

Looking back then over this review we see that the mind is at
every stage a theatre of simultaneous possibilities. Consciousness
consists in the comparison of these with each other, the selection of
some, and the suppression of the rest by the reinforcing and inhibiting agency of Attention. The highest and most elaborated
mental products are filtered from the data chosen by the faculty
next beneath out of the mass offered by the faculty below that,
which mass in turn was sifted from a still larger amount of yet simpler material, and so on. The highest distillate thus *represents* in
the last analysis nothing but sensational elements. But this is far
from meaning that it implies nothing but passive faculty of sensation. As well might one say that the sculptor is passive, because the
statue stood from eternity within the stone. So it did, but with a
million different ones beside it. The world as a Goethe feels and
knows it all lay embedded in the primordial chaos of sensations,
and into these elements we may analyze back every thought of the
poet. We may even, by our reasonings, unwind things back to that
black and jointless continuity of space and moving clouds of swarming atoms which science calls the only real world. But all the while
the world we feel and live in, will be that which our ancestors and
we, by slowly cumulative strokes of choice, have extricated out of
this, as the sculptor extracts his statue by simply rejecting the other

portions of the stone. Other sculptors, other statues from the same stone! Other minds, other worlds from the same chaos! Goethe's world is but one in a million alike embedded, alike real to those who may abstract them. Some such other worlds may exist in the consciousness of ant, crab and cuttle-fish.

After this perhaps too long analysis let us now look back. We have found that the unaided action of the cerebral hemispheres would probably be random and capricious; that the nerve-process likely to lead to the animal's interests would not necessarily predominate at a given moment. On the other hand, we have found that an impartial consciousness is a nonentity, and that of the many items that ever occupy our mental stage Feeling always selects one as most congruous with the interests it has taken its stand upon. Collating these two results, an inference is unavoidable. The "items" on the mental stage are the subjective aspects of as many nerve-processes, and in emphasizing the representations congruous with conscious interest and discouraging all others, may not Attention actually reinforce and inhibit the nerve-processes to which the representations severally correspond?

This of course is but a hypothetical statement of the verdict of direct personal feeling—a verdict declared mendacious by Professor Clifford. But the intricate analysis by which it has been reached gives it great plausibility. I shall strengthen the probability by further facts in a moment. But I beg the reader to notice here the limitations of the power of Feeling, if power there be. All the possibilities of representation, all the images are furnished by the brain. Consciousness produces nothing, it only alters the proportions. Even the miraculous action of free-will can only consist in the quantitative reinforcement of representations already given qualitatively. A sonorous plate has no proper note of its own. It is almost impossible by scraping it to reproduce twice an identical tone. The number of Chladni's sand-figures it will furnish is as inexhaustible as the whimsies which may turn up in a brain. But as the physicist's finger pressing the plate here or there determines nodal points that throw the sand into shapes of relative fixity, so may the accentuating finger of consciousness deal with the fluctuating eddies in the cerebral cortex.

That these eddies are stirred by causes that have no connection with either dominant interests or present impressions seems manifest from the phenomena of dreaming. The chaotic imagery there appears due to the unequal stimulus of nutrition in different localities. But if an accidental variation in nutrition is sufficient to determine the brain's action, what safeguard have we at any time against its random influence? It may of course be reasonably objected that the exceptional state of sleep can afford no proper clue to the brain's operations when awake. But Maury in his classic work, *Le Sommeil*, has conclusively proved the passage of dreams through "hypnagogic hallucinations" into that meteoric shower of images and suggestions, irrelevant to the main line of thought, the continual presence of which everyone who has once had his *interest awakened* in the subject, will without difficulty recognize in himself. Ordinarily these perish in being born, but if one by chance saunters into the mind, which *is* related to the dominant pursuit of the moment, presto! it is pounced upon and becomes part of the empirical *Ego*. The greatest inventions, the most brilliant thoughts often turn up thus accidentally, but may mould for all that the future of the man. Would they have gained this prominence above their peers without the watchful eye of consciousness to recognize their value and emphasize them into permanence?

> Nur allein der Mensch
> Vermag das Unmögliche:
> Er unterscheidet,
> Wählet und richtet;
> Er kann dem Augenblick
> Dauer verleihen.

The hypothesis we are advocating might, if confirmed, considerably mitigate one of the strongest objections to the credibility of the Darwinian theory. A consciousness which should not only determine its brain to prosperous courses, but also by virtue of that hereditary influence of habit (nowadays so generally believed in by naturalists) should organize from generation to generation a nervous system more and more mechanically incapable of wandering from the lines of interest chosen for it at first, would immensely shorten the time and labor of natural selection. Mr. Darwin regards animated nature as a sort of table on which dice are continually being thrown. No intention presides over the throwing, but lucky numbers from time to time fortuitously turn up and are preserved. If the ideas we have advanced concerning the instability of a complicated cerebrum be true, we should have a sort of extension of this reign of accident into the functional life of every individual animal whose brain had become sufficiently evolved. As his body morphologically was the result of lucky chance, so each of his so-called acts of intelligence would be another; and ages might elapse before out of this enormous lottery-game a brain should emerge both complex and secure. But give to consciousness the power of exerting a constant pressure in the direction of survival, and give to the organism the power of growing to the modes in which consciousness has trained it, and the number of stray shots is immensely reduced, and the time proportionally shortened for Evolution. It is, in fact, hard to see how without an effective super-intending ideal the evolution of so unstable an organ as the mammalian cerebrum can have proceeded at all.

That consciousness should only be intense when nerve-processes are retarded or hesitant, and at its minimum when nerve-action is rapid or certain, adds color to the view that it is efficacious. Rapid, automatic action is action through thoroughly excavated nerve-tracks which have not the defect of uncertain performance. All instincts and confirmed habits are of this sort. But when action is hesitant there always seem several alternative possibilities of nervous discharge. The feeling awakened by the nascent excitement of each nerve-track seems by its attractive or repulsive quality to determine whether the excitement shall abort or shall become complete. Where indecision is great, as before a dangerous leap, consciousness is agonizingly intense. Feeling, from this point of view, may be likened to a cross-section of the chain of nervous discharge, ascertaining the links already laid down, and groping among the fresh ends presented to it for the one which seems best to fit the case.

The remarkable phenomena of "vicarious function" in the nervous centres form another link in our chain of circumstantial evidence. A machine in working order functions fatally in one way. Our consciousness calls this the right way. Take out a valve, throw a wheel out of gear or bend a pivot, and it becomes a different machine, functioning just as fatally in another way which we call the wrong way. But the machine itself knows nothing of wrong or right: matter has no ideals to pursue. A locomotive will carry its train through an open drawbridge as cheerfully as to any other destination.

A brain with part of it scooped out is virtually a new machine, and during the first days after the operation functions in a thoroughly abnormal manner. Why, if its performances blindly result from its structure, undirected by any feeling of purpose, should it not blindly continue now to throw off inappropriate acts just as before its mutilation it produced appropriate ones? As a matter of fact, however, its performances become from day to day more normal, until at last a practised eye may be needed to suspect anything wrong. If we suppose the presence of a mind, not only taking cognizance of each functional error, but able to exert an efficient pressure to inhibit it if it be a sin of commission, to lend a strengthening hand if the nerve-defect be a weakness or sin of omission—nothing seems more natural than that the remaining parts of the brain, assisted in this way, should by virtue of the principle of habit grow back to the old teleological modes of exercise for which they were at first incapacitated. Nothing, on the contrary, seems at first sight more unnatural than that they should vicariously take up the duties of a part now lost without those *duties as such* exerting any persuasive or coercive force.[8]

There is yet another set of facts which seem explicable by the supposition that consciousness has causal efficacity. It has long been noticed that pleasures are generally associated with beneficial, pains with detrimental, experiences. All the fundamental vital processes illustrate this law. Starvation, suffocation, privation of food, drink and sleep, work when exhausted, burns, wounds, inflammation, the effects of poison, are as disagreeable as filling the hungry stomach, enjoying rest and sleep after fatigue, exercise after rest, and a sound skin and unbroken bones at all times, are pleasant. Mr. Spencer, in the chapter of his *Psychology* entitled "Pleasures and Pains," has suggested that these coincidences are due, not to any pre-established harmony, but to the mere action of natural selection which would certainly kill off in the long run any breed of creatures to whom the fundamentally noxious experience seemed enjoyable. An animal that should take pleasure in a feeling of suffocation would, if that pleasure were efficacious enough to make him immerse his head in water, enjoy a longevity of four or five minutes. But if

---

[8] This argument, though so striking at first sight, is perhaps one which it would be dangerous to urge too dogmatically. It may be that restitution of cerebral function is susceptible of explanation on drainage-principles, or, to use Stricker's phrase, by "collateral innervation." As I am preparing a separate essay on this subject, I will say no more about the matter here.

pleasures and pains have no efficacy, one does not see (without some such *a priori* rational harmony as would be scouted by the "scientific" champions of the Automaton-theory) why the most noxious acts, such as burning, might not give a thrill of delight, and the most necessary ones, such as breathing, cause agony.[9] The exceptions to this law are, it is true, numerous, but relate to experiences that are either not vital or not universal. Drunkenness, for instance, which though noxious is to many persons delightful, is a very exceptional experience. But, as the excellent physiologist Fick remarks, if all rivers and springs ran alcohol instead of water, either all men would hate it or our nerves would have been selected so as to drink it with impunity. The only very considerable attempt, in fact, that has ever been made to explain the *distribution* of our feelings is that of Mr. Grant Allen in his suggestive little work *Physiological Æsthetics*; and his reasoning is based exclusively on that causal efficacity of pleasures and pains which the "double-aspect" partisans so strenuously deny.

Thus, then, from every point of view the circumstantial evidence against that theory is very strong. *A priori* analysis of both brain and conscious action shows us that if the latter were efficacious it would, by its selective emphasis, make amends for the indeterminateness of the former; whilst the study *a posteriori* of the *distribution* of consciousness shows it to be exactly such as we might expect in an organ added for the sake of steering a nervous system grown too complex to regulate itself. The conclusion that it is useful is, after all this, more than justifiable. But, if it is useful, it must be so

---

[9] I do not overlook an obvious objection suggested by such an operation as breathing. It, like other motor processes, results from a tendency to nervous discharge. When this takes place immediately, hardly any feeling but the rather negative one of ease results. When, however, a nervous discharge is checked it is a universal law that consciousness of a disagreeable kind is awakened, reaching in the case of suffocation the extremity of agony. An Automatist may then say that feeling here, so far from playing a dynamic part, is a mere passive index or symptom of certain mechanical happenings; and if here, then elsewhere. It may be replied that even were this true of completely habitual acts like breathing, where the nervous paths have been thoroughly organized for generations, it need not be true of hesitant acts not yet habitual; it need not be true of pains and pleasures, such as hunger and sleep, *not* connected with motor discharge; and even in the instance chosen it leaves out the possibility that the nervous mechanism, now automatically perfect, may have become so by slowly organized habit acquired under the guidance of conscious feeling.

through its efficaciousness, and the Conscious-Automaton-theory must succumb to the theory of Common Sense.

Our discussion might fairly stop here save for the possible difficulty some readers may have in appreciating the full utility of having certain nervous possibilities emphasized above the rest. The measure of all utility is, as we have seen, some standard posited by Desire. The standard of survival or self-preservation is most potent. But there exist a host of other standards, æsthetic and moral, imperative so long as they do not conflict with this one and sometimes imperative over this one. In the preliminary selection by the senses of certain objective orders of movement, it is difficult to see what standard is subserved. The utility of not having a sense for magnetism when we have one for heat, is not obvious. We may at most suspect a possible æsthetic brightness and clearness to result from the wide intervals. But passing by this obscure region we see without the least difficulty why we ignore those ingredients of sensation which are not signs of things. What the peculiarity is in itself which makes Smith's voice so different from Brown's, we need never inquire so long as whenever we hear it we say, "There is Smith." For our practical interest in recognizing whom we have to deal with outweighs our interest in the shades of sound *per se.* The selection again of certain attitudes, expressions, etc., in Smith, to stand as characteristic of him so that when others are present we say, "He does not look like himself," and if he is sitting to us for his portrait we spend an hour perhaps in placing him and lighting him so as to bring out with the utmost clearness these selected traits—this selection, I say, is equally explicable by various æsthetic standards, permanency, simplicity, harmony, clearness, and the like. Passing now from traits to *things,* the utility of selection is obviously created and measured by the interests the man has made his own. If Edward never walks out without finding a four-leafed clover, while Oliver dies of old age without having seen one, this is merely due to the fact that Edward has somehow been led to stake his happiness on that particular branch of discovery, and out of a visual field identical with that of Oliver has picked the details that minister to this somewhat arbitrary interest. Granted the interest, we cannot deny the use of the picking-out power. That Edward, having this interest in common with many others, should finally succeed in emphasizing certain of those others and suppressing this, would be an example of the utility of selection in the ethical field, supposing always that the new interest chosen were of a higher order and not, like making puns, for example, as trivial an end as the one forsaken.

In the ethical field the importance of choosing one's paramount interest is universally recognized. But it is not so commonly known how, when the interest is once fixed upon, the selective activity must ceaselessly work to detect its presence or absence in each emergency that turns up. Take, for example, an inebriate struggling with temptation. The glass is before him, and the act of drinking has an infinity of aspects and may be defined in as many ways. If he selected the aspect of its helping him to write an article, of its being only lager-beer, of its being the fourth of July, of his needing it as medicine, of his never having formally signed the pledge, of this particular drink "not counting," or else of its giving him the strength to make a much more powerful resolution for the future than any of his previous ones, or whatever other sophistries his appetite may instigate, he does but accentuate some character really contained in the act, but needing this emphasizing pressure of his attention to be erected into its essence. But if, out of all the teeming suggestions with which the liquor before him inspires his brain, respectively saying, "It is a case of this good, of that interest, of yonder end," his mind pounces on one which repeats, *"It is essentially a case of drunkenness!"* and never lets that go, his stroke of classification becomes his deed of virtue. The power of choosing the right name for the case is the true moral energy involved, and all who posit moral ends must agree in the supreme utility of, at least, this kind of selective attention.

But this is only one instance of that substitution for the entire phenomenon of one of its partial aspects which is the essence of all reasoned thought as distinguished from mere habitual association. The utility of reasoned thought is too enormous to need demonstration. A reasoning animal can reach its ends by paths on which the light of previous experience has never shone. One who, on the contrary, cannot break up the total phenomenon and select its essential character must wait till luck has already brought it into conjunction with his End before he can guess that any connection obtains between the two. All this is elaborated in the article "On Brute and Human Intellect" to which I have ventured to refer the reader. In that article (p. 274 [*ed.*, 35]) I stated that I had found it impossible to symbolize by any mechanical or chemical peculiarity that tendency of the human brain to focalize its activity on small points which seems to constitute the essence of its reasoning power. But if such focalization be really due not so much to structural peculiarity as to the emphasizing power of an efficacious consciousness superadded, the case need no longer perplex us.

Of course the materialist may still say that the emphasized attention obeys the strongest vibration and does not cause it, that we will what we do, not do what we will—that, in short, interest is passive and at best a *sign* of strength of nerve-disturbance. But he is immediately confronted by the notorious fact that the strongest tendencies to automatic activity in the nerves often run most counter to the selective pressure of consciousness. Every day of our lives we struggle to escape some tedious tune or odious thought which the momentary disposition of the brain keeps forcing upon us. And, to take more extreme cases, there are murderous tendencies to nervous discharge which, so far from involving by their intensity the assent of the will, cause their subjects voluntarily to repair to asylums to escape their dreaded tyranny. In all these cases of *voluntas paradoxa* or *invita*, the individual selects out of the two possible selves yielded by his cerebral powers one as the true *Ego*; the other he regards as an enemy until at last the brain-storm becomes too strong for the helmsman's power. But even in the depths of mania or of drunkenness the conscious man can steady himself and be rational for an instant if a sufficient motive be brought to bear. He is not dead, but sleepeth.

I should be the last to assert that the Common-Sense-theory leaves no difficulties for solution. I feel even more strongly than Professors Huxley and Clifford that the only *rational nexus* is that of identity, and that feeling and nerve-tremor are disparate. I feel too that those who smile at the idea of calling consciousness an "organ," on a par with other organs, may be moved by a fundamentally right instinct. And I moreover feel that that unstable equilibrium of the cerebrum which forms the pivot of the argument just finished may, with better knowledge, be found perfectly compatible with an average appropriateness of its actions taken in the long run. But with all these concessions made, I still believe the Common-Sense-theory to merit our present credence. Fragmentary probabilities supported by the study of details are more worthy of trust than any mere universal conceptions, however tempting their simplicity. Science has won all her credit by the former kind of reasoning, Metaphysics has lost hers by the latter. The impossibility of motion, of knowledge, either subjective or objective, are proved by arguments as good as that which denies causality to feeling, because of its disparity with its effects. It is really monstrous to see the *prestige* of "Science" invoked for a materialistic conclusion, reached by methods which, were they only used for spiritualistic ends, would be hooted at as antiscientific in the extreme. Our argument, poor as it is, has kept at any rate upon the plane of concrete facts. Its circumstantial evidence can hardly be upset until the Automaton-theorists shall have condescended to make or invoke some new discoveries of detail which shall oblige us to reinterpret the facts we already know. But in that case I feel intimately persuaded that the reinterpretation will be so wide as to transform the Automaton-theory as thoroughly as the popular one. The Automaton-theory in its present state contents itself with a purely negative deliverance. There is a chasm, it says, between feeling and act. Consciousness is impotent. It exists, to be sure, but all those *manners* of existence which make it seem relevant to our outward life are mere meaningless coincidences, inexplicable parts of the general and intimate irrationality of this disjointed world. What little continuity and reason there seems to be, it says, lies wholly in the field of molecular physics. Thither Science may retreat and hump her strong back against the mockeries and phantasms that people the waste of Being around.

Now the essence of the Common-Sense-theory, I take it, is to negate these negations. It obstinately refuses to believe Consciousness irrelevant or unimportant to the rest. It is there for a purpose, it has a meaning. But as all meaning, relevancy and purpose are symbolized to our present intelligence in terms of action and reaction and causal efficacy, Common Sense expresses its belief in the worth of Feeling by refusing to conceive of it out of these relations. When a philosophy comes which, by new facts or conceptions, shall show how particular feelings may be destitute of causal efficacy without the genus Feeling as a whole becoming the sort of *ignis fatuus* and outcast which it seems to be to-day to so many "scientists" (loathly word!), we may hail Professors Huxley and Clifford as true prophets. Until then, I hold that we are incurring the slighter error by still regarding our conscious selves as actively combating each for his interests in the arena and not as impotently paralytic spectators of the game.

The Spatial Quale

Mr. Cabot, in his acute and suggestive article on the notion of space in the July number of this journal [*The Journal of Speculative Philosophy*], argues that, as it forms a system of relations, it cannot be given in any one sensation, and concludes that it is a symbol of the general relatedness of objects constructed by thought from data which lie below consciousness. However Mr. Cabot may differ in detail from the authors whom he criticises, he and they are generically one; for the starting-point of their whole industry, in endeavoring to *deduce* space, lies in their regarding as the fundamental characteristic thereof the fact that any one spatial *position* can only be defined by its relation to other positions, and in their assumption that position, until thus defined, is not felt at all.

Mr. Cabot begins his article with the hegelian thesis that extension has only negative predicates; that it signifies only the indefinite "*otherness*" of all objects of perception to each other. I am at a loss to see how such an inaccurate identification of a species with its entire genus can ever have been in favor. Otherness is not space; otherness is just—otherness, and nothing else; a logical relation between ideas of which *spatial* otherness supplies us with a very peculiar and distinct sort of instance. The ground of its distinctness from other kinds of otherness I hold to be the special form of sensibility which objects spatially comparable *inter se* awaken in us; and I shall endeavor in the following pages to prove that this form of sensibility—this quality of extension or spatial *quale,* as I have called it—exists at the outset in a simple and unitary form. The *positions* which ultimately come to be determined within it, in mutual relation to each other, are later developments of experience, guided by attention. These *relations* of position differ in no respect from the logical relations between items thought of in nonspatial regards. If I say A is farther to the left than B, my relating thought is the same as when I say a nasturtium is nearer to vermilion than a rose. When I say "An ox is larger than a sheep," my relating thought is the same as when I say "Napoleon was more ambitious than Washington." The difference in the two cases lies wholly in the sensible *data* on which the thought works. In the one case these are spatial, in the other chromatic, in the third moral; and would be what the Germans call *intensiv* in a fourth case, if I were to say, "Camphor smells milder than ammonia."

It seems to me that the differences of opinion to which the question has given rise, have arisen in the failure to discriminate between the mere sensible quality of extensiveness, as such—the spatial *quale,* as we may call it—and the subdivision and measurement of this extension. By holding fast to this discrimination, I believe that empiricism and nativism can be reconciled, and all the facts on which they severally lay most stress receive equal justice. Almost all those who have written on the subject hitherto have seemed to regard it as axiomatic that our consciousness of the whole of space is formed by adding together our perceptions of particular spaces; that there can be no perception of any extent at all without a perception of particular positions within that extent, and of their distances and directions from each other. Extension becomes thus what the English psychologists have called it, an "aggregate of coexisting positions," and we find intelligent writers like Mr. Sully[1] speaking of "the *fallacious assumption* that there can be an idea of distance in general apart from particular distances"; whilst Wundt similarly says:[2] "An indefinite localization, which waits for experience to give it its reference to real space, stands in contradiction with the very idea of localization, which means the reference to a determinate point of space."

If all this be true, Mr. Cabot is perfectly right in saying that we

[1] *Mind,* vol. iii [1876], p. 177.
[2] *Grundzüge der physiologischen Psychologie* [1874], p. 480.

cannot be aware of space at all without being aware of it as a distinctly apprehended system of *relations* between a multitude of parts—without, in a word, performing a mental synthesis. But that we are originally aware of it without all this, can, I think, be easily shown; and this vague original consciousness of a space in which separate positions and directions have not, as yet, been mentally discriminated, deserves, if it exists at all, the name of sensation quite as much as does the color, "blue," or the feeling, "warm"; especially since, like "blue" or "warm," it seems a simple form of retinal or cutaneous sensibility, involving no muscular element whatever.

I will try first to show that into our cognition of space there necessarily enters what must be called a specific quality of sensibility, *sui generis*, the spatial *quale*. This cannot possibly be analyzed into the mere notion of order or relation. Mill, Bain, and Spencer, who so strangely keep repeating that space is nothing but "the order of coexistences," forget the fact that we have coexistences which are arranged in no spatial order. The sound of the brook near which I write, the odor of the cedars, the feeling of satisfaction with which my breakfast has filled me, and my interest in writing this article, all simultaneously coexist in my consciousness without falling into any sort of spatial order. If, with my eyes shut, these elements of consciousness give me any spatial feeling at all, it is that of a teeming muchness or abundance, formed of their mutual interpenetration, but within which they occupy no positions. For the "order of coexistences" to become the order of space, the coexistences must, in the first place, be evenly gradated, or ordered, in themselves; and, in the second place, their gradations must be enveloped in the unity of the peculiar spatial feeling.

The mind can arrange its ingredients in many orders. The order of positions in space is evenly gradated in three dimensions, but neither the even gradation, nor the three dimensions, nor both together, suffice by themselves to constitute its spatiality. We may have an evenly gradated order of luminosities from white to black; of tints from yellow, through green, to blue; of loudnesses of all intensities; of good and evil, and so on; but the position of any item in these orders, although it may be metaphorically expressed on a spatial scale, is not directly intuited by the mind as objectively existing in such a scale. The order is really a logical one, *constructed* out of the mutual relations of the various items by the mind, which compares them. It lacks the sensible matrix, so to speak, of a unifying intuition, in which they lie embedded as the equally logical order of related positions lies in space. Just so we may arrange items of experience in three dimensions; tones may be arranged on scales of intensity, pitch and *timbre*; colors in the orders of hue, intensity, and purity; and the entire system of all possible color and tone, thus constructed, has been symbolized to the imagination by cubes, pyramids, spheres, and the like. But no one dreams that they exist as such, for everyone is conscious that the construction is a logical one, involving a conscious comparison of remembered items and their relations. These exist separately, and to the *system* which they unitedly form there corresponds no sensible, unifying quality which the mind can immediately intuit as a unifying background, like that yielded by space to the bidimensional order of objective positions.

Space, then, as we know it, is something additional to mere co-existence and mere continuous order. The space in which items are arranged when they are intuited by us as objectively existing in spatial order, and not simply so symbolically figured, is an entirely peculiar kind of feeling, indescribable except in terms of itself. Why should we hesitate to call it an ingredient of the *sensation* yielded to us by the retina or skin, which intuits the items? Everyone will admit the degree of *intensity* of a sensation to be a part of its sensible quality. The brightness of the blue sky, as I now look at it, betrays its intensity by pricking, as it were, my retina. The *extent* of the blue which I at this moment see, seems to be an attribute given quite as immediately. A broad blueness differs from a narrow blueness as immediately as a bright blueness from a sombre blueness. I may, it is true, in the exercise of conscious comparison, identify this particular brightness and blueness with a certain remembered number in a conventional scale of colors, and then think of the neighboring tints as they evenly shade away from this one. So I may, by taking thought, estimate in square feet the breadth of the blue surface, and locate by my imagination its position in that total system of real spaces which I have learnt to know as the geographic world, but which no single retinal sensation can ever give me all at once, because no single retinal image is large enough. For the *intuition* of a given objective space, with its peculiar *quale*, must not be confounded with the *notion* of the total space, in which that and all other particular spaces lie in determinate order. The latter is a real construction out of separate, but related, elements. The former is a sensation—given all at once, if at all. Any space which I can take in at one glance comes to me as an undivided *plenum*. Were it built up, as the empiricists say, out of a vast number of perceptions of position fused together, I do not see how its quality could escape retaining something of the jerky, granulated character of its composite source. The spaces we *do* construct by adding together related positions—those, namely, which are too vast to be taken in at one glance—are, in fact, presented to consciousness in this jerky manner. The thought of the space between me and the opposite wall is perfectly smooth. The thought of the space between me and San Francisco has to be imagined as a successive number of hours and days of riding or railroading, filled with innumerable stoppings and startings, none of which can be omitted without falsifying the imagination. But if, as the empiricists say, all our space consciousness were compounded of innumerable ideas of motion and position, even the shortest space we perceive ought to be as coarse-grained, if one may so express it, as the distance from here to San Francisco.

We are thus forced to conclude that it is a simple, specific quality of retinal or cutaneous sensation. The quality of muchness or vastness, which envelops the separate positions and particular extensions which we learn to discriminate, clings to them always, colors their order, and makes it the special kind of order we call spatial. *Quâ* order, the spatial order is truly the product of relating thought; but *quâ* spatial it is a *datum* of simple sensibility. In the individual's psychic history the sensation, space, as a simple vague consciousness of vastness, comes first. The field of vision—or better, the sensation of light—can no more exist without it than without its *quantum* of intensity. But just as the degree of intensity, to be cognized as such or such a degree, requires a long education, involving memory, comparison, and recognition; so the quantity of extension, to be perceived—as a given number of feet, rods, or miles—presupposes a like education. The standard of intensity is the intensity of some remembered sensation which we choose for our absolute unit. The standard of extension is the remembered spatial sensation of vastness, or *absolute size*, which we get when certain amounts of our cutaneous surface are excited, or when on our retina we feel the image of our hand, foot, and so forth, at a certain average or habitual distance selected as the norm.

The spatial *quale* is, then, primitively a very vague *quantum*, but it is a *spatial quantum*. The word vague means that of which the external limits are uncertain, or that which is without internal subdivisions, or both; in the technical language of logic, that which is neither "clear" nor "distinct." The vaguely spatial field of vision is made clear and distinct by being subdivided. To subdivide it means to have the attention called now to one point, now to another within its limits and upon its borders. This is a process which, amongst other things, undoubtedly involves different local sensations at different points, and feelings resulting from muscular motion. Its result is the *measurement* of the field of vision. We may admit the coincidences which Helmholtz, Wundt, and others have shown between visual space thus *measured* and the laws of muscular movement of the eye-ball; we may even allow that the measurement is almost exclusively due to an intellectual elaboration of sensations of motion or innervation. But for all that, we need not in the least suppose that the *spatiality* of the thing measured does not pre-exist as a simple sensible quality.

It seems to me that all our sensations, without exception, have this spatial *quale*. I am surprised that Riehl, whose article is in other respects so just, should regard it as an exclusive endowment of the retina. What I mean by the spatial quality is what Professor Bain so often refers to as the "massiveness" of a feeling. The squeaking of a slate-pencil is less spatial than the voluminous reverberations of a thunderstorm; the prick of a pin less so than the feeling of a warm bath; a little neuralgic pain, fine as a cobweb, in the face, far less so than the heavy soreness of a boil or the vast discomfort of a colic or lumbago.[3]

---

[3] Should anyone object that such terms as "voluminous" and "massive," applied to sound and pain, are but metaphorical, and involve no literal spatial import, we may ask him why this peculiarly spatial metaphor is used rather than any other. Evidently because of some quality in the sound or pain which distinctly *reminds us of space*. If we furthermore hold, as I do, that the only possible foundation of an analogy is a partial identity in the analogous things, we must suppose the voluminousness and massiveness in question to be, at least partially, the same with spatial bulk. Now, the category of *muchness* is the only *partial* ingredient common to all the several terms. But *muchness* is generic, and embraces temporal, numerical and intensive, as well as extensive muchness. But that peculiarity in the pain and sound which makes us call them voluminous is quite different from that which would make us call them protracted, numerous, or intense. They must, then, have some other characteristic which determines their muchness as spatial; and this, being otherwise indescribable, is what I call the simple spatial *quale*.

The vastness of the retinal sensation seems in no essential respect, but only perhaps in amount, to differ from these. It need not surprise us to find an objectively small surface yielding, when excited, a more massive sensation than a much larger, but less sensitive, surface. How disproportionately great does the crater of a newly-extracted tooth feel! A midge buzzing against our tympanum often feels as big as a butterfly. Degree of nerve-disturbance, and extent thereof, seem to a certain extent to stand mutually in vicarious relation. The retina, then, by the mere fact of being excited, gives us the feeling of extent, and it differs from other sensitive surfaces only in the fact that we are able to fix our attention successively on its different points, to discriminate their directions, and so to measure it.

If one should admit that the first two dimensions of space may thus be called part of the simple retinal sensation, but that the intuition of depth cannot be so given, I would not only reply, with Stumpf, that we cannot feel plane space *as a plane* without in some way cognizing the cubic spaces which the plane separates, but I also would propose the following simple experiment: Let the objector sit with closed eyes, and let a friend approximate some solid object, like a large book, noiselessly to his face. He will immediately become aware of the object's presence and position—likewise of its departure. The perception here seems due to the excessive tactile sensibility of the tympanic membrane, which feels the pressure of the air differently according as an object is near it or not. To certain blind persons this sensation is a surprisingly accurate revealer of surrounding facts, and a friend of the author, making the experiment for the first time, discriminated unhesitatingly between the three degrees of solidity of a board, a lattice-frame, and a sieve, held close to his ear. Now as this sensation is never used by ordinary persons as a means of perception, we may fairly assume that its felt quality in those whose attention is called to it for the first time, belongs to it *quâ* sensation, and owes nothing to educational suggestions. Now this felt quality is most distinctly and unmistakably one of vague spatial vastness in three dimensions—quite as much so as is the felt quality of the retinal sensation when we lie on our back and fill the entire field of vision with the empty blue sky. When an object is brought near the ear we immediately feel shut in, contracted; when the object is removed, we suddenly feel as if a transparency, clearness, openness, had been made outside of us.[4] And the feeling will, by anyone who will take the pains to observe it, be acknowledged to involve the third dimension in a vague, unmeasured state.

On the peripheral parts of the retina discrimination is very imperfect, although practice may make it much less so. If the reader will fix his eye steadily on a distant point, and bring his hand gradually into the field of view, he will first see the hand, and see it as extended and possessing parts, but will be wholly unable to count the fingers. He will see objects on the same portions of the retina without recognizing what they are. In like manner if he turn his head upside down, or get into some unnatural position, the spatial *relations* of what he sees—distances, directions, and so forth —will be very uncertain, positions and measurements vague; but who will pretend that the picture, in losing its *order*, has become any the less spatial?

Just as the current psychologies assume that there can be no space before separate positions have been accurately distinguished, so they assume the perception of motion to be impossible until the positions of terminus *a quo* and terminus *ad quem* are severally cognized, and their successive occupancies by the moving body are perceived to be separated by a distinct interval of time. As a matter of fact, however, we cognize only the very slowest motions in this way. Seeing the hand of a clock at XII, and afterwards at VI, I judge that it has moved through the interval. Seeing the sun now in the east and again in the west, I infer it to have passed over my head. But we can only *infer* that which we already generically know in some more direct fashion, and it is experimentally certain that we have the feeling of motion given us as a direct and simple *sensation*. Czermak long ago pointed out the difference between seeing the motion of the second-hand of a watch, when we look directly at it, and noticing the fact of its having altered its position when we fix our gaze upon some other point of the dial-plate. In the first case we have a specific quality of sensation which is absent in the second. If the reader will find a portion of his skin—the arm, for example

---

[4] I may remark parenthetically, upon the thoroughly objective reference of this uneducated sensation. The observer is not aware of his feeling as such, but of the immediate presence or removal in space of an object. The blind persons whom I have examined with reference to their use of this sensation were entirely ignorant that it resided in the tympanum at all. They did not know how they came to feel the objects, but only that they were there.

—where a pair of compass-points an inch apart are felt as one impression, and if he will then trace lines a tenth of an inch long on that spot with a pencil-point, he will be distinctly aware of the point's motion and vaguely aware of the direction of the motion. The perception of the motion here is certainly not derived from a pre-existing knowledge that its starting and ending points are separate positions in space, because positions in space ten times wider apart fail to be discriminated as such when excited by the dividers. It is the same with the retina. One's fingers when cast upon its peripheral portions, cannot be counted—that is to say, the five retinal tracts which they occupy are not distinctly apprehended by the mind as five separate positions in space—and yet the slightest movement of the fingers is most vividly perceived as movement, and nothing else. It is thus certain that our sense of movement, being so much more delicate than our sense of position, cannot possibly be derived from it. A curious observation by Exner[5] completes the proof that movement is a primitive form of sensibility, by showing it to be much more delicate than our sense of succession in time. This very able young physiologist caused two electric sparks to appear in rapid succession, one beside the other. The observer had to state whether the right hand one or the left hand one appeared first. When the interval was reduced to as short a time as 0.045″ the discrimination of temporal order in the sparks became impossible. But Exner found that if the sparks were brought so close together in space that their irradiation circles overlapped, the eye then felt their flashing as if it were the motion of a single spark from the point occupied by the first to the point occupied by the second, and the time interval might then be made as small as 0.014″ before the mind began to be in doubt as to whether the apparent motion started from the right or left. On the skin similar experiments gave similar results.

We are accordingly compelled to admit a sensation of motion as such, prior to our discriminations of position in either time or space. But motion, even in this primitive state, occurs in spatial form. It thus follows that we have a feeling of space, distinct enough at any rate for motion to be apprehended as such, before we have anything like the perception of a system of related positions, dis-

5 *Sitzungsberichte der kaiserlichen Akademie der Wissenschaften*, Wien, Bd. LXXII, Abth. 3 (1875), pp. 156–190.

tances, or directions. This feeling of space, involving as it does no consciousness of relations (though it may later evolve such consciousness), can only be called a kind of sensation.

Whether the feelings of muscular contraction and innervation, or whether the vertiginous sensation yielded by the semi-circular canals of the ear involve also a cognition of motion of this "distinct," though not "clear," kind may be left an open question. It seems, at least, not improbable that they do.[6] We should thus have a certain spatial quantification given as a universal datum of sensibility. These primitive movement spaces may be at first wholly ambiguous.

Vierordt has, in fact, tried in a striking essay[7] to show that we are originally not aware whether a given movement sensation is performed by us or by something else upon us. Objectivity and subjectivity, direction, extent, and all other relative determinations are subsequent intellectual acts, presupposing memory and comparison. But these latter functions could never work their data into the spatial form unless that form already clove to the latter as sensations.

To sum up briefly my thesis: I say that the feeling arising from the excitement of any extended part of the body is felt as extended —why, we cannot say. The primary retinal sensation is a simple

[6] I have not seen Cyon's late work on the semi-circular canals, but I cannot believe him to have succeeded in proving these to be the principal space-giving organ. That they give, when excited, a vague sense of motion through a vague room is undeniable, and they make us acutely sensible of different directions and velocities in this motion. I imagine they subserve the finished structure of objective space more by their delicate discrimination of direction than in any other way. Right and left, up and down, are elementary sensations. If we take a cube and label one side *top*, another *bottom*, a third *front*, and a fourth *back*, there remains no form of words by which we can *describe* to another person which of the remaining sides is *right* and which *left*. We can only point and say here is right and there is left, just as we should say this is red and that blue, without being able to give an idea of them in words. Now when we move our heads to the left or right new objects dart into those respective sides of the field of vision, and thus the sides of this field have their intrinsic contrast augmented by the still intenser contrast of the two feelings of direction in movement severally associated with them. Up and down, and intermediate directions, have their differentiation in consciousness improved in the same way. It may be also that our visual feeling of depth, the third dimension, is reenforced by an associated semi-circular canal feeling of floating forwards. Where the third dimension is abysmal—as in looking up to, or down from, a height—the association of a swimming, floating, or falling element is very manifest.

[7] *Zeitschrift für Biologie*, 1876.

vastness, a teeming muchness. The perception of positions within it results from subdividing it. The measurement of distances and directions comes later still.

The vastness is subdivided by the attention singling out particular points within it. How this discrimination occurs we shall see later; but when it has occurred, every subdivision thus separately noticed appears as occupying a separate position within the total bigness. Several subdivisions of a sensitive surface, excited together, fuse into a broader position or bigger space than that of any one of them excited or noticed alone,[8] but smaller than the total bigness which they help constitute. A and B, two points simultaneously discriminated by attention, are *ipso facto* felt as outside or alongside of each other; but the amount of separating interval and the direction are at first quite vague. It is only when a third point, C, has been noticed, or rather a large number of additional points, all outside of each other, that the comparison of their distances and directions fixes and determines the distance and direction of A from B. We then feel A and B to be closer together than B and C. We feel C to be in the same direction from B as B is from A, and the like. And this gradual education determines for the first time a system of fixed positions within the total space. In a word, accurate perception of any two positions as such, presupposes separate acquaintance with other positions. The mapping out of retinal space involves much experience; the mere perception of it as spatial, none. All these are ultimate facts not deducible from anything simpler. He who believes them is certainly to be called a "Nativist," or a "Sensationalist."

It follows, from these propositions, that if a sensitive surface is affected *in its totality* by each of many different outward causes, each cause will appear with the vastness given by the surface, but the several causes will not appear alongside of each other, not even if they all excite the surface at once. The olfactory and gustatory surfaces seem to be in this predicament. Whatever excites them at all excites the whole extent of them at once; though, even in the

[8] The single sensation yielded by two compass-points, although it seems simple, is yet felt to be much bigger and blunter than that yielded by one. The touch of a single point may always be recognized by its quality of sharpness. This page looks much smaller to the reader if he closes one eye than if both eyes are open. So does the moon, which latter fact shows that the phenomenon has nothing to do with parallax.

tongue there seems to be a determination of bitter flavors to the back, and of acids to the front, edge of the organ. Spices likewise affect its sides and front, and a taste like that of alum localizes itself, by its styptic effect on the portion of mucous membrane which it immediately touches, more sharply than roast pork, for example, which stimulates all parts alike. The pork, therefore, tastes more spacious than the alum or the pepper. In the nose, too, certain smells, of which vinegar may be taken as the type, seem less spatially extended than heavy, suffocating odors, like musk. The reason of this appears to be that the former inhibit inspiration by their sharpness, whilst the latter are drawn into the lungs, and thus excite an objectively larger surface. I will, however, not venture to dogmatize on this point.

In like manner, a sensitive surface, excited everywhere homogeneously, might only feel its total vastness without discerning positions therein. A fœtus bathed in *liquor amnii* discerns no one part of its skin more than another. But if we wet a portion of the skin, the wet part is strongly contrasted with the rest, and, with the general contrast of excitement, the contrast of local feeling simultaneously awakes. Adventitious sensations, occurring on special points of a sensitive surface, certainly call attention to the diversities of local feeling resident in the points, and make us notice their separateness in a way impossible when the surface was unexcited. In the spatial muchness of a colic—or, to call it by a more spacious-sounding vernacular, belly-ache—I can with difficulty distinguish the north-east from the south-west corner, but can do so much more easily if, by pressing my finger against the former, I am able to make the pain there more intense. I cannot feel two local differences on my skin by a pure mental act of attention, unless the local feelings are very strongly contrasted indeed, and belong to quite distinct parts of the body. But I can get the contrast of local feelings in spots much closer together by exciting them, even though each be excited in an identical way, as by compass-points. In cases of this sort, where points receiving an identical kind of excitement are, nevertheless, felt to be locally distinct, and the objective irritants are also judged multiple—*e.g.*, compass-points on skin, or stars on retina—the ordinary explanation of psychologists is no doubt just: We judge the outward causes to be multiple because we have discerned the local feelings of their sensations to be different. Granted none but homogeneous irritants, that organ would then distinguish the greatest multiplicity of irritants—would count most stars or compass-points, or best compare the size of two wet surfaces—whose local sensibility was the least even. A skin whose sensibility shaded rapidly off from a focus, like the apex of a boil, would be better than a homogeneous integument for spatial perception. The retina, with its exquisitely sensitive *fovea*, has this peculiarity, and undoubtedly owes to it a great part of the minuteness with which we are able to subdivide the total bigness of the sensation it yields. On its periphery the local differences do not shade off very rapidly, and we can count there fewer subdivisions.

But I believe that the psychologists, in making the judgment of discrete cause, *always* depend on perception of discrete position, have only stated half the truth.[9] I fancy that the breaking up of the sensitive surfaces into positions depends quite as much on our recognition of the heterogeneity and multiplicity of simultaneously impinging sensations as the latter recognition depends on our noticing the positions.

Positions which would not be distinguished if excited by homogeneous stimuli have their local feelings awakened when the stimuli show a strong contrast of quality. Whatever emphasizes the quality of the adventitious feeling turns the attention more exclusively to it, and makes us, in the same act, aware of its place. Qualitative contrasts are counted *where* they belong. On the retinal margin color contrast is very imperfect. A motley object gives us nothing but a blurred perception of "something there." The *there* is as blurred as the *something*, but the moment the object breaks into two colors the *there* breaks into two spots.

It follows, from all this, that the psychologic problem which the study of space-perception suggests is not what has generally been assumed. How, after noticing certain simultaneous differences, do we come to make a spatial construction of them? That problem is unanswerable; extent cleaves immediately to every simultaneity,

9 I do not refer to the explanations of double image by misjudged doubleness of position, where two organs are used—the double pea felt with crossed fingers (see Robertson, in *Mind*, vol. i) and double optic images (see Wundt, *Psychologie*). These delusions are no doubt due to the fact that the simultaneous excitements in question most habitually come from two objects differently located. The objective judgment, however, may be readily corrected by experience without the duplicity of the local sensation, as such, being in the least altered. I deal in the text only with the local discriminations made within the continuous bigness yielded by a single organ, retina, or finger.

and position to every difference we notice within it—all by an ultimate law. Our real problem is: How come we to notice the simultaneous differences at all? How can we ever evolve parts from a
confused unity, if the latter did not yield them at first? How, in a
word, does a vague muchness ever become a sum of discrete constituents? This is the problem of Discrimination, and he who will
have thoroughly answered it will have laid the keel of psychology.

I can only suggest here that the history of discrimination is to a
great extent a history of interaction between sensations. It is due
to the play of association and dissociation. In the case that now
concerns us, local contrasts which would never be noticed, *per se*,
are emphasized in consciousness in many ways by the addition of
other feelings to them. In addition to what we have noticed already, I may make the following remarks.

In the first place, it is a law that sensations experienced in immutable association are apt not to be discriminated. We do not
discriminate the feeling of contraction of the diaphragm from that
of expansion of the lungs. Experienced always together, they form
the simple feeling called "drawing breath." Now, the purely local
peculiarities of feeling in different parts of a sensitive surface are
locked into an invariable order in our experience. We should
therefore naturally expect to have great difficulty in picking out
any one point on the retinal surface; for example, if that surface
never became the seat of other contrasts than these immutable, local
differences. The difficulty would be still farther increased by the
fact that, considered *in abstracto*, local differences are utterly insipid, and carry with them no difference of emotional interest.
But emotional interests are the great guides to selective attention.
One retinal position, therefore, could hardly be singled out from
any other before an interesting object had come to occupy it. It
might then share the interest of the object, and be noticed. Again,
the local differences, *per se*, may be very slight quantitatively, and
require an adventitious sensation, superinduced upon them, to
awaken the attention. But after the attention has once been awakened in this way, it may continue to be conscious of the unaided
difference; just as a sail on the horizon may be too faint for us to
notice until someone's finger placed against the spot has pointed it
out to us, but may then remain visible after the finger has been
withdrawn.

On the skin the purely local contrasts of feeling seem slight, whilst the adventitious sensations, that may simultaneously come and perch in different near spots, are few in kind. But who can doubt that if, instead of receiving the same kind of sensation from the outer world at each point, a square inch of the skin might be checkered all over with spots of heat and cold, of itching, throbbing, stinging, pressure, and suction, our local analysis of it would be far more delicate. But this imaginary condition of the skin is the actual condition of the retina, with its power to be simultaneously impressed by the most widely contrasted and most sharply diversified adventitious feelings. The retina can at once feel white and black, but the ear cannot so feel sound and silence. The addition of mobility to these two peculiarities of the retina multiplies enormously their separate effects as aids to discrimination. A luminous point, moving from *a* to *b* on the retina, will awaken the perception of movement in space which we saw above to be primordial; which, in fact, excites the attention more than any other retinal sensation, so that the marginal parts of the retina may be said to be mere sentinels, saying, "Who goes there?" and calling the *fovea* to the spot. The tract moved over is thus most vividly accentuated and marked off from the environment. Moreover, a sensation but dimly segregated whilst on the margin of the field of view has its quality distinctly contrasted with all the rest the moment we turn the *fovea* upon it, and may then remain distinguished when it resumes its marginal position. The number of forms and colors we learn to separate from each other is thus increased, whilst the incessant wandering of the forms and colors from point to point must inevitably, by that "law of dissociation by varying concomitants" of which I have spoken in a previous article,[10] drag the purely local feelings, not only apart from each other in consciousness, but also apart from any constant association with particular forms and colors, and end by letting them roll out isolatedly upon the table of the mind, where they then are felt as so many positions, pure and simple.

In yet another way the local feelings, if very slight, may be discriminated by the aid of motion. It seems to be one of the laws of discrimination that two feelings, whose contrast is so slight as to pass unnoticed, may end by becoming distinguished, in case they severally form associations with other bodies of feeling whose con-

10 On "Brute and Human Intellect." This *Journal* [*of Speculative Philosophy*], vol. xii, p. 236 [*Essays in Psychology*, p. 1 above].

trast is more massive. The massive contrast takes, as it were, the smaller one in its tow. The slightly differing feelings are dragged asunder, and afterwards, by a process we cannot explain, remain segregated and discernibly *in se*. Thus, Madeira and sherry may be indistinguishable at first to my taste; but, if I get to associate the taste of one with Brown's table and the taste of the other with Smith's, I will presently, on tasting Madeira, be reminded of Brown's dining-room by *something* in the wine, and will then use the name Madeira, which is also associated with the same experiences. Later still, the "something" itself is cognized as a characteristic flavor. To apply this to the eye, each peripheral retinal point becomes habitually associated with the one peculiar feeling of movement necessary to bring the object which occupies it to the *fovea*. If two feelings of movement are more massively contrasted, *inter se*, than two retinal local feelings, they may drag these out from their first confounded state, just as Brown's table and Smith's drag sherry apart from Madeira.

It is no wonder then that the retina, whose peculiarities of structure so enormously facilitate the intricacy of association and dissociation, should be the organ in which all discrimination, local as well as qualitative, is at its maximum.

I have said nothing yet about the quantitative measurement of retinal distances. It seems quite certainly performed by the aid of movement, which, superimposing the same line or figure on different tracts of the retinal surface, marks them off as tracts equal to each other. Feelings of innervation and contraction, quantitatively compared with each other in consciousness, may also be used to estimate the equivalence of retinal tracts on which the same image cannot be successively superposed. I assuredly have nothing to add to the admirable labors of the German physiologist on the *Ausmessung des Seefeldes*, and do not venture to decide between Classen's views and those of Wundt and Helmholtz. I merely call attention to the fact that these quantitative equivalencies are woven by the muscles into a previously existing spatial surface, in which the general bearing of the several included positions is already defined. The equivalencies have no more to do with constituting the spatiality, as such, than the numbers on a block of houses have to do with constituting their habitability. Most authors assume that without muscular feelings the spatial form of consciousness could not exist at all. They either constitute it or help create it. M. Delbœuf more clearly than anyone, says, in his *Psychologie comme science naturelle*, that they constitute it; and in his brilliant and original article on Vision[11] he maintains that a punctiform sense organ, which could only be excited by a line of force vertical to its surface, would, if made to move from the point A (which sends one such line down upon it) to the point B (which sends another), affect us with the consciousness that A and B were situated beside each other in space, at a distance measured by the intervening movement. If, for instance, we have a punctiform ear at the bottom of a tube which admits only such air waves as coincide with its axis, we should, according to M. Delbœuf, by rotating this tube, first upon the trombone, then upon the drum, and then upon other instruments of the orchestra, acquire a perfectly topographic field of sound, as spatial as that of the retina, the position of each sonorous ingredient being defined by the movement which calls it into existence. The reason why the actual ear gives us no such distinct field is, according to M. Delbœuf, because our ear is so constructed that, no matter which way we move it, we are always conscious of the same sounds, the utmost alteration being a slight change in relative intensity. Now I believe this is entirely incorrect, and that we have not the shadow of a reason to suppose that, were the trombone to become silent the moment we moved our ear from it towards the drum, and the latter not to sound until, so to speak, we had accurately sighted it, we should form any notion that they coexisted, separated by an interval of space. Sounds and motions would form pure succession in time, like the succession of notes separated by muscular feelings in the larynx when we sing a scale.[12]

The only organ which can give a feeling of space is an extended, not a punctiform organ. When the retina fixates, first A and then B, B comes into the field without A vanishing. For a time they are actually felt to coexist as simultaneous retinal sensations, distinguished from each other by the analytic attention. This form of presence, and no mere linking by motion, makes their arrangement spatial. All that motion can do is to help us distinguish A from B

---

[11] *Revue Philosophique*, T. iv, pp. 173, 183. "*La faculté de se mouvoir en sachant qu'on se meut.*"

[12] The ascription of height and depth to certain notes seems due, not to any localization of the sounds, but to the fact that a feeling of vibration in the chest and tension in the gullet accompanies the singing of a bass note, whilst when we sing high the palatine mucous membrane is drawn upon by the muscles which move the larynx, and awakens a feeling in the roof of the mouth.

as they lie side by side. In the retina it does this by rapidly altering their sensible quality. When the *fovea* is on A, A is bright; when it moves to B, B is bright. In this way it breaks A and B apart, and we perceive their separate positions. A motion which should occur without in any way altering the relative intensity or quality of the coexistent feelings would in no way aid us to distinguish them. It would help our space perception quite as little as the motion of M. Delbœuf's punctiform organ, which, by altogether annihilating A the moment B was attended to, might be considered as occupying the opposite extreme. The retina forms the golden mean.

So far, it seems to me, we have met with no great difficulties. What has made students of the subject disinclined to admit that the retinal sensations, purely as such, have a primitive, spatial collaterality in consciousness, has been the fact that the same amount of excited retina can suggest the most various, absolute, and relative direction and size in the object whose image occupies it, according to the circumstances. If the native determinations of space by the retina be so overpowered by the suggestions of experience, there can, these authors think, be nothing intuitive about them.

But this difficulty is easily cleared away by reflecting that the determinations of size, shape, and so forth, in question, pertain to the objective world of things, as we deem them absolutely to exist. These objective spaces may very well not be intuitive, but constructed by Association and Selection, out of various subjective spatial experiences, partly tactile, partly locomotor, partly retinal experiences taken from other points of view than the present. And the present retinal sensation, with its spatial characteristics, may quite as well be used as a sign of these other spatial characteristics as the sound *bang* may be the sign of the widely different sound made by the explosion of a cannon. Underneath all this complex and varying objective import of the retinal sensation, the subjective sensation itself persists, with all its parts, alongside each other, in the full spatial collaterality which nativists claim for them. It is true, that most men overlook it, because the import is of more practical moment to them than the sign. But artists and physiologists train their attention to observe the sensation *in se*, and I am not aware that any one of them has ever professed to find it devoid of the spatial *quale*.

Such abundant room thus appears to be left for the achievements of empiricists in the study of this objective construction that they need not grudge to the nativists the little gift of primordial bigness and collateral subdivision which the latter are contented to "beg" at the outset of their task. The only point which, in my mind, casts the least doubt on their assumption is drawn from the ear. Though we are able by that organ to discriminate coexistent voices, or pitches, we do not necessarily arrange them alongside of each other. At most, the high tone is felt as a thin, bright streak on a broader, darker background. It may be, however, that the terminal organs of the acoustic nerve are excited all at once by sounds of any pitch, as the whole retina would be by every luminous point if there were no dioptric apparatus affixed. Notwithstanding the brilliant conjectures of the last few years which assign different acoustic end-organs to different rates of air-wave, we are still greatly in the dark about the subject; and I, for my part, would much more confidently reject a theory of hearing which violated the principles advanced in this article than give up those principles for the sake of any hypothesis hitherto published about either organs of corti or basilar membrane.

There are but three possible kinds of theory concerning space. Either (1) there is no spatial *quale* at all, and space is a mere symbol of succession; or (2) there is a *quale* given immediately in sensation; or, finally (3), there is a *quale produced* out of the inward resources of the mind, to envelop sensations which, as given originally, are not spatial, but which, on being cast into the spatial form, become united and orderly. This last is the Kantian view. Stumpf admirably designates it as the "psychic stimulus" theory, the crude sensations being considered as goads to the mind to put forth its slumbering power. Wundt, who calls space a synthesis containing properties which its elements lack, explicitly adopts the third view, and so does Lotze. Helmholtz is so sententious (and vacillating?) that it is a little hard to class him distinctly, but there is no doubt that visual space, at any rate, is constructed for him out of non-spatial sensations of sight. The word "empiricist" in his optics means just the opposite of its ordinary signification. Mill, Bain, and Spencer seem all to have gone astray, like lost sheep. Mill, with his mental chemistry, would sometimes seem to hold the third view, but sometimes again the first. Bain sticks most to the first, but sometimes implies the third. These authors are bent on making a triumphant use of their all-sufficing principle of association. They wish, therefore, if possible, to *account* for space by it.

But, between the impossibility of getting from mere association anything not contained in the sensations associated, and the dislike to allow any spontaneous mental productivity, they flounder in a dismal dilemma. Spencer joins them there. He most explicitly denies the spatial quality to any of the elementary sensations. In his *Psychology*, volume 2, page 168, he says: "No idea of extension can arise from a *simultaneous* excitation" of a multitude of nerve terminations like those on the skin or the retina, since this would imply a "knowledge of their relative positions,"—that is "a pre-existent idea of a special extension: which is absurd." On page 172 he says, "No relation between *successive* states of consciousness gives in itself any idea of extension"; and, on page 218, "the *muscular* sensations accompanying motion are quite distinct from the notions of Space and Time associated with them."

He nevertheless vociferously inveighs against the Kantian position, that space is a spontaneous mental product. And yet he does not anywhere explicitly deny space to have a specific *quale* different from that of time.

Such abject incoherency is really pitiful. The fact is, that all these English authors are really psychical stimulists, or Kantists, at bottom. The space they speak of is a new mental product not given in the sensations. I repudiate this position because it appears to me thoroughly mythological. I have no direct experience of any such mental act of creation or production. My spatial intuitions do not occur in two times, but in one. My mind is woven of one tissue, and not chopped into joints. There is not a moment of passive non-spatial sensation, succeeded by one of active spatial perception, but the form I look at is as immediately felt as the color which fills it. If one can be called a sensation, so can the other. That higher parts of the mind are also involved in spatial perception, who can deny? They fill it with intellectual relations, as Mr. Cabot has well pointed out. But these relations, when they obtain between elements of the spatial order, do in no whit differ from the same intellectual relations when they join elements in the orders of number, intensity, quality, and the like. The spatiality comes *to* the intellect, not from it.

One word more about Kant. Helmholtz says:[13] "By Kant the proof that space is an *a priori* form is based essentially on the posi-

13 *Mind*, vol. iii, p. 213.

tion that the axioms are synthetic propositions *a priori*. But even if this position be dropped, the space-representation might still be the necessary *a priori* form in which every co-extended manifold is perceived. This [*i.e.*, dropping the axioms] is not surrendering any essential feature of the Kantian position."

I make bold to differ from this. The mere innateness of the spatial form of sensibility is surely not the essence of the Kantian position. Every sensationalist empiricist must admit a wealth of native forms of sensibility. The important question is: Do they, or do they not, yield us *a priori propositions*, synthetic judgments? If our "sensation" space does this, we are still Kantians in a deeper sense by far than if we merely call the spatial *quale* a form of *Anschauung*, rather than an *Empfindung*. But if the new geometry of Helmholtz and others has upset the necessity of our axioms (and this appears to be the case; see, especially, the article just quoted), then the Kantian doctrine seems literally left without a leg to stand upon.

The Feeling of Effort

> La locomotion animale . . . n'a nul rapport direct
> avec ce qu'on appelle volonté . . . . L'effort, le *nisus*,
> ne doit pas être fixé dans le rapport de la volition
> . . . avec l'acte propre du mobile matériel.
>
> . . . L'effort, dans l'acception rationnelle de ce
> mot, est le rapport de la représentation avec elle-
> même.   RENOUVIER

I propose in the following pages to offer a scheme of the physiology
and psychology of volition, more completely worked out and satisfactory than any I have yet met with. The matter is a little intricate,
and I shall have to ask the reader to bear patiently a good deal of
detail for the sake of the importance of the result.

That we *have* a feeling of effort there can be no doubt. Popular
language has sufficiently consecrated the fact by the institution of
the word effort, and its synonyms exertion, striving, straining. The
difference between a simply passive sensation, and one in which
the elements of volition and attention are found, has also been
recorded by popular speech in the difference between such verbs
as to see and to look; to hear and to listen; to smell and to scent;
to feel and to touch. Effort, attention, and volition are, in fact,
similar elements of Feeling differing all in the same generic manner from its receptive, or simply sensational elements; and forming
the active as distinguished from the passive parts of our mental
nature. This distinction is styled by Bain the most vital one within
the sphere of mind; and at all times psychologists of the *a priori*
school have emphasized the utter opposition between our consciousness of spontaneity or out-going energy, and the consciousness
of any mere *impression* whatever.

Fully admitting the feelings of active energy as mental facts, our question simply is *of what nervous processes are they the concomitants?* As the feeling of effort is nowhere more coarsely and obviously present than in the phenomenon of muscular exertion, let us limit our inquiry first to that.

I. Muscular Exertion an Afferent Feeling

Johannes Müller was, so far as I know, the first to say[1] that the nerve-process accompanying the feeling of muscular exertion, is the discharge from the motor centre into the motor nerve. The supposition is a most natural and plausible one; for if afferent nerve processes are felt, each in its characteristic way, why should not efferent processes be felt by equal right, and with equally characteristic qualities? Accordingly we find in writers of all nations since Müller's time, repetitions implicit or explicit, of his suggestion. But the authors who have most emphatically insisted on it, and raised it to the position of a fundamental doctrine, are Bain, Hughlings Jackson and Wundt.

Bain says: "The sensibility accompanying muscular movement coincides with the *outgoing* stream of nervous energy, and does not, as in the case of pure sensation, result from any influence passing inwards, by incarrying or sensitive nerves."[2]

Jackson writes: " 'Sensations,' in the sense of 'mental states,' arise, I submit, during energising of motor as well as of 'sensory' nerve processes—with the 'out-going,' as well as with the 'in-going' current."[3]

Wundt separates the feeling of force exerted, from the feeling of effected movement.[4] And in later writings he adopts the term *Innervationsgefühl* to designate the former in relation to its supposed cause, the efferent discharge. Feelings of innervation have since then become household words in psychological literature. Two English writers only, so far as I know, Dr. Charlton Bastian, and Dr. Fer-

---

[1] *Physiologie*, 1840, Bd. ii, p. 500.

[2] *The Senses and the Intellect*, 3d edition, p. 77.

[3] "Clinical and Physiological Researches on the Nervous System." (Reprinted from the *Lancet*, 1873.) London, J. & A. Churchill, p. xxxiv. See also this author's very original though somewhat obscure paper on Aphasia in *Brain* for October, 1879, p. 351.

[4] *Beiträge zur Theorie der Sinneswahrnehmung*, p. 420. *Physiologische Psychologie*, p. 316.

rier, have expressed skepticism as to the existence of any feelings connected with the efferent nervous discharge. But their arguments being imperfect, and in the case of Bastian rather confusedly expressed, have passed unnoticed. Lotze in Germany has also raised a skeptical voice, but has not backed his doubts by many arguments.[5] The notorious existence of the *feeling* of effort in muscular exertion; the fact that the efferent discharge there plays the principal *rôle*, and the plausibility of the postulate so often insisted on by Lewes that identity of structure involves identity of function, have all conspired to make us almost believe, as a matter of course, that motor cells when they discharge into motor fibres, should have their own "specific energy" of feeling, and that this should be no other than the sense of energy put forth.

In opposition to this popular view, I maintain that the feeling of *muscular* energy put forth is a complex *afferent* sensation coming from the tense muscles, the strained ligaments, squeezed joints, fixed chest, closed glottis, contracted brow, clenched jaws, etc., etc. That there is over and above this another feeling of effort involved, I do not deny; but this latter is purely moral and has nothing to do with the motor discharge. We shall study it at the end of this essay, and shall find it to be essentially identical with the effort to remember, with the effort to make a decision, or to attend to a disagreeable task.

First then, let us disprove the notion that there is any feeling connected with the motor or efferent nervous discharge. We may begin by asking: Why should there be? Even accepting Lewes's postulate in the abstract, what degree of "identity" should be demanded between the afferent and efferent nerve apparatus, to insure their being both alike, "sentient"? Even to our coarse optical examination, the sensory and the motor cells are widely different. But apart from *a priori* postulates, and however strange to logic it may appear, it is a fact that the motor apparatus is absolutely insentient in an afferent direction, although we know that the fibres of the anterior root will propagate a disturbance in that direction as well as in the other. Why may not this result from a true insentiency in the motor cell, an insentiency which would accompany

---

[5] See his *Metaphysik*, 1879, p. 589. See also *Revue Philosophique*, t. iv, p. 359.

all action there, and characterize its normal discharges as well as the unnatural irritations made by the knife of the surgeon or the electrodes of the physiologist upon the motor nerve.

Plausibility accrues to this presumption when we call to mind this general law: that consciousness seems to desert all processes where it can no longer be of any use. The tendency of consciousness to a minimum of complication is in fact a dominating law in Psychology. The logical law of parsimony is only its best known case. We grow unconscious of every feeling which is useless as a sign to lead us to our ends, and where one sign will suffice, others drop out, and that one remains to function alone. We observe this in the whole history of sense perception, and in the acquisition of every art. We ignore which eye we see with, because a fixed mechanical association has been formed between our motions and each retinal image. Our motions are the ends of our seeing, our retinal images the signals to these ends. If each retinal image, whichever it be, can suggest automatically a motion in the right direction, what need for us to know whether it be in the right eye or the left? The knowledge would be superfluous complication. So in acquiring any art or voluntary function. The marksman thinks only of the exact position of the goal, the singer only of the perfect sound, the balancer only of the point in space whose oscillations he must counteract by movement. The associated mechanism has become so perfect in all these persons, that each variation in the thought of the end, is functionally correlated with the one movement fitted to bring the latter about. Whilst they were tyros, they thought of their means as well as their end; the marksman of the position of his gun or bow, or the weight of his stone, the pianist of the visible position of the note on the keyboard, the singer of his throat or breathing, the balancer of his feet on the rope, or his hand or chin under the pole. But little by little they succeeded in dropping all this supernumerary consciousness, and they became secure in their movements exactly in proportion as they did so.

Now if we analyze the nervous mechanism of voluntary action, we shall see that by virtue of this principle of parsimony in consciousness, the motor discharge *ought* to be devoid of sentience. The essentials of a voluntary movement, are: 1, a preliminary idea of the end we wish to attain; 2, a *"fiat"*; 3, an appropriate muscular contraction; 4, the end felt as actually accomplished. In man, at any rate, it is admitted that the idea of the end and the muscular contraction were originally coupled by empirical association; that is to say, the child with his end in view, made random movements until he accidentally found one to fit. This movement awakened its own characteristic feeling which thenceforward remained with him as the idea of the movement appropriate to that particular end. If the man should acquire a million distinct ends, he must acquire a million such motor ideas and a million connexions between them and the ends. But one such connexion, subserved by an exclusive nerve tract used for no other purpose, will be enough for each end. The end conceived will, when these associations are formed, always awaken its own proper motor idea. As for the manner in which this idea awakens its own proper movement—the one which will convert it from an idea into an actual sensation—the simplest possible arrangement would be to let it serve *directly* (through its peculiar neural process) as a stimulus to the special motor centre, the ultimate sensible effect of whose discharge it prefigures and represents.

The ordinary theory, however, makes the matter much more complicated. The idea of the end is supposed to awaken first a *feeling* of the proper motor innervation, and *this*, when adjudged right, to discharge the muscular combination.

Now what can be gained by the interposition of this second relay of feeling between the idea and the movement? Nothing on the score of economy of nerve tracts; for it takes just as many of them to associate a million ideas with a million motor feelings,[6] each specific, as to associate the same million ideas with a million insentient motor centres. And nothing on the score of precision; for the only conceivable way in which they might further precision would be by giving to a mind whose notion of the end was vague, a sort of halting stage with sharper imagery on which to collect its wits before uttering its *fiat*. But not only are the conscious discriminations between "ends" much sharper than anyone pretends the shades of difference between feelings of innervation to be, but even were this not the case, it is impossible to see how a mind with its end vaguely conceived, could tell out of a lot of *Innervationsgefühle*, were they never so sharply differentiated, which one fitted that end exactly, and which did not. A sharply conceived end will

---

[6] The association between the two orders of feeling being of course brought about by a separate neural connexion between the tracts supporting each.

on the other hand directly awaken a distinct movement as easily as it will awaken a distinct feeling of innervation. If feelings can go astray through vagueness, surely the fewer steps of feeling there are interposed, the more securely we shall act. We ought then on *a priori* grounds alone to regard the *Innervationsgefühl* as a pure encumbrance.

Let us turn now to *a posteriori* evidence.

It is a notorious fact, recognized by all writers[7] on voluntary motion, that the will seems concerned only with results and not with the muscular details by which they are executed. But when we say "results," what is it exactly that we mean? We mean, of course, the movements objectively considered, and revealing themselves (as either accomplished or in process of being accomplished), to our sensible perceptions. Our idea, notion, thought, of a movement, what we *mean*, whenever we speak of the movement, is this sensible perception which we get of it when it is taking place, or has completely occurred.

What then is this sensible perception?

What does it introspectively seem to be? I unhesitatingly answer: an aggregate of *afferent* feelings, coming primarily from the contraction of muscles, the stretching of tendons, ligaments and skin, and the rubbing and pressing of joints; and secondarily, from the eye, the ear, the skin, nose or palate, any or all of which may be indirectly affected by the movement as it takes place in another part of the body. The only idea of a movement which we *can* possess is composed of images of these, its afferent effects. By these differences alone, are movements mentally distinguished from each other, and these differences are sufficient for all the discriminations we can possibly need to make, when we intend one movement rather than another.

The recent writers who have been prompt to recognize the fact that volition is directed only to results, have hardly been sensible of the far-reaching consequences of this admission—consequences which will develop themselves as our inquiry proceeds. Meanwhile one immediate conclusion follows: namely, that there are no such things as efferent feelings, or feelings of innervation. These are wholly mythological entities. Whoever says that in raising his arm

---

[7] By no one more clearly set forth than by Hume himself in his essay "Of the Idea of Necessary Connexion." The best recent statement I know is by Jaccoud: *Les Paraplégies et l'ataxie du mouvement*, Paris, 1864, p. 591.

he is ignorant of how many muscles he contracts, in what order of sequence, and in what degrees of intensity, expressly avows a colossal amount of unconsciousness of the processes of motor discharge. Each separate muscle at any rate cannot have its distinct feeling of innervation. Wundt,[8] who makes such enormous use of these hypothetical feelings in his psychologic construction of space, is himself led to admit that they have no differences of quality, but feel alike in all muscles, and vary only in their degrees of intensity.[9] They are used by the mind as guides, not of *what* movement, but of *how strong* a movement it is making, or shall make. But does not this virtually surrender their existence altogether?

For if anything be obvious to introspection it is that the degree of strength of our muscular contractions is completely revealed to us by afferent feelings coming from the muscles themselves and their insertions, from the vicinity of the joints, and from the general fixation of the larynx, chest, face and body, in the phenomenon of effort, objectively considered. When a certain degree of energy of contraction rather than another is thought of by us, this complex aggregate of afferent feelings, forming the material of our thought, renders absolutely precise and distinctive our mental image of the exact strength of movement to be made, and the exact amount of resistance to be overcome.

Let the reader try to direct his will towards a particular movement, and then notice what *constituted* the direction of the will. Was it anything over and above the notion of the different feelings to which the movement when effected, would give rise? If we abstract from these feelings, will any sign, principle, or means of orientation be left, by which the will may innervate the right muscles with the right intensity, and not go astray into the wrong ones? Strip off these images of result,[10] and so far from leaving us with a complete assortment of directions into which our will may launch itself, you leave our consciousness in an absolute and total vacuum. If I will to write "Peter" rather than "Paul," it is the thought of cer-

[8] Leidesdorf und Meynert's *Vierteljahrsschrift für Psychiatrie*, Bd. i, Heft i, S. 36–7, 1867. *Physiologische Psychologie*, 1st ed., S. 316.

[9] Harless, in an article which in many respects forestalls what I have to say ("Der Apparat des Willens," in Fichte's *Zeitschrift für Philosophie und philosophische Kritik*, Bd. 38, 1861), uses the convenient word *Effektbild* to designate our idea of this sensory result of a movement.

[10] We speak here only of the *muscular* exertion, properly so called. The difficulty often involved in making the *fiat* still remains a reserved question.

tain digital sensations, of certain alphabetic sounds, of certain appearances on the paper, and of no others, which immediately precedes the motion of my pen.

If I will to utter the word *Paul* rather than *Peter*, it is the thought of my voice falling on my ear, and of certain muscular feelings in my tongue, lips and larynx, which guide the utterance. All these feelings are afferent, and between the thought of them, by which the act is mentally specified with all possible completeness, and the act itself, there is no room for any third order of mental phenomenon. Except, indeed, what I have called the fiat, the element of consent, or resolve that the act shall ensue. This, doubtless, to the reader's mind, as to my own, constitutes the essence of the voluntariness of the act. This fiat will be treated of in detail farther on. It may be entirely neglected here, for it is a constant coefficient, affecting all voluntary actions alike, and incapable of serving to distinguish them. No one will pretend that its quality varies according as the right or the left arm, for example, is used.

So far then, we seem free to conclude that an anticipatory image of the sensorial consequences of a movement, hard or easy, *plus the fiat* that these consequences shall become actual, ought to be able to discharge *directly* the special movement with which in our past experiences the particular consequences were combined as effects. Furthermore, there is no introspective evidence whatever of the existence of any intermediate feelings, possessing either qualitative or quantitative differences, and accompanying the efferent discharge.[11]

Is there, notwithstanding, any circumstantial evidence? At first sight, it appears as if the circumstantial evidence in favor of efferent feelings were very strong. Wundt says,[12] that were our motor feelings of an afferent nature, "it ought to be expected that they would increase and diminish with the amount of outer or inner work actually effected in contraction. This, however, is not the case, but the strength of the motor sensation is purely proportional to the strength of the *impulse* to movement, which starts from the central organ innervating the motor nerves. This may be proved by observations made by physicians in cases of morbid alteration in the

11 The various degrees of difficulty with which the fiat is given form a complication of the utmost importance, reserved for discussion further on.
12 *Vorlesungen über die Menschen- und Thierseele*, Bd. i, p. 222.

muscular effect. A patient whose arm or leg is half paralyzed, so that he can only move the limb with great effort, has a distinct feeling of this effort: the limb seems to him heavier than before, appearing as if weighted with lead; he has, therefore, a sense of more work effected than formerly, and yet the effected work is either the same or even less. Only he must, to get even this effect, exert a stronger innervation, a stronger motor impulse than formerly.''

In complete paralysis also, patients will be conscious of putting forth the greatest exertion to move a limb which remains absolutely still upon the bed, and from which of course no afferent muscular or other feelings can come.[13]

Dr. Ferrier in his *Functions of the Brain* (Am. Ed., pp. 222–4) disposes very easily of this line of argument. He says: "It is neces-

---

[13] In some instances we get an opposite result. Dr. H. Charlton Bastian (*British Medical Journal*, 1869, p. 461, note) says:

"Ask a man, whose lower extremities are completely paralysed, whether, when he ineffectually wills to move either of these limbs, he is conscious of an expenditure of energy in any degree proportionate to that which he would have experienced if his muscles had naturally responded to his volition. He will tell us rather that he has a sense only of his own utter powerlessness, and that his volition is a mere mental act, carrying with it no feelings of expended energy, such as he is accustomed to experience when his muscles are in powerful action, and from which action and its consequences alone, as I think, he can derive any adequate notion of resistance."

Dr. J. J. Putnam has quite recently reported to me a case of this sort of only a few months' standing. Many amputated patients who still feel their lost limbs are unable to make any conscious effort to move them. One such case informs me that he feels more able to will a distant table to move, than to exert the same volition over his acutely-felt lost leg. Others, on the contrary (*Vide* Weir Mitchell's book on Gunshot Injuries to Nerves), say they cannot only will, but, as far as their feeling is concerned, *execute*, movements of their amputated limbs. It would be extremely interesting to unravel the causes of these divergences. May it be that in recent cases with the recollection of varied movements fresh in the mind, the patient has a stock of distinct images of position on which to base his fiat; while in an inveterate case, either of paralysis with contraction, or of amputation with consciousness of the limb in an invariable position, reminiscences of other positions have through long desuetude become so incapable of revival that there is no preliminary idea of an End for the fiat to knit itself to. Such a supposition conforms well to the utterances of two amputated persons with whom I have conversed. They said it was like "willing into the void," they "did not know how to set about it," and so forth. The recency of Dr. Putnam's case above mentioned seems, however, to conflict with such an explanation and I only make the suggestions in the hope that someone with better opportunities for observation than I possess, may become interested in the matter. I may add that in teaching a new and unnatural movement, the starting point is to awaken by its passive production a distinct sense of what the movement, if effected, would feel like. This defines the direction of the exertion the pupil is to make.

sary, however, to exclude movements *altogether* before such an explanation [as Wundt's] can be adopted. Now, though the hemiplegic patient cannot move his paralysed limb though he is conscious of trying hard, yet he will be found to be making powerful muscular exertion of some kind. Vulpian has called attention to the fact, and I have repeatedly verified it, that when a hemiplegic patient is desired to close his paralysed fist, in his endeavours to do so he unconsciously performs this action with the sound one. It is, in fact, almost impossible to exclude such a source of complication, and unless this is taken into account very erroneous conclusions as to the cause of the sense of effort may be drawn. In the fact of muscular contraction and the concomitant centripetal impressions, even though the action is not such as is desired, the conditions of the consciousness of effort exist without our being obliged to regard it as depending on central innervation or outgoing currents.

"It is, however, easy to make an experiment of a simple nature, which will satisfactorily account for the sense of effort, even when these unconscious contractions of the other side, such as hemiplegics make, are entirely excluded.

"If the reader will extend his right arm and hold his forefinger in the position required for pulling the trigger of a pistol, he may without actually moving his finger, but by simply making believe, experience a consciousness of energy put forth. Here, then, is a clear case of consciousness of energy without actual contraction of the muscles either of the one hand or the other, and without any perceptible bodily strain. If the reader will again perform the experiment, and pay careful attention to the condition of his respiration, he will observe that his consciousness of effort coincides with a fixation of the muscles of his chest, and that in proportion to the amount of energy he feels he is putting forth, he is keeping his glottis closed and actively contracting his respiratory muscles. Let him place his finger as before, and *continue breathing* all the time, and he will find that however much he may direct his attention to his finger, he will experience not the slightest trace of consciousness of effort until he has actually moved the finger itself, and then it is referred locally to the muscles in action. It is only when this essential and ever present respiratory factor is, as it has been, overlooked, that the consciousness of effort can with any degree of plausibility be ascribed to the outgoing current. In the contrac-

The Feeling of Effort

tion of the respiratory muscles there are the necessary conditions of centripetal impressions, and these are capable of originating the general sense of effort. When these active efforts are withheld, no consciousness of effort ever arises, except in so far as it is conditioned by the local contraction of the group of muscles towards which the attention is directed, or by other muscular contractions called unconsciously into play in the attempt.

"I am unable to find a single case of consciousness of effort which is not explicable in one or other of the ways specified. In all instances the consciousness of effort is conditioned by the actual fact of muscular contraction. That it is dependent on centripetal impressions generated by the act of contraction, I have already endeavoured to show. When the paths of the centripetal impressions, or the cerebral centres of the same, are destroyed, there is no vestige of a muscular sense. That the central organs, for the apprehension of the impressions originating from muscular contraction, are different from those which send out the motor impulse, has already been established. But when Wundt argues that this cannot be so, because then the sensation would always keep pace with the energy of muscular contraction, he overlooks the important factor of the fixation of the respiratory muscles, which is the basis of the general sense of effort in all its varying degrees."

To these remarks of Ferrier's I have nothing to add. Anyone may verify them, and they prove conclusively that the consciousness of muscular exertion, being impossible without movement *effected somewhere*, must be an afferent and not an efferent sensation, a consequence, and not an antecedent of the movement itself. An idea of the amount of muscular exertion requisite to perform a certain movement can consequently be nothing other than an anticipatory image of the movement's sensible effects.

Driven thus from the body at large, where shall the circumstantial evidence for the feeling of innervation lodge itself? Where but in the muscles of the eye, from which last small retreat it judges itself inexpugnable. And, to say the truth, it may well be excused for its confidence; for Ferrier alone, so far as I know, has ventured to attack it there, and his attack must be deemed a very weak failure. Nevertheless, that fastness too must fall, and by the lightest of bombardments. But, before trying the bombardment, let us examine the position with a little care, laying down first a few general principles about optical vertigo, or illusory appearance of movement in objects.

We judge that an object moves under two distinct sets of circumstances:

1. When its image moves on the retina, and we know that the eye is still.

2. When its image is stationary on the retina, and we know that the eye is moving. In this case we feel that we *follow* the object.

In either of these cases a mistaken judgment about the state of the eye will produce optical vertigo.

If in case 1, we think our eye is still when it is really moving, we shall get a movement of the retinal image which we shall judge to be due to a real outward motion of the object. This is what happens after looking at rushing water, or through the windows of a moving railroad car, or after turning on one's heel to giddiness. The eyes, without our intending to move them, go through a series of involuntary rotations, continuing those they were previously obliged to make to keep objects in view. If the objects had been whirling by to our right, our eyes when turned to stationary objects will still move slowly towards the right. The retinal image upon them will then move like that of an object passing to the left. We then try to catch it by voluntarily and rapidly rotating the eyes to the left, when the involuntary impulse again rotates the eyes to the right, continuing the apparent motion, and so the game goes on.

If in case 2, we think our eyes moving when they are in reality still, we shall judge that we are following a moving object when we are but fixating a steadfast one. Illusions of this kind occur after sudden and complete paralysis of special eye muscles, and the partizans of feelings of efferent innervation regard them as *experimenta crucis*. Helmholtz writes:[14] "When the external rectus muscle of the right eye, or its nerve, is paralyzed, the eye can no longer be rotated to the right side. So long as the patient turns it only to the nasal side it makes regular movements, and he perceives correctly the position of objects in the visual field. So soon, however, as he tries to rotate it outwardly, *i.e.*, towards the right, it ceases to obey his will, stands motionless in the middle of its course, and

14 *Physiologische Optik*, p. 600.

94

the objects appear flying to the right, although position of eye and retinal image are unaltered.[15]

"In such a case the exertion of the will is followed neither by actual movement of the eye, nor by contraction of the muscle in question, nor even by increased tension in it. The act of will *produced absolutely no effects* beyond the nervous system, and yet we judge of the direction of the line of vision as if the will had exercised its normal effects. We believe it to have moved to the right, and since the retinal image is unchanged, we attribute to the object the same movement we have erroneously ascribed to the eye. . . . These phenomena leave no room for doubt that we only judge the direction of the line of sight by the effort of will with which we strive to change the position of our eyes. There are also certain weak feelings in our eyelids, . . . and furthermore in excessive lateral rotations we feel a fatiguing strain in the muscles. But all these feelings are too faint and vague to be of use in the perception of direction. We feel then what impulse of the will, and how strong a one, we apply to turn our eye into a given position."

Partial paralysis of the same muscle, *paresis,* as it has been called, seems to point even more conclusively to the same inference, that the will to innervate is felt independently of all its afferent results. I will quote the account given by a very recent authority,[16] of the effects of this accident:

"When the nerve going to an eye muscle, *e.g.,* the external rectus of one side, falls into a state of paresis, the first result is that the same volitional stimulus, which under normal circumstances would have perhaps rotated the eye to its extreme position outwards, now is competent to effect only a moderate outward rotation, say of 20°. If now, shutting the sound eye, the patient looks at an object situated just so far outwards from the paretic eye that this latter must turn 20° in order to see it distinctly, the patient will feel as if he had moved it not only 20° towards the side, but into its extreme lateral position, for the impulse of innervation requisite for bringing it into view is a perfectly conscious act, whilst the diminished state of contraction of the paretic muscle lies for the

---

15 The left and sound eye is here supposed covered. If both eyes look at the same field there are double images which still more perplex the judgment. The patient, however, learns to see correctly before many days or weeks are over.   W. J.

16 Alfred Graefe, in *Handbuch der gesammten Augenheilkunde,* Bd. vi, S. 18.

present out of the ken of consciousness. The test proposed by von Graefe, of localization by the sense of touch, serves to render evident the error which the patient now makes. If we direct him to touch rapidly the object looked at, with the forefinger of the hand of the same side, the line through which the finger moves will not be the line of sight directed 20° outwards, but will approach more nearly to the extreme possible outward line of vision."

A stone cutter with the external rectus of the left eye paralyzed, will strike his hand instead of his chisel with his hammer, until experience has taught him wisdom.

It appears as if here the judgment of direction *could* only arise from the excessive innervation of the rectus when the object is looked at. All the afferent feelings must be identical with those experienced when the eye is sound, and the judgment is correct. The eyeball is rotated just 20° in the one case as in the other, the image falls on the same part of the retina, the pressures on the eyeball and the tensions of the skin and conjunctiva are identical. There is only one feeling which *can* vary, and lead us to our mistake. That feeling must be the effort which the will makes, moderate in the one case, excessive in the other, but in both cases an efferent feeling, pure and simple.

Beautiful and clear as this reasoning seems to be, it is based on an incomplete inventory of the afferent data. The writers have all omitted to consider what is going on in the *other eye*. This is kept covered during the experiments to prevent double images, and other complications. But if its condition under these circumstances be examined, it will be found to present changes which must result in strong afferent feelings. And the taking account of these feelings demolishes in an instant all the conclusions which the authors from whom I have quoted, base upon their supposed absence. This I will now proceed to show.

Take first the case of complete paralysis and assume the right eye affected. Suppose the patient desires to rotate his gaze to an object situated in the extreme right of the field of vision. As Hering has so beautifully shown, both eyes move by a common act of innervation, and in this instance both move towards the right. But the paralyzed right eye stops short in the middle of its course, the object still appearing far to the right of its fixation point. The left sound eye, meanwhile, although covered, continues its rotation until the extreme rightward limit thereof has been reached. To an observer looking at both eyes the left will seem to squint. Of course this continued and extreme rotation produces afferent feelings of rightward motion in the eyeball, which momentarily overpower the faint feelings of central position in the diseased and uncovered eye. The patient feels by his left eyeball as if he were following an object which by his right retina he perceives he does not overtake. All the conditions of optical vertigo are here present: the image stationary on the retina, and the erroneous conviction that the eyes are moving.

The objection that a feeling in the left eyeball ought not to produce a conviction that the right eye moves, will be considered in a moment. Let us meanwhile, turn to the case of simple paresis with apparent translocation of the field.

Here the right eye succeeds in fixating the object, but observation of the left eye will reveal to an observer the fact that it squints just as violently inwards as in the former case. The direction which the finger of the patient takes in pointing to the object, is the direction of this squinting and covered left eye. As Graefe says (although he fails to seize the true import of his own observation), "It appears to have been by no means sufficiently noticed how significantly the direction of the line of sight of the secondarily deviating eye [*i.e.*, of the left], and the line of direction of the pointed finger agree."[17]

The translocation would, in a word, be perfectly explained, could we suppose that the sensation of a certain degree of rotation in the left eyeball were able to suggest to the patient the position of an object whose image falls on the right retina alone. Can then, a feeling in one eye be confounded with a feeling in the other?

Not only Donders and Adamük, by their vivisections, but Hering by his exquisite optical experiments, have proved that the apparatus of innervation for both eyes is single, and that they function as one organ—a double eye, according to Hering, or what Helmholtz calls, a *Cyclopenauge*. Now the retinal feelings of this double organ, singly innervated, are also to a great extent absolutely indistinguishable, namely, where they fall in corresponding points. But even where they are *numerically* distinguishable, they are indistinguishable with respect to our knowing whether they belong to the left retina or to the right. When, as so often happens, part

17 *Ibid.*, p. 21.

97

of a distant object is hidden from one eye by the edge of an intervening body, and seen only by the other eye, we rarely know by our spontaneous feeling that this is the case, nor when we have noticed the fact can we tell which eye is seeing and which is eclipsed. If the reader will hold two needles in front of his nose, one of them behind the other, and look at the distant one with both eyes, the near one will appear to him double. But he will be quite unable by his mere feeling, to say to which eye either of the double images belongs. If he gives an opinion, he will probably say the right image belongs to the right eye, the reverse being really the case.[18] In short, we use our retinal sensations indifferently, and only to tell us where their objects lie. It takes long practice directed specially *ad hoc*, to teach us on which retina the sensations respectively fall.

Now the different sensations which arise from the positions of the eyeballs are also used exclusively as signs of the position of objects; an object directly fixated, being localized habitually at the intersection of the two optical axes, but without any separate consciousness on our part that the position of one axis is different from another. All we are aware of is a consolidated feeling of a certain "strain" in the eyeballs, accompanied by the perception that just so far in front and so far to the right or to the left, there is an object which we see. This being the case, our patient paretic of the right external rectus, might be expected to see objects, not only transposed to the right, but also nearer because the intersection of his squinting axes is nearer, and smaller because a retinal image of fixed size awakens the judgment of an object small in proportion as it is judged near. Whether paretic patients of this kind are subject to this additional illusion remains to be discovered by examinations which ophthalmologists in large practice alone have the opportunity of making.[19] It is worth while to observe, however,

[18] See also W. B. Rogers, Silliman's *Journal*, 1860, for other curious examples of this incapacity.

[19] In three recent cases examined for me by ophthalmological friends this additional delusion seemed absent, and I also found it absent in a case of paralysis of the external rectus with translocation which, by Dr. Wadsworth's kindness, I lately examined at the hospital. The "absence" spoken of was in all these cases a vacillating and uncertain judgment rather than a steadfastly positive judgment that distance and size were unaltered.

The extraordinary vacillation of our judgments of size and distance will be noticed by anyone who has experimented with slightly concave, convex or prismatic glasses.

that the feeling of accommodation and the knowledge of the true size of the object conspire with the feeling of convergence to give the judgment of distance. And where the convergence is an altogether abnormal one, as in the paretic squint, the feeling of the left eyeball being excessive, might well simply overpower all other feelings and leave no clear impression whatever save a general one of looking far towards the right.

The only thoroughly crucial test of the explanation here proposed of the paretic translocation, would be a case in which the left eye alone looked at the object whilst the right, looking at nothing, strongly converged. Since, however, the only way of making a normal eye converge, is to give it an object to look at, it would seem at first sight as if such a case could never be obtained. It has occurred to me, notwithstanding, that slight atropinization of one eye might cause such strong accommodative innervation, that the convergent muscles might sympathetically contract, and a squint tend to occur. The squint would be steadfast, and situated in the non-atropinized eye, if it were covered and the poisoned eye alone made to fixate a near object. And if under these circumstances the object thus monocularly seen were translocated outwardly, we should have a complete verification of the explanation I present. The innervation is wholly different from that in paresis, and the only point the two cases have in common is the covered eye rotated nasalwards. Probably it would not be easy to find the patient, or the dose of atropia just fitted for producing the squint. But one positive instance would outweigh a hundred negative ones. I have had

---

The most familiar example is that of looking at the moon through an opera glass. It looks larger, so its details are more distinctly seen; being so distinct it looks nearer, and because it seems nearer it is also judged smaller. (Aubert's *secundare Urtheilstäuschung.*) Many experiments may be devised by which the left eye may be made to converge by a prism whilst the right looks either at the same object or sees one of the double images of a more distant object whose other double image is cut off by a screen from the left retina. Under these circumstances we get translocations which may be similar to those in paresis but they prove nothing to our purpose, for the moment the prism is introduced before the left eye, altering its convergence, the right eye moves sympathetically, giving rise to a translation of its retinal image, which of course suggests translocation of the object. The only experiment capable of proving the theory advanced in the text would be one in which *no* shifting of the image on the right retina accompanied the turning inwards of the left eye. The experiment without prisms mentioned by Hering (*Lehre vom binocularen Sehen*, pp. 12–14), seems the nearest approach which we can make to this, but there both eyes fixate the same objects, and there is some translation of the image.

a chance to experiment on but one person. A large needle was stuck in a horizontal board, whose edges touched the face, the needle being from eight to twelve inches in front of the right atropinized eye. The subject was told to touch with her finger the under surface of the board, just beneath the needle. The results were negative—no well-marked squint being perceptible—but on the third day after the atropinization, the patient regularly placed her finger from one-half to three-quarters of an inch too far to the right. Other observations ought to be made.

There seems meanwhile to be a very good negative instance by which to corroborate our arguments. If we whirl about on our heel to the right, objects will, as above-mentioned, seem to whirl about us to the left as soon as we stand still. This is due to the fact that our eyes are unwittingly making slow movements to the right, corrected at intervals by quick voluntary ones to the left. There is then in the eyes a permanent excess of rightward innervation, the reflex resultant of our giddiness. The intermittent movements to the left by which we correct this, simply confirm and intensify the impression it gives us of a leftward whirling in the field of view: we seem to ourselves to be periodically pursuing and overtaking the objects in their leftward flight. Now if we convert this periodic voluntary action into permanent action, by holding the eyeballs still in spite of their reflex tendency to rotate (*i.e.*, by using such an excess of leftward voluntary innervation as would keep us fixating one object), we ought, if truly conscious of the degree of our voluntary innervation, to feel our eyes actually moving towards the left. And this feeling should produce in us the judgment that we are steadily following with our gaze a leftward moving field of view. As a matter of fact, however, this never happens. What does happen is that the field of view stops its motion the moment our eyes stop theirs.[20] Nothing could more conclusively prove the inability of

[20] The subject of optical vertigo has been best treated by Breuer in Stricker's *Medizinische Jahrbücher*, Jahrgang, 1874, 1 Heft. (See also 1875, 1 Heft.) Hoppe's more recent work *Die Schein-Bewegungen*, I have not seen. I ought to say that Mach (*Grundlinien der Lehre von den Bewegungsempfindungen*, 1875, pp. 83–5) denies that in his case fixating a point causes the apparent movement of objects to stop. His case is certainly exceptional, but need not invalidate in the least our theory. The eye-motions in all cases are reflex results of a sensation of subjective whirling of the body due most probably to excitement of the semi-circular canals. *This* is not arrested in anyone by fixing the eyes; and persisting in Mach with a constant field

mere innervation (however complex or intense) to influence our perception. Nothing could more completely vindicate the idea that *effected* movements, through the afferent sensations they give rise to, are alone what serve as premises in our motor judgments.[21]

II. IDEO–MOTOR ACTION

So far then, so good. We have got rid of a very obstructive complication in relegating the feeling of muscular exertion, properly so called, to that vast and well known class of afferent feelings, none of whose other members are held by anyone to be especially connected with the mysterious sentiments of effort and power, which are the subjects of our study. All muscle feelings eliminated, the question stands out pure and simple: What is the volitional effort proper? What makes it easy to raise the finger, hard to get out of bed on a cold morning, harder to keep our attention on the insipid image of a procession of sheep when troubled with insomnia, and hardest of all to say No to the temptation of any form of instinctive pleasure which has grown inveterate and habitual. In a word what is the nature of this *fiat* of which we have so often spoken?[22]

---

of view, may in him be sufficient to suggest the judgment that the field follows him in his flight, whilst in the average observer the further addition of a moving retinal image may be requisite for the full production of that psychic impression. All the feelings in question are rather confused and fluctuating, while the nausea which rapidly supervenes stands in the way of our becoming adepts in their observation.

[21] Let it not be objected that the involuntary rightward motion of the eyeballs which misled us, after standing still, into the impression that the world was moving, was "effected" and ought to have given us afferent sensations strong enough to prevent our being deluded by the image passing over the retina. No doubt we get these afferent sensations and *with sufficient practice* would rightly interpret them. But as the experiment is actually made, neither they nor the moving image on the retina (which far overpowers them in vivacity of impression) are *expected*. When we *intend* a movement of the eyes, the world being supposed at rest, we always expect both these sensations. Whenever the latter has come unexpectedly we have been in presence of a really moving object, and every moment of our lives moving objects are giving us unexpectedly this experience. Of prolonged unexpected movements of the eyes we never under normal circumstances have any experience whatever. What wonder then that the intense and familiar sensation of an unexpectedly moving retinal image should wholly overpower the feeble and almost unknown one of an unexpected and prolonged movement of the eyeballs and be interpreted as if it existed alone. I cannot doubt however that with sufficient practice we should all learn so to attend to and interpret the feelings of the moving eyeballs as to reduce the retinal experience to its proper signification.

[22] The philosophic importance of clearing the ground for the question may be shown by the example of Maine de Biran. This thoroughly original writer's whole

In our bed we think of the cold, and we feel the warmth and lie still, but we all the time feel that we can get up with no trouble *if we will.* The difficulty is to will. We say to our intemperate acquaintance, "You can be a new man, *if you will.*" But he finds the willing impossible. One who talks nonsense under the influence of hasheesh, realizes all the time his power to end his sentences soberly and sensibly, *if he will.* But his will feels as yet no sufficient reason for exerting itself. A person lying in one of those half-trance like states of immobility not infrequent with nervous patients, feels the *power* to move undiminished, but cannot resolve to manifest it. And cases might be multiplied indefinitely in which the fiat is not only a distinct, but a difficult and effort-requiring moment in the performance.

On the other hand cases may be multiplied indefinitely of actions performed with no distinct volitional fiat at all—the mere presence of an intellectual image of the movement, and the absence of any conflicting image, being adequate causes of its production. As Lotze says:[23] "The spectator accompanies the throwing of a billiard ball, or the thrust of the swordsman with slight movements of his arm;

---

life was devoted to the task of showing that the primordial fact of conscious personality was the sentiment of volitional effort. This intimate sense *is the self* in each of us. "It becomes the self by the sole fact of the distinction which establishes itself between the subject of the effort and the term which resists by its own inertia. The ego cannot begin to know itself or to exist for itself, except in so far as it can distinguish itself as subject of an effort, from a term which resists." (*Œuvres inédites,* Vol. 1, pp. 208, 212.) Maine de Biran makes this resisting term the muscle, though it is true he does not, like so many of his successors, think we have an *efferent* sense of its resistance. Its resistance is known to us by a muscular sensation proper, the *effect* of the contraction (p. 213). We shall show in the sequel that this sensation resists our fiat or volitional effort proper in no degree *quâ* muscular, but simply *quâ* disagreeable. Any other disagreeable sensation whatever may equally well serve as the term which resists our fiat that it become real. M. de B.'s giving such a monstrous monopoly to the muscular feelings is a consequence of his not having completed the discrimination I make in the text between all afferent sensations together on the one hand, and the fiat on the other. Muscle feelings for him still occupy an altogether singular, hybrid and abnormal sort of position.

23 *Medicinische Psychologie,* 1852, p. 293. In his admirably acute chapter on the will this author has most explicitly maintained the position that what we call muscular exertion is an afferent and not an efferent feeling: "We must affirm universally that in the muscular feeling we are not sensible of the *force* on its way to produce an effect, but only of the *sufferance* already produced in our moveable organs, the muscles, after the force has, in a manner unobservable by us, exerted upon them its causality" (p. 311). How often the battles of psychology have to be fought over again, each time with heavier armies and bigger trains, though not always with so able generals.

the untaught narrator tells his story with many gesticulations; the reader while absorbed in the perusal of a battle scene feels a slight tension run through his muscular system, keeping time as it were with the actions he is reading of. These results become the more marked the more we are absorbed in thinking of the movements which suggest them; they grow fainter exactly in proportion as a complex consciousness, under the dominion of a crowd of other representations, withstands the passing over of mental contemplation into outward action. . . . We see in writing or piano-playing a great number of very complicated movements following quickly one upon the other, the instigative representations of which remained scarcely a second in consciousness, certainly not long enough to awaken any other volition than the general one of resigning oneself without reserve to the passing over of representation into action. All the actions of our daily life happen in this wise: Our standing up, walking, talking, all this never demands a distinct impulse of the will, but is adequately brought about by the pure flux of thought."

Dr. Carpenter has proposed the name *ideo-motor* for these actions without a special fiat. And in the chapter of his *Mental Physiology* bearing this title may be found a very full collection of instances.[24] It is to be noted that among the most frequent cases of this sort are those acts which result from ideas or perceptions, intercurrent as it were to the main stream of our thought, and it may be logically disconnected therewith. I am earnestly talking with a friend, when I notice a piece of string on the floor. The next instant I have picked it up, with no deliberate resolve to do so, and with no check to my conversation. Or, I am lying in my warm bed, engrossed in some revery or other, when the notion suddenly strikes me "it is getting late," and before I know it, I am up in the cold, having executed without the smallest effort of resolve, an action which, half an hour previous, with full consciousness of the *pros* and the *cons*, the warm rest and the chill, the sluggishness and the manliness, time lost and the morning's duties, I was utterly unable to decide upon.

I then lay it down as a second corner-stake in our inquiry, that *every representation of a motion awakens the actual motion which*

[24] Prof. Bain has also amply illustrated the subject in his work on the *Senses and Intellect*, 3d edition, pages 336 to 343. He considers that these facts prove that the ideas of motion inhabit identical nerve tracts with the actualized motions.

is its object, unless inhibited by some antagonistic representation simultaneously present to the mind.

It is somewhat dangerous to base dogmatic conclusions on the experiments so far made on the cerebral cortex, nevertheless they may help to confirm conclusions already probable on other grounds. Munk's vivisectional experiments on the cortical centres seem much the most minute and elaborate which have yet been reported. Now Munk concludes from them that the so-called motor centres of Hitzig and Ferrier, each of which, when electrically irritated, provokes a characteristic movement in some part of the body, are sensory centres—the centres for the feelings of touch, pressure, position, and motion of the bodily parts in question. The entire zone which contains them is called by him the *Fühlsphäre* of the cerebral surface, and is made coördinate with the *Sehsphäre* and *Hörsphäre*.[25]

Electric excitement of the fore paw centre can then only give us an image of the paw in some resultant state of flexion or extension. And the reason why motor effects occur like clock-work when this centre is irritated, would be that this image is awakened with such extraordinary vivacity by the stimulus that no other idea in the animal's mind can be strong enough to inhibit its discharging into the insentient motor centres below.

Now the reader may still shake his head and say: "But can you seriously mean that all the wonderfully exact adjustment of my action's strength to its ends, is not a matter of outgoing innervation? Here is a cannon ball, and here a pasteboard box: instantly and accurately I lift each from the table, the ball not refusing to rise because my innervation was too weak, the box not flying abruptly into the air because it was too strong. Could representations of the movement's different sensory effects in the two cases be so delicately foreshadowed in the mind? or being there, is it credible that they should, all unaided, so delicately graduate the stimulation of the unconscious motor centres to their work?" Even so! I reply to both queries. We have a most extremely delicate foreshadowing of the

[25] H. Munk (Du Bois-Reymond's *Archiv für Physiologie*, 1878, pp. 177–8 and 549). It is true that Munk still believes in the *Innervationsgefühl*, only he supposes it to be a result of the activity of the lower motor centres, not coming to consciousness *in situ*, but transmitted upwards by fibres to the zone in question, and there perceived along with the passive feelings of the part involved. It is needless to say that there is not an atom of objective ground for the belief in these afferent innervation feelings—even less than for the efferent ones ordinarily assumed.

sensory effects. Why else the start of surprise that runs through us, if someone has filled the light seeming box with sand before we try to lift it, or has substituted for the cannon ball which we know, a painted wooden imitation? *Surprise* can only come from getting a sensation which differs from the one we expect. But the truth is that when we know the objects well, the very slightest difference from the expected weight will surprise us, or at least attract our notice. With unknown objects we begin by expecting the weight made probable by their appearance. The expectation of this sensation innervates our lift, and we "set" it rather small at first. An instant verifies whether it is too small. Our expectation rises, *i.e.*, we think in a twinkling of a setting of the chest and teeth, a bracing of the back, and a more violent feeling in the arms. Quicker than thought we have them, and with them the burden ascends into the air. Bernhardt[26] has shown in a rough experimental way that our estimation of the amount of a resistance is as delicately graduated when our wills are passive, and our limbs made to contract by direct local faradization, as when we ourselves innervate them. Ferrier[27] has repeated and verified the observations. They admit of no great precision, and too much stress should not be laid upon them either way, but at the very least, they tend to show that no added delicacy would accrue to our perception from the consciousness of the efferent process, even if it existed.

III. The Inscrutable Psycho-Physic Nexus Is Identical in All Innervation and Lies outside the Sphere of the Will

On the ordinary theory, the movements which accompany emotion, and those which we call voluntary, are of a fundamentally different character. The emotional movements are admitted to be discharged without intermediary by the mere presence of the exciting idea. The voluntary motions are said to follow the idea only after an intermediate conscious process of "innervation" has been

[26] *Archiv für Psychiatrie,* III, 618–635. Bernhardt strangely enough seems to think that what his experiments disprove is the existence of afferent muscular feelings, not those of efferent innervation—apparently because he deems that the peculiar thrill of the electricity ought to overpower all other afferent feelings from the part. But it is far more natural to interpret his results the other way, even aside from the certainty yielded by other evidence that passive muscular feelings exist. This other evidence is compendiously summed up by Sachs in Reichert und Du Bois-Reymond's *Archiv,* 1874, pp. 175–195.

[27] *Functions of the Brain* (Am. ed.), p. 228.

aroused. On the present theory the only difference lies in the fact that the emotions show a peculiar congenital connexion of certain forms of idea with certain very specially combined movements, largely of the "involuntary" muscles, but also of the others—as in fear, anger, etc.—such connexion being non-congenital in voluntary action; and in the further fact that the discharge of idea into movement is much more readily inhibited by other casually present ideas in the case of voluntary action, and less so in the case of emotions; though here too inhibition takes place on a large scale.[28]

That one set of ideas should compel the vascular, respiratory, and gesticulatory symptoms of shame, another those of anger, a third those of grief, a fourth those of laughter, and a fifth those of sexual excitement, is a most singular fact of our organization, which the labors of a Darwin have hardly even begun to throw light upon. Where such a prearrangement of the nerve centres exists, the way to awaken the motor symptoms is to awaken first the idea and then to dwell upon it. The thought of our enemy soon brings with it the bodily ebullition, of our loss the tears, of our blunder the blush. We even read of persons who can contract their pupils voluntarily by steadily imagining a brilliant light—that being the sensation to which the pupils normally respond.

"It is possible to weep at will by trying to recall that peculiar feeling in the trigeminal nerve which habitually precedes tears. Some can even succeed in sweating voluntarily, by the lively recollection of the characteristic skin sensations, and the voluntary reproduction of an indescribable sort of feeling of relaxation, which ordinarily precedes the flow of perspiration. Finally, it is well known how easily the thought of gustatory stimuli excites the activity of the salivary glands. This capacity to indirectly excite activities usually involuntary, is much more pronounced in certain diseases. Hypochondriacs know well how easily the heart-beat may be made to alter, or even cramps of single muscles, feelings of *aura*, and so forth, be brought about in this way, which no doubt in the religious epidemics of the Middle Ages, led to the imitative spread of ecstatic convulsions, from one person to another."[29] It suffices to think steadily of the feeling of yawning, to provoke the act in

[28] Witness the evaporation of manifestations of disgust in the presence of fear, of lust in the presence of respect, etc., etc.

[29] Lotze, *Medicinische Psychologie*, p. 303.

most persons; and in everyone in certain states, to imagine vomiting is to vomit.

The great play of individual idiosyncracy in all these matters, shows that the following or not following of action upon representation is a matter of connexions among nervous centres, which connexions may fluctuate widely in extent. The ordinary "voluntary" act results in this way: First, some feeling produces a movement in a reflex, or as we say, accidental way. The movement excites a sensorial tract, causing a feeling which, whenever the sensorial tract functions again, revives as an idea. Now the sensorial and motor tracts, thus associated in their actions, remain associated forever afterwards, and as the motor originally aroused the sensory, so the sensory may now arouse the motor (provided no outlying ideational tracts in connexion with it prevent it from so doing). Voluntary acts *are* in fact nothing but acts whose motor centres are so constituted that they *can* be aroused by these sensorial centres, whose excitement was originally their effect. Acts, the innervation of which cannot thus run up its primal stream, are not voluntary. But the line of division runs differently in different individuals.

Now notice that in all this, whether the act do follow or not upon the representation is a matter quite immaterial so far as the *willing* of the act represented goes. I will to write, and the act follows. I will to sneeze, and it does not. I will that the distant table slide over the floor towards me; it also does not. My willing representation can no more instigate my sneezing centre, than it can instigate the table, to activity. But in both cases, it is as true and good willing as it was when I willed to write. In a word, volition is a psychic or moral fact pure and simple, and is absolutely completed when the *intention* or *consent* is there. The supervention of motion upon its completion is a supernumerary phenomenon belonging to the department of physiology exclusively, and depending on the organic structure and condition of executive ganglia, whose functioning is quite unconscious.

In St. Vitus' dance, in locomotor ataxy, the representation of a movement and the consent to it take place normally. But the inferior executive centres are deranged, and although the ideas discharge them, they do not discharge them so as to reproduce the precise sensations which they prefigure. In aphasia the patient has an image of certain words which he wishes to utter, but when he opens his mouth, he hears himself making quite unintended sounds. This may fill him with rage and despair—which passions only show how intact his will remains.[30]

Paralysis only goes a step farther. The associative mechanism is not only deranged but altogether broken through. The volition occurs, but the hand remains as still as the table. The paralytic is made aware of this by the absence of the expected change in his afferent sensations. He tries harder, *i.e.*, he mentally frames the sensation of muscular "effort" with consent that it shall occur. It does so: he frowns, he heaves his chest, he clenches his other fist, but the palsied arm lies passive.[31] It may then be that the thought of his impotence shall make his will, like a Rarey-tamed horse, forever afterwards cowed, inhibited, impossible, with respect to that particular motion.[32]

The special case of the limb being completely anæsthetic, as well as atactic, curiously illustrates the merely external and quasi-accidental connexion between muscular motion and the thought which instigates it. We read of cases like this:

"Voluntary movements cannot be estimated the moment the patient ceases to take note of them by his eyes. Thus after having made him close his eyes, if one asks him to move one of his limbs either wholly or in part, he does it but cannot tell whether the effected movement is large or small, strong or weak, or even if it

[30] In ataxy it is true that the sensations resultant from movement are usually disguised by anæsthesia. This has led to false explanations of the symptom (Leyden, *Die graue Degeneration der hinteren Rückenmarksstränge*, 1863). But the undeniable existence of atactics without a trace of insensibility proves the trouble to be due to disorder of the associating machinery between the centres of ideation and those of discharge. These latter cases have been used by some authors in support of the Innervationsgefühl theory: (Classen: *Ueber das Schlussverfahren des Sehactes*, 1863, p. 50); the spasmodic irregular movements being interpreted as the result of an imperfect *sense* of the amount of innervation we are exerting. There is no subjective evidence whatever of such a state. The undoubtedly true theory is best expounded by Jaccoud: *Les Paraplégies et l'ataxie motrice*, 1864, part iii, chapter ii.

[31] A normal palsy occurs during sleep. We will all sorts of motions in our dreams, but seldom perform any of them. In nightmare we become conscious of the non-performance, and will the "effort." This seems then to occur in a restricted way, limiting itself to the occlusion of the glottis and producing the respiratory anxiety which wakes us up.

[32] *Vide supra*, note 13.

has taken place at all. And when he opens his eyes after moving his leg from right to left, for example, he declares that he had a very inexact notion of the extent of the effected movement. . . . If, having the intention of executing a certain movement, *I prevent him*, he does not perceive it, and supposes the limb to have taken the position he intended to give it."[33] Or this:

"The patient when his eyes were closed in the middle of an unpractised movement, remained with the extremity in the position it had when the eyes closed and did not complete the movement properly. Then after some oscillations the limb gradually sank by reason of its weight (the sense of fatigue being absent). Of this the patient was not aware, and wondered when he opened his eyes, at the altered position of his limb."[34]

In the normal state of man there is always a possibility that action may not occur in this simple ideo-motor way. The motor ideas may awaken other ideas which inhibit the discharge into the executive ganglia. But in the state called hypnotism we have a condition analogous to sleep in so far forth that the ideas which turn up do not awaken their habitual and most reasonable associates. Their motor effects are therefore not inhibited, and the hypnotized subject not only believes everything that is told him, however improbable, but he acts out every motor suggestion which he receives. The eminent French philosopher, Renouvier, as early as 1859, expressly assimilated these facts of hypnotism to the ordinary ideo-motor actions, and to those effects of moral vertigo and fascination which make us fall when we are on heights, laugh from the fear of laughing, etc., etc. His account of the psychology of volition[35] is the firmest, and in my opinion, the truest connected treatment yet given to the subject by any author with whom I am acquainted.

33 Landry: "Mémoire sur la paralysie du sens musculaire," in *Gazette des Hôpitaux,* 1855, p. 270.

34 Takács: "Untersuchungen über die Verspätung der Empfindungsleitung," *Archiv für Psychiatrie,* Bd. x, Heft 2, p. 533.

35 *Essais de critique générale;* 2me Essai, "Psychologie rationelle," pp. 273 and following. 2me Édition, 1875. Tome I, pp. 367–408. Heidenhain, in an interesting pamphlet (*Der sogenannte thierische Magnetismus,* Leipzig, 1880), has recently propounded the opinion that in hypnotized subjects the hemispheres are thrown entirely out of gear and no *ideas* whatever awakened. This opinion is so much at variance with that of English and French observers that further corroboration is required.

IV. THE WILL CONNECTS TERMS IN THE MENTAL SPHERE ONLY

We must now leave behind us the cases of extremely uncom-
plicated mental motivation, which we have hitherto considered,
and take up others where the tendency of a particular motor idea
to take effect is arrested or delayed. These are the cases where the
fiat, the distinct decision, or the volitional effort, come in; and we
find them of many degrees of complexity.

First there are cases with no effort properly so called, either of
muscle or resolution: Shall I put on this hat or that? Shall I draw
a horse or a man on the sheet of paper which this amusement-
craving child brings me? Shall I move my index finger, or my little
finger to show my *"liberum arbitrium indifferentiæ"*? In the moun-
tains, in youth, on some intoxicating autumn morning, after in-
vigorating slumber, we feel strong enough to jump over the moon,
and casting about us for a barrier, a rock, a tree, or any object on
which to measure our bodily prowess, we perform with perfect
spontaneity feats which at another time might demand an almost
impossible exertion of muscle and of will.

Both of these exertions are present in a vast class of actions. Exhausted with fatigue and wet and watching, the sailor on a wreck
throws himself down to rest. But hardly are his limbs fairly relaxed,
when the order "to the pumps!" again sounds in his ears. Shall he,
can he, obey it? Is it not better just to let his aching body lie, and
let the ship go down if she will? So he lies on, till, with a desperate
heave of the will, at last he staggers to his legs, and to his task again.

Again, there are instances where the volitional fiat demands great
effort though the muscular exertion be insignificant, *e.g.*, the getting out of bed and bathing oneself on a cold morning.

Finally, we may have the fiat in all its rigor, with no motor representation whatever involved, or one so remote as not to count
directly at all in the mental motivation.

Of the former class are all resolutions to be patient rather than
to act. Such a one we have to make in the dentist's chair: The alternatives are a state of inward writhing, and mental swearing,
coupled with spasmodic respiration, and all sorts of irregularly
antagonistic muscular contractions—a state of shrinking and protest
in a word, on the one hand; and on the other a state of muscular
relaxation and free breathing, a sort of mental welcoming of the

pain, and the elated consciousness that be it never so savage, we can stand it. This is a state of *consent*, and the passage from the former state to it, not the passage the other way, is in this instance the one requiring the fiat, and characterized by the mental "click" of resolve.

As examples of the last class, take Regulus returning to Carthage, the priest who decides to break with his church, the girl who makes up her mind to live single with her ideal, rather than accept the good old bachelor who is her only suitor, the embezzler who fixes a certain day on which to make public confession, the deliberate suicide, yea the wretch who after long hesitation, resolves that he will put arsenic into his wife's cup. These pass through one moment which like a knife-edge parts all their past from all their future, but which leads to no *immediate* muscular consequences at all.

Now if we analyze this great variety of cases, we shall find that the knife-edge moment where it exists, has the same identical constitution in all. It is literally a *fiat*, a state of mind which consents, agrees, or is willing, that certain represented experiences shall continue to be, or should now for the first time become, part of Reality. The consent comes after hesitation. The hesitation came because something made us imagine another alternative. When both alternatives are agreeable, as in the intoxication of the mountain morning, or the *liberum arbitrium indifferentiæ*, the hesitation is but momentary; for either course is better than delay, and the one which lies nearest when the sense that we are uselessly delaying becomes pungent, is the one which discharges into act—thus no mental tension has time to arise.

But in other cases both alternatives are images of mixed good and evil. Whatever is done has to be done against some inhibitory agency, whether of intrinsic unpleasantness in the doing, or of represented odiousness of the doing's fruits: the fiat has to occur against resistance. Volition then comes hand in hand with the sentiment of effort, and the proper problem of this essay lies before us.

What does the effort seem to do? To bring the decisive volition. What is this volition? The stable victory of an idea, although it may be disagreeable, the permanent suppression of an idea although it may be immediately and urgently pleasant.

What do we mean by "victory"? The survival in the mind in such form as to constitute unwavering contemplation, expectation, assent, or affirmation. What do we mean by "suppression"? Either complete oblivescence, or such presence as to evoke the steady sentiment of aversion or negation.

Volition with effort is then incidental to the conflict of ideas of what our experience may be. Conflict involves those strange states or general attitudes of feeling, which when we speak logically or intellectually, we call affirmation and negation, but when we speak emotionally, we call assent and refusal. Psychologically of course, like every other mental modification, these attitudes are feelings *sui generis*, not to be described, but only labelled and pointed out. What they are *in se*, what their conflict is, and what its decision and resolution are, we know in every given case introspectively with an absolute clearness that nothing can make clearer. But what forms of cerebral nerve-process correspond to these mind-processes is an infinitely darker matter, and one as to which I will here make no suggestion except the simple and obvious one that they and volition with them are subserved by the ideational centres exclusively and involve no downward irradiation into lower parts. The irradiation only comes when they are completed.

In the dentist's chair, one idea is that of the manliness of enduring the pain, the other is that of its intolerable character. We assent to the manliness, saying, "let it be the reality," and behold, it becomes so, though with a mental effort exactly proportionate to the sensitiveness of our nerves. To the sailor on the wreck, one idea is that of his sore hands, and the nameless aching exhaustion of his whole frame which further pumping involves. The other, is that of a hungry sea ingulfing him. He says: "rather the former!" and it becomes reality, in spite of the inhibiting influence of the comparatively luxurious sensations of the spot in which he for the moment lies.

To the sinner in the agony of his mind, one idea is of the social shame and all the outward losses and degradations to which confession will expose him, the other is that of the rescue from the damned unending inward foulness to which concealment seems to doom him. He says to the confession, "*fiat!* with all its consequences," and sure enough, when the times comes, *fit*, but not without mental blood and sweat.

Everywhere the difficulty is the same: to keep affirming and adopting a state of mind of which disagreeableness is an integral factor. The disagreeableness need not be of the nature of pain; it may be the merely relative disagreeableness of insipidity. When the spontaneous course of thought is to exciting images, whether sanguine or lugubrious, loving or revengeful, all reasonable representations come with a deadly flatness and coldness that strikes a chill to the soul. To cling to them however, as soon as they show their faces, to consent to their presence, to affirm them, to negate all the rest, is the characteristic energy of the man whose will is strong. If on this purely mental plane his effort succeeds, the outward consequences will take care of themselves, for the representation will work unaided its motor effects. The simplest cases are the best for illustrating the point, and in the case of a man afflicted with insomnia, and to whose body sleep comes through the persistent successful diversion of the mind from the train of whirling thoughts, to the monotonous contemplation of one letter after another of a verse of poetry, spelled out synchronously with the acts of respiration, we have all the elements that can anywhere be found: a struggle of ideas, a victory of one set and certain bodily effects automatically consequent thereon. *To sustain a representation, to think,* is what requires the effort, and is the true moral act. Maniacs know their thoughts to be insane, but they are too pressing to be withstood. Again and again sober notions come, but like the sober instants of a drunken man, they are so sickeningly cadaverous, or else so still and small and imperceptible, that the lunatic can't bear to look them fully in the face and say: "let these alone represent my realities." Such an extract as this will illustrate what I mean:

"A gentleman of respectable birth, excellent education, and ample fortune, engaged in one of the highest departments of trade .... [and being] induced to embark in one of the plausible speculations of the day .... was utterly ruined. Like other men, he could bear a sudden overwhelming reverse better than a long succession of petty misfortunes, and the way in which he conducted himself on the occasion met with unbounded admiration from his friends. He withdrew however into rigid seclusion, and, being no longer able to exercise the generosity and indulge the benevolent feelings which had formed the happiness of his life, made himself a substitute for them by day-dreams, gradually fell into a state of irritable despondency, from which he only gradually recovered with the loss of reason. He now fancied himself possessed of immense wealth, and gave without stint his imaginary riches. He has ever since been under gentle restraint, and leads a life not merely of happiness, but of bliss; converses rationally, reads the newspapers, where every tale of distress attracts his notice, and being furnished with an abundant supply of blank checks, he fills up one of them with a munificent sum, sends it off to the sufferer, and sits down to his dinner with a happy conviction that he has earned the right to a little indulgence in the pleasures of the table; and yet, on a serious conversation with one of his old friends, he is quite conscious of his real position, but the conviction is so exquisitely painful that *he will not let himself believe it.*" [36]

Now to turn to the special case of the decision to make a muscular movement. This decision may require a volitional effort, or it may not. If I am well, and the movement is a light one (like the brushing of dust from my coat-sleeve), and suggests no consequences of an unpleasant nature, it is effortless. But if unpleasant consequences are expected, that effective sustaining of the idea which results in bringing the motion about, and which is equivalent to mental consent that those consequences become real, involves considerable effort of volition. Now the unpleasant consequences may be immediate—my body may be weary, or the movement violent, and involve a great amount of that general and special afferent feeling which we learned above to constitute *muscular* exertion. Under these circumstances the idea of the movement *is* the imagination of these massively unpleasant feelings, and nothing else. The willing of the movement is the consent to these imagined feelings becoming real—the saying of them, "*fiant.*" The effort which the willing requires is the purely mental transition from the mere *conception* of the feelings to their *expectation*, steadfastly maintaining itself before the mind, disagreeable though it be. The motor idea, assuming at last this victorious *status*, not only uninhibited by remote associations, but inhibited no longer even by its own unpleasantness, discharges by the preappointed mechanism into the right muscles. Then the motor sensations accrue in all their expected severity, and the *muscular* effort as distinguished from the *volitional* effort has its birth.

It is needless after this to say what absolutely different phenomena these two efforts are, or to expatiate upon the unfortunateness of their being confounded under the same generic name. Muscular feelings whenever they are massive, and the body is not

[36] *The Duality of the Mind*, by A. L. Wigan, M. D., pp. 122–123.

"fresh," are rather disagreeable, especially when accompanied by stopped breath, congested head, bruised skin of fingers, toes, or shoulders, and strained joints. And it is only *as thus disagreeable* that the mind has difficulty in consenting to their reality. That they happen to be made real by our bodily activity is a purely accidental circumstance. A soldier standing still to be fired at, expects disagreeable sensations engendered by his bodily passivity. The action of his will, *in consenting to the expectation*, is identical with that of the sailor rising to go to the pumps. What is hard for both is *facing an idea as real.*

The action of the will must not be limited to the willing of an act. To exert the will and to make soft muscles hard, are not one thing, but two entirely different things. Extremely frequent association may account for, but not excuse their confusion by the psychologist. The represented disagreeableness of a muscular motion may often be that which an exertion of will is called on to overcome; but as well might a cook, who daily associates the burning of the fire with the boiling of the potatoes, define the inward essence of combustion as the making of hard potatoes soft.

The action of the will is the reality of consent to a *fact* of any sort whatever, a fact in which we ourselves may play either an active, or a suffering part. The fact always appears to us in an idea: and it is willed by its idea becoming victorious over inhibiting ideas, banishing negations, and remaining affirmed. The victorious idea is in every case whatsoever built up of images of feelings afferent in their origin. And the first philosophical conclusion properly so called, into which our inquiry leads us, is a confirmation of the older sensationalist view that all the mind's materials without exception are derived from passive sensibility. Those who have thought that sensationalism abdicated its throne and mental spontaneity came in when Prof. Bain admitted a "sensation of energy exerted by the outgoing stream," have rejoiced in the wrong place altogether. There *is* a feeling of mental spontaneity, opposed in nature to all afferent feelings; but it does not, like the pretended feeling of muscular innervation, sit among them as among its peers. It is something which dominates them all, by simply choosing from their midst. It may reinforce either one in turn—a retinal image by attending to it, a motor image by willing it, a complex conception, like that of the world having a divine meaning, by believing it. Whatever mental material this element of spontaneity comes and perches on, is sustained, affirmed, selected from the rest; though but for the feeling of spontaneous psychic effort, which thus reinforces it, we are conscious every moment that it might cease to be. The whole contrast of *a priori* and empirical elements in the mind lies, I am fully convinced, in this distinction. All our mind's contents are alike empirical. What is *a priori* is only their accentuation and emphasis. This greeting of the spirit, this acquiescence, connivance, partiality, call it what you will, which seems the inward gift of our selfhood, and no essential part of the feelings, to either of which in turn it may be given—this psychic effort pure and simple, is the fact which *a priori* psychologists really have in mind when they indignantly deny that the whole intellect is derived from sense.

V. No Conscious Dynamic Connection between the Inner and Outer Worlds

Now if we take this psychic fact for just what on the face of it it seems to be, namely, the giving to an idea the full degree of reality it can have in and for the mind, we are led to a curious view of the relations between the inner and the outer worlds. The ideas, as mere representatives of possibility, seem set up midway between them to form a sort of atmosphere in which Reality floats and plays. The mind can take any one of these ideas and make it *its* reality—sustain it, adopt it, adhere to it. But the mind's state will be Error, unless the outer force "backs" the same idea. If it backs it, the mind is cognitive of Truth; but whether in error, or in truth, the mind's espousal of the idea is called Belief. The outer force seems in no wise constrained to back the mind's adoptions, except in one single kind of case—where the idea is that of bodily movement. Here the outer force (with certain reservations) obeys and follows the mind's lead, agreeing to father as it were every child of that sort which the mind may conceive. And the act by which the mind thus takes the lead is called a Volition.

The ideas backed by both parties are the Reality; those backed by neither, or by the mind alone, form a residuum, a sort of limbo or no-man's land, of wasted fancies and aborted possibilities.

But is it not obvious from this that the difference between Belief and Volition is not intrinsic? What the mind does in both cases is the same. It takes an image, and says, "so far as I am concerned, let this stand; let it be real for me." The behavior of the outer force is what makes all the difference. Generally constrained in the case of the motor volition, it is independent in the case of the belief. It is true that volition may be impotent and belief delusive;—but be they however never so false or powerless, by their inward nature they are *ejusdem farinæ*—beliefs and volitions still.

Belief and Will are thus concerned immediately only with the relation between possibilities *for the mind*, and realities *for the mind*. The notion of *reality for the mind*, becomes thus the pivotal notion in the analysis of both. To analyze this notion itself seems at present an impossible task. Professor Bain has exerted his utmost powers upon it, but, to our mind, without avail; and what J. S. Mill says[37] still remains true, that when we arrive at the element which makes a belief differ from a mere conception, "we seem to have reached, as it were, the central point of our intellectual nature, presupposed and built upon in every attempt to explain the more recondite phenomena of our being."

The sense of reality must then be postulated as an ultimate psychic fact. But we know that it may come with effort, or without, in the theoretic as well as in the motor sphere; and the reader who has had the patience to follow our study of effort as far as this, will not object to going on now to consider it in both spheres together.

Hume said that to believe an idea, was simply to *have* it in a lively manner. We, on our part, have seen the ideo-motor cases in which to will an idea is simply to have it. But a moment's reflection shows that such spontaneous belief and will are possible only where the mind's contents are at a minimum of complication. In the trance-subject's mind any simple suggestion will be both believed and acted on, because none of its usual associates are awakened. Bain[38] and Taine[39] have beautifully shown how in the normal subject all ideas taken *per se* are hallucinatory or held as true. Doubt never comes from any intrinsic insufficiency in a thought, but from the manner in which extrinsic ideas conflict with it, or in Taine's phrase, serve as its reductive. Before they come we have the primal state of theoretic and practical innocence.

[37] His edition of James Mill's *Analysis*, Vol. i, p. 423. Bain's reply is in the section on Belief in the 3d edition of his *Emotions and Will*.
[38] *Emotions and Will*, 3d Ed., pp. 511–517.
[39] *De l'intelligence*, Part i, Book ii, Chap. i.

But wider suggestions bring the fall, and turn the simple credulity to doubt and the fearless spontaneity to hesitation. A stable faith, a firm decree, can then only come after reflection, and be its fruits. What is reflection? A conflict between many ideas of possibility. During the conflict the sense of reality is lost or rather the connexion between it and each of the ideas in turn. The conflict is over when the sense of reality returns, like the tempered steel, ten times more precious and invincible for its icy bath in the waters of uncertainty. But why and how does it return? and why does it so often return with the symptom of effort by its side? Is it an independent entity which merely took its flight at the first alarm of the battle, and which now with effort as its ally and affirmation at its right hand and negation at its left, comes back to *give* the victory to one idea? Or is it a simple resultant of the victory which was a foregone conclusion decided by the intrinsic strength of the conflicting ideas alone?

We stand here in the presence of another mighty metaphysical problem. If the latter alternative be true there is no genuine spontaneity, no ambiguous power of decision, no real freedom either of faith or of act. The effort which seems to come and reinforce one side, endowing it with the feeling of reality, can be no new force adding itself to those already in the arena. It can only be a sort of eddy or derivative from their movement, whose semblance of independent form is illusory, and whose amount and direction are implicitly given the moment they are posited.

This has been the doctrine of powerful schools. The ideas themselves and their conflict have been held to constitute the total history of the mind, with no unaccounted-for phenomenon left over. Long before mutual inhibition by nerve processes had been discovered, the inhibitions and furtherances of one idea by another, had by Herbart been erected into a completely elaborated system of psychic statics and dynamics. The English associationist school, without using the word inhibition, and in a much less outwardly systematic, though by no means less successful way, had also represented choice and decision as nothing but the resultant of different ideas failing to neutralize each other exactly. Doubt, fear, contradiction, curiosity, desire, assent, conviction, affirmation, negation and effort, are all alike, on this view, but collateral products, incidents of the form of equilibrium of the representations, as they pass from the oscillating to the stable state.

This is of course conceivable;—and to have the conception in a lively manner (as Hume says), may well in us as in so many others, carry the sense of reality with it, and command conviction. But still the other alternative conflicts, and *may* reduce this conception to one of mere possibility, degrading it from a creed to an hypothesis. It seems impossible, if our minds are in this open state, to find any crucial evidence which may decide. I shall, therefore, not pretend to dogmatize myself, but close this essay by a few considerations, which may give at least an appearance of liveliness to the alternative notion, that the mental effort with which the affirmation of reality so often comes conjoined, may be an adventitious phenomenon, not wholly given and pre-determined by the ideas of whose struggle it accompanies the settlement.

A little natural history becomes here necessary. When outer forces impinge upon a body we say that its resultant motion follows the line of least resistance, or of greatest traction. When we deliberately symbolize the mental drama in mechanical language, we also say that belief and will follow the lines of least resistance, or of most attractive motivation. But it is a curious fact that our *spontaneous* language is by no means compatible with the law that mental action always follows lines of least resistance. Of course, if we proceed *a priori* and define the line of least resistance, as the line that is followed, the law must hold good. But in all hard cases either of belief or will, it seems to the agent as if one line were easier than another, and offered least resistance, even at the moment when the other line is taken. The sailor at the pumps, he who under the surgeon's knife represses cries of pain, or he who exposes himself to ostracism for duty's sake, feels as if he were following the line of greatest temporary resistance. He speaks of conquering and overcoming his impulses and temptations.

But the sluggard, the drunkard, the coward, never talk of their conduct in that way or say they resist their energy, overcome their sobriety, conquer their courage and so forth. If in general we class all motives as sensual on the one hand and moral on the other, the sensualist never says of his behavior that it results from a victory over his conscience, but the moralist always speaks of his as a victory over his appetite. The sensualist uses terms of inactivity, says he forgets his ideal, is deaf to duty and so forth; which terms seem to imply that the moral motives *per se* can be annulled without energy or effort, and that the strongest mere traction lies in the line of the sensual impulse. The moral one appears in comparison with this, a still small voice which must be artificially reinforced to prevail. Effort is what reinforces it, making things seem as if, while the sensual force were essentially a fixed quantity, the moral might be of various amount. But what determines the amount of the effort when by its aid moral force becomes victorious over a great sensual resistance? The very greatness of the resistance itself. If the sensual impulses are small, the moral effort is small. The latter is *made great* by the presence of a great antagonist to overcome. And if a brief definition of moral action were required, none could be given which would better fit the appearances than this: It is action in the line of the greatest resistance.

The facts may be most briefly symbolized thus, S standing for the sensual motive, M for the moral and E for the effort:

$$M \ per \ se < S.$$
$$M + E > S.$$

In other words, if E adds itself to M, S immediately offers the least resistance, and motion occurs in spite of it.

But the E does not seem to form an integral part of the M. It appears adventitious and indeterminate in advance. We can make more or less as we please, and *if* we make enough we can convert the greatest mental resistance into the least.

Now the question whether this appearance of ambiguity is illusory or real, is the question of the freedom of the will. Many subtle considerations may be brought to prove that the amount of effort which a moral motive comports as its ally, is a fixed function of the motive itself, and like it, determined in advance. On the other hand, there is the notion of an absolute ambiguity in the being of this thing, and its amount, sun-clear to the consciousness of each of us. He who loves to balance nice doubts and probabilities, need be in no hurry to decide. Like Mephistopheles to Faust, he can say to himself, *"dazu hast du noch eine lange Frist,"* for from generation to generation the evidence for both sides will grow more voluminous, and the question more exquisitely refined. But if his speculative delight is less keen, if the love of a *parti pris* outweighs that of keeping questions open, or if, as a French philosopher of genius[40] says, *"l' amour de la vie qui s'indigne de tant de discours,"* awakens in him, craving the sense of either peace or power;

40 J. Lequier: *La Recherche d'une première vérité*, 1865, p. 90.

then taking the risk of error on his head, he must project upon one of the alternatives in his mind, the attribute of *reality for him*. The present writer does this for the alternative of freedom. May the reader derive no less contentment if he prefer to take the opposite course!

Only one further point remains, but that is an important one philosophically. There is no commoner remark than this, that resistance to our muscular effort is the only sense which makes us aware of a reality independent of ourselves. The reality revealed to us in this experience takes the form of a *force* like the force of effort which we ourselves exert, and the latter after a certain fashion serves to measure.[41] This force we do not similarly exert when we receive tactile, auditory, visual and other impressions, so the same reality cannot be revealed by those passive senses.

Of course if the foregoing analysis be true, such reasoning falls to the ground. The "muscular sense" being a sum of afferent feelings is no more a "force-sense" than any other sense. It reveals to us hardness and pressure as they do colour, taste, smell, sonority, and the other attributes of the phenomenal world. To the *naïve* consciousness all these attributes are equally objective. To the critical all equally subjective. The physicist knows nothing whatever of force in a non-phenomenal sense. Force is for him only a generic name for all those *things* which will cause motion. A falling stone, a magnet, a cylinder of steam, a man, just as they appear to sense, *are* forces. There is no supersensible force *in* or *behind* them. Their force is just their sensible pull or push, if we take them naturally, and just their positions and motions if we take them scientifically. If we aspire to strip off from Nature all anthropomorphic qualities, there is none we should get rid of quicker than its "Force." How illusory our spontaneous notions of force grow when projected into the outer world becomes evident as soon as we reflect upon the phenomenon of muscular contraction. In pure objective dynamic terms (*i.e.*, terms of position and motion), it is the *relaxed* state of the muscle which is the state of stress and tension. In the act of

41 See for example, Spencer's *Psychology*, Part VII, Chaps. XVI and XVII; Herschel's *Familiar Lectures*, Lecture XII; an article on "The Force behind Nature," by Dr. Carpenter, reprinted in the *Popular Science Monthly* for March, 1880; Martineau's Review of Bain in *Essays, Philosophical and Theological*, 1866, pp. 244 ff.; Mansel's *Metaphysics*, pp. 105, 346.

contraction, on the contrary, the tension is resolved, and disappears. Our feeling about it is just the other way—which shows how little our feeling has to do with the matter.

The subject has an interest in connexion with the free-will controversy. It is an admitted mechanical principle that the resultant movement of a system of bodies linked together in definite relations of energy, may vary according to changes in their collocation, brought about by moving them at right angles to their pre-existing movements; which changes will not interfere with the conservation of the system's energy, as they perform no work upon it. Certain persons desiring to harmonize free-will with the theory of conservation, have used this conception to symbolize the dynamic relations of will with brain, by saying that the mental effort merely determines the moment and the spot at which a certain molecular *vis viva* shall start, by a sort of rectangular pressure which plays the part of an independent variable in the equations of movement required by the principles of conservation. Thus free-will may be conceived without any of the internal energy of the system being either augmented or destroyed.

Now so long as mental effort in general was supposed to have a particular connexion with muscular effort, and so long as muscular effort was supposed to reveal to us behind the resistance of bodies, a "force" which they contained, there was a ready reply to all this speculation. Your will, it could be said, *is* doing "work" upon the system. "Work" is defined in mechanics as movement done against resistance, and your will meets with a resistance which it has to overcome by moral effort. Were the molecular movements brought about by the will, rectangular to pre-existing movements, they would not resist, and the volition would be effortless. But the volition involves effort, and since according to the will-muscle-force-sense theory, its effort is an inner force which overcomes a real outer force, since, indeed, without this antagonism we should be without the notion of outer force altogether, why then the effort, if free, must be an absolutely new contribution and creation so far as the sum of cosmic energy is concerned. The only alternative then (if one still held to the will-muscle-force-sense theory) was either with Sir John Herschel,[42] frankly to avow that "force" may be created anew, and that "conservation" is only an approximate law;

[42] *Loc. cit.*, p. 468.

or else to drop free-will, in favor of conservation, and suppose the ego in willing, to be merely cognitively conscious, in the midst of the universal force-stream, of certain currents with which it was mysteriously fated to identify itself.

To my mind all such discussions rest on an anthropomorphization of outward force, which is to the last degree absurd. Outward forces so far as they are anything, are masses in certain positions, or in certain movements, and nought besides. The muscular "force-sense" reveals to us nothing but hardness and pressure, which are subjective sensations, like warmth or pain. The moral effort is not transitive between the inner and the outer worlds, but is put forth upon the inner world alone. Its point of application is an idea. Its achievement is "reality for the mind," of that idea. That, when the idea is realized, the corresponding nerve tracts should be modified, and so *de proche en proche*, the muscles contract, is one of those harmonies between inner and outer worlds, before which our reason can only avow its impotence. If our reason tries to interpret the relation as a dynamic one, and to conceive that the neural modification is brought about by the idea shoving the molecules of the ganglionic matter sideways from their course, well and good! Only we had better assume ourselves unconscious of the dynamism. We are unconscious of the molecules as such, and of our lateral push as such. Why should we be conscious of the "force" as such, by which the molecules resist the push? They are one thing, and the consciousness which they subserve is always an idea of another thing. *The only resistance which the force of consciousness feels or can feel, is the resistance which the idea makes to being consented to as real.*

Conclusions

1. Muscular effort, properly so called, and mental effort properly so called, must be distinguished. What is commonly known as "muscular exertion," is a compound of the two.

2. The only feelings and ideas connected with muscular motion are feelings and ideas of it *as effected*. Muscular effort proper, is a sum of feelings in afferent nerve tracts, resulting from motion being *effected*.

3. The pretended feeling of efferent innervation does not exist— the evidence for it drawn from paralysis of single eye muscles, van-

ishing when we take the position of the sound eye into account.

4. The philosophers who have located the human sense of force and spontaneity in the *nexus* between the volition and the muscular contraction, making it thus join the inner and the outer worlds, have gone astray.

5. The point of application of the volitional effort always lies within the inner world, being an idea or representation of afferent sensations of some sort. From its intrinsic nature or from the presence of other ideas, this representation may spontaneously tend to lapse from vivid and stable consciousness. Mental effort may then accompany its maintenance. That (being once maintained) it should by the connexion between its cerebral seat and other bodily parts, give rise to movements in the so-called voluntary muscles, or in glands, vessels, and viscera, is a subsidiary and secondary matter, with which the psychic effort has nothing immediately to do.

6. Attention, belief, affirmation and motor volition are thus four names for an identical process, incidental to the conflict of ideas alone, the survival of one in spite of the opposition of others.

7. The surviving idea is invested with a sense of reality which cannot at present be further analyzed.

8. The question whether, when its survival involves the feeling of effort, this feeling is determined in advance or absolutely ambiguous and matter of chance as far as all the other data are concerned, is the real question of the freedom of the will, and explains the strange intimateness of the feeling of effort to our personality.

9. To single out the sense of muscular resistance as the "force-sense" which alone can make us acquainted with the reality of an outward world is an error. We cognize outer reality by every sense. The muscular makes us aware of its hardness and pressure, just as other afferent senses make us aware of its other qualities. If they are too anthropomorphic to be true, so is it also.

10. The ideational nerve tracts alone are the seat of the feeling of mental effort. It involves no discharge downwards into tracts connecting them with lower executive centres; though such discharge may follow upon the completion of the nerve processes to which the effort corresponds.

Notes on the Sense of Dizziness in Deaf-Mutes

An immense amount of evidence, collected within the last few years, tends to show that the semicircular canals of the internal ear have nothing to do with the function of hearing, but are organs of a special sense hitherto unrecognized as such: the sense, namely, of translation through space, which in its more extreme degrees becomes the feeling of dizziness or vertigo. It occurred to me that, if this theory were true, some, at least, of the inmates of deaf and dumb institutions ought to prove insusceptible of experiencing this latter sensation, for in some either the whole auditory nerve is probably degenerated, or else its ampullar terminations will have shared the local fate, whatever it be, which has abolished the hearing functions of the cochlea. An inquiry was accordingly set on foot, of which the results already most beautifully confirm the modern theory. A very large number of the deaf-mutes examined are either wholly incapable of being made dizzy by the most violent rotations, or experience but a slight and transient giddiness. Others, as was to be expected, are strongly and normally affected. The difference in the demeanor of the two extreme classes of patients is so striking as to leave no room for mistake, and to banish doubt from the most sceptical spectator's mind. In the Horace Mann School in Boston, where 54 children were whirled in a rotary swing (by far the purest and most powerful means of inducing vertigo), only two were made dizzy. At the Hartford Asylum, out of 155 pupils, 49 are reported not dizzy, and 49 hardly dizzy. At the National College for Deaf-mutes in Washington, out of 62 persons examined, 19 are not at all dizzy, and 2 hardly dizzy. I have also received 58 answers to a printed circular of questions: 18 of these report complete absence, 12 a slight degree of dizziness; in all, 326 cases, of whom 131 were not dizzy, and 63 but slightly so. The deficiency in question seems quite independent of the age at which deafness began, semi-mutes and congenitals being found indifferently in all three classes. The number of deaf-mutes who are afflicted with disorders of locomotion seems never to have attracted the attention of physiologists, although it has long been notorious in asylums. The connection of these disorders with the loss of the semicircular canal sense becomes now a most interesting problem, into which I have begun to inquire. The matter is evidently complicated by the fact that the disease causing deafness may also leave central disorders expressing themselves in anæsthesia of the legs or by ataxia. That this is so appears from the number of semi-mutes who stagger and zigzag in walking, especially in the dark, but who are normal as respects dizziness. Congenital mutes are hardly ever found with disorders of locomotion. The evidence I already have in hand justifies the formation of a tentative hypothesis, as follows: The normal guiding sensation in locomotion is that from the semicircular canals. This is co-ordinated in the cerebellum (which is known to receive auditory nerve fibres) with the appropriate muscles, and the nervous machinery becomes structurally organized in the first few years of life. If, then, this guiding sensation be suddenly abolished by disease, the machinery is thrown completely out of gear, and must form closer connections than before either with sight or touch. But the cerebellar tracts, being already organized in another way, yield but slowly to the new co-ordinations now required, and for many years make the patient's gait uncertain, especially in the dark. Where the defect of the auditory nerve is congenital the cerebellar machinery is organized from the very outset in co-ordination with tactile sensations, and no difficulty occurs. To prove this hypothesis a minute medical examination of many typical cases will be required. If this prove confirmatory, it will then appear probable that many of the so-called paralyses after diphtheria, scarlet-fever, etc., may be nothing but sudden anæsthesiæ of the semicircular canals.

A complete discussion, with further details, is reserved for future publication.

The Sense of Dizziness in Deaf-Mutes

Prevented by outward circumstances from completing an investigation into the above subject which I would willingly have made more thorough, I publish the facts I have already obtained, in the hope that some one with better opportunities may carry on the work. The regular medical attendants of deaf-mute institutions seem particularly well fitted for such a task.

So far as I can make out, the immunity from dizziness which is characteristic of deaf-mutes has never been remarked or commented on before, even at asylums. Another illustration of how few facts "experience" will discover unless some prior interest, born of theory, is already awakened in the mind.

The modern theory, that the semicircular canals are unconnected with the sense of hearing, but serve to convey to us the feeling of movement of our head through space, a feeling which, when very intensely excited, passes into that of vertigo or dizziness, is well known.[1] It occurred to me that deaf-mute asylums ought to offer

[1] For the benefit of possible readers who may not be physiologists I would say that a summary of the evidence for this view is given in Foster's *Text Book of Physiology*, Book III, chap. vi, § 2. An attack on this theory has recently been made by Baginsky, a very full abstract of whose article appeared in the number of this [*American*] *Journal* [*of Otology*] for last January. Baginsky's experiments seem to me far from conclusive; and his argument has been satisfactorily replied to by

some corroboration of the theory in question, if a true one. Among their inmates must certainly be a considerable number in whom either the labyrinths or the auditory nerves in their totality have been destroyed by the same causes that produced the deafness. We ought therefore to expect, if the semicircular canals be really the starting-points of the sensation of dizziness, to find, on examining a large number of deaf-mutes, a certain proportion of them who are completely insusceptible of that affection, and others who enjoy immunity in a less complete degree.

The number of deaf-mutes who have been examined to test this suggestion is in all 519. Of these 186 are reported as totally insusceptible of being made dizzy by whirling rapidly round with the head in any position whatever.[2] Nearly 200 students and instructors in Harvard College were examined for purposes of comparison, and but a single one remained exempt from the vertigo. Of the deaf-mutes, 134 are set down as dizzy in a very slight degree; whilst 199 were normally, and in a few cases abnormally, sensitive.

The surmise with which I started is thus proved, and the theory that the semicircular canals are organs of equilibrium receives renewed corroboration.

Of course the cases observed represent every kind of ear disease, and it is impossible to analyze them so as to show why exemption from vertigo should be associated with the deafness in one case and in another not. "Congenital" mutes are found in all three classes, and so are "semi-mutes," so that the age at which the deafness comes on has nothing to do with it. The diseases which are the most fertile causes of deafness, meningitis, scarlet-fever, typhoid fever, etc., are as apt to leave the patient's sensibility to vertigo normal as they are to abolish it.

The cases from which the above aggregate conclusions are drawn are from several distinct sources: the Hartford Asylum; the National College at Washington, and its primary department; the Horace Mann School in Boston; the Clarke Institution at Northampton; the Indiana Institution; the answers to a printed circular I distributed, and a number of separate voluntary reports I received. In tabular form the statistics run as follows:

Högyes in Pflüger's *Archiv*, vol. xxvi, page 558, and by Spamer, *Ibid.*, vol. xxv, page 177.

[2] It is well known that with the head leaning forwards or backwards, or towards one shoulder, the dizziness is much more intense.

Institution.	Not dizzy.	Slightly.	Dizzy.
National College.	18	5	38
Its Primary Department	11	1	19
Hartford	49	49	57
Boston	45	20	4
Northampton	35	30	20
Indiana	6	6	4
Circulars	28	19	46
Various	4	4	11
	186	134	199

Total 519 cases.[3]

The same case was often reported through more than one channel. I have tried as well as I could, though I fear without perfect success, to eliminate these reduplications. As regards the accuracy of the reports, there is this to be said. Among normal people it is well known how individuals differ in their sensitiveness to whirling about or swinging. The cases marked "slight" may *possibly* therefore fall within the normal limits. It is more probable however that the majority of them represent a more or less abnormally reduced susceptibility. In the cases I myself examined, every one where the presence of vertigo was at all doubtful was recorded as "slight," so as not to overload the column of figures favorable to my hypotheses. In the Harvard College records, in which each man inscribed his own result, the expressions "slightly" and "somewhat" occur, but they do so very few times indeed. Where the vertigo was slight, it has often happened that a deaf-mute examined one day or by one person was reported "not dizzy," whilst another day or another examiner caused the case to be recorded either as "slightly dizzy" or as "dizzy." I am disposed to think that both normal and abnormal subjects differ somewhat in their sensibility to vertigo

---

[3] I add the following communication in a note because it is less exactly reported, and the observations were perhaps made more cursorily than those set down in the text. Mr. Fosdick, of the Institution at Danville, Ky., writes in March, 1881: "I selected twenty boys about half of whom had been born deaf, the other half had lost hearing. . . . I applied to them our test in the three ways. . . . With those who had lost hearing from disease the result was uniform. No dizziness could be produced. . . . With those who had been born deaf the results were equally uniform. A few seconds of spinning were in most cases sufficient to produce dizziness."

from one day to another. Löwenfeld[4] says that this is markedly the case with the vertigo induced by galvanic currents across the head, of which I shall have something to say anon.

A certain lack of rigorous accuracy in individual instances ought then to throw no discredit whatever on the main result of the investigation, which is that disease of the internal ear is likely to confer immunity from dizziness. Nobody could possibly confound the extreme cases, nor could any difference of opinion arise concerning them. We see on the one hand an affection which may nauseate the patient or make it impossible for him to stand on his feet at all; on the other, absolute and total indifference to the whirling in every respect whatsoever.

As regards the method of examination, active spinning about on the feet with the head successively upright, bent forwards, and inclined on one shoulder, is of course the simplest way of testing the matter. The eyes must be closed to eliminate optical vertigo pure and simple, but opened when the spinning is over, so that the patient may have every advantage for walking straight. Except in the Boston and Northampton Schools this was the method generally used. It is likely to give an unduly small number of total exemptions, from the fact that if the whirling has been long and violent, some feeling of confusion will remain for a few moments as a consequence of head congestion, and some irregularity of gait as a consequence of involuntary continuance of muscular action. This latter may be called muscular vertigo—it probably figures in many of the cases marked "slight."

The muscular vertigo may be entirely eliminated by *passive* rotation. The children of the Boston and Northampton Schools were seated on a square board, each angle whereof had a rope affixed to it. The ropes were kept parallel up to a height above the head of the inmate by a cross-shaped brace of wood which kept them asunder at that point. Above the cross-brace they rapidly converged to the point of suspension of the apparatus. The apparatus is rotated by the examiner's hands till the ropes above the brace are tightly twisted. The child is then seated on the board, with closed eyes, and head in any position desired, and the torsion of the ropes is left to work its effects freely. These consist in a rapid revolution of the whole apparatus, including its inmate. The moment the

---

4 *Experimentelle und kritische Untersuchungen zur Electrotherapie des Gehirns,* München, 1881.

speed of rotation slackens, the examiner stops the rotation, and sets the child, who has been instructed previously, to open his eyes and walk as straight as possible towards a distant point on the floor. I examined all the Northampton children myself in this way, and (with my brother's assistance) repeated thus the examinations made of the children of the Horace Mann School by their teachers a year before.[5] The Harvard students were also examined in this way.

It is difficult to be sure, in many of the cases marked "slightly dizzy," whether the sensation experienced by the subject was a mild degree of true vertigo, or a slight confusion arising from the effects of centrifugal movement of the intracranial fluids and viscera. That changes of intracranial pressure will give rise to dizziness by directly influencing the brain independently of the semicircular canals is evident from the number of subjects who are of reduced sensibility as respects dizziness from whirling, but who say that they feel dizzy when their head is suddenly raised from a bent position, or when they get up after stooping to the ground. In reply to a question in the circular, "Do you ever experience dizziness under any other circumstances?" [than whirling] two of the "not dizzy" class, six of the "slightly dizzy" class, and five of the "dizzy" class speak of experiencing this feeling.

In the light of all these facts it became an interesting question to ascertain whether the dizziness produced by galvanic currents through the head be due to irritation of the vertigo centres themselves or of their peripheral organ the semicircular canals. Hitzig, as is well known, made a careful study of these phenomena on normal persons; it may be found in his *Untersuchungen über das Gehirn*. With its theoretical conclusions it is impossible to agree. The objective facts however, which I believe he first accurately analyzed, are these: If the subjects' eyes are open, they move slowly towards the side of the anode when the current is strong, then

---

[5] In a preliminary report of these inquiries published in the *Harvard University Bulletin*, No. 18 (1881), the figures are different from those I give here. The differences are due to later observations. I regret very much that owing to a rather incomprehensible degree of thoughtlessness, it never occurred to me to test the pupils' sense of rotation after the original Crum Brown and Mach method: that is, to seat them in the swing with closed eyes, to rotate it gently through a comparatively small number of degrees, and to see how accurately they could afterwards assign the direction and amount of rotation. It is to be hoped that any one repeating the observations will not leave this one out. We should expect that non-dizzy deaf-mutes would be quite unaware of the rotation if it were absolutely frictionless and slow.

rapidly recover themselves by a quick movement towards the side of the kathode. At the same time the world appears to swim towards the kathode, and the head and body incline over towards the anode.

At the Northampton School we tested forty-three pupils with a galvanic current strong enough to make four normal adults, on whom it was tried, bend body and head strongly over. Of twenty-three deaf-mutes of the "not dizzy" class, only five showed this phenomenon. Of twenty pupils of the "dizzy" class ("slight" cases were not tried) fourteen showed it in a greater or less degree. At the Boston School the girls became so nervous that the few results I obtained with them were valueless. Of the boys, fifteen "not dizzy" cases were tried, and but one swayed towards the anode. Three "slight" cases were tried; one swayed, the other two did not. One "quite dizzy" case had the current passed, but did not sway.

With respect to the subjective feelings accompanying the current's passage, they are so numerous and often so intense that a deaf-mute child experiencing them for the first time can hardly be expected to give a very lucid account of them. Stinging of the skin over the mastoid processes, subjective noises (often very loud), flashes before the eyes, strange cerebral confusion, are prominent among them. Nevertheless, it seemed evident that many of the patients whose body did not sway at all and whose eyes showed no perceptible nystagmus, *did* have some sort of a vertiginous feeling, which they expressed by moving the hand wavingly across the forehead, by saying they were "dizzy" or felt like "falling." I regard the experiments, therefore, as almost inconclusive. To be of value they should be repeated many times with the same subjects on different days, and with non-polarizable electrodes fastened by a spring arc behind the ears, so as to follow the head in its movements without modifying the contact. The current should also be measured, which was not done accurately in the above cases.

Taken as they stand, all I feel like saying of them is that they make it appear *not improbable* that both the vertigo centre and its peripheral organ are galvanically excitable; but that the peripheral organ is much more sensitive to the current than is the centre. There was certainly a marked difference of demeanor, on the whole, between the "dizzy" and the "not dizzy" pupils of the Northampton School, when under the current, even though in many cases the difference were only one of degree.

In view of the great probability that sea-sickness is due to an over-excitement of the organs of vertigo, propagated to the cerebellum or whatever other "centres" of nausea there may be, I inquired of many deaf-mutes whether they had been exposed to rough weather at sea and suffered in the usual way. The majority, of course, had not been exposed. Fifteen of the "not dizzy" or "scarcely dizzy" classes had been exposed, and of these not one had been sea-sick. This, it is true, is negative evidence, and might easily be upset by two or three cases of exemption from dizziness with susceptibility to sea-sickness.[6] As it stands, however, it affords a presumption that non-dizzy deaf-mutes *may, ipso facto,* enjoy immunity from sea-sickness. And it suggests the application of small blisters behind the ears as a possible counter-irritant to that excitement of the organs beneath, in which that most intolerable of all complaints *may* take its rise.

Perhaps the most interesting of all the results to which our inquiries have led is the following. A certain number of non-dizzy deaf-mutes when plunged under water seem to be affected by an indescribable alarm and bewilderment, which only ceases when they find their heads above the surface. Every one who has lost himself in the woods, or wakened in the darkness of the night to find the relation of his bed's position relatively to the doors and windows of his room forgotten, knows the altogether peculiar discomfort and anxiety of such "disorientation" in the horizontal plane. In ordinary life, however, the sense of what is the *vertical* direction is never lost. Even with eyes closed, and the "static" sense, as Breuer calls it, of the semicircular canals lost, *gravity* exerts its never-ceasing influence on our limbs, and tells us where the ground is and where the zenith, no matter what our movements may be. "So shakes the magnet, and so stands the pole." Helmholtz, who wrote his *Optics* before the semicircular canal sense was discovered, ascribes much of the sea-sick vertigo to the sufferers' sense of the

---

[6] I have three such possible counter-cases, but in all the record is so imperfect (and no address being given farther inquiry cannot be made) that they cannot be used. To question 8 in the circular, "Have you been exposed to sea-sickness and been sea-sick since losing your hearing?" one, forty-two years old, not dizzy, replies, "Yes, but once in my childhood." Another, slightly dizzy, thirty-nine years old, deaf at thirteen years, says, "Was greatly nauseated by my first ride in the rail cars when fourteen years old." The third, not dizzy, writes, "Was on a coast steamer for three days out of sight of land in a storm; felt slightly uncomfortable in state-room, but was all right in the open air of the deck." The state-room sickness may have been due to smell.

direction of gravity being thrown out of gear: "One feels the traction of gravity [on board ship] now apparently to the right, now to the left, now forwards and now backwards, because one is no longer able to find [with his eyes] the direction of the vertical. Only after long practice, as I can myself testify, does one come to use gravity as an exclusive means of orientation, and only then does the vertigo cease."[7]

But imagine a person without even the sense of gravity to guide him, and the "disorientation" ought to be complete—a sort of bewilderment concerning his relations to his environment in all three dimensions will ensue, to which ordinary life offers absolutely no parallel. Now this case seems realized when a non-dizzy deaf-mute dives under water with his eyes closed. He hears nothing (except perhaps subjective roaring); sees nothing; his semicircular canal sense tells him nothing of motion up or down, right or left, or round about; the water presses on his skin equally in each direction; he is literally cut off from all knowledge of their relations to outer space, and ought to suffer the maximum possible degree of bewilderment to which in his mundane life a creature can attain.

I have received information bearing on this point, and distinct enough to be quoted, from thirty-three cases in all. Curious exceptions occur which I cannot understand, and which I will presently state. Meanwhile here are some extracts from my correspondents' replies which show the condition above described to be no fiction. Professor Samuel Porter, of the College at Washington, from whom I have derived most of my information on this point, says, "I am told it is the case with some deaf-mutes that they sometimes find a difficulty in rising after a dive from uncertainty as to up and down."

L. G. (not dizzy) writes:

"A year after I lost my hearing, on a day when the sun was shining brightly, I dove from a high place, and immediately after entering the water had no knowledge of locality. In what direction the top was I

---

[7] *Physiologische Optik*, page 604. One of my colleagues, an eminent geologist, with a good topographical instinct, tells me that whenever he "loses his bearings" in the country, he becomes nauseated. I myself became distinctly nauseated one night after trying for a long time to imagine the right position of my bed in the dark, it having been changed a day or two previous. These facts seem to show that a purely ideal excitement of images of "direction," when strong and confused, such images being probably faint repetitions of semicircular canal feelings, may engender precisely the same physical consequences as would an equally strong and confused excitement of the canals themselves.

could not determine, and it was the same as respects the bottom. I endured agonies in searching for the surface. At last, when I had given up all hope, my head was fortunately at the surface, and I was soon master of the situation. I was told that I had been swimming on the surface with the back of my head sometimes out of water, and at other times completely immersed. For years I could not summon up courage to dive again. I never feel at my ease under water."[8]

W. H. (scarcely dizzy) writes:

"Since I became deaf it has been difficult to control myself under water. . . . When I undertake to dive into the water I immediately lose all control over my movements, and cannot tell which way is *up* or which is *down*. . . . Once I struck against something, but I am not able to say whether it was the bottom of the river or the steep rocks near the shore."

A. S. L. (not dizzy):

"If I get my head under water it is impossible for me to tell which is the top or bottom of the river or pond, and there is a great roaring and buzzing in my head."

G. M. T. (not dizzy):

"Before I lost my hearing I was a good diver, but after that time I could never trust my head under water."

M. C. (not dizzy):

"Difficult to swim or dive without being frightened terribly. . . . I generally close eyes till under water, then open them till top is reached. If eyes are kept closed I become confused."

J. L. H. (doubtfully dizzy):

"It is very seldom that any deaf-mute can escape drowning when his head has got under water. Persons with such heads as mine are rendered unable to come out of the water in the right direction."

J. C. B. (not dizzy):

"Dare not go under water at all unless by day and with eyes open. . . . Must keep the eyes open. Impossible to swim in the dark."

C. S. D. (not dizzy):

"Can't dive at all. As soon as water gets in my eyes, I can't get them open; get confused, and do not know whether I am standing on my head or my feet."

[8] Says eyes were closed.

A. B. (not dizzy):

"Gets perfectly bewildered under water. Dives with closed eyes."

C. P. F. (not dizzy):

"I undertook on one occasion to turn a summersault in water only two feet deep. It was done in such a way that I came down on my hands and knees on the bottom with my head under water. Instantly I seemed to be in water fathoms deep, facing a cliff which I was trying to climb up with my hands and feet. I pawed and pawed but could not rise, neither could I sink. There was no sensation to prove to me that I was in a horizontal position; every sensation was that of standing upright in water above my head. It seemed hours before I could climb that cliff, though it was only a second or two before my pawing brought me into water so shallow that my head appeared above the surface. Instantly the sensation of being in an upright position vanished, and I felt myself to be where I really was, on my hands and knees in the water."

Of this class of cases there are fifteen out of the thirty-three. The remaining ten "not dizzy" say they can dive perfectly well. Two of them report that they do so equally well with eyes closed or open, and of two others Professor Porter sends me the same account. Of the residual eight there are five normal as respects dizziness. One complains of losing equilibrium, another of turning giddy, a third of "not knowing which way I am going," a fourth of "losing presence of mind," the fifth of having "lost power of directing movements." Closer inquiry of this last case showed that the perplexity only happened once, and that its cause was then the bright sunshine on the bottom of the bathing tank which he mistook for the light of the sky.[9]

Finally three cases, "slightly dizzy," complain of noises in the ears, and peculiar feelings which make diving difficult of performance.

Obviously the conditions are very complicated. In the eight last cases the symptoms might be due (in all but the fifth) to the entrance of water through a perforated tympanum. This is well known to cause both dizziness and roaring, but the presence of tympanic perforation in the subjects in question is unknown. It is impossible

[9] The same cause seems to have increased the bewilderment of Mr. L. G. on the occasion described in the first quotation above (page 134). He informs Professor Porter that he always keeps his eyes open under water, and that they were open on that occasion. He speaks of the sun shining brightly.

to say whether some of the "bewilderment" of the first fourteen may not be due to this cause, but as they report themselves "not dizzy" to whirling, this seems in the main unlikely.

The intermediate class of ten "not dizzy," four of whom we know to be able to dive with closed eyes without being bewildered, is the hardest to deal with, and threatens even to upset our pretty little theory. The only reason why we do not immediately confess that it does so is the suspicion (always possible) of some error in the report, which a minute personal examination would reveal. I can therefore only hand the matter over to those with opportunities for investigation, as an as yet unsolved mystery upon which it is to be hoped, they may throw some farther light.

A noteworthy fact (which shall be immediately explained) is that the non-dizzy patients who got bewildered under water were all more or less afflicted with ataxia or some other disorder of movement. A natural explanation of their trouble would then be that they had simply lost control of their limbs for swimming movements. This may be true of some: two report trouble under water soon after loss of hearing, but not now, the ataxia having meanwhile improved. But the ten non-dizzy who *can* dive happen also all to be ataxic. So that ataxia *per se* cannot be held to be an all-sufficient reason for the phenomenon in question.

The reason for the great predominance of locomotor disorders in the persons who answered my circulars is this: one of the first things I discovered on beginning my inquiries was the fact, notorious at deaf and dumb institutions but apparently not much known to the outer world, that large numbers of deaf-mutes stagger and walk zigzag, especially after dark, and are unable to stand steady with their eyes closed. To such deaf-mutes as these were most of my circulars purposely sent. I do not refer to the awkward gait and shuffling of the feet which are so commonly exhibited at asylums,[10] but to a real difficulty in controlling their equilibrium. Congenital deaf-mutes appear hardly ever to show this peculiarity. I have only heard of two or three cases of their doing so. The bulk of those that stagger were made deaf by scarlet-fever or some form

[10] This seems little more than a bad habit produced by two causes: (1) When they walk with each other their eyes are occupied in looking at each other's fingers and faces, and cannot survey the ground which then is, as it were, explored by the feet; and (2) Their deafness makes them insensitive to the disagreeable noise that their feet make.

of meningeal inflammation. When the facts first began to come in I naturally thought that the staggering,[11] which usually improves in course of time, might be due to the loss of the afferent sense most used in locomotor muscular co-ordination, supposing the semi-circular canal feelings to constitute this afferent sense. In the pre-liminary note published in the *Harvard University Bulletin,* I wrote as follows:

"The evidence I already have in hand justifies the formation of a tentative hypothesis, as follows: The normal guiding sensation in locomotion is that from the semicircular canals. This is co-ordinated in the cerebellum (which is known to receive auditory nerve fibres) with the appropriate muscles, and the nervous machinery becomes structurally organized in the first few years of life. If, then, this guiding sensation be suddenly abolished by disease, the machinery is thrown completely out of gear, and must form closer connections than before either with sight or touch. But the cerebellar tracts, being already organized in another way, yield but slowly to the new co-ordinations now required, and for many years make the patient's gait uncertain, especially in the dark. Where the defect of the au-ditory nerve is congenital the cerebellar machinery is organized from the very outset in co-ordination with tactile sensations, and no difficulty occurs. To prove this hypothesis a minute medical ex-amination of many typical cases will be required. If this prove confirmatory, it will then appear probable that many of the so-called paralyses after diphtheria, scarlet-fever, etc., may be nothing but sudden anæsthesiæ of the semicircular canals."

The minute medical examination I spoke of, I have been pre-vented by circumstances from making or getting made. What ought to be done would be to carefully test the staggering patients for such anæsthesiæ of the body or limbs, losses of tendon reflex, and various locomotor symptoms of ataxia, as would show the presence of cen-tral nervous disorder independent of the labyrinthine trouble, but joint results with it of the disease that left the subject deaf. If a cer-tain residuum of patients were found without any signs of such nerve-central disorder, the hypothesis quoted would receive cor-roboration. I must confess, however, that the very large number of staggering and zigzagging deaf-mutes, who are *free* from any

---

[11] Moos, quoted by M'Bride (*Edinburgh Medical Journal,* February, 1882), says the staggering is cured in twenty-seven months after cerebro-spinal meningitis. I find it to have often lasted much longer.

labyrinthine lesion (as evidenced by their being normal as respects dizziness), and whose cases have been made known to me since the preliminary report was written, make it seem plausible that the ataxic disorders usually flow directly from lesions of the locomotor centres, sequelæ of the meningitis, scarlet-fever, or whatever other disease the patient may have had. Whether they do so exclusively cannot now be decided. I know of no more interesting problem for a physician with good opportunities for observation to solve, than that of the relation of the semicircular canal sense to our ordinary locomotor innervation. And certainly fresh cases of deafness coupled with loss of sensibility to rotation seem the most favorable field of study.

It has been suggested, I no longer know by whom, that the mysterious topographic instinct which some animals and certain classes of men possess, and which keeps them continuously informed of their "bearings," of which way they are heading, of the "lay of the land," etc., might be due to a kind of unconscious dead reckoning of the algebraic sum of all the angles through which they had twisted and turned in the course of their journey. If the semicircular canals are the organs of sensibility for angular rotation, the abolition of their function ought to injure the topographic faculty. I accordingly asked in my circular the question: "Have you a good bump of locality?" A rather stupidly expressed phrase, but one which I supposed would be popularly intelligible. Forty-seven persons, not dizzy, or scarcely dizzy, answered this question distinctly, forty with a "yes," and seven with a "no." So that in this (truly vague enough) matter, my inquiries give no countenance to the suggestion alluded to.[12]

"Dizziness" on high places was also made the subject of one of my questions. This feeling, in those who experience it normally, is a compound of various muscular, cutaneous, and visceral sensations with vertigo; and of course the answers of my correspondents, not being of an analytical sort, would be of very little value, even were they much more numerous than they are. They stand as follows:

---

[12] In a long and interesting article in the *Revue Philosophique* for July, 1882 ("Le Sens de l'orientation et ses organes"), M. C. Viguier maintains the view that the semicircular canals are organs in whose endolymph terrestrial magnetism determines induced currents which vary with the position of the canals, and (apparently) enable the animal to recognize a lost direction as soon as he finds it again. Clever and learned as are M. Viguier's arguments, I confess they fail to awaken in me any conviction that their thesis is true.

"Are you dizzy on high places?"

Of those not or scarcely dizzy on whirling, sixteen say "yes," twenty-nine "no."

Of those dizzy on whirling, twenty-nine say "yes," and fourteen "no."

Taken in their crudity these answers suggest the bare possibility that anæsthesia of the semicircular canals *may* confer some little immunity from that particularly distressing form of imaginative weakness. The centres of imagination of falling may grow weak with the disuse of the sense for falling, and the various reflex results (feelings in the calves, hypogastrium, skin, respiratory apparatus, etc.), which help to constitute the massive feeling of dread, not following upon the sight of the abyss, as they normally should do, the subject may remain cool-headed, when in former times he would have been convulsed with emotion.

One more point, of perhaps greater interest. The following letter from Dr. Beard, of New York, speaks for itself:

NEW YORK, *July* 2, 1881.

DEAR DR. JAMES,—Acting upon your suggestion, I have succeeded in abolishing the sense of vertigo in my trance subjects. I have accomplished this in two ways. First, by means of the swing which you have used in your experiments. I find that persons when put into trance sleep and placed in a swing which is twisted up tightly, so that it untwists rapidly, and for a considerable time, feel no dizziness or nausea, but when brought out of the trance, at once walk away without the least difficulty.

I find—as you did—that the great majority of individuals cannot in the normal state do this; but are made very dizzy and sick, and sometimes even fall out of the swing.

Secondly, by having the subject look at some limited space on the ceiling, holding his head up, and turning around rapidly four or five times. Scarcely any one can do this, in the normal condition, and walk off straight. They will stagger, as though intoxicated or suffering from ataxia. These trance subjects, when put into that condition with their eyes open, can go through this test, and immediately walk off without any difficulty whatever.

These experiments—I may say—have been witnessed by a large number of physicians in this city, and have been confirmed independently by some of them. There is no difficulty in confirming these experiments, when you have trained subjects to coöperate with you.

I regard these experiments as of a demonstrative character; that is, as belonging to the class of experiments that prove the genuineness of the trance phenomena, since there are very few indeed who can simulate them.

I have no doubt whatever that sea-sickness could be cured entirely by putting persons into trance.

Yours, truly,
GEORGE M. BEARD.

Finally (to wring the last drop from an inquiry which, however slender may be its basis of fact, will be accused by no one of not having had the maximum possible number of theoretic conclusions extracted from it!), I will subjoin the following extract from one of my correspondents' letters as a crumb for vivisectional physiologists to whom the fact narrated may be unknown:

"If a dog *grows up* and his tail is cut off suddenly, he staggers so badly he cannot cross a foot log."[13]

To all my correspondents I owe thanks for the facts imparted in this paper. Without the most painstaking co-operation of Professor Samuel Porter, in particular, it could hardly have been written. To Principal Williams, of the Hartford School; Miss Fuller, of the Boston School; and Miss Rogers, of Northampton, my best thanks are also due. Dr. J. J. Putnam has assisted me with counsel and aid in the galvanic observations. Dr. Clarence J. Blake examined the condition of the ears of the Northampton children, but not being able to deduce any conclusions relevant to my own inquiry from his observations, I leave them unrecorded here.

[13] Experiment made by a preacher in East Tennessee, a friend of the writer.

On Some Omissions of Introspective Psychology

As is well known, contradictory opinions about the value of introspection prevail. Comte and Maudsley, for example, call it worthless; Ueberweg and Brentano come near calling it infallible. Both
opinions are extravagances; the first for reasons too obvious to be
given, the second because it fails to discriminate between the immediate *feltness* of a mental state and its perception by a subsequent
act of reflection. The *esse* of a mental state, the advocates of infallibility say, is its *sentiri*; it has no recondite mode of being "in-
itself." It must therefore be felt as it really is, without chance of
error. But the feltness which is its essence is its own immanent and
intrinsic feltness at the moment of being experienced, and has nothing to do with the way in which future conscious acts may feel about
it. Such *sentiri* in future acts is not what is meant by its *esse*. And
yet such *postmortem sentiri* is the only way in which the introspective psychologist can grasp it. In its bare immediacy it is of no use
to him. For his purposes it must be more than experienced; it must
be remembered, reflected on, named, classed, known, related to
other facts of the same order. And as in the naming, classing, and
knowing of things in general we are notoriously fallible, why not
also here? Comte is quite right in laying stress on the fact that a
feeling, to be named, judged, or perceived, must be already past.
No subjective state, whilst present, is its own object; its object is
always something else. There are, it is true, cases in which we ap-

pear to be naming our present feeling, and so to be experiencing and observing the same inner fact at a single stroke, as when we say "I feel tired," "I am angry," etc. But these are illusory, and a little attention unmasks the illusion. The present conscious state, when I say "I feel tired," is not the direct feeling of tire; when I say "I feel angry," it is not the direct feeling of anger. It is the feeling of *saying-I-feel-tired*, of *saying-I-feel-angry*—entirely different matters, so different that the fatigue and anger apparently included in them are considerable modifications of the fatigue and anger directly felt the previous instant. The act of naming them has momentarily detracted from their force.

The only sound grounds on which the infallible veracity of the introspective judgment might be maintained, are empirical. If we have reason to think it has never yet deceived us, we may continue to trust it. This is the ground actually maintained by Herr Mohr in a recent little work.[1] "The illusions of our senses," says this author, "have undermined our belief in the reality of the outer world; but in the sphere of inner observation our confidence is intact, for we have never found ourselves to be in error about the reality of an act of thought or feeling. We have never been misled into thinking we were *not* in doubt or in anger when these conditions were really states of our consciousness."

But, sound as the reasoning here is, I fear the premises are not correct; and I propose in this article to supplement Mr. Sully's chapter on the Illusions of Introspection, by showing what immense tracts of our inner life are habitually overlooked and falsified by our most approved psychological authorities.

When we take a rapid general view of the wonderful stream of our consciousness, what strikes us first is the different *pace* of its different portions. Our mental life, like a bird's life, seems to be made of an alternation of flights and perchings. The rhythm of language expresses this, where every thought is expressed in a sentence, and every sentence closed by a period. The resting-places are usually occupied by sensorial imaginations of some sort, whose peculiarity is that they can be held before the mind for an indefinite time, and contemplated without changing; the places of flight are filled with thoughts of relations, static or dynamic, that for the most part obtain between the matters contemplated in the periods of comparative rest.

---

[1] *Grundlage der empirischen Psychologie*, Leipzig, 1882, p. 47.

Let us call the resting-places the "substantive parts," and the places of flight the "transitive parts," of the stream of thought. We may then say that the main end of our thinking is at all times the attainment of some other "substantive" part than the one from which we have just been dislodged. And we may say that the main use of the transitive parts is to lead us from one substantive conclusion to another. Of this perhaps more hereafter.

Now the first difficulty of introspection is that of seeing the transitive parts for what they really are. If they are but flights to a conclusion, stopping them to look at them before the conclusion is reached is really annihilating them. Whilst if we wait till the conclusion *be* reached, it so exceeds them in vigor and stability that it quite eclipses and swallows them up in its glare. Let anyone try to cut a thought across in the middle and get a look at its section, and he will see how difficult the introspective observation of the transitive tracts is. The rush of the thought is so headlong that it almost always brings us up at the conclusion before we can arrest it. Or if our purpose is nimble enough and we do arrest it, it ceases forthwith to be itself. As a snowflake caught in the warm hand is no longer a flake but a drop, so, instead of catching the feeling of relation moving to its term, we find we have caught some substantive thing, usually the last word we were pronouncing, statically taken, and with its function, tendency and particular meaning in the sentence quite evaporated. The attempt at introspective analysis in these cases is in fact like seizing a spinning top to catch its motion, or trying to turn up the gas quickly enough to see how the darkness looks. And the challenge to *produce* these psychoses, which is sure to be thrown by doubting psychologists at anyone who contends for their existence, is as unfair as Zeno's treatment of the advocates of motion, when, asking them to point out in what place an arrow *is* when it moves, he argues the falsity of their thesis from their inability to make to so preposterous a question an immediate reply.

If holding fast the transitive parts of thought's stream, so as to observe them, be the first great difficulty of introspection, then its first great fallacy must necessarily be a failure to register them and give them their due, and a far too great emphasis laid on the more substantive parts of the stream. Accordingly we find that the orthodox empirical psychologists, whether of England, Germany, or France, record under the name of images, *Vorstellungen*, or ideas, only such representations as have objects that can be brought to the distinct focus of attention and there stably held in view. Hume's fantastical assertion that we can form no idea of a thing with either quality or quantity without representing its exact degrees of each, has remained an undisputed dogma in nominalistic minds, until Mr. Galton and Prof. Huxley, or perhaps M. Taine, first called it in question. Strange that so patent an inward fact as the existence of "blended" images could be overlooked! Strange that the assertion could virtually be made that we cannot imagine a printed page without at the same time imagining every letter on it—and made too by a school that prided itself particularly on its powers of observation! However, of such blunders is the history of psychology composed.

But if blurred and indistinct substantive states could be systematically denied, *a fortiori* was it easy to deny that *transitive* states, considered as segments of the stream of sentiency, have any existence at all. The principal effort of the Humian school has been to abrogate relations, not only from the sphere of reality, but from the sphere of consciousness; most of them being explained as words, to which no definite meanings, inner or outer, attach. The principal effort of the Platonizing schools has been to prove that, since relations are unquestionably perceived to obtain between realities, but as unquestionably cannot be perceived through any modifications of the stream of subjective sentiency comparable in nature with those through which the substantive qualities of things are perceived, they must needs be perceived by the immediate agency of a supersensible Reason, the omission to do homage to which is for the Platonists the vital defect in the psychological performances of the opposite school.

The second great fallacy of introspection, then, is the ignoring of the fact that a peculiar modification of our subjective feeling corresponds to our awareness of each objective relation, and is the condition of its being known. To Mr. Spencer belongs the honor of having exploded this fallacy, in a few pages that seem to have made but small impression on his contemporaries, but which I cannot help regarding as by far the most important portion of his *Principles of Psychology*. In §65 of that work it is distinctly laid down that, subjectively considered, "a relation proves to be itself a kind of feeling—the momentary feeling accompanying the transition from one conspicuous feeling to another conspicuous feeling";

and that, "notwithstanding its extreme brevity, its qualitative character is appreciable." The phrase "feeling of relation" will be sure to shock certain fastidious ears, but I nevertheless think we had better use it. Surely if any objective truth whatever can come to be known during, and through the instrumentality of, a feeling, there seems no *a priori* reason why a relation should not be that truth; or why, since the feeling has no proper subjective name of its own, we should hesitate to psychologize about it as "the feeling of that relation." There is no other way of talking about it at all.

But, though I have praised Mr. Spencer for being the first to use the phrase, I cannot praise him for having seen very deeply into the doctrine. Like most English psychologists, he tries to reduce the number of relations among things to a minimum; and in other passages says they are limited to likeness and unlikeness, coexistence in space and sequence in time. Whether this be true of *real* relations, does not here concern us. But it is certainly false to say that our *feelings* of relation are of only these four kinds. On the contrary, there is not a conjunction or a preposition, and hardly an adverbial phrase, syntactic form, or inflection of voice, in human speech, that does not express some shading or other of relation which we at some moment actually feel to exist between the larger objects of our thought. If we speak objectively, it is the real relations that appear revealed; if we speak subjectively, it is the stream of consciousness that matches each of them by an inward coloring of its own. In either case the relations are numberless, and no existing language is capable of doing justice to all their shades.

We ought to say a feeling of *and*, a feeling of *if*, a feeling of *but*, and a feeling of *by*, quite as readily as we say a feeling of *blue* or a feeling of *cold*. Yet we do not: so inveterate has our habit become of recognizing the existence of the substantive parts alone, that language almost refuses to lend itself to any other use. In a later place we shall see how the analogy of speech misleads us in still other ways. The Empiricists have always dwelt on its influence in making us suppose that where we have a separate name, a separate thing must needs be there to correspond with it; and they have rightly denied the existence of the mob of abstract entities, principles and forces, in whose favor no other evidence than this could be brought up. But they have said nothing of the obverse error, which in psychology is just as bad, the error, namely, of supposing that where there is *no* name no entity can exist. All *dumb* psychic states have, owing to this error, been coolly suppressed; or, if recognized at all, have been named after the substantive perception they led to, as thoughts "about" this object or "about" that, the stolid word *about* engulfing all their delicate idiosyncrasies in its monotonous sound. Thus the greater and greater accentuation and isolation of the substantive parts have continually gone on.

But the worst consequence of this vicious mode of mangling thought's stream is yet to come. From the continuously flowing thing it is, it is changed into a "manifold," broken into bits, called discrete; and in this condition, approved as its authentic and natural shape by the most opposite schools, it becomes the topic of one of the most tedious and interminable quarrels that philosophy has to show. I do not mean to say that the "Associationist" manner of representing the life of the mind as an agglutination in various shapes of separate entities called ideas, and the Herbartian way of representing it as resulting from the mutual repugnancies of separate entities called *Vorstellungen*, are not convenient formulas for roughly symbolizing the facts. So are the fluid-theories of electricity, the emission-theory of light, the archetype-theory of the skeleton, and the theory that curves are composed of small straight lines. But, if taken as literal truth, I say that any one of these theories is just as false as any other, and leads to as pernicious results. The Associationist and the Herbartian psychologies are both false and for one and the same reason, that what God has joined together they resolutely and wantonly put asunder. It would be calamitous for us, *à propos* of this matter, to get embogged in a metaphysical discussion about what real unity and continuity are. So I hasten to say that, by the continuity of the mental stream, all I here contend for is the absence of *separate* parts in it. It is for the assertors of separate parts to tell us what they mean by their separateness—a thing which (so far as I know) they have never done, except when the Kantians say it is something that nothing short of the agency of categories working under a transcendental Ego can overcome. But, be the definition of the separateness of the parts what it may, the burden of proving its existence lies with its friends. For the stream of our feeling is sensibly continuous, like time's stream.[2] This is surely the natural way of viewing it in the first instance, and as an empirical fact. It presents itself as a continuum. It is true that

---

[2] Of course I speak only of tracts of it uninterrupted by sleep or other unconsciousness.

by it are revealed to us a multiplicity of what we are pleased to consider separate *objects*; but it ought to be proved, not simply assumed, that the proper way of describing this fact is to say we have *a cluster of feelings* as numerous as the objects, and not to say that we have a *feeling of the cluster* of objects, however numerous these may be. The whole cluster is, if apprehended at all, apprehended in one *something*. Why not as well in one subjective modification or pulse of feeling, as in one Ego? Of course this *naïve* and natural way of describing the stream of knowledge ought not to prejudge the results of analysis made later on, and such analysis might show an Ego, and ever so much besides. But the ordinary plan of talking of a plurality of separate feelings from the first does prejudge the question, and abandon altogether the empirical and natural-history point of view.

And see the fruits of prejudging a matter like this, see the two schools at work!

The Empiricists, whether English or German, start with their pluralism of psychic entities, ideas or *Vorstellungen*; show their order and connection with each other; and then treat this order—which in the first instance appears as an object visible only to the psychologist, and recorded by him as a sort of physical fact—as equivalent to a mental fact apprehensible from within the series, and resulting in a modification of the manner in which the entities feel *themselves*.

The Rationalists immediately protest that the conclusions in this account are not warranted by the premises, that the ideas or *Vorstellungen*, assumed as distinct psychic factors out of which mind is to be built up, must be kept *pure* during all the processes through which the psychologist leads them; and, that if kept pure, the reciprocal order or relation in which they may happen objectively to exist, will in no degree affect their manner of *being felt*. If the idea red is the idea red, it will be just that idea and nothing farther, whether the idea green has preceded it or not. The bald external fact of its sequence to green and its contrast to green will not make it aware of itself *as a fact* so sequent and so contrasted. Such awareness, if realized at all, could only be realized by a third psychic entity, to which the green and the red in their purity should be alike external and yet alike present; be known as separate and contrasted, and yet have the separateness overcome and the contrast removed by the way in which they lie together in the synthetic unity of the relation in which they are perceived. Such a third psychic entity cannot be a compound of the ideas themselves; for ideas cannot compound themselves, and if they could the result would be a merging into a "mean" and not, as here, a preservation of individuality intact; it cannot be a link or hyphen[3] or any sort of *intermediary* to make the ideas *continuous*, for that, though between, would be really external to, both ideas, and be merely a third feeling on its own account, as ignorant of the other two as they are ignorant of each other. Not any of these things can it be; not any fact of sensibility whatever, but a fact of an altogether higher order, to which all facts of sensibility are as the dust it treads on, an *act*, unnameable but by its own name, which is *intelligence*, inimitable in its function, which is *relating*, unique in its agent, which is the *Ego, self,* or *me.*

Both schools make then the same baseless hypothesis at the outset—the hypothesis that feeling is discontinuous by nature. The Kantians, Platonizers, or whatever one may please to call them, make another hypothesis to neutralize it, and so save the appearances.[4] The Sensationalists, unwilling to admit the supernatural principle, end with the philosophical melancholy of a Hume at

---

[3] Such "hyphens," it may be said in passing, seem to be the feelings of relation Mr. Spencer has in mind in the section of his *Psychology* to which reference was made a short time back.

[4] Our hegelian Platonizers will of course protest that *their* withers are unwrung by this indictment, and that the Ego they contend for is no quasi-mechanical power working from without on detached materials, but only a name for the fact that what we have called the segments of the stream are consciously *for* each other. The question is a delicate one to decide. My own impression is that practically they are often tempted; and that the form the temptation takes is that of dropping into the old-fashioned psychic dualism. The Platonizing mood is essentially dualistic, for it is essentially worshipful; and every object of worship needs the foil of a principle of evil to set off its lustre. Sentiency as a detached principal is therefore almost indispensable to this habit of philosophizing. Every church needs its devil, and sense and its works are the devil of the Platonic congregation. The most amusing proof of the Platonic demand for a dualistic psychology is given by the always delicious Ferrier, who, in Proposition 10 of his *Institutes*, affirms Plato to have meant nothing more by his intelligible world than ordinary men mean by their sensible world; but who, instead of remaining satisfied with this promising reduction, immediately adds: "but then his sensible world must be moved a peg downwards. It must be thrust down into the regions of nonsense. It must be called, as we have properly called it, . . . the nonsensical world, the world of pure infatuation, of downright contradiction, of unalloyed absurdity." Why? Not for any evidence he gives that such a world as this *exists*, any more *intra* than *extra mentem*; but apparently for the sole reason that an evil principle may never fail to be at hand, on which our higher nature may, when occasion requires, exert its powers of disdain.

the conclusion of his treatise, or with Mill's dismal confession of failure at the close of his chapter on the Psychological Theory of Mind.

But if we descend to the root of the trouble and deny the initial hypothesis, all difficulties and all need of discussion disappear at a stroke. And in truth there is no evidence whatever for supposing the pure atomic ideas of red and yellow, and the other elements of mental structure, to exist at all. They are abstractions, mere fictitious psychic counterparts to those elementary qualities of which we come to believe the real world is made up, but no one of them is an actual psychic fact. Whenever an elementary quality of the outer world is thought by us, the vehicle of the thinking is a feeling representing a highly complex object, that quality in relation with something else. Let us consider the mental stream and try to see what its constituents are like. Everyone will admit that, as he thinks, a procession of varying objects, now simple, now complex in the extreme, passes before his attention, and that each one of these objects, whatever be its character, is accompanied by some sort of modification of his mental condition, of his subjective feeling, of the *wie ihm zu Muthe ist*, as Lotze would say. Even the advocates of an eternally identical Ego will confess that it must know its objects, *quâ* changing, in and by and through changing states, affections, acts, or attitudes, which are modifications, however superficial, of its identity. We can then represent, if not the whole, at least the changing part of the subjective stream by a continuous line, and if, as psychologists, we wish to isolate any portion of it for examination, we can symbolize that isolation by making cross-strokes. But, as Mr. Hodgson has so admirably shown, the cross-strokes do not pre-exist. They are *"artefacta"*; and the natural function of every segment of the line is to lead continuously into the next segment and carry consciousness along unbroken.

Now what differences obtain between the segments of the subjective stream—between the intervals scored off upon the line? Their differences of character must at least be as great as the differences of the objects they severally are aware of, or help to make known—whichever form of expression one prefer; otherwise there would be a difference of perception without any subjective sign or symptom, which is absurd.

If then the fact known be the-sequence-of-green-to-red-and-the-contrast-of-these-two-colors, the state of mind in which that fact comes to knowledge must be quite other than the state of mind in which either pure red or pure green comes to knowledge. In other words, if we start the stream with a feeling of pure red as its first segment, we must follow that up with a second segment which is a feeling of green-as-sequent-upon-the-red-and-contrasted-with-it; or, if we insist on having a "pure" feeling of green, we may let it come in the second segment, and then follow with a third in which the complex relation of the objects of the first two segments is perceived. In either case, the stream must contain segments that are not "pure" elementary feelings. It must contain feelings of qualities-in-relation as well as of qualities absolute. But these feelings do not cease for that to be consubstantial with the rest of the stream. They can all be figured in the same straight line. They involve no new psychic dimension, as when the transcendentalists, after letting a number of "pure" feelings successively go "bang," bring their *deus ex machinâ* of an Ego swooping down upon them from his Olympian heights to *make* a cluster of them with his wonderful "relating thought."

The only thing that can see the pure feelings as a cluster (if pure feelings there be) is a later segment of the stream, to which the "pure" segments and their content appear as objects. It is a peculiarity of the stream that its several parts are susceptible of becoming objects for each other. We cannot explain this peculiarity any more than we can explain any other cognition. As a matter of fact, *every* segment of the stream is cognitive, and seems to look at an object other than itself; and when this object turns out to be a past segment, we say the present one remembers it. The present one in our supposed case is the remembrance of something complex, but that does not keep it from being a single segment. All the arguments used by the transcendentalists to prove the real unity of the Ego, the oneness of the relating principle, apply perfectly to the case before us, and forbid us for an instant to suppose that the segment in which a complex fact is remembered is not just one feeling and no more. Whatever is known *together* is and must be known through a single modification of thought's stream. When I think the seven colors of the rainbow, I do not have seven thoughts of a color, and then a thought of a bow; that would be eight thoughts. What I have is just one thought of the whole object. And the first reasonable word has yet to be said to prove that such a "thought" as this is not, when considered in its subjective constitution, and apart from its cognitive function, also a "feeling," as specific and unique as the simplest affection of consciousness.

The demand for atoms of feeling, which shall be real units, seems a sheer vagary, an illegitimate metaphor. Rationally, we see what perplexities it brings in its train; and empirically, no fact suggests it, for the actual contents of our minds are always representations of some kind of an *ensemble*. From the dawn of an individual consciousness to its close, we find each successive pulse of it capable of mirroring a more and more complex object, into which all the previous pulses may themselves enter as ingredients, and be known. There is no reason to suppose that the same feeling ever does or can recur again. The same *thing* may recur and be known in an indefinite number of successive feelings; but does the least proof exist that in any two of them it is represented in an identical subjective state? All analogy points the other way. For when the identical thing recurs, it is always thought of in a fresh manner, seen under a somewhat different angle, apprehended in different relations from those in which it last appeared. And the feeling cognizant of it is the unitary feeling of it-in-those-relations, not a feeling of it-pure *plus* a second feeling, or a supernatural "thought," of the relations. We are so befogged by the suggestions of speech that we think a constant thing, known under a constant name, ought to be known by means of a constant mental affection. The ancient languages, with their elaborate declensions, are better guides. In them no substantive appears "pure," but varies its inflection to suit the way it is known. However it may be of the stream of real life, of the mental river the saying of Herakleitos is probably literally true: we never bathe twice in the same water there.

How could we, when the structure of our brain itself is continually growing different under the pressure of experience? For an identical feeling to recur, it would have to recur in an unmodified brain, which is an impossibility. The organ, after intervening states, cannot react as it did before they came.

If we are ever to be entitled to make psychological inferences from brain-processes, we should make them here in favor of the view I defend. The whole drift of recent brain-inquiry sets towards the notion that the brain always acts as a whole, and that no part of it can be discharging without altering the tensions of all the other parts. The best symbol for it seems to be an electric conductor, the amount of whose charge at any one point is a function of the total charge elsewhere. Some tracts are always waning in tension, some waxing, whilst others actively discharge. The states of tension, however, have as positive an influence as the discharges in determining the total condition, and consequently in deciding what the *psychosis* shall be to which the complex *neurosis* corresponds. All we know of submaximal nerve-irritations, and of the summation of apparently ineffective stimuli, tends to show that *no* changes in the brain are really physiologically ineffective, and that presumably none are bare of psychological result. But as the distribution of brain-tension shifts from one relative state of equilibrium to another, like the aurora borealis or the gyrations of a kaleidoscope, now rapid and now slow, is it likely that the brain's faithful psychic concomitant is heavier-footed than itself, that its rate of change is coarser-grained, that it cannot match each one of the organ's irradiations by a shifting inward iridescence of its own? But if it can do this, its inward iridescences must be infinite, for the brain-redistributions are in infinite variety. If so coarse a thing as a telephone-plate can be made to thrill for years and never reduplicate its inward condition, how much more must this be the case with the infinitely delicate brain?

As, in the senses, an impression feels very differently according to what has preceded it; as one color succeeding another is modified by the contrast, silence sounds delicious after noise, and a note, when the scale is sung up, sounds unlike itself when the scale is sung down; as the presence of certain lines in a figure changes the apparent form of the other lines, and as in music the whole æsthetic effect comes from the manner in which one set of sounds alters our feeling of another; so, in thought, we must admit that those portions of the brain that have just been maximally excited retain a kind of soreness which is a condition of our present consciousness, a co-determinant of how and what we now shall feel.

I am sure that this concrete and total manner of regarding the mind's changes is the only true manner, difficult as it may be to carry it out in detail. Associationism and Herbartianism are only schematisms which, the moment they are literally taken, become mythologies, and had much better be dropped than retained.[5]

---

[5] In an article on the "Association of Ideas" published in the *Popular Science Monthly* of New York for March, 1880, I have myself tried to reinterpret the various

Let me, by a few examples, bring the fact home for which I contend; let me show how a state of mind may be quite specific and at the same time quite inarticulate; let me exhibit some of the modifications that are probably due to nascent and waning excitements of the brain.

Suppose three successive persons say to us: "Wait!" "Hark!" "Look!" Our consciousness is thrown into three quite different attitudes of expectancy, although no definite object is before it in any one of the three cases. Counting out different actual bodily attitudes, and counting out the reverberating images of the three words, which are of course diverse, probably no one will deny the existence of a residual conscious affection, a sense of the direction from which an impression is about to come, although no positive impression is yet there. Meanwhile we have no names for the psychoses in question but the names hark, look, and wait.

Suppose we try to recall a forgotten name. The state of our consciousness is peculiar. There is a gap therein; but no mere gap. It is a gap that is intensely active. A sort of wraith of the name is in it, beckoning us in a given direction, making us at moments tingle with the sense of our closeness, and then letting us sink back without the longed-for term. If wrong names are proposed, this singularly definite gap acts immediately so as to negate them. They do not fit into its mould. And the gap of one word does not feel like the gap of another, all empty of content as both might seem necessarily to be when described as gaps. When I vainly try to recall the name of Spalding, my consciousness is far removed from what it is when I vainly try to recall the name of Bowles. Here some ingenious persons will say: "How *can* the two consciousnesses be different when the terms which might make them different are not there? All that is there, so long as the effort to recall is vain, is the bare effort itself. How should that differ in the two cases? You are making it seem to differ by prematurely filling it out with the different names, although these, by the hypothesis, have not yet come. Stick to the two efforts as they are, without naming them after facts not yet existent, and you'll be quite unable to designate any point in which they differ." Designate, truly enough. We can only designate the difference by borrowing the names of objects not yet in the mind. Which is to say that our psychological vocabulary is wholly

---

varieties of association as due to quantitative alterations in what is always an integral action of the brain.

inadequate to name the differences that exist, even such strong differences as these. But namelessness is compatible with existence. There are innumerable consciousnesses of emptiness, no one of which taken in itself has a name, but all different from each other. The ordinary way is to assume that they are all emptinesses of consciousness, and so the same state. But the feeling of an absence is *toto cœlo* other than the absence of a feeling. It is an intense feeling. The rhythm of a lost word may be there without a sound to clothe it; or the evanescent sense of something which is the initial vowel or consonant may mock us fitfully, without growing more distinct. Everyone must know the tantalizing effect of the blank rhythm of some forgotten verse, restlessly dancing in one's mind, striving to be filled out with words.

Again, what is the strange difference between an experience tasted for the first time and the same experience recognized as familiar, as having been enjoyed before, though we cannot name it or say where or when? A tune, an odor, a flavor sometimes carry this inarticulate feeling of their familiarity so deep into our consciousness that we are fairly shaken by its mysterious emotional power. But strong and characteristic as this psychosis is—it probably is due to the submaximal excitement of wide-spreading associational brain-tracts—the only name we have for all its shadings is "sense of familiarity."

When we read such phrases as "naught but," "either one or the other," "*a* is *b*, but," "although it is, nevertheless," "it is an excluded middle, there is no *tertium quid*," and a host of other verbal skeletons of logical relation, is it true that there is nothing more in our minds than the words themselves as they pass? What then is the meaning of the words which we think we understand as we read? What makes that meaning different in one phrase from what it is in the other? "Who?" "What?" "When?" "Where?" Is the difference of felt meaning in these interrogatives nothing more than their difference of sound? And is it not (just like the difference of sound itself) known and understood in an affection of consciousness correlative to it, though so impalpable to direct examination? Is not the same true of such negatives as "no," "never," "not yet"?

The truth is that large tracts of human speech are nothing but signs of direction in thought, of which direction we nevertheless have an acutely discriminative sense, though no definite sensorial image plays any part in it whatsoever. Sensorial images are stable psychic facts; we can hold them still and look at them as long as we like. These bare images of logical movement on the contrary are psychic transitions, always on the wing, so to speak, and not to be glimpsed except in flight. Their function is to lead from one set of images to another. As they pass, we feel both the waxing and the waning images in a way altogether peculiar and a way quite different from the way of their full presence. If we try to hold fast the feeling of direction, the full presence comes and the feeling of direction is lost. The blank verbal scheme of the logical movement gives us the fleeting sense of the movement as we read it, quite as well as does a rational sentence awakening definite imaginations by its words.

What is that first instantaneous glimpse of someone's meaning which we have, when in vulgar phrase we say we "twig" it? Surely an altogether specific affection of our mind. And has the reader never asked himself what kind of a mental fact is his *intention of saying a thing* before he has said it? It is an entirely definite intention, distinct from all other intentions, an absolutely distinct state of consciousness therefore; and yet how much of it consists of definite sensorial images, either of words or of things? Hardly anything! Linger, and the words and things come into the mind; the anticipatory intention, the divination is there no more. But as the words that replace it arrive, it welcomes them successively and calls them right if they agree with it, it rejects them and calls them wrong if they do not. It has therefore a nature of its own of the most positive sort, and yet what can we say about it without using words that belong to the later mental facts that replace it? The *intention-to-say-so-and-so* is the only name it can receive. One may say that a good third of our psychic life consists in these rapid premonitory perspective views of schemes of thought not yet articulate. How comes it about that a man reading something aloud for the first time is able immediately to emphasize all his words aright, unless from the very first he have a sense of at least the form of the sentence yet to come, which sense is fused with his consciousness of the present word, and modifies its emphasis in his mind so as to make him give it the proper accent as he utters it? Emphasis of this kind is almost altogether a matter of grammatical construction. If we read "no more" we expect presently to come upon a "than"; if we read "however" at the outset of a sentence it is a "yet," a "still," or a "nevertheless," that we expect. A noun in a certain position demands a verb in a certain mood and number, in another position it expects a relative pronoun. Adjectives call for nouns, verbs for adverbs, etc., etc. And this foreboding of the coming grammatical scheme combined with each successive uttered word is so practically accurate, that a reader incapable of understanding four ideas of the book he is reading aloud can nevertheless read it with the most delicately modulated expression of intelligence.

Some will interpret these facts by calling them all cases in which certain images, by laws of association, awaken others so very rapidly that we think afterwards we felt the very *tendencies* of the nascent images to arise before they were actually there. For this school the only possible materials of consciousness are images of a perfectly definite nature. Tendencies exist, but they are facts for the outside psychologist rather than for the subject of the observation. The tendency is thus a *psychical* zero; only its *results* are felt.

Now what I contend for, and accumulate examples to show, is that "tendencies" are not only descriptions from without, but that they are among the *objects* of the stream, which is thus aware of them from within, and must be described as in very large measure constituted of *feelings of tendency*, often so vague that we are unable to name them at all. It is in short the re-instatement of the vague to its proper place in our mental life which I am so anxious to press on the reader's attention. Mr. Galton and Prof. Huxley have made one step in advance in exploding the ridiculous theory of Hume and Berkeley that we can have no images but of perfectly definite things. Mr. Spencer has made another in overthrowing the equally ridiculous notion that, whilst simple objective qualities are revealed to our knowledge in feelings, relations are not. But these reforms are not half sweeping and radical enough. What must be admitted is that the definite images of traditional psychology form but the very smallest part of our minds as they actually live. The traditional psychology talks like one who should say a river consists of nothing but pailsful, spoonsful, quartpotsful, barrelsful, and other moulded forms of water. Even were the pails and the pots all actually standing in the stream, still between them the free water would continue to flow. It is just this free water of consciousness that psychologists resolutely overlook. Every definite image in the mind is steeped and dyed in the free water that flows round it. With it goes the sense of its relations, near and remote, the dying echo of whence it came to us, the dawning sense of whither it is to lead. The significance, the value, of the image is all in this halo or penumbra, that surrounds and escorts it—or rather that is fused into one with it and has become bone of its bone and flesh of its flesh; leaving it, it is true, an image of the same *thing* it was before, but making it an image of that thing newly taken and freshly understood.

What is that shadowy scheme of the "form" of an opera, play, or book, which remains in our mind and on which we pass judgment when the actual thing is done? What is our notion of a scientific or philosophical system? Great thinkers have vast premonitory glimpses of schemes of relation between terms, which hardly even as verbal images enter the mind, so rapid is the whole process. We all of us have this permanent consciousness of whither our thought is going. It is a feeling like any other, a feeling of what thoughts are next to arise, before they have arisen. This field of view of consciousness varies very much in extent, depending largely on the degree of mental freshness or fatigue. When very fresh, our minds carry an immense horizon with them. The present image shoots its perspective far before it, irradiating in advance the regions in which lie the thoughts as yet unborn. Under ordinary conditions the halo of felt relations is much more circumscribed. And in states of extreme brain-fag the horizon is narrowed almost to the passing word—the associative machinery, however, providing for the next word turning up in orderly sequence, until at last the tired thinker is led to some kind of a conclusion. At certain moments he may find himself doubting whether his thoughts have not come to a full stop; but the vague sense of a *plus ultra* makes him ever struggle on towards a more definite expression of what it may be; whilst the slowness of his utterance shows how difficult, under such conditions, the labor of thinking must be.

In the light of such considerations as these, the old dispute between Nominalism and Conceptualism seems to receive the simplest of solutions. The Nominalists say that, when we use the word *man*, meaning *mankind*, there is in the mind nothing more than either a sound or a particular image, *plus* certain tendencies which those elements have to awaken an indefinite number of images of particular men, or of other images (verbal or not) which "make sense" with *mankind*, but not with any individual. These "tendencies" are, however, for them mere physical facts, and not modes of feeling the word as it is uttered. The Conceptualists, on the other hand, see perfectly well that at the very moment of uttering the word, or even before uttering it, we know whether it is to be taken in a universal or a particular sense; and they see that there is some actual present modification of the mind which is equivalent to an *understanding* of the sense. But they call this modification, or conceptual character of the word, an act of pure intelligence, ascribe it to a higher region, and deem it not only other than, but even opposite to, all "facts of feeling" whatsoever.

Now why may we not side with the Conceptualists in saying that the universal sense of the word does correspond to a mental fact of *some* kind, but at the same time, agreeing with the Nominalists that all mental facts are modifications of subjective sensibility, why may we not call that fact a "feeling"? *Man* meant for *mankind* is in short a different feeling from *man* as a mere noise, or from *man* meant for *that* man, to wit, John Smith alone. Not that the difference consists simply in the fact that, when taken universally, the word has one of Mr. Galton's "blended" images of man associated with it. Many persons have seemed to think that these blended, or, as Prof. Huxley calls them, "generic," images are equivalent to concepts. But, in itself, a blurred thing is just as particular as a sharp thing; and the generic character of either sharp image or blurred image depends on its being felt *with its representative function*. This function is the mysterious *plus*, the understood meaning. But it is nothing applied to the image from above, no pure act of reason inhabiting a supersensible and semi-supernatural plane. It can be diagrammatized as continuous with all the other segments of the subjective stream. It is just that staining, fringe or halo of obscurely felt relation to masses of other imagery about to come, but not yet distinctly in focus, which we have so abundantly set forth.

If the image come unfringed it reveals but a simple quality, thing, or event; if it come fringed it reveals something expressly taken universally or in a scheme of relations. The difference between thought and feeling thus reduces itself, in the last subjective analysis, to the presence or absence of "fringe." And this in turn reduces itself, with much probability, in the last physiological analysis, to the absence or presence of sub-excitements of an effective degree of strength in other convolutions of the brain than those whose discharges underlie the more definite nucleus, the substantive ingredient, of the thought—in this instance, the word or image it may happen to arouse.[6]

I wish that space were here afforded to show what, in most cases of rapid thinking, the fringe or halo is with which each successive image is enveloped. Often it cannot be more than a sense of the mutual affinity or belonging together of the successive images, and

[6] The contrast is not, as the Platonists would have it, between certain subjective facts called images and sensations, and others called acts of relating intelligence; the former being blind perishing things, knowing not even their own existence as such, whilst the latter combine past and future, the north pole and the south, in the mysterious synthesis of their cognitive sweep. The contrast is really between two *aspects*, in which all mental facts without exception may be taken; their structural aspect, as being subjective, and their functional aspect, as being cognitions. In the former aspect, the highest as well as the lowest is a feeling, a peculiarly tinged segment of the stream. This tingeing is its sensitive body, the *wie ihm zu Muthe ist*, the way it feels whilst passing. In the latter aspect, the lowest mental fact as well as the highest grasps some bit of universal truth as its content, even though that truth were as relationless a matter as a bare unlocalized and undated quality of pain. From the cognitive point of view, all mental facts are intellections. From the subjective point of view all are feelings. Once admit that the passing and evanescent are as real parts of the stream as the distinct and comparatively abiding; once allow that fringes and haloes, inarticulate perceptions, whereof the objects are as yet unnamed, mere nascencies of cognition, premonitions, awarenesses of direction, are thoughts *sui generis*, as much as articulate imaginings and propositions are; once restore, I say, the *vague* to its psychological rights, and the matter presents no further difficulty.

And then we see that the current opposition of Feeling to Knowledge is quite a false issue. If every feeling is at the same time a bit of knowledge, we ought no longer to talk of mental states differing by having more or less of the cognitive quality; they only differ in knowing more or less, in having much fact or little fact for their object. The feeling of a broad scheme of relations is a feeling that knows much; the feeling of a simple quality is a feeling that knows little. But the knowing itself, whether of much or of little, has the same essence, and is as good knowing in the one case as in the other. Concept and image, thus discriminated through their objects, are consubstantial in their inward nature, as modes of feeling. The one, as particular, will no longer be held to be a relatively base sort of an entity, to be taken for granted, whilst the other, as universal, is celebrated as a sort of standing miracle, to be adored but not explained. Both concept and image, *quâ* subjective, are singular and particular. Both are moments of the stream which come, and in an instant are no more. The word universality has no meaning as applied to their psychic body or structure, which is always finite. It only has a meaning when applied to their use, import, or reference to the kind of object they may reveal. The representation, as such, of the universal object is as particular as that of an object about which we know so little that the interjection "Ha!" is all it can evoke from us in the way of speech. Both should be weighed in the same scales, and have the same measure meted out to them, whether of worship or of contempt.

of their continuity with the main topic. This is the minimal perception of rational sequence, and can obtain between pure series of words, as well as between pictorial images, or between these and words. It gives us a lulling sense that we are "all right"; and when we have it, we let the image before us "pass" without demur. We feel that the topic is gradually being enriched, and that we are making towards the right conclusion. When we listen with relaxed attention, this vague perception that all the words we hear belong to the same language and to the same special vocabulary in that language, and that the grammatical sequence is familiar, is practically equivalent to an admission that what we hear is sense. But if an unusual foreign word be introduced, if the grammar trip, or if a term from an incongruous vocabulary suddenly appear, such as "rat-trap" or "plumber's bill" in a philosophical discourse, the sentence detonates, as it were, we receive a shock from the incongruity, and the drowsy assent is gone. The feeling of rationality in these cases seems rather a negative than a positive thing, being the mere absence of shock, or sense of discord, between the terms of thought. Provided only the right substantive conclusion be reached, the train of images that lead us to it is comparatively indifferent. They may be purely verbal, they may be mixed verbal and pictorial, or they may not be verbal at all, as in the interesting account by Mr. Ballard of his deaf-mute philosophizing. They may be what they please;—but if they only bring us out right, they are rational operations of thinking.[7]

Let us now pass to another introspective difficulty and source of fallacy, different from the one hitherto considered, but quite as baleful to psychology. I mean the *confusion between the psychologist's standpoint and the standpoint of the feeling* upon which he is supposed to be making his report.

The standpoint of the psychologist is external to that of the consciousness he is studying. Both itself and its own object are objects for him. They form a couple which he sees in relation, and compares together, and it follows from this that he alone can verify

---

[7] Hegel's celebrated dictum that pure being is identical with pure nothing, results from his taking the words statically, or without the fringe they wear when in a context. Taken in isolation, they agree in the single point of awakening no sensorial images. But taken dynamically, or as significant—as *thought*—their fringes of relation, their affinities and repugnances, their function and meaning, are felt and understood to be absolutely opposed.

the cognitive character of any mental act, through his own assumed *true* knowledge of its object. Now he may err either by foisting his own knowledge of the object into the feeling, and representing the latter as aware of it just as he is. Or he may err by representing the feeling as if it felt *itself* to be what he knows it to be. Thus the psychologist may misrepresent the feeling in either of two ways, or in both.

I may mention immediately that the doctrine of the post-Kantians, that all knowledge is also self-knowledge, seems to flow from this confusion. Empirically, of course, an awareness of self accompanies most of our thinking. But that it should be needed to *make* that thinking "objective" is quite another matter. "Green-after-red-and-other-than-it" is an absolutely complete object of thought, ideally considered, and needs no added element. The fallacy seems to arise from some such reflection as this, that since the feeling *is* what it feels itself to be, so it must feel itself to be what it *is*, namely, related to each of its objects. That the last *is* covers much more ground than the first, the philosopher here does not notice. The first *is* signifies only the feeling's inward quality; the last *is* covers all possible facts *about* the feeling, relational facts, which can only be known from outside points of view like that of the philosopher himself.[8]

But the great *Tummelplatz* of the confusion of the standpoints is the question of perception, and the whole problem of the manner in which the object is present to the mind in cognition. Distinguishing the standpoints explicitly leads us here to a very simple solution; and at the same time it clears up the subjective constitution of great tracts of our thinking, on which introspection hitherto has thrown but the most insufficient of lights.

The psychologist, studying this question, stands, as aforesaid, outside of the cognitive state-of-consciousness he is analyzing, and compares it with its supposed object, which he thinks he *really* knows. Let us call the object as known to him "the reality." Then the question is: Is the reality directly present to the feeling under observation, or is it represented by a mental substitute? And, if the latter: Is the representative *like* the reality, a copy of it, or is it not?

[8] The criticisms of the late Professor T. H. Green on empiricist writers seem to me to be so saturated with this confusion of the two standpoints, that their in many respects excellent teaching sadly loses its effectiveness.

A word about the back-bone of the human mind, the psychological principle of identity, will help us here. Logic and ontology both have their principles of identity, but the psychological principle is different from either, being a highly synthetic proposition, which affirms that different mental acts can contemplate, mean to contemplate, and know that they mean to contemplate, the same objective matter, quality, thing or truth. The notion of sameness-with-something-else is in fact one of the "fringes" in which a substantive mental kernel-of-content can appear enveloped. The same reality, as we call the kernel, can, then, by virtue of this principle, be thought in widely differing ways. Some of these ways are complete ways, the others are relatively incomplete ways. As a rule, the more substantive and sensational a way is, the more complete we usually suppose it to be.

When now, as psychologists, we undertake to describe any one of these ways of thinking, we call them all "thoughts *about* that reality," ticketing them with its substantive name. For instance, whether I say "I write with steel pens," having such a pen in my hand, and seeing it move over the paper; or whether I say "I write with them," in a conversation whose general topic is steel-pens; or whether I say "Quills are better"; or whether I simply *intend* to say any one of these things, but no image verbal or other arises, because my attention is suddenly diverted;—whichever of these facts occur, most people would describe my mental state as "thought about steel-pens." They would name a substantive kernel, and call that the "object" of each of the several thoughts. And the professed psychologists would agree with them. But the psychologists would then begin, as the laymen do not, to wonder how thought *can* be "about" an "object," which may be present to the thought neither in its own sensible shape, nor by its name, nor even by a pronoun, or any sort of an articulate representative whatever—for these seem to be the predicaments of the last three thoughts about the pen. And the psychologists would then after their several fashions spin ingenious theories as to the typical and normal mode of "presence" to the mind of the "object" of its thoughts; each one finding in some *one* of the cases observed a warrant for his own peculiar views.

The whole puzzle arises from the wrong mode of describing the several cases, by which the layman and the psychologist alike substitute the "reality," which is their own object, and which happens to be also the substantive kernel of the object of the first thought instanced, for the several objects of the other three thoughts. Clearing up our ideas of "the object" brings us out of the wood.

The object of any thought is its entire content or deliverance, neither more nor less. It is a vicious use of speech to take out a substantive kernel from its content and call that its object; and it is an equally vicious use of speech to add a substantive kernel not articulately included in its content, and to call that its object. Yet either one of these two sins we commit, whenever we content ourselves with saying that a given thought is simply "about" a certain topic, or that that topic is its "object." The object of my thought in the previous sentence, for example, is not simply "the sins we commit," nor "the sins we commit as psychologists," nor "the sins we commit as psychologists naming the objects of thoughts." Its object is nothing short of the entire sentence; and if we wish to speak of it substantively, we must make a substantive of it by writing it out in full with hyphens between all its words. Nothing short of this can possibly name its delicate idiosyncrasy. And if we wish to *feel* that idiosyncrasy we must reproduce the thought as it was uttered, with every word fringed and the whole sentence bathed in that original halo of obscure relations, which, like an horizon, then spread about its meaning.

In this "fringing" may be included a feeling of *continuity with the previous thoughts*, of there having been no breach of topic, but of the main interest and problem being unchanged. This would justify us psychologists in saying that the "topic" of the successive thoughts was still steel-pens, even although steel-pens as substantive images had long ceased to be present, and were not represented verbally even in pronominal form.

But can anyone pretend, in strict psychology, that the "topic" these incomplete thoughts are said to be "of" or "about," stands in the same relation to the thoughts themselves as that in which the "reality," steel-pens, stood to the complete thought we began with? Does it hold the same relation to them that the steel-pen holds to me, as I now take it in my hand and watch it write? Most assuredly not: the so-called topic is the *immediate object* of the complete thought, and of my thought. Each of the incomplete thoughts, whilst we say it is "of" that same topic, has all the time its *own* immediate object, which stands in the place the topic stands in in the complete thought and in mine. Exactly what that object is, is a question very hard to answer introspectively, when the thought is incomplete and transitive, and it has sped, and its light is out. We may safely say, however, that *continuity-with-the-complete-thought*, or with whatever previous thought first brought the topic on the *tapis*, enters *into* the object of each of the incomplete thoughts, so far as they can be truly said to be "about" that topic. They do not envelop the topic in a substantive manner, they are thrown *at* it merely. Their relation to it is that of a sense of the direction in which it lies. That directions unmarked by explicit and substantive termini are among the most frequently discriminated objects of our thinking, is a point that needs no proof. When a child, asked for the reason of something, says simply *"Because . . . ,"* and is satisfied; or when a man, after hearing a long plan, says "No! we cannot do it *so*, . . ."; each of them draws a line of definite relation between some substantive thing and a term not realized in the thought, but hidden out of sight and towards which the thinker merely points or looks.

Let us continue to use the name "topic" to designate the substantive reality *towards* which each of the incomplete thoughts looks, and to some conclusion from or about which the whole procession of them will probably lead. We, as outside observers of the thoughts, knowing them in this their function of being connected with it, have a perfect right to say that they are "thoughts concerning this topic." But we are absolutely wrong if we say that their *object* is the topic, or that the topic is *present* to them, or that they are in any *direct* way "of" or "about" it. We then not only thrust into them *our* object, and the object of another thought with which they are only remotely connected; but we by the same act excuse ourselves from seeking—and if we chance to seek, prevent ourselves from finding—what their own immediate objects really are.

Every thought has its *own* object immediately present to it; and the only question in each particular case is as to *what* that object is. For the traditional psychologists, however, who say that many differing thoughts may have the same object, the great question is, *how* is that object present to them all, since they seem to resemble each other as little as they do. And the difficulties of answering that question are such that we find as clear-headed writers on the whole as Reid and Stewart throwing up the sponge. Even in sense-perception, they say, the reality is no more represented by our feeling than it is in our most remotely and indirectly referential thought. There is never the least resemblance or consanguinity between the thing we know and the feeling's content. The latter is merely a signal to awaken the *knowledge* of the thing, which knowledge is an act of pure intelligence, of which absolutely nothing can be said, and whose connection with the signal is for us an arbitrary and unintelligible fact.

Now the truth is that in certain selected cases the signal *is* the reality. In complete sense-perception, for example, we normally believe that we see the latter face to face. Of what we have called the incomplete thoughts, however, this reality is only the "topic"; that is, a whole procession of them may occur without the reality's features being once directly present therein; but yet be a procession that takes note of its existence after a fashion, and is aware of itself *as* a procession leading to or from it as a terminus.

That there is a semblance of paradox here cannot be denied. Grant the procession to know its own existence as a procession; still how can it know itself as a procession to or from *that* reality —or even in the direction of that reality—without also knowing that reality itself immediately and face to face? But this apparent paradox comes from the confusion of the incomplete thought's standpoint with our own. We think the reality must be known in the procession as it is known to us, when—naming the procession —we call it a procession to or from that reality—also explicitly naming and imagining the latter too. *We* cannot *name* the topic without the reality becoming a direct present object to *us*. But the procession can and does feel its topic in an entirely different way. To substitute our way for this way is a complete falsification of the data into which, as psychologists, we are supposed to inquire. What the actual way is, is excessively difficult to make out, on account of the elusive character of those transitive and relational elements of subjectivity on which we commented at the outset of our essay, and of which the procession is mainly composed. Considering our feeling of a tune may make the matter a little clearer. A tune is a processional feeling, in which the idea of the whole is present to each note, so far as to tinge or "fringe" that note differently from the way in which it finds itself tinged or fringed in any other tune. Now the "topic" is to each incomplete thought in the procession what the "tune" is to each note. *We* have to name

166

the topic and the tune explicitly whenever we speak of them; but as we do not pretend that each note in the tune names and hums the entire tune on its own account, at the same time that it hears itself; so we ought not to pretend that each thought in the procession names and knows the topic of the procession in the same articulate and explicit way that we do, when we try to define just which procession it is.

What *sort* of a feeling each thought in the procession has of which procession it is, is as much a mystery for us to-day as what sort of a sense each note has of the tune it is in. These are the problems for the introspection of the future. I have said enough to show, I hope, their difficulty, and some of the causes on which that difficulty depends—the main one being that our thought is a teleological organism, of which large tracts exist only for the attainment of others; and that our perception of these others, which were called its substantive parts, tends to spread itself everywhere in our reflective memory and obscure and replace the perception of the more evanescent parts that intervened. I hope I have made the reader feel how crude a thing that is which even our best textbooks seek to pass off as "analysis of the human mind," and how deeply our current opinions on the subject demand revision.[9]

---

[9] One word on my attitude towards the Ego may avert misconception. All I have urged against it in this article, is against it in its alleged exclusive capacity of "relating" agent. I have said there is no need of an agent to relate together what never was separate, and that it is an unnecessary hypothesis for explaining *cognition*. That feelings can be "for" each other when they do not belong to the same Ego, is proved whenever one person knows what another person thinks. That their being "for" each other when they do belong to the same Ego, is not *a consequence* of such belonging—but may be more simply formulated by saying that each segment of the stream has its objects, and that the earlier segments become objects for the later—is what I have sought to show. If this "solidarity" of the stream of feelings is all that is meant by the Ego—if the Ego is merely a name for that fact—well and good—we seem agreed! For myself, however, there are certain material peculiarities about the way in which segments of the stream are *for* each other when they belong to the *same* Ego, that call for a deeper study of the question, and rather lead us to reserve the word Ego until they are quite cleared up. What is the difference between *your* feeling cognized by me, and a feeling expressly cognized by me as *mine*? A difference of intimacy, of warmth, of continuity, similar to the difference between a sense-perception and something merely imagined—which seems to point to a special *content* in each several stream of consciousness, for which Ego is perhaps the best specific name.

What Is an Emotion?

The physiologists who, during the past few years, have been so industriously exploring the functions of the brain, have limited their attempts at explanation to its cognitive and volitional performances. Dividing the brain into sensorial and motor centres, they have found their division to be exactly paralleled by the analysis made by empirical psychology, of the perceptive and volitional parts of the mind into their simplest elements. But the *æsthetic* sphere of the mind, its longings, its pleasures and pains, and its emotions, have been so ignored in all these researches that one is tempted to suppose that if either Dr. Ferrier or Dr. Munk were asked for a theory in brain-terms of the latter mental facts, they might both reply, either that they had as yet bestowed no thought upon the subject, or that they had found it so difficult to make distinct hypotheses, that the matter lay for them among the problems of the future, only to be taken up after the simpler ones of the present should have been definitively solved.

And yet it is even now certain that of two things concerning the emotions, one must be true. Either separate and special centres, affected to them alone, are their brain-seat, or else they correspond to processes occurring in the motor and sensory centres, already assigned, or in others like them, not yet mapped out. If the former be the case we must deny the current view, and hold the cortex to be something more than the surface of "projection" for every sensitive spot and every muscle in the body. If the latter be the case, we must ask whether the emotional "process" in the sensory or motor centre be an altogether peculiar one, or whether it resembles the ordinary perceptive processes of which those centres are already recognized to be the seat. The purpose of the following pages is to show that the last alternative comes nearest to the truth, and that the emotional brain-processes not only resemble the ordinary sensorial brain-processes, but in very truth *are* nothing but such processes variously combined. The main result of this will be to simplify our notions of the possible complications of brain-physiology, and to make us see that we have already a brain-scheme in our hands whose applications are much wider than its authors dreamed. But although this seems to be the chief result of the arguments I am to urge, I should say that they were not originally framed for the sake of any such result. They grew out of fragmentary introspective observations, and it was only when these had already combined into a theory that the thought of the simplification the theory might bring to cerebral physiology occurred to me, and made it seem more important than before.

I should say first of all that the only emotions I propose expressly to consider here are those that have a distinct bodily expression. That there are feelings of pleasure and displeasure, of interest and excitement, bound up with mental operations, but having no obvious bodily expression for their consequence, would, I suppose, be held true by most readers. Certain arrangements of sounds, of lines, of colors, are agreeable, and others the reverse, without the degree of the feeling being sufficient to quicken the pulse or breathing, or to prompt to movements of either the body or the face. Certain sequences of ideas charm us as much as others tire us. It is a real intellectual delight to get a problem solved, and a real intellectual torment to have to leave it unfinished. The first set of examples, the sounds, lines, and colors, are either bodily sensations, or the images of such. The second set seem to depend on processes in the ideational centres exclusively. Taken together, they appear to prove that there are pleasures and pains inherent in certain forms of nerve-action as such, wherever that action occur. The case of these feelings we will at present leave entirely aside, and confine our attention to the more complicated cases in which a wave of bodily disturbance of some kind accompanies the perception of the interesting sights or sounds, or the passage of the exciting train of ideas. Surprise, curiosity, rapture, fear, anger, lust, greed, and the like, become then the names of the mental states with which the person is possessed. The bodily disturbances are said to be the "manifestation" of these several emotions, their "expression" or "natural language"; and these emotions themselves, being so strongly characterized both from within and without, may be called the *standard* emotions.

Our natural way of thinking about these standard emotions is that the mental perception of some fact excites the mental affection called the emotion, and that this latter state of mind gives rise to the bodily expression. My thesis on the contrary is that *the bodily changes follow directly the* PERCEPTION *of the exciting fact, and that our feeling of the same changes as they occur* IS *the emotion*. Common sense says, we lose our fortune, are sorry and weep; we meet a bear, are frightened and run; we are insulted by a rival, are angry and strike. The hypothesis here to be defended says that this order of sequence is incorrect, that the one mental state is not immediately induced by the other, that the bodily manifestations must first be interposed between, and that the more rational statement is that we feel sorry because we cry, angry because we strike, afraid because we tremble, and not that we cry, strike, or tremble, because we are sorry, angry, or fearful, as the case may be. Without the bodily states following on the perception, the latter would be purely cognitive in form, pale, colorless, destitute of emotional warmth. We might then see the bear, and judge it best to run, receive the insult and deem it right to strike, but we could not actually *feel* afraid or angry.

Stated in this crude way, the hypothesis is pretty sure to meet with immediate disbelief. And yet neither many nor far-fetched considerations are required to mitigate its paradoxical character, and possibly to produce conviction of its truth.

To begin with, readers of this Journal do not need to be reminded that the nervous system of every living thing is but a bundle of predispositions to react in particular ways upon the contact of particular features of the environment. As surely as the hermit-crab's abdomen presupposes the existence of empty whelk-shells somewhere to be found, so surely do the hound's olfactories imply the existence, on the one hand, of deer's or foxes' feet, and on the other, the tendency to follow up their tracks. The neural machinery is but a hyphen between determinate arrangements of matter outside the body and determinate impulses to inhibition or discharge within its organs. When the hen sees a white oval object on the ground, she cannot leave it; she must keep upon it and return to it, until at last its transformation into a little mass of moving chirping down elicits from her machinery an entirely new set of performances. The love of man for woman, or of the human mother for her babe, our wrath at snakes and our fear of precipices, may all be described similarly, as instances of the way in which peculiarly conformed pieces of the world's furniture will fatally call forth most particular mental and bodily reactions, in advance of, and often in direct opposition to, the verdict of our deliberate reason concerning them. The labors of Darwin and his successors are only just beginning to reveal the universal parasitism of each special creature upon other special things, and the way in which each creature brings the signature of its special relations stamped on its nervous system with it upon the scene.

Every living creature is in fact a sort of lock, whose wards and springs presuppose special forms of key—which keys however are not born attached to the locks, but are sure to be found in the world near by as life goes on. And the locks are indifferent to any but their own keys. The egg fails to fascinate the hound, the bird does not fear the precipice, the snake waxes not wroth at his kind, the deer cares nothing for the woman or the human babe. Those who wish for a full development of this point of view, should read Schneider's *Der thierische Wille*—no other book shows how accurately anticipatory are the actions of animals, of the specific features of the environment in which they are to live.

Now among these nervous anticipations are of course to be reckoned the emotions, so far as these may be called forth directly by the perception of certain facts. In advance of all experience of elephants no child can but be frightened if he suddenly find one trumpeting and charging upon him. No woman can see a handsome little naked baby without delight, no man in the wilderness see a human form in the distance without excitement and curiosity. I said I should consider these emotions only so far as they have bodily movements of some sort for their accompaniments. But my first point is to show that their bodily accompaniments are much more far-reaching and complicated than we ordinarily suppose.

In the earlier books on Expression, written mostly from the artistic point of view, the signs of emotion visible from without were the only ones taken account of. Sir Charles Bell's celebrated *Anatomy of Expression* noticed the respiratory changes; and Bain's and Darwin's treatises went more thoroughly still into the study of the visceral factors involved—changes in the functioning of glands and muscles, and in that of the circulatory apparatus. But not even a Darwin has exhaustively enumerated *all* the bodily affections characteristic of any one of the standard emotions. More and more, as physiology advances, we begin to discern how almost infinitely numerous and subtle they must be. The researches of Mosso with the plethysmograph have shown that not only the heart, but the entire circulatory system, forms a sort of sounding-board, which every change of our consciousness, however slight, may make re-verberate. Hardly a sensation comes to us without sending waves of alternate constriction and dilatation down the arteries of our arms. The blood-vessels of the abdomen act reciprocally with those of the more outward parts. The bladder and bowels, the glands of the mouth, throat, and skin, and the liver, are known to be affected gravely in certain severe emotions, and are unquestionably affected transiently when the emotions are of a lighter sort. That the heart-beats and the rhythm of breathing play a leading part in all emotions whatsoever, is a matter too notorious for proof. And what is really equally prominent, but less likely to be admitted until special attention is drawn to the fact, is the continuous co-operation of the voluntary muscles in our emotional states. Even when no change of outward attitude is produced, their inward tension alters to suit each varying mood, and is felt as a difference of tone or of strain. In depression the flexors tend to prevail; in elation or belligerent excitement the extensors take the lead. And the various permuta-tions and combinations of which these organic activities are sus-ceptible, make it abstractly possible that no shade of emotion, however slight, should be without a bodily reverberation as unique, when taken in its totality, as is the mental mood itself.

The immense number of parts modified in each emotion is what makes it so difficult for us to reproduce in cold blood the total and integral expression of any one of them. We may catch the trick with the voluntary muscles, but fail with the skin, glands, heart, and other viscera. Just as an artificially imitated sneeze lacks something of the reality, so the attempt to imitate an emotion in the absence of its normal instigating cause is apt to be rather "hollow."

The next thing to be noticed is this, that every one of the bodily changes, whatsoever it be, is *felt*, acutely or obscurely, the moment it occurs. If the reader has never paid attention to this matter, he will be both interested and astonished to learn how many different local bodily feelings he can detect in himself as characteristic of his various emotional moods. It would be perhaps too much to expect him to arrest the tide of any strong gust of passion for the sake of any such curious analysis as this; but he can observe more tranquil states, and that may be assumed here to be true of the greater which is shown to be true of the less. Our whole cubic capacity is sensibly alive; and each morsel of it contributes its pulsations of feeling, dim or sharp, pleasant, painful, or dubious, to that sense of personality that every one of us unfailingly carries with him. It is surprising what little items give accent to these complexes of sensibility. When worried by any slight trouble, one may find that the focus of one's bodily consciousness is the contraction, often quite inconsiderable, of the eyes and brows. When momentarily embarrassed, it is something in the pharynx that compels either a swallow, a clearing of the throat, or a slight cough; and so on for as many more instances as might be named. Our concern here being with the general view rather than with the details, I will not linger to discuss these but, assuming the point admitted that every change that occurs must be felt, I will pass on.[1]

I now proceed to urge the vital point of my whole theory, which is this. If we fancy some strong emotion, and then try to abstract from our consciousness of it all the feelings of its characteristic bodily symptoms, we find we have nothing left behind, no "mind-stuff" out of which the emotion can be constituted, and that a cold and neutral state of intellectual perception is all that remains. It is true, that although most people, when asked, say that their introspection verifies this statement, some persist in saying theirs does

---

[1] Of course the physiological question arises, *how* are the changes felt?—*after* they are produced, by the sensory nerves of the organs bringing back to the brain a report of the modifications that have occurred? or *before* they are produced, by our being conscious of the outgoing nerve-currents starting on their way downwards towards the parts they are to excite? I believe all the evidence we have to be in favor of the former alternative. The question is too minute for discussion here, but I have said something about it in a paper entitled "The Feeling of Effort," in the *Anniversary Memoirs of the Boston Society of Natural History*, 1880 (translated in *La Critique Philosophique* for that year, and summarized in MIND, V [No. 20], 582). See also G. E. Müller's *Grundlegung der Psychophysik*, § 110.

not. Many cannot be made to understand the question. When you beg them to imagine away every feeling of laughter and of tendency to laugh from their consciousness of the ludicrousness of an object, and then to tell you what the feeling of its ludicrousness would be like, whether it be anything more than the perception that the object belongs to the class "funny," they persist in replying that the thing proposed is a physical impossibility, and that they always *must* laugh, if they see a funny object. Of course the task proposed is not the practical one of seeing a ludicrous object and annihilating one's tendency to laugh. It is the purely speculative one of subtracting certain elements of feeling from an emotional state supposed to exist in its fulness, and saying what the residual elements are. I cannot help thinking that all who rightly apprehend this problem will agree with the proposition above laid down. What kind of an emotion of fear would be left, if the feelings neither of quickened heart-beats nor of shallow breathing, neither of trembling lips nor of weakened limbs, neither of goose-flesh nor of visceral stirrings, were present, it is quite impossible to think. Can one fancy the state of rage and picture no ebullition of it in the chest, no flushing of the face, no dilatation of the nostrils, no clenching of the teeth, no impulse to vigorous action, but in their stead limp muscles, calm breathing, and a placid face? The present writer, for one, certainly cannot. The rage is as completely evaporated as the sensation of its so-called manifestations, and the only thing that can possibly be supposed to take its place is some cold-blooded and dispassionate judicial sentence, confined entirely to the intellectual realm, to the effect that a certain person or persons merit chastisement for their sins. In like manner of grief: what would it be without its tears, its sobs, its suffocation of the heart, its pang in the breast-bone? A feelingless cognition that certain circumstances are deplorable, and nothing more. Every passion in turn tells the same story. A purely disembodied human emotion is a nonentity. I do not say that it is a contradiction in the nature of things, or that pure spirits are necessarily condemned to cold intellectual lives; but I say that for *us*, emotion dissociated from all bodily feeling is inconceivable. The more closely I scrutinize my states, the more persuaded I become, that whatever moods, affections, and passions I have, are in very truth constituted by, and made up of, those bodily changes we ordinarily call their expression or consequence; and the more it seems to me that if I were to become corporeally anæsthetic, I should be excluded from the life of the affections, harsh and tender alike, and drag out an existence of merely cognitive or intellectual form. Such an existence, although it seems to have been the ideal of ancient sages, is too apathetic to be keenly sought after by those born after the revival of the worship of sensibility, a few generations ago.

But if the emotion is nothing but the feeling of the reflex bodily effects of what we call its "object," effects due to the connate adaptation of the nervous system to that object, we seem immediately faced by this objection: most of the objects of civilized men's emotions are things to which it would be preposterous to suppose their nervous systems connately adapted. Most occasions of shame and many insults are purely conventional, and vary with the social environment. The same is true of many matters of dread and of desire, and of many occasions of melancholy and regret. In these cases, at least, it would seem that the ideas of shame, desire, regret, etc., must first have been attached by education and association to these conventional objects before the bodily changes could possibly be awakened. And if in *these* cases the bodily changes follow the ideas, instead of giving rise to them, why not then in all cases?

To discuss thoroughly this objection would carry us deep into the study of purely intellectual Æsthetics. A few words must here suffice. We will say nothing of the argument's failure to distinguish between the idea of an emotion and the emotion itself. We will only recall the well-known evolutionary principle that when a certain power has once been fixed in an animal by virtue of its utility in presence of certain features of the environment, it may turn out to be useful in presence of other features of the environment that had originally nothing to do with either producing or preserving it. A nervous tendency to discharge being once there, all sorts of unforeseen things may pull the trigger and let loose the effects. That among these things should be conventionalities of man's contriving is a matter of no psychological consequence whatever. The most important part of my environment is my fellow-man. The consciousness of his attitude towards me is the perception that normally unlocks most of my shames and indignations and fears. The extraordinary sensitiveness of this consciousness is shown by the bodily modifications wrought in us by the awareness that our fellow-man is noticing us *at all*. No one can walk across the platform at a public meeting with just the same muscular innervation he uses to walk across his room at home. No one can give a message to such a meeting without organic excitement. "Stage-fright" is only the extreme degree of that wholly irrational personal self-consciousness which everyone gets in some measure, as soon as he feels the eyes of a number of strangers fixed upon him, even though he be inwardly convinced that their feeling towards him is of no practical account.[2] This being so, it is not surprising that the additional persuasion that my fellow-man's attitude means either well or ill for me, should awaken stronger emotions still. In primitive societies "Well" may mean handing me a piece of beef, and "Ill" may mean aiming a blow at my skull. In our "cultured age," "Ill" may mean cutting me in the street, and "Well," giving me an honorary degree. What the action itself may be is quite insignificant, so long as I can perceive in it intent or *animus*. *That* is the emotion-arousing perception; and may give rise to as strong bodily convulsions in me, a civilized man experiencing the treatment of an artificial society, as in any savage prisoner of war, learning whether his captors are about to eat him or to make him a member of their tribe.

But now, this objection disposed of, there arises a more general doubt. Is there any evidence, it may be asked, for the assumption that particular perceptions *do* produce wide-spread bodily effects by a sort of immediate physical influence, antecedent to the arousal of an emotion or emotional idea?

The only possible reply is, that there is most assuredly such evidence. In listening to poetry, drama, or heroic narrative, we are often surprised at the cutaneous shiver which like a sudden wave flows over us, and at the heart-swelling and the lachrymal effusion that unexpectedly catch us at intervals. In listening to music, the same is even more strikingly true. If we abruptly see a dark moving form in the woods, our heart stops beating, and we catch our breath instantly and before any articulate idea of danger can arise. If our friend goes near to the edge of a precipice, we get the well-known feeling of "all-overishness," and we shrink back, although we posi-

---

[2] Let it be noted in passing that this personal self-consciousness seems an altogether bodily affair, largely a consciousness of our attitude, and that, like other emotions, it reacts on its physical condition, and leads to modifications of the attitude—to a certain rigidity in most men, but in children to a regular twisting and squirming fit, and in women to various gracefully shy poses.

tively *know* him to be safe, and have no distinct imagination of his fall. The writer well remembers his astonishment, when a boy of seven or eight, at fainting when he saw a horse bled. The blood was in a bucket, with a stick in it, and, if memory does not deceive him, he stirred it round and saw it drip from the stick with no feeling save that of childish curiosity. Suddenly the world grew black before his eyes, his ears began to buzz, and he knew no more. He had never heard of the sight of blood producing faintness or sickness, and he had so little repugnance to it, and so little apprehension of any other sort of danger from it, that even at that tender age, as he well remembers, he could not help wondering how the mere physical presence of a pailful of crimson fluid could occasion in him such formidable bodily effects.

Imagine two steel knife-blades with their keen edges crossing each other at right angles, and moving to and fro. Our whole nervous organization is "on-edge" at the thought; and yet what emotion can be there except the unpleasant nervous feeling itself, or the dread that more of it may come? The entire fund and capital of the emotion here is the senseless bodily effect the blades immediately arouse. This case is typical of a class: where an ideal emotion seems to precede the bodily symptoms, it is often nothing but a representation of the symptoms themselves. One who has already fainted at the sight of blood may witness the preparations for a surgical operation with uncontrollable heart-sinking and anxiety. He anticipates certain feelings, and the anticipation precipitates their arrival. I am told of a case of morbid terror, of which the subject confessed that what possessed her seemed, more than anything, to be the fear of fear itself. In the various forms of what Professor Bain calls "tender emotion," although the appropriate object must usually be directly contemplated before the emotion can be aroused, yet sometimes thinking of the symptoms of the emotion itself may have the same effect. In sentimental natures, the thought of "yearning" will produce real "yearning." And, not to speak of coarser examples, a mother's imagination of the caresses she bestows on her child may arouse a spasm of parental longing.

In such cases as these, we see plainly how the emotion both begins and ends with what we call its effects or manifestations. It has no mental *status* except as either the presented feeling, or the idea, of the manifestations; which latter thus constitute its entire material, its sum and substance, and its stock-in-trade. And these cases ought to make us see how in all cases the feeling of the manifestations may play a much deeper part in the constitution of the emotion than we are wont to suppose.

If our theory be true, a necessary corollary of it ought to be that any voluntary arousal of the so-called manifestations of a special emotion ought to give us the emotion itself. Of course in the majority of emotions, this test is inapplicable; for many of the manifestations are in organs over which we have no volitional control. Still, within the limits in which it can be verified, experience fully corroborates this test. Everyone knows how panic is increased by flight, and how the giving way to the symptoms of grief or anger increases those passions themselves. Each fit of sobbing makes the sorrow more acute, and calls forth another fit stronger still, until at last repose only ensues with lassitude and with the apparent exhaustion of the machinery. In rage, it is notorious how we "work ourselves up" to a climax by repeated outbreaks of expression. Refuse to express a passion, and it dies. Count ten before venting your anger, and its occasion seems ridiculous. Whistling to keep up courage is no mere figure of speech. On the other hand, sit all day in a moping posture, sigh, and reply to everything with a dismal voice, and your melancholy lingers. There is no more valuable precept in moral education than this, as all who have experience know: if we wish to conquer undesirable emotional tendencies in ourselves, we must assiduously, and in the first instance cold-bloodedly, go through the *outward motions* of those contrary dispositions we prefer to cultivate. The reward of persistency will infallibly come, in the fading out of the sullenness or depression, and the advent of real cheerfulness and kindliness in their stead. Smooth the brow, brighten the eye, contract the dorsal rather than the ventral aspect of the frame, and speak in a major key, pass the genial compliment, and your heart must be frigid indeed if it do not gradually thaw!

The only exceptions to this are apparent, not real. The great emotional expressiveness and mobility of certain persons often lead us to say "They would feel more if they talked less." And in another class of persons, the explosive energy with which passion manifests itself on critical occasions, seems correlated with the way in which they bottle it up during the intervals. But these are only eccentric types of character, and within each type the law of the last paragraph prevails. The sentimentalist is so constructed that "gushing" is his or her normal mode of expression. Putting a stopper on the "gush" will only to a limited extent cause more "real" activities to take its place; in the main it will simply produce listlessness. On the other hand the ponderous and bilious "slumbering volcano," let him repress the expression of his passions as he will, will find them expire if they get no vent at all; whilst if the rare occasions multiply which he deems worthy of their outbreak, he will find them grow in intensity as life proceeds.

I feel persuaded there is no real exception to the law. The formidable effects of suppressed tears might be mentioned, and the calming results of speaking out your mind when angry and having done with it. But these are also but specious wanderings from the rule. Every perception must lead to *some* nervous result. If this be the normal emotional expression, it soon expends itself, and in the natural course of things a calm succeeds. But if the normal issue be blocked from any cause, the currents may under certain circumstances invade other tracts, and there work different and worse effects. Thus vengeful brooding may replace a burst of indignation; a dry heat may consume the frame of one who fain would weep, or he may, as Dante says, turn to stone within; and then tears or a storming-fit may bring a grateful relief. When we teach children to repress their emotions, it is not that they may *feel* more, quite the reverse. It is that they may *think* more; for to a certain extent whatever nerve-currents are diverted from the regions below, must swell the activity of the thought-tracts of the brain.[3]

The last great argument in favor of the priority of the bodily symptoms to the felt emotion, is the ease with which we formulate by its means pathological cases and normal cases under a common scheme. In every asylum we find examples of absolutely unmotived fear, anger, melancholy, or conceit; and others of an equally unmotived apathy which persists in spite of the best of outward reasons why it should give way. In the former cases we must suppose the nervous machinery to be so "labile" in some one emotional direction, that almost every stimulus, however inappropriate, will

[3] This is the opposite of what happens in injuries to the brain, whether from outward violence, inward rupture or tumor, or mere starvation from disease. The cortical permeability seems reduced, so that excitement, instead of propagating itself laterally through the ideational channels as before, tends to take the downward track into the organs of the body. The consequence is that we have tears, laughter, and temper-fits, on the most insignificant provocation, accompanying a proportional feebleness in logical thought and the power of volitional attention and decision.

cause it to upset in that way, and as a consequence to engender the particular complex of feelings of which the psychic body of the emotion consists. Thus, to take one special instance, if inability to draw deep breath, fluttering of the heart, and that peculiar epigastric change felt as "precordial anxiety," with an irresistible tendency to take a somewhat crouching attitude and to sit still, and with perhaps other visceral processes not now known, all spontaneously occur together in a certain person; his feeling of their combination *is* the emotion of dread, and he is the victim of what is known as morbid fear. A friend who has had occasional attacks of this most evil of all maladies, tells me that in his case the whole drama seems to centre about the region of the heart and respiratory apparatus, that his main effort during the attacks is to get control of his inspirations and to slow his heart, and that the moment he attains to breathing deeply and to holding himself erect, the dread, *ipso facto*, seems to depart.[4]

The account given to Brachet by one of his own patients of her opposite condition, that of emotional insensibility, has been often quoted, and deserves to be quoted again:—

"I still continue (she says) to suffer constantly; I have not a moment of comfort, and no human sensations. Surrounded by all that can render life happy and agreeable, still to me the faculty of enjoyment and of feeling is wanting—both have become physical impossibilities. . . . In everything, even in the most tender caresses of my children, I find only bitterness. I cover them with kisses, but there is something between their lips and mine; and this horrid something is between me and all the enjoyments of life. My existence is incomplete. The functions and acts of ordinary life, it is true, still remain to me; but in every one of

---

[4] It must be confessed that there are cases of morbid fear in which objectively the heart is not much perturbed. These however fail to prove anything against our theory, for it is of course possible that the cortical centres normally percipient of dread as a complex of cardiac and other organic sensations due to real bodily change, should become *primarily* excited in brain-disease, and give rise to an hallucination of the changes being there—an hallucination of dread, consequently, coexistent with a comparatively calm pulse, etc. I say it is possible, for I am ignorant of observations which might test the fact. Trance, ecstasy, etc., offer analogous examples—not to speak of ordinary dreaming. Under all these conditions one may have the liveliest subjective feelings, either of eye or ear, or of the more visceral and emotional sort, as a result of pure nerve-central activity, with complete peripheral repose. Whether the subjective strength of the feeling be due in these cases to the actual energy of the central disturbance, or merely to the narrowing of the field of consciousness, need not concern us. In the asylum cases of melancholy, there is usually a narrowing of the field.

them there is something wanting—to wit, the feeling which is proper to them, and the pleasure which follows them. . . . *Each of my senses, each part of my proper self, is as it were separated from me and can no longer afford me any feeling; this impossibility seems to depend upon a void which I feel in the front of my head, and to be due to the diminution of the sensibility over the whole surface of my body, for it seems to me that I never actually reach the objects which I touch. . . . I feel well enough the changes of temperature on my skin, but I no longer experience the internal feeling of the air when I breathe. . . .* All this would be a small matter enough, but for its frightful result, which is that of the impossibility of any other kind of feeling and of any sort of enjoyment, although I experience a need and desire of them that render my life an incomprehensible torture. Every function, every action of my life remains, but deprived of the feeling that belongs to it, of the enjoyment that should follow it. My feet are cold, I warm them, but gain no pleasure from the warmth. I recognize the taste of all I eat, without getting any pleasure from it. . . . My children are growing handsome and healthy, everyone tells me so, I see it myself, but the delight, the inward comfort I ought to feel, I fail to get. Music has lost all charm for me, I used to love it dearly. My daughter plays very well, but for me it is mere noise. That lively interest which a year ago made me hear a delicious concert in the smallest air their fingers played— that thrill, that general vibration which made me shed such tender tears —all that exists no more."[5]

Other victims describe themselves as closed in walls of ice or covered with an india-rubber integument, through which no impression penetrates to the sealed-up sensibility.

If our hypothesis be true, it makes us realize more deeply than ever how much our mental life is knit up with our corporeal frame, in the strictest sense of the term. Rapture, love, ambition, indignation, and pride, considered as feelings, are fruits of the same soil with the grossest bodily sensations of pleasure and of pain. But it was said at the outset that this would be affirmed only of what we then agreed to call the "standard" emotions; and that those inward sensibilities that appeared devoid at first sight of bodily results should be left out of our account. We had better, before closing, say a word or two about these latter feelings.

They are, the reader will remember, the moral, intellectual, and æsthetic feelings. Concords of sounds, of colors, of lines, logical

[5] Quoted by Semal: *De la sensibilité générale dans les affections mélancoliques,* Paris, 1875, pp. 130–134.

consistencies, teleological fitnesses, affect us with a pleasure that seems ingrained in the very form of the representation itself, and to borrow nothing from any reverberation surging up from the parts below the brain. The Herbartian psychologists have tried to distinguish feelings due to the *form* in which ideas may be arranged. A geometrical demonstration may be as "pretty," and an act of justice as "neat" as a drawing or a tune, although the prettiness and neatness seem here to be a pure matter of sensation, and there to have nothing to do with sensation. We have then, or some of us seem to have, genuinely *cerebral* forms of pleasure and displeasure, apparently not agreeing in their mode of production with the so-called "standard" emotions we have been analyzing. And it is certain that readers whom our reasons have hitherto failed to convince, will now start up at this admission, and consider that by it we give up our whole case. Since musical perceptions, since logical ideas, can immediately arouse a form of emotional feeling, they will say, is it not more natural to suppose that in the case of the so-called "standard" emotions, prompted by the presence of objects or the experience of events, the emotional feeling is equally immediate, and the bodily expression something that comes later and is added on?

But a sober scrutiny of the cases of pure cerebral emotion gives little force to this assimilation. Unless in them there actually be coupled with the intellectual feeling a bodily reverberation of some kind, unless we actually laugh at the neatness of the mechanical device, thrill at the justice of the act, or tingle at the perfection of the musical form, our mental condition is more allied to a judgment of *right* than to anything else. And such a judgment is rather to be classed among awarenesses of truth: it is a *cognitive* act. But as a matter of fact the intellectual feeling hardly ever does exist thus unaccompanied. The bodily sounding-board is at work, as careful introspection will show, far more than we usually suppose. Still, where long familiarity with a certain class of effects has blunted emotional sensibility thereto as much as it has sharpened the taste and judgment, we do get the intellectual emotion, if such it can be called, pure and undefiled. And the dryness of it, the paleness, the absence of all glow, as it may exist in a thoroughly expert critic's mind, not only shows us what an altogether different thing it is from the "standard" emotions we considered first, but makes us suspect that almost the entire difference lies in the fact that the bodily sounding-board, vibrating in the one case, is in the other mute. "Not so very bad" is, in a person of consummate taste, apt to be the highest limit of approving expression. *"Rien ne me choque"* is said to have been Chopin's superlative of praise of new music. A sentimental layman would feel, and ought to feel, horrified, on being admitted into such a critic's mind, to see how cold, how thin, how void of human significance, are the motives for favor or disfavor that there prevail. The capacity to make a nice spot on the wall will outweigh a picture's whole content; a foolish trick of words will preserve a poem; an utterly meaningless fitness of sequence in one musical composition set at naught any amount of "expressiveness" in another.

I remember seeing an English couple sit for more than an hour on a piercing February day in the Academy at Venice before the celebrated "Assumption" by Titian; and when I, after being chased from room to room by the cold, concluded to get into the sunshine as fast as possible and let the pictures go, but before leaving drew reverently near to them to learn with what superior forms of susceptibility they might be endowed, all I overhead was the woman's voice murmuring: "What a *deprecatory* expression her face wears! What self-abnega*tion*! How *unworthy* she feels of the honor she is receiving!" Their honest hearts had been kept warm all the time by a glow of spurious sentiment that would have fairly made old Titian sick. Mr. Ruskin somewhere makes the (for him) terrible admission that religious people as a rule care little for pictures, and that when they do care for them they generally prefer the worst ones to the best. Yes! in every art, in every science, there is the keen perception of certain relations being *right* or not, and there is the emotional flush and thrill consequent thereupon. And these are two things, not one. In the former of them it is that experts and masters are at home. The latter accompaniments are bodily commotions that they may hardly feel, but that may be experienced in their fulness by *Crétins* and Philistines in whom the critical judgment is at its lowest ebb. The "marvels" of Science, about which so much edifying popular literature is written, are apt to be "caviare" to the men in the laboratories. Cognition and emotion are parted even in this last retreat—who shall say that their antagonism may not just be one phase of the world-old struggle known as that between the spirit and the flesh?—a struggle in which it seems pretty certain that neither party will definitively drive the other off the field.

To return now to our starting-point, the physiology of the brain. If we suppose its cortex to contain centres for the perception of changes in each special sense-organ, in each portion of the skin, in each muscle, each joint, and each viscus, and to contain absolutely nothing else, we still have a scheme perfectly capable of representing the process of the emotions. An object falls on a sense-organ and is apperceived by the appropriate cortical centre; or else the latter, excited in some other way, gives rise to an idea of the same object. Quick as a flash, the reflex currents pass down through their pre-ordained channels, alter the condition of muscle, skin and viscus; and these alterations, apperceived like the original object, in as many specific portions of the cortex, combine with it in consciousness and transform it from an object-simply-apprehended into an object-emotionally-felt. No new principles have to be invoked, nothing is postulated beyond the ordinary reflex circuit, and the topical centres admitted in one shape or another by all to exist.

It must be confessed that a crucial test of the truth of the hypothesis is quite as hard to obtain as its decisive refutation. A case of complete internal and external corporeal anæsthesia, without motor alteration or alteration of intelligence except emotional apathy, would afford, if not a crucial test, at least a strong presumption, in favor of the truth of the view we have set forth; whilst the persistence of strong emotional feeling in such a case would completely overthrow our case. Hysterical anæsthesias seem never to be complete enough to cover the ground. Complete anæsthesias from organic disease, on the other hand, are excessively rare. In the famous case of Remigius Leims, no mention is made by the reporters of his emotional condition, a circumstance which by itself affords no presumption that it was normal, since as a rule nothing ever *is* noticed without a pre-existing question in the mind. Dr. Georg Winter has recently described a case somewhat similar,[6] and in reply to a question, kindly writes to me as follows:—"The case has been for a year and a half entirely removed from my ob-

---

[6] "Ein Fall von allgemeiner Anæsthesie," *Inaugural-Dissertation*. Heidelberg, Winter, 1882.

servation. But so far as I am able to state, the man was characterized by a certain mental inertia and indolence. He was tranquil, and had on the whole the temperament of a phlegmatic. He was not irritable, not quarrelsome, went quietly about his farm-work, and left the care of his business and housekeeping to other people. In short, he gave one the impression of a placid countryman, who has no interests beyond his work." Dr. Winter adds that in studying the case he paid no particular attention to the man's psychic condition, as this seemed *"nebensächlich"* to his main purpose. I should add that the form of my question to Dr. Winter could give him no clue as to the kind of answer I expected.

Of course, this case proves nothing, but it is to be hoped that asylum-physicians and nervous specialists may begin methodically to study the relation between anæsthesia and emotional apathy. If the hypothesis here suggested is ever to be definitively confirmed or disproved it seems as if it must be by them, for they alone have the data in their hands.

P.S.—By an unpardonable forgetfulness at the time of dispatching my MS. to the Editor, I ignored the existence of the extraordinary case of total anæsthesia published by Professor Strümpell in Ziemssen's *Deutsches Archiv für klinische Medicin*, xxii, 321, of which I had nevertheless read reports at the time of its publication. [*Cf.* first report of the case in MIND, III (No. 10), 263, translated from Pflüger's *Archiv.* ED.] I believe that it constitutes the only remaining case of the sort in medical literature, so that with it our survey is complete. On referring to the original, which is important in many connections, I found that the patient, a shoemaker's apprentice of 15, entirely anæsthetic, inside and out, with the exception of one eye and one ear, had shown *shame* on the occasion of soiling his bed, and *grief*, when a formerly favorite dish was set before him, at the thought that he could no longer taste its flavor. As Dr. Strümpell seemed however to have paid no special attention to his psychic states, so far as these are matter for our theory, I wrote to him in a few words what the essence of the theory was, and asked him to say whether he felt sure the grief and shame mentioned were real feelings in the boy's mind, or only the reflex manifestations provoked by certain perceptions, manifestations that an outside observer might note, but to which the boy himself might be insensible.

Dr. Strümpell has sent me a very obliging reply, of which I translate the most important passage.

"I must indeed confess that I naturally failed to institute with my

Anæsthetiker observations as special as the sense of your theory would require. Nevertheless I think I can decidedly make the statement, that he was by no means completely lacking in emotional affections. In addition to the feelings of *grief* and *shame* mentioned in my paper, I recall distinctly that he showed *e.g., anger*, and frequently quarrelled with the hospital attendants. He also manifested *fear* lest I should punish him. In short, I do not think that my case speaks exactly in favor of your theory. On the other hand, I will not affirm that it positively refutes your theory. For my case was certainly one of a very centrally conditioned anæsthesia (perception-anæsthesia, like that of hysterics) and therefore the conduction of outward impressions may in him have been undisturbed."

I confess that I do not see the relevancy of the last consideration, and this makes me suspect that my own letter was too briefly or obscurely expressed to put my correspondent fully in possession of my own thought. For his reply still makes no explicit reference to anything but the outward manifestations of emotion in the boy. Is it not at least conceivable that, just as a stranger, brought into the boy's presence for the first time, and seeing him eat and drink and satisfy other natural necessities, would suppose him to have the feelings of hunger, thirst, etc., until informed by the boy himself that he did all these things with no feeling at all but that of sight and sound—is it not, I say, at least possible, that Dr. Strümpell, addressing no direct introspective questions to his patient, and the patient not being of a class from which one could expect voluntary revelations of that sort, should have similarly omitted to discriminate between a feeling and its habitual motor accompaniment, and erroneously taken the latter as proof that the former was there? Such a mistake is of course possible, and I must therefore repeat Dr. Strümpell's own words, that his case does not yet refute my theory. Should a similar case recur, it ought to be interrogated as to the inward emotional state that coexisted with the outward expressions of shame, anger, etc. And if it then turned out that the patient recognized explicitly the same mood of feeling known under those names in his former normal state, my theory would of course fall. It is, however, to me incredible that the patient should have an *identical* feeling, for the dropping out of the organic sounding-board would necessarily diminish its volume in some way. The teacher of Dr. Strümpell's patient found a mental deficiency in him during his anæsthesia, that may possibly have been due to the consequences resulting to his general intellectual vivacity from the subtraction of so important a mass of feelings, even though they were not the whole of his emotional life. Whoever wishes to extract from the next case of total anæsthesia the maximum of knowledge about the emotions, will have to interrogate the patient with some such notion as that of my article in his mind. We can define the pure psychic emotions far better by starting from such an hypothesis and modifying it in the way of restriction and subtraction, than by having no definite hypothesis at all. Thus will the publication of my article have been justified, even though the theory it advocates, rigorously taken, be erroneous. The best thing I can say for it is, that in writing it, I have almost persuaded *myself* it may be true.

The Latest Cure for Sea-Sickness

Sir,—On turning over the leaves of a copy of the *Pall Mall Budget* for August 1, which had penetrated the wilderness in which I have been spending the past fortnight, I was startled by a jocose little paragraph about a certain Dr. James of Boston, who has been proposing to cure sea-sickness by stopping the ears with wax, and who fortifies his reasoning by referring to Ulysses and the sirens. As I cannot but think this mythological doctor to be a travesty of my humble self—how he came to wander into your pages heaven only knows!—I trust your readers will regard the provocation as sufficient to justify me in emerging from my obscurity and addressing them in authentic form. I have long wished to get the matter experimented on on a large scale, but have shrunk from addressing a communication to a popular journal. Your paragraph, however, unbinds my modesty and elicits the following statement:—

The semi-circular canals of the internal ear are nowadays pretty well understood not to be organs of hearing, but of equilibrium. The sensation they normally give us is that of change of direction and speed in the movements of our head through space. When over-excited they give rise to vertigo and nausea. A large percentage of deaf mutes (in whom these canals are presumably thrown out of function) are insusceptible of being made dizzy. Of a considerable number of such deaf mutes who had been exposed to sea-sickness, none (with the exception of two doubtful cases) had ever suffered. All these facts lead to the hypothesis that sea-sickness may arise in the first instance from the over-excitement of these sensitive organs; and finally they lead to the practical suggestion that such over-excitement might be warded off or allayed by that method of "counter irritation" which succeeds so well in other analogous cases of irritability. The counter-irritation here could only consist in blistering or otherwise reddening the skin above and behind the ears. The experiment is so simple a one, and would be, if successful, so pregnant of relief to travelling man's estate, that it seems a shame it should not be tested by a large number of persons. I have tried it myself twice, being a very bad sailor. The first time was on the British Channel, on a very rough day, when every one around me was violently sick. I simply rubbed the skin behind my ears with my fingers till it was slightly excoriated. An incipient nausea, which was felt at the end of the first half-hour, completely vanished as the sensation of cutaneous burning became strong. In crossing the Atlantic I was less successful, but my sea-sickness there was rather anomalous, its principal symptom being a high fever and no nausea, and I do not consider the failure to be a refutation of the method. It may be that the latter will serve for short exposures, like Channel voyages, but not for longer ones. At any rate the scientific presumption in favour of its utility is certainly large enough to warrant experimentation by any one who dreads the direst of all forms of misery. If this letter induce any of your readers to take the matter up practically, I shall be very glad; and shall be particularly obliged if they will be kind enough to report their results, whether favourable or unfavourable, to your obedient servant,

WM. JAMES

Cambridge, Mass., U.S., Sept. 11.

Report of the Committee on Hypnotism

Many hours have been spent in work upon this subject by the members of the committee, for the most part singly. Mr. Cory has no report to make at present. Messrs. James and Carnochan's experiments were confined almost entirely to students of Harvard College. Out of between fifty or sixty of these, who were operated on, a dozen, more or less, were influenced at the first sitting, being a proportion of about one in five. Two men were so much better subjects than the rest, that they ended by receiving almost exclusive attention.

The comparatively small amount of time at our disposition for these investigations, and the variations of some of the subjects from one day to another, necessitating many repetitions of the same experiment, make it impossible to report anything definitive this year. A few of our notes may, however, be of interest, although nothing essentially novel is contained therein.

The need of "guiding sensations" for voluntary motion was proved by the artificial reproduction of a rare pathological state. In two persons (one of them being the Mrs. P. who is mentioned in the report on mediumistic phenomena) an arm was made absolutely anæsthetic, whilst retaining its muscular contractility. Under these circumstances, the subject could execute a commanded movement, —such as raising the arm, clenching the fist, writing the name, etc., —but only when the eyes were used to superintend. With closed eyes the movements were feeble and ineffectual, and the patient quite uncertain whether the purpose had been accomplished or not. Passive movements communicated to the arm and hand were then unrecognized or misunderstood.

Much time was spent in a quest (as yet only advanced enough to show how far from simple the conditions are) of what the psychical modification is in the hypnotic trance. Is the anæsthesia, for example, produced by suggestion, due to an abolition of sensation or an abolition of "apperception"? Does the subject not *feel*? or is he become incapable of *noticing* what he feels? or is his state something more peculiar still?

That the sensorial process[1] occurs, seems proved by after-images. Two of our subjects who were made completely blind to a red patch laid on a piece of paper immediately saw a bluish-green patch when the red patch was removed.[2]

That the process of apperception, assimilation, or recognition of what the impression is, does also occur, seems proved by observations of a somewhat similar sort on the same two subjects. Make a stroke on paper or blackboard, and tell the subject it is not there, and he will see nothing but the clean paper or board. Next, he not looking, surround the original stroke with other strokes exactly like it, and ask him what he sees. He will point out one by one all the new strokes, and omit the original one every time, no matter how numerous the new strokes may be, or in what order they are arranged. Similarly, if the original single stroke to which he is blind be *doubled* by a prism of sixteen degrees placed before one of his eyes (both being kept open), he will say that he now sees *one* stroke, and point in the direction in which the image seen through the prism lies.

Obviously, then, he is not blind to the *kind* of stroke in the least.

---

[1] By sensorial I do not necessarily mean retinal exclusively. M. Binet, in his excellent little *Psychologie du raisonnement*, considers that after-images involve cerebral as well as retinal processes. If, namely, the right eye look fixedly at a colored stripe whilst the left eye is closed, the left eye will get an after-image of the stripe when we open it and look at the background, closing in turn the right eye. A student, Mr. R. W. Black, to whom I was showing the experiment, suggested that the after-image might still belong to the shut right eye, combining its darkened field of view with the open left eye's brighter one. This objection to Mr. Binet's interpretation of the process as non-retinal is, at least, plausible. I have as yet been unable to devise an experimental combination for deciding conclusively between the two views.—W. J.

[2] That this was not due to suggestion or expectation, seems proved by its not invariably taking place with the same subject.

He is blind only to one individual stroke of that kind in a particular position on the board or paper,—that is, to a particular complex object; and, paradoxical as it may seem to say so, he must distinguish it with great accuracy from others like it, in order to remain blind to it when the others are brought near. He "apperceives" it, as a preliminary to not seeing it at all![3] How to conceive of this state of mind, is not easy. It would be much simpler to understand the process, if adding new strokes made the first one visible. There would then be two different objects apperceived as totals,—paper with one stroke, paper with two strokes; and, blind to the former, he would see all that was *in* the latter, because he would have apperceived it as a different total in the first instance.

A process of this sort occurs sometimes (not always) when the new strokes, instead of being mere repetitions of the original one, are lines which combine with it into a total object, say, a human face. The subject of the trance then may regain his sight of the line to which he had previously been blind, by seeing it as part of the face.

When by a prism before one eye a previously invisible line has been made visible to that eye, and the other eye is closed or screened, *its* closure makes no difference; the line still remains visible. But if *then* the prism is removed, the line will disappear even to the eye which a moment ago saw it, and both eyes will revert to their original blind state.[4]

We have, then, to deal in these cases neither with a sensorial anæsthesia, nor with a mere failure to notice, but with something much more complex; namely, an active counting out and positive exclusion of certain objects. It is as when one "cuts" an acquaintance, "ignores" a claim, or "refuses to be influenced" by a consideration of whose existence one remains aware. This, at least, expresses a provisional hypothesis which may reveal new facts by suggesting new observations to test its truth.

The delicacy of discrimination shown in recognizing the invisible line is often very great. The extraordinary mixture, in the hypnotic trance, of preternatural refinement of discrimination with the grossest insensibility, is one of the most remarkable features

[3] M. Ch. Féré was, so far as I know, the first to make this remark.

[4] The phenomenon is described as it most frequently happens. There have been some exceptions, and there are some curious variations in the visibility of the finger with which the subject points out the line he sees when he looks at it with both eyes open and the prism before one; but these we reserve for further study.

of the condition. A blank sheet of paper with machine-cut edges, without water-mark or anything which could lead to the recognition of one side or edge from the other, is shown to the subject, with the statement that it is a photograph of a well-known face. As soon as he distinctly sees the photograph upon its surface, he is told that it will float off from the paper, make a voyage round the walls of the room, and then return to the paper again. During this imaginary performance, he sees it successively on the various regions of the wall; but if the paper is meanwhile secretly turned over, and handed to him upside down, or with its under surface on top, he instantly recognizes the change, and, seeing *the portrait* in the altered position of the paper, turns the latter about "to get the portrait right." Here, then, is an hallucination, which, in traversing the room, can conquer the most discrepant backgrounds, but which peculiarities in the look of a sheet of paper, perceivable by no normal eye, can turn upside down! Sheets of paper absolutely indistinguishable by the bystanders, or by the subject himself when awake, are identified in trance, no matter how much they may be shuffled and mixed together, by the imaginary pictures they are supposed to bear. The hallucination is presumably determined by minute peculiarities in the paper, and yet it negates completely the paper's most flagrant characteristic, which is the blankness of its surface.[5] We have no comment to make on the psychic condition here, except to suggest its complexity, and its analogy to the psychic blindness previously described. Both states imply a preliminary process of discrimination and identification of the object really present, *followed* by its *apperception* or *conception* in falsified form. The conception is what the subject believes, and on it he acts. To what degree it carries actual *sensorial* brain-processes with it, is a matter for future research. That it *can* carry them is evident; for, as we have verified, the hallucination of a colored patch on a real white ground will sometimes be followed by a negative after-image when the gaze is transferred to another place. But, on the other hand, when subjects are asked to trace their hallucinations

[5] This reminds us a little of the state of mind in those perceptions called by Aubert "*secondäre Urtheilstäuschungen.*" The moon, e.g., appears to most people *small* through a telescope. The instrument enlarges all its details so that it seems *near*,—so near that we apparently think its retinal image ought to be larger if it were the same moon. *Ergo*, we deem it a smaller moon. In other words, our conclusion turns round and destroys its own premises.

with a pencil, or even to describe them minutely, they often show a vagueness and uncertainty which their previous expressions and actions would hardly have led one to expect.

Another very simple observation shows the delicacy of visual discrimination in the trance state. If a sheet of ruled foolscap paper, or a paper with a fine monotonous ornamental pattern printed on it, be shown to the subject, and *one* of the ruled lines or elements of the pattern be pointed to for an instant, and the paper immediately removed, he will then almost always, when after a short interval the paper is presented to him again, pick out the indicated line or element with infallible correctness. The operator, meanwhile, has either to keep his eye fixed upon it, or to make sure of its position by counting, in order not to lose its place.

This puts us on the track of a distinction between the normal and the trance mode of perception, which partly explains the latter. The evolution of man's mind is altogether in the analytic direction. He deals with objects by picking out their "essential" character, tracing its consequences, and ignoring other features. He remembers a house in a street by the one little inconspicuous detail of its number, very likely observing nothing else about it; and similarly he retains the line on the foolscap paper by not dispersing his attention over the sheet, but counting the number of lines between the one selected and the nearest edge. The number thus obtained is a permanent part of the mind's possession, and is obviously for practical purposes more exact than any reminiscence of the "general look" of the line in its place would be.

The trance-subject, however, surrenders himself to the general look. He disperses his attention impartially over the sheet. The place of the particular line touched is part of a "general effect" which he gets in its entirety, and which would be distorted if another line were touched instead. This general effect is lost upon the normal looker-on, bent as he is on concentration, analysis, and emphasis. What wonder, then, that, under these experimental conditions, the trance-subject excels him in touching the right line again? If he has time given him to count the line, he will excel the trance-subject; but, if the time be too short to count, he will best succeed by following the trance method, abstaining from analysis, and being guided by the "general look" of the line's place on the sheet. One is surprised at one's success in this the moment one gives up one's habitually analytic state of mind.

Is it too much to say that we have in this dispersion of the attention and subjection to the "general effect" something like a relapse into the state of mind of brutes? The trance-subject never gives any other reason for his optical discriminations, save that it "looks so." So a man, on a road once traversed inattentively before, takes a certain turn for no reason except that he *feels* as if it must be right. He is guided by a sum of impressions, not one of which is emphatic or distinguished from the rest, not one of which is essential, not one of which is conceived, but all of which together drive him to a conclusion to which nothing but *that* sum-total leads. Are not some of the wonderful discriminations of animals explicable in the same way? The cow finds her own stanchions in the long stable, the horse stops at the house he has once stopped at in the monotonous street, because no other stanchions, no other house, yield impartially *all* the impressions of the previous experience. The man, however, by seeking to make some one impression characteristic and essential, prevents the rest from having their effect. So that, if the (for him) essential feature be forgotten or changed, he is too apt to be thrown out altogether. The brute or the trance-subject may then seem to outstrip him in sagacity.

It ought to be said, that, in trying to verify in other ways this hypothesis of the trance-subject's non-analytic state of mind, we have met with exceptions which invite to further study. Certain it is that, when expressly stimulated thereto, trance-subjects will reason and analyze acutely. We therefore publish the above notes as suggestions to inquiry rather than as records of results.

The habitual psychic stagnancy of the trance-subject is shown by another simple test. If a lot of dots or strokes on a piece of paper be exhibited for a moment to a person in normal condition, with the request that he say how many are there, he will find that they break into groups in his mind's eye, and that whilst he is analyzing and counting one group the others dissolve. In short, the impression made by the dots changes rapidly into something else. In the trance-subject, on the contrary, it seems to *stick*; and, if the dots did not much exceed twenty, our patients counted them off in their mind's eye with ease.[6]

---

[6] The stagnancy of mind is also shown by the tranquil way in which the most incongruous suggestions are adopted A large silk handkerchief was made invisible by suggestion to one of our subjects, and then thrown over the body of a gentleman so as to hide all between his head and his knees. Naturally, as it was opaque as

This is all we can say at present of the hypnotic subject's mental state,—a topic whose investigation will tax the wit, but certainly reward the industry, of the most ingenious psychologist who may devote himself to its elucidation.

There was no sign of any sort of clairvoyance in either of the two advanced subjects above mentioned, nor, as tested by card guessing, in Mrs. P., the medium, when in the hypnotic condition. A very good student-subject, discovered by one of his comrades, was reported, on what seemed not bad evidence, to have named in his trance objects hidden from his sight; but, in the two sittings we had with him, nothing of the sort occurred. Indeed, on the second of these occasions, he was with difficulty kept entranced at all.

The only quite mysterious case of perception we found was with another subject, who in either six or seven different trials picked out from a heap of silver and copper change, consisting of from fourteen to twenty-two pieces, the one coin which had been contributed by his operator to the heap. He never made a false guess on the evenings when these successes occurred; and the only reason he could give for his choice was either that the coin *felt as if* it were the right one, or that it "felt heavy." The coins were of course arranged out of his sight; and in some of the later trials, though not in the whole series, express care was taken to see whether he might not have been guided to his choice by the right coin being *warmer* than the rest, but with a negative result. On *one* evening he altogether failed in this experiment. With handkerchiefs he was less uniformly successful. We shall continue these experiments, so as to ascertain, if possible, the nature of the clew which determined the subject's choice.

A direct difference in the effects of upward and downward passes, independent of suggestion or expectation, has always been part of the orthodox "magnetic" creed. But the recent flood of "scientific" literature on the subject is almost mute on this point. Dr. J. K. Mitchell of Philadelphia, a contemporary of Braid, whose caution, clearness, and cool head ought ere now to have secured for him a prominent name in the history of hypnotism,[7] admitted that the different effects of upward and downward passes were the only sign

---

well as invisible, it made invisible whatever it covered. "Is C. still in the room?" the subject was then asked. "His *head* is here," was the reply, made in a perfectly indifferent tone: "I don't know where his body is."

[7] See his *Five Essays*, edited by Dr. S. Weir Mitchell, Philadelphia [1859].

of a direct physical influence of operator upon subject which he was able to find. Our own experiments verified the difference in question in cases too numerous to be plausibly ascribed to accident. The young men upon whom the passes were made knew nothing of what we were seeking to test, and as often as not answered wrongly when asked later if they knew the direction in which the passes had been made. Yet in five or six individuals, upward passes, the first time they were tried, awoke the patient, or restored his hand, arm, etc., to its natural state, whilst downward passes had a precisely opposite effect. It is a curious thing to see the face of a man whose eyes and mouth have been shut tight by suggestion, and over whose face the operator makes passes in an upward direction on the right side, whilst he makes downward passes on the left. On being told to open their eyes and whistle, two or three such patients have opened upon us only the right eye, and whistled out of the right corner of their mouth. Others showed no difference whatever in their reaction to the different passes. The matter must be prosecuted further. Obviously, so long as it is under dispute, experiments, to prove anything, must be made with ignorant subjects, and must succeed the first time they are tried.

Besides the observations we have recorded, we verified most of the now classical and familiar phenomena of trance. A few curious observations on the *rapport* between operator and subject, and on the influence of magnets, had better be treated as coincidences for the present, because not found in the subject at different times. Our experience has impressed upon us the variability of the same subject's trance from one day to another. It may occur that a phenomenon met with one day, but not repeated, and therefore accounted a mere coincidence, is really due to a particular phase of the trance, realized on that occasion, but never again when sought for. To decide definitely between these alternatives, in the case of any special phenomenon, would obviously require many sittings and consume much time.

WILLIAM JAMES
GOUVERNEUR M. CARNOCHAN

A Suggestion for the Prevention of
Sea-Sickness

Harvard College,
Cambridge, Mass., May 12, 1887.

Mr. Editor,—Some years ago, whilst studying the feeling of dizziness, I was led to discover the singular immunity from it which deaf-mutes, as a class, possess; and in an article published in the *American Journal of Otology*, for October of that year, I ascribed this immunity to the destruction either of the auditory nerves or of their labyrinthine termination. I found, moreover, in deaf-mutes what seemed signs of a possible immunity from sea-sickness; and ventured the suggestion that the semi-circular canals were probably the starting-point of that affection also, and that its symptoms in an ordinary sufferer might perhaps be alleviated by blistering or otherwise counter-irritating the skin around the ears. Later, I thought, that in crossing the English Channel I had prevented an attack of sea-sickness in myself by simply rubbing my mastoid processes with my fingers. I have been unable to get any one else (such is the inertia of the human beings amongst whom our lot is cast!) even to try the experiment—which I should think might succeed in a short voyage even if it failed in a long one. Later, a New York physician (whose pamphlet I have mislaid, and whose name I am ashamed to say I cannot momentarily recall) defended the same theory in a very interesting manner, and, if I remember aright, drew from it similar therapeutic consequences. My present object in writing is to take advantage of a newspaper article which has been sent me, to bring the matter once more before the attention of the profession, and to stimulate experimentation, if possible. The editor of the *Gulf View*, of Cedar Key, Florida, in the number for April 2d, of that Journal, gives the following interesting account of his own case:

"In the year 1859 he received a blow from behind on the mastoid process, just behind the right ear, crushing the outer table of the skull and destroying the delicate nervous portion of the internal ear, including these same semi-circular canals, alluded to, as being absent or negative in deaf-mutes. The immediate consequences of the injury were, first, the most distressing nausea of a character identical with that of seasickness, which lasted with intervals of ease for two or three days, and secondly, complete destruction of the function of the organ, the ear of that side being totally dead ever after. Shortly after convalescence, the writer made a voyage to Cuba and back, in rough weather, exposed to a very rough sea for six days on the voyage over, and the same time returning, and to his agreeable surprise, though previously very susceptible, he found himself to be proof against seasickness, and the immunity has continued to this day, nearly, twenty-eight years."

This editor adds, having seen some chance allusion to my suggestion in another paper, that, "It would be queer, if from these incidents and inductions, we should arrive at a knowledge of a sure means of obviating the horrors of the *mal du mer*, which seems not improbable, and the suggestions made by Dr. James of the use of friction, or counter irritation as a remedy, is surely worthy of careful and extended trial, coupled with such other remedies as our improved knowledge of the causes of the disease may suggest. We shall await the result with interest."

Will not you and other leaders of opinion give publicity to this subject and urge travellers to try so simple an experiment? The yachting and travelling season is about to begin. It would seem, if public attention were well attracted to the matter, that by next autumn we ought to have enough cases of trial either to prove or to disprove what at present remains a mere hypothesis. I need not say how glad I should be to receive information either of distinct failure or distinct success.   Very truly yours,

                                                        WM. JAMES

Reaction-Time in the Hypnotic Trance

The time which intervenes between the giving of an expected signal and the making of a movement (previously determined upon) in response thereto, is called in the works on physiology, "the simple reaction-time" of the subject experimented on. This reaction-time varies from one subject to another, and varies in the same subject when certain conditions vary. It ranges, in ordinary subjects, from one-tenth to three-tenths of a second, or more.

One of the conditions which makes it vary seems to be the hypnotic state. In a suggestive paper published in *Mind* (Vol. VIII, p. 170, 1883) by Professor G. Stanley Hall, the normal and hypnotic reaction-times of a certain subject are given (averaged) as follows:

Before hypnotization.	Hypnotized.	After waking.
0.328 Sec.	0.193 Sec.	0.348 Sec.

In the spring of 1885 I made similar measurements on three different hypnotic subjects, with results different from Professor Hall's. I have kept them until now, hoping to be able to add to them; but as there seems small immediate prospect in that direction, I publish what I have ascertained.

The subjects were Seniors in Harvard College, intelligent, and apparently quite normal men. I will call them A, C, and M, respectively. I had hypnotized them all several times before these observations were made, and they went off easily when a few "passes" were made before their face. The signal was the sound of a smart stroke which closed a galvanic circuit. The reaction consisted in raising the hand from a telegraph key and thereby opening the same circuit. A magnetic pen, interposed on the circuit, marked the instants of its closing and opening upon the smoked paper of a revolving drum (Baltzar's Kymograph); whilst a tuning-fork, vibrating fifty times a second, transmitted to the same paper a line of waves which served as measurer of time. With A, three experiments were made on three different days. C and M were each tried twice, on different days. In all, 810 reactions were traced. The results are as follows, times being expressed in thousandths of a second:

"Subject" and Date.	Number of Reactions.	Average times before Trance.	Number of Reactions.	Average times during Trance.	Number of Reactions.	Average times after Trance.
A. May 1 . . .	27	306	32	294		
May 5 . . .	63	207	74	203		
May 19 . . .	53	204	54	304	52	163
C. May 1 . . .	21	199	51	340		
May 19 . . .	45	282	21	546 [1]	55	166
M. May 5 . . .	31	214	75	292		
May 15 . . .	46	224	53	286	57	209

What one first remarks upon reading these figures is the irregularity of the results. In five of the seven observations made, the reaction-time during trance was considerably longer than the normal reaction-time taken before hypnotizing the subject. In the other two observations it was a very little shorter. The two trances in which it was shortened occurred in the same subject, A, in whom, on another occasion, it was considerably lengthened. This shows that the idiosyncrasy of the subject has nothing to do with the matter, but that it depends on some change of inward condition.

[1] This figure is less than the real average, as the 21 reactions counted were only a part of those made and embraced all the shorter ones, the rest being omitted to save the toil of the counting.

In the three observations in which the reaction-time after trance was recorded, it fell not only below the trance-time but below the normal time before trance. In one subject, C, the fall was very marked. In Professor Hall's subject, the reactions were made half-an-hour after waking the subject, whilst mine were made but five or six minutes later. Taking my three observations as they stand, one might well interpret them by saying that the hypnotic trance inhibits neural processes, and makes them slower, and that when the trance goes off the release from the inhibited condition expresses itself in a proportionate acceleration. This would sound pretty. But the case of A on May 19 forbids one to range it under any such simple conception. In point of fact, A seemed wide-awake when he began his reactions after the trance. But we found, after he had ended them, that he had relapsed into the trance during their performance. It was not outwardly apparent at what moment the relapse occurred, for all the reactions I am describing were executed with closed eyes, so as not to interfere with the concentration of the attention on the acoustic signal. If we average the first and second halves of the record separately, we find 0.175 seconds for the time of the first 26 reactions and 0.152 for the last 26 reactions. The rapider half of the record must have contained the trance-reactions. The slowest reactions after trance of all were in this case at the very beginning of the record, namely (counted in vibrations of the fork): 33, 26½, 20, 21, 22½, 17, 22, 21. Only two reactions later among the whole 54 rose into the twenties.

To sum up, it is clear that there is no simple hypnotic state which can be quoted as having a determinate effect on the reaction-time. There are hypnotic and post-hypnotic *states* which vary very much, and some of which retard, whilst others quicken, the reactions.[2] These states may very likely shade rapidly into each other. Of other marks, by which to discriminate them, we know nothing.

Professor Hall found the deviations from the average time to be less when his subject was hypnotized, than when awake. In my observations the opposite was the case, so far as I have made the calculations. In C's record on May 19 one need only look at the

---

[2] For instance, Professor Hall's subject was an admirably prompt and varied histrionic subject, who would copiously act out every suggestion. But my subject C, although he could easily be hallucinated in any desired way, seemed always very drowsy and slow of response during his trance. If left to himself he invariably fell fast asleep.

tracings to see how much more the several trance-reactions differ from each other than do the several normal actions from each other. The least average error in C's record on this day is when his times were shortest, namely, after waking from the trance. A bare inspection of the record shows this. I averaged all the deviations above (+) and all those below (—) the average reaction-time of the case of A on May 19. They run as follows in seconds:

Before Trance.	During Trance.	After Trance.
$+0.032$	$+0.095$	$+0.023$
-0.018	-0.053	-0.075

I can thus, so far as I have examined my data, draw no general conclusions from them about the average deviation. The only lesson of the facts I report seems to be that we should beware of making rash generalizations from few cases about the hypnotic state. That name probably covers a very great number of different neural conditions. The general drift of recent investigation has tended to bring this into clearer and clearer light; and the little peppercorn of testimony which I herewith offer will perhaps not be regarded as entirely worthless if it be considered as corroborative of what more important investigations have in their way shown.

The Consciousness of Lost Limbs

Many persons with lost limbs still seem to feel them in their old place. This illusion is so well known, and the material for study is so abundant, that it seems strange that no more systematic effort to investigate the phenomenon should have been made. Dr. Weir Mitchell's observations in his work on *Injuries of Nerves* (1872) are the most copious and minute with which I am acquainted. They reveal such interesting variations in the consciousness in question, that I began some years ago to seek for additional observations, in the hope that out of a large number of data, some might emerge which would throw on these variations an explanatory light.

The differences in question are principally these:

1. Some patients preserve consciousness of the limb after it has been lost; others do not.

2. In some it appears always in one fixed position; in others its apparent position changes.

3. In some the position can be made to seem to change by an effort of will; in others no effort of will can make it change; in rare cases it would even seem that the very attempt to will the change has grown impossible.

I have obtained first-hand information from a hundred and eighty-five amputated persons. Some of this was gained by personal interviews; but much the larger portion consists of replies to a

circular of questions of which I sent out some eight hundred copies
to addresses furnished me by some of the leading makers of artificial
limbs.[1]

The results are disappointing, in that they fail to explain the
causes of the enumerated differences. But they tell certain things
and suggest reflections which I here set down for the use of future
inquirers.[2]

First, as to the relative frequency of the feeling of the lost parts.
It existed at the time of answering my interrogatories in about
three-quarters of the cases of which I have reports. I say in *about*
the proportion of cases, for many of the answers were not quite
clear. It had existed in a much larger proportionate number, but
had faded out before the time of answering. Some had ceased to
feel it "immediately," or "an hour or two" after the amputation.
In others it had lasted weeks, months, or years. The oldest case I
have is that of a man who had had a thigh amputation performed
at the age of thirteen years, and who, after he was seventy, affirmed
his feeling of the lost foot to be still every whit as distinct as his
feeling of the foot which remained. Amongst my one hundred and
seventy-nine cases only seven are of the upper extremity. In all of
these, the sense of the lost hand remained.

The consciousness of the lost limb varies from acute pain, pricking, itching, burning, cramp, uneasiness, numbness, etc., in the
toes, heel, or other place, to feelings which are hardly perceptible,
or which become perceptible only after a good deal of "thinking."
The feeling is not due to the condition of the stump, for in both
painful and healthy stumps it may be either present or absent.
Where it is distinct both the lost foot or hand and the stump are
felt simultaneously, each in its own place. The hand and foot are
usually the only lost parts very distinctly felt, the intervening tracts

[1] For these addresses I have to thank Messrs. Fisk & Arnold, of Boston; Marks, and
Wicket & Bradley, of New York; Clement, and Osborne, of Philadelphia; and
Douglass, of Springfield, Mass.

[2] One lesson from them is that in a delicate inquiry like this, little is to be
gained by distributing circulars. A single patient with the right sort of lesion and a
scientific mind, carefully cross-examined, is more likely to deepen our knowledge
than a thousand circulars answered as the average patient answers them, even
though the answers be never so thoroughly collated by the investigator. This is
becoming apparent in many lines of psychological inquiry; and we shall probably,
ere long, learn the limits within which the method of circulars is likely to be used
with fruit.

seeming to disappear. A man, for example, whose arm was cut off at the shoulder-joint told me that he felt his hand budding immediately from his shoulder. This is, however, not constantly the case by any means. Many patients with thigh amputation feel, more or less distinctly, their knee, or their calf. But even where they do not, the foot may seem separate from the stump, though possibly located nearer it than natural. A second shoulder-joint case says his arm seems to lie on his breast, centrally with fingers closed on palm just as it did eight or ten hours before amputation.

It is a common experience, during the first weeks after amputation, for the patient to forget that his leg is gone. Many patients tell how they met with accidents, by rising suddenly and starting to walk as if their leg were still there, or by getting out of bed in the same way. Others tell how they have involuntarily put down their hand to scratch their departed foot. One man writes that he found himself preparing with scissors to cut its nails, so distinctly did he feel them. Generally the position of the lost leg follows that of the stump and artificial leg. If one is flexed the other seems flexed; if one is extended so is the other; if one swings in walking the other swings with it. In a few correspondents, however, the lost leg maintains a more or less fixed position of its own, independent of the artificial leg. One such man told me that he felt as if he had three legs in all, getting sometimes confused, in coming down stairs, between the artificial leg which he put forwards, and the imaginary one which he felt bent backwards and in danger of scraping its toes upon the steps just left behind. Dr. Mitchell tells of certain arms which appeared fixedly in the last painful attitude they had occupied before amputation. One of my correspondents writes that he feels constantly a blister on his heel which was there at the time of his accident; another that he had chilblains at the time of the accident, and feels them still on his toes.

The differences in the apparent mobility of the lost part, when felt, are strange. About a hundred of the cases who feel (say) their feet, affirm that they can "work" or "wiggle" their toes at will. About fifty of them deny that they have any such power. This again is not due to the condition of the stump, for both painful and healthy stumps are found equally amongst those who can and amongst those who cannot "work their toes." Almost always when the will is exerted to move the toes, actual contraction may be perceived in the muscles of the stump. One might, therefore, expect that where the toe-moving muscles were cut off, the sense of the toes being moved might disappear. But this is not the case. I have cases of thigh amputation, in which all the foot-moving muscles are gone, and yet in which the feet or toes seem to move at will. And I have cases of lower-leg amputation in which, though the foot-moving muscles contract in the stump, the toes or feet feel motionless.

But although, in a gross sense, we are thus forced to conclude that neither the state of the stump nor the place of the amputation absolutely determines the differences of consciousness which different individuals show, it is nevertheless hard to believe that they are not amongst the more important influencing conditions of the illusion which we are studying. On *a priori* grounds it seems as if they must be so. What is the phenomenon? It is what is commonly known as the extradition, or projection outwards, of a sensation whose *immediate* condition is the stimulation of a central organ of perception by an incoming nerve or nerves. As the optical centres respond to stimulation by the feeling of forms and colors, and the acoustic centres by that of sounds, so do certain other centres respond by the feeling of a foot, with its toes, heel, etc. This feeling is what Johannes Müller called the "specific energy" of the neural tracts involved. It makes no difference how the tracts are excited, that feeling of a foot is their only possible response. So long as they feel at all, what they feel is the foot.[3] In the normal state the foot thus felt is located where the eye can see and the hand touch it. When the foot which the eye sees and the hand touches is cut off,

---

[3] It would seem that, even in the case of congenital defect of the extremities, the brain-centres might feel in the usual ancestral way. "A nineteen-year-old girl and a man in the forties, who had each but one normal hand, the other, instead of fingers, having only little prominences of skin without bones or muscles, thought they bent their absent fingers when they bent the deformed stump. Tickling these eminences, or binding a string about the fore-arm, caused the same sensations as in amputated persons, and a pressure on the ulnar nerve made the outer fingers tingle. In the same way persons born with a much shortened arm have stated the length of this member to be greater than it really was. An individual whose right fore-arm almost entirely failed, so that the dwarfed hand seemed to spring from the elbow, was conscious of the misshapen arm as normal and almost as long as the other." I quote this remarkable passage from Valentin's *Lehrbuch der Physiologie des Menschen*, Vol. II, p. 609. Valentin gives a number of references to the contemporaneous literature of the subject, and his own remarks, which occupy several pages, are well worth reading, even now.

still the immediate inner feeling of it persists so long as the brain-centres retain their functions; and, *in the absence of any counter-motive*, it ought, one would think, to continue located about where it used to be. There would be a counter-motive, if nerves which in the unamputated man went to the foot and were excited every time the foot was touched, were to find themselves, after the amputation, excited every time the *stump* was touched. The foot-feeling (which the nerves would continue to give) being then associated with the stump-contacts, would end (by virtue of a law of perception of which I made mention in *Mind* for 1887, p. 196) by locating itself at the place at which those contacts were believed, on the testimony of the eye and the hand, to occur. In other words, the foot-feeling would fuse with the feeling resident in the stump. In but few cases does this seem to occur;[4] and the reason is easily found. At the places where the amputation is apt to be made, the nerves which supply the foot are all buried deeply in the tissues. Superficial contact with the stump never excites, therefore, the sensibility of the foot-nerves. All ordinary contacts of the stump, thus failing to awaken the foot-feeling in any noticeable way, that feeling fails to grow associated with the stump's experiences; and when (on exceptional occasions) deep pressure of the stump awakens not only its own local cutaneous feeling but the foot-feelings due to the deeper-lying nerve, the two feelings still keep distinct in location as in quality.

There is, usually, in fact, a positive reason against their local fusion. More than one of my correspondents writes that the lost foot is best felt when the end of the stump receives the thrust of the artificial leg. Whenever the old foot is thus most felt at the moment when the artificial foot is seen to touch the ground, *that* place of contact (being both important and interesting) should be the place with which the foot-feeling would associate itself (by virtue of the mental law already referred to). In other words, we should project our foot-feeling upon the ground, as we used to before we lost the member, and we should feel it follow the movements of the artificial limb.[5] An observation of Dr. Mitchell's corroborates this view. One

---

[4] I have found none. Dr. Mitchell reports one at least, in which the lost hand lay "seemingly *within* the stump" (p. 356. Cf. also p. 351). This was an upper-arm amputation.

[5] The principle here is the same as that by which we project to the extremity of any instrument with which we are probing, tracing, cutting, etc., the sensations

of his patients "lost his leg at the age of eleven, and remembers that the foot by degrees approached, and at last reached, the knee. When he began to wear an artificial leg it reassumed, in time, its old position, and he is never, at present, aware of the leg as shortened, unless for some time he talks and thinks of the stump and of the missing leg, when . . . the direction of attention to the part causes a feeling of discomfort, and the subjective sensation of active and unpleasant movement of the toes. With these feelings returns at once the delusion of the foot as being placed at the knee."[6]

The latter half of this man's experience shows that the principles I have invoked (though probably quite sound as far as they go) are not exhaustive, and that, between fusion with the stump and projection to the end of the artificial limb, the intermediate positions of the foot remain unaccounted for. It will not do to call them vague remains of the old normal habit of projection, for often they are not vague, but quite precise. Leaving this phenomenon on one side, however, let us see what more our principles can do.

In the first place they oblige us to invert the popular way of looking at the problem. The popular mind wonders how the lost feet can still be felt. For us, the cases for wonder are those in which the lost feet are not felt. The first explanation which one clutches at, for the loss, is that the nerve-centres for perception may degenerate and grow atrophic when the sensory nerve-terminations which normally stimulate them are cut off. Extirpation of the eyeballs causes such atrophy in the occipital lobes of the brain. The spinal cord has been repeatedly found shrunken at the point of entrance of the nerves from amputated limbs. And there are a few carefully reported cases in which the degeneration has been traced ascending to the cortical centres, along with an equal number of cases in which no such ascending degeneration could be found.[7] A degenerated centre can of course no longer give rise to its old feelings; and where the centres are degenerated, that fact explains all-sufficiently why the lost member can no longer be felt. But it is impossible to range all the cases of non-feeling under this head. Some of them date from the first hours after the operation, when degeneration is out of the question. In some the perceptive centres are proved to

---

which the instrument communicates to our hand when it presses the foreign matter with which it is in contact.

[6] *Injuries of Nerves*, Philadelphia, 1872, p. 352.

[7] François-Franck: *Leçons sur les fonctions motrices du cerveau*, 1887, p. 291.

be there by exciting electrically the nerve-trunks buried in the stump. "I recently faradised," says Dr. Mitchell, "a case of dis-articulated shoulder without warning my patient of the possible result. For two years he had altogether ceased to feel the limb. As the current affected the brachial plexus of nerves, he suddenly cried aloud, 'Oh, the hand, the hand!' and attempted to seize the missing member. The phantom I had conjured up swiftly disappeared, but no spirit could have more amazed the man, so real did it seem."[8]

In such a case as this last, the only hypothesis that remains to us is to suppose that the nerve-ends are so softly embedded in the stump as, under ordinary conditions, to carry up no impressions to the brain, or none strong enough to be noticeable. Were they carried, the patient would feel, and feel a foot. Not feeling the foot, and yet being capable of feeling it (as the faradization proves), it must be either that no impressions are carried, or else that for some reason they do not appeal to consciousness. Now it is a general law of consciousness that feelings of which we make no practicable use tend to become more and more overlooked. Helmholtz has explained our habitual insensibility to double images, to the so-called *muscæ volitantes* caused by specks in the humors of the eye, to the upper harmonics which accompany various sounds, as so many effects of the persistent abstraction of our attention from impressions which are of no use. It may be that in certain subjects this sort of abstraction is able to complete our oblivescence of a lost foot; our feeling of it has been already reduced almost to the vanishing point, by reason of the shielded condition of the nerve-ends, just assigned. The feeling of the lost foot tells us absolutely nothing which can practically be of use to us.[9] It is a superfluous item in our conscious baggage. Why may it not be that some of us are able to cast it out of our mind on that account? Until a few years ago all oculists believed that a similar superfluity, namely, the second set of images seen by the squinting eye in squinters, was cast out of consciousness so persistently that the eye grew actually blind. And, although the competency of the explanation has probably been disproved as regards the blindness, yet there is no doubt that it is quite competent to prove an almost invincible *unconsciousness* of the images cast upon a squinting eye.

[8] *Op. cit.*, p. 349.
[9] Except the approach of storms; but then it is in cases where the feeling is preserved.

Unconsciousness from habitual inattention is, then, probably one factor in the oblivescence of lost extremities,—a factor which, however, we must regard as unavailing where impressions from the nerve-ends are strong.[10]

Let us next consider the differences in regard to the illusion of voluntary movement in the lost parts. Most of the patients who seem to themselves able to move their lost feet, hands, etc., at will, produce a distinct contraction of the muscles of the stump whenever they make the voluntary effort. As the principle of specific energies easily accounted for the consciousness of the lost limb being there at all, so here another principle, almost as universally adopted by psychologists, accounts as easily for the consciousness of movement in it, and leaves the real puzzle to reside rather in those cases in which the illusion of movement fails to exist.

The principle I refer to is that of the inheritance of ancestral habit. It is all but unanimously admitted at the present day that any two experiences, which during ancestral generations have been invariably coupled together, will have become so indissolubly associated that the descendant will not be able to represent them in his mind apart. Now of all possible coupled experiences it is hard to imagine any pair more uniformly and incessantly coupled than the feeling of effected contraction of muscles, on the one hand, and that of the changed position of the parts which they move, on the other. From the earliest ancestors of ours which had feet, down to the present day, the movement of the feet must always have accompanied the contraction of the muscles; and here, if anywhere, habit's hereditary consequences ought to be found, if the principle that habits are transmitted from one generation to another is sound at

---

[10] I have quoted my hundred and forty-odd patients as feeling their lost member, as if they all felt it *positively*. But many of those who say they feel it seem to feel it *dubiously*. Either they only feel it occasionally, or only when it pains them, or only when they try to move it; or they only feel it when they "think a good deal about it" and make an effort to conjure it up. When they "grow inattentive," the feeling "flies back," or "jumps back to the stump." Every degree of consciousness, from complete and permanent hallucination, down to something hardly distinguishable from ordinary fancy, seems represented in the sense of the missing extremity which these patients say they have. Indeed I have seldom seen a more plausible lot of evidence for the view that imagination and sensation are but differences of vividness in an identical process, than these confessions, taking them altogether, contain. Many patients say they can hardly tell whether they feel or fancy the limb.

all.[11] No sooner then should the brain-centres for perceiving muscular contractions be excited, than those other centres functionally consolidated with them ought to share the excitement, and produce a consciousness that the foot has moved. If it be objected to this that this latter consciousness ought to be ideal rather than sensational in character, and ought therefore not to produce a fully developed illusion, it is sufficient to point to what happens in many illusions of the same type. In these illusions the mind, sensibly impressed by what seems a part of a certain probable fact, forthwith *perceives* that fact in its entirety. The parts supplied by the mind are in these cases no whit inferior in vividness and reality to those actually impressing the sense.[12] In all perception, indeed, but half of the object comes from without. The larger half usually comes out of our own head. We can ourselves produce an illusion of movement similar to those which we are studying by putting some unyielding substance (hard rubber, *e.g.*) between our back teeth and biting hard. It is difficult not to believe that our front teeth approach each other, when we feel our biting muscles contract.[13] In ourselves the feeling of the real position of the jaws persists unchanged to contradict the false suggestion. But when we recall that in the amputated no such positive contradiction can occur, since the parts are gone, we see how much easier it must be in their case for the false sense of movement to flourish unchecked.[14]

[11] In saying that if it is sound, then the explanation which I offer follows, I wish to retain reserved rights as to the general question of its soundness, regarding which evidence seems to me as yet somewhat incomplete. But the explanation which I offer could base itself on the invariable associations of the individual's experience, even if the hereditary transmission of habitual associations proved not to be a law of nature.

[12] They are vivid and real in proportion to the inveterateness of their association with the parts which impress the sense. The most perfect illusions are those of false motion, relief, or concavity, changed size, distance, etc., produced when, by artificial means, an object gives us sensations, or forces us to move our eyes in ways ordinarily suggestive of the presence of an entirely different object. We *see* then the latter object directly, although it is not there. The after-image of a rectangular cross, of a circle, change their shapes when we project them on to an oblique surface; and the new shape, which is demonstrably a reproduction of earlier sense-impressions, feels just like a present sense-impression.

[13] See for another example Sternberg, in Pflüger's *Archiv*, Bd. 37, S. 1. The author even goes so far as to lay it down as a general rule that we ordinarily judge a movement to be executed as soon as we have given the impulse.

[14] Out of the ninety-eight of my cases who feel their limbs to move, there are forty-three who can produce no feeling of movement in the lost extremity without

But how, then, comes it that there can be any patients who lack the false sense in question? In one hundred and forty of my cases, about fifty lacked it completely; and even when the stump-muscles contract violently, many patients are unable to feel any change at all in the position of the imaginary extremity. This is not due to the fact that the amputation is made above the origin of the hand-or-foot-moving muscles; for there are eleven cases where these muscles remain and contract, but yet no sense of movement exists. I must say that I can offer no clear solution of this anomaly. It must be left over, together with those obstinate cases of partial apparent shortening of which we spoke above, for future investigators to treat.

One reflection, however, seems pertinent to the entire set of phenomena we have studied. They form a group in which the variations from one individual to another, if they exist at all, are likely to become extreme. Darwin notices that no organs in animals are so subject to variation as rudimentary organs. Being functionless, selection has no hold on them, the environment exerts no influence to keep them up (or down) to the proper standard, and the consequence is that their aberrations are unchecked. Now phantasms of lost legs and arms are to the mental organism just what rudimentary organs are to the bodily organism. They have no longer any real relations with the environment, being mere vestiges of something which formerly had real relations. The environment does not correct such a phantasm for any odd course it may get into. If it slips away altogether, the environment lets it go, and doesn't call it back. If it happen "by accident" to harden itself in a fixed position, or shorten itself, or to dissolve connection with its ancestral associates in the way of muscular feeling, the accident is not repaired; and experience, which throughout the rest of our mental life puts prompt bounds to too great eccentricity, here lets it luxuriate unrebuked. I do not know how far one ought to push this idea. But

---

visibly contracting the muscles of the stump. But (leaving out doubtful cases) twelve of the others positively affirm that, after the most careful examination, no contractions can be detected in the stump, whilst yet the extremity seems to move at will. One such case I observed myself. The man had an amputation of the upper arm. He seemed to himself to flex his fingers at will; but I could perceive no change whatever in the stump. The thought of the movement seemed here a sufficient suggestion; as in those anæsthetic cases where the patient thinks of a movement and wills it, and then (if his eyes are closed) fancies it executed, even though the limb be held still by the bystanders.

(what we can call by no better name but) accident or idiosyncrasy certainly plays a great part in all our neural and mental processes, especially the higher ones. We can never seek amongst these processes for results which shall be invariable. Exceptions remain to every empirical law of our mental life, and can only be treated as so many individual aberrations. It is perhaps something to have pointed out the department of lost-limb-consciousness as that in which the aberrant individuals are likely to reach their maximum number.

The apparent changes of temperature of the lost parts form an interesting chapter, which, however, I will not discuss. Suffice it to say, that in many patients the lost foot can be made to feel warm or cold by warming or cooling the stump. A draught of air on the stump produces the feeling of a draught on the foot. The lost foot also sympathizes sometimes with the foot which remains. If one is cold, the other feels cold. One man writes that whenever he walks through puddles and wets his sound foot, his lost foot feels wet too.

My final observations are on a matter which ought to interest students of "psychic research." Surely if there be any distant material object with which a man might be supposed to have clairvoyant or telepathic relations, that object ought to be his own cut-off arm or leg. Accordingly, a very wide-spread belief will have it, that when the cut-off limb is maltreated in any way, the man, no matter where he is, will feel the injury. I have nearly a score of communications on this point, some believing, more incredulous. One man tells of experiments of warming, etc., which the doctor in an adjoining room made on the freshly cut-off leg, without his knowledge, and of which his feelings gave him no suspicion. Of course, did such telepathic *rapport* exist, it need not necessarily be found in every case. But in none of the cases of my collection in which the writers seek to prove it does their conclusion inspire confidence. All (with perhaps one exception which, unfortunately, I have lost) are vaguely told; and, indeed, amongst all the pains which come and go in the first weeks of amputation, it would be strange if some did not coincide with events happening to the buried or "pickled" limb. One man writes me that he has dug up his buried leg eight times, and changed its position. He asks me to advise him whether to dig it up again, saying he "dreads to."

In concluding, I repeat that I have been able to throw no new light of a positive sort on those individual differences, the explanation of which was the aim of my inquiry. I have, perhaps, by invoking certain well-known principles, succeeded in making the fundamental illusions, that of the existence, and that of the movement of the lost part, seem less paradoxical, and the exceptions to these illusions less odd than they have hitherto appeared. But, on the whole, I leave the subject where I took it up from Dr. Weir Mitchell's hands; and one of the main effects of the investigation on my own mind is admiration for the manner in which he wrote about it fifteen years ago.

What the Will Effects

The science of Man in our generation has started on a new career. Our ancestors considered him as something set over against Nature and opposed to all her laws and ways. We, on the contrary, are beginning to regard him as Nature's flower, possessing nothing not ultimately drawn from her influences—her showers, her breezes and her soil. Psychology has shared in the general awakening. We begin to hear the phrase "the new Psychology." "Physiological Psychology," "Psychophysics" have become the titles of accredited departments of literature. To know how to handle a chronograph, or a Bunsen cell, and to dissect out a frog's sciatic nerve, even if not a dog's, are beginning to be held as important requisites in a professor of mental science, as that polite learning and power of introspection, which were formerly an all-sufficient equipment for his work.

Rich as are already in some respects the results of this natural-history method of studying human nature, it must be confessed that, in the main, what it has brought forth is more an accumulation of materials from which to draw future conclusions than any very important new conclusion itself. None of the old classical problems of Psychology have received their definitive quietus at the hands of the zoological school; and what animates the enthusiasm of us disciples is less the sense of the great things which we have already done than of those which we are probably upon the eve of doing. In many departments of psychology, however, genuine progress has been made, not only in the way of collecting materials, but in that of clearly conceiving their relations. The Psychology of Volition is an example; and, if the reader is so disposed, we will spend an hour together in asking what happens according to recent Psychology, whenever we exert our will.

The only conception at the same time renovating and fundamental with which Biology has enriched Psychology, the only *essential* point in which "the new Psychology" is an advance upon the old, is, it seems to me, the very general, and by this time very familiar notion, that all our activity belongs at bottom to the type of reflex action, and that all our consciousness accompanies a chain of events of which the first was an incoming current in some sensory nerve, and of which the last will be a discharge into some muscle, blood-vessel, or gland. This chain of events may be simple and rapid, as when we wink at a blow; or it may be intricate and prolonged, as when we hear a momentous bit of news and deliberate before deciding what to do. But its normal end is always some activity. Viewed in this light the thinking and feeling portions of our life seem little more than half-way houses towards behavior; and recent Psychology accordingly tends to treat consciousness more and more as if it existed only for the sake of the conduct which it seems to introduce, and tries to explain its peculiarities (so far as they can be explained at all) by their practical utility. Mr. Spencer, by his broad description of mental life as "adjustment to the environment" has done more than any English writer to popularize this view. My writing of this article is just as much a self-maintaining reaction of mine upon my environment as my flinching from a blow would be.

Some reactions are involuntary and others are voluntary; and the first point which "the new Psychology" scores, is that the voluntary reactions are all derived from the involuntary. This is a point easy to make clear. In a former article (see "What Is an Instinct?" vol. I, p. 355) I discussed the involuntary reactions. They are commonly divided into three kinds, reflex acts, manifestations of emotion, and instinctive or impulsive performances. But from a scientific point of view these distinctions are unmeaning, for the physiological process is in all our involuntary actions essentially one and the same. The other day I was standing at a railroad station with a little child, when an express-train went thundering by.

The child, who was near the edge of the platform, started, winked, had his breathing convulsed, turned pale, burst out crying, and ran frantically towards me and hid his face. Here were so many involuntary discharges let loose by the same stimulus. But there was no essential difference between them from the point of view of their causation and mode of execution. The winking and starting we name reflex, the effects on pulse, breathing and tear-glands emotional, and the running and hiding, instinctive acts; but these terms are obviously mere practical conveniences; and in all concrete cases of reaction upon an impression organs of all classes, glands, blood-vessels, and muscles of every description, are affected at one and the same time.

Now in these involuntary reactions the creature can know what he is going to do only after he has done it, if I may express myself by such an Irish bull. Every time we first perform an action of this sort, it takes us by surprise. I have no doubt that that child was almost as astonished by his own behavior as he was by the train, and more than I was who stood by. Of course, if such a reaction has already many times occurred, we learn what to expect of ourselves, and can then foresee our conduct even though it remain as involuntary and uncontrollable as it was before.

But in *voluntary* action properly so called the act is foreseen from the very first. The idea of it always precedes its execution. This, as all will admit, is the *sine quâ non* and essence of every voluntary action. And it is an immediate consequence of this that no act can possibly be voluntary the first time it is performed. Until we have done it at least once, we can have no idea of what sort of a thing it is like, and do not know in what direction to set our will to bring it about. One cannot will into the void. Most of us have never moved our ears; none of us have stopped our hearts. If we knew how to start we might set to work to learn these feats. But we can't tell in which direction to begin, or what particular sort of effort to make. It is like suddenly telling a man to utter any sentence he pleases in the Ethiopian tongue. The problem is altogether indeterminate. What we need is a more definite idea of just what we are to do. Now what constitutes our definite idea of just what any movement is? If the reader will carefully consider the matter, he will be able, I think, to give only one answer. Our idea of a movement is our image of the way in which we shall feel when it is in process of doing or is done. Our idea of raising our arm for example, or of crooking our finger, is a sense, more or less vivid, of how the raised arm, or the crooked finger, feels. There is no other idea than this, or any other mental material out of which an idea might be made. We cannot possibly have any idea of our ears' motion until our ears have moved. This is why most of us cannot make even a vain effort to move these organs. They have never moved. If we wished to learn to move them (and many of us might learn, with perseverance) the first thing would be to move them passively with our fingers in the right direction, until we had a pretty clear idea of how the movement felt. Only then could we begin to train our voluntary power. This is why we begin to teach children to write by "holding their hand," to look through a telescope by telling them to hold one eyelid closed; and in general why the acquisition of all feats of address is accelerated by a bystander helping our recalcitrant members into position. Without such aid we must wait for some random contortion to hit the right attitude and give us an idea of just what it is at which we are to aim.

It thus appears that voluntary activity must be regarded as always of a secondary and never of a primary sort. It must come consecutively to activity of an involuntary kind. The movements which it consciously intends must once have been performed with no intention, or it could not intend them. Our forefathers were hazy as to this. They thought the will could exert its effects *ex abrupto*. We now see clearly that it can only go to work on reminiscences of earlier movement; that a creature without memory can have no will; and that all the contractions of which the most complex volitional utterances are composed must originally have been random or instinctive expressions of our automatic life.[1] The works of Bain, Maudsley and Sully copiously illustrate this dependence of voluntary action upon a pre-existing machinery, and the growth of the will out of a blind impulsive soil.

So much for the first point in the Psychology of the Will. The second point which modern Psychology scores, is one which may strike the reader as less obviously true. Having made him see that

[1] Of course I do not mean that a man cannot commit a murder voluntarily until he has committed one involuntarily. Such acts as murders are *complex combinations* of movements, crouching, springing, stabbing and the like. What I mean is that he can perform no one elementary movement voluntarily unless it has been already involuntarily performed.

before the Will can go to work it needs a store of recollections of how various movements may feel, I must now make him see that *it needs nothing else,* and that such ideas of movement are not only indispensable conditions of volition, but sufficient conditions as well.

Dr. Carpenter long ago gave the name of "ideo-motor actions" to a class of performances with which all of us are familiar; and which, if I mistake not, he seemed to place among the curiosities of our volitional life. The truth is that these ideo-motor actions are not curiosities, but true types and patterns of normal volition, simply stripped of complication and disguise. The actions I have in mind are such as these. Whilst talking, I become conscious of a pin on the floor, or of some dust on my sleeve. Without interrupting the conversation I brush away the dust or pick up the pin. I make no express resolve, but the mere perception of the object and the fleeting notion of the act seem of themselves to bring the latter about. Similarly, I sit at table after dinner and find myself from time to time taking nuts or raisins from the dish and eating them. So far as deliberate resolution goes my repast is long since done; but the sight of the dish awakens a rapid idea of the possibility of eating the fruit, and this idea, *not meeting any express contradiction,* fatally passes over into action. It needs for this no separate *fiat* of the will; it is enough that no positively hindering idea should be there.

We all know what it is to get out of bed on a freezing morning in a room without a fire, and how the very vital principle within us protests against the ordeal. Probably most of us have lain on certain mornings for an hour at a time unable to brace ourselves to the resolve. We think how late we shall be, how the duties of the day will suffer; we say "I *must* get up, this is ignominious," etc.; but still the warm couch feels too delicious, the cold outside too cruel, and resolution faints away and postpones itself again and again just as it seemed on the verge of bursting the resistance and passing over into the decisive act. Now how do we *ever* get up under such circumstances? If I may generalize from my own experience, we more often than not get up without any struggle or decision at all. We suddenly find that we *have* got up. A fortunate lapse of consciousness occurs; we forget both the warmth and the cold; we fall into some revery connected with the day's life, in the course of which the idea flashes across us, "Hollo! I must lie here no longer"—an idea which at that lucky instant awakens no contradictory or paralyzing suggestions, and consequently produces immediately its appropriate motor effects. It was our acute consciousness of both the warmth and the cold during the period of struggle, which paralyzed our activity then and kept our idea of rising in the condition of *wish* and not of *will*. The moment these inhibitory ideas ceased, the original idea exerted its effects.

This case seems to me to contain in miniature form the data for an entire psychology of volition. If we wisely generalize its teachings we shall say that anywhere and everywhere *the sole known cause for the execution of a movement is the bare idea of the movement's execution*, and that if the idea occurs to a mind *empty of other ideas*, the movement will fatally and infallibly take place.

The hypnotic subject passively acting out every motor suggestion which his operator makes, seems to embody this simplest of all possible cases. Ask him what he is thinking of before you make the suggestion, and he will say "nothing." But seldom are our minds as empty as his. Usually they contain other ideas in addition to that of the movement in question, and according as these additional ideas are of one sort or another, we get one or another kind of result. If they are entirely irrelevant to the idea of the movement they neither help nor hinder its effects;—such were presumably the topics of our conversation when we picked up the string from the floor. If they *harmonize* with the idea of the movement, they reenforce its efficacy over the muscles;—when the idea of rising comes in the midst of an exciting vision of what is to be done when we are dressed, we fairly leap from bed. But if the additional ideas *conflict* with the idea of the movement, they block the path of its discharge and inhibit its motor efficacy altogether. The thought of the cold room thus blocked the discharge of the idea of rising. The thought "We have eaten enough!" would have checked the raising of our hand, had it come whilst we were about to extend the latter towards the confectionery on the dinner table.

There is nothing paradoxical about this blocking of one process in the nerve-centres by another. The physiology of recent years has shown that any and every process, almost, may, under certain conditions, arrest activities going on elsewhere; and "inhibition" now figures, in text-books of nervous science, as a function almost as wide-spread and characteristic as stimulation itself. Just which are the processes which will inhibit, and which are those which will re-enforce each other, are matters for delicate experimentation to decide. *All* our thoughts correspond to processes in the cerebral hemispheres. We know that certain thoughts conflict with others and that certain acts are only possible so long as objections to them do not pop into our minds. This seems, introspectively, to be a logical consequence of the contrasted inner natures of the ideas themselves. The "new Psychology" is, of course, far from denying this; but she insists that the logical law is a mechanical law as well, and that the brain-processes to which the contrasted ideas severally correspond, are such as dam each other up and stop each other's discharge.

The immense complicacy and subtilty of these mutually inhibitory processes appears from the number of actions that are thought of every hour of the day by an ordinarily active mind, and which yet give rise to no sensible movement. The other things which are thought of at the same time do not naturally conspire with these actions. They are not consented to. *Consent*, in short, is a word which describes most of our activity far more accurately than *volition* does. Volition implies something positive, energetic, and akin to effort. Consent is passive; and three-fourths of our daily conduct consists in simply taking off the brakes, and letting ideas and impulses have their way. Volition, properly so called, if there were any, would in these cases lie in refusing consent. I think every man's consciousness will bear witness to the truth of this.

Not that the refusing of consent need imply energetic volition either. Quite as little as the execution of a movement does its inhibition always require an express effort or command. Either of them *may* require it, as we shall presently see. But in all simple and ordinary cases, just as the bare presence of one idea will prompt a movement, so the bare presence of another idea will prevent its taking place. Try to feel as if you were crooking your finger, whilst keeping it straight. In a minute it will fairly tingle with the imaginary change of position; yet it will not sensibly move; because *its not really moving* is also a part of what you have in mind. Drop *this* idea, think of the movement purely and simply, with all brakes off, and presto! it takes place with no effort at all.[2]

---

[2] It always takes place insensibly even when the brakes are on. The skill of such muscle-readers as Mr. Irving Bishop depends on the fact that hardly anyone in

A waking man's behavior is thus at all times the resultant of two opposing neural forces. With unimaginable fineness some currents among the cells and fibres of his brain are playing on his motor nerves, whilst other currents, as unimaginably fine, are playing on the first currents, damming or helping them, altering their direction or their speed. The upshot of it all is that whilst the currents must always end by being drained off through *some* motor nerves, they are drained off sometimes through one set and sometimes through another; and sometimes they keep each other in equilibrium so long that a superficial observer may think they are not drained off at all. Such an observer must remember, however, that from the physiological point of view a gesture, an expression of the brow, or an expulsion of the breath, are movements as much as an act of locomotion is. A king's breath slays as well as an assassin's blow; and the outpouring of those currents which the magic imponderable streaming of our ideas accompanies need not always be of an explosive or otherwise physically conspicuous kind.

The ideas which perhaps more generally than any others inhibit muscular activity, and keep us quiet, are those of pains and pleasures; the pains of movement and the pleasures of the *status quo*. The paralyzing effects of the bed's warmth and of the cold in the room are cases in point. And conversely, the ideas which more generally than any others incite to movement are those of the pleasures to be gained by action, and the pains connected with repose. A hasty philosophy has universalized these facts, and gravely insisted that the only *possible* inciter to voluntary action is the idea of pleasure, and its only *possible* inhibitor the idea of pain. Ethically, this might be true; that is, it might be (as utilitarians contend) that the ideas of pleasure and of pain are the only *rational* motives for acting or for desisting from activity. I will express no opinion as to whether this be true or not in ethics; but I know that its counterpart in psychology is absolutely false. Be it or be it not admitted that the idea of pleasure *ought* to be, it certainly cannot be admitted that it *is* the only idea which moves a man to action. If there is any one point which "the new Psychology," with its derivation of the will from involuntary impulse, makes plain,

---

thinking of a movement is able entirely to suppress the tendency to carry it out. The muscle-reader feels this tendency in the "Agent's" hand which is laid upon his person.

it is that. Our first acts, of every sort, are blind, made for no motive, properly so called, but fatally stimulated into being by sensations due to determinate outer things or inner states. Our next acts are from ideas or representations of these things and states. Our last acts (as we see them in the thoroughly cultivated man) are from ideas of some abstract good, be the good pleasure, or something which may exclude pleasure, as "duty" is often felt to do. Pleasure is apt to be throughout a secondary complication to the drama of stimulation and desire.[3] It regulates, but need not operate; it steers, but need not propel. And when the idea of it does propel, and becomes itself the motive, it is only as one among many ideas which have this privilege coequally. If one idea, such as that of pleasure, may let loose the springs of action, surely other ideas may; and experience alone can decide which ideas have this power. It decides that their actual name is legion. Innumerable objects of desire and passion innervate our limbs just as they light up a fever in our breasts; and ninety-nine times out of a hundred we no more act for the pleasure connected with the action, than we frown for the pleasure of the frowning, or blush for the pleasure of the blush. Blind reactive impulse at the beginning, ideational coercion of some sort at the end, such are the poles between which the evolution of human conduct swings. Ask the common drunkard why he falls so often a prey to temptation. He will say that half the time he cannot tell. It is a sort of vertigo. His nerve-centres are a sluiceway, pathologically unlocked by every passing conception of a bottle and a glass. He does not thirst for the beverage; the taste of it

---

[3] An activity prompted by any cause or motive whatsoever brings a certain pleasure with it when successfully completed (especially if the completion involves the overcoming of obstacles), and an activity prompted by any cause or motive whatsoever, if frustrated, brings pain. It is painful to have our breathing stopped, and pleasant to have the activity of listening to a lecture ended by the lecturer getting through. The pleasure is an incident or concomitant of such acts, just as coal-consumption is a concomitant of a steamer's locomotion. As long as the locomotion continues the coal-consumption goes on; when it stops, the coal-consumption ends. But habitually we no more go to lectures for the mere relief of getting through, or breathe for the mere sake of escaping pain, than steamers go to sea or stop for the mere sake of consuming or not consuming coal. Of course we may occasionally make these our express motive for breathing or lecture-going, just as steamers *may* go to sea for the express sake of getting rid of coal. But the hedonist in psychology is like one who should say that no steamer can possibly go to sea for any other motive than to burn its coal. The incidental consequence of the activity, which only sometimes may be the deliberately proposed purpose of the activity, is made everywhere and always to usurp the proposed purpose's place.

may even appear repugnant; and he perfectly foresees the morrow's remorse. But when he thinks of the liquor or sees it, he finds himself preparing to drink, and does not stop himself; and more than this he cannot say.

This is why volcanic natures like the Mahomets, the Luthers, and the Bonapartes are usually fatalists. They find themselves bursting into action with an energy at which they are themselves astonished, as if some god or demon had released a spring. But there is an intoxication in this outpour which makes them welcome and adopt it, whithersoever it may lead, coupled, in men of the heroic mould, with an ability to meet its consequences whatever they may be.

To sum up our results so far. We are an organized machinery for muscular explosion, placed in an environment full of things which pull and clamp the triggers of the machinery in various pre-appointed ways. This is our involuntary life. But the things leave images behind them, and so do the discharges themselves, with their consequences in the way of pleasure and of pain. All these images in turn incite to new discharges, and re-enforce and inhibit each other just as their originals did. This is our voluntary life, so far as we have studied it; and the great conclusion we now reach is, that *the only thing which can either incite or check a voluntary movement is the cerebral process which corresponds to an idea.* A priori, of course, there is nothing strange in an ideational process doing this. For, in our ignorance of the intimate nature of nerve-action, it seems as likely that an ideational centre should discharge into a motor-nerve as that any other sort of centre should.

So much for the middle stage of volition, which we will call, for convenience, the *volition of consent.* In the volition of consent the idea which serves as motive or temptation is sufficient of itself to engender action if no other idea stands in the way. But there remains a *volition of effort,* which seems a widely different thing. Often the idea which serves as our motive or reason for action seems too weak to produce action unless aided by another force. Of this force we seem conscious in the effort of will which we have to make whenever we do a difficult thing. This seems the act of will *par excellence*; and it would be the play of Hamlet with the Prince left out, were I to end my tale here, and not give some account of this last and most mysterious feature of the case.

The older psychologists treated the effort of will as the only spiritual force which can influence immediately the material world. Its point of application might be muscles or brain-cells—that was an inessential part of their theory, but the *mode* of its application, its relation to the bodily process with which it is connected, was altogether different from the relation of any bare idea to the bodily process to which it corresponds. The idea was inert and passive, a mere concomitant. The effort, on the contrary, was a *force*, which passed from the mental to the physical world.

Now it seems to me that if there is anything which recent advances in psychology ought to teach, it is that this is a mistaken view, and that the feeling of effort has no such exceptional position between the inner and the outer worlds. Either all states of consciousness are forces, or none are; either all feelings react upon the brain-states which they accompany, or none do. Ideas react as much as efforts. What effort does when it comes to the aid of ideas is not to *supplant the ideas* in making the bodily machine obey, but to *hold the ideas fast*, so that *they* may acquire strength and stability enough to make the machine obey. The ideas are the spiritual things which the body obeys quite as much when the effort is, as when it is not, there. A very few words ought, it seems to me, to make this clear.

Every man alive knows what it is to be under the empire of passion. Either he has had a fever of desire upon him for the acquisition of a possession—a horse, or boat, or house, or land; or he has loved a woman's eyes; or some ambition or other has seized him in its fiery grasp. Let us now suppose a man with a passion the circumstances of which make it thoroughly unwise, and then ask ourselves what constitutes the difficulty for him of acting as if this were the case—for difficulty there is, as we all well know. Certainly there is no physical difficulty. It is as easy physically to pocket one's money as to pay it out, and as easy to walk away from as in the direction of a coquette's door. The difficulty is mental; it is that of getting the idea of the wise action to stay before our mind at all. When any strong emotional state whatever is upon us the tendency is for no images but such as are congruous with it to come up. If others by chance offer themselves, they are instantly smothered and crowded out. If we be joyous we cannot keep thinking of that tomb which certainly awaits us—try it now, sanguine reader! If lugubrious, we cannot think of new triumphs, flowers and spring;

nor if vengeful, of our oppressor's community of nature with ourselves. The cooling advice which we get from others when the fever-fit is on us is the most jarring and exasperating thing in life. Reply we cannot, so we get angry; for by a sort of self-preserving instinct which our passion has, it feels that these chill ideas, if they once but gain a lodgement, will work and work until they have frozen the very vital spark from out of all our mood and brought our airy castles in ruin to the ground. Such is the inevitable effect of reasonable ideas over others—*if they can once get a quiet hearing*; and passion's cue accordingly is always and everywhere to prevent their still small voice from being heard at all. "Let me not think of that! Don't speak to me of that!" This is the sudden cry of all those who in a passion perceive some sobering considerations about to check them in mid career. *"Hæc tibi erit janua leti,"* we feel. There is something so icy in this cold-water bath, something which seems so hostile to the movement of our life, so purely negative, in Reason, when she lays her corpse-like finger on our heart and says "Halt! give up! leave off! go back! sit down!" that it is no wonder that to most men the steadying influence seems, for the time being, like a very minister of death.

The strong-willed man, however, is the man who hears the still small voice unflinchingly, and who, when the death-bringing consideration comes, looks at its face, consents to its presence, clings to it, affirms it, and holds it fast, in spite of the host of exciting mental images which rise in revolt against it and would expel it from the mind. Sustained in this way by a resolute effort of attention, the moral idea erelong succeeds in calling up its own congeners and associates, and ends by changing the man's consciousness altogether. And with his consciousness his actions change. The new ideas, as soon as they are stably in possession of the mental field, infallibly produce their motor effects. The struggle, the difficulty is all in their getting possession of the field. The strain of the will lies in keeping the attention firmly fixed upon them, in spite of the fact that the spontaneous drift of thought is all the other way. That is what takes the moral effort. And when the moral effort has victoriously maintained the presence of the moral ideas, its work is over. The mysterious tie between the ideas and the cerebral motor-centres next comes into play, and, in a way which we cannot even guess at, the obedience of the bodily organs follows as a matter of course.

In all this one sees that the immediate point of application of the voluntary effort does not lie in the physical world at all, but in the mental world. It is *an idea* to which our will applies itself, an idea which, if we let it go, would slip away, but which we will not let go. Consent to the idea's undivided presence, this is effort's sole achievement. Its only function is to get this feeling of consent into the mind. And for this there is but one way. The idea to be consented to must be kept from flickering and going out. It must be held steadily before the mind until it *fills* the mind. Such filling of the mind by an idea, with its congruous associates, *is* consent to the idea, and to the fact which the idea represents. There is no other possible sort of consent than this. If the idea be that of the beginning or stopping of some bodily movement of our own, we call the consent, thus laboriously gained, a volition. The movement in this case becomes real as soon as we agree to the notion that it shall be real. Nature here "backs" us instantaneously and follows up our inward willingness by outward changes of her own. Nature does this in no other instance than this one of our own bodily movements. I may consent to the table dancing across this room; but that will not make it dance, as my legs would dance if the consent applied to them. My legs themselves will refuse to dance if my spinal cord be diseased. But these differences in the way in which nature acts at different places and times do not affect the *psychology* of my volition in the least degree. As far as my *mind* is concerned, it is just as good and true willing when I say to the table's moving "*fiat*," as when I say "*fiat*" to the movement of my own legs. The will, mentally considered, is consent to a *fact* of any kind, a fact in which we ourselves may play an active, a neutral, or a suffering part. The fact always appears to us in an idea: and it is willed by its idea becoming victorious over internal and external difficulties, banishing contradictory ideas and remaining in stable possession of the mind.

I think it will not be possible to find a single case of voluntary effort to which this description does not apply. Take violent muscular exertion for example. The feeling of muscular exertion consists of an immense number of in-coming sensations, due to the contraction of the muscles of our glottis, chest, jaws, body and limbs, and to our strained joints and ligaments and squeezed or twisted skin. The only volition which is required to bring about the actual state of muscular exertion is a sincere and genuine consent that all these sensations shall be real. But when we are lazy, or exhausted with fatigue, the sensations in question are very unwelcome, and the idea of being filled with their reality is repugnant to the mind. When once we have brought ourselves to face it, however, to say to the muscular sensations, "Be our reality, however disagreeable you may prove," to utter our "*fiat*," in a word, the contractions and their effects occur, and the muscular exertion is realized to its full extent. The effort of will required for muscular exertion consists then, like all other efforts of will, in the forcible holding fast to an incongenial idea.

It is a strange fact, this, that the fixed idea of a set of muscular feelings should immediately be followed by bodily changes which make those feelings real. But it is not an unexampled fact, because there is no idea whatever which is not immediately followed by *some* bodily change. We call many of these changes emotional. The peculiarity of the emotional changes is that the sight or idea of some *object* is needed to produce them. We cannot weep, for example, by dint of thinking of the feeling of our tears, but only by dint of thinking of an outward cause of grief. The odd thing about the changes called *voluntary* is that we provoke them by thinking of how they themselves are going to feel. This is no doubt due to some anatomical cause. The brain-centres for imagining the con-traction of our voluntary muscles, etc., must be connected with the motor-nerves in an altogether special way. But, neglecting all these variations, there results from the aggregate of facts which we have reviewed a lesson for brain-physiology which is as simple as it is important: *There can be no centres in the upper brain which are exclusively motor.* All its parts must be motor and sensory alike—sensory at all times, motor when not inhibited by each other.[4] In other words, they all have a permanent sensory *property*, and in-termittent motor *functions*. Their sensory property is ideation.

When they inhibit each other, there is no outer movement, but in the mind a conflict of ideas. All that consciousness embraces is the swaying to and fro of the ideas, and the final repose of the

[4] The hinder part of the brain does not respond to electrical stimulation by the production of any muscular movements. This may be due to inhibitions. Goltz and his pupil Loeb have noticed that when the frontal lobes are cut off, the animal's mobility becomes extreme, as if habitual inhibitions were removed. It would be interesting to try whether, in an animal so operated on, direct stimulation of the occipital lobes might not give rise to movements, similar in general character to those discharged from the so-called motor zone.

attention in the one which gains the day. Now this repose of the attention may come about spontaneously, or it may come with moral effort. The work of moral effort then, when we come to reduce it to its simplest expression, is neither more nor less than the work of attending to a difficult idea. Effort of volition and effort of attention, psychologically considered, are, in short, two names for an identical thing. Muscular discharges and arrests are all consecutive to the central phenomenon in volition, which is this bare attention to the idea. The only sort of resistance which our will can possibly experience is the resistance which certain ideas offer to being attended to at all. This resistance may come from an intrinsic and more or less permanent uncongeniality in the ideas. I know a person who, on some days, will turn to anything rather than to the noon-day lesson in logic which he has to get up, poke the fire, set chairs straight, dust the floor, snatch the newspaper, trim his nails, take down any book which catches his eye, waste the morning anyhow and everyhow, in short, rather than attend to that tedious and accursed thing. Or the resistance may come from an *extrinsic* uncongeniality, due to the temporary possession of the mind by ideas of an incompatible sort. Such are the cases of passion we talked of a while ago; such would be the thought of an ordeal we must go through on the morrow, visiting us in the midst of a dinner party, at a theatre, or other scene of pleasure, where our cares had temporarily been lulled to sleep. Under such circumstances we shy away like frightened horses from the incongruous topic, the moment we get a glimpse of its ugly profile on the threshold of our thought.

To attend to it, under such circumstances, is, however, the moral act; and it is the only moral act which, as spirits, we are ever called upon to perform. The effort which such attention implies seems to be indeterminate in quantity, as if we might make more or less as we chose. If it be really indeterminate, our future acts are ambiguous, or unpredestinate: in common parlance our wills are free. If the amount of effort be not indeterminate, but be related in a fixed manner to the ideas themselves, in such wise that whatever idea at any time fills our consciousness was from eternity bound to fill it then and there, and compel from us the exact effort of attention, neither more nor less, which we bestow upon it; then our wills are not free, and all our acts are foreordained. The question of fact in the free-will controversy is thus extremely simple. It relates solely to the amount of effort of attention which we can at any time put forth. Are the duration and intensiy of this effort fixed functions of the idea attended to or not? Now as I just said, it *seems* as if the attention were an independent variable, as if we might exert more or less of it in any given case. When a man has let his thoughts go for days and weeks until at last they culminate in some particularly dirty or cowardly or cruel act, it is hard to persuade him in the midst of his remorse, that he might not have reined them in; hard to make him believe that this whole goodly universe (which his act so jars upon) required and exacted it of him at that fatal moment, and from eternity made aught else impossible. I must confess that I sympathize with such a man, and favor the free-will belief. But the question will never be decided by purely empirical or scientific evidence; and free-will and determinism, as actual creeds, will probably always be just what they are to-day, postulates of rationality, namely, different assumptions which different thinkers make, because so each of them is able to cast the world into what seems to him personally the most intelligible form.

We have thus answered the question with which we started, of what happens when we exert our will. *We simply fill our mind with an idea which, but for our effort, would slip away.* But it is impossible before we close not to look for a moment into the vista of moral reflections which this reply throws open to the view.

In the first place it makes it plain that the will has as much to do with our beliefs and faiths as with our movements. It is, in fact, only in consequence of a faith that our movements themselves ensue. We think of a movement and say, *"let* it ensue! so far as we are concerned let it be part of reality!"* This is all that our *mind* can do—physical nature must do the rest. And this is all that our mind does in any theoretic belief, such as that in the divine or undivine nature of the essence of life. In espousing any such belief, who can do more than say of it "as far as I am concerned, let that view of life stand. Let it be real. Let my mind be filled up with the thought of it, let no difficulties drive it from my sight"? But, as all sober-minded thinkers know, there are great difficulties in the way of holding any unwavering view of life. The unutterable complexity of this huge world that girdles us about, seems sometimes as if it were expressly meant to defy our attempts to conceive it as a unity. Beliefs and unbeliefs shake us by fits.[5] The thoughts of the day-spring and the thoughts of midnight drive each other out. No sooner are we settled in the mood of spiritual trust than some new brutality on the part of Nature overturns our peace; no sooner at ease in a materialistic *parti pris* than we catch a phrase of music, or a friend dies, or we see some dewy morning break over the hilltops of the world, and then the ice cracks, and all our questions and hopes are afloat and alive again.

Now whereas in all practical affairs, in all matters where the willing produces an immediate result, it is universally admitted that the men who can will, who can hold on to unwelcome or elusive ideas, are a higher kind of men than those who cannot—more evolved, more fit for life, more helpful to the race; it is a singular fact that in these theoretic questions it is commonly supposed to be a sign of weakness and inferiority if one let one's will have anything to say. One's ideal attitude towards *Truth*, we are carefully taught, should be that of utter passivity. The truth must come and stamp itself in its own person authentically upon our unaiding and unresisting minds. If we let our satisfactions or dissatisfactions influence the manner of our reception of it, we shall surely fail to get it pure.

Now if one had a perfectly single set of interests, it would be tolerably easy to live up to the professions of this creed. If one were a pure sentimentalist, with no sense for Nature's cold mechanics, one might keep an utterly cloistered faith and live with one's head in the sand of some creed which utterly defied physiology and physics, and yet have a perfectly good intellectual conscience, and consider that this was nothing but yielding to evidence of an objective sort. So too if one were a good bull-necked materialist by nature. Having no yearnings for the Infinite, it would cost nothing to give the Infinite up, nor to say that the mechanical philosophy had written itself in characters of living light on the virgin tablets of one's pure intelligence. But these ostrich-like attitudes are both of them getting harder than ever to maintain. With civilization, sympathy and sensibility and the love of life are ever growing more acute and exacting; and, tolling obstinately within us like never to be silenced bells, they demand that the element which we call

[5] Compare the immortal Blougram in Browning's verse.

divine in things shall be an essential and eternal element as well. But there too, on the other hand, like a great ocean spread outside of us, lies the world without a purpose of the mechanical philosophy, in which what is divine appears as a mere accident; and no modern man's ears can be quite deaf to the tumbling of that ocean's waves.

So long as our mind is assailed in two such different ways, it is quite idle to talk of its being passive and will-less until the objective truths shall have written themselves down. They write down no messages which are both coherent and universal. Nor if (conscious of the immensity of our ignorance) we resolve to go without a universal message for the present, and to wait till more light comes, can we be passive and will-less any more easily. For one must always wait in some dominant mood or attitude; and the mere resolve itself of waiting and not making what is called a snap-decision, often demands volition of the most energetic sort. The theoretic life of a cultivated modern man requires, in fact, as vigorous a co-operation of his will as his practical life does. Look at the men who at the present day feel life on all its sides, and yet who are incapable of volition in intellectual affairs, and imagine that there ought to be some sort of truth with which they can remain in passive equilibrium. Their feelings make them shiver at the materialistic facts; whilst their loyalty to science makes them dread to be dupes of their feelings. They become one mass of indecision, plaintiveness and defeat, so far as they take the philosophic life seriously at all; and remain facing the same urgencies and the same difficulties to the end, unable to deal with them, unable to drop them, and worrying their span of time away between disconsolately wishing certain things were true, yet dreading to affirm them in the teeth of other facts.

But the men of will do not let "I dare not wait upon I would," in any such sorry fashion. They choose their attitude and know that the facing of its difficulties shall remain a permanent portion of their task. Whether it be the materialistic idea, the spiritualistic idea, or the waiting idea, which they adopt, they do it resolutely and strike the major key. They hold fast to it in the teeth of the opposite ideas which ever urge them to let go their grasp. They find a zest in this difficult clinging to truth, or a lonely sort of joy in pressing on the thorns and going without it, which no passively warranted possession of it can ever confer. And thereby they be-

come the masters and the lords of life. They must be counted with
henceforth; they form a part of human destiny. No more in the
theoretic than in the practical sphere do we care for, or go for help
to, those who have no head for risks, or sense for living on the
perilous edge. But just as surely as time flows on and as our consciousness grows more complex, so surely does our theoretic life
lie more and more upon the perilous edge. And, just as in every
siege and shipwreck, there is found some dauntless heart, whose
example pours new life into his company; so in the wars of speculation and the shipwrecks of faith it is the same. Ever there rises
up the prophet, the hero of belief, who drinks more deeply than
any of the cup of bitterness; but his countenance is so unshaken and
he speaks such mighty words of cheer, that his thought becomes
our thought, and to later generations he seems a being half divine.

But if we ask how this is possible, and how one may one's self
set about it to get this sovereign mood of will, the only answer is to
point to the hero who can hold to ideas that are difficult and elusive, and say "lo, be as this man!" *Velle non discitur*, said Seneca.
The only thing which no theory, no printed directions, can teach
us, is how to will. What it *might* do, what it *might have done*, we
can be taught; what it *shall* do depends on the inalienable essence
of each individual man.

Réponse de M. W. James aux remarques de M. Renouvier, sur sa théorie de la volonté[1]

Cher monsieur,

Je suis extrêmement sensible à l'honneur grand et peu mérité que vous m'avez fait en présentant au public français mon petit article sur la volonté, et en le faisant suivre d'un commentaire si flatteur. Je suis cependant un si pauvre faiseur de phrases que je n'essaierai pas d'exprimer ma gratitude; je vous prierai simplement de m'accorder une page ou deux de votre revue des explications à donner au sujet de vos *Remarques*. Je serai aussi bref que je le pourrai.

Premièrement, en ce qui concerne mon originalité, Lotze a été, autant que je sache, le premier à formuler clairement la relation entre représentation, volition et mouvement effectué. On trouvera les passages dans les §§ 266-7-8 de sa *Medicinische psychologie*, publiée en 1852. Votre propre formulation, qui n'est pas essentiellement plus profonde, à ce qu'il me semble, mais qui est beaucoup plus explicite, a été publiée sept ans plus tard, mais obtenue d'une manière indépendante. Mes propres idées se sont formées bien postérieurement, par la lecture et de votre ouvrage et de celui de

---

[1] Voyez les numéros 6 et 8 de la *Critique philosophique* de la présente année.— L'insertion de l'aimable et intéressante lettre de M. William James a été retardée par le désir que nous avons eu d'y joindre une traduction des passages importants signalés par ce dernier dans la *Medicinische psychologie* de Lotze.

Lotze; de sorte que je n'ai sur ce point ni indépendance ni originalité quelconque.

Secondement, touchant *l'espèce* de représentation d'un mouvement à laquelle le mouvement actuel fait suite, je m'en suis expliqué, dans mon article, comme si elle devait se composer des souvenirs des sensations *internes* engendrées par les mouvements passés dans les parties mouvantes elles-mêmes. Mon article, ayant été écrit pour un recueil populaire, a dû être simplifié outre mesure, comme de coutume en pareil cas; et, dans ce cas-ci, j'ai pris une des espèces de l'idée motrice pour tenir la place du genre tout entier. Vous avez absolument raison de protester contre cette vue étroite. Il est certain, ainsi que vous y insistez, que le dernier phénomène psychique qui précède un mouvement peut être et est souvent une image des effets *externes* du mouvement sur l'œil, l'oreille ou quelque partie éloignée du corps. Nos mouvements volontaires de vocalisation paraissent être instigués par des images acoustiques. Ceux des mouvements de nos membres qui nous sont le plus habituels sont dûs ordinairement à des images optiques. Lorsque je désire tout d'un coup toucher du doigt un point dans l'espace, j'ai plus fortement conscience de l'endroit (*of where*) où la place de ce point paraît être, à mon œil, que de la manière (*of how*) dont mon bras et ma main doivent sentir quand je le touche. On pourrait objecter qu'il y a des faits ici qui échappent à notre conscience introspective; qu'une image tactile des sensations internes attendues dans le membre doit intervenir entre l'image optique de cette place et le mouvement exécuté; mais que cette image tactile est si rapidement supplantée par les sensations internes actuelles, pendant que le mouvement s'effectue, que nous manquons à en prendre connaissance comme d'un phénomène indépendant. Ceci est une hypothèse qui mérite considération; elle doit avoir un résultat expérimentalement vérifiable. Si une personne à laquelle un signal est donné fait un mouvement qui laisse une marque sur un appareil chronographique, elle obtient une mesure de ce qu'on appelle le «temps physiologique» de ce mouvement particulier. Or, si l'on compare deux mouvements (semblables d'ailleurs) dont l'un est représenté d'avance pour nous en termes optiques, ou «externes», l'autre en termes tactiles, ou «internes», le premier doit avoir le temps physiologique le plus long, dans la théorie que nous discutons, parce que la suggestion rapide qu'elle suppose de l'image tactile est un événement auquel rien ne correspond dans le cas où la représentation est consciemment tactile dès le début. Je me suis occupé quelque temps, il y a plusieurs années, d'exécuter des mesures comparatives de ce genre. Je regrette de dire qu'il ne m'a pas été possible de découvrir une forme d'expérience assez affranchie de complications secondaires pour me donner des résultats utilisables.

Toutefois, je dirai que je n'ai trouvé aucune raison de soupçonner que le temps fût allongé lorsque l'idée motrice était optique; non plus que l'attention introspective que j'ai dû alors accorder à l'opération n'a tendu à me confirmer dans l'idée qu'une image tactile latente y intervient toujours. Loin de là, c'est alors que pour la première fois je me suis mis fortement à douter de cette idée.

Pendant ce temps, mon collègue la professeur Bowditch a fait avec le docteur Southard des expériences qui semblent montrer que, quelquefois au moins, il n'intervient aucune image tactile. Ces physiologistes ont trouvé qu'ils pouvaient, les yeux fermés, toucher *avec plus de précision* un point marqué sur la table, lorsqu'ils l'avaient simplement *regardé* que lorsqu'ils l'avaient simplement *touché* un moment auparavant. Pour le docteur S. l'erreur moyenne, avec le toucher, était de 17 millimètres contre 12 millimètres avec la vue.[2] Il est certain qu'ici une rapide image tactile ne pouvait s'être placée comme moyen de passage entre l'image optique et la décharge motrice. Comment la physiologie du cerveau s'accommodera de ces faits, c'est une question qui regarde les physiologistes; ils devront dans tous les cas admettre que le procès idéationnel qui précède immédiatement et provoque un procès moteur peut quelquefois être un procès d'imagination optique.

Troisièmement, je voudrais dire un mot de ma réduction de toutes les actions psychiques au type réflexe. Je ne suis pas sûr que, quand j'affirme et que vous niez, nous prêtions aux mêmes mots les mêmes significations. J'entends, pour le faire bref, que l'objet de la pensée, à tout instant donné, fait partie d'une chaîne d'objets successivement suggérés qui peuvent être suivis, en remontant, jusqu'à quelque sensation reçue, et qui se termineront tôt ou tard à quelque modification de notre mouvement. Par exemple, mes pensées présentes peuvent être suivies, en remontant, jusqu'à l'impression causée dernièrement sur ma rétine par vos paroles imprimées, et se déchargent, en ce moment même, en des mouvements de mes doigts qui tiennent la plume. La succession de nos objets

[2] Ce travail a été publié dans le *Journal of Physiology*, vol. III, n° 3.

mentaux est, je le crois fermement, expliquée par le fait physiologique qu'un procès cérébral en éveille un autre, suivant des voies en partie organisées par une formation interne, et en partie tracées par l'expérience externe;—expliquée, dis-je, en ce sens que nous ne pouvons avoir un objet, duquel ces voies ne soient la condition de *possibilité*. Mais cette dépendance par rapport à des voies matérielles, pour la possibilité de nos objets, n'implique pas nécessairement que la succession de ces derniers soit entièrement déterminée par des lois matérielles. On n'a simplement qu'à admettre que la conscience qui accompagne les procès matériels peut réagir de telle manière qu'elle ajoute à volonté à l'intensité ou à la durée de certains procès particuliers; un champ de *sélection* s'ouvre aussitôt, qui nous mène bien loin de la détermination mécanique. Un procès appuyé et accentué par la conscience éveillera ses propres associés et produira ses conséquences, à l'exclusion des autres, et l'enchaînement des pensées prendra de la sorte une forme entièrement différente de celle qu'elle aurait pu prendre si la conscience n'eût été là avec son efficacité. Soit qu'il existe ou non une volonté-force, avec des variations indépendantes, il me semble qu'un parfait *théâtre pour son activité* est fourni par un système de voies dans lesquelles des courants se meuvent et produisent des tensions et des décharges. La force indépendante n'a besoin que d'altérer par augmentation ou par diminution la tension donnée en un point, pour changer entièrement la résultante en direction de la décharge. Tout ce que notre libre vouloir peut légitimement revendiquer, c'est de disposer des possibilités qui nous sont offertes en manière d'alternatives par le flux mécanique des choses. J'espère qu'en ce sens-là, vous ne verrez nulle objection à étendre la notion de l'action réflexe à notre vie supérieure. Si librement qu'un acte puisse se produire, sa suggestion première est certainement due à des courants réflexes, et des courants réflexes sont ce qui le rend actuel. L'action régulatrice de tels courants par la volonté ne peut être autre chose qu'une sélection de certains d'entre eux, déjà tout près d'être un peu plus forts que les autres.

Croyez-moi, cher monsieur, etc...

WILLIAM JAMES

Cambridge (Mass.) U. S. of A., 23 septembre 1888.

"The Psychological Theory of Extension"

Since even the worm will 'turn,' the space-theorist can hardly be expected to remain motionless when his Editor stirs him up. Had I seen my July MIND earlier than I did, these remarks would have been in time for the October number. Appearing in January, I can only hope that the reader may not regard them as reviving an issue that is stale. The Editor, in his observations on "The Psychological Theory of Extension" in No. 51, made, as it seems to me, some *admissions* that ought to be recorded, as well as some *assumptions* that ought to be questioned, in the interests of clear thinking, in this dark field. One admission (if I rightly understand page 420) amounts to nothing less than giving up the whole positive and constructive part of the Brown-Bain-Spencer-Mill theory of Space-perception, and confessing that the criticisms usually made upon it are fatal. That theory contends that a variety of intensive elements can, by grouping [association] assume in consciousness the appearance of an extended order. "How is the transformation to be effected? Or, rather, can it any way be effected?" asks the Editor. "I do not know that it can," he replies, "if sought for upon that line." As the account of Space-perception by these authors is usually reckoned one of the greatest triumphs of the Analytic School of Psychology, this defection, by a writer whose general tendencies are loyal to the school, is worthy of emphatic notice. The Editor's second admission is, that, if we could suppose ourselves reduced to the eye with its exploratory movements as our sole and only means of constructing a spatial order, such a construction might come to pass (p. 424)—an admission quite at variance with the widely prevalent notion that analytic psychology has proved the space-perceptions of the eye to be but reproduced experiences of touch and locomotion. So many doctrines reign by the mere inertia of supposed authority, that when, as in these two points, the chain of authority gets broken, public attention should be drawn to the fact.

The chief *assumption* of the Editor's which I wish to question is his proposition that, although experiences of an intensive order will not by *themselves* acquire the extensive character, they will yet, if so experienced as to be referred to an *object* (in the sense of "bare obstacle to muscular activity of a touching organ"), begin to assume that character. If we construe this view definitely, everything about it seems to me questionable. Either the obstacle feels big originally or it does not. If it have originally no bigness, the same difficulty arises which the Editor admits to be fatal to ordinary theory: how can intensive elements be transformed into an extensive result? If, on the contrary, the obstacle have a sensible bigness, then, of course, that would explain how the touch of it, the look of it, or any other sensation which the mind incorporates in it, should share the bigness and appear itself extended. But then the question would arise—Why on earth should this feeling of muscular resistance be the only one which originally comes to us with a bigness? What grounds *a posteriori* or *a priori* can we show for assigning to it so pre-eminent an advantage, in the teeth of all the spontaneous appearances, which make us feel as if the blueness of the sky were spread out in itself, and as if the rolling of the thunder or the soreness of an abscess were intrinsically great? But the Editor keeps his whole account so studiously and cautiously vague that I confess I find it hard to construe his obstacle-object as definitely as this. It must, he says, not be treated as external "at the outset," for the mere experience of resisted muscular activity is analyzable into elements which "are found to be merely intensive—intensity of passive touch varying with intensity of effort" (p. 421). Nevertheless touch and effort are so related as to "suggest a cleft in conscious experience, which has but to be widened and defined for the opposition of self and not-self to become established." It is when referred to the "not-self" of the experience thus defined that the originally intensive qualities of touch, look, sound, etc., begin, according to the Editor, to appear extended, and finally become more definitely extended in proportion as the resisting body gets more definitely to seem external.

Such accounts, however vaguely expressed, are indubitably true, if one goes far enough back in time. Since things are perceived later which were not perceived earlier, it is certain *a priori* that there was a moment when the perception of them began; and we are, therefore, sure in advance, of being right, if we say of any perception that first it didn't exist, and that then there was a mere suggestion and nascency of it, which grew more definite, until, at last, the thing was fully established. The only merit of such statements lies in getting them historically exact, and in determining the very moment at which each successive element of the final fact came in. Science can never *explain the qualities* of the successive elements, if they show new qualities, appearing then for the first time. It can only name the moment and conditions of their appearance, and its whole problem is to name these aright. Now, we probably all agree that the *condition* of our perceiving the quality of bigness, the extensive quality, in any sensible thing is some peculiar process in our brain at the moment. But whereas, in the articles which the Editor criticizes, I maintained that the *moment* is the very first moment in which we get a sensation of any sort whatever, the Editor contends possibly that it is the first time we have the feeling of resisted muscular effort, but more probably (as I read his text) that it is much later in the day, after many sensations, all purely "intensive," have come and gone. In my articles I have given (with probably far too great prolixity) the grounds for the date which I assign, and criticized the grounds given by Wundt and Helmholtz for the later one which they prefer. I miss in the Editor's remarks (as in all English writings upholding the same view) any attempt at explicit proof that the earlier date is impossible, and that sensations cannot come with any apparent bigness when they first appear. May not the supposed impossibility be rather an assumption and a prejudice, due to uncriticized tradition? If there be definite reasons for it in the Editor's mind, I hope sincerely that he will publish them without delay. But if, on the contrary, a mere dim bigness *can* appear in all our first sensations, then the date of its appearance is most probably then; for discriminations, associations and selections among the various bignesses, occurring later on, will perfectly explain (as I have tried to show) how the definitive perception of real outer space and of the bodies in it grows up in the mind. Eye-experience, touch-experience and muscular experience go on abreast in this evolution, and their several objects grow intimately identified with each other. But I fail to see in this fact any reason for that *dependence* of the visual space-feelings on a "tactile base," such as my critic in his last paragraph seems to find. One who asks a blind person to compare pasteboard angles and the directions of their sides with each other, and who observes the extraordinary inferiority of his tactile perceptions to our visual ones, will be very loath to believe that the latter have the former for their base.

I am at a loss to know who the Editor means by the theorists ("space-theorists, generally," he calls them) who commit the mistake of seeking "for an extension that is extension of nothing at all." Certainly this mistake cannot be imputed to anyone who, like myself, holds extension to be coeval with sensation. The matter of the sensation must always be there to fill the extension felt. The extension is of the warmth, the noise, the blue luminosity, the contact, the muscular mass contracting, or whatever else the phenomenon may be.

Still other points do I find obscure in the Editor's remarks—obscure, I am sure, from no other reason but the brevity to which he has confined them. May he be enabled soon to set them forth at fairer length!

The Congress of Physiological Psychology at Paris

Professor William James of Harvard has kindly thrown off, at request, the following brief report of proceedings at the Paris Congress of Physiological Psychology, referred to in the last No. of MIND:—

"The first meeting was on Tuesday, August 6, and morning and evening sessions were continued during the week. Five sub-sections were formed to discuss special subjects and bring them before the general sessions in the afternoon. One of these sub-sections debated the Muscular Sense; another, Heredity; another, Hypnotism; the fourth, a project for an international census of Hallucinations on lines proposed by the English Society for Psychical Research; whilst the fifth dealt with the subject of Abnormal Association of Sensations of one kind with those of another, M. Grüber of Jassy having reported a very extraordinary case of 'colored hearing.' Finally, a supplementary committee reported a permanent plan of organization.

"The attendance at the general meetings varied from about 120 to 60 or 70. A medical congress, devoted especially to Hypnotism, of which M. Bérillon was the moving spirit, seemed to form a powerful derivative in the last few days. M. Charcot, president of the Société de psychologie physiologique, which had issued the invitations to the Congress, did not appear at all. Professor Ribot was present on the first day, and gave the opening address, on the *status* of contemporary psychology; showing in simple but impressive words how it advances by combining physiological and pathological observation and experiment with the older introspective method, and urging the investigators of all countries to share in the work now become common. Professor Charles Richet, the general secretary, was present at all the meetings, and his tact and good sense proved most useful at times in steering the devious course of discussion; his hospitality also will not easily be forgotten by the foreign visitors. MM. Gley and Marillier played an indispensable part in the proceedings.

"The committee of arrangements had prepared a program of subjects with a rather full printed syllabus of conclusions and suggestions. Of these subjects, several, for lack of time, failed to come to a full discussion. Such were (1) the part played by movements in the formation of mental images; (2) the appetites in idiots and imbeciles; (3) psychic poisons; (4) automatic writing and other unconscious movements; (5) the action of magnets on the organism. The subjects more thoroughly debated have been mentioned above. Largely under Mr. Galton's guidance, a circular of questions relative to Heredity was adopted by the Congress, and an international committee appointed to take charge of it. Similar action was taken upon the census of Hallucinations. The result of the discussions on Attention and the Muscular Sense was to show the need of a better understanding than we yet possess of the feeling of mental effort, the study of which was recommended as a *desideratum* to all psychologists. In the numerous questions relative to Hypnotism, great diversities of view came out, showing how much more work has still to be done in this field. The partisans of the Nancy School were decidedly in the majority at the meetings; and everyone seemed to think that the original Salpêtrière doctrine of hypnotism, as a definite pathological condition with its three stages and somatic causes, was a thing of the past. Dr. Bernheim even expressed doubt whether any such thing as hypnotism distinct from sleep and suggestion existed at all.

"The most striking feature of the discussions was, perhaps, their tendency to slope off to some one or other of those shady horizons with which the name of 'psychic research' is now associated. Amongst those who took a more active part in debate may be named MM. Marillier, Gley, Binet, Pierre Janet, Bertrand, Espinas, Bernheim, Liégeois, Ochorowicz, Danilewsky, Grote of Moscow, Delbœuf, Forel, Galton, Sidgwick, F. W. H. Myers. The open results were, however (as always happens at such gatherings), secondary in real importance to the latent ones—the friendships made, the intimacies deepened, and the encouragement and inspiration which came to everyone from seeing before them in flesh and blood so large a part of that little army of fellow-students, from whom and for whom all contemporary psychology exists. The individual worker feels much less isolated in the world after such an experience. The entire number of persons who gave their 'adhesion' to the Congress (the membership-fee being 10 francs) was not far from 400, the majority naturally French. From England the only persons present were Mr. Galton, Prof. and Mrs. Henry Sidgwick, Mr. F. W. H. Myers and Dr. A. T. Myers. The United States furnished Profs. James and Jastrow and Mr. Riley. Russia counted more 'adherents.' From the German Empire, though many eminent men sent in their names, Baron von Schrenck-Notzing and Drs. Münsterberg and Sperling were (I think) alone present. This is the more to be regretted, as the absent ones can now never realize how altogether gracious and hospitable a welcome they would have received. The Congress wound up on Saturday night with a feast of other things than reason and a flow of something besides soul on the platform of the Eiffel Tower, where, amongst other toasts, one was proposed by Prof. Lombroso to the health of Prof. Richet as the *"représentant de l'anti-chauvinisme dans la Science."* Reason and soul were there too, however; and hardly could finer subjects of contemplation for both of them have been found than the wonderfully illuminated landscape of exhibition grounds, palaces and fountains spread out below, with all the lights and shadows of nocturnal Paris framing it in.

"The Congress decided to institute a permanent organization, under the name of the *International Congress of Experimental Psychology.* It voted that its next meeting should take place in England three years hence. A permanent Committee of Organization was named, with members in the principal countries which had taken part; and a vote was passed expressing the hope that every member who was engaged in investigating a particular subject would put himself through this Committee into communication with psychologists similarly employed in other countries. The Committee is constituted as follows:—MM. Beaunis, Bernheim, Bertrand, Espinas, Ferrari, Gley, Marillier, Ribot, Richet (France, 9); Galton, F. W. H. Myers, Sidgwick (England, 3); Münsterberg, v. Schrenck-Notzing, Sperling (Germany, 3); Danilewski, Grote, Ochorowicz (Russian, 3); Forel, Herzen (Switzerland, 2); Benedikt (Austria); Delbœuf (Belgium); Neiglick (Finland); Lombroso (Italy); Grüber (Roumania); James (United States): in all, 26."

The Hidden Self

"The great field for new discoveries," said a scientific friend to me the other day, "is always the Unclassified Residuum." Round about the accredited and orderly facts of every science there ever floats a sort of dust-cloud of exceptional observations, of occurrences minute and irregular, and seldom met with, which it always proves less easy to attend to than to ignore. The ideal of every science is that of a closed and completed system of truth. The charm of most sciences to their more passive disciples consists in their appearing, in fact, to wear just this ideal form. Each one of our various *ologies* seems to offer a definite head of classification for every possible phenomenon of the sort which it professes to cover; and, so far from free is most men's fancy, that when a consistent and organized scheme of this sort has once been comprehended and assimilated, a different scheme is unimaginable. No alternative, whether to whole or parts, can any longer be conceived as possible. Phenomena unclassifiable within the system are therefore paradoxical absurdities, and must be held untrue. When, moreover, as so often happens, the reports of them are vague and indirect, when they come as mere marvels and oddities rather than as things of serious moment, one neglects or denies them with the best of scientific consciences. Only the born geniuses let themselves be worried and fascinated by these outstanding exceptions, and get no peace till they are brought within the fold. Your Galileos, Galvanis, Fresnels, Purkinjes, and Darwins are always getting confounded and troubled by insignificant things. *Anyone* will renovate his science who will steadily look after the irregular phenomena. And when the science is renewed, its new formulas often have more of the voice of the exceptions in them than of what were supposed to be the rules.

No part of the unclassed residuum has usually been treated with a more contemptuous scientific disregard than the mass of phenomena generally called *mystical*. Physiology will have nothing to do with them. Orthodox psychology turns its back upon them. Medicine sweeps them out; or, at most, when in an anecdotal vein, records a few of them as "effects of the imagination," a phrase of mere dismissal whose meaning, in this connection, it is impossible to make precise. All the while, however, the phenomena are there, lying broadcast over the surface of history. No matter where you open its pages, you find things recorded under the name of divinations, inspirations, demoniacal possessions, apparitions, trances, ecstasies, miraculous healings and productions of disease, and occult powers possessed by peculiar individuals over persons and things in their neighborhood. We suppose that mediumship originated in Rochester, N. Y., and animal magnetism with Mesmer; but once look behind the pages of official history, in personal memoirs, legal documents, and popular narratives and books of anecdote, and you will find that there never was a time when these things were not reported just as abundantly as now. We college-bred gentry, who follow the stream of cosmopolitan culture exclusively, not infrequently stumble upon some old-established journal, or some voluminous native author, whose names are never heard of in *our* circle, but who number their readers by the quarter-million. It always gives us a little shock to find this mass of human beings not only living and ignoring us and all our gods, but actually reading and writing and cogitating without ever a thought of our canons, standards, and authorities. Well, a public no less large keeps and transmits from generation to generation the traditions and practices of the occult; but academic science cares as little for its beliefs and opinions as you, gentle subscriber to this MAGAZINE, care for those of the readers of the *Waverley* and the *Fireside Companion*. To no one type of mind is it given to discern the totality of Truth. Something escapes the best of us, not accidentally, but systematically, and because we have a twist. The scientific-academic mind and the feminine-mystical mind shy from each other's facts, just as they fly from each other's temper and spirit. Facts are there only for those who have a mental affinity with them. When once they are indisputably ascertained and admitted, the academic and critical minds are by far the best fitted ones to interpret and discuss them—for surely to pass from mystical to scientific speculations is like passing from lunacy to sanity; but on the other hand if there is anything which human history demonstrates, it is the extreme slowness with which the ordinary academic and critical mind acknowledges facts to exist which present themselves as *wild* facts with no stall or pigeon-hole, or as facts which threaten to break up the accepted system. In psychology, physiology, and medicine, wherever a debate between the Mystics and the Scientifics has been once for all decided, it is the Mystics who have usually proved to be right about the *facts*, while the Scientifics had the better of it in respect to the theories. The most recent and flagrant example of this is "animal magnetism," whose facts were stoutly dismissed as a pack of lies by academic medical science the world over, until the non-mystical theory of "hypnotic suggestion" was found for them, when they were admitted to be so excessively and dangerously common that special penal laws, forsooth, must be passed to keep all persons unequipped with medical diplomas from taking part in their production. Just so stigmatizations, invulnerabilities, instantaneous cures, inspired discourses, and demoniacal possessions, the records of which were shelved in our libraries but yesterday in the alcove headed "Superstitions," now, under the brand-new title of "Cases of hystero-epilepsy," are republished, reobserved, and reported with an even too credulous avidity.

Repugnant as the mystical style of philosophizing may be (especially when self-complacent), there is no sort of doubt that it goes with a gift for meeting with certain kinds of phenomenal experience. The writer has been forced in the past few years to this admission; and he now believes that he who will pay attention to facts of the sort dear to mystics, while reflecting upon them in academic-scientific ways, will be in the best possible position to help philosophy. It is a circumstance of good augury, that scientifically trained minds in all countries seem drifting to the same conclusion. Nowhere is this the case more than in France. France always was the home of the study of character. French literature is one long loving commentary on the variations of which individual human nature is capable. It seems fitting, therefore, that where minute and faithful observation of abnormal personal peculiarities is the order of the day, French science should take the lead. The work done at Paris and Nancy on the hypnotic trance is well known. Grant any amount of imperfection, still the essential thing remains, that here we have a mass of phenomena, hitherto outlawed, brought within the pale of sober investigation—the rest is only an affair of time. Last summer there appeared a record of observations made at Havre on certain hysterical somnambulists, by M. Pierre Janet, Professor of Philosophy in the Lycée of that town, and published in a volume of five hundred pages, entitled *L'Automatisme psychologique* (Paris, Alcan), which, serving as the author's thesis for the Doctorate of Science in Paris, made quite a commotion in the world to which such things pertain.

The new light which this book throws on what has long been vaguely talked about as unconscious mental life seems so important that I propose to entertain the readers of SCRIBNER'S with some account of its contents, as an example of the sort of "psychical research" which a shrewd man with good opportunities may now achieve. The work bristles with facts, and is rather deficient in form. The author aims, moreover, at generalizing only where the phenomena force him to, and abstract statements are more embedded, and, as it were, interstitial, than is the case in most Gallic performances. In all this M. Janet's mind has an English flavor about it which it is pleasant to meet with in one otherwise so good a Frenchman. I shall also quote some of the observations of M. Binet,[1] the most ingenious and original member of the Salpêtrière school, as these two gentlemen, working independently and with different subjects, come to conclusions which are strikingly in accord.

Both may be called contributors to the comparative science of trance-states. The "Subjects" studied by both are sufferers from the most aggravated forms of hysteria, and both authors, I fancy, are consequently led to exaggerate the dependence of the trance-conditions upon this kind of disease. M. Janet's subjects, whom he calls Léonie, Lucie, Rose, Marie, etc., were patients at the Havre Hospital, in charge of doctors who were his friends, and who allowed him to make observations on them to his heart's content.

---

[1] M. Binet has contributed some of his facts to the Chicago *Open Court* for 1889.

One of the most constant symptoms in persons suffering from hysteric disease in its extreme forms consists in alterations of the natural sensibility of various parts and organs of the body. Usually the alteration is in the direction of defect, or anæsthesia. One or both eyes are blind, or blind over one half of the field of vision, or the latter is extremely contracted, so that its margins appear dark, or else the patient has lost all sense for color. Hearing, taste, smell may similarly disappear, in part or in totality. Still more striking are the cutaneous anæsthesias. The old witch-finders, looking for the "devil's seals," well learned the existence of those insensible patches on the skin of their victims, to which the minute physical examinations of recent medicine have but lately attracted attention again. They may be scattered anywhere, but are very apt to affect one side of the body. Not infrequently they affect an entire lateral half, from head to foot, and the insensible skin of, say the left side, will then be found separated from the naturally sensitive skin of the right by a perfectly sharp line of demarcation down the middle of the front and back. Sometimes, most remarkable of all, the entire skin, hands, feet, face, everything, and the mucous membranes, muscles, and joints, so far as they can be explored, become *completely* insensible without the other vital functions being gravely disturbed. These anæsthesias and hemianæsthesias, in all their various grades, form the nucleus of M. Janet's observations and hypotheses. And, first of all, he has an hypothesis about the anæsthesia itself, which, like all provisional hypotheses, may do excellent service while awaiting the day when a better one shall take its place.

The original sin of the hysteric mind, he thinks, is the *contractions of the field of consciousness*. The attention has not sufficient strength to take in the normal number of sensations or ideas at once. If an ordinary person can feel ten things at a time, an hysteric can feel but five. Our minds are all of them like vessels full of water, and taking in a new drop makes another drop fall out; only the hysteric mental vessel is preternaturally small. The unifying or synthetizing power which the Ego exerts over the manifold facts which are offered to it is insufficient to do its full amount of work, and an ingrained habit is formed of neglecting or overlooking certain determinate portions of the mass. Thus one eye will be ignored, one arm and hand, or one half of the body. And apart from anæsthesia, hysterics are often extremely *distraites*, and unable to attend

to two things at once. When talking with you they forget everything else. When Lucie stopped conversing directly with anyone,
she ceased to be able to hear anyone else. You might stand behind
her, call her by name, shout abuse into her ears, without making
her turn round; or place yourself before her, show her objects,
touch her, etc., without attracting her notice. When finally she
becomes aware of you, she thinks you have just come into the room
again, and greets you accordingly. This singular forgetfulness
makes her liable to tell all her secrets aloud, unrestrained by the
presence of unsuitable auditors. This contracted mental field (or
state of monoideism, as it has been called) characterizes also the
hypnotic state of normal persons, so that in this important respect
a waking hysteric is like a well person in the hypnotic trance. Both
are wholly lost in their present idea, its normal "reductives" and
correctives having lapsed from view.

The anæsthesias of the class of patients we are considering can
be made to disappear more or less completely by various odd processes. It has been recently found that magnets, plates of metal, the
electrodes of a battery, placed against the skin, have this peculiar
power. And when one side is relieved in this way, the anæsthesia is
often found to have transferred itself to the opposite side, which,
until then, was well. Whether these strange effects of magnets and
metals be due to their direct physiological action, or to a prior
effect on the patient's mind ("expectant attention" or "suggestion") is still a mooted question.[2] A still better awakener of sensibility in most of these subjects is the *hypnotic state*, which M.
Janet seems to have most easily induced by the orthodox "magnetic" method of "passes" made over the face and body. It was in
making these passes that he first stumbled on one of the most
curious facts recorded in his volume. One day, when the subject
named Lucie was in the hypnotic state, he made passes over her
again for half an hour, just as if she were not already "asleep." The
result was to throw her into a sort of syncope from which, after
another half hour, she revived in a second somnambulic condition
entirely unlike that which had characterized her hitherto—different
sensibilities, a different memory, a different person, in short. In

[2] M. Janet seems rather to incline to the former view, though suggestion may at
times be exclusively responsible, as when he produced what was essentially the
same phenomenon by pointing an orange-peel held out on the end of a long stick
at the parts!

the waking state the poor young woman was anæsthetic all over, nearly deaf, and with a badly contracted field of vision. Bad as it was, however, sight was her best sense, and she used it as a guide in all her movements. With her eyes bandaged she was entirely helpless, and, like other persons of a similar sort whose cases have been recorded, she almost immediately fell asleep in consequence of the withdrawal of her last sensorial stimulus. M. Janet calls this waking or primary (one can hardly, in such a connection, say "normal") state by the name of Lucie 1. In Lucie 2, her first sort of hypnotic trance, the anæsthesias were diminished but not removed. In the deeper trance, "Lucie 3," brought about as just described, no trace of them remained. Her sensibility became perfect, and instead of being an extreme example of the "visual" type, she was transformed into what, in Professor Charcot's terminology, is known as a motor. That is to say, that whereas, when awake, she had thought in visual terms exclusively, and could imagine things only by remembering how they *looked*, now, in this deeper trance, her thoughts and memories seemed largely composed of images of movement and of touch—of course I state summarily here what appears in the book as an induction from many facts.

Having discovered this deeper trance in Lucie, M. Janet naturally became eager to find it in his other subjects. He found it in Rose, in Marie, and in Léonie; and, best of all, his brother, Dr. Jules Janet, who was *interne* at the Salpêtrière Hospital, found it in the celebrated subject Witt. whose trances had been studied for years by the various doctors of that institution without any of them having happened to awaken this very peculiar modification of the personality.

With the return of all the sensibilities in the deeper trance, the subjects are transformed, as it were, into normal persons. Their memories, in particular, grow more extensive; and here comes in M. Janet's first great theoretic generalization, which is this: When a certain kind of sensation is abolished in an hysteric patient, there is also abolished along with it all recollection of past sensations of that kind. If, for example, hearing be the anæsthetic sense, the patient becomes unable even to imagine sounds and voices, and has to speak, when speech is still possible, by means of motor or articulatory cues. If the motor sense be abolished, the patient must will the movements of his limbs by first defining them to his mind in visual terms, and must innervate his voice by premonitory ideas of the way in which the words are going to sound. The practical effects of this law of M. Janet's upon the patient's recollections would necessarily be great. Take things touched and handled, for example, and bodily movements. All memories of such things, all records of such experiences, being normally stored away in tactile terms, would have to be incontinently lost and forgotten so soon as the cutaneous and muscular sensibility should come to be cut out in the course of disease. Memory of them would be restored again, on the other hand, so soon as the sense of touch came back. Experiences, again, undergone during an anæsthetic condition of touch (and stored up consequently in visual or auditory terms exclusively), can have contracted no "associations" with tactile ideas, for such ideas are, for the time being, forgotten and practically non-existent. If, however, the touch-sensibilities ever are restored, and their ideas and memories with them, it may easily happen that they, with their clustered associations, may temporarily keep out of consciousness things like the visual and other experiences accumulated during the anæsthetic period which have no connections with them. If touch be the dominant sense in childhood, it would thus be explained why hysterical anæsthetics, whose tactile sensibilities and memories are brought back again by trance, so often assume a childlike deportment, and even call themselves by baby-names. Such, at least, is a suggestion of M. Janet's to explain a not infrequent sort of observation. MM. Bourru and Burot found, for instance, in their extraordinary male somnambulist Louis V., that reviving by suggestion a certain condition of bodily feeling in him would invariably transport him back to the epoch of his life when that condition had prevailed. He forgot the later years, and resumed the character and sort of intellect which had characterized him at the earlier time.

M. Janet's theory will provoke controversy and stimulate observation. You can ask little more than that of any theory. My own impression is that the law that anæsthesias carry "amnesias" with them, will not come out distinctly in every individual case. The intricacy of the associative processes, and the fact that comparatively few experiences are stored up in one form of sensibility alone, would be sufficient to prevent this. Perfect illustrations of the law will therefore be met with only in privileged subjects like M. Janet's own. *They* indeed seem to have exemplified it beautifully. M. Janet says:

"It seems to me, that if I were to awake some morning with no muscular or tactile feelings, if, like Rose, I should suddenly lose my sense of color, and distinguish nothing in the universe but black and white, I should be terrified, and instantly appeal for help. These women, on the contrary, find their state so natural that they never even complain. When I, after some trials, proved to Rose that she could perceive no color, I found her ignorant of the fact. When I showed Lucie that she could feel neither pain nor contact, she answered, 'All the better!' When I made her conscious that she never knew where her arms were till she saw them, and that she lost her legs when in bed, she replied, '*C'est tout naturel*, as long as I don't see them; everyone is like that.' In a word, being incapable of comparing their present state of sensibility with a former one of which all memory is lost, they suffer no more than we do at not hearing the 'music of the spheres.' "

M. Janet restored their tactile sense temporarily by means of electric currents, passes, etc., and then made them handle various objects, such as keys and pencils, or make particular movements, like the sign of the cross. The moment the anæsthesia returned, they found it impossible to recollect the objects or the acts. "They had had nothing in their hands, they had done nothing," etc. The next day, however, sensibility being again restored by similar processes, they remembered perfectly the circumstance, and told what they had handled or had done.

It is in this way that M. Janet explains the general law that persons forget in the waking state what has happened to them in trance. There are differences of sensibility, and consequently breaches in the association of ideas. Certain of his hysterics (as we have seen) regained complete sensibility in their deeper trance. The result was such an enlargement of their power of recollecting that they could then go back and explain the origin of many of their peculiarities which would else be inexplicable. One stage in the great convulsive attack of hystero-epilepsy is what the French writers call *la phase des attitudes passionnelles*, in which the patient, without speaking or giving any account of herself, will go through the outward movements of fear, anger, or some other emotional state of mind. Usually this phase is, with each patient, a thing so stereotyped as to seem automatic, and doubts have even been expressed as to whether any consciousness exists whilst it lasts. When, however, the patient Lucie's tactile sensibility came back in her state of Lucie 3, she explained the origin of her hysteric crises in a great fright which she had had when a child, on a day when certain men, hid behind the curtains, had jumped out upon her; she told how she went through this scene again in all her crises; she told of her sleep-walking fits through the house when a child, and how, for several months, she had been shut in a dark room because of a disorder of the eyes. All these were things of which she recollects nothing when awake, because they were records of experiences mainly of motion and of touch, and when awake her feelings of touch and movement disappeared.

But the case of Léonie is the most interesting, and shows beautifully how, with the sensibilities and motor impulses, the memories and character will change.

"This woman, whose life sounds more like an improbable romance than a genuine history, has had attacks of natural somnambulism since the age of three years. She has been hypnotized constantly, by all sorts of persons, from the age of sixteen upwards, and she is now forty-five. Whilst her normal life developed in one way in the midst of her poor country surroundings, her second life was passed in drawing-rooms and doctors' offices, and naturally took an entirely different direction. To-day, when in her normal state, this poor peasant-woman is a serious and rather sad person, calm and slow, very mild with everyone, and extremely timid; to look at her one would never suspect the personage which she contains. But hardly is she put to sleep hypnotically than a metamorphosis occurs. Her face is no longer the same. She keeps her eyes closed, it is true, but the acuteness of her other senses supplies their place. She is gay, noisy, restless, sometimes insupportably so. She remains good-natured, but has acquired a singular tendency to irony and sharp jesting. Nothing is more curious than to hear her, after a sitting when she has received a visit from strangers who wished to see her asleep. She gives a word-portrait of them, apes their manners, pretends to know their little ridiculous aspects and passions, and for each invents a romance. To this character must be added the possession of an enormous number of recollections whose existence she does not even suspect when awake, for her amnesia is then complete. . . . She refuses the name of Léonie, and takes that of Léontine (Léonie 2), to which her first magnetizers had accustomed her. 'That good woman is not myself,' she says, 'she is too stupid.' . . . To herself Léontine (or Léonie 2), she attributes all the sensations and all the actions; in a word, all the conscious experiences, which she has undergone *in somnambulism*, and knits them together to make the history of her already long life. To Léonie 1, on the other hand, she exclusively ascribes the events lived through in waking hours. I was at first struck by an important exception to the rule, and was disposed to think that there might be something arbitrary in this partition of her recollections. In the normal state Léonie has a husband and children. But Léonie 2, the somnambulist, whilst acknowledging the children as her own, attributes the husband to 'the other.' This choice was perhaps explicable, but it followed no rule. It was not till later that I learned that her magnetizers in early days, as audacious as certain hypnotizers of recent date, had somnambulized her for her first *accouchements*, and that she had lapsed into that state spontaneously in the later ones. Léonie 2 was thus quite right in ascribing to herself the children—since it was she who had had them—and the rule that her first trance-state forms a different personality was not broken. But it is the same with her second state of trance. When after the renewed passes, syncope, etc., she reaches the condition which I have called Léonie 3, she is another person still. Serious and grave, instead of being a restless child, she speaks slowly and moves but little. Again she separates herself from the waking Léonie 1. 'A good but rather stupid woman,' she says, 'and not me.' And she also separates herself from Léonie 2. 'How can you see anything of me in that crazy creature?' she says. 'Fortunately I am nothing for her!' "

Léonie 1 knows only of herself; Léonie 2 of herself and of Léonie 1; Léonie 3 knows of herself and of both the others. Léonie 1 has a visual consciousness; Léonie 2 has one both visual and auditory; in Léonie 3 it is at once visual, auditory, and tactile. Professor Janet thought at first that he was Léonie 3's discoverer. But she told him that she had been frequently in that condition before. Dr. Perrier, a former magnetizer, had hit upon her just as M. Janet had, in seeking by means of passes to deepen the sleep of Léonie 2. "This resurrection of a somnambulic personage, who had been extinct for twenty years, is curious enough; and in speaking to Léonie 3 I naturally now adopt the name of Léonore, which was given her by her first master."

The reader easily sees what surprises the trance-state may prepare, not only for the subject but for the operator. For the subject the surprises are often inconvenient enough, especially when the trance comes and goes spontaneously. Thus Léonie 1 is overwhelmed with embarrassment when, in the street, Léonie 2's gentlemen-friends (who are not hers) accost her. Léonie 2 spontaneously writes letters, which Léonie 1, not understanding, destroys when she finds them. Léonie 2 proceeds to thereupon hide them in a photograph album, into which she knows Léonie 1 will never look, because it contains the portrait of her former magnetizer, the sight of whom may put her to sleep again, which she dislikes. Léonie 1 finds herself in places known only to Léonie 2, to which the latter has led her, and then taken flight, etc. One sees the possibility of a new kind of "Comedy of Errors," to which it would take the skill of a Parisian *vaudevilliste* to do justice.

I fear that the reader unversed in this sort of lore will here let his growing impatience master him, and throw away my article as the work of either a mystifier or a dupe. These facts seem so silly and unreal, these "subjects" so contrary to all that our education has led us to expect our fellow-creatures to be! Well, our education has been too narrow, that is all. Let one but once become familiar with the behavior of that not very rare personage, a good hypnotic subject, and the entire class of phenomena which I am recording come to seem not only possible but probable. It is, after all, only the fulfilment of what Locke's speculative genius suggested long ago, when, in that famous chapter on "Identity and Diversity" which occasioned such scandal in its day, after saying that personality extended no farther than consciousness, he went on to affirm that there would be two different selves or persons in one man, if the experiences undergone by that man should fall into two groups, each gathered into a distinct focus of recollection.

But still more remarkable things are to come, so I pray the reader to be patient and hear me a little longer, even if he means to give me up at last. These different personalities, admitted as possible by Locke, which we, under M. Janet's guidance, have seen actually succeeding each other under the names of Lucie 1, 2, and 3; and under those of Léonie 1, 2, and 3 mutually disowning and despising each other; are proved by M. Janet not only to exist in the successive forms in which we have seen them, but to *coexist*, to exist simultaneously; in such wise that while Lucie 1, for example, is apparently the only Lucie, anæsthetic, helpless, yet absorbed in conversation, that other Lucie—Lucie 3—is all the time "alive and kicking" inside of the same woman, and fully sensible and wide awake, and occupied with her own quite different concerns. This simultaneous coexistence of the different personages into which one human being may be split is the *great* thesis of M. Janet's book. Others, as Edmund Gurney, Bernheim, Binet, and more besides, have had the same idea, and proved it for certain cases; but M. Janet has emphasized and generalized it, and shown it to be true universally. He has been enabled to do this by *tapping* the submerged consciousness and making it respond in certain peculiar ways of which I now proceed to give a brief account. He found in several subjects, when the ordinary or primary consciousness was fully absorbed in conversation with a visitor (and the reader will remember how absolutely these hysterics then lapse into oblivion of surrounding things), that the submerged self would hear his voice if he came up and addressed the subject in a whisper; and would respond either by obeying such orders as he gave, or by gestures, or, finally, by pencil-writing on a sheet of paper placed under the hand. The *ostensible* consciousness, meanwhile, would go on with the conversation, entirely unaware of the gestures, acts, or writing performances of the hand. These latter, in turn, appeared quite as little disturbed by the upper consciousness's concerns. This proof by automatic writing of the secondary consciousness's existence is the most cogent and striking one; but a crowd of other facts prove the same thing. If I run through them all rapidly, the reader will probably be convinced.

The apparently anæsthetic hand of these subjects, for one thing, will often adapt itself discriminatingly to whatever object may be put into it. With a pencil it will make writing movements; into a pair of scissors it will put its fingers, and will open and shut them, etc. The primary consciousness, so to call it, is meanwhile unable to say whether or no *anything* is in the hand, if the latter be hidden from sight. "I put a pair of eye-glasses into Léonie's anæsthetic hand; this hand opens it and raises it towards the nose, but halfway thither it enters the field of vision of Léonie, who sees it and stops stupefied. 'Why,' says she, 'I have an eye-glass in my left hand!' " M. Binet found a very curious sort of connection between the apparently anæsthetic skin and the mind in some Salpêtrière subjects. Things placed in the hand were not felt, but *thought* of (apparently in visual terms), and in no wise referred by the subject to their starting-point in the hand's sensation. A key, a knife, placed in the hand occasioned *ideas* of a key or a knife, but the hand felt nothing. Similarly the subject thought of the number 3, 6, etc., if the hand or finger was bent three or six times by the operator, or if he stroked it three, six, etc., times.

In certain individuals there was found a still odder phenomenon, which reminds one of that curious idiosyncrasy of "colored hearing" of which a few cases have been lately described with great care by foreign writers. These individuals, namely, *saw* the impression received by the hand, but could not feel it; and the things seen appeared by no means associated with the hand, but more like an independent vision, which usually interested and surprised the patient. Her hand being hidden by a screen, she was ordered to look at another screen and to tell of any visual image which might project itself thereon. Numbers would then come, corresponding to the number of times the insensible member was raised, touched, etc. Colored lines and figures would come, corresponding to similar ones traced on the palm; the hand itself, or its fingers, would come when manipulated; and, finally, objects placed in it would come; but on the hand itself nothing could ever be felt. Of course, simulation would not be hard here; but M. Binet disbelieves this (usually very shallow) explanation to be a probable one of the cases in question.[3]

The usual way in which doctors measure the delicacy of our touch is by the compass-points. Two points are normally felt as one whenever they are too close together for discrimination; but what is "too close" on one part of the skin may seem very far apart on another. In the middle of the back or on the thigh less than three inches may be too close; on the finger-tip a tenth of an inch is far enough apart. Now, as tested in this way, with the appeal made to the primary consciousness, which talks through the mouth, and seems to hold the field alone, a certain person's skin may be entirely anæsthetic and not feel the compass-points at all; and yet this same skin will prove to have a perfectly normal sensibility if the appeal be made to that other secondary or sub-consciousness which expresses itself automatically by writing or by movements of the hand. M. Binet, M. Pierre Janet, and M. Jules Janet have all found this. The subject, whenever touched, would signify "one point" or "two points," as accurately as if she were a normal person. But she would signify it only by these movements; and of the movements themselves her primary self would be as unconscious as of the facts they signified, for what the submerged consciousness makes the hand do automatically is unknown to the upper consciousness, which uses the mouth.

---

[3] This whole phenomenon shows how an idea which remains itself below the threshold of a certain conscious self may occasion associative effects therein. The skin-sensations, unfelt by the patient's primary consciousness, awaken, nevertheless, their usual visual associates therein.

Messrs. Bernheim and Pitres have also proved, by observations too complicated to be given here, that the hysterical blindness is no real blindness at all. The eye of an hysteric which is totally blind when the other, or seeing eye, is shut, will do its share of vision perfectly well when *both* eyes are open together. But even where both eyes are semi-blind from hysterical disease, the method of automatic writing proves that their perceptions exist, only cut off from communication with the upper consciousness. M. Binet has found the hand of his patients unconsciously writing down words which their eyes were vainly endeavoring to "see," *i.e.*, to bring to the upper consciousness. Their submerged consciousness was, of course, seeing them, or the hand couldn't have written as it did. Similarly the sub-conscious self perfectly well perceives colors which the hysterically color-blind eyes cannot bring to the normal consciousness. Again, pricks, burns, and pinches on the anæsthetic skin, all unnoticed by the upper self, are recollected to have been suffered, and complained of, as soon as the under self gets a chance to express itself by the passage of the subject into hypnotic trance.

It must be admitted therefore that, in certain persons at least, the total possible consciousness may be split into parts which co-exist, but mutually ignore each other and share the objects of knowledge between them, and—more remarkable still—are complementary. Give an object to one of the consciousnesses, and by that fact you remove it from the other or others. Barring a certain common fund of information, like the command of language, etc., what the upper self knows, the under self is ignorant of, and *vice versa*. M. Janet has proved this beautifully in his subject Lucie. The following experiment will serve as the type of the rest: In her trance he covered her lap with cards, each bearing a number. He then told her that on waking she should *not see* any card whose number was a multiple of three. This is the ordinary so-called "post-hypnotic suggestion," now well known, and for which Lucie was a well-adapted subject. Accordingly, when she was awakened and asked about the papers on her lap, she counted and picked up only those whose number was not a multiple of 3. To the 12, 18, 9, etc., she was blind. But the hand, when the sub-conscious self was interrogated by the usual method of engrossing the upper self in another conversation, wrote that the only cards in Lucie's lap were those numbered 12, 18, 9, etc., and on being asked to pick up all the cards which were there, picked up these and let the others lie.

Similarly, when the sight of certain things was suggested to the sub-conscious Lucie, the normal Lucie suddenly became partially or totally blind. "What is the matter? I can't see!" the normal personage suddenly cried out in the midst of her conversation, when M. Janet whispered to the secondary personage to make use of her eyes. The anæsthesias, paralyses, contractions, and other irregularities from which hysterics suffer seem, then, to be due to the fact that their secondary personage has enriched itself by robbing the primary one of a function which the latter ought to have retained. The curative indication is evident: Get at the secondary personage by hypnotization, or in whatever other way, and make her *give up* the eye, the skin, the arm, or whatever the affected part may be. The normal self thereupon regains possession, sees, feels, and is able to move again. In this way M. Jules Janet easily cured the subject Witt. of all sorts of afflictions which, until he had discovered the secret of her deeper trance, it had been difficult to subdue. "*Cessez cette mauvaise plaisanterie,*" he said to the secondary self, and the latter obeyed. The way in which the various personages share the stock of possible sensations between them seems to be amusingly illustrated in this young woman. When awake, her skin is insensible everywhere except on a zone about the arm where she habitually wears a gold bracelet. This zone has feeling; but in the deeper trance, when all the rest of her body feels, this particular zone becomes absolutely anæsthetic.

Sometimes the mutual ignorance of the selves leads to incidents which are strange enough. The acts and movements performed by the sub-conscious self are withdrawn from the conscious one, and the subject will do all sorts of incongruous things, of which he remains quite unaware.

"I order Lucie [by the method of *distraction*] to make a *pied de nez*, and her hands go forthwith to the end of her nose. Asked what she is doing, she replies that she is doing nothing, and continues for a long time talking, with no apparent suspicion that her fingers are moving in front of her nose. I make her walk about the room, she continues to speak, and believes herself sitting down."

M. Janet observed similar acts in a man in alcoholic delirium. Whilst the doctor was questioning him, M. Janet made him, by whispered suggestion, walk, sit, kneel, and even lie down on his face on the floor, he all the while believing himself to be standing beside his bed. Such *bizarreries* sound incredible until one has seen their like. Long ago, without understanding it, I myself saw a small example of the way in which a person's knowledge may be shared by the two selves. A young woman, who had been writing automatically, was sitting with a pencil in her hand, trying to recall, at my request, the name of a gentleman whom she had once seen. She could only recollect the first syllable. *Her hand*, meanwhile, without her knowledge, wrote down the last two syllables. In a perfectly healthy young man who can write with the planchette, I lately found the hand to be entirely anæsthetic during the writing act. I could prick it severely without the subject knowing the fact. The planchette, however, accused me in strong terms of hurting the hand. Pricks on the *other* (non-writing) hand, meanwhile, which awakened strong protest from the young man's vocal organs, were denied to exist by the self which made the planchette go.

We get exactly similar results in post-hypnotic suggestion. It is a familiar fact that certain subjects, when told during a trance to perform an act or to experience an hallucination after waking, will, when the time comes, obey the command. How is the command registered? How is its performance so accurately timed? These problems were long a mystery, for the primary personality remembers nothing of the trance or the suggestion, and will often trump up an improvised pretext for yielding to the unaccountable impulse which comes over him so suddenly, and which he cannot resist. Edmund Gurney was the first to discover, by means of automatic writing, that the secondary self was awake, keeping its attention constantly fixed on the command and watching for the signal of its execution. Certain trance-subjects, who were also automatic writers, when roused from trance and put to the planchette—not knowing then what they wrote, and having their upper attention fully engrossed by reading aloud, talking, or solving problems in mental arithmetic—would inscribe the orders they had received, together with notes relative to the time elapsed and the time yet to run before the execution. It is therefore to no "automatism," in the mechanical sense, that such acts are due: a self presides over them, a split-off, limited, and buried, but yet a fully conscious self. More than this, the buried self often comes to the surface and drives out the other self whilst the acts are performing. In other words, the subject lapses into trance again when the moment arrives for execution, and has no subsequent recollection of the act which he has done. Gurney and Beaunis established this fact, which has since been verified on a large scale; and Gurney also showed that the patient became *suggestible* again during the brief time of the performance. M. Janet's observations, in their turn, well illustrate the phenomenon.

"I tell Lucie to keep her arms raised after she shall have awakened. Hardly is she in the normal state when up go her arms above her head, but she pays no attention to them. She goes, comes, converses, holding her arms high in the air. If asked what her arms are doing, she is surprised at such a question and says, very sincerely: 'My hands are doing nothing; they are just like yours.' . . . I command her to weep, and when awake she really sobs, but continues in the midst of her tears to talk of very gay matters. The sobbing over, there remains no trace of this grief, which seemed to have been quite sub-conscious."

The primary self often has to invent an hallucination by which to mask and hide from its own view the deeds which the other self is enacting. Léonie 3 writes real letters, whilst Léonie 1 believes that she is knitting; or Lucie 3 really comes to the doctor's office, whilst Lucie 1 believes herself to be at home. This is a sort of delirium. The alphabet, or the series of numbers, when handed over to the attention of the secondary personage, may, for the time being, be lost to the normal self. Whilst the hand writes the alphabet, obediently to command, the "subject," to her great stupefaction, finds herself unable to recall it, etc. Few things are more curious than these relations of mutual exclusion, of which all gradations exist, between the several partial consciousnesses.

How far this splitting up of the mind into separate consciousnesses may obtain in each one of us is a problem. M. Janet holds that it is only possible where there is abnormal weakness, and consequently a defect of unifying or co-ordinating power. An hysteric woman abandons part of her consciousness because she is too weak nervously to hold it all together. The abandoned part, meanwhile, may solidify into a secondary or sub-conscious self. In a perfectly sound subject, on the other hand, what is dropped out of mind at one moment keeps coming back at the next. The whole fund of experiences and knowledges remains integrated, and no split-off portions of it can get organized stably enough to form subordinate selves. The stability, monotony, and stupidity of these latter is often very striking. The post-hypnotic self-consciousness seems to think of nothing but the order which it last received; the cataleptic sub-consciousness, of nothing but the last position imprinted on the limb. M. Janet could cause definitely circumscribed reddening and tumefaction of the skin, on two of his subjects, by suggesting to them in hypnotism the hallucination of a mustard-poultice of any special shape. "*J'ai tout le temps pensé à votre sinapisme,*" says the subject, when put back into trance after the suggestion has taken effect. A man, N——, whom M. Janet operated on at long intervals, was between whiles tampered with by another operator, and when put to sleep again by M. Janet, said he was "too far away to receive orders, being in Algiers." The other operator, having suggested that hallucination, had forgotten to remove it before waking the subject from his trance, and the poor, passive, trance-personality had stuck for weeks in the stagnant dream. Léonie's sub-conscious performances having been illustrated to a caller by a *pied de nez*, executed with her left hand in the course of conversation, when, a year later, she meets him again up goes the same hand to her nose again, without Léonie 1 suspecting the fact.

And this leads me to what, after all, is the really important part of these investigations—I mean their possible application to the relief of human misery. Let one think and say what one will about the crudity and intellectual barbarism of much of the philosophizing of our contemporary nerve-doctors; let one dislike as much as one may please the thoroughly materialistic attitude of mind which many of them show; still, their work, as a whole, is sanctified by its positive, practical fertility. Theorems about the unity of the thinking principle will always be, as they always have been, *barren*; but observations of fact lead to new issues *in infinitum*. And when one reflects that nothing less than the cure of insanity—that direst of human afflictions—lies possibly at the end of such inquiries as those which M. Janet and his *confrères* are beginning, one feels as if the disdain which some spiritualistic psychologists exhibit for such researches were very poorly placed. The way to redeem people from barbarism is not to stand aloof and sneer at their awkward attempts, but to show them how to do the same things better. Ordinary hypnotic suggestion is proving itself immensely fertile in the therapeutic field; and the subtler knowledge of sub-conscious states which we are now gaining will certainly increase our powers in this direction many fold. Who knows how many pathological states (not simply nervous and functional ones, but organic ones too) may be due to the existence of some perverse buried fragment of consciousness obstinately nourishing its narrow memory or delusion, and thereby inhibiting the normal flow of life? A concrete case will best exhibit what I mean. On the whole, it is more deeply suggestive to me than anything in Janet's book.

The story is that of a young girl of nineteen named Marie, who came to the hospital in an almost desperate condition, with monthly convulsive crises, chill, fever, delirium, attacks of terror, etc., lasting for days, together with various shifting anæsthesias and contractures all the time, and a fixed blindness of the left eye. At first M. Janet, divining no particular psychological factor in the case, took little interest in the patient, who remained in the hospital for seven months, and had all the usual courses of treatment applied, including water-cure and ordinary hypnotic suggestions, without the slightest good effect.

She then fell into a sort of despair, of which the result was to make M. Janet try to throw her into a deeper trance, so as to get, if possible, some knowledge of her remoter psychologic antecedents, and of the original causes of the disease, of which, in the waking state and in ordinary hypnotism, she could give no definite account. He succeeded even beyond his expectations; for both her early memories and the internal memory of her crises returned in the deep somnambulism, and she explained three things: Her periodical chill, fever, and delirium were due to a foolish immersion of herself in cold water at the age of thirteen. The chill, fever, etc., were consequences which then ensued; and now, years later, the experience then stamped in upon the brain for the first time was *repeating itself* at regular intervals in the form of an hallucination undergone by the sub-conscious self, and of which the primary personality only experienced the outer results. The attacks of terror were accounted for by another shocking experience. At the age of sixteen she had seen an old woman killed by falling from a height; and the sub-conscious self, for reasons best known to itself, saw fit to believe itself present at this experience also whenever the other crises came on. The hysterical blindness of her left eye had the same sort of origin, dating back to her sixth year, when she had been forced, in spite of her cries, to sleep in the same bed with another child, the left half of whose face bore a disgusting eruption. The result was an eruption on the same parts of her own face, which came back for several years before it disappeared entirely, and left behind it an anæsthesia of the skin and the blindness of the eye.

So much for the origin of the poor girl's various afflictions. Now for the cure! The thing needed was, of course, to get the subconscious personality to leave off having these senseless hallucinations. But they had become so stereotyped and habitual that this proved no easy task to achieve. Simple commands were fruitless; but M. Janet at last hit upon an artifice, which shows how many resources the successful mind-doctor must possess. He carried the poor Marie back in imagination to the earlier dates. It proved as easy with her as with many others when entranced, to produce the hallucination that she was again a child, all that was needed being an impressive affirmation to that effect. Accordingly M. Janet, replacing her in this wise at the age of six, made her go through the bed-scene again, but gave it a different *dénouement*. He made her believe that the horrible child had no eruption and was charming, so that she was finally convinced, and caressed without fear this new object of her imagination. He made her re-enact the scene of the cold immersion, but gave it also an entirely different result. He made her live again through the old woman's accident, but substituted a comical issue for the old tragical one which had made so deep an impression. The sub-conscious Marie, passive and docile as usual, adopted these new versions of the old tales; and was apparently either living in monotonous contemplation of them or had become extinct altogether when M. Janet wrote his book. For all morbid symptoms ceased as if by magic. "It is five months," our author says, "since these experiments were performed. Marie shows no longer the slightest mark of hysteria. She is well; and, in particular, has grown quite stout. Her physical aspect has absolutely changed." Finally, she is no longer hypnotizable, as often happens in these cases when the health returns.

The mind-curers and Christian scientists, of whom we have lately heard so much, unquestionably get, by widely different methods, results, in certain cases, no less remarkable than this. The ordinary medical man, if he believes the facts at all, dismisses them from his attention with the cut-and-dried remark that they are "only effects of the imagination." It is the great merit of these French investigators, and of Messrs. Myers, Gurney, and the "psychical researchers," that they are for the first time trying to read some sort of a definite meaning into this vaguest of phrases. Little by little the meaning will grow more precise. It seems to me a very great step to have ascertained that the secondary self, or selves, coexist with the primary one, the trance-personalities with the normal one, during the waking state. But just what these secondary selves may be, and what are their remoter relations and conditions of existence, are questions to which the answer is anything but clear. My own decided impression is that M. Janet's generalizations are based on too limited a number of cases to cover the whole ground. He would have it that the secondary self is always a symptom of hysteria, and that the essential fact about hysteria is the lack of synthetizing power and consequent disintegration of the field of consciousness into mutually exclusive parts. The secondary and the primary consciousnesses added together can, on M. Janet's theory, never exceed the normally total consciousness of the individual. This theory certainly expresses pretty well the facts which have fallen under its author's own observation, though even here, if this were a critical article, I might have something to say. But there are trances which obey another type. I know a non-hysterical woman who, in her trances, knows facts which altogether transcend her *possible* normal consciousness, facts about the lives of people whom she never saw or heard of before. I am well aware of all the liabilities to which this statement exposes me, and I make it deliberately, having practically no doubt whatever of its truth. My *own* impression is that the trance-condition is an immensely complex and fluctuating thing, into the understanding of which we have hardly begun to penetrate, and concerning which any very sweeping generalization is sure to be premature. *A comparative study of trances and subconscious states* is meanwhile of the most urgent importance for the comprehension of our nature. It often happens that scattered facts of a certain kind float around for a long time, but that nothing scientific or solid comes of them until some man writes just enough of a book to give them a possible body and meaning. Then they shoot together, as it were, from all directions, and that book becomes the centre of crystallization of a rapid accumulation of new knowledge. Such a book I am sure that M. Janet's ought to be; and I confidently prophesy that anyone who may be induced by this article to follow the path of study in which it is so brilliant a pioneer will reap a rich reward.

Notes on Ansel Bourne

May 30th, 1890.

He was tried during this afternoon by Drs. Wadsworth and Jack, both in and out of the trance. No difference of vision or hearing was discovered in the two states. He recognized tobacco and vinegar in the trance by their smell, and also salt and sugar on his tongue, though the sugar was recognized slowly. I found, to my surprise, that he discriminated points about as well on the palmar surface of hands or fingers when in as when out of the trance. The tardiness of his replies made it seem as if he must be more insensitive. The only difference between trance and waking as to sensibility seems then to be a not very pronounced analgesia during trance.

Produced hallucination of red cross in trance. No after image. Waked him by upward passes made without warning.

A Plea for Psychology as a 'Natural Science'

In the first number of this journal, Professor Ladd takes my *Principles of Psychology* as a text for certain critical reflections upon the cerebralistic point of view which is becoming so popular in psychology to-day. I appreciate fully the kind personal tone of the article, and I admit that many of the thrusts strike home, though it shocks me a bit, I confess, to find that in some particulars my volumes have given my critic so false an impression of my beliefs. I have never claimed, for instance, as Professor Ladd seems to think I claim, that psychology as it stands to-day, *is* a natural science, or in an exact way a science at all. Psychology, indeed, is to-day hardly more than what physics was before Galileo, what chemistry was before Lavoisier. It is a mass of phenomenal description, gossip, and myth, including, however, real material enough to justify one in the hope that with judgment and good-will on the part of those interested, its study may be so organized even now as to become worthy of the name of natural science at no very distant day. I hoped that my book would leave on my readers an impression somewhat like this of my own state of mind. I wished, by treating Psychology *like* a natural science, to help her to become one. But what one book may have said or not said is a matter of small moment. My two volumes are doubtless uncouth enough; and since Professor Ladd wrote his article my general position has probably been made more clear in the abridgement of them, which Messrs. Holt & Co. have recently published under the name of *Psychology: Briefer Course*.[1] Let us drop the wearisome book, therefore, and turn to the question itself, for that is what we all have most at heart. What may one lawfully mean by saying that Psychology ought to be treated after the fashion of a 'natural science'? I think that I can state what I mean; and I even hope that I can enlist the sympathy of men like Professor Ladd in the cause, when once the argument is fairly set forth.

What is a natural science, to begin with? It is a mere fragment of truth broken out from the whole mass of it for the sake of practical effectiveness exclusively. *Divide et impera.* Every special science, in order to get at its own particulars at all, must make a number of convenient assumptions and decline to be responsible for questions which the human mind will continue to ask about them. Thus physics assumes a material world, but never tries to show how our experience of such a world is 'possible.' It assumes the inter-action of bodies, and the completion by them of continuous changes, without pretending to know how such results can be. Between the things thus assumed, now, the various sciences find definite 'laws' of sequence; and so are enabled to furnish general Philosophy with materials properly shaped and simplified for her ulterior tasks. If, therefore, psychology is ever to conform to the type of the other natural sciences, it must also renounce certain ultimate solutions, and place itself on the usual common-sense basis by uncritically begging such data as the existence of a physical world, of states of mind, and of the fact that these latter take cognizance of other things. What the 'physical world' may be in itself, how 'states of mind' can exist at all, and exactly what 'taking cognizance' may imply, are inevitable further questions; but they are questions of the kind for which general philosophy, not natural science, is held responsible.

Now if there is any natural science in possession of a subject-matter well set off and contrasted with all others, it is psychology. However much our self-consciousness, our freedom, our ability to conceive universals, or what not, may ally us with the Infinite and Absolute, there is yet an aspect of our being, even of our mental

[1] See especially the chapters headed 'Introductory' and 'Epilogue.'

being, which falls wholly within the sphere of natural history. As constituting the inner life of individual persons who are born and die, our conscious states are temporal *events* arising in the ordinary course of nature—events, moreover, the conditions of whose happening or non-happening from one moment to another, lie certainly in large part in the physical world. Not only this; they are events of such tremendous practical moment to us that the control of these conditions on a large scale would be an achievement compared with which the control of the rest of physical nature would appear comparatively insignificant. All natural sciences aim at practical prediction and control, and in none of them is this more the case than in psychology to-day. We live surrounded by an enormous body of persons who are most definitely interested in the control of states of mind, and incessantly craving for a sort of psychological science which will teach them how to *act*. What every educator, every jail-warden, every doctor, every clergyman, every asylum-superintendent, asks of psychology is practical rules. Such men care little or nothing about the ultimate philosophic grounds of mental phenomena, but they do care immensely about improving the ideas, dispositions, and conduct of the particular individuals in their charge.

Now out of what may be called the biological study of human nature there has at last been precipitated a very important mass of material strung on a guiding conception which already to some degree meets these persons' needs. The brain-path theory based on reflex action, the conception of the human individual as an organized mass of tendencies to react mentally and muscularly on his environment in ways which may be either preservative or destructive, not only helps them to analyze their cases, but often leads them to the right remedy when perversion has set in. How much more this conception may yet help them these men do not know, but they indulge great hopes. Together with the physiologists and naturalists they already form a band of workers, full of enthusiasm and confidence in each other, and are pouring in materials about human nature so copious that the entire working life of a student may easily go to keeping abreast of the tide. The 'psychical researchers,' though kept at present somewhat out in the cold, will inevitably conquer the recognition which their labors also deserve, and will make, perhaps, the most important contributions of all to the pile. But, as I just remarked, few of these persons have any aptitude or fondness for general philosophy; they have quite as little as the pure-blooded philosophers have for discovering particular facts.

The actual existence of two utterly distinct types of mind, with their distinct needs, both of them having legitimate business to transact with psychology, must then be recognized; and the only question there can be is the practical one of how to distribute the labor so as to waste it least and get the most efficient results. For my part, I yield to no man in my expectations of what general philosophy will some day do in helping us to rational conceptions of the world. But when I look abroad and see how almost all the fresh life that has come into psychology of recent years has come from the biologists, doctors, and psychical researchers, I feel as if their impulse to constitute the science in their own way, as a branch of biology, were an unsafe one to thwart; and that wisdom lies, not in forcing the consideration of the more metaphysical aspects of human consciousness upon them, but, on the contrary, in carefully rescuing these aspects from their hands, and handing them over to those of the specialists in philosophy, where the metaphysical aspects of physics are already allowed to belong. If there could be, after sufficient ventilation of the subject, a generally expressed consent as to the kind of problems in psychology that were metaphysical and the kind that were analogous to those of the natural sciences, and if the word 'psychology' could then be restricted so as to cover as much as possible the latter and not the former problems, a psychology so understood might be safely handed over to the keeping of the men of facts, of the laboratory workers and biologists. We certainly need something more radical than the old division into 'rational' and 'empirical' psychology, both to be treated by the same writer between the covers of the same book. We need a fair and square and explicit *abandonment* of such questions as that of the soul, the transcendental ego, the fusion of ideas or particles of mind stuff, *etc.*, by the practical man; and a fair and square determination on the part of the philosophers to keep such questions out of psychology and treat them only in their widest possible connections, amongst the objects of an ultimate critical review of all the elements of the world.

Professor Andrew Seth has put the thing excellently in his late inaugural address at Edinburgh, on the *Present Position of the Philosophical Sciences*.[2] "Psychology," he says, "has become more scientific, and has thereby become more conscious of her own aims, and, at the same time, of her necessary limitations. *Ceasing to put herself forward as philosophy*, she has entered upon a new period of development as science; and in doing so she has disarmed the jealousy, and is even fast conquering the indifference, of the transcendental philosopher." Why should not Professor Ladd, why should not any 'transcendental philosopher,' be glad to help confirm and develop so beneficial a tendency as this? In Professor Ladd's own book on *Physiological Psychology*, that "real being, proceeding to unfold powers that are *sui generis*, according to laws of its own," for whose recognition he contends, plays no organic part in the work,[3] and has proved a mere stumbling-block to his biological reviewers. Why force it on their attention, and perpetuate thereby a sort of wrangle from which physics and chemistry have long since emerged, and from which psychology, if left to the 'facts of experience' alone, promises so soon to escape?

Now the sort of 'fact of experience' on which in my book I have proposed to compromise, is the so-called 'mental state,' in whose existence not only common men but philosophers have uniformly believed. Whatever conclusions an ultimate criticism may come to about mental states, they form a practically admitted sort of object whose habits of coexistence and succession and relations with organic conditions form an entirely definite subject of research. Cannot philosophers and biologists both become 'psychologists' on this common basis? Cannot both forego ulterior inquiries, and agree that, provisionally at least, the mental state shall be the ultimate datum so far as 'psychology' cares to go? If the 'scientific monists' would only agree to say nothing of the states being produced by the integration and differentiation of 'psychic units,' and the 'transcendental metaphysicians' agree to say nothing of their

2 Blackwood, 1891.

3 I mean that such a being is quite barren of particular consequences. Its character is only known by its reactions on the signals which the nervous system gives, and these must be gathered by observation after the fact. If only it were subject to successive reincarnations, as the theosophists say it is, so that we might guess what sort of a body it would unite with next, or what sort of persons it had helped to constitute previously, those would be great points gained. But even those gains are denied us; and the real being is, for practical purposes, an entire superfluity, which a *practical* psychology can perfectly well do without.

being acts of spiritual entities developing according to laws of their own, peace might long reign, and an enormous booty of natural laws be harvested in with comparatively no time or energy lost in recrimination and dispute about first principles. My own volumes are indeed full of such recrimination and dispute, but these un-fortunate episodes are for the most part incidental to the attempt to get the undivided 'mental state' once for all accepted by my colleagues as the fundamental datum for their science. To have proposed such a useful basis for united action in psychology is in my own eyes the chief originality and service of the book; and I cannot help hoping that Professor Ladd may himself yet feel the force of the considerations now urged. Not that to-day we *have* a 'science' of the correlation of mental states with brain states; but that the ascertainment of the laws of such correlation forms the *program* of a science well limited and defined. Of course, when such a science is formed, the whole body of its conclusions will fall a prey to philosophical reflection, and then Professor Ladd's 'real being' will inevitably have the best possible chance to come to its rights.

One great reason why Professor Ladd cares so little about set-ting up psychology as a natural science of the correlations of men-tal with cerebral events, is that brain states are such desperately inaccessible things. I fully admit that any *exact* account of brain states is at present far beyond our reach; and I am surprised that Professor Ladd should have read into my pages the opinion that psychology as a natural science must aim at an account of brain states exclusively, as the correlates of states of mind. Our mental states are correlated *immediately* with brain states, it is true; but, more remotely, they are correlated with many other physical events, peripheral nerve currents for example, and the physical stimuli which occasion these. Of these latter correlations we have an extensive body of rather orderly knowledge. And, after all, may we not exaggerate the degree of our ignorance of brain states them-selves? We don't know exactly what a nerve current is, it is true; but we know a good deal *about* it. We know that it follows a path, for instance, and consumes a fraction of a second of time in doing so. We know that, physically considered, our brain is only a mass of such paths, which incoming currents must somehow make their way through before they run out. We even know something about the consciousness with which particular paths are specially 'correlated,' those in the occipital lobes, *e.g.*, being connected with the consciousness of *visible* things. Now the provisional value of such knowledge as this, however inexact it be, is still immense. It sketches an entire program of investigation, and defines already one great *kind* of law which will be ascertained. The *order in time* of the nerve currents, namely, is what determines the *order in time*, the coexistences and successions of the states of mind to which they are related. Professor Ladd probably does not doubt the nerve-current theory of motor habits; he probably does not doubt that our ability to learn things 'by heart' is due to a capacity in the cerebral cortex for organizing definitely successive systems of paths of discharge. Does he then see any radical reason why the *special time-order* of the 'ideas' in any case whatever of 'association' may not be analogously explained? And if not, may he not go on to admit that the most characteristic features of our faculty of memory,[4] of our perception of outer things,[5] of our liability to illusion,[6] *etc.*, are most plausibly and naturally explained by acquired organic habitudes, stamped by the order of impressions on the plastic matter of the brain? But if he will admit all this, then the diagrams of association-paths of which he preserves so low an opinion are not absolutely contemptible. They do represent the *sort* of thing which determines the order of our thoughts quite as well as those diagrams which chemists make of organic molecules represent the sort of thing which determines the order of substitution when new compounds are made.

It seems to me, finally, that a critic of cerebralism in psychology ought to do one of two things. He ought either to reject it in principle and entirely, but then be willing to throw over, for example, such results as the entire modern doctrine of aphasia—a very hard thing to do; or else he ought to accept it in principle, but then cordially admit that, in spite of present shortcomings, we have here an immense opening upon which a stable phenomenal science must some day appear. We needn't pretend that we have the science already; but we can cheer those on who are working for its future,

---

4 Such as the need of a 'cue'; the advantages, for recall, of repetition and multiple association; the fact of obliviscence, *etc.*

5 That the ideas of all the thing's attributes arise in the imagination, even when only a few of them are felt, *etc.*

6 That, *e.g.*, the most *usual* (and therefore *probable*) associates of the present sensation are mentally imagined even when not actually there.

and clear metaphysical entanglements from their path. In short, we can aspire.

We never ought to doubt that Humanity will continue to produce all the types of thinker which she needs. I myself do not doubt of the 'final perseverance' or success of the philosophers. Nevertheless, if the hard alternative were to arise of a choice between 'theories' and 'facts' in psychology, between a merely rational and a merely practical science of the mind, I do not see how any man could hesitate in his decision. The kind of psychology which could cure a case of melancholy, or charm a chronic insane delusion away, ought certainly to be preferred to the most seraphic insight into the nature of the soul. And that is the sort of psychology which the men who care little or nothing for ultimate rationality, the biologists, nerve-doctors, and psychical researchers, namely, are surely tending, whether we help them or not, to bring about.

Thought Before Language: A Deaf-Mute's Recollections

On page 266 [WORKS, p. 257] of the first volume of my work, *The Principles of Psychology*, I quoted an account of a certain deaf-mute's thoughts before he had the use of any signs for verbal language. The deaf-mute in question is Mr. Melville Ballard, of the Institution for the Deaf and Dumb at Washington; and his narrative shows him to have had a very extensive command of abstract, even of metaphysical conceptions, when as yet his only language was pantomime confined to practical home affairs. Professor von Giżycki of Berlin, whose nominalistic prepossessions were apparently startled by Mr. Ballard's account, wrote to me to ask if I had made sure of his being trustworthy. This led me to make inquiry amongst those who knew Mr. Ballard intimately, and the result was to show that they all regarded him as an exceptionally good witness.[1] Mr.

[1] Professor Samuel Porter (who first published Mr. Ballard's statement in the *Princeton Review* for January, 1881) says: "I regard him as a person quite remarkable for the clearness and accuracy of his recollection of matters of fact, especially such as have occurred under his own observation or in his own experience, and as scrupulously honest and truthful. Indeed his traits of character, both intellectual and moral, are such that I cannot conceive of a case in which testimony of the kind in question could be less open to suspicion and objection."—Mr. Edward Allen Fay writes: "Mr. Ballard is an exceptionally conscientious person in making statements. There is nobody whose testimony with respect to any facts of which he might have knowledge I should more readily accept than his. I place implicit confidence in his honesty as a witness. Is it possible that he is himself deceived, and that, as Prof. v. G. suggests, he 'verlegt sein jetziges gebildetes Denken in die Seele jenes Kindes

Fay (the gist of whose statement about Mr. Ballard I print below) was kind enough to refer me to another printed account of a deaf-mute's cosmological ideas before the acquisition of language; and this led me to correspond with its author, Mr. Theophilus H. d'Estrella, instructor in drawing (I understand) at the California Institution for the Deaf and Dumb, and the Blind. The final result is that I have Mr. d'Estrella's permission to lay before the readers of the PHILOSOPHICAL REVIEW a new document which, whilst it fully tends to corroborate Mr. Ballard's narrative, is much more interesting by its intrinsic content.[2]

The printed account just referred to appeared in the *Weekly News* (a paper published at the Institution at Berkeley, California, and printed by the pupils) for April 27, 1889. Although expressed in the third person, Mr. d'Estrella informs me that it was prepared by himself. I give it here as it stands, in the form of a note to a

---

zurück'? I suppose it is possible, but it does not seem to me probable. His recollection of those early years is so distinct, he recalls so vividly other circumstances which are directly associated with the train of thought described, and about which there could be no mistake, that I am compelled to accept his statement as 'unconditionally trustworthy.' "—Mr. J. C. Gordon says: "Mr. B. is peculiarly qualified to relate incidents interesting to him in the order in which they originally occurred, and with extreme accuracy. His perceptions are acute, and his power of recollection of facts within the range of his experience I consider quite extraordinary. He is not a great students of books, and probably has no idea of the bearing of his statements on metaphysical speculations."

[2] Mr. W. Wilkinson, Superintendent of the Institution, writes to me of Mr. d'Estrella that "he is a man of the highest character and intellectual honesty. He was the first pupil that ever entered this Institution, and when I took charge of the school in 1865 he was about fourteen years old. It was *at that time* that I became specially interested in his account of his explanations of the various physical phenomena as they presented themselves to his untutored mind. At that time I wrote out many pages of his story, but this account, with a good deal of other material, was destroyed in our great fire of 1875. It very often occurs that deaf-mutes are not able to distinguish between the concepts obtained before and after education. By the time they have obtained education enough to express themselves clearly, the memory of things happening before education has become dim and untrustworthy; but Mr. d'Estrella was, and is, unusually bright and of a very inquiring turn of mind, so that before coming to school he endeavored to explain to his own satisfaction the reason of many things, and it is quite surprising how similar his explanations were to the explanations which are found in the childhood of many races. Mr. d'Estrella is imaginative, but quite as much so before education as since, and the early age at which he gave me the account of himself forbids the notion that he could have been influenced by mythologies, and the nearness of time, taken with his honesty, is sufficient assurance of the accuracy of his statement. You may trust Mr. d'Estrella perfectly for any statement he may make."

paper by Mr. J. Scott Hutton on the notions of deaf-mutes before instruction:

This interesting extract reminds Mr. d'Estrella of his similar notions. Nothing stimulated his curiosity like the moon. He was afraid of the moon but he always loved to watch her. He noticed the shadowy-face in the full moon. Then he supposed that she was a living being. So he tried to prove whether the moon was alive or not. It was accordingly done in four different ways. First, he shook his head in a zig-zag direction with his eyes fixed on the moon. She appeared to follow the motions of his head now rising and then lowering, turning forward and backward. He also thought that the lights were alive, too, because he repeated similar experiments. Secondly, while walking out, he watched if the moon would follow him. The orb seemed to follow him everywhere. Thirdly, he wondered why the moon appeared regularly. So he thought that she must have come out for to see him alone. Then he talked to her in gestures and fancied that he saw her smile or frown. Fourthly, he found out that he had been whipped oftener when the moon was visible. It was as though she were watching him and telling his guardian (he being an orphan boy) all about his bad capers. He often asked himself who she could be. At last he became sure that she was his mother, because while his mother lived, he had never seen the moon. Afterwards every now and then he saw the moon and behaved well towards his friends. The little boy had some other notions. He believed that the earth was flat and the sun was a ball of fire. At first he thought that there were many suns, one for each day. He could not make out how they could rise and set. One night he happened to see some boys throwing and catching burning oil-soaked balls of yarn. He turned his mind to the sun and thought that it must have been thrown up and caught just the same—but by what force? So he supposed that there was a great and strong man, somehow hiding himself behind the hills (San Francisco being a hilly city.) The sun was his ball of fire as a toy, and he amused himself in throwing it very high in the sky every morning and catching it every evening.

After he began to convince himself about the possible existence of such a mighty god, he went on with his speculations. He supposed that the god lit the stars for his own use as we do the gas-lights in the street. When there was wind, he supposed that it was the indication of his passions. A cold gale bespoke his anger, and a cool breeze his happy temper. Why? Because he had sometimes felt the breath bursting out from the mouth of angry people in the act of quarreling or scolding. When there were clouds, he supposed that they came from the big pipe of the god. Why? Because he had often seen with childish wonder how the smoke curled from lighted pipes or cigars. He was often awed by the fantastic shapes of the floating clouds. What strong lungs the god had! When there was a fog, the boy supposed that it was his breath in the cold morning. Why? Because he had often seen his own breath in such weather. When there was rain, he did not doubt that the god took in much water and spued it from his big mouth in the form of a shower. Why? Because he had several times watched how cleverly the heathen Chinese spued the water from his mouth over the washed clothes. The boy did not suppose that the people grew. He seldom saw a baby, but when he did, he hated it and thought it a horrid-looking thing. He had contempt for girls. He was never bad on Sundays. In fair weather he would always go to church and Sunday-School. Why? Because he fancied that the moon wanted him to go as he had been in the habit of going to the Catholic church with his mother. He was in rags sometimes, but the church people and Sunday-School children were generally kind to the homeless little boy. He had some faint idea of death. He saw a dead baby in a little coffin. He was told that it could not eat, drink or speak, and so it would go into the ground and never, never come back home. Again he was told that he would get sick and go down into the ground. He got angry. He said that he would go up to the sky where his moon mother wanted him.

Mr. d'Estrella's autobiographic letter to me runs as follows:

The history of my parents is a very little known. I never saw my father. He was a French-Swiss. My mother—a native of Mexico—died when I was five years old. Then I had no other living relative known to me. It is about seven years ago when I first learned that I had one aunt and two cousins yet living. I am now forty years old.

I was born quite deaf. However, I have been able to hear a little in the left ear only. About eight years ago my ears were examined, and it was said that the external ear and the drum as well as the nerves going to the brain were perfect, but the trouble was the inner ear or the mechanism of the internal ear. Suppose, if I were not born deaf, it must then be that I became deaf somehow in my infancy. My two friends who saw me in my infancy said that I was not born deaf. They remembered that everybody would speak to me, and I should immediately turn towards them. The doctors attributed my deafness to a fall or fright. I cannot see that either the fall or the fright had anything to do with my deafness. It is said that those who are born deaf never hear in their dreams. I am strongly subjected to dreams, but I never heard any sound in my dreams until once in 1880. Since then I had not heard again till 1890. Later, since, I have heard three times—making up five times in all my life hitherto. However I do not believe that fact, because I know that a good many deaf mutes who lost their hearing at five or six years have never heard in their dreams.

The first recollection is that I cried. I think I was four years old then. One morning my mother left me alone for the first time in a room and locked the door. I was afraid because I had never remained alone in a closed room. So I cried. She came back in soon and ran laughing to me. She comforted and caressed me with kisses of love. This only is all what I can think instinctively of a mother's love. Probably the next recollection is one of the few I have cherished through years of memory. I remember it as though this had occurred yesterday. While walking one sunny Sunday morning with my mother to a Catholic convent, it took me by surprise when I heard the bell tolling. Rapture seized me at once. I cried joyfully. Then I felt a dreamy, wandering sensation amid the bustle of the people. Even after the good bell ceased tolling, the vibrations continued ringing in my over-excited brain for a while. Often do I think of this undying recollection—sometimes with awe, sometimes with delight. When I think of it, I feel as though I were *actually* hearing the bell toll—toll slowly and sweetly. Even, while writing this part, I feel apparently paralyzed in my senses as if my soul were giving way to the mesmeric spell of the very recollection.

I have several other early recollections, more or less perfect. I remember that I saw a priest burning a number of Bibles; that I attended a Catholic spelling-school (I often wonder if I learned to say 'papa' there. I can say 'papa' as plainly as any one can—this is the only word I have ever lisped); that I saw much excitement in moving the furnitures and other household articles in a hurried and confused manner, because there was an earthquake (which I afterwards learned in the Annals of S. F.—I was born in S. F.); that I saw a great red comet; that my mother told me that we all should be knocked down if the comet struck the ground; that I watched the comet every night until it disappeared; that I saw a man lassoing another, both on horseback at full speed through the street; that I saw two fires near my home; that my mother took me to church on Sundays and on other days oftener early in the morning. If I was restless during the service, she would give me something to eat. (Although I am not a Catholic, yet now and then I go to the Catholic church, and enjoy my meditation mainly to keep the memory of my mother.) While my mother was alive, I did not know that I was deaf. I did not see the sun and stars figuratively. I remember that I had never observed the moon but once with a sort of wonder,—the moon was new. I seldom went out by myself and played with the children. I was then passively quiet and good, almost an intellectual blank.

I know almost nothing about my mother's death. While she was sick, she gave me some marmalade and kissed me, for the last time. I was then put away. I do not remember if I saw her corpse or attended her funeral, nor how I felt about her death. Only that my friends said that she had gone to the sky to rest.

What then became of me after my mother's death? I remember at best that I was taken to the house of my god-mother. Since she was my mother's best friend, I did not miss my mother consciously at all. A short time afterwards, a French consul (I believe, my father's brother) took me to the house of a Mexican woman and left me there, with a box of Noah's animals, in her charge. I did not feel homesick. She continued as my guardian until I was taken to school (I was the first pupil, then, in the California institution). I remained about four years with her. She, I learned when in school, was my mother's bitter enemy out of jealousy in love affairs.

Hitherto till this time I had but a little, if ever possible, of instinctive language. I could hardly make intelligible signs; but my mother might understand my gestures, that is, such as were moved by feelings for what I should either wish or deny. For example, the idea of food was aroused in my mind by the feeling of hunger. This simply constitutes the Logic of Feeling; bear in mind that it is different from the Logic of Signs. I could neither think nor reason at all, yet I could recognize the persons either with delight or with dislike. Still, nearly all the human emotions were absent, and even the faculty of conscience was wanting. Everything seemed to appear blank around me except the momentary pleasures of perception. What happened at home had not come back within my memory until I went to school. The state of my mental isolation, I believe, is wholly due to my confinement at home. I was then five years old, though.

But no sooner had I been left in charge of my guardian than the knowledge of good and evil was opened to me slowly but surely. As Minerva the goddess of wisdom was said to have leaped forth out of the brain of her father Jupiter, full grown and full armed for the business of life, so was my new life formed apparently mature and complete. The unwomanly treatment of my guardian was, in truth, the direct cause of the evolution of my instinctive—or better speaking—latent feelings for the higher. Not only could I think in pictures, but almost spontaneously I was also able to learn how to think and reason. Thinking in pictures or images is prevalent among most of the congenitally deaf children at different degrees in proportion to the different powers of perception. That faculty predominates in this class, and consequently compensates for the loss of hearing, no matter even if they do not think at all. I learned to know that there was a difference between right and wrong, and to understand that there was a relation between cause and effect. This proves that my conscience must have been in the act of developing. My mental condition was favorably elaborated and properly reduced to the Logic of Signs.

How were the essential signs acquired? My mother must have known my wants beforehand, without any forced attempt on my part. But my guardian was a stranger to me, and could not understand my desires. It was necessary that she or I would seek something rational or conventional to make us understand each other. So we made signs, one after another. Imitation constitutes the foundation of the sign language. We traced as intelligibly as possible the shapes and peculiarities of the objects and the actions of the bodily movements. The language thus acquired was greatly augmented by the expression and play of the features to emphasize the meanings of the signs. She soon made herself a good sign-maker. The Mexicans, as well as the people of the Romance races, are expert in pantomimic gestures which they are in the habit of using while speaking to one another. How natural all the imitative signs are! When I came to school, I had no difficulty in understanding the true deaf and dumb language of signs—the conventional language. The sign language is the universal one. (I do not pretend to say that I am about the best sign-maker in this institution. This must be attributed to the early training of the mind during my ante-speech days.)

My guardian let me go about in the rear yard. There I learned to love hens, ducks, turkeys, parrots, canary-birds, dogs, cats. Quite a bustle of life. A novelty of observation.

The woman often went out shopping. I sometimes accompanied her. As I had learned to remember the places she frequented—within a radius of two or three blocks—she sent me to the grocery to get something, such as bread, milk, potatoes, etc. I enjoyed it, because she would not let me go otherwise. While out on errand, I now and then might make acquaintances with boys and play with them for a little time. One morning I was carrying a pitcher of milk. A boy accidentally broke it and let the milk spill. I cried and went home with the broken vessel. I told the woman honestly about it. She would not listen, but she got angry and whipped me. I believe that this was the first whipping I had ever got from any person. Because I thought that it was not good, my blood rose in protest. She whipped me harder, and I yielded reluctantly.

I now began to notice the gambols of the boys out on streets. So new and keen was my instinct for sport that I envied their play. Then I slipped stealthily out of the yard to the gate and looked at their pranks with delight. At last I went out to play. The woman caught and whipped me. I played again. She whipped me again. Well, I then began to think why. I thought and thought. She could not make me understand that I was a bad boy. Playing seemed to be *good*. I soon learned to hate her. If she had scolded me gently and gave me decently to understand her command, it might have been all right. But it was too late. I made up my mind that I would have my own way, regardless of consequences. I did not want to be whipped so often. I all at once hated whipping. It would make me anything but good. I played out whenever I liked. She whipped me nearly every time. It did me no good. It hardened my body as well as my heart. She desired some other way of punishment by taking off my hat. It failed. She then took off my shoes. It met the same fate. She took off my jacket. I still played only with pants and a shirt on. It availed nothing. I had already determined that she would be revenged. She found it useless to break down my obstinacy. Now and then she would whip me very long and hard when I was out too long. I saw it rationally, but I delighted in following the boys on the alert far from home—say, ten blocks. One day I was playing with two larger boys. There was a large miry pond across the alley. We wanted to cross it. They succeeded, but I was unfortunate. While I was walking along the picket fence, one of the pickets gave way and I lost my balance, falling flat into the mire. I, from head to foot, was covered with the mud. I waddled and cried until I got out of the pond. By chance, my guardian, who had made a call, saw and took me. It was quite a far way off. The children out at recess stared at me and laughed 'wickedly' like the imps. What a funny picture it must be! As soon as we got home, she made me strip off my clothes and wash them. I was then completely naked—still worse, I was made to do the washing out in the yard. It meant punishment. Several of the boys peeped over the yard and made faces at me. I rebelled, but the woman was the more determined, and the boys were the most delighted. I had to remain so in this uncomfortable place for hours until the clothes got dry enough.

A good many of the neighbors knew from the hearsay of the children and by hearing my cries that I must have been cruelly treated. They were kind to me, and would let me come in and have something nice to eat. Several of them dared to see the bad woman, and tell her not to be so hard on me. But she had her own way.

Her new husband was an American captain and owned some barges. The woman sometimes took me with her to his office at the wharf where she usually got meat. Afterwards she sent me alone to the wharf and bring the meat. What a long journey it would take for a small boy to cross a dozen of blocks—alone! However, what a splendid tramp it was! How much I loved to go to the bay! The sea was a wonder to me—nay, a wonder of wonders, since even a boat was a marvel. What a variety of life along the wharves! Such a life with such a variety awakened in me a vague feeling of mystery—sadness(?)—loneliness(?). At my request, the woman would let me go to the wharf early in the morning to get the meat. As soon as I brought it home, I made haste to the bay, and spent many long hours to view the cosmopolitan sights. I made acquaintance with the rough-looking though good-natured sailors. They taught me many good and bad ways. I was quick to see and understand. I learned from them how to draw a picture of a ship. I made very good pictures, indeed, for a boy of my age. I sometimes doubt if I can draw a ship with her details so good now as I did that time, because I used to notice all the parts of the whole ship. (I am now an amateur artist and photographer. I teach drawing at school.)

I loved money. I liked best to have dimes and half-dimes. The love of money led me to steal some little money. I was an adept in theft. I could steal some small thing easily, most without being detected. Yet my friends or some other person knew from hearing my steps that I had taken something, usually eatables. But I never confessed it, even by threats, nay, by ready force. That habit was mainly owing to the condition of hunger; this was an excusable necessity, I say. I was often ill-fed at home. It meant punishment for staying away too long. This stung me dearly towards stubbornness, and I became worse and worse. It shows plainly that there is no greater fallacy than 'the child's will must be broken!' Will forms the production of character. Without strength of will there will be no strength of purpose.

I began to find a new kind of pleasure in being out at night, because I could see more vicissitudes of evil amid the din of dissipation peculiar to the early days of California, then before the sixties. I was as a moth midst the dazzling lights of the night revels. I became quite a nocturnal being. In this way I contracted many bad things during my abandoned youth,—a period of four years. The influence of this evil has still retained some fascinating but unhealthy influence over my imagination. On this account I sometimes ask myself, with a certain sense of mystery and gratitude, if I had left school twenty years ago, and gone somewhere for a living, what might have become of me? I have been connected with this school thirty-one years. My long, home-like stay prevents me from ever returning to that pernicious life too soon.

More about stealing. Often did I go out at night with an empty stomach. I had to find something to satiate my hunger. Sometimes I returned home at midnight without a morsel, and entered the kitchen quietly. I took bread or meat, or what else I could hold, and slipped away. Sometimes it was done at the different houses of my friends. They would be too glad to give me some food, but I was too proud or ashamed to beg. Sometimes I took a loaf of fresh bread off the doorsteps where the baker put it. Sometimes, while passing close to the fruit-stand, I slipped one apple or two into my pockets or shirt. I had no intuitive conscience at all. There might possibly be a mote of it when I thought of the moon (you have already known my cosmology). Of course, hunger was stronger than conscience. Yet that faculty seemed to be more or less active. I shall say how I was cured of stealing. I frequented a meat-shop. The good-natured butcher let me go about at large. I happened to see some money in a box under the counter behind. I thought of getting some little money there. So I went back and crept slowly to the box and took a dime. I feasted on its worth of candy. Fond of sweets I was. I stole another dime in a few days. I wanted more money, so I stole a quarter of a dollar. My conscience worked up as though saying that it was too much. I knew that it cost two dimes and one half-dime together. As long as I had it with me I felt peculiarly unhappy. I turned around to see if it was all right. I spent all of it, and saw how much more good time I could have with one of greater value. I did not come back to the shop so soon for the money. A good while later I stole the other quarter, and so on about weekly I took the quarters, piece after piece. That never-forgotten morning I wanted a quarter. While behind under the counter, I was about to put my hand into the box. The man opened it. I was quite frightened, but remained still. I would not leave, but I waited and slipped my hand into the box. So nervous was I that I took whatever piece I could touch first. I took one, and thought from the size of the piece that it was a quarter. I made haste to the nearest grocery-store and asked for candy. I put the money on the counter. It was gold!—ten dollars!! I felt as though I were a fish out of the water, with my eyes shooting out. At once I took it back and ran out. I could see nothing but gold everywhere. My heart beat. Did I know that I was guilty? If so, how could I know? Simply by seeing that I had stolen *too much*. Although I did not know the relative value of gold, yet I knew that gold cost more than silver. Because it was heavy, bright, and could be had only by the rich. I felt that it was too much for me. I never saw gold among the poorer people, and always noticed it in the hands of the more respectable ones. How could I get rid of the gold? I ran and ran with the gold tight in my hand until I returned to the senses. Then I went to the confectionery and bought much candy, regardless of the consequences about the change. The man looked surprised, but yet, knowing that I was deaf, he might not suspect anything ill with me. He gave me the change all in silver, many halves. I was quite bewildered, but I tried well to be still. The silver was now too heavy for me to carry along as easily. The conscience came, saw, and conquered. I went some way with caution, and hid all the money under a saloon. I felt free. I thought of going to the minstrels in the evening. When the time came I went back for the money. I found it all gone. I was momentarily disappointed, but in fact I felt happier than sorry for conscience's sake. Strange to say, anybody, even the butcher, never gave me to understand that I had been suspected of the theft. Still more strange, I have never stolen money again. Besides, I did not steal as many other things, particularly food, as I used to. My conscience must have become keen enough. It began developing more and more, mainly owing to the influence of the moon. (Then the moon was full, when I found the money gone.) Therefore my cosmological speculations came out, as those already given in the Annals.

Let me add as to the origin of the ocean. One day I went with some boys to the ocean. They went bathing. I first went into the ocean, not knowing how it tasted and how strong the waves rolled. So I was knocked around, with my eyes and mouth open. I came near being drowned. I could not swim. I went to the bottom and instinctively crawled up on the sand. I spit the salt water out of my mouth, and wondered why the water was so salty. I thought that it was the urine of that mighty god.

I hated girls with contempt. I never played with them. I would not visit my friends who had girls at home. Why? Because from my accidental observation I found out the difference between the girls and boys,—not in dress, but in sex. This led me to despise female animals. When I was hungry, I might occasionally go to the women for foods, but I could not stay long with them. While at school, I retained this dislike three years before I could like a girl.

I cannot remember if I ever knew that I was deaf. I knew that I could not talk, but I never asked myself why, not because I was satisfied with my condition, but because I was too wide awake to think of my own self. I often wondered how others could speak, particularly while they were quarrelling. I believed that the people could never grow. I had never wanted to be a man, because I could do enough what I liked to. I seldom saw a baby. I hated it and thought it a dirty thing. I have still retained the dislike for babies. (I am single.)

This is all what I can say for the present. Mr. Wilkinson, when he was my teacher, used to make me write about what I did before I came to school. It helped me much thus to repeat the memory. Ever since my recollections have been the same, though the words have changed now and then to get better style and more definite meanings in language.

It shows that I thought in pictures and signs before I came to school. The pictures were not exact in details, but were general. They were momentary and fleeting in my mind's eye. The signs were not extensive but somewhat conventional after the Mexican fashion—not at all like the symbols of the deaf and dumb language. I used to tell my friends about some of my cosmology. Several of them encouraged me.

Thought Before Language

One always took so much interest in me that he attempted to teach me. But he knew almost nothing, only he could say yes or no with more or less emphasis in gestures, when I said in pantomimic what I did or what I saw, or what I thought. He was the means of sending me to school as soon as he learned that the school started. He was an Italian. Some of the signs I used were beard for *man*, breast for *woman*, moustache with spelling papa for *papa*, the hand moving over the face and one finger of each hand meeting parallel (alike, meaning that some one looked like me) for *mother*, the hand down over the shoulder moving like a bell for *Sunday*, two hands open before the eyes for *book* or *paper*, one hand stretching sideway for *going*, the hand moving backwards for *coming*, the hand moving slant for *whipping*, the fingers whirling for *stealing*, the rubbing of the thumb and one of the fingers for *money*, two hands turned opposite for *breaking*, one finger stretching from the eye for *seeing*, one finger stretching from the mouth for *speaking*, one finger stretching from the forehead for *understanding*, one finger rapping lightly on the forehead for *knowing*, ditto with negation for *not knowing*, one finger resting on the forehead with the eyes shut for *thinking*, one finger now resting on the forehead and then stretching with emphasis for *understanding*, etc., etc. The signs for meat, bread, milk, water, chocolate, horse, cow, were as natural as the Mexicans make nowadays. The Mexicans generally ask with facial gestures, 'What do you do?' 'How do you do?' 'What is the matter?' 'What is the news?' It is natural. I could then understand these questions.

The reader will have noticed that many of the signs which Mr. d'Estrella reports himself to have used are regular conventional gestures of the deaf-mute sign language. Some of these may be used habitually by the Mexicans, others the poor boy probably captured out of the social atmosphere, so to speak, in the way in which needy creatures so generally find a way to the object which can satisfy their want. It will be observed, however, that his cosmological and ethical reflections were the outbirth of his solitary thought; and although he tried to communicate the cosmology to others, it is evident, since the most receptive of his friends could only say 'yes' or 'no' to him in return, that the communion must have been very incomplete. He surely had no conventional gestures for the causal and logical relations involved in his inductions about the moon, for example. So far as it goes, then, his narrative tends to discountenance the notion that no abstract thought is possible without words. Abstract thought of a decidedly subtle kind, both scientific and moral, went on here in advance of the means of expressing

289

it to others. To a great extent it does so in all of us to-day, for nothing is commoner than to have a thought, and then to seek for the proper words in which to clothe its most important features. The only way to defend the doctrine of the absolute dependence of thought on language is so to enlarge the sphere of this latter word as to make it cover every possible sort of mental imagery, whether communicable to others or not. Of course no man can think without some kind of mind-stuff to think in. Our general meanings and abstract conceptions must always have for their vehicle images more or less concrete, and 'fringes' of tendency and relation which we feel between them. To a solitary untaught individual (could such a one exist) such unverbalized images would be rationally significant, and a train of them might be called a monologue. But such a monologue is not what any one naturally means by speech; and it is far better to drop the language-doctrine altogether than to evaporate its meaning into triviality like this.

Mr. d'Estrella's reminiscences also help to settle the question of whether moral propositions are 'intuitive' or not. He begins life as a thief, with, as he says, "no intuitive conscience at all," and yet with a knowledge that what he does is an outward social offence, since he must needs do it secretly. At last he is converted to honesty—by what? Not by the teachings of others, not by detection and punishment, but by the very magnitude of his own crimes. He steals so much that the burden becomes too heavy to bear. It sobers him; and a success which would have turned a non-moral or an immoral boy into a confirmed criminal, produces in him a reaction towards honesty. This would seem to be a common experience. A youth tries dissipation, or indulges himself in tyranny or meanness, till at last an experience supervenes which tastes too strong, even for him, the agent. He didn't intend quite *that*! It casts a 'lurid light' on all the rest of the performances, so he cries 'halt' and 'turns over a new leaf.' Now I take it that the doctrine of an innate conscience in morals, as opposed to the pure associationist doctrine of nursery-teaching *plus* prudential calculation, means no more than this, that bad deeds will end by *tasting* bad, even to the agent who does them successfully, if you let him experience them concretely enough, with all the circumstances that they comport. They will, in short, beget an intrinsic disgust; the need of stealthiness in our tread, the satiety which our orgies leave, the looks and cries of our victims lingering obstinately behind, spoil the fun for us and end by undermining it altogether. For the poor deaf and dumb boy the fun of thieving stopped as soon as the ill-gotten gold-piece saddled him with so important a responsibility that even his moon-mother in the sky grew mixed up with the affair.

Few documents, it seems to me, cast more light on our unsophisticated intellectual and moral instincts than the sincere and unpretending narrative which Mr. d'Estrella has allowed me to print.

The Original Datum of Space-Consciousness

Under this title Mr. E. Ford, in the last MIND, propounds to Mr. Ward and myself an alternative which he considers fatal to our doctrines of space-perception. May I make a reply to the criticism so far as it concerns my own view?

Mr. Ford says that 'local signs' are "utterly inadequate to furnish a foundation for the perception of position." If 'to furnish a foundation' mean 'to *explain*,' I entirely agree with our critic. The word 'local sign' has perhaps come to be abused in recent literature on the space-question. Lotze's original intent with it (if I am not mistaken) was rather negative than positive. He needed a term which would denote a numerically distinctive quality in each point of our sensitive surfaces, and yet which would not connote any positive explanation of the relative positions in which the objects perceived by the points appear arranged. But one now notices a tendency to use the term local sign as if it were meant to cover some mysterious explanation. I am not sure that Mr. Ford does not take it in this way, for he assumes that Mr. Ward and I 'deduce' or 'develop' space from the local sign system. I, for one, certainly disclaim anything of the kind. By defending what I call a sensationalist theory of space-perception, I mean expressly to deny that we can logically or rationally deduce the features of the finished phenomenon. Its antecedents are physiological. Mr. Ford asks: "How much does the conception of extensity involve?" As a matter of *fact*, extensity involves all that comes out of it in the way of finished space-determinations. But as a mere *conception*, I do not see that extensity necessarily involves any exact system of points with their relations or distances, for we may empirically be conscious of spaces that are exceedingly confused and vague as to their inner content. This is especially marked in dozing and in recovery from syncope or anæsthesia. Neither, on the other hand, do any number of distinct feelings, susceptible of serial arrangement, such as 'local signs' are assumed to be, necessarily 'involve' extensity, for we find in every department of our sensibility feelings which, when we arrange them serially, never appear spread out before us in space. That certain organs give us sensations of extensity, and that parts of these organs contribute objects which when separately attended to appear definitely placed within the extensity, are facts which seem to me insusceptible of any logical explanation. All we can say is, that these organs act in this way, and others do not.

Take, to illustrate, the cases of the eye and the ear. When we first hear a musical chord, it has a certain richness and volume, but no distinct parts are apprehended within it yet. By setting the attention in a certain way, however, we discern first one, and then another of the notes. There is a quality in each note which identifies, individualizes and distinguishes it from the rest. Moreover, if we 'compare' the notes, we feel a relation between them, which Prof. Stumpf has well called their 'distance.' One pair have more distance between them than another, so that we can arrange them serially. In the case of the notes, however, no one would seriously pretend that the distance was a *sound*, like that of the notes themselves. Most people would call it a relation intellectually and not sensibly apprehended; and if asked *why* it is not sensibly perceived, would simply say that we have no sense-organ for such relations. Now the field of vision is both like and unlike the chord. It is something rich and voluminous, within which presently, by setting the attention, we discern first one and then another spot, and then, by comparing, define the distance between them. Only here the distance is a thing *seen*, and not a relation apprehended merely intellectually; for in the eye we have, as in the ear we have not, a sense-organ for such distances. Simultaneously with the spots, their distance is optically felt, the physiological condition of the feeling being the excited retinal tract which stretches between the retinal points on which the spots fall.

But, says Mr. Ford, if the seen distance, or line, "is a feeling, what is the relation between this feeling and the two points which it connects? Our reply of course would be: That of 'besideness,' of local contact, which we consider must be postulated as a primary datum. We do not see what answer would be open to Mr. James."

To which I can only reply that the answer 'primary datum' is as open to me as to Mr. Ford. That two seen things, when distinguished, appear 'beside' each other, and that two heard things do not, seem to me two inexplicable facts. The usual explanation that we pass from the one seen thing to the other by a muscular 'sweep,' the feeling of which is absent in the case of the heard things, is quite inadequate; for (even if the facts were strictly true, which they are not) one does not see why the end of a muscular feeling *should* appear separated in space from its beginning any more than one sees why the beginning and end of a sound should *not* so appear. Nor can the Mills' phrase of 'mental chemistry' or Wundt's of 'psychic synthesis' be held to have explanatory value. On the contrary, they but re-name the mystery. Whatever the intrinsic character of the qualities known as local signs may be, if they are susceptible of serial gradation, they must appear more or less 'distant' from each other, and some will appear next each other. But the distance will be space-distance, and the nextness will be 'besideness,' only when the whole system of qualities aroused together appears with spread-outness or extent. Serial position then becomes sensible and palpable as *place*. Behind this 'ultimate fact' we cannot go.

When then Mr. Ford offers his final dilemma: "The local sign is either given as a relation or as a quality. If the former, the relation of position must be original and the development theory is superfluous. If the latter, the theory fails"; I can only say that I know of no development-theory for which I am responsible, for I never tried 'to develop' either extensity or position out of local signs. The local sign is of course a quality, and one local sign by itself cannot be given as a relation. But that, when many local signs, or rather the sensitive organic points which correspond to them, are excited together, the objects tinged by the local signs appear *in* relation, and eke in relations of position, is a fact which no theory of mine ever attempted rationally to explain.

Professor Wundt and Feelings of Innervation

A note to page 432 of Vol. I of the fourth edition of Wundt's *Physiologische Psychologie* quotes an opinion of mine and corrects it in a manner that seems to demand a word of reply. When the external rectus-muscle of a man's eye (say the left eye) is wholly or partly paralyzed, objects lying in the left half of the field of view appear to that left eye to lie farther to the left than they really are. In Prof. Wundt's earlier writings he agreed with von Graefe and others in explaining this phenomenon by the man's consciousness of the excessive leftward innervation which he must employ in turning his diseased eye towards the object. The existence of feelings of innervation was attacked presently by Bastian, Ferrier, and others, and this particular supposed case of it was explained away by G. E. Müller and myself. We pointed out that the true cause of the object's false leftward location was rather to be found in the inward squint of the right eye when the left one vainly or successfully turns to look at the object. The leftward innervation is indeed increased, but there is no need of assuming the *feeling* of it to be increased, when the feeling of its *results* in the turning of the *right* eyeball (even when its lid is closed or it is screened from the object) explains sufficiently why the man should think himself looking farther to the left with both eyes than he really is.

Professor Wundt, in the third edition of his book, definitively abandoned the theory of feelings of innervation. In the present fourth edition he adds to what he has to say upon the subject some novel remarks of detail. *Inter alia* he says that it is impossible to explain the false location of the object in the case before us by the position of the sound, or right, eye. It seems to me, however, that he has failed to understand correctly the facts and his authorities for them, and that Müller's and my explanation stands as firm as it did before.

Wundt says (p. 424): "To the movement of the sound eye the false localization cannot be ascribed, for the images seen by the two eyes are distinct, and only that of the lame eye is falsely placed." In the note to p. 432 he quotes a passage from Alfred Graefe and thereupon makes the remark that more particularly provokes the present note from me. I must leave Graefe's passage in the transparency and elegance of the original: "*Die Richtung in welcher sich das [dem, paralytischen Auge angehörende] Scheinbild von dem [vom normalen Auge herrührenden] wahren Bilde entfernt, liegt stets in der nach aussen projicirten Wirkungsbahn des gelähmten Muskels, d. h. in der Ebene, welche die Sehlinie um die Drehungsaxe desselben beschreibt.*" Wundt's remark hereupon is: "When therefore W. James (*Psychology*, ii, 506) [WORKS, p. 1116] and others aver that the displacement of the false image comes from the movement of the normal eye, they would seem to ascribe to this latter the marvellous capacity of a simultaneous twofold localization, first a normal one coming from the said eye's real position, and second an abnormal one, corresponding to the position which the paralytic eye is striving to reach."

What meaning the special quotation from Graefe may have for Prof. Wundt's mind I cannot tell, but the rest of Graefe's text, and the facts themselves are so simple that one wonders how there can be two opinions about them. The case Wundt is considering is apparently that in which both eyes are open, the object lies or moves towards the left, and the sound right eye turns to it and sees it where it is, whilst the lame left eye fails to rotate so as to fixate it and consequently gets its image on the nasal half of the retina or, in other words, sees the object in indirect vision to the left of the point at which it directly looks. During all this there is a convergent squint, the right eye being turned in and looking farther to the left than does the left eye.[1] The question now is: *where* do the

---

[1] For simplicity's sake I omit the variation in which the left eye succeeds in rotating so as to fixate the object, whilst the right eye turns violently in, and, fixating

two images appear? The left eye's image must in any case appear to the left of the right eye's image, because whilst the latter falls on the right fovea, the former falls on the nasal half of the left retina. But where does the right eye's image appear? In its real place, or thereabouts, according to all accounts. *Thus the position of the right eye is what determines a place, to the left of which the left eye's image is falsely referred.* There is no question of any twofold localization here by the right or normal eye. That eye sees in the direction of its own line of sight, of which direction it would appear to be made conscious by its feelings of rotation. The left eye also has feelings of rotation, but they would appear to be over-powered by those of the right eye, first because the actual rotations of the latter eye are the stronger, and second because (as a host of similar pathological examples show) we are liable (until trained by contrary experience) to suppose, when we have intended a move-ment, that the movement has taken place. The patient intends to move both his eyes considerably to the left. He does so move his right eye only; but failing, in the novelty of the whole experience, to discriminate in his orbital feelings just what new and strange things have occurred, he thinks he has performed the entire move-ment as usual in spite of the fact that he has not. He sees double; he locates the left eye's image according to the fatal laws of retinal projection; and he gets a strong vertigo as the result of the unusual behavior of the field of view. How Professor Wundt himself would explain the wrong localization by the left eye without invoking either the right eye's position or the feelings of innervation in which he formerly believed, he does not deign to say.

The point is a minute one, certainly in itself not worthy of notice; and the existence or non-existence of feelings of innervation is an alternative on which, so far as I can see at present, no general theoretic consequences seem to hinge. I should consequently not have been stirred to write this note were it not that Professor Wundt's peculiar manner of revising his opinions is objectionable from the point of view of literary ethics, and is beginning, I fancy, to arouse in other readers besides myself an irritation to which it is but just that some expression should be given.

First, it would seem better, in issuing revised editions of works

---

a point leftward of the object, gets the image of the latter on the nasal half of its retina, or sees it in indirect vision to the right of the spot which it fixates. The principles of explanation are here the same.

as weighty as those of this author, to name explicitly in the new prefaces the pages where modifications of doctrine are to be found. No one ought to be forced to read a thousand pages merely to ascertain what an author's newest formulations are. Second, it would seem well, in parts of the text where a change of view has occurred, to announce that fact explicitly in the text. And third, it would be fair, if one cited authors already identified with the new view, to cite them so as to award to them some degree of credit. In this overburdened age the reader has a right to clearness on every point. But Prof. Wundt's new prefaces contain no reference by pages to what is revised; his text habitually lacks any indication that his thought may once have been different from what it is; and his citations are almost always by way of discrediting the predecessors quoted and clearing their opinions out of the way. No one, I think, who should be introduced to Psychology by Wundt's third edition could come to any other conclusion than that Bastian, Ferrier, and others were adherents of a foolish theory of innervation-feelings to which Wundt himself now and ever stood opposed. In the fourth edition Münsterberg, one of the most original opponents of innervation-feelings, is quoted only once and then actually so as to make the reader think that he might most naturally have got his views from Wundt himself (see p. 431, note).

The mania for a plausible smoothness, the shrinking from an appearance of fallibility, seem in fact in Wundt's later writings to be driven so far as seriously to neutralize the clearness and value of the work. A thinker so learned, so intelligent, before whose encyclopædic capacity an entire generation bows down with cordial admiration, ought to be above such foibles. Not in such ways were the best parts of the reputation of a Fechner, a Mill, a Darwin, made.

The Physical Basis of Emotion

In the year 1884 Prof. Lange of Copenhagen and the present writer published, independently of each other, the same theory of emotional consciousness. They affirmed it to be the effect of the organic changes, muscular and visceral, of which the so-called 'expression' of the emotion consists. It is thus not a primary feeling, directly aroused by the exciting object or thought, but a secondary feeling indirectly aroused; the primary effect being the organic changes in question, which are immediate reflexes following upon the presence of the object.

This idea has a paradoxical sound when first apprehended, and it has not awakened on the whole the confidence of psychologists. It may interest some readers if I give a sketch of a few of the more recent comments on it.

Professor Wundt's criticism may be mentioned first.[1] He unqualifiedly condemns it, addressing himself exclusively to Lange's version. He accuses the latter of being one of those *psychologischen Scheinerklärungen* which assume that science is satisfied when a psychic fact is once for all referred to a physiological ground.

His own account of the matter is that the immediate and primary result of 'the reaction of Apperception[2] on any conscious-content'

[1] *Philosophische Studien*, VI, 349 (1891).

[2] In this article, as in the 4th edition of his *Psychology*, Wundt vaguely completes his *volte-face* concerning 'Apperception' and dimly describes the latter in associa-

or object is a *Gefühl* (364). *Gefühl* is an unanalyzable and simple process corresponding in the sphere of *Gemüth* to sensation in the sphere of intellection (359). But *Gefühle* have the power of altering the course of ideas—inhibiting some and attracting others, according to their nature; and these ideas in turn produce both secondary *Gefühle* and organic changes. The organic changes in turn set up additional *sinnliche Gefühle* which fuse with the preceding ones and strengthen the volume of feeling aroused. This whole complex process is what Wundt calls an *Affect* or Emotion—a state of mind which, as he rightly says, 'has thus the power of intensifying itself' (358–363). I shall speak later of what may be meant by the primary *Gefühl* thus described. Wundt in any case would seem to be certain both that it is the essential part of the emotion, and that currents from the periphery cannot be its organic correlate. I should say, granting its existence, that it falls short of the emotion proper, since it involves no *commotion*, and that such currents *are* its cause. But of these points later on. The rest of Wundt's criticism is immaterial, dealing exclusively with certain rash methodological remarks of Lange's; emphasizing the 'parallelism' of the psychical and the physical; and pointing out the vanity of seeking in the latter a causal explanation of the former. As if Lange ever pretended to do this in any intimate sense! Two of Wundt's remarks, however, are more concrete.

How insufficient, he says, must Lange's explanation of emotions from vaso-motor effects be, when it results in making him put joy and anger together in one class! To which I reply both that Lange has laid far too great stress on the vaso-motor factor in his explanations, and that he has been materially wrong about congestion of the face being the essential feature in anger, for in the height of that passion almost every one grows pale—a fact which the expression 'white with rage' commemorates. Secondly, Wundt says, whence comes it that if a certain stimulus be what causes emotional expression by its mere reflex effects, another stimulus almost iden-

---

tionist terms. "Apperception is nothing really separable from the effects which it produces in the content of representation. In fact it consists of nothing but these concomitants and effects. [A thing that 'consists' of its concomitants!] . . . In each single apperceptive act the entire previous content of the conscious life operates as a sort of integral total force" (364, 365), etc. The whole account seems indistinguishable from pure Herbartism, in which Apperception is only a name for the interaction of the old and the new in consciousness, of which interaction feeling may be one result.

tical with the first will fail to do so if its *mental* effects are not the same? (355). The mental motivation is the essential thing in the production of the emotion, let the 'object' be what it may.

This objection, in one form or another, recurs in all the published criticisms. "Not the mere object as such is what determines the physical effects," writes Mr. D. Irons in a recent article[3] which, if it were more popularly written, would be undeniably effective, "but the subjective feeling towards the object. . . . An emotional class is not something objective; each subject to a great extent classifies in this regard for itself, and even here time and circumstance make alteration and render stability impossible. . . . *If I were not afraid the object would not be an object of terror*" (p. 84). And Dr. W. L. Worcester, in an article[4] which is both popularly written and effective, says: "Neither running nor any other of the symptoms of fear which he [W. J.] enumerates is the necessary result of seeing a bear. A chained or caged bear may excite only feelings of curiosity, and a well armed hunter might experience only pleasurable feelings at meeting one loose in the woods. It is not, then, the perception of the bear that excites the movements of fear. We do not run from the bear unless we suppose him capable of doing us bodily injury. Why should the expectation of being eaten, for instance, set the muscles of our legs in motion? 'Common sense' would be likely to say it was because we object to being eaten, but according to Professor James, the reason we dislike to be eaten is because we run away" (287).

A reply to these objections is the easiest thing in the world to make if one only remembers the force of association in psychology. 'Objects' are certainly the primitive arousers of instinctive reflex movements. But they take their place, as experience goes on, as elements in total 'situations,'[5] the other suggestions of which may prompt to movements of an entirely different sort. As soon as an object has become thus familiar and suggestive, its emotional consequences, *on any theory of emotion*, must start rather from the total situation which it suggests than from its own naked presence. But whatever be our reaction on the situation, in the last resort

---

[3] "Prof. James' Theory of Emotion," *Mind*, n.s., III, 77–97 (1894).

[4] "Observations on Some Points in James's Psychology. II. Emotion."—*The Monist*, III, 285–298 (1893).

[5] In my nomenclature it is the total situation which is the 'object' on which the reaction of the subject is made.

it is an instinctive reaction on that one of its elements which strikes us for the time being as most vitally important. The same bear may truly enough excite us to either fight or flight, according as he suggests an overpowering 'idea' of his killing us, or one of our killing him. But in either case the question remains: Does the emotional excitement which follows the idea follow it immediately, or secondarily and as a consequence of the 'diffusive wave' of impulses aroused?

Dr. Worcester finds something absurd in the very notion of acts constituting emotion by the consciousness which they arouse. How is it, he says, with voluntary acts? "If I see a shower coming up, and run for a shelter, the emotion is evidently of the same kind, though perhaps less in degree, as in the case of the man who runs from the bear. According to Professor James, I am afraid of getting wet because I run. But supposing that, instead of running, I step into a shop and buy an umbrella. The emotion is still the same. I am afraid of getting wet. Consequently, so far as I can see, the fear, in this case, consists in buying the umbrella. Fear of hunger, in like manner, might consist in laying in a store of provisions; fear of poverty, in shoveling dirt at a dollar a day, and so on indefinitely. Anger, again, may be associated with many other actions than striking. Shylock's anger at Antonio's insults induced him to lend him money. Did the anger . . . consist in the act of lending the money?" (291). I think that all the force of such objections lies in the slap-dash brevity of the language used, of which I admit that my own text set a bad example when it said 'we are frightened because we run.' Yet let the word 'run' but stand for what it was meant to stand for, namely, for many other movements in us, of which invisible visceral ones seem by far the most essential; discriminate also between the various grades of emotion which we designate by one name, and our theory holds up its head again. 'Fear' of getting wet is not the same fear as fear of a bear. It may limit itself to a pre-vision of the unpleasantness of a wet skin or of spoiled clothes, and this may prompt either to deliberate running or to buying an umbrella with a very minimum of properly emotional excitement being aroused. Whatever the fear may be in such a case it is not constituted by the voluntary act.[6] Only the details of the concrete case can inform us whether it be, as above suggested, a mere ideal

---

[6] When the running has actually commenced, it gives rise to *exhilaration* by its effects on breathing and pulse, etc., in this case, and not to *fear*.

vision of unpleasant sensations, or whether it go farther and involve also feelings of reflex organic change. But in either case our theory will cover all the facts.

Both Dr. Worcester and Mr. Irons are struck by this variability in the symptoms of any given emotion; and holding the emotion itself to be constant, they consider that such inconstant symptoms cannot be its cause. Dr. Worcester acutely remarks that the actions accompanying all emotions tend to become alike in proportion to their intensity. People weep from excess of joy; pallor and trembling accompany extremes of hope as well as of fear, etc. But, I answer, do not the subject's feelings also then tend to become alike, if considered in themselves apart from all their differing intellectual contexts? My theory maintains that they should do so; and such reminiscences of extreme emotion as I possess rather seem to confirm than to invalidate such a view.

In Dr. Lehmann's highly praiseworthy book, *Die Hauptgesetze des menschlichen Gefühlslebens*,[7] much is said of Lange's theory; and in particular this same alleged identity of the emotion in the midst of such shifting organic symptoms seems to strike the critic as a fact irreconcilable with its being true. The emotion ought to be different when the symptoms are different, if the latter *make* the emotion; whereas if we lay a primary mental feeling at its core its constancy with shifting symptoms is no such hard thing to understand (p. 120). *Some* inconstancy in the mental state itself, however, Dr. Lehmann admits to follow from the shifting symptoms; but he contrasts the small degree of this inconstancy in the case of 'motived' emotions where we have a recognized mental cause for our mood, with its great degree where the emotion is 'unmotived,' as when it is produced by intoxicants (alcohol, haschisch, opium) or by cerebral disease, and changes to its opposite with every reversal of the vaso-motor and other organic states. I must say that I cannot regard this argument as fatal to Lange's and my theory so long as we remain in such real ignorance as to what the subjective variations of our emotions actually are. Exacter observation, both introspective and symptomatic, might well show in 'motived' emotions also just the amount of inconstancy that the theory demands.

Mr. Irons actually accuses me of self-contradiction in admitting that the symptoms of the same emotion vary from one man to

---

[7] Leipzig, 1892.

another, and yet that the emotion has them for its cause. How can any definite emotion, he asks, exist under such circumstances, and what is there then left to give unity to such concepts as anger or fear at all (82)? The natural reply is that the bodily variations are within limits, and that the symptoms of the angers and of the fears of different men still preserve enough *functional* resemblance, to say the very least, in the midst of their diversity to lead us to call them by identical names. Surely there *is* no definite affection of 'anger' in an 'entitative' sense.

Mr. Irons finds great difficulty in believing that both intellectual and emotional states of mind, both the cognition of an object and the emotion which it causes, contrasted as they are, can be due to such similar neural processes, viz., currents from the periphery, as my theory assumes. "How," he asks, "can one perceptive process of itself suffuse with emotional warmth the cold intellectuality of another? . . . If perceptions can have this warmth, why is it the exclusive property of perception of organic disturbance?" (85). I reply in the first place that it is not such exclusive property, for all the higher senses have warmth when 'æsthetic' objects excite them. And I reply in the second place that even if secondarily aroused visceral thrills were the only objects that had warmth, I should see no difficulty in accepting the fact. This writer further lays great stress on the vital difference between the receptive and the reactive states of the mind, and considers that the theory under discussion takes away all ground for the distinction. His account of the inner contrast in question is excellent. He gives the name of 'feeling-attitude' to the whole class of reactions of the self, of which the experiences which we call emotions are one species. He sharply distinguishes feeling-attitude from mere pleasure and pain—a distinction in which I fully agree. The line of direction in feeling-attitude is from the self outwards, he says, while that of mere pleasure and pain (and of perception and ideation) is from the object to the self. It is impossible to feel pleasure or pain *towards* an object; and common language makes a sharp distinction between being pained and having bad feelings towards somebody in consequence. These attitudes of feeling are almost indefinitely numerous; some of them must always intervene between cognition and action, and when in them we feel our whole Being moved (93–96). Of course one must admit that any account of the physiology of emotion that should be inconsistent with the possibility of this strong contrast within consciousness would thereby stand condemned. But on what ground have we the right to affirm that visceral and muscular sensibility cannot give the direction from the self outwards, if the higher senses (taken broadly, with their ideational sequelæ) give the direction from the object to the self? We do, it is true, but follow a natural analogy when we say (as Fouillée keeps saying in his works on *Idées-forces,* and as Ladd would seem to imply in his recent *Psychology*) that the former direction in consciousness ought to be mediated by outgoing nerve-currents, and the latter by currents passing in. But is not this analogy a mere superficial fancy, which reflection shows to have no basis in any existing knowledge of what such currents can or cannot bring to pass? We surely know too little of the psycho-physic relation to warrant us in insisting that the similarity of direction of two physical currents makes it impossible that they should bring a certain inner contrast about.

Both Dr. Worcester and Mr. Irons insist on the fact that consciousness of bodily disturbance, taken by itself, and apart from its combination with the consciousness of an exciting object, is not emotional at all. "Laughing and sobbing, for instance," writes the former, "are spasmodic movements of the muscles of respiration, not strikingly different from hiccuping, and there seems no good reason why the consciousness of the former two should usually be felt as strong emotional excitement, while the latter is not. . . . Shivering from cold, for instance, is the same sort of a movement as may occur in violent fright, but it does not make us feel frightened. The laughter excited in children and sensitive persons by tickling of the skin is not necessarily accompanied by any mirthful feelings. The act of vomiting may be the accompaniment of the most extreme disgust, or it may occur without a trace of such emotion" (289). The facts must be admitted; but in none of these cases where an organic change gives rise to a mere local bodily perception is the reproduction of an emotional diffusive wave complete. Visceral factors, hard to localize, are left out; and these seem to be the most essential ones of all. I have said that where they also from any inward cause are added, we *have* the emotion; and that then the subject is seized with objectless or pathological dread, grief, or rage, as the case may be. Mr. Irons refuses to accept this interpretation. The bodily symptoms do not here, he says, when felt, constitute the emotion. In the case of fear they constitute rather the object of which we are afraid. We fear *them,* on account of their unknown or indefinite evil consequences. In the case of morbid rage, he suggests, the movements are probably not the expression of a genuine inner rage, but only frantic attempts to relieve some inward pain, which outwardly look like rage to the observer (80). These interpretations are ingenious, and may be left to the reader's judgment. I confess that they fail to convert me from my own hypothesis.[8]

Messrs. Irons and Wundt (and possibly Baldwin and Sully, neither of whom accept the theory in dispute, but to whose works I have not access where I write, so that I cannot verify my impression) think that the theory carries with it implications of an objectionable sort philosophically. Irons, for example, says that it belongs to a psychology in which feeling can have no place, because it ignores the self and its unity, etc. (92). In my own mind the theory has no philosophic implications whatever of a general sort. It assumes (what probably every one assumes) that there must be a process of some sort in the nerve-centres for emotion, and it simply defines that process to consist of afferent currents. It does this on no general theoretic grounds, but because of the introspective appearances exclusively.

The objective qualities with which perception acquaints us are considered by psychologists to be results of sensation. When these qualities affect us with pleasure or displeasure, we say that the sensations have a 'tone of feeling.' Whether this tone be due to a mere form of the process in the nerve of sense, as some authors (e.g. Mr. Marshall) think, or to additional specific nerves, as others (e.g. Dr. Nichols) opine, is immaterial. The pleasantness or unpleasantness,

[8] Mr. Irons elsewhere says that "an object on being presented suddenly may cause intense fear. On being recognised as familiar the terror may vanish instantly, and, while the mental mood has changed, for a measurable time at least, all the bodily effects of the former state are present" (86). Their dying phase certainly is present for a while; but *has* the emotion then 'vanished instantly'? I should rather say that there is then a very mixed emotional state, in which something of the departing terror still blends with the incoming joy of relief. The case of waking from nightmare is for us civilizees probably the most frequent experience in point. On such occasions the horror with me is largely composed of an intensely strong but indescribable feeling in my breast and in all my muscles, especially those of the legs, which feel as if they were boiled into shreds or otherwise inwardly decomposed. This feeling fades out slowly and until it is gone the horror abides, in spite of the fact that I am already enjoying the incomplete relief which comes of knowing that the bad experience is a dream, and that the horror is on the wane. It were much to be wished that many persons should make observations of this sort, for individual idiosyncrasy may be great.

once there, seems immediately to inhere in the sensible quality it-self. They are beaten up together in our consciousness. But in addi-tion to this pleasantness or painfulness of the content, *which in any case seems due to afferent currents,* we may also feel a general seizure of excitement, which Wundt, Lehmann, and other German writers call an *Affect,* and which is what I have all along meant by an emotion. Now whenever I myself have sought to discover the mind-stuff of which such seizures consist, it has always seemed to me to be additional sensations often hard to describe, but usually easy to identify, and localized in divers portions of my organism. In addition to these sensations I can discern nothing but the 'ob-jective content' (taking this broadly so as to include judgments as well as elements judged), together with whatever agreeableness or disagreeableness the content may come tinged by.[9] *Such organic sensations being also presumably due to incoming currents, the result is that the whole of my consciousness* (whatever its inner contrasts be) *seems to me to be outwardly mediated by these.* This is the length and breadth of my 'theory'—which, as I apprehend it, is a very unpretending thing.

It may be, after all, that the difference between the theory and the views of its critics is insignificant. Wundt admits tertiary feel-ings, due to organic disturbance, which must fuse with the primary and secondary feelings before we can have an 'Affect'; Lehmann

---

[9] The disagreeableness, etc., is a very mild affection, not drastic or grasping *in se* in the case of any objective content except localized bodily *pain,* properly so called. Here the feeling seems in itself overpowering in intensity apart from all secondary emotional excitement. But I think that even here a distinction needs to be made between the primary consciousness of the pain's *intrinsic quality,* and the con-sciousness of its degree of *intolerability,* which is a secondary affair, seeming con-nected with reflex organic irradiations. I recently, while traversing a little surgical experience, had occasion to verify once more the fact that it is not the mere *bigness* of a pain that makes it most unbearable. If a pain is honest and definite and well localized it may be very heavy and strong without taxing the extreme of our endur-ance. But there are pains which we feel to be faint and small in their intrinsic amount, but which have something so poisonous and non-natural about them that consent to their continuance is impossible. Our whole being refuses to suffer them. These pains produce involuntary shrinkings, writhings, sickness, faintness, and dread. For such emotion superadded to the pain itself there is no distinctive name in English. Prof. Münsterberg has distinguished between *Schmerz* as an original 'content' of consciousness and *Unlust* as due to flexor reactions provoked thereby; and before his Essay appeared, I remember hearing Dr. D. S. Miller and Dr. Nichols maintain in conversation that painfulness may be always a matter of 'intolerability,' due to the reflex irradiations which the painful object may arouse. Thus might even the mildest *Gemüthsvorgänge* be brought under the terms of my theory.

writes: "Constrained by the facts, we are obliged to concede to the organic sensations and tones of feeling connected with them an essential participation in emotion (wesentliche Bedeutung für die Affekte)" (p. 115); and Professor Ladd also admits that the 'rank' quality of the emotions comes from the organic repercussions which they involve. So far, then, we are all agreed; and it may be admitted, in Dr. Worcester's words, that the theory under attack 'contains an important truth,' and even that its authors have 'rendered a real service to psychology' (p. 295). Why, then, is there such strong opposition? When the critics say that the theory still contradicts their consciousness (Worcester, p. 288), do they mean that introspection acquaints them with a part of the emotional excitement which it is psycho-physically impossible that incoming currents should cause? Or, do they merely mean that the part which introspection can *localize* in the body is so small that when abstracted a large mass of unlocalizable emotion remains? Although Mr. Irons professes the former of these two meanings, the only prudent one to stand by is surely the latter; and here, of course, every man will hold by his own consciousness. I for one shall never deny that individuals may greatly differ in their ability to localize the various elements of their organic excitement when under emotion. I am even willing to admit that the primary *Gefühlston* may vary enormously in distinctness in different men. But speaking for myself, I am compelled to say that the only feelings which I cannot more or less well localize in my body are very mild and, so to speak, platonic affairs. I allow them hypothetically to exist, however, in the form of the 'subtler' emotions, and in the mere intrinsic agreeableness and disagreeableness of particular sensations, images, and thought-processes, where no obvious organic excitement is aroused.[10]

This being the case, it seems almost as if the question had become a verbal one. For which sort of feeling is the *word* 'emotion' the more proper name—for the organic feeling which gives the rank

---

[10] Mr. Irons contends that in admitting 'subtler' forms of emotion, I throw away my whole case (88, 89); and Dr. Lehmann enters into an elaborate argument to prove (as he alleges, against Lange and me) that primary feeling, as a possible accompaniment of any sensation whatever, must be admitted to exist (§§ 157–164). Such objections are a complete *ignoratio elenchi*, addressed to some imaginary theory with which my own, as I myself understand it, has nothing whatever to do, all that I have ever maintained being the dependence on incoming currents of the *emotional seizure* or *Affect*.

character of commotion to the excitement, or for that more primary pleasure or displeasure in the object, or in the thought of it, to which commotion and excitement do not belong? I myself took for granted without discussion that the word 'emotion' meant the rank feeling of excitement, and that the special emotions were names of special feelings of excitement, and not of mild feelings that might remain when the excitement was removed. It appears, however, that in this assumption I reckoned without certain of my hosts.

Dr. Worcester's quarrel with me at the end of his article becomes almost exclusively verbal. All pleasure and pain, he says, whether primary and of the higher senses and intellectual products, or secondary and organic, should be called 'emotion' (296).[11] Pleasure or pain revived in idea, as distinguished from vivid sensuous pleasure and pain, he suggests to be what is meant by emotion 'in the sense in which the word is commonly used' (297); and he gives an array of cases in point:

"Suppose that I have taken a nauseous dose, and made a wry face over it. No one, I presume, would question that the disagreeableness lay in the unpleasant taste, and not in the distortion of the countenance. Now, suppose I have to repeat the dose, and my face takes on a similar expression at the anticipation to that which it wore when I took it originally. How does this come about? If I can trust my own consciousness, it is because the vivid reproduction, in memory, of the unpleasant taste is itself unpleasant. . . . If this be the fact, what can be more natural than that it should excite the same sort of associated movements that were excited by the original sensation? I cannot make it seem any more credible that my *repugnance* to a repetition of the dose is due to my involuntary movements than my discomfort in taking it originally was due to the similar movements that occurred then. . . . I hardly think that any one who will consult his own consciousness will say that the reason he likes the taste of an orange is that it makes him laugh or smile to get it. He *likes* it because it tastes good, and is sorry to lose it for the same reason" (296–297).

---

[11] 'The essence of emotion is pleasure or pain,' he adds. This is a hackneyed psychological doctrine, but on any theory of the seat of emotion it seems to me one of the most artificial and scholastic of the untruths that disfigure our science. One might as well say that the essence of prismatic color is pleasure and pain. There are infinite shades and tones in the various emotional excitements, which are as distinct as sensations of color are, and of which one is quite at a loss to predicate either pleasant or painful quality.

Now, accepting Dr. Worcester's description of the facts, I remark immediately that the nauseousness and pleasantness are due to incoming nerve-currents—at any rate in the cases which he selects—and the feeling of the involuntary movements as well; so whatever name we give to the phenomena, so far they fall comfortably under the terms of my theory. The only question left over is what may be covered by the words 'repugnance' and 'liking,' which I have italicized, but which Dr. Worcester does not emphasize, as he describes his instances. Are *these* a third sort of affection, *not* due to afferent currents, and interpolated between the gustatory feelings and reactions which are so due? Or are they a name for what, when carefully considered, resolves itself into more delicate reactions still? I privately incline to the latter view, but the whole *animus* of my critic's article obliges me to attribute to him the opinion, not only that the like and dislike must be a third sort of affection not grounded on incoming currents, but that they form the distinctive elements of the 'emotional' state of mind.

The whole discussion sharpens itself here to a point. We can leave the lexicographers to decide which elements the word 'emotional' belongs to; for our concern is with the facts, and the question of fact is now very plain. Must we (under any name) admit as an important element in the emotional state of mind something which is distinct both from the intrinsic feeling-tone of the object and from that of the reactions aroused—an element of which the 'liking' and 'repugnance' mentioned above would be types, but for which other names may in other cases be found? The belief that some such element does exist, and exist in vital amount, is undoubtedly present in the minds of all the rejectors of the theory in dispute. Dr. Worcester rightly regrets the deadlock when one man's introspection thus contradicts another's (288), and demands a more objective sort of umpire. Can such a one be found? I shall try to show now that it possibly has been found; and that Dr. Sollier's recent observations on complete anæsthetics show that in some persons at least the supposed third kind of mental element may exist, if it exists at all, in altogether inappreciable amount.

In my original article I had invoked cases of generalized anæsthesia, and admitted that if a patient could be found who, in spite of being anæsthetic inside and out, could still suffer emotion, my case would be upset. I had quoted such cases as I was aware of at the time of writing, admitting that so far as appearances went they made against the theory; but I had tried to save the latter by distinguishing between the objective reaction which the patient makes and the subjective feeling which it gives him. Since then a number of cases of generalized anæsthesia have been published, but unfortunately the patients have not been interrogated from the proper point of view. The famous 'theory' has been unknown to the reporting doctors. Two such cases, however, described by Dr. Berkley of Baltimore,[12] are cited by Dr. Worcester 'for what they are worth' in its refutation (294). The first patient was an Englishwoman, with complete loss of the senses of pain, heat and cold, pressure and equilibrium, of smell, taste, and sight. The senses of touch and of position were not completely gone, but greatly impaired, and she could hear a little. As for visceral sensations, she had had no hunger or thirst for two years, but she was warned by feeling of the evacuative needs. She laughts at a joke, shows definitely grief, shame, surprise, fear, and repulsion. Dr. Berkley writes to Dr. Worcester as follows: "My own impression derived from observation of the patient is, that all mental emotional sensibilities are present and only a little less vivid than in the unanæsthetic state; and that emotions are approximately natural, and not at all coldly dispassionate."

The second case was that of a Russian woman with complete loss of cutaneous, and almost complete loss of muscular, sensibility. Sight, smell, hearing preserved, and nothing said of visceral sensation (in Dr. Worcester's citation). She showed anger and amusement, and not the slightest apathy.

This last case is obviously too incompletely reported to serve; and in the preceding one it will be noticed that certain degrees of visceral and of muscular sensibility remained. As these seem the important sorts emotionally, she may well have felt emotion. Dr. Berkley, however, writes of her 'apathy'; and it will be noticed that he thinks her emotions 'less vivid than in the unanæsthetic state.'

In Dr. Sollier's patient the anæsthesia was far more complete, and the patient was examined for the express purpose of testing the dependence of emotion on organic sensibility. Dr. Sollier, moreover, experimented on two other subjects in whom the anæsthesia

[12] *Brain*, Part IV, 1891.

was artificially induced by hypnotic suggestion. The spontaneous case was a man aged forty-four; the hypnotic cases were females of hysteric constitution.[13] In the man the anæsthetic condition extended so far that at present every surface, cutaneous and mucous, seems absolutely insensible. The muscular sense is wholly abolished; the feelings of hunger and satiety do not exist; the needs of defecation and micturition are unfelt; taste and smell are gone; sight much enfeebled; hearing alone is about normal. The cutaneous and tendinous reflexes are lacking. The physiognomy has no expression; speech is difficult; the entire muscular apparatus is half paralyzed, so that locomotion is almost impossible.

" 'I *know*,' this patient says, 'that I have a heart, but I do not feel it beat, except sometimes very faintly.' When an event happens which ought to affect it [the heart, as I understand the text], he fails equally to feel it. He does not feel himself breathe, or know whether he makes a strong or a weak inspiration. 'I do not feel myself alive,' he says. Early in his illness he several times thought himself dead. He does not know whether he is asleep or awake. . . . He often has no thoughts. When he does think of anything it is of his home or of the war of 1870, in which he took part. The people whom he sees come and go about him are absolutely indifferent to him. He does not notice what they do. 'They do not appear,' he says, 'like natural men to me, but more like mechanisms.' Similar perturbations of perception occur also in hearing. 'I do not hear in the old way; it is as if it sounded in my ear, but did not enter into my head. It does not stay there long.' His *aprosexia* is complete, and he is incapable of interest in anything whatever. Nothing gives him pleasure. 'I am insensible to everything; nothing interests me. I love nobody; neither do I dislike anybody.' He does not even know whether it would give him pleasure to get well, and when I tell him that his cure is possible it awakens no reaction—not even one of surprise or doubt. The only thing that seems to move him a little is the visit of his wife. When she appears in the room 'it gives me a stroke in the stomach,' he says; 'but as soon as she is there I wish her away again.' He often has a fear that his daughter may be dead. 'If she should die I believe I should not survive her, although if I never were to see her again it would make no difference to me.' His visual images are nonexistent, and he has no representation of his wife when she is gone. The weakness of the sensations remaining to him gives him a sense of

13 The paper, entitled "Recherches sur les rapports de la sensibilité et de l'émotion," will be found in the *Revue Philosophique* for March of this year, vol. XXXVII, pp. 241–266.

uncertainty about all things: 'I am never sure of anything.' Nothing surprises or astonishes him. His state of apathy, of indifference, of extreme emotionlessness, has developed slowly *pari passu* with the anæsthesia. His case realizes, therefore, as completely as possible the experiment desiderated by W. James."

In the hypnotic experiments, Dr. Sollier provoked in his subjects sometimes visceral and sometimes peripheral anæsthesia, and sometimes both at once. He registered the organic reactions (by pneumograph, etc.) as far as possible, and compared them with those produced in the same subject when an emotion-exciting idea was suggested, first in the anæsthetic and then in the normal state. Finally, he questioned the subject on the impressions she had received. For the detailed results the reader must consult the original paper. I will only mention those which seem most important, as follows:

(1) Complete peripheral anæsthesia abolishes completely the power of movement. At the same time the limbs grow cold and sometimes blue (247).

(2) When visceral anæsthesia is added, the patient says she feels as if she no longer were alive (*ibid.*).

(3) When totally anæsthetic she feels no normal emotion whatever at the suggestion of hallucinations and delusions which have the power of moving her strongly when the sensibility is restored. When the anæsthesia is less complete she may say that she feels not the usual emotion, but a certain stroke in the head or stomach at the reception of the moving idea (250, 254).

(4) When the anæsthesia is solely peripheral, the emotion takes place with almost normal strength.

(5) When it is solely visceral, the emotion is abolished almost as much as when it is total, so that the emotion depends almost exclusively on visceral sensations (258).

(6) There is sometimes a very slight motor reaction shown by the pneumograph in visceral anæsthesia when an exciting idea is suggested (Figs. 2, 7 *bis*), but M. Sollier thinks (for reasons of a highly speculative kind) that in complete *inemotivity* the visceral reactions themselves do not take place (265).

The reader sees that M. Sollier's experimental results go on the whole farther than 'my theory' ever required. With the visceral sensibility not only the 'coarser' but even the 'subtler' forms of emotion depart. Some people must then be admitted to exist in whom the amount of supposed feeling that is not due to incoming currents is a negligible quantity. Of course we must bear in mind the fallibility of experiments made by the method of 'suggestion.' We must moreover remember that the male patient's inemotivity may have been a co-ordinate result with the anæsthesia, of his neural lesions, and not the anæsthesia's mere effect. But nevertheless, if many cases like those of M. Sollier should be found by other observers, I think that Prof. Lange's theory and mine ought no longer to be treated as a heresy, but might become the orthodox belief. That part, if there be any, of emotional feeling which is not of afferent origin should be admitted to be insignificant, and the name 'emotion' should be suffered to connote organic excitement as the distinctive feature of the state.

Person and Personality: From
Johnson's Universal Cyclopædia

Person and Personality [*person* is viâ O. Fr. from Lat. *perso'na*, theater-mask, part (in a play), personage, person; loan-word from Gr. πρόσωπον, mask, face, adapted to presumed etymology of *per*, through + *sona're*, sound (i.e. speak)]: the word person is still sometimes used to denote the corporeal appearance of a man rather than his inner attributes, as when we say that he possesses an agreeable person, or is personally repulsive. Later, the relations that a man might sustain in the world as a "personage," *personam agens*, or *gerens*, became prominent, and later still the spiritual functions became the essential content of the notion. In common parlance to-day "person" means an individual man in his typical completeness as uniting a human body to a free and rational soul. From this point of view personality has been denied to pure spirits and to the souls of the departed awaiting the resurrection, because they are bodiless; also to idiots because they are irrational; to maniacs because they are not free; and to animals, however intelligent, because they are not human. By emphasizing one feature of the conception or another, psychology, ethics, law, and theology have all developed the conception of personality in different ways.

In psychology "personality" designates individuality, or what is called "personal identity," and various opinions have been held concerning the foundations of this. It is either an ultimate and self-subsistent principle at the core of a man, or it is a result de-

315

rived from other principles. Already in Hindu philosophy we have this opposition in the contrast between the Sankhya system, with its absolute plurality or independent finite souls, and the Vedanta system, for which there exists only one self, the supreme Brahman, with whom all particular selves (Atman) are really coidentical, but (until they are redeemed by knowledge) dwell in the illusion of finite personality through not distinguishing themselves from the organisms with which they are severally conjoined. These organisms have their psychic as well as their physical side. Their grosser body is resolved at death into its elements, but a finer body, together with the senses and active powers, the *manas*, or organ of consciousness and will, the breath, and the *karma*, or moral worth acquired, form principles of continued individuality which ever enter into other bodies, so that through an indefinite series of transmigrations the finite personal life is kept up. The *modern theosophists'* doctrine of personality is derived from the Vedantic system.

Among the Jews the spiritual principle of personality was the "spirit" (*Ruach*) or warm breath of life which animated the dust, when breathed thereinto by Jehovah. This breath-spirit, which we find as the ruling conception in all primitive thought, maintains its place in both Greek and Christian philosophy, developing into the more physiological conception of "animal spirits" on the one hand, and into the Pauline doctrine of the "Spirit," or *pneuma*, on the other. The animal spirits filling the arteries, nerve-tubes, and brain cavities were supposed to mediate between the rational soul and the body; the theological "spirit" mediates between God and the soul or *psyche*.

In the Greek philosophy, passing over the confused utterances of the pre-Socratic masters, we find the *pneuma* or fiery air-current to play a great part in the systems of the *Stoics*. Being of a nature both material and immaterial, it was well calculated to serve as the animating principle of the world at large as well as of the individual person in it. *Plato and Aristotle* subordinated the principle of the breath to the immaterial and rational *psyche*. In Plato we find the germ of later spiritualistic conceptions of personality. The man is composed of two almost hostile principles, of which the soul is the one that is essential, being superior to Nature, pre-existing to the body, and possessing an immortal destiny to be attained by a course of rational and moral development.

The body here is the soul's vessel or prison, and, although its necessary servant, is also the source of its errors and faults. This dualistic view was in Aristotle's psychology developed into that wonderful conception of soul as "form" and body as "matter" which dominated all Christian philosophy until the time of Descartes. For Aristotle the person is this organic unity of form and matter, this animated body in its completeness, this subject of biology and psychology in one; and nutrition becomes a function of the soul as much as thinking is. *Scholastic peripateticism* here, as elsewhere, elaborated the Aristotelian ideas into greater hardness and articulateness. Soul and body, separately taken, are incomplete substances. Only their union is a concretely *subsistent* substance, *suppositum* or *hypostasis*; and since in the case of the human soul the nature of the substance is rational, the *suppositum rationale* thus composed is what is meant by *person*. *Individua substantia naturæ rationalis* is the definition of "a person," often quoted from Boethius.

It is not till Descartes's time that we find consummated with perfect sharpness the distinction, now so familiar to us, of Consciousness and the Unconscious. In the Cartesian philosophy the Conscious and the Extended, having absolutely nothing in common with each other, were raised to the rank of two mutually exclusive substances, and the commerce of soul and body in the human person, mediated for Descartes himself by the animal spirits, had to be carried on for Malebranche and other Cartesians by a perpetual miracle of "divine assistance." The person was thus broken in two, or rather became a purely spiritual entity, while the rest of nature, including the body, was materialistically treated. In Cartesianism, however, as in Peripateticism, the finite souls still constitute a multitude of distinct substances, and are not, as with Spinoza, lost in the one substance of God. Personal identity, in a word, is *real*— a principle, not a result.

In Locke's *Essay Concerning Human Understanding* the great revolution toward empiricism begins. Personality is now explained as a result, and not assumed as a principle. It is not something which, by simply being, gives rise to consequences, but something which is made from moment to moment by a cause which can be assigned. Locke believes, indeed, in souls as substances and in their identity; but the mere ontological self-identity of such a soul would, he says, make no *personal* identity unless a recollecting consciousness were joined thereto. "Consciousness" is what makes a *person*, when it remembers past experiences, as having been also its own. If the same consciousness with its memories could migrate from one soul to another, we should have personal identity without identity of substance. And conversely, if one man were to have distinct incommunicable consciousnesses at different times, he would make different persons. As personality is annexed to consciousness, so punishment ought to be annexed to personality, and in the great day, wherein the secrets of all hearts are laid open, no one should be made to answer for what he knows nothing of, but should receive his doom, his conscience accusing or excusing. The importance of Locke's doctrine lay in this, that he eliminated "substantial" identity as transcendental and unimportant, and made of "personal" identity (the only practically important sort) a directly verifiable empirical phenomenon. Where not actually experienced, it *is* not. Hume went beyond Locke in discarding substances, whether spiritual or material, altogether. Our sense of *gradual* change in the succession of our particular "ideas," in which "there is properly no simplicity at one time, nor identity in different," is what Hume means by our personal identity. Locke's and Hume's views have been carried out both in Germany and England by the *associationist psychology*, which in consequence has been dubbed a "psychology without a soul."

Since Kant's time the consciousness of subjection to moral law, and the autonomy and freedom implied by such a consciousness, have often been referred to as the specific marks of personality. On this view "person" means a being with inner ideal ends, to which it freely acknowledges responsibility. Here the psychological notion passes over into the ethical and juridical conceptions of personality.

Recent psychology has, in the main, elaborated itself on Lockian lines. The succession of associated ideas inwardly held together by memory is regarded by all schools to constitute the content of the *empirical self*. For some writers these ideas themselves are compounds of simpler psychic units, so that the psychic person is a purely secondary result, with no special principle of unity. Others contend for such a primordial principle, either in the shape of a real spiritual being or soul, which owns the ideas, or in that of a "transcendental Ego" which performs their synthesis.

Multiple Personality.—That something beyond the mere contemporaneous connection of many ideas with one organism is needed to make one personal consciousness result, is shown by certain phenomena which psychologists are but just beginning to study with care. In a variety of ways one and the same "man" may successively or simultaneously have different consciousnesses that are, in Locke's words, incommunicable. The most familiar cases of this are ordinary forgetfulness, absence of mind, and rapid oblivescence of dreams, where subsequent recollection proves the apparently lost ideas to have been there all the time. In somnambulism, either natural or "hypnotic," the rule is for the subject to forget on waking all that he has done, but to remember it again on re-entering the somnambulistic state. He may thus live two alternating personal lives with a distinct system of memory in each. It was first proved by Edmund Gurney that the memories of the hypnotic consciousness may coexist, after waking, with the normal consciousness of the subject, but be unknown to the latter. Taking subjects to whom it had been "suggested" in trance that they must perform certain acts after waking when a signal should be given (see HYPNOTISM), but whose waking consciousness ignored the suggestion, he set their hands, when they woke, upon a *planchette* and got the order automatically and "unconsciously" written, while their normal consciousness was occupied in reading aloud, or in conversation. At about the same time Janet, Binet, and others found phenomena in connection with the anæsthetic surfaces of hysteric patients, which proved the anæsthesia to be relative only to the subject's principal consciousness, another consciousness appearing present which took cognizance of the apparently lost sensations. Thus one patient's anæsthetic hand can feel her toilet articles and handle them skillfully; in others, if the attention be distracted, the anæsthetic hand adapts its movements to objects that are placed in it, as scissors, matches, etc. Or if figures be traced on the anæsthetic palm, the patient will *see* them, vicariously, as it were; but the chief proof, as with Gurney, is by automatic writing. Janet used what he calls the "method of distraction" in these cases. In this the patient is kept absorbed in conversation with a third party, while the operator, approaching her quietly, whispers questions in her ear. The consciousness engaged in talking ignores the questions, but, if a pencil be placed in the hand, answers to them are automatically written. It is as if one consciousness animated the speaking mouth and another the writing hand, both, however, using the ear. Myers has given the name of *subliminal selves* to consciousnesses supernumerary to the principal one; and Janet and others have found that painful reminiscences split off from the principal consciousness, persisting thus subliminally and revealing themselves in the hypnotic trance, are prime factors of the hysteric condition. Cases of *alternating personality,* in which the man or woman passes at intervals into a "second" state with its own peculiarities, of which the normal state, when resumed, knows nothing, have been recorded at great length. "Léonie," "Félida X.," "Lurancy Vennum," "Ansel Bourne," and "Louis V.," may be named as types. In the last-named case there were as many as five different personalities with exclusive systems of memory and peculiarities both of bodily sensibility and character. A very large number of men and women can readily become *automatic* writers, either with *planchette* or pencil. The writing hand becomes sometimes anæsthetic, sometimes not; and there are all degrees of detachment of the principal consciousness from what is written. In no case, however, is the subject's "will" felt to be concerned. These writings tend in most cases to assume the character of messages from spirits who sign their names; and in its most developed degree automatic writing passes into *mediumistic trance* and may be succeeded by *"speaking under control."* Here again there are degrees; but the medium's normal consciousness usually remembers nothing of the trance-utterances, which may assume a character very unlike the medium's own. (See SPIRITUALISM.) The phenomena of *demoniacal possession,* so rife in ancient times and in primitive societies, seems to be essentially the same thing as our trance-mediumship, obeying, however, a different inspiration as regards its moral content. In both phenomena the "attacks" are short, no memory of them remains, and the patient between them is well. The subjects have nothing in common with the insane, technically so called.

All these facts have brought the question of what is the unifying principle in personality to the front again. It is certain that one human body may be the home of many *consciousnesses,* and thus, in Locke's sense, of many *persons*; but much in the temperament of the secondary persons seems unaccountable if they are only accidental improvisations, produced by certain groups of the patient's "ideas" separating from the rest and leading a quasi-independent life. They have a generic similarity in many cases, as in automatic writing and trance-speaking, which suggests some common cause as yet imperfectly known, or at any rate a context which if explored might make the phenomena, with their peculiar regularity, appear more rational. It is clear already that the margins and outskirts of what we take to be our personality extend into unknown regions. Cures and organic effects, such as blisters, produced by hypnotic suggestion show this as regards our bodily processes; while the utterances of mediums and automatic writers reveal a widespread tendency, in men and women otherwise sane, to personifications of a determinate kind; and these again, though usually flimsy and incoherent in the extreme, do, as the present writer believes, occasionally show a knowledge of facts not possessed by the primary person. The significance and limits of these phenomena have yet to be understood, and psychology is but just beginning to recognize this investigation as an urgent task.

BIBLIOGRAPHY.—For opinions before Locke see all the histories of philosophy, especially Siebeck's *Geschichte der Psychologie*; and for Hindu ideas, see Deussen's *System des Vedânta*. Locke's statements are in book II, chap. xxvii, of his *Essay*; Hume's in part iv, § vi, of his *Treatise of Human Nature*. In modern psychology Ladd's *Physiological Psychology*, part iii, and James's *Principles of Psychology*, chap. x, may be referred to, the one defending a Real Being as the principle of personal unity, the other placing it in the function of memory. General defenses of the spiritual view are A. W. Momerie's book *Personality*, and F. A. Shoup's *Mechanism and Personality*. The theosophic doctrine is conveniently expressed in Blavatsky's *Key to Theosophy, passim*. Binet's *Altérations de la personnalité* and various essays by Myers in the *Proceedings of the Society for Psychical Research* give the facts of multiple personality in much detail.

Consciousness Under Nitrous Oxide

An English correspondent sends me the following account of his subjective experiences during nitrous-oxide intoxication. I place it (with his permission) on record in the PSYCHOLOGICAL REVIEW. Normal human consciousness is only a narrow extract from a great sea of possible human consciousness, of whose limits we know nothing, but of the nature of portions of which such documents as the following may help to inform us. It were greatly to be wished that they might be multiplied.   W. J.

The note in your book, entitled 'The Will to Believe,' upon the above subject, recalls to my mind a strange experience which I had in June, 1895, while still an undergraduate at Oxford.

I had been studying philosophy, and had about as much acquaintance with it as a man gets in two years, who has a good deal of natural interest in abstract speculation, but very little natural talent for it. The ideas of Hegel, though exercising a tolerable fascination over my mind, were only known to me at second or third hand, through English and Scotch writers and casual conversation.

One morning in June, 1895, or certainly not later than the end of May, I went round to a dentist's opposite Balliol College, to have a tooth out. I had never 'taken gas' before, and never have since. My experience was, as accurately as I can remember it at this distance of time, as follows:

Either of set purpose, or to distract my mind from the intensely uncomfortable process of 'going off,' I determined to observe very carefully the changes in my conscious states.

What happened, I found, was that the contents of consciousness, the feelings, gradually became reduced, till I came down nearly, though not quite, to the bare uncolored fact of consciousness of existence almost divorced from sensation. By this time, of course, I was hardly in a position to observe accurately, but when I came afterwards to think the matter over, it seemed that I had spent an absurdly long time in this state, and then suddenly, when I was hoping for it, but least expecting it, had 'gone out,' like a snuffed candle.

The next experience I became aware of, who shall relate! my God! *I knew everything!* A vast inrush of obvious and absolutely satisfying solutions to all possible problems overwhelmed my entire being, and an all-embracing unification of hitherto contending and apparently diverse aspects of truth took possession of my soul by force. The odd thing, and one that sent a ripple of merriment through my consciousness, was that I seemed to have reconciled Hegelianism itself with all other schools of philosophy in some higher synthesis. The biter bit!

Then, in a flash, this state of intellectual ecstasy was succeeded by one that I shall never forget, because it was still more novel to me than the other—I mean a state of moral ecstasy. I was seized with an immense yearning to take back this truth to the feeble, sorrowing, struggling world in which I had lived. I pictured to myself with justifiable pride how they could not fail to recognize it as being the real truth when they heard it, and I saw that previous prophets had been rejected only because the truths they brought were partial and on that account not convincing. I had a balm for all hurts, and the prospect of how entire humanity would crowd around to bless the bringer nearly intoxicated me. But I thought I was dying and should not be able to tell them. I had never cared much for life, but it was then that I prayed and strove to live for the world's sake, as I had never prayed and striven before. It seemed in vain, however, that I battled for life, and I was just resigning myself to extinction when an immense sense of relief and of some obstacle having given way broke in upon me. This was, of course, succeeded by another fit of philanthropic ecstasy. Five or ten seconds more, and I should be able to speak, and the world would *really* be redeemed, whether I lived on or not. It was a moment of the supremest bliss, exceeding those former ones. Suddenly I saw standing on a little pink stage a little pink man with a kindly face which I seemed to recognize. Who could it be? Then, as the little pink man grew rapidly larger and less pink, and I steamed into the position of normal consciousness (for that was the sensation) I heard a voice, apparently not that of the little pink man, but coming from some one out of my range of vision, say: "That would have been a tough job without the elevator." These words gave me power to speak out, and I shouted aloud: "That would have been a tough job without the elevator; I've found out some metaphysics!" Hardly had I said the words, however, than they mocked me. The truth had evaporated, like a forgotten dream, and left me with half-formed phrases on my lips and an ashen-gray delight in my heart. The dentist asked me whether I wasn't suffering from a sluggish liver, and the little pink man, the doctor, recommended me to go away for a change of air. Shades of the prison-house have since closed about me, and Professor Caird still reigns unchallenged at Balliol.

Introduction to *The Psychology of Suggestion*
by Boris Sidis

I am glad to contribute to this book of Dr. Boris Sidis a few words of introduction, which may possibly gain for it a prompter recognition by the world of readers who are interested in the things of which it treats. Much of the experimental part of the work, although planned entirely by Dr. Sidis, was done in the Harvard Psychological Laboratory, and I have been more or less in his confidence while his theoretic conclusions, based on his later work in the Pathological Institute of the New York State Hospitals, were taking shape.

The meaning of personality, with its limits and its laws, forms a problem which until quite recently had to be discussed almost exclusively by logical and metaphysical methods. Within the past dozen years, however, an immense amount of new empirical material had been injected into the question by the observations which the "recognition" by science of the hypnotic state set in motion. Many of these observations are pathological: fixed ideas, hysteric attacks, insane delusions, mediumistic phenomena, etc. And altogether, although they are far from having solved the problem of personality, they must be admitted to have transformed its outward shape. What are the limits of the consciousness of a human being? Is "self" consciousness only a part of the whole consciousness? Are there many "selves" dissociated from one another? What is the medium of synthesis in a group of associated ideas? How can certain systems of ideas be cut off and forgotten? Is personality a product, and not a principle? Such are the questions now being forced to the front—questions now asked for the first time with some sense of their concrete import, and questions which it will require a great amount of further work, both of observation and of analysis, to answer adequately.

Meanwhile many writers are seeking to fill the gap, and several books have been published seeking to popularize the new observations and ideas and present them in connected form. Dr. Sidis' work distinguishes itself from some of these by its originality, and from others by the width of its scope.

It is divided into three parts: Suggestibility; the Self; Man as One of a Crowd. Under all these heads the author is original. He tries by ingenious experiments to show that the suggestibility of waking persons follows an opposite law to that of hypnotic subjects. Suggestions must be *veiled*, in the former case, to be effective; in the latter case, the more direct and open they are the better. By other ingenious experiments Dr. Sidis tries to show that the "subliminal" or "ultra-marginal" portions of the mind may in normal persons distinguish objects which the attentive senses find it impossible to name. These latter experiments are incomplete, but they open the way to a highly important psychological investigation.

In Part II, on "The Self," a very full account is given of "double personality," subliminal consciousness, etc. The author is led to adopt as an explanation of the dissociations which lie at the root of all these conditions the physiological theory of retraction of the processes of the brain cells, which in other quarters also seems coming to the front. He makes an elaborate classification of the different degrees of dissociation or amnesia, and, on the basis of a highly interesting and important pathological case, suggests definite methods of diagnosis and cure. This portion of the book well deserves the attention of neurologists.

In Part III the very important matter of "crowd psychology" is discussed, almost for the first time in English. There is probably no more practically important topic to the student of public affairs. Dr. Sidis illustrates it by fresh examples, and his treatment is highly suggestive.

I am not convinced of all of Dr. Sidis' positions, but I can cordially recommend the volume to all classes of readers as a treatise both interesting and instructive, and original in a high degree, on a branch of research whose importance is daily growing greater.

HARVARD UNIVERSITY, *November 1, 1897.*

Introduction to *The Elements of Psychology*
by Edward L. Thorndike

I have been invited to contribute a preface to this book, though when I ask myself, why any book from Professor Thorndike's pen should need an introduction to the public by another hand, I find no answer. Both as an experimental investigator, as a critic of other investigators, and as an expounder of results, he stands in the very forefront of American psychologists, and his references to my works in the text that follows will, I am sure, introduce me to more readers than I can introduce him to by my preface.

In addition to the monographs which have been pouring from the press for twenty years past, we have by this time, both in English and in German, a very large number of general text-books, some larger and some smaller, but all covering the ground in ways which, so far as students go, are practical equivalents for each other. The main subdivisions, principles, and features of descriptive psychology are at present well made out, and writers are agreed about them. If one has read earlier books, one need not read the very newest one in order to catch up with the progress of the science. The differences in them are largely of order and emphasis, or of fondness on the authors' parts for certain phrases, or for their own modes of approach to particular questions. It is one and the same body of facts with which they all make us acquainted.

Some of these treatises indeed give much more prominence to the details of experimentation than others—artificial experimentation, I mean, with physical instruments, and measurements. A rapid glance at Professor Thorndike's table of contents might lead one to set him down as not belonging to the experimental class of psychologists. He ignores the various methods of proving Fechner's psycho-physic law, and makes no reference to chronoscopes, or to acoustical or optical technics. Yet in another and psychologically in a more vital sense his book is a laboratory manual of the most energetic and continuous kind.

When I first looked at the proofs and saw each section followed by a set of neatly numbered exercises, problems, and questions in fine print, I confess that I shuddered for a moment. Can it be, I thought, that the author's long connection with the Teachers College is making even of him a high-priest of the American "text-book" Moloch, in whose belly living children's minds are turned to ashes, and whose ritual lies in text-books in which the science is pre-digested for the teacher by every expository artifice and for the pupil comminuted into small print and large print, and paragraph-headings, and cross-references and examination questions, and every other up-to-date device for frustrating the natural movement of the mind when reading, and preventing that irresponsible rumination of the material in one's own way which is the soul of culture? Can it be, I said, that Thorndike himself is sacrificing to machinery and discontinuity?

But I had not read many of the galleys before I got the opposite impression. There are, it is true, discontinuities in the book which might slightly disconcert a critic with a French turn of taste, but that is because of the intense concreteness with which the author feels his subject and wishes to make his reader feel it. The problems and questions are uniquely to that end. They are laboratory work of the most continuous description, and the text is like unto them for concreteness. Professor Thorndike has more horror of vagueness, of scholastic phrases, of scientific humbug than any psychologist with whom I am acquainted. I defy any teacher or student to go through this book as it is written, and not to carry away an absolutely first-hand acquaintance with the workings of the human mind, and with the realities as distinguished from the pedantries and artificialities of psychology. The author's supera-bounding fertility in familiar illustrations of what he is describing amounts to genius. I might enter into an exposition of some of the other peculiarities of his treatise, but this quality of exceeding realism seems to cap the others and to give it eminence among the long list of psychology-books which readers now-a-days have to choose from.

It is not a work for lazy readers, however; and lazy reading also has a sacred place in the universe of education. But I seem to foresee for it a powerful anti-pedantic influence, and I augur for it a very great success indeed in class-rooms. So, with no more prefatory words, I heartily recommend it to all those who are interested in spreading the knowledge of our science.

On Some Mental Effects of the Earthquake

NOTE.—From the opening sentence of this article the reader will truly infer that Professor James dropped his work at Harvard University not long ago to deliver a course of lectures at Leland Stanford, Jr., University. Some one has aptly described him as "the psychologist who writes like a novelist." Certainly his many writings have won him a distinguished place as a student of the human mind and character. It was fortunate that such a man had so remarkable an opportunity to study the workings of human nature in a crisis almost unique; and it is fortunate that *The Companion* can give its readers the results of such a study.—*The Editors*.

When I departed from Harvard for Stanford University last December, almost the last good-by I got was that of my old Californian friend B.: "I hope they'll give you a touch of earthquake while you're there, so that you may also become acquainted with *that* Californian institution."

Accordingly, when, lying awake at about half past five on the morning of April 18th in my little "flat" on the campus of Stanford, I felt the bed begin to waggle, my first consciousness was one of gleeful recognition of the nature of the movement. "By Jove," I said to myself, "here's B.'s old earthquake, after all!" And then, as it went *crescendo*, "And a jolly good one it is, too!" I said.

Sitting up involuntarily, and taking a kneeling position, I was thrown down on my face as it went *fortior* shaking the room exactly as a terrier shakes a rat. Then everything that was on anything else slid off to the floor, over went bureau and chiffonier with a crash, as the *fortissimo* was reached, plaster cracked, an awful roaring noise seemed to fill the outer air, and in an instant all was still again, save the soft babble of human voices from far and near that soon began to make itself heard, as the inhabitants in costumes *negligés* in various degrees sought the greater safety of the street and yielded to the passionate desire for sympathetic communication.

The thing was over, as I understand the Lick Observatory to have declared, in forty-eight seconds. To me it felt as if about that length of time, although I have heard others say that it seemed to them longer. In my case, sensation and emotion were so strong that little thought, and no reflection or volition, were possible in the short time consumed by the phenomenon.

The emotion consisted wholly of glee and admiration; glee at the vividness which such an abstract idea or verbal term as "earth-quake" could put on when translated into sensible reality and veri-fied concretely; and admiration at the way in which the frail little wooden house could hold itself together in spite of such a shaking. I felt no trace whatever of fear; it was pure delight and welcome.

"Go it," I almost cried aloud, "and go it *stronger!*"

I ran into my wife's room, and found that she, although awak-ened from sound sleep, had felt no fear, either. Of all the persons whom I later interrogated, very few had felt any fear while the shaking lasted, although many had had a "turn," as they realized their narrow escapes from bookcases or bricks from chimney-breasts falling on their beds and pillows an instant after they had left them.

As soon as I could think, I discerned retrospectively certain pe-culiar ways in which my consciousness had taken in the phenome-non. These ways were quite spontaneous, and, so to speak, in-evitable and irresistible.

First, I personified the earthquake as a permanent individual entity. It was *the* earthquake of my friend B.'s augury, which had been lying low and holding itself back during all the intervening months, in order, on that lustrous April morning, to invade my room, and energize the more intensely and triumphantly. It came, moreover, directly to *me*. It stole in behind my back, and once inside the room, had me all to itself, and could manifest itself convincingly. Animus and intent were never more present in any human action, nor did any human activity ever more definitely point back to a living agent as its source and origin.

What Was "It"?

All whom I consulted on the point agreed as to this feature in their experience. "It expressed intention," "It was vicious," "It was bent on destruction," "It wanted to show its power," or what not. To me, it wanted simply to manifest the full meaning of its *name*. But what was this "It"? To some, apparently, a vague demonic power; to me an individualized being, B.'s earthquake, namely.

One informant interpreted it as the end of the world and the beginning of the final judgment. This was a lady in a San Francisco hotel, who did not think of its being an earthquake till after she had got into the street and some one had explained it to her. She told me that the theological interpretation had kept fear from her mind, and made her take the shaking calmly. For "science," when the tensions in the earth's crust reach the breaking-point, and strata fall into an altered equilibrium, earthquake is simply the collective *name* of all the cracks and shakings and disturbances that happen. They *are* the earthquake. But for me *the* earthquake was the *cause* of the disturbances, and the perception of it as a living agent was irresistible. It had an overpowering dramatic convincingness.

I realize now better than ever how inevitable were men's earlier mythologic versions of such catastrophes, and how artificial and against the grain of our spontaneous perceiving are the later habits into which science educates us. It was simply impossible for untutored men to take earthquakes into their minds as anything but supernatural warnings or retributions.

A good instance of the way in which the tremendousness of a catastrophe may banish fear was given me by a Stanford student. He was in the fourth story of Encina Hall, an immense stone dormitory building. Awakened from sleep, he recognized what the disturbance was, and sprang from the bed, but was thrown off his feet in a moment, while his books and furniture fell round him. Then, with an awful, sinister, grinding roar, everything gave way, and with chimneys, floor-beams, walls and all, he descended through the three lower stories of the building into the basement. "This is my end, this is my death," he felt; but all the while no trace of fear. The experience was too overwhelming for anything but passive surrender to it. (Certain heavy chimneys had fallen in, carrying the whole center of the building with them.)

Arrived at the bottom, he found himself with rafters and débris round him, but not pinned in or crushed. He saw daylight, and crept toward it through the obstacles. Then, realizing that he was in his nightgown, and feeling no pain anywhere, his first thought was to get back to his room and find some more presentable clothing. The stairways at Encina Hall are at the ends of the building. He made his way to one of them, and went up the four flights, only to find his room no longer extant. Then he noticed pain in his feet, which had been injured, and came down the stairs with difficulty. When he talked with me ten days later he had been in hospital a week, was very thin and pale, and went on crutches, and was dressed in borrowed clothing.

IN SAN FRANCISCO

So much for Stanford, where all our experiences seem to have been very similar. Nearly all our chimneys went down, some of them disintegrating from top to bottom; parlor floors were covered with bricks; plaster strewed the floors; furniture was everywhere upset and dislocated; but the wooden dwellings sprang back to their original position, and in house after house not a window stuck or a door scraped at top or bottom. Wood architecture was triumphant! Everybody was excited, but the excitement at first, at any rate, seemed to be almost joyous. Here at last was a *real* earthquake after so many years of harmless waggle! Above all, there was an irresistible desire to talk about it, and exchange experiences.

Most people slept outdoors for several subsequent nights, partly to be safer in case of a recurrence, but also to work off their emotion, and get the full unusualness out of the experience. The vocal babble of early-waking girls and boys from the gardens of the campus, mingling with the birds' songs and the exquisite weather, was for three or four days a delightful sunrise phenomenon.

Now turn to San Francisco, thirty-five miles distant, from which an automobile ere long brought us the dire news of a city in ruins, with fires beginning at various points, and the water-supply interrupted. I was fortunate enough to board the only train of cars—a very small one—that got up to the city; fortunate enough also to escape in the evening by the only train that left it. This gave me and my valiant feminine escort some four hours of observation. My business is with "subjective" phenomena exclusively; so I will say nothing of the material ruin that greeted us on every hand—the daily papers and the weekly journals have done full justice to that topic. By midday, when we reached the city, the pall of smoke was vast and the dynamite detonations had begun, but the troops, the police and the firemen seemed to have established order, dangerous neighborhoods were roped off everywhere and picketed, saloons closed, vehicles impressed, and every one at work who *could* work.

It was indeed a strange sight to see an entire population in the streets, busy as ants in an uncovered ant-hill scurrying to save their eggs and larvæ. Every horse, and everything on wheels in the city, from hucksters' wagons to automobiles, was being loaded with what effects could be scraped together from houses which the advancing flames were threatening. The sidewalks were covered with well-dressed men and women, carrying baskets, bundles, valises, or dragging trunks to spots of greater temporary safety, soon to be dragged farther, as the fire kept spreading!

In the safer quarters, every door-step was covered with the dwelling's tenants, sitting surrounded with their more indispensable chattels, and ready to flee at a minute's notice. I think every one must have fasted on that day, for I saw no one eating. There was no appearance of general dismay, and little of chatter or of incoördinated excitement.

Every one seemed doggedly bent on achieving the job which he had set himself to perform; and the faces, although somewhat tense and set and grave, were inexpressive of emotion. I noticed only three persons overcome, two Italian women, very poor, embracing an aged fellow countrywoman, and all weeping. Physical fatigue and *seriousness* were the only inner states that one could read on countenances.

With lights forbidden in the houses, and the streets lighted only by the conflagration, it was apprehended that the criminals of San Francisco would hold high carnival on the ensuing night. But whether they feared the disciplinary methods of the United States troops, who were visible everywhere, or whether they were themselves solemnized by the immensity of the disaster, they lay low and did not "manifest," either then or subsequently.

The only very discreditable thing to human nature that occurred was later, when hundreds of lazy "bummers" found that they could keep camping in the parks, and make alimentary storage-batteries of their stomachs, even in some cases getting enough of the free rations in their huts or tents to last them well into the summer. This charm of pauperized vagabondage seems all along to have been

Satan's most serious bait to human nature. There was theft from the outset, but confined, I believe, to petty pilfering.

Cash in hand was the only money, and millionaires and their families were no better off in this respect than any one. Whoever got a vehicle could have the use of it; but the richest often went without, and spent the first two nights on rugs on the bare ground, with nothing but what their own arms had rescued. Fortunately, those nights were dry and comparatively warm, and Californians are accustomed to camping conditions in the summer, so suffering from exposure was less great than it would have been elsewhere. By the fourth night, which was rainy, tents and huts had brought most campers under cover.

I went through the city again eight days later. The fire was out, and about a quarter of the area stood unconsumed. Intact skyscrapers dominated the smoking level majestically and superbly— they and a few walls that had survived the overthrow. Thus has the courage of our architects and builders received triumphant vindication!

Two Impressions

The inert elements of the population had mostly got away, and those that remained seemed what Mr. H. G. Wells calls "efficients." Sheds were already going up as temporary starting-points of business. Every one looked cheerful, in spite of the awful discontinuity of past and future, with every familiar association with material things dissevered; and the discipline and order were practically perfect.

As these notes of mine must be short, I had better turn to my more generalized reflections.

Two things in retrospect strike me especially, and are the most emphatic of all my impressions. Both are reassuring as to human nature.

The first of these was the rapidity of the improvisation of order out of chaos. It is clear that just as in every thousand human beings there will be statistically so many artists, so many athletes, so many thinkers, and so many potentially good soldiers, so there will be so many potential organizers in times of emergency. In point of fact, not only in the great city, but in the outlying towns, these natural order-makers, whether amateurs or officials, came to the front immediately. There seemed to be no possibility which there was not some one there to think of, or which within twenty-four hours was not in some way provided for.

A good illustration is this: Mr. Keith is the great landscape-painter of the Pacific slope, and his pictures, which are many, are artistically and pecuniarily precious. Two citizens, lovers of his work, early in the day diverted their attention from all other interests, their own private ones included, and made it their duty to visit every place which they knew to contain a Keith painting. They cut them from their frames, rolled them up, and in this way got all the more important ones into a place of safety.

When they then sought Mr. Keith, to convey the joyous news to him, they found him still in his studio, which was remote from the fire, beginning a new painting. Having given up his previous work for lost, he had resolved to lose no time in making what amends he could for the disaster.

The completeness of organization at Palo Alto, a town of ten thousand inhabitants close to Stanford University, was almost comical. People feared exodus on a large scale of the rowdy elements of San Francisco. In point of fact, very few refugees came to Palo Alto. But within twenty-four hours, rations, clothing, hospital, quarantine, disinfection, washing, police, military, quarters in camp and in houses, printed information, employment, all were provided for under the care of so many volunteer committees.

Much of this readiness was American, much of it Californian; but I believe that every country in a similar crisis would have displayed it in a way to astonish the spectators. Like soldiering, it lies always latent in human nature.

The second thing that struck me was the universal equanimity. We soon got letters from the East, ringing with anxiety and pathos; but I now know fully what I have always believed, that the pathetic way of feeling great disasters belongs rather to the point of view of people at a distance than to the immediate victims. I heard not a single really pathetic or sentimental word in California expressed by any one.

The terms "awful," "dreadful" fell often enough from people's lips, but always with a sort of abstract meaning, and with a face that seemed to admire the vastness of the catastrophe as much as it bewailed its cuttingness. When talk was not directly practical, I might almost say that it expressed (at any rate in the nine days I was there) a tendency more toward nervous excitement than toward grief. The hearts concealed private bitterness enough, no doubt, but the tongues disdained to dwell on the misfortunes of self, when almost everybody one spoke to had suffered equally.

Surely the cutting edge of all our usual misfortunes comes from their character of loneliness. We lose our health, our wife or children die, our house burns down, or our money is made way with, and the world goes on rejoicing, leaving us on one side and counting us out from all its business. In California every one, to some degree, was suffering, and one's private miseries were merged in the vast general sum of privation and in the all-absorbing practical problem of general recuperation. The cheerfulness, or, at any rate, the steadfastness of tone, was universal. Not a single whine or plaintive word did I hear from the hundred losers whom I spoke to. Instead of that there was a temper of helpfulness beyond the counting.

It is easy to glorify this as something characteristically American, or especially Californian. Californian education has, of course, made the thought of all possible recuperations easy. In an exhausted country, with no marginal resources, the outlook on the future would be much darker. But I like to think that what I write of is a normal and universal trait of human nature. In our drawing-rooms and offices we wonder how people ever *do* go through battles, sieges and shipwrecks. We quiver and sicken in imagination, and think those heroes superhuman. Physical pain, whether suffered alone or in company, is always more or less unnerving and intolerable. But mental pathos and anguish, I fancy, are usually effects of distance. At the place of action, where all are concerned together, healthy animal insensibility and heartiness take their place. At San Francisco the need will continue to be awful, and there will doubtless be a crop of nervous wrecks before the weeks and months are over, but meanwhile the commonest men, simply because they *are* men, will go on, singly and collectively, showing this admirable fortitude of temper.

Notes

Appendixes

A Note on the Editorial Method

The Text of
Essays in Psychology

Apparatus

Index

Notes

The William James Collection is housed in the Houghton Library of Harvard University. It can be identified by the call number 'MS Am 1092', with, sometimes, either 'b' or 'f' as a prefix and a decimal following the numeral '2'. Many books from James's library are also preserved there; many of these are sufficiently identified by their call numbers which begin either with 'WJ' or 'AC'. Other books from his library are in Harvard's Widener Library and elsewhere, and in such cases their location is stated. Still others were sold and have not been located. Ralph Barton Perry made a list, however, noting markings and annotations; this unpublished list can be consulted at Houghton.

Since work on this edition began, the Houghton Library has reclassified the manuscripts and many letters in the James Collection. A new and more detailed guide has been prepared. The new call numbers are used in the present notes. Apparently, in time, the 'WJ' class will be eliminated, but thus far only a few books have been affected. Some books have been transferred recently from Widener to Houghton, while others, reported by Perry as sold or not listed at all, have turned up in the Widener stacks and other collections. The concluding volumes of this edition will contain a complete account of James's library and will give the then current call numbers and locations. Since the same volumes will contain James's annotations, extensively indexed, only those annotations that appear to have a direct bearing upon the text at hand are noted in the present volume.

James was a very active reader who filled his books with annotations and markings. The term 'markings' refers to underlining, vertical lines in margins, exclamation points, question marks, the notation 'N.B.', and 'Qu' for 'quote'. James's style of marking is distinctive: the N.B.'s are such that the same vertical stroke serves for both the 'N' and the 'B', while his underlining often has a peculiar waver. Furthermore, James habitually filled the flyleaves of his books with indexes, in some cases simply jotting down a page number or two, in others, noting numerous subjects and marking passages for attention or quotation. Pages singled out in this fashion usually have markings. Thus, for books protected in Houghton, the risk of error in attributing a given marking to James is slight. The risk is greater for materials in open stacks such as those in Widener, where the only claim made is that the book was owned or used by James and that there are markings. Where the books have been sold, we are totally dependent upon Perry's reports.

Many of the essays in the present volume were cannibalized for *The Principles of Psychology*. Collations for the essays drawn on are given in Professor Bowers's textual introduction.

Notes

Works by James already published in the present edition are cited in this edition, identified as WORKS, while others are cited in the original editions.

1.1 Everyone] Possible evidence that James retained an interest in animal intelligence is provided by a report in the *Harvard Graduates' Magazine*, 5 (June 1897), 611, to the effect that on April 12 James made experiments on an orangoutan and on a chimpanzee from the Boston Zoo. The experiments are not described.

1.20 It] That the animal consciousness can be imagined by imagining men dreaming was suggested by Ralph Waldo Emerson in "Demonology," *North American Review*, 124 (March 1877), 180–181, reprinted in *Lectures and Biographical Sketches* (Boston: Houghton, Mifflin, 1884) (WJ 424.25.8), p. 12. The view that animals do not form abstract ideas could be derived from Aristotle, for example, *Nicomachean Ethics*, bk. VII, ch. 3, 1147^b, line 5. The Cartesian view that animals are automata implies that they lack self-consciousness. It is discussed by Thomas Henry Huxley, "On the Hypothesis That Animals Are Automata, and Its History," *Fortnightly Review*, n.s. 16 (November 1, 1874), 555–580, reprinted in *Method and Results: Essays* (London: Macmillan, 1893), and in *Science and Culture, and Other Essays* (New York: D. Appleton, 1882). James's copy of the last mentioned work remained in the James house until the summer of 1978 when it was sold to the Pangloss Bookshop, Cambridge, Mass., and is now in my possession. In part V of the *Discourse on Method*, Descartes argues that animals lack language.

3.14 solar] Friedrich Max Müller (1823–1900), German-born philologist, in *Comparative Mythology* (1856), *Introduction to the Science of Religion* (1873), and other writings, argued on the basis of etymology that most myths originated as stories about the sun.

4.23 Bain's] Alexander Bain (1818–1903), Scottish philosopher and psychologist, *Mental and Moral Science* (London: Longmans, Green, 1868) (WJ 506.41.2), p. 85. In James's copy, this and the passage from p. 127 are marked.

7.18 logical] Diagrams that could have served James as models for his own appear in William Stanley Jevons (1835–1882), British logician and economist, *Elementary Lessons in Logic* (London: Macmillan, 1870) (WJ 542.25). In 1885 and later years, James used this as a text in his logic classes; but the work had been used by others at Harvard in previous years.

8.8 redintegrate] For the term see *The Principles of Psychology*, WORKS, p. 537.

10.2 Mill] James could be referring to James Mill (1773–1836), British philosopher and historian, *Analysis of the Phenomena of the Human Mind*, new edition, ed. John Stuart Mill, 2 vols. (London: Longmans, Green, Reader, and Dyer, 1869) (WJ 550.50), I, 224: "And to say I am conscious of a feeling, is merely to say that I feel it." In note 75 (I, 229–232), John Stuart Mill (1806–1873) discusses this doctrine with some reservations.

15.2 Kingsley] Charles Kingsley (1819–1875), English clergyman and author.

15.13 Martineau] James Martineau (1805–1900), English clergyman, *Essays, Philosophical and Theological* (Boston: William V. Spencer, 1866), p. 273, from the essay "Cerebral Psychology: Bain." A copy of this work, with pp. 268–273 heavily marked, was sold from James's library. In later editions additional volumes of essays were added, and the 1866 *Essays* were identified as vol. I.

16.34 Spencer] Herbert Spencer (1820–1903), *The Principles of Psychology*, 2nd ed., 2 vols. (New York: D. Appleton, 1871–1873) (WJ 582.24.6), I, 345 (sec. 157). In his copy next to the quoted text, James has "Fuller example on p. 464" (see p. 20).

17.32 Helmholtz] Hermann Ludwig Ferdinand von Helmholtz (1821–1894), German physiologist and physicist. In *The Principles of Psychology*, Works, p. 755n, James cites the *Handbuch der physiologischen Optik* (Leipzig: Voss, 1867), pp. 430, 447, and also notes with approval (Works, p. 171n) that in *Die Thatsachen in der Wahrnehmung* (Berlin: A. Hirschwald, 1879) (WJ 737.51), p. 27, Helmholtz changed his mind.

18.40 Spencer] James develops his criticism that Spencer overlooks interest and selection in "Remarks on Spencer's Definition of Mind as Correspondence," *Journal of Speculative Philosophy*, 12 (January 1878), 1–18, reprinted in *Essays in Philosophy*, Works. For additional references see *The Principles of Psychology*, Works, note to 19.24.

20.29 page] On I, 464 (sec. 207) of his copy James writes: "In other words the 'note books' of a scientific man will of themselves evolve the results. The accumulation of tables of data will per se produce statistical laws &."

21.28 Mill's] The four methods are described in John Stuart Mill, *A System of Logic Ratiocinative and Inductive*, 8th ed., 2 vols. (London: Longmans, Green, Reader, and Dyer, 1872) (WJ 555.51), I, 448–471. James omits the "Method of Residues." In his copy on I, 448, James comments: "Mill treats these as if they were mainly methods of *discovering* causes. 9 times out of 10 they are used merely for *testing* causes hypothetically conceived."

23.1 Darwin] Charles Darwin, *The Descent of Man, and Selection in Relation to Sex*, 2 vols. (London: John Murray, 1871), I, 46, citing Isaac Israel Hayes (1832–1881), American explorer. James's copy of this work was sold.

26.5 *Coriolanus*] From Shakespeare's *Coriolanus*, act 5, scene 4, lines 30–31.

27.40 Bleek] Wilhelm Heinrich Immanuel Bleek (1827–1875), South African linguist and folklorist, *On the Origin of Language*, trans. Thomas Davidson (New York: L. W. Schmidt, 1869), pp. 48–49.

28.1 Howe] Samuel Gridley Howe (1801–1876), American educator and philanthropist, Laura Bridgman's teacher. His account of the teaching of Laura Bridgman is found in the reports of the Perkins Institution for the Blind. Excerpts from the reports are included in the *Letters and Journals of Samuel Gridley Howe*, ed. Laura E. Richards, 2 vols. (Boston: Dana Estes, ᶜ1909). The lowering of the line image is found on I, 58.

29.39 Wright] Chauncey Wright (1830–1875), American philosopher, *Philosophical Discussions*, ed. Charles Eliot Norton (New York: Henry Holt, 1877), pp. 199–266. For the relations between Wright and James see Ralph Barton Perry, *The Thought and Character of William James*, 2 vols. (Boston: Little, Brown, 1935), I, 520–532.

30.9 Bain] Alexander Bain, *On the Study of Character, Including an Estimate of Phrenology* (London: Parker, Son, and Bourn, 1861), p. 327. James inverts the order of sentences. Perry reports that a marked copy of this work (1861) was sold.

31.5 Homer] *Odyssey*, bk. XXII, lines 381–389; *Iliad*, bk. IV, lines 141–147. In *The Principles of Psychology*, WORKS, p. 985n, James attributes the translation to George Herbert Palmer (1842–1933), American philosopher, James's colleague at Harvard. The quoted text is quite different in Palmer's *The Odyssey of Homer* (Boston: Houghton, Mifflin, 1891), p. 354.

31.24 Taine] Hippolyte Adolphe Taine (1828–1893), French philosopher and psychologist, *De l'intelligence*, 2 vols. (Paris: Hachette, 1870) (WJ 684.41), I, 44. James reviewed the English translation of this work in the *Nation*, 15 (August 29, 1872), 139–141.

32.39 Renouvier] Charles Renouvier (1815–1903), French philosopher, "De la ressemblance mentale de l'homme et des autres animaux selon Darwin," *Critique Philosophique*, 5th year, vol. 2 (October 19, 1876), pp. 184–191 (anecdote on p. 191). Renouvier cites no source for David Livingstone (1813–1873), British explorer and missionary. Renouvier comments on James's use of the anecdote in "De la caractéristique intellectuelle de l'homme, d'après M. Wm. James," pt. 3, *Critique Philosophique*, 8th year, vol. 2 (August 13, 1879), p. 22n. For a note on the relations between James and Renouvier see *Essays in Philosophy*, WORKS, note to 23.1.

36.5 Spencer's] Spencer's theory is discussed by James at greater length in the section on "The Origin of Instincts," *The Principles of Psychology*, WORKS, pp. 1270–1280. James provides extensive quotations from Spencer's writings.

36.11 Brown-Séquard's] Charles Édouard Brown-Séquard (1817–1894), Mauritian physiologist. Brown-Séquard reports his observations of guinea pigs in "Hereditary Transmission of an Epileptiform Affection Accidentally Produced," *Proceedings of the Royal Society*, 10 (1860), 297–298.

38.1 Everyone] On March 11, 1879, James wrote to Shadworth Hodgson: "My article in *Mind* was written against the swaggering dogmatism of certain medical materialists, good friends of mine, here and abroad. I wanted to show them how many empirical facts they had overlooked. *In petto* I hold myself liable to future conversion by such as you" (Perry, I, 616–617). In a letter to James Jackson Putnam, January 17, 1879, James insists that in this essay he only attributed causal power to consciousness and did not deal with the question of free will: "I did not pretend in my article to say that when things happen by the intermediation of consciousness they do not happen by law. The dynamic feelings which the nerve processes give rise to, and which enter in consciousness into comparison with each other and are selected, may in every instance be fatally selected. All that my article claims is that this additional stratum which complicates the chain of cause and effect also gives it determinations not identical with those which would result if it were left out. . . . I don't see if one has a fatalistic faith how it can ever be driven out, even from applying to the phenomena of consciousness. I equally fail to see on the other hand how free-will faith can be forcibly driven out, but I meant expressly to steer clear of all such complications in my article" (Nathan G. Hale, Jr., *James*

Jackson Putnam and Psychoanalysis [Cambridge, Mass.: Harvard University Press, 1971], p. 70).

38.2   Huxley]   Thomas Henry Huxley (1825–1895), English biologist and essayist; for the address see note to 1.20. Huxley's paper was delivered in 1874 at Belfast before a meeting of the British Association for the Advancement of Science.

38.3   Spalding]   Douglas Alexander Spalding (c.1840–1877), British naturalist. The author of Spalding's obituary in *Mind*, 3 (1878), 153–154, accuses Spalding of believing himself to be the first to propose, in scattered contributions to *Nature*, that "animals and men are conscious automata."

38.4   Clifford]   William Kingdon Clifford (1845–1879), British mathematician and philosopher, "Body and Mind," *Fortnightly Review*, n.s. 16 (December 1, 1874), 714–736; reprinted in *Lectures and Essays*, ed. Leslie Stephen and Frederick Pollock, 2 vols. (London: Macmillan, 1879), II, 31–70. Perry reports that both volumes of this edition were sold.

38.6   Hodgson's]   Shadworth Hollway Hodgson (1832–1912), British philosopher, *The Theory of Practice: An Ethical Inquiry*, 2 vols. (London: Longmans, Green, Reader, and Dyer), 1870. Perry reports that James's annotated set was sold. For a note on the relations between James and Hodgson see *The Principles of Psychology*, WORKS, note to 7.23.

39.1   Huxley]   Huxley discusses Hume's view of causality in *Hume* (New York: Harper & Brothers, 1879), pp. 118–126. Perry reports that a copy of an 1879 edition was sold.

39.12   Huxley]   Huxley discusses decapitated frogs in "On the Hypothesis," *Science and Culture*, pp. 227, 235.

39.16   Lewes's]   George Henry Lewes (1817–1878), English philosopher and writer. Perry reports that four volumes of the five making up the three series of *Problems of Life and Mind* were sold. Lewes discusses the presence of consciousness in the spinal cord in *Problems*, second series, *The Physical Basis of Mind* (London: Trübner, 1877), pp. 413–493, problem IV on "The Reflex Theory"; and in *The Physiology of Common Life*, 2 vols. (Edinburgh: William Blackwood and Sons, 1859–1860), II, 81–272, on "The Mind and the Brain." James's review of *The Physical Basis of Mind* is sharply critical, *Nation*, 25 (November 8, 1877), 290.

41.10   consciousness]   The physiological side of James's argument is developed in Chapter II, "The Functions of the Brain," *The Principles of Psychology*, WORKS, pp. 25–87.

41.23   frog]   In *Principles* for experiments on frogs James relied on Friedrich Leopold Goltz (1834–1902), German physiologist, *Beiträge zur Lehre von den Functionen der Nervencentren des Frosches* (Berlin: A. Hirschwald, 1869). James's copy was given to Harvard but has not been located. James himself is known to have dissected frogs.

43.16   *useful*]   In the analogous discussion in *Principles*, WORKS, p. 144, James depicts consciousness as striving to realize purposes: "Every actually existing consciousness seems to itself at any rate to be a *fighter for ends*."

43.38 Mill] James could have in mind Mill's doctrine that to be aware of a succession we need the presence of both states, the consequent as a sensation, the antecedent as an idea revived by association with the consequent (*Analysis of the Phenomena of the Human Mind*, II, 20–22).

44.32 "Spencer's] Reprinted in *Essays in Philosophy*, WORKS.

45.32 Renouvier] Renouvier discusses the category of personality in *Traité de logique générale*, 2nd ed., 3 vols. (Paris: Bureau de la *Critique Philosophique*, 1875) (WJ 675.61.2), II, 482–493. The *Traité* is the first of his *Essais de critique générale*.

46.6 Ulrici] Hermann Ulrici (1806–1884), German philosopher, *Leib und Seele. Grundzüge einer Psychologie des Menschen*, 2nd ed., 2 vols. (Leipzig: Weigel, 1874), II, 19–20. *Leib und Seele* is part I of Ulrici's *Gott und der Mensch*.

46.28 Spencer] James's index to volume one of Spencer's *Principles of Psychology* contains "Continuity of ego 190, 248, 105, 483, 435" and " 'Without break'! 294," references to sections 76, 110, 43, 213, 195, 131.

46.35 Lange] Friedrich Albert Lange (1828–1875), German philosopher, *Geschichte des Materialismus und Kritik seiner Bedeutung in der Gegenwart*, 2nd ed., 2 vols. (Iserlohn: J. Baedeker, 1873–1875), II, 421–422. Perry reports that both volumes, with annotations, were sold from James's library.

47.15 Rogers] William Barton Rogers (1804–1882), American naturalist, "On Our Inability from the Retinal Impression Alone to Determine Which Retina is Impressed," *American Journal of Science and Arts*, 2nd series, 30 (November 1860), 404–409.

47.19 Helmholtz] See *The Principles of Psychology*, WORKS, pp. 274, 487–488, 666.

47.41 "all] From Tennyson's "The Flower," *The Works of Alfred Lord Tennyson* (London: Macmillan, 1905), p. 235.

47.43 correct.] In his file of *Mind* in Houghton (Phil 22.4.6*) James adds a reference to Franciscus Cornelis Donders (1818–1889), Dutch ophthalmologist, abstract of "Die Grenzen des Gesichtsfeldes in Beziehung zu denen der Netzhaut," *Jahresberichte über die Fortschritte der Anatomie und Physiologie*, physiological series for 1877, 6 (1878), 164–165.

49.31 Green] Thomas Hill Green (1836–1882) English philosopher, in his Introduction to David Hume, *A Treatise of Human Nature*, ed. T. H. Green and T. H. Grose, 2 vols. (London: Longmans, Green, 1874) (WJ 540.54.2). For other works by Green from James's library see *A Pluralistic Universe*, WORKS, note to 8.37.

50.31 Taine] In his *Philosophie de l'art* published in 1865 and 1880, in an enlarged second edition, Taine holds that artists select what is most typical of a thing and use all the elements of their art to make it prominent (*Philosophie de l'art*, 13th ed., 2 vols. [Paris: Hachette, 1909], II, 345).

51.12 Schopenhauer] Arthur Schopenhauer (1788–1860), in *Die Welt als Wille und Vorstellung*, 2 vols. (Leipzig: F. A. Brockhaus, 1859) (*AC 85.J2376.

Zz859s), II, 362–363, summarizes his claim that human actions flow from character and motive and states that the full argument is in his *Preisschrift über die Freiheit des Willens.*

52.32 Chladni's] Ernst Florens Friedrich Chladni (1756–1827), German physicist, noted for experiments in which metal plates covered with sand were vibrated and produced nodal figures.

53.7 Maury] In *The Principles of Psychology*, WORKS, p. 767n, James cites Louis Ferdinand Alfred Maury (1817–1892), French scholar, *Le Sommeil et les rêves: Études psychologiques sur ces phénomènes et les divers états qui s'y rattachent*, 3rd ed. (Paris: Didier, 1865), chs. 3–4 (pp. 35–79).

53.21 Nur] From Goethe's poem "Das Göttliche," *Goethes Werke*, I (Hamburg: Christian Wegner, 1948), 148.

55.27 Spencer] *The Principles of Psychology*, I, 272–288, see especially p. 280 (sec. 125).

55.38 Stricker's] Salomon Stricker (1834–1898), Hungarian pathologist, "Über die collaterale Innervation," *Medizinische Jahrbücher*, 1877, pp. 415–424.

55.39 essay] The essay was not identified. The note does not appear in *The Principles of Psychology*, WORKS, p. 146.

56.9 Fick] Probably Adolf Fick (1829–1901), German physiologist.

56.14 Allen] Charles Grant Blairfindie Allen (1848–1899), Canadian-born naturalist and writer. James's index to *Physiological Æsthetics* (London: Henry S. King, 1877) (WJ 503.49) contains the entries "Rebuts objection from noxious pleasures 27" and "*Pain* a sign of destruction; *displeasure* of merely excessive waste, 40." For James's review and the correspondence between them see *The Will to Believe*, WORKS, note to 174.36.

58.15 "not] In *The Principles of Psychology*, WORKS, p. 131, James refers to similar excuses offered by Rip Van Winkle as played by Joseph Jefferson (1829–1905), American actor.

62.1 Cabot] James Elliot Cabot (1821–1903), American scholar, biographer of Emerson, "Some Considerations on the Notion of Space," *Journal of Speculative Philosophy*, 12 (July 1878), 225–236. Cabot corresponded with Henry James, James's father, and was a participant with James and others in a series of philosophical clubs in Cambridge in the 1870's. (See Max H. Fisch, "Philosophical Clubs in Cambridge and Boston: From Peirce's Metaphysical Club to Harris's Hegel Club," *Coranto*, vol. 2, no. 1 [Fall 1964], pp. 12–23; vol. 2, no. 2 [Spring 1965], pp. 12–25; vol. 3, no. 1 [Fall 1965], pp. 16 29). In his "Thomas Davidson: A Knight-Errant of the Intellectual Life," *Memories and Studies* (New York: Longmans, Green, 1911), p. 81, James recalls that "whatever topic was formally appointed for the day, we invariably wound up with a quarrel about Space and Space-perception." Cabot replied to James in "The Spatial Quale: An Answer," *Journal of Speculative Philosophy*, 13 (April 1879), 199–204.
  In his Preface to *The Principles of Psychology*, WORKS, pp. 5–6, James states that "The Spatial Quale" can be substituted for the much longer chapter on space of the book.

62.3 argues] In "Some Considerations on the Notion of Space" (pp. 234–235) Cabot writes: "The notion of Space, like all our notions, and like the whole content of our experience, is the workmanship of the mind operating with *data* of which, because they lie below consciousness, we know nothing directly. If we call these *data* sensations, then it is clear that there is no sensation of Space as an objective fact, because there is no sensation of any *object*—because Sensation is its own object, and has no other. 'There is something there,' means something *else* than my sensation. If we say (as we may) that to be conscious of a feeling is to be conscious that it has relation to *something* beyond itself, then there is no objection to the position that we have a feeling, or a sense, of Space, which needs only to be clearly set before the mind and to have its implications made explicit, in order to become the notion of Space; only that, as it differs from those organic feelings which we commonly call sensations precisely in this, that it *can* be made more explicit—in other words, that we can discriminate those operations of the mind for which it stands—it becomes superfluous and misleading to insist on the fact that it is *also* a sensation."

Cabot argues that "no simple feeling of any kind can be conceived as giving us by itself the impression of Extent; we cannot suppose it constituting a surface, or consisting of parts arranged above or below, or on the right or left hand of each other. Our feelings are by their very nature internal; occupy no room, and exist, as Hume said, *nowhere* but only in being felt. Nor can any assemblage of these zeroes give us what they do not themselves contain" (p. 227).

62.7 authors] In "Some Considerations" Cabot writes: "Assuming, then, that Extension is not a sensible quality, but a relation which may subsist among impressions of any quality, or, at any rate, of various qualities, the next question is how we become aware of it" (p. 227). Cabot criticizes writers such as Thomas Brown (1778–1820), Scottish philosopher, and John Stuart Mill, who attempt to "evolve Extension from purely intensive feelings, with the help of the consciousness of movement" (p. 229). Equally unacceptable for Cabot are theories of Lotze, Helmholtz, and Wundt.

62.10 *position*] In "The Spatial Quale: An Answer" Cabot responds: "I do not say that it is a conscious construction, in which separate positions are first distinguished and then brought into relations with each other. On the contrary, I hold the perception that the positions cannot exist without the relations, or the relations without the positions, to be the perception of Space; and that this confused, self-contradictory feeling, when it is accounted for and its contradictions solved by means of an adequate hypothesis, becomes the notion of Space" (p. 203). Cabot accuses the "physiological psychologists" of resting content with mere feeling. "We may, and often do, stop at the fact that each is an impression, a something felt—and this being sufficient for our purpose, we may neglect to inquire farther into what is implied in this fact. Only, I say, this is not philosophizing. It is not the office of philosophy to lead us to feel our thoughts . . . but to teach us to understand our feelings—to find out what they signify, what notions they imply, or what conclusions they oblige us to adopt" (p. 203).

62.13 Cabot] In "Some Considerations" Cabot writes: "Yet, although Extension is the most general character of bodies, when we ask ourselves what it is, we find only negative predicates; it is pure indifference to every one of the sensible qualities; they may all be changed without touching the extension of the body; and we can at last only define this extension as the *otherness*, the mutual externality, of the parts" (p. 225). In his reply Cabot comments: "It is not, he says, the indefinite *otherness* of the objects of perception, but a quite distinct sort of *otherness*, due to a special form of sensibility which certain objects awaken in us. As to this, I do not see that we disagree; indeed, I think he ought to go still further than he does, and make his distinction deeper—a distinction of categories, and not merely of kinds within the same category. For I hold the feeling of Space to be the first appearance of Quantity, and thus the first intimation of external reference among feelings previously qualitative" (p. 199).

63.21 empiricism] For the terms empiricism and nativism see *The Principles of Psychology*, WORKS, pp. 907–910.

63.29 "aggregate] In *First Principles of a New System of Philosophy* (New York: D. Appleton, 1877) (WJ 582.24.4), p. 164 (sec. 47), Spencer writes: "Our consciousness of Space is a consciousness of co-existent positions." Similar remarks can be found in his *Principles of Psychology*, II, 184 (sec. 331).

63.30 Sully] James Sully (1842–1923), British philosopher and psychologist, "The Question of Visual Perception in Germany," *Mind*, 3 (January 1878), 1–23; (April 1878), 167–195. The article is marked in James's annotated set of *Mind* (Phil 22.46*) in Houghton, but there is only one brief annotation. Sully is referring to the nativism of Ewald Hering (1834–1918), German physiologist and psychologist, *Beiträge zur Physiologie* (Leipzig: W. Engelmann, 1861–1864) (WJ 737.76). Hering's views are discussed in *The Principles of Psychology*, WORKS, pp. 854n–855n. For the relations between James and Sully see *Principles*, WORKS, note to 7.17.

63.32 Wundt] Wilhelm Wundt (1832–1920), German psychologist and philosopher, *Grundzüge der physiologischen Psychologie* (Leipzig: W. Engelmann, 1874) (WJ 796.59.2), p. 480. Also preserved is the second edition, 2 vols. (Leipzig: W. Engelmann, 1880) (WJ 796.59.4). Both volumes of the fourth edition (Leipzig: W. Engelmann, 1893) were sold, while neither volume of the third (Leipzig: W. Engelmann, 1887) has been located.

64.15 Mill] In *The Principles of Psychology*, WORKS, p. 912n, in his list of the "ablest works" in English which treat the subject of space perception, James includes John Stuart Mill's "Bailey on Berkeley's Theory of Vision," *Dissertations and Discussions: Political, Philosophical, and Historical*, II (New York: Henry Holt, 1873), 162–197; and chapter XIII of *An Examination of Sir William Hamilton's Philosophy*. For a note on James's copies of the latter work see *The Principles of Psychology*, WORKS, note to 166.37. James's *Index Rerum* (bMS Am 1092.9 [4520]), a notebook begun in 1864 with entries into the 1890s, on pp. 28–29 of the appendix, contains a somewhat critical summary of the Bailey review.

64.15 Bain] In *The Principles of Psychology*, WORKS, p. 912n, James recommends chapter 1 of the section on "Intellect" of *The Senses and the Intellect*, 3rd ed. (London: Longmans, Green, 1868) (WJ 506.41.4), pp. 321–456.

67.12 Helmholtz] For a more detailed discussion with quotations from the *Handbuch der physiologischen Optik* see *The Principles of Psychology*, WORKS, pp. 867, 897–898.

67.12 Wundt] For a more detailed treatment see *The Principles of Psychology*, WORKS, pp. 868, 906–907, 1110.

67.20 Riehl] In "Some Considerations," p. 225n, Cabot cites Alois Riehl (1844–1924), Austrian philosopher, "Der Raum als Gesichtsvorstellung," *Vierteljahrsschrift für wissenschaftlicher Philosophie*, 1 (1877), 215–223.

67.23 Bain] For 'massive' and similar terms see *The Senses and the Intellect*, pp. 111, 199, 227.

68.14 dimensions] In "Bailey on Berkeley's Theory of Vision," *Dissertations and Discussions*, II, 164–165, Mill affirms that the colored appearances, which is all that the eye senses by itself, "have existence only in two dimensions." According to him, this is the view of Berkeley and is among the doctrines least disputed by "modern metaphysicians."

68.17 Stumpf] Carl Stumpf (1848–1936), German psychologist. The correspondence between James and Stumpf is at Houghton (bMS Am 1092.9 [620–642, 3778–3811]), while two letters to Stumpf are at the Staatsbibliothek preussischer Kulturbesitz in Berlin. For the relations between them see Perry, II, 173–204. James could be referring to *Über den psychologischen Ursprung der Raumvorstellung* (Leipzig: S. Hirzel, 1873) (WJ 783.89.2), pp. 178–183. James's copy is dated July 1876.

68.24 tympanic] See note to 127.1–2.

69.29 Czermak] Johann Nepomuk Czermak (1828–1873), Czechoslovakian laryngologist-phoneticist. In the paper cited below, Exner makes a similar remark and cites Czermak's "Ideen zu einer Lehre vom Zeitsinn," *Sitzungsberichte der kaiserlichen Akademie der Wissenschaften* (Vienna), mathematisch-naturwissenschaftliche Classe, 24 (1857), 231–236.

70.16 Exner] Sigmund Exner (1846–1926), Austrian physiologist, "Über das Sehen von Bewegungen und die Theorie des zusammengesetzten Auges," *Sitzungsberichte der kaiserlichen Akademie der Wissenschaften* (Vienna), mathematisch-naturwissenschaftliche Classe, vol. 72, pt. 3 (1875), pp. 156–190. For works by Exner from James's library see *The Principles of Psychology*, WORKS, note to 46.13.

71.12 Vierordt] Karl von Vierordt (1818–1884), German physician, "Die Bewegungsempfindungen," *Zeitschrift für Biologie*, 12 (1876), 226–240. For works by Vierordt from James's library see *The Principles of Psychology*, WORKS, notes to 192.4, 795.38.

71.23 Cyon's] Élie de Cyon (1843–1912), Russian-born physician and writer, *Recherches expérimentales sur les fonctions des canaux semi-circulaires et sur leur rôle dans la formation de la notion de l'espace* (Paris: Martinet, 1878).

73.16 fœtus] According to the Secretary's Records of the Harvard Natural History Society in the Harvard University Archives (HUD 3599.505), on December 7, 1875, James gave a paper on the dissection of a three-month old foetus.

74.35 Robertson] George Croom Robertson (1842–1892), British philosopher, "Sense of Doubleness with Crossed Fingers," *Mind*, 1 (January 1876), 145–146 (*Philosophical Remains of George Croom Robertson*, ed. Alexander Bain and

T. Whittaker [London: Williams and Norgate, 1894], pp. 133–134). Robertson cites Aristotle's *Metaphysics*, 1011ᵃ. The *Métaphysique d'Aristote*, ed. Jules Barthélemy-Saint-Hilaire, 3 vols. (Paris: Baillière, 1879) with the note "crossed fingers 69" in volume II was sold from James's library. Robertson's experiments were made with a penholder. James discusses this illusion in *The Principles of Psychology*, WORKS, pp. 731–732. The correspondence between James and Robertson is at Houghton (bMS Am 1092.9 [504–528, 3536–3552]).

74.35 Wundt] The question of double images is discussed in the *Grundzüge*, 1st ed., p. 586. In the back of his copy of Wundt's *Beiträge zur Theorie der Sinneswahrnehmung* (Leipzig: C. F. Winter, 1862) (WJ 796.59), James has "correspondirenden Stellen doppelt 266 etc." James's copy is dated Dresden, June 15, 1868.

77.30–31 *Ausmessung*] In *The Principles of Psychology*, WORKS, p. 897, James writes that "Helmholtz's analysis of the facts of our *'measurement of the field of view'* is, bating a lapse or two, masterly"; see Helmholtz's *Handbuch*, pp. 550–554. The phrase is also used by Wundt, *Grundzüge*, 2nd ed., II, 85.

77.31 Classen's] August C. Classen (1835–1889), German physician. Preserved from James's library is Classen's *Physiologie des Gesichtssinnes zum ersten Mal begründet auf Kant's Theorie der Erfahrung* (Braunschweig: Friedrich Vieweg und Sohn, 1876) (WJ 713.5). Helmholtz in the *Handbuch* and Wundt in the *Grundzüge* refer to Classen only a few times and with no indications of major disagreement. In his *Index Rerum*, beginning under Helmholtz and continuing on pp. 20–21 of the appendix, James summarizes Helmholtz's essay "The Recent Progress of the Theory of Vision" (1868), reprinted in *Popular Lectures on Scientific Subjects*, trans. E. Atkinson (London: Longmans, Green, 1873), pp. 197–316.

77.40 Delbœuf] Joseph Remi Léopold Delbœuf (1831–1896), Belgian philosopher and psychologist, *La Psychologie comme science naturelle: Son présent et son avenir* (Paris: Germer Baillière, 1876) (WJ 617.48), especially pp. 64–75. Thirteen letters from Delbœuf to James are at Houghton (bMS Am 1092, letters 152–164). For works sold from James's library see *Some Problems of Philosophy*, WORKS, note to 76.19. On p. 226 of "Some Considerations," Cabot discusses Delbœuf's book.

78.3 article] Joseph Remi Léopold Delbœuf, "Du rôle des sens dans la formation de l'idée d'espace," *Revue Philosophique de la France et de l'Étranger*, 4 (August 1877), 167–184. The term 'punctiform' is not used by Delbœuf. The italics are James's.

78.29 punctiform] In "The Spatial Quale: An Answer" Cabot comments: "By a punctiform organ he means, I suppose, one whereby we should receive sensations having position, but no extent; a sensation say of blue, which is not spread out upon a surface, a feeling of warmth not pervading any body. But then, I ask, what would be wanting to such a sensation—what would have to be added in order that it should give us the impression of extent? Only, it seems to me, that the relation to other points, which is implied in its position, should be made explicit and visible, or tangible. It cannot really *have* position except by relation to other things, and all that is needed is that this fact should be felt. And such is our actual case" (pp. 201–202).

79.19 authors] See *The Principles of Psychology*, WORKS, pp. 852–853.

79.35 sign] In *The Principles of Psychology*, WORKS, p. 873, James attributes this view to Helmholtz. In "The Spatial Quale: An Answer" Cabot interprets James as holding that "in every sensation, over and above the particular quality of blue, warm, etc., a sign is given to us, which we are apt to overlook because the import is of more practical moment to us than the sign, but which indicates objective determinations of things" (p. 202). Cabot then adds: "But if this, or anything like it, is Dr. James's position, as I gather from page 84 [p. 79] of his article that it is, then I do not see why he should expect to find in the sign, as one of its native qualities, before it becomes a sign, the objective determinations of the thing signified, any more than he would expect to find in the wood of a finger-post the native tendency to set people on the right road. The thing does not exist until it is so used. And so of extent, it does not exist until those relations of which it consists are in some degree determined by the mind" (p. 203).

80.11–12 conjectures] In his lecture "On the Physiological Causes of Harmony in Music" (1857) Helmholtz writes: "Now if we venture to conjecture . . . that every such appendage is tuned to a certain tone like the strings of a piano, then the recent experiment with a piano shows you that when (and only when) that tone is sounded the corresponding hair-like appendage may vibrate, and the corresponding nerve-fibre experience a sensation" (*Popular Lectures on Scientific Subjects*, p. 85). Helmholtz developed this view in *Die Lehre von den Tonempfindungen, als physiologische Grundlage für die Theorie der Musik* (1863). Perry reports that an annotated copy of the 3rd ed. (Braunschweig: Vieweg, 1870) was sold. The anatomy of the ear was studied by Alfonso Corti (1822–1876), Italian anatomist.

80.26 Stumpf] James's index to Stumpf's *Über den psychologischen Ursprung* contains the entry "Psychischer Reiz theorie 28." On p. 28 Stumpf discusses Kant's view of space.

80.28 Wundt] James's index to the *Grundzüge*, 1st ed., contains "630, Synthese u. Association." For a more extended discussion of Wundt's views see *The Principles of Psychology*, WORKS, pp. 906–908.

80.30 Lotze] Rudolph Hermann Lotze (1817–1881), German philosopher. For Lotze's view of space see *The Principles of Psychology*, WORKS, pp. 797n–798n, 906. The numerous works by Lotze preserved from James's library will be listed in the volume of manuscript remains.

80.30 Helmholtz] See *The Principles of Psychology*, WORKS, pp. 908–910.

80.34 Mill] For references to the works of John Stuart Mill see *The Principles of Psychology*, WORKS, p. 901, and note to 163.32. In *Principles* (p. 902) James refers to both Mills in this place.

80.35 Bain] See *The Principles of Psychology*, WORKS, p. 901.

81.6 Psychology] In his copy of Spencer's *Principles of Psychology*, on II, 168 (sec. 327), next to the passage quoted, James has cross-references to pp. 272, 225, 219, 272, and a deleted reference to p. 168; on II, 172 (sec. 327), to pp. 182, 186, 204–5; on p. 218 (sec. 341), the quoted text is marked N.B.

81.37 Helmholtz] Hermann Helmholtz, "The Origin and Meaning of Geometrical Axioms," *Mind*, 3 (April 1878), 212–225.

83.7 RENOUVIER] Charles Renouvier, *Traité de psychologie rationnelle d'après les principes du criticisme*, 2nd ed., 3 vols. (Paris: Bureau de la *Critique Philosophique*, 1875) (WJ 675.61.4), I, 396, 399.

83.24 Bain] In *The Senses and the Intellect*, p. 77, Bain affirms that those who suppose that feelings of movement are "impressions passing to the brain by sensitive nerves" deprive of physiological support "the most vital distinction within the sphere of mind." In James's copy parts of the text are marked.

84.6 Müller] Johannes Müller (1801–1858), German physiologist, *Handbuch der Physiologie des Menschen*, vol. II, pt. 3 (Coblenz: J. Hölscher, 1840), p. 500.

84.21 Jackson] John Hughlings Jackson (1835–1911), British neurologist. Jackson published "On the Anatomical & Physiological Localisation of Movements in the Brain," *Lancet*, vol. 1 for 1873, pp. 84–85 (January 18), pp. 162–164 (February 1), pp. 232–234 (February 15), reprinted with the addition of a Preface (London: J. and A. Churchill [n.d.]). James is quoting from the Preface, pp. xxxiv–xxxv (*Selected Writings of John Hughlings Jackson*, ed. James Taylor, I [London: Hodder and Stoughton, 1931], 55). Jackson's paper in *Brain*, 1 (October 1878), 304–330; 2 (July 1879), 203–222; (October 1879), 323–356, is titled "On Affections of Speech from Disease of the Brain."

84.30 Bastian] For both Bastian and Ferrier see pp. 91–92.

84.37 *Physiologische*] 1st ed.

85.4 Lotze] Hermann Lotze, *Metaphysik* (Leipzig: S. Hirzel, 1879) (WJ 751.88.8), p. 589 (sec. 301); "De la formation de la notion d'espace," *Revue Philosophique de la France et de l'Étranger*, 4 (1877), 345–365.

85.9 Lewes] *The Physical Basis of Mind*, p. 77: *"Identity of organic connection everywhere implies identity of function; and similarity of organic connection similarity of function."*

88.38 Hume] David Hume, *A Treatise of Human Nature*, I, 450–466 (pt. III, sec. 14).

88.39 Jaccoud] Sigismond Jaccoud (1830–1913), Swiss-born physician, *Études de pathogénie et de sémiotique. Les Paraplégies et l'ataxie du mouvement* (Paris: Delahaye, 1864), p. 591.

89.34 Leidesdorf] Wilhelm Wundt, "Neuere Leistungen auf dem Gebiete der physiologischen Psychologie," *Vierteljahrsschrift für Psychiatrie*, vol. 1, no. 1 (1867), pp. 23–56. The Widener copy (Phil 31.2) is from James's library. It is dated Berlin, 1868; the Wundt article is annotated. The periodical was edited by Max Leidesdorf and Theodor Meynert.

89.36 Harless] Emil Harless (1820–1862), German physiologist, "Der Apparat des Willens," *Zeitschrift für Philosophie und philosophische Kritik*, n.s. vol. 38 (1861), pp. 50–73; 'ein Effectbild' is found on p. 66. The *Zeitschrift* was edited by Immanuel Hermann Fichte. James's *Index Rerum*, under 'Harless', contains an extensive summary of this paper.

90.29 Wundt] Wilhelm Wundt, *Vorlesungen über die Menschen- und Thierseele*, 2 vols. (Leipzig: Voss, 1863), I, 222. Only vol. II is preserved from James's library (WJ 796.59.8).

Notes

91.12 Ferrier] David Ferrier (1843–1928), British physician and neurologist, *The Functions of the Brain* (New York: G. P. Putnam's Sons, 1876), pp. 222–224. Preserved in Widener is James's annotated copy of the second edition (London: Smith, Elder, 1886) (Phil 6115.3.6). In the second edition, pp. 382n–383n, Ferrier quotes with approval James's remarks at 87.22–89.11.

91.14 Bastian] Henry Charlton Bastian (1837–1915), British physician and biologist, "Remarks on the 'Muscular Sense', and on the Physiology of Thinking," *British Medical Journal*, vol. 1 for 1869 (May 1), pp. 394–396; (May 15), pp. 437–439; (May 22), pp. 461–463; (June 5), pp. 509–512.

91.24 Putnam] James Jackson Putnam (1846–1918), Boston physician, a student with James in the Harvard Medical School. For the correspondence between James and Putnam see *The Principles of Psychology*, WORKS, note to 7.25–26.

91.28 Mitchell's] Silas Weir Mitchell (1829–1914), American neurologist and author, *Injuries of Nerves and Their Consequences* (Philadelphia: J. B. Lippincott, 1872), pp. 350, 356–357. The amputation did not always result from a gunshot wound. Six letters from Mitchell to James are at Houghton (bMS Am 1092, letters 553–558). For works by Mitchell from James's library see *The Principles of Psychology*, WORKS, note to 359.36. Mitchell is coauthor of *Gunshot Wounds and Other Injuries of Nerves* (1864), but amputations are not discussed in the book.

92.5 Vulpian] Edme Félix Alfred Vulpian (1826–1887), French physiologist and physician. Ferrier does not cite a source.

93.35 Ferrier] Ferrier discusses feelings of innervation and eye muscles in *Functions*, 1st ed., p. 222.

94.38 *Physiologische*] Pp. 600–601.

95.39 Graefe] Alfred Karl Graefe (1830–1899), "Motilitätsstörungen" in *Handbuch der gesammten Augenheilkunde*, VI (Leipzig: W. Engelmann, 1880), 18–19.

96.2 Graefe] Graefe does not cite a source for Albrecht von Graefe (1828–1870), German ophthalmologist.

96.34 Hering] See especially Ewald Hering, *Die Lehre vom binocularen Sehen* (Leipzig: W. Engelmann, 1868). An annotated copy was sold from James's library.

97.29 Adamük] E. Adamük, "Über die Innervation der Augenbewegungen," *Zentralblatt für die medizinischen Wissenschaften*, 8 (1870), 65–67.

97.32–33 Helmholtz] In the *Handbuch*, pp. 611–612, Helmholtz discusses the cyclopean eye in reference to Hering's view and cites Hering's *Beiträge zur Physiologie*, pp. 254–256.

97.39 *Ibid.*] VI, 21.

98.32 Rogers] See note to 47.15.

98.36 Wadsworth's] Perhaps Oliver Fairfield Wadsworth (1838–1911), American physician.

Notes

99.29 Aubert's] In *The Principles of Psychology*, WORKS, p. 868n, James cites Hermann Aubert (1826–1892), German physiologist, *Grundzüge der physiologischen Optik* (Leipzig: W. Engelmann, 1876) (WJ 705.7), pp. 601, 615, 627.

99.42 objects] In a copy of "The Feeling of Effort" in Widener (Phil 5300. 2A), given by James on February 25, 1881, there is a note in an unidentified hand: "Blunder! One eye is shut, and Hering's expt. then completely proves my position. Read espy. Helmholtz's account: Phy. Opt. pp. 607–8. W.J." The fact that in *Principles* (WORKS, p. 1120n) after citing Hering James goes on to quote the appropriate text from Helmholtz is evidence in favor of the authenticity of the note.

100.32 Breuer] Josef Breuer (1842–1925), Austrian psychoanalyst, "Über die Function der Bogengänge des Ohrlabyrinthes," *Medizinische Jahrbücher*, no. 1 for 1874, pp. 72–124; "Beiträge zur Lehre vom statischen Sinne (Gleichgewichtsorgan, Vestibularapparat des Ohrlabyrinths)," part 2, *Medizinische Jahrbücher*, no. 1 for 1875, pp. 87–156. The *Jahrbücher* were edited by Salomon Stricker.

100.33 Hoppe's] Johann Ignaz Hoppe (1811–1891), *Die Schein-Bewegungen* (Würzburg: A. Stuber, 1879).

100.34 Mach] Ernst Mach (1838–1916), Austrian physicist and philosopher, *Grundlinien der Lehre von den Bewegungsempfindungen* (Leipzig: W. Engelmann, 1875) (WJ 753.13.4), pp. 83–85. For a note on the relations between James and Mach see *The Principles of Psychology*, WORKS, note to 91.41.

101.43 Maine] François Pierre Maine de Biran (1766–1824), French philosopher, *Œuvres inédites de Maine de Biran*, ed. Ernest Naville, I (Paris: Dezobry, E. Magdeleine et Cie, 1859), 208, 212.

102.17 Lotze] Hermann Lotze, *Medicinische Psychologie oder Physiologie der Seele* (Leipzig: Weidmann, 1852) (WJ 751.88.4), pp. 293–294 (sec. 260). James's copy is dated Berlin, January 1867 and Dresden, July 1868.

102.39 "We] In his copy opposite the text quoted James has: "Warum denn nicht alle beide, da wir doch auch der Willensimpulse bewusst sind?"

103.19 Carpenter] William Benjamin Carpenter (1813–1885), British physiologist, *Principles of Mental Physiology, with Their Applications to the Training and Discipline of the Mind, and the Study of Its Morbid Conditions* (New York: D. Appleton, 1874) (WJ 511.77), in ch. 6 (pp. 220–315) titled "Of Ideation and Ideo-Motor Action."

103.38 Bain] Part of section on "Ideal Feelings of Movement." On p. 338 of his copy James marked the following: "*The renewed feeling occupies the very same parts, and in the same manner, as the original feeling, and no other parts, nor in any other assignable manner.*"

104.6 Munk's] Hermann Munk (1839–1912), German physiologist, "Weitere Mittheilungen zur Physiologie der Grosshirnrinde," *Archiv für Anatomie und Physiologie*, physiologische Abtheilung, 1878, pp. 162–178, 547–559. On p. 552 Munk has diagrams indicating the location of the three areas mentioned by James.

104.9 Hitzig] Eduard Hitzig (1838–1907), German psychiatrist. Preserved in Widener is James's annotated copy of *Untersuchungen über das Gehirn* (Berlin: A. Hirschwald, 1874) (Phil 6117.35).

104.9 Ferrier] *The Functions of the Brain*, 2nd ed., pp. 346–403.

105.15 Bernhardt] Martin Bernhardt (1844–1915), German neurologist, "Zur Lehre vom Muskelsinn," *Archiv für Psychiatrie und Nervenkrankheiten,* 3 (1872), 618–635.

105.38 Sachs] Carl Sachs (1853–1878), German physician, "Physiologische und anatomische Untersuchungen über die sensiblen Nerven der Muskeln," *Archiv für Anatomie, Physiologie und wissenschaftliche Medicin,* 1874, pp. 175–195. The *Archiv* was edited by Carl Bogislaus Reichert and Emil Du Bois-Reymond.

106.14 Darwin] In *The Principles of Psychology* James frequently cites Darwin on *The Expression of the Emotions in Man and Animals* (New York: D. Appleton, 1873). A marked copy was sold from James's library.

108.14 Rarey-tamed] John Solomon Rarey (1827–1866), American horse trainer, emphasized both firmness and humane treatment.

108.27 Leyden] Ernst Viktor von Leyden (1832–1910), German physician, *Die graue Degeneration der hinteren Rückenmarksstränge* (Berlin: A. Hirschwald, 1863).

108.32 Classen] August C. Classen, *Über das Schlussverfahren des Sehactes* (Rostock: G. B. Leopold's Universitäts-Buchhandlung, 1863), p. 50.

108.36 Jaccoud] Pp. 587–638.

109.31 Landry] O. Landry, French physician, "Mémoire sur la paralysie du sentiment d'activité musculaire," *La Lancette Française, Gazette des Hôpitaux,* 28th year (June 7, 1855), p. 262; (June 12, 1855), pp. 269–271; (June 19, 1855), pp. 282–283; (July 10, 1855), pp. 318–319; (July 19, 1855), pp. 334–335.

109.33 Takács] Andreas Takács, "Untersuchungen über die Verspätung der Empfindungsleitung," *Archiv für Psychiatrie und Nervenkrankheiten,* 10 (1880), 527–533.

109.35 Essais] In its first edition the second essay of the *Essais de critique générale* is titled *L'Homme: La Raison, la passion, la liberté. La Certitude, la probabilité morale* (Paris: Ladrange, 1859). James's original reference to p. 237 seems an error for p. 273. *Traité de psychologie rationnelle* is the title of the second edition.

109.36 Heidenhain] Rudolf Peter Heinrich Heidenhain (1834–1897), German physiologist, *Der sogenannte thierische Magnetismus: Physiologische Beobachtungen* (Leipzig: Breitkopf und Härtel, 1880).

111.6 Regulus] Marcus Atilius Regulus (d. c.250 B.C.), Roman general, was captured by the Carthaginians and sent by them on a mission to Rome. According to legend, he kept his word and returned to Carthage knowing that he would be put to death upon his return.

114.38 Wigan] Arthur Ladbroke Wigan, *The Duality of the Mind Proved by the Structure, Functions, and Diseases of the Brain, and by the Phenomena*

Notes

of *Mental Derangement, and Shewn to be Essential to Moral Responsibility* (London: Longman, Brown, Green, and Longmans, 1844), pp. 122–123.

117.23   Hume]   *Treatise*, I, 396 (bk. I, pt. III, sec. 8).

117.36   Bain's]   Alexander Bain, *The Emotions and the Will*, 3rd ed. (London: Longmans, Green, 1875) (WJ 506.41), pp. 505–538.

117.39   *De*]   Pp. 76–144 on the "Nature et réducteurs de l'image."

118.31   Herbart]   Johann Friedrich Herbart (1776–1841), German philosopher, *Lehrbuch zur Psychologie* (Königsberg: Unzer, 1816), pp. 101–102 (sec. 124).

120.13   symbolized]   William Mackintire Salter (1853–1931), American ethical culture leader, who later married a sister of James's wife, published "Dr. James on the Feeling of Effort," *Unitarian Review*, 16 (December 1881), 544–551. In his letter of December 27, 1881, to Salter (bMS Am 1092.9 [3654]), James thanked him for a copy of the essay and added: "In that paragraph about M + e > S &, I was wrong in talking as if the moral motive alone were reinforcible by the Effort. It seems to me a man can make just the same effort to be diabolic that he makes to be virtuous. And if the Effort be really an independent variable in the Equations, this makes it entirely free in both directions and gives greater consistency to the formulation of freedom as equivalent to indeterminism, and as opposed to the hocus pocus 'freedom to do right' business."

120.31   Faust]   Goethe, *Faust*, ed. Erich Trunz (Hamburg: Christian Vegner, 1963), p. 55 (line 1650).

120.36   philosopher]   Jules Lequier (1814–1862), French philosopher, *La Recherche d'une première vérité: Fragments posthumes*, ed. Charles Renouvier (Saint-Cloud: Belin, 1865), p. 90.

121.35   *Psychology*]   Herbert Spencer, *The Principles of Psychology*, II, 454–466, 467–478.

121.35–36   Herschel's]   John Frederick William Herschel (1792–1871), English astronomer and physicist, *Familiar Lectures on Scientific Subjects* (London: Strahan & Co., 1866), pp. 460–475 "On the Origin of Force."

121.37   Carpenter]   William Benjamin Carpenter, "The Force behind Nature," *Popular Science Monthly*, 16 (March 1880), 614–625; reprinted from the *Modern Review*, 1 (January 1880), 34–50.

121.37–38   Martineau's]   See note to 15.13.

121.39   Mansel's]   Henry Longueville Mansel (1820–1871), English philosopher, *Metaphysics or the Philosophy of Consciousness Phenomenal and Real* (Edinburgh: Adam and Charles Black, 1860), pp. 105, 346. For works by Mansel from James's library see *Some Problems of Philosophy*, note to 33.25. In his *Index Rerum*, under Force, Will, and on p. 7 of the Appendix, James summarizes and discusses numerous writings bearing on the analogy between volition and force.

123.2   conscious]   This could be an allusion to Shadworth Hodgson, see *The Principles of Psychology*, WORKS, p. 133.

125.1 An] All notes related to James's work on vertigo are keyed to "The Sense of Dizziness in Deaf-Mutes."

127.1–2 investigation] The secretary's records of the Harvard Natural History Society (Harvard University Archives, HUD 3599.505) note that James addressed the society on the causes of vertigo on February 1, 1876. The *Boston Medical and Surgical Journal*, 101 (August 7, 1879), 199–200, reports that on February 18, 1879, James spoke at a meeting of the Boston Society of Medical Sciences on the *membrana tympani* and spatial orientation: "After referring to the great power of drawing conclusions of this sort which has been claimed for the blind, and which had been traced to the skin of the face, having been said to be impaired by veiling the head, he gave an account of experiments made on some of the inmates of the Perkins Institution for the Blind at South Boston, as well as upon healthy persons. By them he had traced this faculty almost exclusively to the ear, and had found that absolute closure of the external meatus by cotton and putty annulled it." The James Collection (bMS Am 1092.9 [4411]) contains a report signed by Francis Almy, apparently in his hand, titled "Experiments on Optical Vertigo. April 26–27. 1880." Almy was a graduate of Harvard College and returned for graduate study in 1879–1880. He made sixteen trials, the last two after consulting his "lecture notes." Thus, the notes may be connected with James's graduate course in physiological psychology.

On January 18, 1883, in a letter from London to his wife (bMS Am 1092.9 [1336]), James wrote that Francis Galton took him to the London Atheneum where the "inexpressibly august philosophical club has its fortnightly dinner." James was asked to report on his study of deaf-mutes.

On January 15, 1902, in response to a question by James McKeen Cattell, James listed the "Sense of Dizziness" as one of his four scientific papers (James's letters to Cattell are in the Library of Congress).

127.18 Foster's] Michael Foster (1836–1907), British physiologist. *A Text Book of Physiology* was revised and reprinted numerous times; in the American reprint of the third English edition (Philadelphia: Henry C. Lea's Son, 1880), the section cited by James is on pp. 816–828 and is titled "The Mechanisms of Co-ordinated Movements." The subject of vertigo receives less attention in earlier editions.

127.20 Baginsky] Benno Baginsky (b. 1848), German physician, "Über die Folgen von Drucksteigerung in der Paukenhöhle und die Function der Bogengänge," *Archiv für Anatomie und Physiologie*, physiologische Abtheilung, 1881, pp. 201–235. On November 9, 1882, James wrote his wife that Hermann Munk had introduced him to Baginsky "whose work I treated superficially in my article" (bMS Am 1092.9 [1302]). A notice of Baginsky's article by J. J. B. Vermyne appears in the *American Journal of Otology*, 4 (January 1882), 51–62.

128.12 whirling] The *Psychological Laboratory of Harvard University* (Cambridge, Mass.: Published by the University, 1893) depicts a revolving chair used in the study of dizziness. The chair is said to have been designed by Hugo Münsterberg and manufactured in Freiburg, Germany. No date of acquisition is given.

128.31 Hartford] James probably means the American Asylum in Hartford, now the American School for the Deaf in West Hartford, Conn.; the National

Deaf-Mute College was part of the Columbia Institution which now is Gallaudet College in Washington, D.C.; the Horace Mann School is now located in Allston, Mass.; the Clarke Institution is now the Clarke School for the Deaf in Northampton, Mass.; the Indiana School for the Deaf is located in Indianapolis, Ind.

128.34 circular] Copies of this questionnaire have not been preserved in the James Collection; inquiries at the institutions mentioned by James received negative replies.

128.37 Högyes] Andreas (Endre) Högyes (1847–1906), Hungarian physician, "Über die wahren Ursachen der Schwindelerscheinungen bei der Drucksteigerung in der Paukenhöhle," *Archiv für die gesammte Physiologie*, 26 (1881), 558–568.

128.37 Spamer] Karl Spamer (1842–1892), German physician, "Noch einige Worte zur Frage der Function der halbkreisförmigen Canäle des Ohres," *Archiv für die gesammte Physiologie*, 25 (1881), 177–180. James reviewed Spamer's work in the *American Journal of Otology*, 2 (1880), 341–343.

129.33 Fosdick] Charles Paxton Fosdick (b. 1856), instructor at the Kentucky School for the Deaf in Danville, Ky.

130.1 Löwenfeld] Leopold Löwenfeld (1847–1924), German physician, *Experimentelle und kritische Untersuchungen zur Electrotherapie des Gehirns inbesonders über die Wirkungen der Galvanisation des Kopfes* (Munich: Finsterlin, 1881), pp. 60–68 and elsewhere.

130.16 eyes] Francis Almy reports his first trial as follows: "Body to right, eyes shut. Opened eyes at stopping. Room seemed spinning to left, the motion gradually dying away." Of his sixteen trials, six were made with the eyes open. Almy makes no references to walking.

131.5 brother's] Perhaps Robertson James (1846–1910).

131.25 Hitzig] *Untersuchungen über das Gehirn*, pp. 199–209.

131.36 Brown] Alexander Crum Brown (1838–1922), Scottish chemist, "On the Sense of Rotation and the Anatomy and Physiology of the Semicircular Canals of the Internal Ear," *Journal of Anatomy and Physiology*, 8 (May 1874), 327–331.

131.36 Mach] In working out a theory of the perception of space, Mach repeatedly studied vertigo. His results can be found in his *Grundlinien der Lehre von den Bewegungsempfindungen*. In later editions of *Die analyse der Empfindungen* (1st ed., 1886), Mach surveyed the development of his views and gave a prominent place to James's observations: "But most remarkable of all are the observations of William James" (*The Analysis of Sensations*, trans. C. M. Williams and Sydney Waterlow [Chicago: Open Court, 1914], p. 148).

132.40 sea-sickness] For James's letters on sea-sickness see pp. 188–189, 198–199 of the present volume.

133.26 Breuer] See note to 100.32. Breuer is sometimes credited with having independently developed a theory of vertigo much like Mach's.

134.25 Porter] Samuel Porter (1810–1901), American educator, instructor at the National Deaf-Mute College, Washington, D.C. The documents quoted are not preserved in the James Collection.

134.33 *Physiologische*] Pp. 604–605.

138.38 Moos] Peter M'Bride, "Diseases Which Involve the Organ of Hearing," *Edinburgh Medical Journal*, vol. 27, pt. 2 (February 1882), pp. 699–704, reports (p. 703) the view of Salomon Moos (1831–1895), German physician, and cites *Über meningitis cerebrospinalis epidemica* (Heidelberg: C. Winter, 1881).

139.23 bump] The expression 'bump of locality' was used in allusion to phrenology.

139.36 Viguier] Camille Viguier, "Le Sens de l'orientation et ses organes chez les animaux et chez l'homme," *Revue Philosophique*, 14 (July 1882), 1–36.

140.17 Beard] George Miller Beard (1839–1883), American physician. In Houghton is James's copy of Beard's *American Nervousness: Its Causes and Consequences. A Supplement to Nervous Exhaustion (Neurasthenia)* (New York: G. P. Putnam's Sons, 1881) (Phil 6951.12.10A*), given by James on August 7, 1906, with markings of uncertain origin; the rare book room of the Countway Library of Medicine in Boston has a copy signed by James of *The Study of Trance, Muscle-Reading and Allied Nervous Phenomena in Europe and America, with a Letter on the Moral Character of Trance Subjects and a Defence of Dr. Charcot* (New York: n.p., 1882) (BF 1152.B38); Widener has *The Psychology of the Salem Witchcraft Excitement of 1692 and Its Practical Application to Our Own Time* (New York: G. P. Putnam's Sons, 1882) (Phil 6951.12), with a few marks of uncertain origin. In a letter to his wife of about June 6, 1880 (bMS Am 1092.9 [1211]), James notes that while in New York he called on Beard. Beard treated sea-sickness in *A Practical Treatise on Sea-Sickness: Its Symptoms, Nature and Treatment* (1880).

141.19 Williams] Job Williams (1842–1914), American educator, principal of the American Asylum, Hartford, Conn.; Sarah Fuller (b. 1836), American educator, principal of the Horace Mann School; Harriet Burbank Rogers (1834–1919), American educator, principal of the Clarke Institution from 1867–1886.

141.22 Blake] Clarence John Blake (1843–1919), American physician.

142.2 Comte] Auguste Comte (1798–1857), French philosopher. For the text see *The Principles of Psychology*, WORKS, pp. 187–188.

142.2 Maudsley] Henry Maudsley (1835–1918), British physiologist and psychologist, criticizes the use of introspection in psychology in *The Physiology of Mind* (London: Macmillan, 1876), in ch. 1 "On the Method of the Study of Mind." James's annotated copy is in Widener (Phil 6122.1.15). For additional works from James's library see *The Principles of Psychology*, WORKS, note to 75.36.

142.3 Ueberweg] Friedrich Ueberweg (1826–1871), German philosopher. For the text see *The Principles of Psychology*, WORKS, p. 187.

142.3 Brentano] Franz Brentano (1838–1917), German philosopher. For the text see *The Principles of Psychology*, WORKS, p. 187.

143.6 ¹feeling] For a more extended development of this view see *The Principles of Psychology*, WORKS, pp. 225–250 and elsewhere.

143.15 Mohr] Jakob Mohr, *Grundlage der empirischen Psychologie* (Leipzig: Mutze, 1882) (WJ 756.40), p. 47. The quoted passage is marked in James's copy.

143.24 Sully's] James Sully, *Illusions: A Psychological Study* (New York: D. Appleton, 1881), pp. 189–211 on "Illusions of Introspection." James's copy was sold.

144.29 Zeno's] For more extended discussions of Zeno's paradoxes see *A Pluralistic Universe* and *Some Problems of Philosophy*.

145.2 Hume's] For the text (*Treatise*, I, 326, 327) see *The Principles of Psychology*, WORKS, pp. 691–692.

145.6 Galton] Francis Galton (1822–1911), British geneticist and statistician. For the text see *The Principles of Psychology*, WORKS, pp. 696–702. The term 'blended image' is taken from Galton; see note to 159.18.

145.6 Huxley] For Huxley's text see *The Principles of Psychology*, WORKS, pp. 692–694.

145.6 Taine] For Taine's text see *The Principles of Psychology*, WORKS, pp. 694–695.

145.33 Spencer] *The Principles of Psychology*, I, 164. For the passage in its full context see James's *Principles*, WORKS, pp. 241n–242n.

147.15 Herbartian] For a more detailed treatment of Herbart's view see *The Principles of Psychology*, WORKS, p. 568.

149.20 Hume] *Treatise*, I, 544.

149.36 Ferrier] James Frederick Ferrier (1808–1864), Scottish philosopher, *Institutes of Metaphysic: The Theory of Knowing and Being* (Edinburgh: Wm. Blackwood, 1854), p. 270. Houghton preserves a copy of this edition (WJ 527.78), identified as from James's library, with annotations by Henry James, Sr., and no indications of use by James. The *Institutes* became vol. I of the three-volume *Philosophical Works of the Late James Frederick Ferrier*.

150.1 Mill's] John Stuart Mill, *An Examination of Sir William Hamilton's Philosophy*, 4th ed. (London: Longmans, Green, Reader, and Dyer, 1872), pp. 248–249, in the chapter "The Psychological Theory of the Belief in Matter, How Far Applicable to Mind." For James's copies of this work see *The Principles of Psychology*, WORKS, note to 166.37.

150.28 Hodgson] Shadworth Hodgson, *The Philosophy of Reflection*, 2 vols. (London: Longmans, Green, 1878) (WJ 539.18.4), I, 290–296.

153.38 article] The article appears in a revised form as chapter 14 of *Principles*. The portions not used in the chapter can be found in *The Principles of Psychology*, WORKS, pp. 1431–33.

156.14 "twig"] For the term see *The Principles of Psychology*, WORKS, note to 245.7.

157.25   Berkeley]   For Berkeley's text see *The Principles of Psychology*, WORKS, pp. 443–444.

159.18   Galton's]   In his *Inquiries into Human Faculty and Its Development* (New York: Macmillan, 1883), pp. 340–348, Galton describes "blended" images produced by projecting photographs of different individuals upon a screen to blend them into a single image.

159.20   Huxley]   In his *Hume*, pp. 92–94, Huxley argues that when several complex impressions are experienced, the points of similarity will grow more and more vivid while the points of difference will fade. The resulting image will be generic and not specific. Perry reports that a copy with "generic images 92" was sold. For Huxley's text see *The Principles of Psychology*, WORKS, pp. 692–694.

161.23   Ballard]   Samuel Porter, "Is Thought Possible without Language?" *Princeton Review*, 57th year (January 1881), pp. 104–128, quotes Melville Ballard, instructor at the National Deaf-Mute College. For Ballard's text see *The Principles of Psychology*, WORKS, pp. 257–259. The question of Ballard's reliability is discussed by James in "Thought Before Language," reprinted in the present volume.

161.35   Hegel's]   For works by Hegel from James's library see *The Will to Believe*, WORKS, note to 196.12. James's main discussions of Hegel are "On Some Hegelisms," *The Will to Believe*, WORKS, and "Hegel and His Method," *A Pluralistic Universe*, WORKS.

162.8   doctrine]   James discusses the psychology of the neo-Kantians in *The Principles of Psychology*, WORKS, pp. 345–350.

162.14–15   fallacy]   For a discussion of the psychologist's fallacy see *The Principles of Psychology*, WORKS, pp. 195–196.

165.39   Reid]   Thomas Reid (1710–1796), Scottish philosopher. For works by Reid from James's library see *The Principles of Psychology*, WORKS, note to 162.25.

165.39   Stewart]   Dugald Stewart (1753–1828), Scottish philosopher. Perry reports that an annotated copy of vol. I of an 1818 edition of the *Elements of the Philosophy of the Human Mind* was sold.

168.9   emotions]   The theory of emotion came to be known as the James-Lange theory after Carl Georg Lange (1834–1900), Danish physiologist, who advanced similar views in *Über Gemüthsbewegungen. Eine psycho-physiologische Studie*, trans. H. Kurella (Leipzig: Theodor Thomas, 1887) (WJ 816.48). It evoked numerous criticisms to which James replied in "The Physical Basis of Emotion," reprinted in the present volume. Some of the extensive literature, both polemical and experimental, is listed in Ignas K. Skrupskelis, *William James: A Reference Guide* (Boston: G. K. Hall, 1977). On September 30 [1884], James wrote to Charles Renouvier in response to criticism: "I don't mean that the emotion is the *perception* of bodily changes *as such*, but only that the bodily changes give us a feeling, which is the emotion. We can, it is true, partly analyze this feeling; if we could totally analyze it into local bodily feelings its emotional character would probably change. After all, what my theory has in view is only the determination of the particular nerve process which emotion accompanies. We are bound to suppose that there is *some* such nerve process accompanying every emotion. Now all I say is that the nerve process is the incoming currents, produced by the reflex movements which the perception of the exciting cause engenders" (Perry, I, 698).

171.25 Schneider's] Georg Heinrich Schneider (1846–1904), German educator, *Der thierische Wille. Systematische Darstellung und Erklärung der thierischen Triebe und deren Entstehung, Entwickelung und Verbreitung im Thierreiche als Grundlage zu einer vergleichenden Willenslehre* (Leipzig: Ambr. Abel [1880]) (WJ 779.39.2). James's copy is dated Lausanne, August 1880.

172.1 Bell's] Charles Bell (1774–1842), British physiologist and anatomist, *Essays on the Anatomy of Expression in Painting* (1806); the revised edition appeared as *The Anatomy and Philosophy of Expression as Connected with the Fine Arts* (1844).

172.2 Bain's] In *Principles* in connection with the emotions, James usually cites Bain's *Emotions and the Will*.

172.3 Darwin's] See note to 106.14.

172.9 Mosso] Angelo Mosso (1846–1910), Italian physiologist, describes his plethysmograph, a device for recording variations in the amount of blood in an organ, in *Über den Kreislauf des Blutes im menschlichen Gehirn* (Leipzig: Veit, 1881).

173.39 translated] "Le Sentiment de l'effort," *Critique Philosophique*, vol. 2 for 1880 (September 23), pp. 123–128; (September 30), pp. 129–135; (October 7), pp. 145–148; (October 28), pp. 200–208; (November 4), pp. 220–224; (November 11), pp. 225–231; (December 9), pp. 289–291; in *Mind*, 5 (October 1880), 582, James's ten conclusions (pp. 123–124 above) are quoted.

173.41 Müller's] Georg Elias Müller (1850–1934), German physiologist, *Zur Grundlegung der Psychophysik* (Berlin: T. B. Grieben, 1878), pp. 316–329. An annotated copy was sold.

177.29 Bain] *The Emotions and the Will*, pp. 124–150 on "Tender Emotion."

179.20 Dante] James perhaps is referring to *Purgatorio*, canto XXXIII, line 74.

180.17 Brachet] The account by a patient of Jean Louis Brachet (1789–1858), French physician, is quoted by François Joseph Semal (1835–1896), Belgian physician, *De la sensibilité générale et de ses altérations dans les affections mélancoliques* (Paris: E. Donnaud, 1875), pp. 130–134. Pages "68, 89, 120, 140, 132" are listed in back of James's copy in Widener (Phil 6625.4).

183.25 Ruskin] John Ruskin (1819–1900), English critic and essayist, in the essay "St. Mark's" from *The Stones of Venice*, in *The Works of John Ruskin*, ed. E. T. Cook and Alexander Wedderburn, X (London: George Allen, 1904), 124–125.

184.35 Winter] Georg Winter (1856–1946), German physician, *Ein Fall von allgemeiner Anæsthesie* (Heidelberg: Winter, 1882). No letters between James and Winter have been found.

185.20 Strümpell] Adolf von Strümpell (1853–1925), German physician, "Beobachtungen über ausgebreitete Anästhesien und deren Folgen für die willkürliche Bewegung und das Bewusstsein," *Deutches Archiv für klinische Medicin*, 22 (1878), 321–361; "Ein Beitrag zur Theorie des Schlafs," *Archiv für die gesammte Physiologie*, 15 (October 23, 1877), 573–574, translated in *Mind*, 3 (April 1878), 263–264. No letters between James and Strümpell have been found.

188.1 Sir] James's letter was prompted by the following item: "The ancients have suffered much from the interpretations of modern rationalism; but Dr. James, of Boston, seems determined to outdo all that has been yet done. But he also proves Ulysses to have anticipated modern science. Deaf people, the American doctor has established to his own satisfaction, are free from sea-sickness, and he recommends stopping the ears with wax as an infallible cure. But when he cites Ulysses' ruse with the Ithacan mariners in his favour, he puts rather a strained interpretation, to say the least, on the siren's song" (*Pall Mall Budget*, August 1, 1884, p. 26). This note could refer to "The Sense of Dizziness" (p. 133), if one interprets the reference to Ulysses as exaggeration. No published work by James is known which would fit. In "A Suggestion" (p. 198) James reviews his writings on the subject and there is no evidence of a gap in the bibliography. The prompting note also appeared in the *Pall Mall Gazette*, July 31, 1884, p. 3; James's letter, September 30, 1884, p. 6.

190.2 committee] Following the first meeting of the American Society for Psychical Research, December 18, 1884, James and Henry Pickering Bowditch, making up the committee on work, published a circular suggesting that in accordance with the practice of the English society five permanent committees be established: on thought transference, on hypnotism, on apparitions and haunted houses, on physical phenomena (Spiritualism), and on Reichenbach's experiments (*Proceedings of the American Society for Psychical Research*, 1 [July 1885], 5). James reported for the Committee on Hypnotism at the meeting of January 12, 1886 with forty-one persons present: "Dr. James reported for the Committee on Hypnotism; putting Mr. Carnochan into the hypnotic state in the presence of the audience, and causing him to exhibit various phenomena characteristic of this condition" (*Proceedings*, 1 [July 1886], 62). The published report is apparently the one given by James at the meeting of June 15, 1886.

190.2 Cory] Charles Barney Cory (b. 1857), American ornithologist, attended the Lawrence Scientific School at Harvard in 1876–1878.

190.3 Carnochan's] Gouverneur Morris Carnochan, a student at Harvard in 1881–1886.

190.18 P.] Leonore Piper (1859–1950), American trance medium. Most of James's extensive investigation of Mrs. Piper appear in *William James on Psychical Research*, ed. Gardner Murphy and Robert O. Ballau (New York: Viking, 1960); they will be included in the psychical research volume of the Works. James's attempts to hypnotize her are described in his "Report of the Committee on Mediumistic Phenomena" (*Proceedings of the American Society for Psychical Research*, 1 [July 1886], 104–105).

191.30 Binet] Alfred Binet (1857–1911), French psychologist, *La Psychologie du raisonnement: Recherches expérimentales par l'hypnotisme* (Paris: Alcan,

1886), p. 44. For further discussion of Binet's view see *The Principles of Psychology*, WORKS, 717n. Works by Binet from James's library will be listed in the volume of manuscript remains.

191.35 Black] Ralph Waldo Black (b. 1862), attended Harvard College in 1882–1883, 1884–1886.

192.36 Féré] Alfred Binet and Charles Féré (1852–1907), French psychiatrist, *Le Magnétisme animal* (Paris: Alcan, 1887), p. 236: "*Il faut que le sujet reconnaisse cet objet pour ne pas le voir.*" In the copy in Widener (Phil 6671.7) "after image of hall, 188" and the page numbers 186, 187, 148 are written out in James's hand.

193.36 Aubert] See note to 99.29.

196.33 Mitchell] John Kearsley Mitchell (1793–1858), American physician and psychologist, *Five Essays*, ed. Silas Weir Mitchell (Philadelphia: J. B. Lippincott, 1859), pp. 159–161, 245. A copy was sold from James's library.

196.33 Braid] James Braid (1795?–1860), British hypnotist.

198.5 article] "The Sense of Dizziness," reprinted in the present volume.

198.20 physician] The description would fit George Miller Beard; see note to 140.17.

200.1 The] This paper is included by James in the list of his four scientific papers (see note to 127.1–2).

200.10 Hall] Granville Stanley Hall (1844–1924), American psychologist, a graduate student at Harvard from 1876 to 1878, "Reaction-Time and Attention in the Hypnotic State," *Mind*, 8 (April 1883), 170–182. For the relations between James and Hall see Dorothy Ross, *G. Stanley Hall: The Psychologist as Prophet* (Chicago: University of Chicago Press, 1972). James's letters to Hall are in the Clark University Archives, Worcester, Mass., with copies at Houghton; Hall's letters to James are at Houghton (bMS Am 1092.9 [165–180]).

201.9 Baltzar's] Baltzar was a manufacturer of physiological instruments in Leipzig. The kymograph is a device for recording variations in blood pressure.

202.4 Hall's] Hall gives the time as 15 minutes (p. 172).

204.1 Many] This paper is included by James in the list of his four scientific papers (see note to 127.1–2). In the *Proceedings of the American Society for Psychical Research*, 1 (December 1887), 134, it is reported that on January 11, 1887, James read a paper on "Sensations from Amputated Limbs" at a meeting of the Society to an audience of 150. On February 25, 1885, in a letter to Frederic William Henry Myers (bMS Am 1092.9 [3306]), James remarks that about a year ago he had sent out some 300 questionnaires on amputated limbs. Two forms of the questionnaire survive; the later is reprinted as Appendix II in the present volume with a list of variants from the earlier form following its text. A questionnaire filled out by James Bonds of Mobile, Alabama, is preserved (MS Am 1092.9 [4566]). On the first page James wrote, "no movement. Theory about stump."

205.31 Messrs.] H. A. Fisk of Boston, Mass., advertised itself as a "manufacturer of artificial limbs"; A. A. Marks of New York City advertised "Marks' patent artificial limbs, with rubber hands and feet."

Notes

206.26   Mitchell]   For example *Injuries of Nerves,* p. 356.

207.22   Müller]   *Handbuch der Physiologie,* vol. II, pt. 3, p. 254.

207.39   Valentin's]   Gabriel Gustav Valentin (1810–1883), German-born physiologist, *Lehrbuch der Physiologie des Menschen,* 2 vols. (Braunschweig: Vieweg und Sohn, 1844), II, 609.

208.10   mention]   In "The Perception of Space," included in *The Principles of Psychology* with the omission of most of p. 196. The text referred to can be found in *Principles,* WORKS, p. 1436.

209.40   François-Franck]   Charles Albert François-Franck (1849–1921), French physiologist, *Leçons sur les fonctions motrices du cerveau (réactions volontaires et organiques) et sur l'épilepsie cérébrale* (Paris: Doin, 1887), p. 291.

210.18   Helmholtz]   For the text see *The Principles of Psychology,* WORKS, pp. 489–490.

212.40   Sternberg]   Maximilian Sternberg (1863–1934), Austrian physician, "Zur Lehre von den Vorstellungen über die Lage unserer Glieder," *Archiv für die gesammte Physiologie,* 37 (September 1885), 1–6.

216.10   Bunsen]   An electrical apparatus developed by Robert Wilhelm Bunsen (1811–1899), German chemist.

217.24   Spencer]   James discusses Spencer's view of mind in "Remarks on Spencer's Definition of Mind as Correspondence," reprinted in *Essays in Philosophy,* WORKS.

217.33   article]   "What Is an Instinct?" *Scribner's Magazine,* 1 (March 1887), 355–365; included in *The Principles of Psychology,* WORKS, pp. 1004–22.

219.30   Bain]   *The Emotions and the Will,* pp. 303–304, provides a summary of Bain's arguments.

219.30   Maudsley]   Henry Maudsley, *Body and Mind: An Inquiry into Their Connection and Mutual Influence, Specially in Reference to Mental Disorders* (London: Macmillan, 1870). James's copy (Phil 6122.1C) was discarded by Widener in 1967.

219.30   Sully]   James Sully, *Outlines of Psychology with Special Reference to the Theory of Education* (New York: D. Appleton, 1884) (WJ 584.51.2), pp. 593–604.

220.6   Carpenter]   See note to 103.19.

222.40   Bishop]   *Science,* 8 (December 3, 1886), 506–507, describes experiments involving "Mr. W. I. Bishop, a young American," performed in Boston. James was one of the observers: "Dr. William James looked at the number on a bank-bill which comprised three digits unknown to Mr. Bishop. The latter drew some large squares upon a blackboard, one for each digit. He was again blindfolded, and, taking Dr. James's hand in his, stood in front of the board, and, while his guide fixed his attention upon the squares and the digits, he drew the three digits in succession correctly."

227.14   "*Hæc*]   Perhaps from Virgil, *Aeneid,* bk. II, line 661.

229.36 Goltz] For references to the work of Friedrich Leopold Goltz see *The Principles of Psychology*, WORKS, pp. 75–76, 77.

229.37 Loeb] Jacques Loeb (1859–1924), German-born physiologist, later active in the United States. For the relations between James and Loeb see *The Principles of Psychology*, WORKS, note to 44.23.

232.40 Browning's] "All we've gained is, that belief, | As unbelief before, shakes us by fits" ("Bishop Blougram's Apology," *The Complete Poetic and Dramatic Works of Robert Browning* [Boston: Houghton, Mifflin, 1895], p. 351).

233.31 "I] From Shakespeare's *Macbeth*, act I, scene 7, line 44.

234.18 Seneca] From Seneca's *Epistulae Morales ad Lucilium*, bk. X, letter 1, 14.

235.2 Je] James's "What the Will Effects" was translated by Renouvier and published in the *Critique Philosophique*, vol. I for 1888 (June), pp. 401–420; Renouvier commented in "Quelques remarques sur la théorie de la volonté de M. W. James," vol. II for 1888 (August), pp. 117–126. James's response was directly followed by Renouvier's "Quelques mots sur la lettre qui précède," vol. II for 1888 (December), pp. 404–406.

235.9 Lotze] *Medicinische Psychologie*, pp. 300–303.

235.13 Votre] In "Quelques remarques" Renouvier quotes extensively from the second of his *Essais de critique générale* (see note to 109.35) to point out the similarity between the ideas he had published in 1859 and James's. In "Quelques mots" Renouvier states that he became acquainted with Lotze's views only through James. Directly following his words, Renouvier adds several pages of translation from Lotze, the pages from the *Medicinische Psychologie* cited by James. On March 29, 1888, James responded to Renouvier's offer to translate "What the Will Effects": "It amounts to little more than what you said long ago in your *Psychologie rationnelle*" (Perry, I, 702).

237.13 Bowditch] Henry Pickering Bowditch (1840–1911), American physiologist, professor at the Harvard Medical School, and William Freeman Southard, American physician, "A Comparison of Sight and Touch," *Journal of Physiology*, 3 (January 1882), 232–245. James's correspondence with Bowditch is at Houghton (bMS Am 1092.9 [77–84, 772–818]).

237.29 réflexe] In "Quelques remarks" (p. 122) in reference to the claim that all action is of the reflex type, Renouvier distinguishes between "l'activité de réaction" and "l'activité propre de l'esprit." In "Quelques mots" while recognizing that James leaves room for indeterminism, Renouvier still insists that in the realm of ideas "nous avons là quelque autre chose que ce qu'on entend communément en physiologie par *actions réflexes*" (pp. 404–405).

239.2 Editor] In "The Psychological Theory of Extension," *Mind*, 13 (July 1888), 418–424, George Croom Robertson, editor of *Mind*, criticizes James Ward, Edmund Duncan Montgomery, and James. Ward replied in *Mind*, 14 (January 1889), 109–115, Montgomery in *Mind*, 13 (October 1888), 579–584. Robertson's remarks are directed against James's "Perception of Space," published in *Mind* in 1887 and included with revisions in *The Principles of Psychology*. In James's set of *Mind* (Phil 22.4.6*) the Robertson article is annotated. James's correspondence with Robertson is at Houghton (bMS Am 1092.9 [504–528, 3536–3552]); three of the letters (3547–3549) deal at length with the issues raised in the controversy.

239.12 Brown] For references to Thomas Brown the index to *The Principles of Psychology*, WORKS, should be consulted.

239.18 replies] Robertson begins by asking whether the "spatial form" can be derived "from certain mental data presumably simpler." "Data of the kind usually assigned, at least in the way they are assigned or usually employed, fail to afford a satisfactory explanation. The data are 'muscular sensations'." Following the admission quoted by James, Robertson remarks: "But perhaps there may be no such difficulty, if it should appear that the problem of Extension is one not to be thus directly faced" (p. 420).

239.23 admission] Robertson writes: "Nor, in asking such questions, is it at all implied that the eye does not give, or rather procure, us everything that is highest and most commanding in our space-perception. It is not even implied that, if we could suppose ourselves reduced to the eye with its exploratory movements as our sole and only means of constructing a spatial order, such a construction might not come to pass—however far removed it would be in character from that of our actual experience. All that is meant is that, dependent as we are for all our basal experiences upon locomotive organs that are at the same time tactile, it is impossible for us through the eye to have a perception of space that is not ultimately . . . to be referred to the tactile base" (p. 424).

240.10 *assumption*] Robertson writes: "All psychologists may be said now to be agreed upon this, that it is in the phase of resisted muscular activity that we first become conscious of a 'not-self' as opposed to 'self'." He then continues: "Now the point to be urged is that if only object, as bare obstacle to muscular activity of a touching organ, has already to any degree become differentiated in consciousness, a basis is got by reference to which the conjoined sensible experiences shown by analysis to be involved in any perception of extension may begin to appear—not as the simply intensive experiences, of one kind or other, which they are in themselves, but—as constituents of object (as not-self)" (pp. 421–422).

242.8 One] In his letter of August 22, 1888 (3548), James makes clear that he is thinking of himself.

243.6 Five] The program of the congress as given in the *Congrès international de psychologie physiologique* (Paris: Bureau des Revues, 1890), p. 3, lists nine sections of which five are the ones given by James.

243.10 census] For notes on the census of hallucinations and James's work with it see *The Will to Believe*, WORKS, notes to 230.40 and 231.31. James's reports on the census will be included in the psychical research volume of the WORKS.

243.13 Grüber] Edouard Grüber, from Jassy in Romania.

243.18 Hypnotism] The *Premier congrès international de l'hypnotisme expérimental et thérapeutique* (Paris: Doin, 1889), p. 11, lists James as a member of the congress from England, professor of philosophy at the University of Cambridge. The congress was held on August 8–12, 1889; Edgar Bérillon, editor of the *Revue de l'Hypnotisme*, served as its general secretary.

243.20 Charcot] Jean Martin Charcot (1825–1893), French neurologist. For works by Charcot from James's library see *The Principles of Psychology*, WORKS, note to 60.38.

243.22 Ribot] Théodule Armand Ribot (1839–1916), French psychologist. For the relations between James and Ribot see *The Principles of Psychology*, WORKS, note to 100.39. Ribot's "Discours inaugural" is found in *Congrès international*, pp. 29–32.

244.5 Richet] Charles Robert Richet (1850–1935), French physiologist. For the relations between James and Richet see *The Principles of Psychology*, WORKS, note to 89.39.

244.9 Gley] Eugène Gley (1857–1930), French physiologist.

244.9 Marillier] Léon Marillier (1842–1901), French psychologist. For the relations between James and Marillier see *The Principles of Psychology*, WORKS, note to 421.36.

244.22 Hallucinations] The committee consisted of Henry Sidgwick (1838–1900), British philosopher and psychical researcher, Frederic William Henry Myers, James, N. Grote of the University of Odessa, and Marillier.

244.28 Nancy] For the Nancy school see *The Principles of Psychology*, WORKS, pp. 1194n, 1199; for the Salpêtrière, pp. 1197–1199. The latter school is associated with Charcot.

244.32 Bernheim] Hippolyte Bernheim (1840–1919), French hypnotist. James's annotated copy of *Hypnotisme, suggestion, psychothérapie: Études nouvelles* (Paris: Doin, 1891) is in Widener (Phil 6671.5).

244.38 debate] Only one comment by James was found in the record of the discussions. Following the report by Gley on the muscle sense, James addressed the following question to Pierre Janet: "Je voudrais savoir si M. Janet soutient que l'excitation extérieure ne détermine à aucun degré le champ de conscience qui doit recevoir cette excitation?" (p. 71).

244.39 Janet] See note to 250.10.

244.39 Bertrand] Alexis Bertrand (1850–1923), French philosopher.

244.39 Espinas] Alfred Espinas (1844–1922), French psychologist.

245.1 Liégeois] Jules Liégeois (1833–1908), French jurist.

245.1 Ochorowicz] Julian Ochorowicz (1850–1917), Polish philosopher.

245.1 Danilewsky] B. Danilewsky (Vasilii Iakovlevich Danilevskii) (b. 1852).

245.2 Forel] August Forel (1848–1931), Swiss psychologist.

245.2 Myers] Frederic William Henry Myers (1843–1901), British essayist and psychical researcher. For the relations between James and Myers see *The Will to Believe*, WORKS, note to 225.38.

245.13 Sidgwick] Eleanor Mildred Sidgwick (1845–1936), British educator and psychical researcher.

245.14 ²Myers] Arthur Thomas Myers (1851–1894), British physician and psychical researcher.

245.15 Jastrow] Joseph Jastrow (1863–1944), American psychologist.

245.15 Riley] In the published record Riley is identified only as a delegate from the United States government.

245.17 Schrenck-Notzing] Albert von Schrenk-Notzing (1862–1929), German psychologist.

245.17 Münsterberg] Hugo Münsterberg (1863–1916), German-born psychologist, later James's colleague at Harvard. For the relations between James and Münsterberg see *The Principles of Psychology*, WORKS, note to 84.32.

245.18 Sperling] Perhaps Max Sperling (b. 1864), German psychologist.

245.24 Lombroso] Cesare Lombroso (1835–1909), Italian sociologist and physician.

245.34 England] James did not participate in the congress held in London in 1892.

246.1 Beaunis] Henri Étienne Beaunis (1830–1921), French psychologist.

246.2 Ferrari] H. Ferrari of the Société de Psychologie Physiologique.

246.5 Herzen] Alexandre Herzen (1839–1906), Swiss psychologist.

246.5 Benedikt] Moriz Benedikt (1835–1920), Austrian psychologist.

246.6 Neiglick] Hjalmar Neiglick.

247.23–248.1 Galvanis] Luigi Galvani (1737–1798), Italian physician and physicist.

248.1 Fresnels] Augustin Jean Fresnel (1788–1827), French physicist.

248.1 Purkinjes] Johannes Evangelista Purkinje (1787–1869), Czech physiologist.

248.21 Rochester] American spiritism, which within decades of these events enjoyed several million adherents, originated with ghostly rappings supposedly heard by two teenage sisters, Margaret and Katharine Fox, near Rochester, N.Y., in 1848. Margaret became widely known through sittings she gave at P. T. Barnum's New York Museum. In 1888, she admitted fraud and gave a lecture tour demonstrating how the sounds were produced. However, she later repudiated her confession.

248.21 Mesmer] Friedrich Anton Mesmer (1733–1815), German physician.

248.37 *Waverley*] The *Waverley Magazine* began publication in 1850 in Boston and was devoted primarily to contributions from amateur authors; the *Fireside Companion*, beginning in New York in 1867, published popular fiction.

249.32 writer] James covered the "facts of the sort dear to mystics" in his lectures on abnormal mental states before the Lowell Institute, Boston, in 1896, notes for which are preserved at Houghton (bMS Am 1092.9 [4402]). Much of his reviewing for the *Psychological Review* in the 1890s dealt with such topics.

250.4 Paris] James is referring to Charcot and his school at the Salpêtrière (see *The Principles of Psychology*, WORKS, pp. 1197–1199).

250.10 Janet] Pierre Janet (1859–1947), French psychologist, *L'Automatisme psychologique: Essai de psychologie expérimentale sur les formes inférieures de l'activité humaine* (Paris: Alcan, 1889) (WJ 642.59). Much of the discussion of Janet was used in *The Principles of Psychology*, WORKS, pp. 201–208, 222–224, 363–367, 368–369; the notes provided there should be consulted for additional references to *L'Automatisme*. Works by Janet from James's library will be listed in the volume of manuscript remains.

250.27 Binet] Articles by Binet in the *Open Court* are "Proof of Double Consciousness in Hysterical Individuals," 3 (July 25, 1889), 1739–1741; "The Relations between the Two Consciousnesses of Hysterical Individuals," 3 (August 1, 1889), 1751–1754; "The Graphic Method and the Doubling of Consciousness," 3 (November 7, 1889), 1919–1922.

253.14 Charcot's] For the terms 'motor' and 'visual' see *Œuvres complètes de J. M. Charcot*, III (Paris: Aux bureaux du *Progrès Médical*, 1890), 190–191.

253.24 Janet] Jules Janet (1861–1945), French psychologist, "L'Hystérie et l'hypnotisme, d'après la théorie de la double personnalité," *Revue Scientifique*, 3rd series, vol. 18 (May 19, 1888), pp. 616–623.

254.24 Bourru] Henri Bourru and Prosper Ferdinand Burot, French physicians, *Variations de la personnalité* (Paris: Baillière, 1888). A marked copy of this work was sold.

254.40 Janet] *L'Automatisme*, pp. 97–98.

255.33 *la*] *L'Automatisme*, p. 50.

256.13 "This] *L'Automatisme*, pp. 128–129, 132–133.

258.16 Locke's] James's copy of *An Essay Concerning Human Understanding* (London: William Tegg, 1853) (WJ 551.13) is dated September 1876. He is referring to bk. II, ch. 27 (pp. 217–249).

258.38 Gurney] Edmund Gurney (1847–1888), British aesthetician and psychical researcher, "Peculiarities of Certain Post-Hypnotic States," *Proceedings of the Society for Psychical Research* (English), 4 (May 1887), 268–323. For the relations between James and Gurney see *The Will to Believe*, WORKS, notes to 225.38 and 228.11.

258.38 Bernheim] See note to 244.32.

259.39 "colored] See p. 243.

261.1 Pitres] Albert Pitres (1848–1928), French psychiatrist, *Des anesthésies hystériques* (Bordeaux: Gounouilhou, 1887).

262.17 *"Cessez*] Jules Janet, "L'Hystérie," p. 622.

262.30 "I] *L'Automatisme*, p. 239.

264.1 Beaunis] For the reference see *The Principles of Psychology*, WORKS, note to 206.28.

264.6 "I] *L'Automatisme*, pp. 255–256.

265.6 *"J'ai*] *L'Automatisme*, p. 267.

266.6 Marie] The case of Marie is found in *L'Automatisme*, pp. 436–440. Janet states that the girl was attempting to stop menstrual bleeding.

268.20 woman] See note to 190.18.

269.2 He] In the *Proceedings of the Society for Psychical Research* (English), 7 (April 1891), 1, it is noted that at the general meeting of the Society on March 6, 1891, "A paper by PROFESSOR WILLIAM JAMES and MR. R. HODGSON, on a case of double personality of the ambulatory type (that of the Rev. Ansel Bourne), which it is proposed to publish in a future number of the *Proceedings*, was read by MR. W. LEAF." Presumably it is this paper which appears under Hodgson's name alone as "A Case of Double Consciousness," *Proceedings*, 7 (July 1891), 221–257. Richard Hodgson (1855–1905), who as secretary of the American branch of the Society was associated with James in numerous investigations of psychical phenomena, reports that early in 1890, J. N. Arnold, of Providence, R. I., an associate of the American branch, first drew James's attention to the case and put him in touch with the principals involved (p. 232). Hodgson then continues: "It will have been observed that no account was forthcoming of Mr. Bourne's doings between the time of his disappearance from Providence and his advent in Norristown two weeks later, and Professor James conceived the idea that if Mr. Bourne could be hypnotised we might obtain from him while in the hypnotic trance a complete history of the whole incident, and at the same time, by post-hypnotic suggestion, prevent the recurrence of any such episode."
Bourne was paid to come to Cambridge for questioning under hypnosis by James, Hodgson, and others from time to time. The sessions lasted from May 27 to 31, 1890, with another session in Bourne's home in Greene, R.I., on June 7, 1890. Transcripts of these sessions are given by Hodgson, pp. 241–249. With the exception of the first session (morning of May 28) when he was not present, James hypnotized and asked most of the questions. Hodgson acted as secretary. Both on May 29 and 30, in letters to his wife, James noted that each day he spent four hours with Bourne and the case does not "develope at all" (bMS Am 1092.9 [1723–1724]).
James reported to the Society in Boston on December 2, 1890. A summary by Hodgson appears in the *Journal of the Society for Psychical Research* (English), 5 (January 1891), 5. The hypnotism suggestion "justified the expectation of Professor James. Mr. Bourne was hypnotised repeatedly by Professor James and Mr. Hodgson, and gave an account of his doings during his eight weeks' absence, and verification has been obtained of some of the incidents which he described as having occurred before his arrival at Norristown. In the hypnotic trance he called himself A. J. Brown, and recollected nothing later than going to sleep in the store at Norristown."
Considerable efforts were made to question witnesses and verify the story

Bourne gave under hypnosis. The report of the investigation conducted by William Romaine Newbold is given by Hodgson, pp. 250–253. In *The Principles of Psychology*, WORKS, pp. 369–371, James quotes from an unidentified source an account of the case which should be consulted for more detail.

Ansel Bourne was born in 1826 and at an early age learned the carpenter's trade, making his living in various Rhode Island towns. In 1857 he underwent a conversion described in *A Narrative of the Wonderful Facts in the Case of Ansel Bourne, of West Shelby, Orleans Co, N.Y., Who, in the Midst of Opposition to the Christian Religion, Was Suddenly Struck Blind, Dumb and Deaf; and after Eighteen Days Was Suddenly and Completely Restored, in the Presence of Hundreds of Persons, in the Christian Chapel, at Westerly, on the 15th of November, 1857. Written under His Direction* (Fall River, Mass., 1877). Following his conversion, he became an itinerant preacher. On January 17, 1887, Bourne went from his home to Providence and did not return for several months. Subsequent investigation showed that about February 1, he arrived at Norristown, Pa., and as A. J. Brown opened and operated a store. On March 14, he was found by neighbors denying that his name was Brown and apparently completely unaware of his life in Norristown.

The Widener copy of *A Narrative* (Phil 6990.26.5) is signed by Hodgson; James's copy is reported as given to Widener.

269.2 Wadsworth] Oliver Fairfield Wadsworth and Frederick Lafayette Jack, physicians who examined Bourne on May 30 (Hodgson, p. 255).

270.1 Ladd] George Trumbull Ladd (1842–1921), American philosopher and psychologist. Ladd's review of *Principles* is "Psychology as So-called 'Natural Science'," *Philosophical Review*, 1 (January 1892), 24–53. Preserved from James's library are *Elements of Physiological Psychology* (New York: Charles Scribner's Sons, 1887) (WJ 448.17), *Psychology: Descriptive and Explanatory* (New York: Charles Scribner's Sons, 1894) (WJ 448.17.4), *Philosophy of Mind* (New York: Charles Scribner's Sons, 1895) (WJ 448.17.2). *Philosophy of Knowledge* (1897) was sold. A letter from Ladd asking for a thorough review is pasted in in James's copy of the *Elements*. James's review is in the *Nation*, 44 (June 2, 1887), 473. James also reviewed the *Psychology*, in the *Psychological Review*, 1 (1894), 286–293. Both reviews are reprinted in *Collected Essays and Reviews* (New York: Longmans, Green, 1920). For James's meeting with Ladd see Perry, II, 274–275.

270.12 Lavoisier] Antoine Laurent Lavoisier (1743–1794), French chemist.

271.2 recently] 1892.

273.39 Seth] Andrew Seth Pringle-Pattison (1856–1931), Scottish philosopher, *The Present Position of the Philosophical Sciences* (Edinburgh: Blackwood, 1891), p. 15.

274.11 *Physiological*] P. 632.

275.25 Ladd] Ladd writes: "With our author, psychology as a natural science, without metaphysics, is wholly cerebral psychology. . . . Let it be noted that this conception excludes, as explanatory science, not only all introspective psychology, as such, but also almost the entire domain of what is customarily known as physiological psychology. All of the immense labors of Weber and Fechner, and of their pupils" (p. 30).

278.2 *Principles*] WORKS, pp. 257–259.

278.8 Giżycki] Georg von Giżycki (1851–1895), German philosopher. One letter to James is preserved (bMS Am 1092, letter 296). For James's meeting with Giżycki see *The Letters of William James*, ed. Henry James, 2 vols. (Boston: Atlantic Monthly Press, 1920), I, 214; for their controversy on determinism, *The Will to Believe*, WORKS, pp. 444–465.

278.14 Porter] Samuel Porter, "Is Thought Possible without Language?" *Princeton Review*, 57th year (January 1881), pp. 104–128.

279.1 Fay] Edward Allen Fay, professor of languages at the National Deaf-Mute College.

279.5 d'Estrella] Theophilus d'Estrella (1851–1929), at the time instructor of art at the California Institution for the Education of the Deaf and Dumb, and the Blind in Berkeley, Cal.

279.11 *Weekly*] D'Estrella's account follows a summary of "The Notions of Deaf-Mutes before Instruction," *Weekly News* (April 27, 1889), p. 2, attributed by the editors to "*Hutton in Gallaudet Conference.*" The reference is to J. Scott Hutton (1833–1891), educator of deaf-mutes.

279.20 Gordon] Joseph C. Gordon, professor of mathematics and chemistry at the National Deaf-Mute College.

279.26 Wilkinson] Warring Wilkinson, principal of the Institution.

281.22 letter] Not preserved in the James Collection.

292.1 Ford] E. Ford, "The Original Datum of Space-Consciousness," *Mind*, n.s. 2 (April 1893), 217–218.

292.9 Lotze's] For the doctrine of local signs see *The Principles of Psychology*, WORKS, pp. 798, 906.

293.24 Stumpf] For Stumpf's notion of distance see *The Principles of Psychology*, WORKS, pp. 501–502.

294.16 Mills'] For this notion in John Stuart Mill see *The Principles of Psychology*, WORKS, note to 163.32.

294.16 Wundt's] For this notion in Wundt see *The Principles of Psychology*, WORKS, p. 907.

295.1 Wundt's] On February 1, 1892, in a letter to Edward Bradford Titchener, James discussed his attitude towards Wundt and his reading of the *Grundzüge*: "I admit that I was guilty of ignorance of most of his 3rd edition when I pubd my P. of P. After having read through both 1st & 2nd., it was perhaps natural to flinch from the 3rd. in a world so crowded with new things that one can't read for lack of time. Külpe's articles on the Will first informed me of Wundt's conversion" (Department of Manuscripts and University Archives, Cornell University). James is referring to Ostwald Külpe (1862–1915), Latvian-born psychologist, "Die Lehre vom Willen in der neueren Psychologie," *Philosophische Studien*, 5 (1888–1889), 179–244, 381–446.

295.7 Graefe] Albrecht von Graefe.

295.22   Wundt]   *Grundzüge*, 3rd ed., I, 400–407.

296.13   Graefe's]   Alfred Karl Graefe, "Motilitätsstörungen," VI, 22.

298.2   modifications]   The letter to Titchener of February 1, 1892, places great stress upon the need to indicate changes of view: "With all my gratitude to Wundt for inspiring me with his wide ideals of study, I must say that I think he is getting in his old age into very reprehensible ways. His infernal pretension to be *smooth, e.g.* to advance *without jolt*, makes him smear over everything. Surely if any name has been identified with the innervationsgefühl it is his. Why can't he then say when driven out of it." In the first volume of his copy of the second edition of the *Grundzüge*, James inserted a list of "Some of the Additions to 4th Edition of Wundt's P. P." Titchener who received his doctorate at Leipzig under Wundt published a note on "The *Innervationsempfindung* in Wundt's Psychology," *Mind*, n.s. 2 (January 1893), 143–144, quoting Wundt's current views on the subject.

299.1   Lange]   See note to 168.9.

299.14   Wundt's]   Wilhelm Wundt, "Zur Lehre von den Gemüthsbewegungen," *Philosophische Studien*, 6 (1890), 335–393.

299.22   *Psychology*]   In the list of changes made in the fourth edition (see note to 298.2), one entry refers to emotions, "Schmerzgefühl 560." But the list ends with "etc etc."

301.6   Irons]   David Irons (1870–1907), Scottish psychologist, "Prof. James' Theory of Emotion," *Mind*, n.s. 3 (January 1894), 77–97.

301.11   *If*]   The sentence in italics precedes the text from p. 84 quoted by James.

301.13   Worcester]   William Leonard Worcester (1845–1901), American physician, "Observations on Some Points in James's Psychology," *Monist*, 2 (April 1892), 417–434; 3 (January 1893), 285–298; 4 (October 1893), 129–143. Three letters from Worcester to James, related to the controversy, are at Houghton (bMS Am 1092.9 [712a]; bMS Am 1092, letters 1183–1184). The Robbins Library at Harvard preserves James's copy of volume II of the *Monist*, with extensive annotations in the Worcester article.

301.39   'object']   See *The Principles of Psychology*, WORKS, pp. 265–266.

303.7   Worcester]   P. 290.

303.16   Lehmann's]   Alfred Georg Ludwig Lehmann (1858–1921), Danish psychologist, *Die Hauptgesetze des menschlichen Gefühlslebens*, trans. F. Bendixen (Leipzig: O. R. Reisland, 1892) (WJ 749.39). James discussed a review of this book in the *Psychological Review*, 3 (1896), 113. For James's writings on other aspects of Lehmann's work see *The Principles of Psychology*, WORKS, note to 512.32.

305.6   Fouillée]   Alfred Fouillée (1838–1912), French philosopher, *L'Évolutionnisme des idées-forces* (Paris: Alcan, 1890) (WJ 629.89), *La Psychologie des idées-forces*, 2 vols. (Paris: Alcan, 1893) (WJ 629.89.4). James reviewed the latter work in the *Philosophical Review*, 2 (November 1893), 716–720.

305.7 Ladd] *Psychology: Descriptive and Explanatory*, pp. 173, 544–545. In James's copy, there are some markings on pp. 173 and 544.

306.8 Baldwin] James Mark Baldwin (1861–1934), American psychologist. In "The Origin of Emotional Expression," *Psychological Review*, 1 (November 1894), 610–623, Baldwin provides many references to his own views and in a postscript on "The Physical Basis of Emotion" suggests that James has come to agree with his critics. According to Baldwin, James's paper should now be read instead of the chapter on emotion in *Principles*. For the relations between James and Baldwin see *The Principles of Psychology*, WORKS, note to 7.17–18.

306.8 Sully] In his index to Sully's *Outlines of Psychology*, James has "Emotion 59."

306.26 Marshall] Henry Rutgers Marshall (1852–1927), American architect and writer, *Pain, Pleasure, and Æsthetics: An Essay Concerning the Psychology of Pain and Pleasure, with Special Reference to Æsthetics* (London: Macmillan, 1894) (WJ 453.78), pp. 36, 45–53, 61. Four letters from Marshall to James are at Houghton (bMS Am 1092, letters 546–549); one letter to Marshall is at Yale. James reviewed the book in the *Nation*, 59 (July 19, 1894), 49–51.

306.27 Nichols] Herbert Nichols (b. 1852), American psychologist, an instructor at Harvard, "The Origin of Pleasure and Pain," *Philosophical Review*, 1 (July 1892), 403–432; (September 1892), 518–534.

307.39 Münsterberg] Hugo Münsterberg, *Beiträge zur experimentellen Psychologie*, 4 pts. (Freiburg i. B.: J. C. B. Mohr, 1889–1892) (WJ 757.62), pt. 4, pp. 216–238.

307.41 Miller] Dickinson Sergeant Miller (1868–1963), American philosopher, a graduate student at Harvard in 1890–1892, instructor in 1899–1904, sometimes wrote under the pseudonym of R. E. Hobart.

307.44 *Gemüthsvorgänge*] See Wundt, "Zur Lehre," p. 359.

308.4 Ladd] *Psychology: Descriptive and Explanatory*, p. 545.

308.35 Lehmann] Pp. 121–126.

310.32 Sollier's] Paul Auguste Sollier (1861–1933), French psychologist, "Recherches sur les rapports de la sensibilité et de l'émotion," *Revue Philosophique de la France et de l'Étranger*, 37 (March 1894), 241–266.

311.8 Berkley] Henry Johns Berkley (1860–1940), American physician, "Two Cases of General Cutaneous and Sensory Anæsthesia, without Marked Psychical Implication," *Brain*, 14 (1891), 441–464.

311.17 Berkley] A letter cited by Worcester, p. 294.

312.12 "'I] Pp. 244–245.

317.17 Boethius] *Contra Eutychen et Nestorium*, sec. III, lines 4–5.

318.20 Hume] "The mind is a kind of theatre, where several perceptions successively make their appearance; pass, re-pass, glide away, and mingle in an infinite variety of postures and situations. There is properly no *simplicity* in it at one time, nor *identity* in different," *Treatise*, I, 534 (Bk. I, pt. IV, sec. 6).

James quotes Hume on personal identity at length in *The Principles of Psychology*, WORKS, pp. 332–333.

319.6   Locke's]   *Essay*, p. 227 (Bk. II, ch. 27, sec. 20).

319.14   Gurney]   For one of Gurney's numerous papers on hypnotism see note to 258.38; others will be listed in *Essays in Psychical Research*, WORKS.

319.23   Janet]   See note to 250.10.

319.23   Binet]   See note to 250.27.

319.34   Janet]   For the method of distraction see *The Principles of Psychology*, WORKS, p. 201 and note to 201.6.

320.1   Myers]   See note to 321.27.

320.9   "Léonie]   See pp. 250, 256–258.

320.9   "Félida]   See *The Principles of Psychology*, WORKS, pp. 358–359.

320.9–10   "Lurancy]   For the case of Lurancy Vennum see *The Principles of Psychology*, WORKS, pp. 375–377.

320.10   Ansel]   See p. 269.

320.10   Louis]   See *The Principles of Psychology*, WORKS, pp. 367–368.

321.16   Siebeck's]   Hermann Siebeck (1842–1920), German philosopher, *Geschichte der Psychologie*, 2 vols. (Gotha: Perthes, 1880–1884).

321.17   Deussen's]   Paul Deussen (1845–1919), German philologist and philosopher, *Das System des Vedânta* (Leipzig: F. A. Brockhaus, 1883).

321.17   Locke's]   *Essay*, pp. 217–232.

321.18   Hume's]   *Treatise*, I, 533–543, "Of Personal Identity."

321.20   Ladd's]   *Elements of Physiological Psychology*, pp. 585–688 on "The Nature of the Mind."

321.20   James's]   "The Consciousness of Self," WORKS, pp. 279–379.

321.24   Momerie's]   Alfred Williams Momerie (1848–1900), *Personality: The Beginning and End of Metaphysics and a Necessary Assumption in All Positive Philosophy* (Edinburgh: William Blackwood and Sons, 1879). "Freedom defined 70–1" is written in the back of the Widener copy (Phil 575.2) in James's hand.

321.24   Shoup's]   Francis Asbury Shoup (1834–1896), American physicist, *Mechanism and Personality: An Outline of Philosophy in the Light of the Latest Scientific Research* (Boston: Ginn & Co., 1891).

321.26   Blavatsky's]   Elena Petrovna Blavatsky (1831–1891), Russian traveler and theosophist, *The Key to Theosophy* (London: Theosophical Publishing Society, 1889). James's copy is in Houghton (Phil 978.5.24*).

321.26   Binet's]   Alfred Binet, *Les Altérations de la personnalité* (Paris: Baillière, 1892).

321.27 Myers] Frederic William Henry Myers, "The Subliminal Consciousness," *Proceedings of the Society for Psychical Research* (English), 7 (1891–1892), 298–355; 8 (1892), 333–404, 436–535; 9 (1893–1894), 3–128; 11 (1895), 334–593.

322.1 correspondent] Nothing was found in the James Collection indicating the identity of the correspondent.

322.9 'The] The appendix to "On Some Hegelisms," *The Will to Believe*, WORKS, pp. 217–221.

324.21 Caird] Edward Caird (1835–1908), Scottish philosopher, at the time master of Balliol.

325.1 Sidis] Boris Sidis (1867–1923), Russian-born psychologist, a student at Harvard in 1892–1896, received his doctorate in 1897. Preserved is James's copy of Sidis and Simon Philip Goodhart (1873–1956), American psychologist, *Multiple Personality* (New York: D. Appleton, 1905). James's copy in Widener (Phil 7042.6B) is inscribed to him. The work is dedicated to James. Some of the correspondence between James and Sidis is in Houghton (bMS Am 1092.9 [619, 3768–3777]).

326.29 classification] *The Psychology of Suggestion* (New York: D. Appleton, 1898), pp. 242–244.

328.2 Thorndike's] Edward Lee Thorndike (1874–1949), American psychologist, attracted to psychology by James's *Principles*, a student at Harvard in 1895–1897, professor at the Teachers College of Columbia University. Preserved is James's copy of *The Elements of Psychology* (New York: A. G. Seiler, 1905) (WJ 350.86). Four letters from Thorndike to James are at Houghton (bMS Am 1092, letters 1139–1142); Thorndike was proposing to revise *Psychology: Briefer Course* for James. Some letters from James to Thorndike are given in Geraldine Jonçich, *The Sane Positivist: A Biography of Edward L. Thorndike* (Middletown, Conn.: Wesleyan University Press, c1968). The Thorndike papers subsequently were given to the Library of Congress, but the James letters could not be located.

331.9 Stanford] James was a visiting professor at Stanford for the Spring term of 1906. Henry Rushton Fairclough, a professor of Latin at Stanford, in his *Warming Both Hands: The Autobiography of Henry Rushton Fairclough* (Stanford University Press, c1941), p. 216, writes: "My wife, however, refused to let her light the stove, as slight shocks could still be felt and there was always danger of fire. As we were still debating the question, a familiar figure appeared at the kitchen door, and William James cried out: 'I want all of you to come to breakfast with us. We have an alcohol lamp and can boil our coffee without danger of fire.' We followed him to his house near by and were much amused as James analyzed his sensations of the morning. This analysis he published a few weeks later in *The Youth's Companion*." On April 22, 1906, James wrote out his experiences for Frances R. Morse (*Letters*, II, 247–250). The *Letters*, II, 247n–248n, give some reminiscences of James and the earthquake by William F. Snow.

331.11 B.] Usually identified as Charles Montague Bakewell (1867–1957), American philosopher.

334.35 escort] Lillien Jane Martin (1851–1943), American psychologist, described by James as "our co-habitant here" (*Letters*, II, 249).

336.21 Wells] Herbert George Wells (1866–1949), English writer, *Anticipations of the Reaction of Mechanical and Scientific Progress upon Human Life and Thought* (Leipzig: Bernhard Tauchnitz, 1902), pp. 82, 97.

337.3 Keith] William Keith (1839–1911), Scottish-born artist.

Appendix I
Notes for "The Spatial Quale"

A transcript of bMS Am 1092.9 (4411). Seven leaves of wove unwatermarked paper, 8⅝ x 7⅛", written in ink on rectos only. Folios 1–2 are numbered in brown crayon. On fol. 7 the ink number 2 has been deleted and 'Space' written after it in brown crayon. The other leaves are numbered in ink. Folios 1–2 have continuous text; folios 3–4 (ink numbered 2–3) are continuous as are fols. 5–6 (ink numbered). Folio 7 is discrete. Although the manuscript apparently cannot be dated, it seems to concern itself in part with the conclusion of "The Spatial Quale" starting at 80.19 and so is reprinted here as in some degree pertinent to the article, whether preceding or succeeding it.

There are some inconsistencies in spelling and in what would appear to be typographical errors in James's notes; they have been retained in their original form. Missing letters in words have been supplied in square brackets.

[*fol.* 1]

Space

Several problems: 1 Is it a *quale* at all or only a language? 2. If a quale—is it a part of the sensation or ['only' *del.*] an intellectual form? 3. If sensational is it a priori? 4. If intellectual, is it ['nec' *del.*] apodictic? &c &c.

3 & 4 lead to the question as to the real significance of a priori & empirical representations. There is a sense in which the elements of all representation are a priori. The['y' *del.*] sensations [*intrl.*] are native forms of sensibility— If space be immediately given in sensation it is a priori in this sense. But "a priori" in this sense loses some of its most important connotations—those of apodictic certainty & universality—*or [*ab. del. doubtful* 'or'] at least possesses them only as consequences of the principle of identity: Sensation *a* is always sensation *a*, space is always space, but not on that account *are ['re' *insrtd.*] we ever entitled to pronounce on any neccessary relation between *a* & *b*, between space & time &c. This sort of a priority is therefore [*fol.* 2] barren. The sort asserted by Kant is that of judgments, not elements of judgment. He says that there are native ways of *coupling* these elements, which can never be departed from, and that space is one of these. Whether we say that it is bro't forth *après coup* by a psychic stimulus, or not, is of small account. The question is not as to the fountain, but as to the *properties [*ab. undel.* 'quality'] of its product. ['If it does not cont' *del.*] The emphasis shd. be laid on "synthetic," not on "a priori" in the discussions between Kant & the empiricists. If the a priori forms *are [*alt. fr.* 'as'] merely beds for *supporting [*ab. del.* 'joining'] elements of experience in the way in which they may happen to lie

380

down beside each other, their only interest is that of their having this specific color, rather than that. The question of their a priority is trivial, for it leads to nothing further. If on the contrary they are ['forms' *del.*] frameworks with rigid divisions into which the elements must squeeze themselves in a pre appointed order *if at all,* the properties of this order as well as the co-
[*fol.* 3, *ink numbered* 2]
Now what gives to the system of positions its difference *from [*ab. del.* 'over'] the system of intensities? The intensity of a colour is determined ['abs po' *del.*] perfectly by its *order [*ab. del.* 'position'] in the colour system; and yet when that colour is present ['the' *del.*] to us the total order hardly ever *arises ['r' *ov.* 's'] to *our ['o' *ov.* 'a'] consciousness. The colour say is a green midway between the maximum & the minimum of intensity. It appears detached to our consciousness, does not drag up its nei[g]hbor shades, nor the dim notion of intense light on the one hand or of absolute blackness on the other *into [*ab. del.* 'with'] which it may pass. That is it don't stick stably in its *system [*ab. del.* 'order']. Colours are only artificially & with effort tho't of in order, & lapse spontaneously into *chaos [*alt. fr.* 'chaous'], and independence. We may say that their *system [*ab. del.* 'order'] is only potential, and results literally from the *application* to them of an intellectual form, that of deliberate comparison.

Now with positions it is far other[*fol.* 4, *ink numbered* 3]-wise. A position is determined by its rank in the system just as a colour is. Colour *orange red [*ab. del.* '['pure green' *del. ab. del.* 'green'] ['lavender' *del. insrtd.*] ['midway between ['la' *del.*] ['white & l' *del.*] light & dark,' *del.*] ['position' *del.*] ['gre' *del.*] yellowish green midway'] considerably adulterated with white, position right upwards not far removed from centre of field. The fixed points of sensation in the colour *case [*intrl.*] are the *extremes ['s' *added*] of ['satu-' *del.*] intense saturated quality orange *& [*intrl.*] red on the one hand & white on the other. The fixed points of sensation as I must call it, in the case of position are the extremes of up-ness, & right ness on the one hand and of straight ahead ness on the other. ['The differen' *del.*] The precise definition or judgment of the given colour and position is an estimate of the quantity or number of intervening shades or positions between the extreme and the given sensation. This estimate can be expressed in words, & colour and position constructed by rule. The constructor must start from the
[*fol.* 5]
dont feel the system at the moment in which we define the colours rank. At most we nascently feel one dimension of it. But with the position we have a distinct feeling of the whole system in which it is ranked. We feel it *as [*ov.* 'e'] embedded there—the extremes, rightness, up-ness &c, are sensibly present as soon as it is— Present in their peculiar quale. It and they form an undivided whole, *divisible* only by express acts of the attention & will. In color they are *revivable* only by express acts of will. The color system then ['is a process vol' *del.*] stands for a voluntary intellectual process; the space system ['stands for' *del.*] is a simple passive feeling. Colour *is worked into [*ab. del.* 'becomes a'] system by addition; ['spa' *del.*] position by division. Now the divisions are doubtless imported by muscular action making "marks" as Sp. says. ['H' *del.*] Muscular action itself is an order of intensity which we appreciate quantitatively. When the [*fol.* 6] simple retinal space becomes divided and redivided by these quantitatively appreciated motions itself becomes *measured,* and intricately known. But unless it were first there and *stood [*insrtd.*] always there in itself to receive the superinduced measurements, these, when expressed to

us wd. always have the same ['vague descriptive sound as when we hear of not' *del.*] non-intuitive character which all processes have have as distinguished from instantaneous sensations. Positions are a system instantaneously felt as such. The attention can ['fel' *del.*] feel their divisibility.

Show now how very great spaces [*comma del.*] are built up by processes. Infinite space is the postulation of the possibility of this process. Intuition vs. idea.

So much for *quale*

[*fol.* 7, *ink* 2 *del.*]

I hold to a quale for these reasons:

1. it seems evidently specific.
2. But if denied I can make it appear probable by other considerations. ['In the first place' *del.*] Those who deny its specific intuitive quality must needs consider it a sort of concept or ['in' *del.*] brief mode of denoting a certain kind of order of synthesis among things. Now there are many such concepts; and they all differ from space in the absence of just this sort of intuitive ['sensible' *del.*] quality which space has. They seem logical, it sensible. Coexistence; order überhaupt ['& disorder, quantity' *del.*] embracing ['b' *ov.* 'p'] the subdivisions of evenly gradated or unevenly gradated order; disorder; quantity; most general of all change. Space is an evenly gradated order, but only one, ['sounds may be evenly gra' *del.*] It is not even the only one in three dimensions. Sounds have 2, *colors ['r' *ov. possible* 'u'] 3. But neither ['order' *del.*] sounds nor colours when once arranged in that order stick there stably they fall into chaos again. On the other hand the system of [*broken off*]

Appendix II

Questionnaire on Consciousness of Lost Limbs

15 APPIAN WAY, CAMBRIDGE, MASS.

DEAR SIR OR MADAM,

I am engaged in scientifically studying the peculiarities of sensation experienced by amputated persons in their lost limbs.

As the information I require can only be obtained by the statistical method of collecting and comparing a very large number of the facts in point, I trust you will not deem it too great a liberty if I beg you to communicate to me some details from your personal experience. All such communications shall be regarded as confidential, and no personal details will be published without the express permission of the writers.

In answering the following questions, please bear in mind that an inaccurate answer is, for scientific purposes, a great deal worse than no answer at all. Some of the questions may for certain individuals be difficult to answer with precision. In such cases, a statement that the answer is difficult, and if possible, of the precise nature of the difficulty, will satisfy the purposes of the inquiry quite as much as the most definite reply.

Will you then, to the best of your ability, answer the questions, each in the blank space left below it?

1. Your name, age, and address.

2. Date of amputation, and part lost.

3. Do you still feel the lost part? If you do not feel it now, for how long did you feel it after the amputation?

4. How much of the limb can you feel, and how does the feeling differ from what it would be if the member were present?

5. Does the limb appear shortened?
   Does it appear in a fixed position?
   If not, does the apparent position change from time to time?

6. If the apparent position changes of its own accord, can you assign any cause for such change?
   Does it follow the position of the stump?
   When you walk, does the *lost leg* seem to swing in alternation with the sound leg, just as it would if there?

Do you ever feel as if you had *two* imaginary legs in addition to a real one?

7. Can you, by consciously directing your attention to the lost part, change the intensity or quality of the feeling there?

8. Can you, by *imagining* strongly that it has moved, make yourself really feel as if it *had* moved into a different position?

9. Can you, by making an *effort of the will*, succeed in making it seem to move into a different position? (Do you recognize as two distinct cases, *imagining* the change, and *willing it?*)

10. If you *cannot* make it seem to move, is this because, *in spite of your effort*, the movement seems not to take place?
    Or is it rather because of a difficulty you experience in *making* the voluntary effort towards a part that no longer exists? If you cannot even make the effort, will you kindly take great pains to describe why; and if you can't describe why, try to say what makes such description difficult.

11. *If*, on the other hand, you *can* succeed in voluntarily making the lost part seem to change its position, will you accurately ascertain whether the feeling you get of the change be not perhaps due to actual contractions you are producing in the muscles, "nerves," or "cords," of the stump, and which you mistake for feelings of motion in the lost part? In other words, are you entirely sure that your feeling of change *goes beyond the stump?*

12. If you are entirely sure that your feeling of the moving lost part is *additional* to the feeling you simultaneously get in the stump, will you ascertain whether you can get this feeling of motion in the lost part *without any actual movement occurring in the stump?* (As this is a rather delicate fact to be sure of, it is hoped that you will test it several times, with the stump uncovered, and held in your own or some one else's hand, so that very faint internal movements in it may not escape notice if they exist.)

13. If you *can* make the lost part seem as to move in obedience to your will, whilst the muscles in the stump are absolutely at rest, will you endeavor to describe the difference (if you feel any) between this way of willing an illusory movement, and the way of willing a real movement in the limb on the other side, corresponding to the one you have lost.

14. Will you add any remarks or reflections connected with the subject? In particular, do you believe you felt in any way the situation or condition of your actual diseased limb after it had been cut off, buried, &c.?

Please receive, in advance, the thanks of

WILLIAM JAMES,
Assistant Professor of Philosophy, Harvard University.

The following variants occur in an earlier form of the questionnaire, which is also contained in bMS Am 1092.9 (4566).

383.2   OR MADAM] *om.*

383.8   shall] will

383.12   is, . . . purposes,] $\sim_\wedge$ . . . $\sim_\wedge$

383.15   inquiry] enquiry

383.18   it?] $\sim$.

383.25–27   Does . . . time?] *These 3 questions are set consecutively on 2 lines*

383.27   If not,] Or$_\wedge$

383.28   of . . . accord] *om.*

383.30–384.2   Does . . . one?] *om.*

384.19   , "nerves," or "cords,"] *om.*

384.29   to move] if it moved

384.31   difference$_\wedge$ . . . any)] $\sim$, (if there be any to your consciousness)

384.31   way of willing] voluntary process of producing

384.32   way of willing] process of producing

384.34–36   In . . . &c.?] *om.*

384.39   *Philosophy,*] $\sim$.

A Note on the Editorial Method

These volumes of THE WORKS OF WILLIAM JAMES offer the critical text of a definitive edition of his published and unpublished writings (letters excepted). A text may be called 'critical' when an editor intervenes to correct the errors and aberrations of the copy-text[1] on his own responsibility or by reference to other authoritative documents, and also when he introduces authoritative revisions from such documents into the basic copy-text. An edition may be called 'definitive' (a) when the editor has exhaustively determined the authority, in whole or in part, of all preserved documents for the text; (b) when the text is based on the most authoritative documents produced during the work's formulation and execution and then during its publishing history; and (c) when the complete textual data of all authoritative documents are recorded, together with a full account of the edited text's divergences from the document chosen as copy-text, so that the user may reconstruct these sources in complete verbal detail as if they were before him. When backed by this data, a critical text in such a definitive edition may be called 'established' if from the fully recorded documentary evidence it attempts to reconstruct the author's true and fullest intention, even though in some details the restoration of intention from imperfect sources is conjectural and subject to differing opinion.

The most important editorial decision for any work edited without modernization[2] is the choice of its copy-text, that documentary form on

---

[1] The copy-text is that document, whether a manuscript or a printed edition, chosen by the editor as the most authoritative basis for his text, and therefore one which is reprinted in the present edition subject only to recorded editorial emendations, and to substitution or addition of readings from other authoritative documents, judged to be necessary or desirable for completing James's final intentions.

[2] By 'modernization' one means the silent substitution for the author's of an entirely new system of punctuation, spelling, capitalization, and word-division in order to bring these original old-fashioned 'accidentals' of the text thoroughly up to date for the benefit of a current reader. It is the theory of the present edition, however, that James's turn-of-the-century 'accidentals' offer no difficulty to a modern scholar or general reader and that to tamper with them by 'modernization' would not only destroy some of James's unique and vigorous flavor of presentation but would also risk distortion of his meaning. Since there is every evidence that, in his books at least,

which the edited text will be based. Textual theorists have long distinguished two kinds of authority: first, the authority of the words themselves—the *substantives*; second, the authority of the punctuation, spelling, capitalization, word-division, paragraphing, and devices of emphasis—the *accidentals* so-called—that is, the texture in which the substantives are placed but itself often a not unimportant source of meaning. In an unmodernized edition like the present, an attempt is made to print not only the substantives but also their 'accidental' texture, each in its most authoritative form. The most authoritative substantives are taken to be those that reflect most faithfully the author's latest intentions as he revised to perfect the form and meaning of his work. The most authoritative accidentals are those which are preferential, and even idiosyncratic, in the author's usage even though not necessarily invariable in his manuscripts. These characteristic forms convey something of an author's flavor, but their importance goes beyond aesthetic or antiquarian appreciation since they may become important adjuncts to meaning. It is precisely these adjuncts, however, that are most susceptible to compositorial and editorial styling away from authorial characteristics and toward the uniformity of whatever contemporary system the printing or publishing house fancied. Since few authors are in every respect so firm in their 'accidental' intentions as to demand an exact reproduction of their copy, or to attempt systematically to restore their own system in proof from divergent compositorial styling, their 'acceptance' of printing-house styling is meaningless as an indication of intentions. Thus, advanced editorial theory agrees that in ordinary circumstances the best authority for the accidentals is that of a holograph manuscript or, when the manuscript is not preserved, whatever typed or printed document is closest to it, so that the fewest intermediaries have had a chance to change the text and its forms. Into this copy-text—chosen on the basis of its most authoritative accidentals—are placed the latest revised substantives, with the result that each part of the resulting eclectic text is presented in its highest documentary form of authority.[3] It is recognized, however, that an author may be so scrupu-

---

James was concerned to control the texture of presentation and made numerous nonverbal as well as verbal changes in preparing printer's copy, and later in proof, for an editor to interfere with James's specific, or even general, wishes by modernizing his system of 'accidentals' would upset on many occasions the designedly subtle balances of his meaning. Moreover, it would be pointless to change his various idiosyncrasies of presentation, such as his increasing use of 'reform' spellings and his liking for the reduction of the capitals in words like *darwinism*. Hence in the present edition considerable pains have been devoted to reprinting the authoritative accidentals of the copy-text and also by emendation to their purification, so far as documentary evidence extends, from the housestyling to which they were subjected in print and which was not entirely weeded out in proof. For a further discussion, see below under the question of copy-text and its treatment.

[3] The use of these terms, and the application to editorial principles of the divided authority between both parts of an author's text, was chiefly initiated by W. W. Greg,

lous in supervising each stage of the production of a work that the accidentals of its final version join with the revised substantives in representing his latest intentions more faithfully than in earlier forms of the text. In such special cases a document removed by some stages from a preserved manuscript or from an early intermediary may in practical terms compose the best copy-text.[4]

In a volume like the present, consisting of articles from learned journals and from magazines, the problem of copy-text is solved by the absence of all antecedent manuscripts and of revised editions. Thus when the text is preserved in only one version, as here, that form automatically and by necessity becomes the copy-text since it is the sole known authority. The essays in this volume represent critically edited texts of the original journal articles on the subject of psychology, with two introductions to the books of friends, and a few notes and commentaries in discussion or letter-to-the-editor form. Many of these twenty-nine articles have not been available in collected form, although one was reprinted by Henry James, Jr., in *Memories and Studies* (McDermott 1911:2) and nine by R. B. Perry in *Collected Essays and Reviews* (McD 1920:2).

With the exception of those articles on which James drew, sometimes heavily, for his *Principles of Psychology*, the editorial theory in this volume is relatively simple. The wording, or substantives, is faithfully reproduced from the copy-texts after a minute scrutiny for error, of which there is little that is demonstrable or even suspicious. The accidentals, however, pose a special problem because of the miscellaneous sources of the texts that have thus been subject to a number of different housestylings.

Although James demonstrably made an effort to control the forms of certain of his accidentals in the proofs, even when he had been relatively careless about their consistency in his manuscript printer's copy, he was not always equally attentive to every detail of the housestyling that printers imposed on his work. In some cases he simply did not observe anomalies even in his own idiosyncratic practices; in others he may have been relatively indifferent when no real clash of principles was involved. Thus, when an editor is aware by reason of inconsistencies within the copy-text that certain 'accidental' printing-house stylings have been substituted for James's own practices as established in manu-

---

"The Rationale of Copy-Text," *Studies in Bibliography*, 3 (1950–51), 19–36. For extensions of the principle, see Fredson Bowers, "Current Theories of Copy-Text," *Modern Philology*, 68 (1950), 12–20; "Multiple Authority: New Concepts of Copy-Text," *The Library*, 5th ser., 27 (1972), 81–115; "Remarks on Eclectic Texts," *Proof*, 4 (1974), 31–76, all reprinted in *Essays in Bibliography, Text, and Editing* (Charlottesville: University Press of Virginia, 1975).

[4] An extensive analysis of specific problems in the mechanical application of traditional theories of copy-text to revised modern works may be found in Bowers, "Greg's 'Rationale of Copy-Text' Revisited," *Studies in Bibliography*, 31 (1978), 90–161.

scripts and marked copy (in this case, as established in *Principles*), or have been substituted for relatively neutral journal copy that seems to approximate James's usual practice, he may feel justified in emending to recover by the methods of textual criticism as much of the purity of the Jamesian accidentals as of the substantives—both ultimately contributing to the most complete and accurate expression of James's meaning.

Nevertheless, some principles are required in order to limit editorial discretion in constructing what might too easily become in certain respects an artificial or synthetic accidentals texture. The first limiting principle has been that each essay has been treated as an independent unit. That is, if evidence encourages the emendation of certain accidental forms in one essay, this individual situation would not justify similar emendation in another essay that lacked the evidence found in the first. Thus a narrow view of copy-text authority requires the editor to follow the housestyling in the accidentals of each copy-text, even though varying from James's known characteristics, so long as the system of accidentals in that particular copy-text is consistent. On the other hand, when the copy-text is inconsistent and if—even once—a known Jamesian characteristic slips through the styling, then it is taken that physical evidence is present for the reading of the manuscript in this particular accidental form which the compositor by chance had omitted to regularize; as a consequence the editor has felt free, then, to emend throughout the article to what the evidence of that one irregular accidental suggests was the Jamesian form in the underlying copy. Most of such emendation concerns the spellings, of course, since these are the most readily recognizable and consistent Jamesian characteristics, whereas only a few set pieces of punctuation—such as the association of other punctuation with dashes—are sufficiently identifiable to be subject to such regularizing emendation.

Certain psychological essays that would ordinarily have appeared in this volume were so completely subsumed in *The Principles of Psychology* that the decision was made to omit them on the grounds that their substantive text can be fully recovered from the collational apparatus found in the edition of *Principles* in these WORKS. These omitted essays are "The Association of Ideas" (McD 1880:1), "The Perception of Time" (McD 1886:3), "The Perception of Space" (McD 1887:4), "The Laws of Habit" (McD 1887:5), "What Is an Instinct?" (McD 1887:6), "Some Human Instincts" (McD 1887:8), and "The Psychology of Belief" (McD 1889:4). As remarked, the *Principles* text adjusted by the record of the article variants in the Historical Collation will fully recover the original form of these essays.

Nine other essays, although utilized to different degrees in *Principles*, have been collected in the present volume since in these cases the use in *Principles* was less extensive and still left sufficient unutilized text to justify an independent interest in the original essay as a whole. These comprise "Brute and Human Intellect" (McD 1878:4), "Are We Automata?" (McD 1879:5), "The Spatial Quale" (McD 1879:6), "The Feeling of Effort" (McD 1880:3), "On Some Omissions of Introspective Psychology" (McD 1884:1), "What Is an Emotion?" (McD 1884:2), "Report of the Committee on Hypnotism" (McD 1886:1), "What the Will Effects" (McD 1888:1), and "The Hidden Self" (McD 1890:1). These special essays are reprinted in their original form without the revisions and alterations that sections of their text underwent in the adaptation to *Principles*. The corresponding text in *Principles* has been used only for the correction, therefore, and not for revision of the original wording. One slight change in the treatment of the accidentals has been made from the principle adopted for the other essays in this volume. That is, when any section of its text utilized in *Principles* alters accidentals from the article to characteristic Jamesian forms in the book, these particular accidentals have been emended for regularization throughout the essay regardless of its own consistency. Examples would be Jamesian 'anyone' for an article's 'any one', 'revery' for 'reverie', or 'afterwards' for 'afterward'. On the other hand, since James himself was not completely consistent in such forms as his generally characteristic 'amongst' for 'among', 'whilst' for 'while', or 'farther' for 'further', these linguistic forms are individually emended from parallel text in *Principles* but are not regularized throughout the article in places where the book does not confirm the authority.

Although the articles are printed in their original substantive form and do not contain the textual revision of the wording found in the *Principles* utilization, a reader may well be concerned to know how James may have changed his ideas and modified or refined his statement when the article matter was reworked in the book. As an aid to close study, therefore, the passages of direct use in *Principles*, as well as the major areas of general paraphrase, are identified in the textual discourses. In the first category—the area of direct use—all substantive variants are recorded in the Historical Collation together with the page-line references to the edition of *Principles* in the WORKS. Any emendations drawn from *Principles* are also identified by page and line number. On the contrary, in the stated areas of general paraphrase, the recording of variants was impracticable and has not been attempted.

Except for the small amount of silent alteration listed below, every editorial change in the copy-text has been recorded, with the identification of its immediate source and the record of the rejected copy-text reading. An asterisk prefixed to the page-line reference (always to this edition) indicates that the alteration is discussed in a Textual Note. The formulas for notation are described in the headnotes to the list of Emendations and to the Historical Collation, but it may be well to mention here the use of the term *stet* to call attention in special cases to the retention of the copy-text reading. Textual Notes discuss certain emendations or refusals to emend. The Historical Collation lists all substantive readings in the collated authoritative documents that differ from the edited text except for those recorded in the list of Emendations, which are not repeated in the Historical Collation. The principles for the recording of variants are described in the headnote to this Collation.

A special section of the apparatus treats hyphenated word-compounds, listing the correct copy-text form of those broken between lines by the printer of the present edition and indicating those in the present text, with the form adopted, that were broken between lines in the copy-text and partake of the nature of emendations. Consultation of the first list will enable any user to quote from the present text with the correct hyphenation of the copy-text.

Silent alterations in the text of this work concern themselves chiefly with mechanical presentation. For instance, heading capitals are normalized in the first line of any essay or section, headings may have their final periods removed, the headlines of the originals may be altered for the purposes of the present edition, anomalous typographical conventions or use of fonts may be normalized including roman or italic syntactical punctuation, which here has been made to conform to a logical system. British forms of accidentals in articles printed in English journals have been silently Americanized to the forms customary in the United States at the time unless by chance they happen to coincide with James's own habits. The minutiae of the accidentals of footnote reference have not been recorded as emendations or as rejected readings. For example, in the footnotes book titles are silently italicized from whatever other form present in the copy-text, as within quotation marks; periods are supplied after abbreviations, and the forms of abbreviations are made consistent; the use of roman or italic fonts is normalized as is the general system of punctuating bibliographical references. In short, such matters involving the reference system have been silently brought into conformity with the printing practice of the time and so in general conform to that found in the styling of the period. When unusual features call for unusual treatment, special notice is always given.

All line numbers keyed to the text include section numbers and subheadings but do not include spaces after titles or subheadings or spaces within the text itself. James's references to pages within the same essay are silently adjusted to the present edition; references to other volumes already published in the WORKS are added in brackets after James's original page numbers.

References to McDermott (McD) are to the "Annotated Bibliography," *The Writings of William James*, ed. John J. McDermott (New York: Random House, 1967).

A word may be said about the editorial treatment of quotations. James, and sometimes his wife, Alice, were likely to copy out quotations by hand. In this process the accidentals, as well as some indifferent substantives, of the original would occasionally be inadvertently modified, a departure partly aided, of course, by further compositorial variation and housestyling. Most accidentals in the quotations have been silently restored to their original form; those retained have been given a *stet* entry. The question of substantive variation, always recorded, is a difficult one to adjudicate on occasion. Some of the minor variation may be taken with confidence as inadvertent and therefore can be consistently restored as emendations. However, James had a habit of occasionally altering words in the quoted author if he thought the sense could be improved, and he would sometimes indulge in paraphrase to speed up a quotation. Such variants taken to be intentional are ordinarily honored and retained in the text. But since the reader should be aware of them without recourse to the Historical Collation, they are placed in the list of Emendations as *stet* entries, with the reading of the quoted author also supplied, so that they are textually as prominent in this apparatus as are the actual emendations made in the text.

Although James's own footnotes are preserved in the text as he wrote them (the only footnotes allowed in the present edition), the citations have been expanded and corrected as necessary in Professor Skrupskelis' Notes to provide the full bibliographical detail required by a scholar, this ordinarily having been neglected in James's own sketchy notation. The Notes also provide full information about quotations in the text that James did not footnote.

The intent of the editorial treatment both in large and in small matters, and in the recording of the textual information, has been to provide a clean reading text for the general user, with all specialized material isolated for the convenience of the scholar who wishes to consult it. The result has been to establish in the wording James's fullest intentions in their most authoritative form, divorced from verbal corruption whether in the copy-text or in subsequent printings or editions. To this crucial aim has been added the further attempt to present James's final verbal intentions within a logically contrived system of his own accidentals that in their texture are as close to their most authoritative form as controlled editorial theory can establish from the documentary evidence that has been preserved for each essay.

The Text of *Essays in Psychology*

BRUTE AND HUMAN INTELLECT (1878).

Copy-text: (P21) "Brute and Human Intellect," *Journal of Speculative Philosophy*, 12 (July 1878), 236–276 (McDermott 1878:4).

"Brute and Human Intellect" was extensively drawn on in *The Principles of Psychology*, Chapter XIII, "Discrimination and Comparison," and in Chapter XXII, "Reasoning." In Chapter XIII the paraphrase is so diffused that collation is impracticable, and only the following areas of direct utilization have been recorded:

 16.34–17.16 As . . . one."[6]] Mr. . . . on."₍ *(no fn.)* PP 478.37–479.18
 18.8–30 *Why* . . . in.] *ditto* PP 479.19–480.7.

Unrecorded distinctive areas of paraphrase are:

 16.28–34 This . . . group."] One . . . deserves. PP 478.31–37
 17.17–32 In . . . testify.] The components . . . found. PP 474.30–475.13
 17.36–18.7 We . . . prisms.] We . . . accommodation. PP 478.19–25.

In Chapter XXII the areas of direct utilization are:

 11.11–12.12 Suppose . . . properties.] Suppose . . . properties, PP 966.15–967.13
 12.34–16.19 Each . . . brutes.] every . . . brutes. PP 967.16–970.29
 21.5–37.28 What . . . with.] *ditto* PP 971.1–991.32.

Unrecorded distinctive areas of paraphrase are:

 2.25–3.17 To . . . alphabet.] Much . . . alphabet, etc. PP 952.7–19
 11.6–10 first . . . first.] *First* . . . successively. PP 966.10–14
 12.12–32 Even . . . plans.] Even . . . ignored. PP 959.6–29.

In the preface to his *Briefer Course*, p. v, James states that "with a single exception all the chapters [of *The Principles of Psychology*] were written for the book; and then by an after-thought some of them were sent to magazines, because the completion of the whole work seemed so distant." The 'single exception' intended was "Brute and Human Intellect," which antedated the signing of the contract for *Principles* on June 12, 1878.

On January 20, 1878, James wrote to W. T. Harris, editor of the *Journal of Speculative Philosophy*, "I will send you in a few days another psychological MS entitled 'On Brute & Human Intellect' which

I hope you may be disposed to publish in your April number. I have written it rather lengthily, intending originally for a more popular channel of publication; but perhaps you may think that the Journal of Speculative Philosophy will suffer no harm by occasionally publishing a popular article" ("Pragmatist to Publisher: Letters of William James to W. T. Harris," ed. Wallace Nethery, *The Personalist*, 49 [Autumn 1968], #4, p. 492, dictated). A postcard of April 18 requests the return of the diagram sheet since James will have the blocks made at his own expense and sent to Harris. Nethery conjectures that Harris had objected to the expense of the illustrations that were to accompany the article (p. 506). Then on June 3, James wrote:

> I regret to be obliged to ask you to return my manuscript on "Brute and Human Intellect." [¶] I have some lecturing engagements which it will be very difficult for me to fill without making use of this and other already prepared manuscripts. [¶] I wished to recall it for this purpose a month ago, but as you had already written me that it should appear in your April number, I refrained, thinking that at so late a moment it might embarrass you to lose so much copy. But as the April number has appeared this morning without it, I can see no impropriety in begging you to forward it to me with the electrotype blocks which you no doubt have already received. [¶] I, of course, will pay express charges. [¶] I am very sorry you should have had so much fruitless trouble with the article but necessity knows no law (#6, pp. 492–493, dictated).

As Nethery remarks, if the purpose of this letter were "to apply a little judicious pressure, it was apparently successful." The article appeared in the July issue.

In bMS Am 1092.9 (4565) is a photostat of "Brute and Human Intellect" with three annotations in an unknown hand although this hand has also written the initials WJ after the annotations. At what date the photostat was made and for what purpose, including the circumstances by which the writer of the annotations received (or copied from another offprint) the information, are equally unknown. It is unfortunate for evidence of authority that *Principles* does not take over any of the passages so that we cannot see what its readings would have been. That the annotator intended to indicate that his notes had James's authority is evidenced by his appending of James's initials. There is also the further fact that in another copy of a reprint of the article in the same file a similar annotation, 'Stop here', is in James's own hand. Given this coincidence and also given the general authority of this file of reprints which came from James's own library, it would seem that the document should be taken seriously as providing us with certain of James's final intentions about the text. The phrase 'Stop here' occurs at the foot of the reprint page 261, which in this edition would come at the end of the paragraph concluding with 'never wonders at it at all.' (26.2). The purpose of this order to stop is uncertain, but the odds may favor the hypothesis that an annotated reprint (in one or more copies) was supposed to serve as outside reading for one of James's courses, and that the student responsibility ended at that point. (This hypothesis may be supported by the fact that reprints of his philosophical articles that had been used for reading in his Philosophy 9 course are preserved.)[1]

The first of the three annotations found in the photostat copy is the word 'oxalic' written in the margin of p. 244 opposite line 8 (8.30), containing in the original the phrase 'citric acid remove ink-spots.' The third comes in line 23 of p. 248 (12.18) in which the text word 'time' is deleted and 'turn' written in the margin and brought in by a guideline as a substitute. In view of this procedure for a true substitute, a question may arise whether 'oxalic' was intended to substitute for 'citric' and the annotator did not observe the deletion. Given the conjectured purpose of this document, or its original, it may seem more likely that 'oxalic' was indeed intended as a substitute instead of a note for an alternative possible reading. It has therefore been taken into the edited text, as has 'turn', which may be thought to be slightly superior in sense to 'time', which is an easy compositorial misreading of 'turn' if that had stood in the manuscript. The second annotation presents a serious problem. On p. 246, in line 17 (10.21) the special small-font italic '*a*' is deleted. This must be an error, for the following 'would be the right character to choose' requires a subject which must be a sign, and the special small-font italic '*a*' is the correct sign in context. The passage, we must note, is corrupt and has been emended in this edition by the necessary insertion of the special small-font italic '*a*' sign in line 13 (10.18) before ', for example,' to make it the subject of 'has no connection with it', which cannot be the predicate for the regular italic '*a*' sign in the first clause. Instead of deleting the special small '*a*' in line 17, therefore, this '*a*' should have been added in line 13 of the article, above. Whether it was James or the copyist who was responsible for the confusion here cannot be known, but confusion there was.

Are We Automata? (1879).

Copy-text: (P24) "Are We Automata?" *Mind*, 4 (January 1879), 1–22 (McD 1879:5).

Direct use was made of this article in *Principles*, Chapter V, "The Automaton-Theory," and in Chapter IX, "The Stream of Thought," in the following areas where record is made of the variants:

39.24–40.11 Mental . . . feared.] *ditto* PP 138.6–30
42.13–43.13 It . . . problem.] But . . . problem. PP 142.27–143.28
46.27–47.18 To . . . it.[6]] To . . . fact.ʌ (*no fn.*) PP 273.29–274.20
48.26–51.27 The . . . on.] *ditto* (the) PP 274.39–277.15
51.35–52.5 We . . . -fish.] We . . . crab! PP 277.22–33
54.15–57.2 That . . . Sense.] Consciousness . . . common-sense. PP 145.7–147.15.

[1] See *Essays in Radical Empiricism* in the Works, pp. 200–203.

Some paraphrases in *Principles* are too scattered and brief to be noted specifically.

The flat statement made in the preface to James's *Briefer Course* that with one exception (presumably "Brute and Human Intellect") all the chapters for *Principles* were written for the book even though printed over the course of years in journals may need some qualification for "Are We Automata?" At least, the origin of the article antedates *Principles* decisively, according to James's own statement made in the first volume (Works, p. 134 [I, 130–131]) that in 1869 when still a medical student he "began to write an essay showing how almost everyone who speculated about brain-processes illicitly interpolated into his account of them links derived from the entirely heterogeneous universe of Feeling. . . . The writing was soon stopped because he [James] perceived that the view which he was upholding against these authors was a pure conception, with no proofs to be adduced of its reality. Later it seemed to him that whatever *proofs* existed really told in favor of their view." A private statement to the same effect was made in a letter of October 21, 1889, to Charles A. Strong: "As for the conscious automaton theory, I excogitated it all by myself, and began to write an article about it (my first) whilst still in Medical School. But I ere long saw grounds to doubt it. . . . I tried to criticize it in an article called 'Are We Automata?' in Volume IV of *Mind*," a letter that then continues with a discussion of some of the article's ideas (Ralph Barton Perry, *The Thought and Character of William James* [Boston: Little, Brown, 1935], II, 26).

On March 11, 1879, James had addressed Shadworth Hodgson and in the course of the letter remarked: "My article in *Mind* was written against the swaggering dogmatism of certain medical materials [*stet*], good friends of mine, here and abroad. I wanted to show them how many empirical facts they had overlooked" (bMS Am 1092.9 [969], dictated to his wife, Alice; hereafter correspondence in the bMS Am 1092.9 series will be identified merely by its letter number). Somewhat earlier, on January 17, 1879, he had written, in another letter dictated to Alice, to his friend J. J. Putnam:

I would say that I did not pretend in my article to say that when things happen by the intermediation of consciousness they do not happen by law. The dynamic feelings which the nerve processes give rise to, and which enter in consciousness into comparison with each other and are selected, may in every instance be fatally selected. All that my article claims is that this additional stratum which complicates the chain of cause and effect also gives it determinations not identical with those which would result if it were left out. If a hydraulic ram be interposed on a water-course, a pendulum and escapement on a *wheel[ab. del.* 'clock']-work the results are altered but still obey the laws of cause and effect. Free-will is in short, no necessary corollary of giving causality to consciousness. My phrase about choosing one's whole character is perfectly consistent with fatalism. I dont see if one has a fatalistic faith how it can ever be driven out, even from applying to the phenomena of consciousness. I equally fail to see on the other hand how free-will faith can be forcibly driven out, but I meant expressly to steer clear of all such complications in my article (Harvard Medical Library, The Francis A. Countway Library of Medicine).

We know from a letter of November 20, 1878, from G. Croom Robertson, the editor of *Mind*, that the article was accepted on that date (#505) and that there was insufficient time for James to be sent proof. On January 24, 1879, after the appearance of the article, Robertson wrote James that he hopes James will "not have been dissatisfied with my way of getting over the appearance of an omission on p. 2. As to your reading of Clifford's so-called argument, since you allow that it was rather a gloss and he disallowed its correctness, it seems fairest to have dropt it" (#506).

THE SPATIAL QUALE (1879).

Copy-text: (P21) "The Spatial Quale," *Journal of Speculative Philosophy*, 13 (January 1879), 64–87 (McD 1879:6).
This article lies in general behind James's "The Perception of Space," *Mind*, 12 (January, April 1887), 1–30, 183–211 (McD 1887:4), but "The Spatial Quale" has transmitted a few passages independently to Chapter XX of *The Principles of Psychology* as follows:

    68.19–23   Let . . . departure.]   If . . . departure. PP 781.35–39
    68.27–69.3   a friend . . . state.ʌ]   A friend . . . state.¹⁰ PP 781.39–782.15
    69.16–70.31   Just . . . results.]   *The* . . . results. PP 810.7–811.22
    71.29–33   If . . . blue,]   If . . . blue. PP 791.34–792.2
    72.34–73.12   even . . . surface.]   *ditto* PP 808.24–33
    72.35–40   ⁸The . . . parallax.]   *ditto* PP 785.17–23
    73.24–28   In . . . intense.]   *ditto* PP 807.21–25
    73.40–74.10   Granted . . . subdivisions.]   *ditto* PP 807.5–15
    75.31–39   Again, . . . withdrawn.]   *The* . . . withdrawn. PP 807.26–32
    80.9–18   excited . . . membrane.]   *ditto* PP 809.16–24.
Substantive variants in *Principles* within the above have been recorded in the Historical Collation. However, three brief passages of paraphrase in *Principles* are not susceptible of such listing:

    64.18–22   The . . . order.]   The . . . other. PP 788.7–11
    67.23–28   The . . . lumbago.³]   We . . . lumbago;ʌ *(no fn.)* PP 776.4–9
    68.5–7   How . . . butterfly.]   The . . . butterfly. PP 781.8–11.
"The Spatial Quale" was written at a time when James was being tempted by expressions of interest from Johns Hopkins and when he was concerned to assure himself of a firmer future at Harvard. A passage from a letter of February 3, 1880, to Josiah Royce helps to explain the curious letter he had written to W. T. Harris on August 10, 1878, when offering the article to Harris' *Journal of Speculative Philosophy*. James wrote to Royce: "I despise my own article, which was dashed off for a momentary purpose and published for another. But I don't see why its

main doctrine, from a psychologic and sublunary point of view, is not sound; and I think I can, if my psychology ever gets writ, set it down in decently clear and orderly form. All *deducers* of space are, I am sure, mythologists" (*The Letters of William James*, ed. Henry James [Boston: Atlantic Monthly Press, 1920], I, 205). His letters to the editor, Harris, went as follows:

> I venture to send you by the same mail another of my lucubrations, suggested this time by Mr. Cabot's article on Space. I have dictated it here in the mountains [Keene Valley, N.Y.] at a distance from all books and have been therefore unable to fill out certain quotations and references. Mr. Cabot's article also I left at home and therefore omitted a page and a half of comment on it which should introduce the article.
> I nevertheless send it to you in this imperfect state, in the hope that you may find it worthy of insertion in the October number and that no time may be lost, should that be the case. I can easily supply the missing passages when the proof is sent me for correction (*Personalist*, #7, p. 493, dictated).

James's anxiety to see the article in print continued. On September 9 he sent Harris a postcard inquiring whether Harris had received "a MS entitled 'The Spatial Quale' which I mailed you some weeks ago" (#8, p. 493, dictated). He then discovered that an appearance would be delayed for several issues:

> On returning from the country I find your communication awaiting me. I confess to a little regret at the postponement of which you speak, but if you can do nothing better, I will of course await the April number. I have a couple of other articles written which I destined for your approval after this one on space should have been accepted. If this don't appear till April, the second one of those can't appear till October. . . . [¶] If you will kindly remand me the Space MS. I will make the necessary additions to it, and keep it for possible use here in lecturing, till such time as you are ready for the printer, when I trust you will let me know (#9, p. 494).

Evidently Harris succumbed to James's blandishments, for James's next letter to him, on October 4, reads, in part: "I thank you very much for your most courteous letter. I should rather have my Space article broken into two parts than have none of it appear before your April number. I accordingly send twenty-five pages of the MS, of which you can print as much as you have room for in your January number, and send me back the remaining sheets with the proof. I will keep them with the rest of the article until the printer again needs them" (#10, p. 494, dictated).

On January 12, 1879, James wrote:

> I have received the proof this morning and send it back corrected and with a small addition. I have lopped off the last two paragraphs, which seem better fitted to begin the second installment than to end the first. I have accordingly prefixed them to the beginning of the remainder of my copy, which I send you by the same mail as this. I don't understand very well what you say of your mistake in calculation. I think you wrote me that you could only give

The Feeling of **

me 10 pages in your January number. If you can now give 17, I should be too glad if the rest of my article would fit into them (#13, pp. 495–496, dictated).

Harris relented enough to furnish the requisite pages for the entire article in the January issue, and on a postcard, dated doubtfully as February 9, 1879, James acknowledged receipt of "your bundle of Journals and sheets, for which many thanks. I am very glad the whole article was printed but regret not having seen the proof of the last half" (#14, p. 496, dictated). This account of the proofreading corrects the blanket statement to Royce in a dictated letter of February 16, 1879, "I will send you a corrected copy of Harris's Journal with my article on Space, which was printed without my seeing the proof" (#3595).

THE FEELING OF EFFORT (1880).

Copy-text: (P42) "The Feeling of Effort," *Anniversary Memoirs of the Boston Society of Natural History* (1880), pp. 3–32 (McD 1880:3). The article was reprinted with some necessary corrections but seemingly without authoritative changes in *Collected Essays and Reviews*, ed. Ralph Barton Perry (New York: Longmans, Green, 1920), pp. 151–219 (McD 1920:2).

In the Widener copy at Harvard (Phil 5300.2A), identified as the "Gift of the author Feb 25, 1881," appear several annotations not in James's hand. The errata corrections are written in at 97.10–11 and at 122.10, and a new correction is made at 104.22. However, in addition a note appears at the foot of the article's p. 14 referring back to 'Hering' and 'both eyes fixate the same objects,' which are underlined. Although not in James's hand, his initials are appended. (For the annotation, see Professor Skrupskelis' Note to 99.40.) These same annotations also appear in the offprint at Houghton (bMS Am 1092.9 [4565]), on the title page of which is the note, "Corrections within are copied from the H. U. Library copy. H. J. Jr 1911." Despite the strange hand in the Widener copy, the initialed note on p. 14 appears to be authoritative, as does the non-errata correction at 104.22.

Direct use was made of this article in *Principles*, Chapter XXVI, "Will":

86.4–36   Plausibility . . . sentience.]   It is . . . sentience. PP 1107.7–1108.26

87.22–88.6   Now what . . . encumbrance.]   For what . . . cues. PP 1109.13–37

88.37–97.38   Whoever . . . right.]   *ditto* PP 1110.22–1112.7, 1113.9–1120.20

98.12–23   It . . . see.]   *ditto* PP 1120.20–1121.10

102.17–103.9   As Lotze . . . action.]   To quote Lotze . . . action." PP 1133.18–29

102.37–45   [23]*Medicinische* . . . generals.]   [34]*Medicinische* . . . generals! PP 1131.33–40

103.9–18   We see . . . thought."ʌ]   "We see . . . thought."³⁴ PP 1131.24–32

104.23–105.23   Now . . . existed.]   *ditto* PP 1112.8–1113.8

106.22–27   "It . . . perspiration.]   "It . . . perspiration." PP 1107.21–26

107.21–108.13   whether . . . passive.³¹]   whether . . . before.⁶¹ PP 1165.6–1166.3

108.20–109.13   We . . . limb."³⁴]   Or we . . . limb."⁴ PP 1101.36–1102.15

110.19–28   Exhausted . . . morning.]   *ditto* PP 1167.37–44

113.25–114.8   "A gentleman . . . *it.*"³⁶]   "A gentleman . . . *it.*"ʌ *(no fn.)* PP 1171.26–44

114.36–115.10   Muscular . . . *real.*]   These feelings . . . *real.* PP 1167.24–33

119.14–120.22   When . . . least.]   *ditto* PP 1154.29–1155.37

120.30–121.2   He . . . *him.*]   He . . . creed. PP 1176.20–31.

Unrecorded distinctive areas of paraphrase occur at:

112.23–29   To the . . . lies.]   The exhausted . . . still. PP 1170.9–16

113.10–24   in the case . . . realities."]   If a patient . . . reality!" PP 1170.19–31.

On November 9, 1880, James addressed William Salter in a dictated letter:

I am very glad my stuff seemed plausible to you, and shall be too proud of a notice from your pen.

The thing was never read, but published in the Memorial volume of the B. S. of N. H., and the separate copies are private reprints, consequently not in the market.

As for free-will, I dont see that the principle of causality is in the least interfered with by it. In the double link between a representation of alternatives and the decision to take one of them, you have more causality than you need. The representation can serve as cause to either *of the [intrl.]* alternative [stet] which it prefigures. Until we know a great deal more about causality than we do we are quite as entitled to call the antecedent in free-will a cause with an excess of possible effects as to call the consequent an effect with an insufficiency of cause. Of what effect a thing shall be the cause is not known until the effect has posited itself. A cause whose possible effects are ambiguous is the cause of either one which may become real.

But to discuss free-will in a note is ridiculous (#3650).

Next year, on December 27, 1881, James thanked Salter for his notice in the *Unitarian Review* (December 1881), 544–551, and in an important comment he altered the import of the statement about M + E > S (see Professor Skrupskelis' Note to 120.13). He then added: "The great Delboeuf has also honored my essay by a review in the *Révue philosophique* for November. He is more polemic than you but between you you 'll make me famous. Seriously, it is a very agreeable sensation to find oneself so earnestly dissected in print, and by such learned hands" (#3654).

Charles Renouvier translated the article as "Le Sentiment de l'effort" in the *Critique Philosophique* starting in September 23, 1880, and ending in November 11. As early as August 21, 1880, James addressed Renouvier from London since he had "just found a copy of my essay on Effort" and sent corrections of the errors on 97.10–11 and 122.10, which were subsequently added as errata in the reprints. He added: "In looking over the essay I am conscious of a good many defects of statement which a less rapid mode of composition would doubtless have improved. I only hope that you & M. Pillon will feel free to render the sense in the easiest and most flowing french, without a too scrupulous fidelity to the words I have used. I think the paper will gain by such treatment" (#3521). From Cambridge on December 27, 1880, he again addressed Renouvier in a dictated letter gracefully thanking him for the translation and confessing that the state of his eyes had prevented him from reading "the whole of your translation of the Feeling of Effort, though the passages I have perused have seemed to me excellently well done. My exposition strikes me as rather complicated now. It was written in great haste and were I to rewrite it, it should be simpler. The omissions of which you speak are of no importance whatever" (#3522).

NOTES ON THE SENSE OF DIZZINESS IN DEAF-MUTES (1881).

Copy-text: (P15) *Harvard University Bulletin*, 2 (1881), 173 (McD 1881: 2).

Perhaps as a result of James having sent a clipping to G. Croom Robertson, the editor, the "Notes" were reprinted verbatim under "Notes and Discussions" in *Mind*, 6 (July 1881), 412–413, with the heading "Sense of Dizziness in Deaf-Mutes" and the introduction 'Professor WILLIAM JAMES has the following Note in the *Harvard University Bulletin* No. 18 (1881):—'.

THE SENSE OF DIZZINESS IN DEAF-MUTES (1882).

Copy-text: (P2) "The Sense of Dizziness in Deaf-Mutes," *American Journal of Otology*, 4 (October 1882), 239–254 (McD 1882:3).

As remarked by Professor Skrupskelis in his Notes to this article, James had been investigating the subject of vertigo for several years and had spoken on the subject in 1876 and 1879. As a consequence of his reprinting James's 1881 "Notes," G. Croom Robertson, the editor of *Mind*, wrote him on July 24, 1882: "Has anything more come of your Expᵗˢ with deaf-mutes? They promised a really definite result" (#510).

The article was reprinted in *Collected Essays and Reviews*, ed. R. B. Perry, pp. 220–243 (McD 1920:2). The few variants appear to have no authority.

On Some Omissions of Introspective Psychology *(1884).*

Copy-text: (P24) "On Some Omissions of Introspective Psychology," *Mind*, 9 (January 1884), 1–26 (McD 1884:1).

"On Some Omissions" was extensively drawn on in *The Principles of Psychology*, Chapter VII, "The Methods and Snares of Psychology," Chapter IX, "The Stream of Thought," and Chapter XII, "Conception."

142.18–143.22   And . . . consciousness."ʌ]   And . . . consciousness."[9] PP 189.24–190.17
143.28–144.38   When . . . stream.]   As . . . stream. PP 236.15–237.24
146.17–147.6   On . . . on.]   There . . . on. PP 238.16–239.7
153.2–21   Some . . . brain?]   Ever . . . brain? PP 229.4–20
153.22–32   As . . . feel.ʌ]   And . . . feel.[9] PP 228.30–229.3
154.6–158.30   Suppose . . . be.]   *ditto* PP 243.1–247.23
159.10–160.3,8–48   Now . . . contempt.]   "Why . . . contempt." PP 451.35–453.33–38 *(fn.* 17)
161.7–19   When . . . thought.]   Usually . . . thought. PP 253.21–32
164.4–22   The . . . meaning.]   But . . . meaning. PP 265.28–266.6.

According to R. B. Perry, the ideas that were to compose "On Some Omissions" were first delivered in London on February 9, 1883, at a meeting at Carveth Read's house. The next day James wrote to his wife: "Yesterday I was parturient of psychological truth, being in one of my fevered states you woṭ of, when ideas are shooting together and I can think of no finite things. I wrote a lot at headlong speed, and in the evening, having been appointed, gave an account of it—the difference between feeling and thought—at the Scratch Eight. . . . I am sure the things I said were highly important scientifically."[2] On May 2, 1883, James dictated a letter to Thomas Davidson in which he remarked: "I have half engaged to give some lectures at the Concord School—Jonah among the prophets. [¶] I send you a bill of fare which may interest you. My own subject must be something in the way of an analysis of consciousness into its factors, object, ego, and stream of feelings, but my own thoughts are all muddled and clotted, and if I can't work them into lecturable shape, it is agreed that I shall back out" (#850). After delivery, he wrote again to Davidson, on August 2, 1883:

I scraped through 3 lectures there [at Concord] myself after a fashion, "on some Omissions of Introspective psychology" *of [ab. del. 'the'] which I afterwards wrote down the substance, ['of,' del.] and send [stet] it to Mind, where I hope it may gain your assent,—at any rate your interest. I have been for the past three months in better working trim than for years back at this season— the result apparently of my long immersion in London smoke—and hoped to

2 This passage is reprinted in Perry, *Thought and Character*, II, 38. On p. 39 Perry links the talk to "On Some Omissions." The same talk is apparently referred to a year later on February 14, 1884, in a letter from Shadworth Hodgson to James (I, 625).

give at Concord 3 lectures on "Cognition." But after pegging away at the subject for many weeks I threw up the sponge and confessed myself beaten, and fell back on this more modest task (#851).[3]

The day before he had written to his brother Henry that "t'is a solid comfort to have so unexpectedly got off an article for Mind" (#2612).

More detail comes in a letter of August 5 to Charles Renouvier:

> The most rapid piece of literary work I *ever ['ev' ov. 'di'] did was completed 10 days ago, and sent to *Mind* where it will doubtless soon appear. I had promised to give three lectures at a rather absurd little "Summer School of Philosophy" which has flourished for 4 or 5 years past in the little town of Concord, near Boston, and which has an audience of from 20 to 50 persons, including the lecturers themselves,—&, finding at the last moment that I could do nothing with my much meditated subject of the Object and the Ego, I turned round and lectured "*on some omissions in Introspective Psychology*," and wrote the *substance of the [intrl.] lectures out immediately after giving them—the whole occupying 6 days (#3529).

Finally, on August 6 James remarked to Howison, "I've written off the substance of my lectures after delivery & *sent ['t' ov. 'd'] it to 'Mind' " (#1026).

Shadworth Hodgson wrote to James on February 14, 1884, shortly after publication to congratulate him on the article and to defend his own theories against what he regarded as James's misunderstanding (#195). On September 30, 1884, in a dictated letter to Renouvier James defended himself to Renouvier:

> I don't wish to inflict upon you a defense of all my heresies, so in reply to your ['question' del.] criticism of my Introspective Psychology article I will only say one thing. You accuse me of bringing *To apeiron* into the mind, whose functions are essentially discrete. The categoric concepts you speak of are concepts of *objects*. Any given state of consciousness which we make into an object by reflection, appears to us as a discrete object,—hence the English psychology of "ideas" and their association. But before it is reflected on, consciousness is *felt*, and as such is continuous, that is, it potentially allows us to make sections anywhere in it, and treat the included portion as a unit. It is continuous as space and time are. And I am willing to admit that it is not a *chose en soi*, for this reason, if you like, any more than they. But as *we [ab. del. 'you'] divide *them* arbitrarily, so I say our divisions of consciousness are arbitrary results of conceptual handling of it on our part. The ordinary psychology, on the contrary, insists that it is naturally discrete and that the divisions *belong* in certain places. This seems to me like saying that space exists in cubes or pyramids, apart from our construction (#3530).

---

[3] Earlier in the letter to Renouvier quoted below, James confessed: "I floundered round in the morasses of the theory of cognition,—the Object & the Ego,—tore up almost each day what I had written the day before, and altho I am inwardly of course more aware than I was before of where the difficulties of the subject lie, outwardly I have hardly any manuscript to show for my pains" (#3529).

The Text of Essays in Psychology

WHAT IS AN EMOTION? (1884).

Copy-text: (P24) "What Is an Emotion?" *Mind*, 9 (April 1884), 188–205 (McD 1884:2).

"What Is an Emotion?" was extensively drawn on in *The Principles of Psychology*, Chapter XXV, "The Emotions."

  170.8–31 Our . . . truth.] *ditto* PP 1065.27–1066.12

  172.28–175.6 And the . . . ago.] The various . . . ago. PP 1066.18–1068.26

  176.21–178.3 But now . . . suppose.] Let me now . . . suppose. PP 1072.2–1073.32

  178.4–32 If our theory . . . thaw!] *ditto* PP 1077.9–1078.6

  178.33–179.8 The great . . . proceeds.] It is true . . . proceeds. PP 1081.24–38

  179.17–25 work . . . brain.³] work . . . brain.ₐ (*no fn.*) PP 1080.34–1081.16

  179.26–180.16 The last . . . depart.⁴] One of . . . depart.¹¹ PP 1073.35–1074.22

  181.28–184.20 If our . . . exist.] *ditto* PP 1082.1–1087.31.

A paraphrased passage occurs at:

  179.35–41 ³This . . . decision.] In . . . child. PP 1081.16–24.

In a letter to Thomas Davidson dated December 20, 1883, James remarked, "I sent off to day a sort of a squib to *Mind* ['M' ov. 'm'], to prove that we are sorry because we cry, angry because we strike etc, instead of vice versa" (#853). In return, on January 28, 1884, the editor G. Croom Robertson accepted it, along with "Absolutism and Empiricism," and encouraged James: "Your *Schlagfertigkeit* is altogether admirable, and if, besides the positive value of the stroke (which in this case I think not little), it means that you feel yourself in the best of intellectual trims, I rejoice in it" (#515). On September 11, 1884, Charles Renouvier wrote James to thank him for an offprint and intimated that "I am sorry that you have not made your thought clearer and more complete, at least for me, by developing the ideas of general teleology and of reflex psychical action which, unless I am mistaken, I suppose you to hold. Limiting myself to what you explicitly set forth, I cannot understand how emotion as such and specifically, can consist in a physical, mechanical impression with which it has by definition no kinship,—or be a way of translating the perception we have of that impression. When I try to grasp what this means I am forced back to the principle of former theories such as Cartesian occasionalism, for I cannot rationally think that *fear*, for example, *is* the perception of a certain molecular vibration" (*Thought and Character*, I, 696–697). To this James responded on September 30 (dictated):

I am truly sorry, but not greatly surprised at your not agreeing to *the [intrl.] doctrines I propose. From what you say I fear you may not have caught the precise meaning of my Emotion theory. I don't mean that the Emotion is the *perception* of ['th' *del.*] bodily changes *as such*, but only that the bodily changes give us a feeling, which is the Emotion. We can, it is true, partly analyze this feeling; if we could totally analyze it into local bodily feelings its emotional character would probably change. After all, what my theory has in view is only ['an attempt to' *del.*] the determination of the particular nerve process which emotion accompanies. We are bound to suppose that there is *some* such nerve process accompanying every emotion. Now all I say is that the nerve process is the incoming currents, produced by the reflex movements which the perception of the exciting cause engenders. I feel sure that some part of our emotions is covered by this account; whether the *whole* of them is so covered is a question about which I am still doubtful (#3530).

The essay was reprinted without any authoritative changes in *Collected Essays and Reviews*, ed. R. B. Perry, pp. 244–275 (McD 1920:2).

THE LATEST CURE FOR SEA-SICKNESS (1884).

Copy-text: (P27a) "The Latest Cure for Sea-Sickness," *Pall Mall Budget*, October 3, 1884, p. 26 (McD 1884:6). This letter to the editor, subscribed on September 11, was printed under the heading "Correspondence."

REPORT OF THE COMMITTEE ON HYPNOTISM (1886).

Copy-text: (P31) "Report of the Committee on Hypnotism," *Proceedings of the American Society for Psychical Research*, 1 (July 1886), 95–102 (McD 1886:1).

The Report was drawn on in *The Principles of Psychology*, Chapter XXVII, "Hypnotism," and Chapter XXII, "Reasoning."

191.17–192.29 Make . . . aware.] *ditto* PP 1207.1–1208.3
194.5–195.20 If a . . . sagacity.] *ditto* PP 975.22–976.36 (*part of fn. 16*).

In his Note to 190.2 Professor Skrupskelis observes that James made an initial report to the Society on January 12, 1886, but the published Report appears to represent the statement made by James and Gouverneur M. Carnochan to the Society on June 15, 1886. James's general feelings about his concern with psychical research are reflected in a letter of August 29, 1886, to G. Croom Robertson:

I have wasted a good deal of time on "Psychical Research" during the past year, and Gurney and I have scribbled a number of notes to each other in consequence. "Two lost souls!" you will say—but that is what remains to be seen. Our poor little "Society' will very likely break down for lack of a Gurney or a Myers to devote time to it. But I feel quite convinced at the end of my year's work, such as it has been, that *this sort of work [*ab. del.* 'it'] is as worthy a specialty as a man could take up,—only it *is* a specialty, demanding an enormous sacrifice of time, and in which amateurs will be as inferior to experts as they are in most other departments of experience. Believing this, I shall probably give very little time to it next year, because at the utmost I should be a dabbler and amateur. I wish that by giving up this, I might get ahead with writing, but I'm once for all a lame duck, and might as well accept it. The moment I get interested in anything, bang goes my sleep, and I have to stop for *10 [*ov.* 'a'] days or a fortnight, till everything has grown cold *again, [*comma ov. period*] *and the mood is off. [*intrl.*] One makes very slow progress at that rate (#3538).

A SUGGESTION FOR THE PREVENTION OF SEA-SICKNESS (1887).

Copy-text: (P8) "A Suggestion for the Prevention of Sea-Sickness" printed in the Correspondence section of the *Boston Medical and Surgical Journal,* 116 (May 19, 1887), 490–491 (McD 1887:7).

REACTION-TIME IN THE HYPNOTIC TRANCE (1887).

Copy-text: (P31) "Reaction-Time in the Hypnotic Trance," *Proceedings of the American Society for Psychical Research,* 1 (December 1887), 246–248 (McD 1887:9).

THE CONSCIOUSNESS OF LOST LIMBS (1887).

Copy-text: (P31) "The Consciousness of Lost Limbs," *Proceedings of the American Society for Psychical Research,* 1 (December 1887), 249–258 (McD 1887:10). The article was reprinted without authoritative variation by R. B. Perry, *Collected Essays and Reviews,* pp. 285–302 (McD 1920:2).

As recorded by Professor Skrupskelis (Note to 204.1) the study stemmed from a paper "Sensations from Amputated Limbs" that James read before the Society on January 11, 1887. A questionnaire and a set of responses on which James based his study are preserved in the Houghton Library at Harvard (bMS Am 1092.9 [4566]). For convenience this questionnaire is reprinted as Appendix II. On February 25, 1885, James wrote to F. W. H. Myers: "A year ago I sent out some 300 circulars to ask people with amputated legs about the manner in which they felt them. A number of answers told *circumstantially [*intrl. without caret*] of miraculous awareness of the bent position, cold situation etc of the recently cut off limb, which only disappeared when the actual severed member was put to rights again. I smiled at these cases of traditional folk-lore perpetuating itself. But in issuing a new edition of the circular *now, [*intrl.*] I feel in duty bound to insert a special question *ad hoc,* lest there should be 'something in it after all' " (#3306).

The passage "Either . . . limb." (211.31–41) is quoted without substantive change in a footnote in *The Principles of Psychology,* Chapter XIX, "The Perception of 'Things,' " 749.30–40.

WHAT THE WILL EFFECTS (1888).

Copy-text: (P37) "What the Will Effects," *Scribner's Magazine,* 3 (February 1888), 240–250 (McD 1888:1).

Direct use was made of this article in *Principles*, Chapter XXVI, "Will":

217.39–218.3   The other . . . face.]   *ditto* PP 1099.13–17
218.16–21   I . . . before.]   *ditto* PP 1099.17–22
220.12–18   Whilst . . . them.]   *ditto* PP 1131.6–12
220.25–221.10   We . . . volition.]   *ditto* PP 1132.23–1133.9
222.29–223.17   Either . . . kind.]   *ditto* PP 1135.14–39
226.30–228.19   Certainly . . . movements.]   Certainly . . . instance.
PP 1167.5–1169.14
230.30–231.12   The effort . . . impossible.]   It certainly . . . impossible. PP 1175.13–34.
Paraphrases of more or less closeness may be found as follows:
220.6–12   Dr. . . . these.]   Dr. . . . disguise. PP 1131.2–6
220.19–24   So far . . . there.]   My dinner . . . acts. PP 1131.13–20
224.22–225.4   Ask . . . say.]   *ditto* PP 1147.32–41
233.40–234.5   And . . . edge.]   *ditto* PP 1181.36–40
234.10–14   Ever . . . divine.]   The prophet . . . own. PP 1182.5–8.

Renouvier wrote to James on March 12, 1888, thanking him for a copy of "What the Will Effects" and asking permission to translate it for the *Critique Philosophique* (#502). James replied on March 29: "Of course it will only put me under still farther obligations to you, if you see fit to translate my article on 'What the Will Effects.' It amounts to little more than what you said long ago in your Psychologie Rationelle. But it is in popular form, and it has surprised me to find how many persons here have read it and been struck by it. It has been mentioned to me by readers, more, I think, than all my other articles put together. The publisher has no international rights. . . . I groan under an excessive number of different duties, very small power of work, and excessively slow literary composition. You would hardly credit it as possible were I to tell you of the number of weeks it took me to write that Scribner article or of the number of pages of 'copy' that went into the wastepaper-basket, for every page that survived" (#3531).

RÉPONSE DE M. W. JAMES AUX REMARQUES DE M. RENOUVIER, SUR SA THÉORIE DE LA VOLONTÉ (1888).

Copy text: (P9) "Réponse de M. W. James aux remarques de M. Renouvier, sur sa théorie de la volonté," *Critique Philosophique*, n.s., 4th year, 2 (December 1888), 401–404 (McD 1888:2).

On March 12, 1888, Renouvier thanked James for a copy of "What the Will Effects" and asked permission to translate it (#502). James gave his ready assent on March 29 (#3531), and the translation appeared in due course in the *Critique Philosophique*, n.s., 4th year, 1 (June 1888), 401–420, entitled "Ce que fait la volonté." Renouvier wrote to James on August 7 (in Perry's translation, *Thought and Character*, I, 707): "I have surrendered to you, in the *Critique philosophique*, 'the honors' of the number. But I did not surrender the privilege of making observations, and in part objections, of my own to your theory of *will*, which is in agreement with mine on the essential point, but not throughout. I have therefore kept my remarks and reservations for another number. You will find them in the next one, the one that comes out at the end of the month. I ask your reflection on them, and, if need be, your indulgence. If our way of understanding the *will* could become general, do you know that it would be the greatest revolution in philosophy since Anaxagoras, Socrates and Pyrrho? But it will not become general because to console himself for his evil-doing, man *wishes* to believe that something rules him: *volentem ducunt"* (French original in #503). Renouvier's objections were printed as "Quelques remarques sur la théorie de la volonté, de M. W. James," *Critique Philosophique*, n.s., 4th year, 2 (August 31, 1888), 117–126, and he also added after James's "Réponse" further comments in "Quelques mots sur la lettre qui précède" (pp. 404–406).

The "Réponse" was reprinted without authoritative change in *Collected Essays and Reviews*, ed. R. B. Perry, pp. 303–309 (McD 1920:2).

"THE PSYCHOLOGICAL THEORY OF EXTENSION" (1889).

Copy-text: (P24) " 'The Psychological Theory of Extension,' " *Mind*, 14 (January 1889), 107–109 (McD 1889:1). The article was reprinted without authoritative change by R. B. Perry in *Collected Essays and Reviews*, pp. 310–315 (McD 1920:2).

" 'The Psychological Theory of Extension' " is in the nature of a reply to G. Croom Robertson's criticism in *Mind*, July 1888, of James's article "The Perception of Space," in four installments, in *Mind*, 12 (January, April, July, October 1887), for which see *The Principles of Psychology* and its apparatus in the WORKS. For additional information see Professor Skrupskelis' Note to 239.2.

The preserved correspondence between Robertson and James is worth quoting in full because of its explication of James's ideas. After acknowledging receipt of the offprints of his Space article and commiserating on the state of Robertson's health in a letter of November 9, 1887, James continues:

The saddest blow I've received is *your* sententious and obdurate refusal [in correspondence] to be converted by my space views! Two friends have written me words of adhesion to the first of the four articles—one of them no less a personage that [*stet*] Hodgson. One has praised the whole lot. *Three eulogists [*ab. del.* 'Four [*ov.* 'Five'] critics'] in all—nay *four [*ov.* 'five']—for Royce also read and praised the first article. But what are the four against the still outstanding *one*, who wont even tell me *which* are the points to be condemned? Pray don't think I wish to challenge you to set to work and specify. To tell the sober truth about the matter, I fancy I have done all about space that my poor powers are capable of, in that little essay. Now that *I [*ov.* 'h'] have "extradited" it, I feel no longer any personal connexion with it, and am willing to let it drift and take its chances in the ['ocean of' *del.*] literary *Ocean ['O' *ov.*

'o']. If it have merit it will probably float. If it sink 'tis that it will deserve to. And others may see to it if they will (#3547).

When James received his copy of Robertson's article in *Mind* he contented himself at first with raising objections in a letter to Robertson of August 22, 1888:

Of course you have respect enough for the genuineness of fibre of my philosophic character to know in advance that I ['will be' *del.*] shall oppose steadfast resistance to your opinions, clear as is their expression, and reasonable as is their tone! Seriously speaking, ['however,' *del.*] it seems to me that you have made *such [*intrl.*] concessions, and *zugespitzt* the question so, that the issue is now very narrow and distinct, and I don't see how it can help being decided in *my* way, when once thus stated. For either this sense of a resisting object is of a *big* object or not; and if of a big object, then my contention is ['all' *del.*] granted *as to the "muscular sense"— [*intrl.*] only the question comes, why the deuce are our muscles the only sense-organs whose objects are big?—a question not easy to answer either a priori or a posteriori, methinks. But if this resisting "base" of objectivity, be *not* itself immediately given as big, I'm blest if I can see how "intensive time-clusters" can "take on the new character" of bigness by being "experienced in connexion with" it. In short it is the old dilemma *back [*intrl.*] again: Either space is given immediately, or it is made by the mind. If given it must be given in some sensation. If made it must be made out of non-spatial elements. *In abstracto* you seem to relinquish this *latter [*ov.* 'last'] idea. But *in concreto*, you retain it.—I'm not sure that we mean the same thing by the 'Kantian' view. *I* mean the doctrine of a *supersensational ['atio' *ov.* 'itive'] construction. For Kant there is a non-spatial *sensational [*intrl.*] chaos before there is space in the mind. For me there is no mental object not already spatial. I don't know what you mean by *supposing ['s' *ov.* 'a'] us to have in mind an "extension that is extension of nothing at all," when we ['suppo' *del.*] assume experience of *non [*alt. fr.* 'not'] resistant extension. Experiences of colours are not of nothing at all. Insects crawling over the skin *do [*ov.* 'are'] not give a feeling of nothing at all, etc etc. These *experiences [*intrl.*] seem to me to have just as much and just as little of space in them as our experiences of resistance. And have you tho't how queer it is on your view that our experiences of resistance, if they are the "psychological ['p' *del.*] basis" of our space-perception, should be among the least spatially *discriminative* of all our experiences?—Lastly as to to [*stet*] your last *(1/2) [*insrtd.*] page— thanks for the concession to the eye! I also concede that in the concrete individual all these experiences come ['abreast,' *del.*] abreast [*insrtd. for del. insrtd.* 'abreast'] and are inextricably entwined. In a sense the tactile ones are "basal," i.e. we choose them as the *reals*—but if you have ever seen a blind ['man' *del.*] man (as I have) trying to tell *with his fingers [*intrl.*] which of two angles cut out of pasteboard *is [*ab. del.* 'was'] the larger etc, and compared ['the slowl' *del.*] his slowness and inaccuracy with the instantaneous certainty of the eye dealing with the same objects, I don't see how you *can [*ab. del.* 'could'] doubt the entire *independence* of our ['the' *del.*] eye-space-measurements of those of touch. . . . But hold! enough! I didn't mean to reopen a controversy of *the subject of [*intrl.*] which I'm already pretty sick, and I hope you wont have the burden laid upon you, either by the pugnacious instinct or anything else, of issuing a rejoinder. ['I' *del.*] If you do, however, I promise you it shall be the last word. I ought, [*comma insrtd. and* 'properly to have' *del.*] out of proper

409

respect *for [*ov.* 'to'] you, to have replied in the pages of Mind; and I doubt-less should have managed to do so if I had had sight our [*stet*] your article in time. But now it is too late, and you'll doubtless excuse the dereliction. I have written what precedes so rapidly that I'm afraid you may find it far from clear (#3548).

However, James ultimately changed his mind as a result of further discussion, as shown by the letter to Robertson of October 7 that seems to have accompanied the manuscript of the present article. "Here goes at you with as fatal a series of remarks as I could muster! Why couldn't you let me lie in *peace? ['ea' *ov.* 'ie'; *qst. mk. ov. comma*] I should so gladly have forgotten space and all its contents, and *left [*alt. fr.* 'let'] my articles *as [*ab. del.* 'become'] a prey to the wolves and the ravening vultures, without stirring a finger in *their [*ab. del.* 'its'] defense. [*doubtful* 'Iv' *del.*] I '*spise* the subject, now that I've said my say about it, and *verily ['il' *ov.* 'y'] fear (so quickly reached are the limits of our mental growth) that I am incapable of learning anything more about it than I have there expressed. You shall have your fling hereafter all over it, with never another word of objection from me. . . . But I must stop! I've been all day at this sorry performance, and must send the MS. as it is without copying or more revision" (#3549).

REPORT ON THE CONGRESS OF PHYSIOLOGICAL PSYCHOLOGY AT PARIS (1889).

Copy-text: (P24) "The Congress of Physiological Psychology at Paris," *Mind*, 14 (October 1889), 614–615 (McD 1889:5).
    In *Mind*, 14 (July 1889), 471, was printed the notice:

An International Congress of Physiological Psychology will be held, in con-nexion with the Paris Exhibition, from the 5th to the 10th of August, under the presidency of M. Charcot. The main heads of the program are—Muscular Sense; the part played by Movements in the formation of Images; whether At-tention is always determined by Emotion; Statistics of Hallucinations; the Appetites of Idiots and Imbeciles; whether in Lunatics there are Motor Im-pulses apart from Images and Ideas; Mental Poisons; Heredity; Hypnotism.

On August 15, a few days after the close, James wrote from Liverpool to Karl Stumpf: "The Congress in Paris was delightful. I have written a very short account of it for Mind (not entering into details) which you will see, so I say nothing of it now, except this, that the courtesy of the *Frenchmen [²'e' *ov.* 'a'] was beyond all praise, and that the sight of 120 men all actively interested in psychology has made me feel much ['more' *del.*] less lonely in the world and ready to finish my *book [*ab. del.* 'psychology'] this year with a great deal more *entrain*. *A [*ov.* 'I'] book hanging on so long on one's hands at last gets outgrown, and even disgusting to me. The Congress has remedied that" (#3783).

Notes on Ansel Bourne

THE HIDDEN SELF (1890).

Copy-text: (P37) "The Hidden Self," *Scribner's Magazine*, 7 (March 1890), 361–373 (McD 1890:1).

Direct use was made of this article in *The Principles of Psychology*, Chapter VIII, "The Relations of Minds to Other Things," and Chapter X, "The Consciousness of Self":

251.1–22   One . . . disturbed.]   *ditto* PP 200.9–29
252.1–10   When . . . auditors.]   When . . . auditors." PP 201.15–24
252.16–26   The . . . sensibility]   These . . . sensibility PP 200.30–201.2
252.30–254.9   One . . . back.]   But one . . . back. PP 364.1–365.17
255.29–257.32   The result . . . master."]   *ditto* PP 365.19–367.23
259.15–265.18   This proof . . . fact.]   This *proof* . . . fact. PP 202.1–208.9.

Extensive use was also made in "What Psychical Research Has Accomplished" in *The Will to Believe* (1897). The page-line references are to the edition of *The Will to Believe* in the WORKS (1979):

247.1–249.37   "The great . . . conclusion.]   *ditto* WB 222.1–225.2.

NOTES ON ANSEL BOURNE (1891).

Copy-text: (P32) "A Case of Double Consciousness," by Richard Hodgson, *Proceedings of the (English) Society for Psychical Research*, 7 (July 1891), 221–257 (not noted by McD but assigned as 1891:6). James's "Notes" appear on pp. 254–255 under the heading "Notes by Professor Wm. James, M.D."

The circumstances of the investigation into Ansel Bourne are detailed in Professor Skrupskelis' Note for 269.2. A few comments are preserved in James's letters to his wife, Alice. In the first, on May 17, headed 7:50 p.m., in the midst of news he merely remarks, "Wrote hard pretty much all day [on *Principles*], lectured on Ansel Bourne, etc." (*Letters*, I, 294). In the second, which seems to have been written on May 28, headed "Wednesday 4.15," James writes that "Ansel B. has told us all about his escapade—in the ordinary trance, too. A grand success! It is to continue tomorrow, and will doubtless be more complete" (#1722). On May 29 he starts: "4 hours of Ansel Bourne . . . . The case does n't develope. It is just a split off dejected tired fragment of Ansel Bourne calling itself Brown and remembering nothing either before or after the Norristown escapade. I think we shall get through with him tomorrow, for the present" (#1723). Finally, on May 30, at 5:30 p.m. James wrote: "Four hours with Ansel Bourne. He does n't develope at all; but I had he [*stet*] skin, eyes, ears etc examined in trance and out of trance by specialists, so as to ascertain all that can be ascertained, and to morrow shall bid him farewell" (#1724).

The Text of Essays in Psychology

A PLEA FOR PSYCHOLOGY AS A 'NATURAL SCIENCE' (1892).

Copy-text: (P28) "A Plea for Psychology as a 'Natural Science,' " *Philosophical Review*, 1 (March 1892), 146–153 (McD 1892:4). The essay was reprinted without authoritative alteration by R. B. Perry in *Collected Essays and Reviews*, pp. 316–327 (McD 1920:2). For the occasion of this article, see Professor Skrupskelis' Note to 270.1 and Perry, *Thought and Character*, II, 119 ff.

THOUGHT BEFORE LANGUAGE: A DEAF-MUTE'S RECOLLECTIONS (1892).

Copy-text: (P28) "Thought Before Language: A Deaf-Mute's Recollections," *Philosophical Review*, 1 (November 1892), 613–624 (McD 1892: 5). The copy in the offprint file at Houghton (bMS Am 1092.9 [4565]) has a pencilled 'omit' in the right margin of footnote 1 opposite "I place implicit confidence in his" | at 278.23, and also in the left margin of footnote 2 opposite "At that time I wrote | out many pages of his story, but this account, with a good deal of other material," | at 279.31–32. The hand is probably not James's and the purpose is somewhat obscure except for the possibility that these are notes made by Perry or Henry James, Jr., with a view to a posthumous collection that never took place.

On December 28, 1891, James wrote to Jacob Gould Schurman, editor of the *Review*: "On setting to work at the deaf-mute article I find myself confronted by the fact that my informant's ['letter' *del.*] narrative covers 15 pp. like those of the sheet enclosed, all written on both sides. If you can get your printer to print from such copy, it will very much facilitate matters. Other wise the odd pages will have to be copied. I hate either to do it or to pay for it myself. So I *write ['wr' *ov.* 'as'] to ask you, first, if it be neccessary [*stet*]; and second ['can't the Review do, if so?' *del.*] if it is so, whether the Review can't have it done, either here or at Ithaca. [¶] Pray let me know, re-enclosing the sheet, and I will finish up my part of the article" (#3708). A problem arose in connection with this letter, as indicated by another from James to Schurman dated January 14, 1892: "The loss of my letter is a serious matter, as I don't know how easily my *deaf & dumb [*ab. del.* 'blind'] man can repair the two lost sheets of his text. . . . . . . Put not your trust in the son's [*stet*] of men! A sudden inspiration seizes me. I look in the drawer where the rest of the deaf & dumb MS. lies . . . and *ecco!* the letter sealed, but unmailed, and the U.S.P.O. exonerated. It goes by the same mail as this, and I trust that your printers can use this copy direct" (#3709). This correspondence involves d'Estrella's letter to James 281.23–289.24, but the resolution of what was to constitute printer's copy is not recorded.

Its problem continued, however. James wrote Schurman on May 18, 1892: "Your card is received. As I sail on the 25th, ['I suppose t' *del.*] and as Mr. d'Estrella's contribution is the really important part of that article, I suppose that he had better see the proof. His address is T. H.

d'Es['trella' *del.*]trella, Institution for the Deaf and Dumb, Berkeley, Cal. The only thing I am afraid of is that with some kind friend's assistance he may purge all the naiveté out of his narrative and so deprive ['of' *del.*] it of its extraordinary charm. If you fear this, don't send it, but correct the proof ultra-carefully yourself. [¶] In any case, the *check for payment should be sent to him*, with several copies of the magazine" (#3712). From Lausanne on July 27 he remarked, "I trust that d'Estrella didn't emasculate or sophisticate his invaluable contribution, which I suppose comes out in ['this month's numb' *del.*] the August number" (#3713). Finally, on November 21 from Florence James begins a postcard to Schurman by: "I hope you ordered the fee for the article in Nov. No[.] about deaf-mute sent to *Th [*intrl.*] d'Estrella California Institution for Deaf & Dumb, Berkeley Cal., as ['I' *del.*] I asked you in the Spring. It reads delectably, I think" (Department of Manuscripts and University Archives, Cornell University).

THE ORIGINAL DATUM OF SPACE-CONSCIOUSNESS (1893).

Copy-text: (P24) "The Original Datum of Space-Consciousness," *Mind*, n.s. 2 (July 1893), 363–365 (McD 1893:1). The article was reprinted without authoritative change in *Collected Essays and Reviews*, ed. R. B. Perry, pp. 328–332 (McD 1920:2).

PROFESSOR WUNDT AND FEELINGS OF INNERVATION (1894).

Copy-text: (P34) "Professor Wundt and Feelings of Innervation," *Psychological Review*, 1 (January 1894), 70–73 (McD 1894:1), under the heading "Discussion."
   In two letters to E. B. Titchener, dated respectively January 3 and February 1, 1892, James writes frankly about his opinions of Wundt and Münsterberg on the subjects later to be treated in this article (Department of Manuscripts and University Archives, Cornell University). In the first, he remarks: "I wish I were 20 years younger and had the advantages of you fellows! I am an 'autodidact' in psychology, ['and' *del.*] have no native aptitude for experimental work, and *began [*poss.* 'begin'] to be responsible for a labortory [*stet*] at the age of nearly 50— a bad combination!"

THE PHYSICAL BASIS OF EMOTION (1894).

Copy-text: (P34) "The Physical Basis of Emotion," *Psychological Review*, 1 (September 1894), 516–529 (McD 1894:2), under the heading "Discussion." The article was reprinted without authoritative change by R. B. Perry in *Collected Essays and Reviews*, pp. 346–370 (McD 1920: 2).
   James wrote from Chocorua on July 5, 1894, to George M. Stratton, who had sublet his Cambridge house:

You will find an interleaved copy of my psychology in 4 bound volumes, *in the **shelves [*alt. fr.* 'shelf'] [*intrl.*] at the left of my big writing table. In (I think) the 3rd vol. is the Chapter on Emotions. Either near its beginning or end is a leaf with *a manuscript [*intrl.*] reference or quotation from Dr W. L. Worcester and another medical man, about anaesthetic patients in whom all the emotions seemed preserved. Will you kindly ['tear out the leaf and send it to me, but before doing so' *del.*] notice the reference (possibly elsewhere) to a number of the Open Court in wh. Dr W. has made these statements, either 1892 or 1893. If not in the larger Psychol., it may possibly be found in the smaller one (Chap on Emotion) which is on the west wall of the library about level with your eyes. Or you might, by looking over the numbers of the Open Court behind the leather sofa in the library, discover Dr W's article itself. *Pray send it to me* by mail. There is wrapping paper in the compartment at the base of the bookcase behind the Japanese screen, and some five cent stamps left in the little Japanese metal box on the library table (Bancroft Library, University of California at Berkeley).

The next day, July 6, another letter was sent off to Stratton: "Two more chores, if you can stand it! Perhaps the fair fingers of Mrs. Stratton will wrap up the book? [¶] It is Lehmann's Hauptgesetze des Gefühlsleben's, which I find I need. It *ought* to be in the region of bookshelves just above the leather sofa. It is a rather slim octavo, bound in ['brow' *del.*] darkish cloth (brown or maroon). If you don't find it thereabouts, don't waste time in looking for it, but let me know, and I will send for the library copy. My own copy has notes in it, which I can use" (Bancroft).

The occasion for these requests was certainly "The Physical Basis of Emotion," as suggested by a letter of July 8 to J. Mark Baldwin: "I am glad you are working on the question of emotional expression. I am just writing a discussion on Wundt's, Lehman[n]'s, Iron's[,] Solber's [i.e., Sollier's] comments on Lange's and my theory" (typed copy, Harvard bMS Am 1092.1). The article was finished and sent off on July 14, 1894, as indicated by another letter to Baldwin: "[James McKeen] Cattell writes me that he is now going to visit you so I address my contribution to the September P. R. direct to you, though I suppose it is still poor C's duty to look after it. I hope that it is not too unconscionably long, and that if you deign to read it, it may end by converting you to the truth. Of course, it goes in as "Discussion" in the finer point. . . . Proof should be addressed to me here [Chocorua]" (Bancroft).

That Stratton had some problems before he sent the Worcester review to James may be assumed from the fact that James's memory had played him false, and the piece was in the *Monist*, not the *Open Court* as stated in his letter. In James's interleaved and annotated copy of *The Principles of Psychology* the leaf he referred to was opposite II, 442 (WORKS, p. 1058) and read, "Review of this Chapter by W. L. Worcester in Monist, III, 285 (Jan. '93)."

James made a late change in a postcard to Cattell from Chocorua on August 6:

I am reminded that I should *probably [*intrl.*] have mentioned Munster-berg in my article on Emotions [*doubtful* 'I' *del.*] in the *note* in wh. I mentioned Miller & Nichols as believing pain proper to be a matter of reflex intolerability. In his 4th Beiträge if I recollect rightly, he expressly says this. *Do [*ov. doubtful* 'An'] you or Baldwin remember aught of this? And if I be not certainly incorrect, & if it be not too late, can you *by any modification* [*doubtful* 'f wal' *del.*] *whatever* in the note lug in his name? I am sorry to trouble you, but such an omission might seem queer in me to M. & I haven't his Beiträge here" (Library of Congress).

The latter part of footnote 9 (307.39–43) results from this addition, the form probably shaped in proof.

PERSON AND PERSONALITY (1895).

Copy-text: (J) *Johnson's Universal Cyclopædia* (New York: A. J. Johnson, 1895), 6, 538–540 (McD 1895:15).
   On a postcard dated April 8, 1894, James wrote to J. Mark Baldwin: "I shall not spurn an offer from Johnson's Cyclopaedia to write either on Telepathy or Personality though I doubt whether I can supply them with much more besides" (typed copy, Harvard bMS Am 1092.1). On May 27, 1894, he complained to Baldwin: "I cannot gather the meaning of 'I sent you a letter through the Johnson Cychop. [*stet*] people'—At any rate I have received none, whether 'through', from or to, them" (*ibid.*). However, by May 30 the offer had come since on that date he responded to Baldwin: " 'Personality' and 'telepathy' I'll attend to, if the remuneration tempts. But 'Spiritualism' is too much for me" (*ibid.*). He inquired on July 8: "When must the Cyclopedia article on personality be finished? I have asked the question of Mr.— who wrote me on behalf of the publishers, but I get no reply" (*ibid.*). On July 24: "I have begun 'personality' taking for granted the existence of a short 'person' article. Or shall I write both 'person' and 'personality'?—or run them into one article with two titles? This last would seem best. [¶] Of course, I assume that another hand is to treat of person legally and theologically" (*ibid.*). A letter of September 26 acknowledges a letter from Baldwin already answered verbally; another, on November 13, requests the address of Lilley of the *Cyclopædia*, which he has mislaid. These two letters may concern the article on "Telepathy" instead, for which see *Essays in Psychical Research* in the WORKS.

CONSCIOUSNESS UNDER NITROUS OXIDE (1898).

Copy-text: (P34) "Consciousness Under Nitrous Oxide," *Psychological Review*, 5 (March 1898), 194–196 (McD 1898:1), under the heading "Discussion and Reports."
   From Cambridge on January 6, 1898, James sent a note to James McKeen Cattell, editor of the *Review*, apparently enclosing the article:

"This document seems to me well worthy of being printed among Notes & Discussions. The author permits, anonymously" (Library of Congress).

INTRODUCTION TO *The Psychology of Suggestion* BY BORIS SIDIS (1898).

Copy-text: (S) *The Psychology of Suggestion*, by Boris Sidis (New York: D. Appleton, 1898), pp. v–vii (McD 1898:6).

On May 25, 1897, according to the postmark, James wrote on a post-card to Sidis: "I had hoped to ['f' *del.*] write the preface Sunday before last, but am almost killed with things and fatigue. I will try to do it this week, but am not sure I can, being *saddled [*ab. del.* 'beset'] with an 'oration' which I have to deliver by heart in Music Hall next Monday [the Robert Gould Shaw Oration, reprinted in *Essays in Religion and Morality*, WORKS]. After then, I can do *anything*. Who is the publisher of Renschbug [i.e., Ranschburg] and Hajós?" (#3770). On October 28, 1897, James wrote:

I retain the proof of the preface. I don't know that you want the rest of the proof back so I keep it. It is highly interesting; and I long for more of Mr. Hanna. I think you are too dogmatic about the dendron retraction business, and should have put it more tentatively forward. Of course it stops a gap provisionally; but demands explanation as to its topographic course as much as the raw phenomena do. Your terminology seems to me in spots a little awkward; but the whole thing is bold, original & radical like your self, & I like it, and hope the book will have a first rate sale. I can't strike out the "not convinced" sentence. One must always "hedge"—but it will do the ['boo pr' *del.*] book no harm" (#3772).

INTRODUCTION TO *The Elements of Psychology* BY EDWARD L. THORNDIKE (1905).

Copy-text: (T) *The Elements of Psychology*, by Edward L. Thorndike (New York: A. G. Seiler, 1905), pp. v–vii (McD 1905:10).

The correspondence between James and Thorndike about this Introduction is preserved only in Geraldine Jonçich, *The Sane Positivist: A Biography of Edward L. Thorndike* (Middletown, Conn.: Wesleyan University Press, 1968), to which the page notations refer. On February 26, 1905, James wrote to Thorndike:

Here's your preface, accursed much good may it do you! As I think I said to you before, I don't see why a man of your eminence needs to get any one else to introduce him to the public or to sully the purity of his title page by the intrusion of an interloping name. So if you come round to my way of thinking, you still have your remedy. You can either throw my preface into the fire or frame it as an heirloom for your descendents—in any case you need not print it.

I hope it will seem to you that I have touched on the real heart of all your striving. . . . It gives me a certain pleasure to think that the reason why you turned to me rather than to someone else for a preface (since you had to have one!) was that you felt a community of fundamental attitude.

Your book seems to me extraordinarily vigorous and deserves a big market success. It will probably damage the sales of my briefer course considerably—but all the better if it deserves to (p. 246).

The book was published in May. Jonçich has an account of Thorndike's attempt in December to send James a cheque for $100 when it seemed likely that the *Elements* indeed might injure the sale of *Briefer Course* and James's declination (p. 253).

ON SOME MENTAL EFFECTS OF THE EARTHQUAKE (1906).

Copy-text: (P39) "On Some Mental Effects of the Earthquake," *Youth's Companion*, 80 (June 7, 1906), 283–284 (McD 1906:2). The article was reprinted without authoritative change in *Memories and Studies*, ed. Henry James, Jr. (New York and London: Longmans, Green & Co., 1911), pp. 209–226 (McD 1911:2).

In his diary for Friday, May 11, 1906, James recorded, "Wrote article on Earthquake for Youth's Companion." The next week, on Thursday, May 17, he noted "Spoke of Earthquake at ['Philosoph' *del.*] Graduate Club." Both entries would have been made in Cambridge.

A brief account of James's expedition into San Francisco and an interesting narrative of the afternoon by Dr. William Snow, whom he was searching for, may be found in *Letters*, II, 246–248, together with his own account in a lengthy and vivid letter of April 22 to Miss Frances R. Morse and of May 9 to Henry James (II, 247–251). On April 22 he wrote to Josiah Royce from Stanford: "Henceforward I am prepared to *pose* at afternoon teas and other social gatherings as an authority on earthquakes. The cutter herself was ['a' *del.*] very *vivid*, and the San Francisco story is *historical*. I spent 6 hours there on the morning. No harm done to *us*" (#3632). On April 26 (*alt. fr.* '25') he wrote to Harald Höffding: "Stanford University has all its superfluous portions wrecked, but its funds are all right, and its intellectual apparatus uninjured. I think that this will be a beneficial turning point in its history. San Francisco is practically wiped off the map—the fire burned for four days unchecked, and of course the wooden houses, which stood beautifully against the earthquake offered no resistance to the flames—the water supply having been ruptured by the planetary disturbance. The time of day 5.30 A M., saved countless lives. The thing lasted nearly a minute. The university has closed, and my wife and I go East tomorrow, if we can find a train. There is no ['mo' *del.*] cash anywhere yet, but I have tickets" (#1009). Then back in Cambridge, on May 9 he wrote a brief note to Henry Holt, including: "The sentimental anguish about the earthquake is all in the breasts of outsiders. At the place of action, men don't seem to have much time for pathos, and the 'common lot' of it all takes away the feeling of loneliness that I suppose gives the sharp edge to most usual cases of misfortune" (Henry Holt Archives, Princeton University Library).

Emendations

Every editorial change from the copy-text is recorded for the substantives and every change in the accidentals as well save for such silent typographical adjustments as are remarked in A Note on the Editorial Method. The reading to the left of the bracket, the lemma, represents the form chosen in the present edition, usually as an emendation of the copy-text. (A prefixed superior [1] or [2] indicates which of any two identical words in the same line is intended.) The sigil immediately following the bracket is the identifying symbol for the earliest source of the emendation, followed by the sigla of any later agreeing documents. Readings in parentheses after sigla indicate a difference in the accidental form of the source from that of the emended reading to the left of the bracket. A semicolon follows the last of the sigla for emending sources. To the right of this semicolon appear the rejected readings of the copy-text and of any other recorded documents, followed by their sigla. When emendations need to be made that are not drawn from any authoritative document, for convenience CER, R. B. Perry's *Collected Essays and Reviews* (1920), in which a number of the essays in this volume were reprinted, has been utilized, and failing that, the editor's own alterations marked as H (Harvard). CER is not noted in the list of Emendations except when it is an emending agent or a rejected substantive. Emendations are drawn from PP, *The Principles of Psychology*, where a number of the essays were reprinted in part. It is used as an emending agent only, except in very rare instances where it appears as a rejected reading. A superior number identifies the exact printing of *Principles* in case of need, as PP[1] for the 1890 first printing and PP[4] for the 1893 fourth printing. The word *stet* after the bracket calls special attention to the retention of a copy-text reading. It may be employed to key a Textual Note, as marked by an asterisk before the page-line number. In a quotation it may indicate that James's version (differing from the source in some respect) has been retained in the edited text. It may also be used in rare instances to indicate that a possibly questionable or unusual reading has been retained in the text.

One special feature appearing in the Emendations is the use of *et seq*. When this phrase occurs, all subsequent readings within the essay are to be taken as agreeing with the particular feature of the reading being recorded (save for singulars and plurals and inessential typographical variation, as between roman and italic), unless specifically noted to the contrary by notation within the entry itself. For convenience, certain shorthand symbols familiar in textual notation are employed. A wavy dash ($\sim$) represents the same word that appears before the bracket and is used exclusively in recording punctuation or other accidental variants. An inferior caret ($_\wedge$) indicates the absence of a

418

punctuation mark (or of a footnote superscript) when a difference in the punctuation constitutes the variant being recorded, or is a part of the variant. A vertical stroke (|) represents a line ending, sometimes recorded as bearing on the cause of an error or fault. A hand symbol (🖙) before a page-line reference draws attention to the parenthetical listing of additional lines where the forms of emendation are identical. Quotations within the text are identified in Professor Skrupskelis' Notes. The sigil WJ/ followed by the appropriate symbol (as WJ/P42) indicates James's autograph revisions, usually found in his file sets of private copies of journal articles, and in books, proofs, or clippings.

BRUTE AND HUMAN INTELLECT

The copy-text is P21, "Brute and Human Intellect," *Journal of Speculative Philosophy*, 12 (July 1878), 236–276 (McDermott 1878:4). Reference is made to PP, *The Principles of Psychology*, the page-line numbers drawn from the edition in the WORKS; the note (*em.*) indicates emendation of the first printing of PP by the present editor to the form shown. Two annotations (not in James's hand but initialed 'WJ', also in an unknown hand) are accepted from a photostat of P21 in the James Collection at Harvard and are designated as WJ(?)/P21.

1.1 *et seq.* Everyone] H; Every one P21

2.38 revery] H; reverie P21

4.4 Present] *stet* P21; *ital.* Bain

4.23 Alexander] H; *om.* P21

🖙6.26 embedded] H; imbedded P21 (*also* 8.7–8;10.39;17.34;20.33)

6.40 someone] H; some one P21

8.30 oxalic] WJ(?)/P21; citric P21

9.29 *a priori*] H; *a-priori* P21

9.36 *a priorists*] H; *a-priorists* P21

10.18 *a*] H; *om.* P21

11.31 light-rays] PP (966.31); ~ ∧ ~ P21

12.18 turn] WJ(?)/P21; time P21

15.14(*second*),20 to] Martineau; into P21

15.22 than] Martineau; than in P21

15.22 terms."⁴] H; ~. ∧⁴ P21 (*error*)

16.34 If the] *stet* P21; The Spencer

16.36 and again] *stet* P21; there along Spencer

17.2 bodies."⁵] PP (479.7); ~.⁵" P21

17.7 color] *stet* P21; *rom.* Martineau

17.7 contrast] Martineau;PP (479.14); contract P21

17.9 form] *stet* P21; form Martineau

17.12 and then] Martineau; then P21

17.27 accommodating] H; accomodating P21 (*error*)

17.38 Herbert] H; *om.* P21

17.39 271–272] H; 271, 272 P21

19.1 *Principles of Psychology.*] H; "~ ~ ~." (*rom.*) P21

20.28 coexisted] H; co-existed P21

21.12;23.39–40 embedded] PP (971.8–9;974.18); imbedded P21

23.1 *Descent of Man,*] H; "~ ~ ~," (*rom.*) P21

24.27 immediately] PP (975.7); immdiately P21 (*error*)

26.5 *Coriolanus*] PP(*em.*) (979.25); *rom.* P21

28.14;33.8–9;34.32 embedded] PP(*em.*) (982.14;987.15;988.36); imbedded P21

28.15 these signs,] PP (982.15); ~, ~∧ P21 (*error*)

29.21 different,] PP (983.17); ~; P21

29.39 Chauncey] PP (982.39); Chauncy P21 (*error*)

30.9–10 *Study of Character,*] H; "~ ~ ~," (*rom.*) P21

30.10 leading fact] *stet* P21; *ital.* Bain

30.10 genius . . .] PP(*em.*) (984.15); ~. P21

30.12 an] Bain; *om.* P21

30.13 (p. 327)] H; *om.* P21

30.17 farther] PP (984.22); further P21

30.33 towards] PP(*em.*) (984.37); toward P21

*30.36–37 suggestions] *stet* P21; suggestion PP (985.2)

30.39 On the] H; *om.* P21

31.8 fishermen] PP (985.12); fisherman P21

31.25 *étonnée*] Taine;PP (985.30); *ètonnée* P21 (*error*)

31.29 anyone] PP(*em.*) (985.34); any one P21

32.2 at] PP³ (986.10); from P21,PP¹⁻²

32.14 some time] H; sometime P21

34.7 intuition] PP (988.11); intuiton P21 (*error*)

34.19 latter] PP³(988.23); former P21,PP¹⁻²

35.32 makes] PP (989.35); make P21

ARE WE AUTOMATA?

The copy-text is P24, "Are We Automata?" *Mind*, 4 (January 1879), 1–22 (McD 1879:5). Reference is made to PP, *The Principles of Psychology*, the page-line numbers drawn from the edition in the WORKS; the note (*em.*) indicates emendation of the first printing of PP by the present editor to the form shown.

38.21 N. S.] H; *om.* P24

39.15 coexist] H; co-exist P24

40.5 anyone] PP(*em.*) (138.24); any one P24

40.30 anyone] H; any one P24

41.31 forwards] H; forward P24

42.12 actions] H; action P24

43.8 forever] PP (143.23); for ever P24

44.26 someone's] H; *some one's* P24

46.24 the] H; the | the P24 (*error*)

47.26 *a*] H; *à* P24

48.33 but] PP (275.6); not P24

49.8 ones;] PP (275.18); ∼: P24

50.19 it.] PP (276.14); ∼? P24 (*error*)

52.28 free-will] H; ∼ₐ∼ P24

53.11 everyone] H; every one P24

53.21 Mensch] Goethe; *ital.* P24

55.11 omission–] H; ∼,– P24

56.2 *a*] PP(*em.*) (146.28); *à* P24

56.22 *a*] PP (147.9); *à* P24

59.10 will–] H; ∼,– P24

THE SPATIAL QUALE

The copy-text is P21, "The Spatial Quale," *Journal of Speculative Philosophy*, 13 (January 1879), 64–87 (McD 1879:6). Reference is made to P24, "The Perception of Space," *Mind*, 12 (January, April 1887), 1–30, 183–211 (McD 1887:4) from which emendations are drawn, and to PP, *The Principles of Psychology*, the page-line numbers drawn from the edition in the WORKS; the note (*em.*) indicates emendation of the first printing of PP by the present editor to the form shown.

62.13 hegelian] H; *cap.* P21

63.2 exists] H; exist P21 (*error*)

63.10 the] H; the | the P21 (*error*)

63.14 fourth] H; foruth P21 (*error*)

63.29–30 coexisting] H; co-existing P21 (*also* 64.17,17–18,21,26,27; 65.16–17)

63.31 *fallacious assumption*] *stet* P21; *rom.* Sully

63.39 *Grundzüge der physiologischen*] H; *om.* P21

*64.35 loudnessesₐ] H; ∼, P21

64.36 intensities;] H; ∼, P21

65.2 embedded] H; imbedded P21

65.7 has] H; have P21 (*error*)

65.9,22–23 everyone] H; every one P21

67.17 pre-exist] H; preëxist P21

67.29;78.1 anyone] H; any one P21

67.42 *quale.*] H; ∼ ₐ P21 (*error*)

69.1 anyone] PP(*em.*) (782.14); any one P21

69.11 upside] H; up side P21

Emendations

[*begin* P24]

69.19 *a*] P24;PP (810.8); *ad* P21 (*error*)

70.6 pre-existing] P24;PP (810.29–30); preëxisting P21

*70.23 0.045″] Exner (Secunden); PP(*em.*) (811.13); 0.044ᴧ P21

70.29 0.014″] Exner (Secunden); PP(*em.*) (811.19); 0.015ᴧ P21

70.38–39 *Sitzungsberichte* . . . –190.] H; Wiener Sitzungs Berichte, LXXII., Bd. III., Abth., § 156. 1875ᴧ P21

[*end* P24]

71.40 forwards] H; forward P21

72.2 subdividing] H; sub-dividing P21

[*begin* P24]

72.35 compass-points] P24;PP (785.18); ∼ᴧ∼ P21

[*end* P24]

73.36–37 multiple– . . . retina–] H; ∼,– . . . ∼,– P21

75.37 someone's] PP (807.30); some one's P21

81.6 *Psychology*] H; *rom.* P21

81.7 a *simultaneous*] stet P21; the simultaneous Spencer

81.11 No] stet P21; Not that such Spencer

81.11 *successive*] stet P21; *rom.* Spencer

81.12 extension] Spencer; succession P21

81.12–13 *muscular*] stet P21; *rom.* Spencer

81.13 motionᴧ] stet P21; the motion, Spencer

81.13 distinct] stet P21; distinct in nature Spencer

81.34 intensity] H; in tensity P21

81.37 ²Kant] stet P21; Kant, indeed, Helmholtz

82.2 position be dropped] stet P21; assertion with the dependent inference is dropt Helmholtz

82.5 position] stet P21; system Helmholtz

THE FEELING OF EFFORT

The copy-text is P42, "The Feeling of Effort," *Anniversary Memoirs of the Boston Society of Natural History* (1880), pp. 3–32 (McD 1880:3). Reference is made to PP, *The Principles of Psychology*, the page-line numbers drawn from the edition in the WORKS; the note (*em.*) indicates emendation of the first printing of PP by the present editor to the form shown. Though not in James's hand, identical annotations (designated as P42 [*errata*]) are accepted from two copies of P42 at Harvard. The one authoritative annotation is noted as WJ/P42. Reference is also made to the reprint in CER, *Collected Essays and Reviews*, edited by R. B. Perry, pp. 151–219 (McD 1920:2).

83.1 animale . . .] H; ∼ ᴧ P42

83.3–4 volition . . .] H; ∼ ᴧ P42

83.5 rationnelle] Renouvier; rationelle P42 (*error*)

84.30 Bastian] CER; Bastion P42 (*error*)

85.37 1879] H; 1869 P42,CER (*error*)

86.25 correlated] PP(1108.15);CER; correllated P42 (*error*)

☛87.7 connexions] H; connections P42 (*also* 87.8;106.2,5;107.5,5–6,14; 108.19;122.4,21;124.12)

87.10 conceived will,] CER; ∼, ∼ᴧ P42

87.14 *directly*ᴧ] CER; ∼, P42

87.32;93.23 anyone] PP(*em.*) (1109.25; 1115.31); any one P42

88.11 mean,] CER; ∼ᴧ P42

☛88.33 admission–] H; ∼,– P42 (*similar* 100.6[*twice*];102.15;104.11; 114.24;116.10,28;117.6;122.2)

88.38–39 "Of . . . Connexion."] H; ᴧon . . . Connection.ᴧ P42,CER

88.40;108.36 Les . . . *l'ataxie*] H; Des . . . de l'Ataxie P42,CER

*89.2 expressly] stet P42; expressively PP (1110.24)

89.35 1st ed.] PP (1110.37); *om.* P42,CER

89.38 *Effektbild*] Harless; *Effectsbild* P42

421

91.12 *Brain*$_\wedge$] PP (1114.3);CER; $\sim$, P42

91.15 says:$_\wedge$] PP (1114.35);CER; $\sim$:– P42

91.20 own] Bastian;PP(*em.*) (1114.40); *om.* P42,CER

91.25 months'] CER; months P42

91.29 cannot] H; can not P42

91.41 someone] H; some one P42

92.1 *altogether*] stet P42; *rom.* Ferrier

95.31 20°$_\wedge$] PP (1118.5);CER; $\sim$, P42

96.4 forefinger] PP(*em.*) (1118.13); CER; fore finger P42

96.6 outwards] PP (1118.15); outward P42

96.7 vision."$_\wedge$] PP (1118.16); $\sim$."[1] P42,CER (*error*)

96.8 paralyzed] PP (1118.17);CER; paralysed P42

96.15 eyeball] PP (1118.24);CER; eye ball P42

97.5 eyeball] PP (1119.14);CER; $\sim$-$\sim$ P42

97.10 left] P42 (*errata*);PP (1119.19); right P42 (*text*);CER

97.11 right] P42 (*errata*);PP (1119.20); left P42 (*text*);CER

97.22 eye$_\wedge$] PP (1120.6);CER; $\sim$, P42

97.22 left],] PP(*em.*) (1120.6); $\sim$,] P42

97.23 agree."[17]] H; $\sim$."$_\wedge$ P42; PP (*page reference in fn. 17 of P42 included in fn. 21 [1117.41]*);CER

98.9 belongs] H; belong P42,CER

98.34 ophthalmological] CER; opthalmological P42 (*error*)

98.41;100.40;101.9 anyone] H; any one P42

100.23 rotate$_\wedge$] CER; $\sim$, P42

101.1 innervation$_\wedge$] CER; $\sim$, P42

101.7 exertion,] H; $\sim_\wedge$ P42

101.29-30 retina$_\wedge$ . . . impression$_\wedge$] CER; $\sim$, . . . $\sim$, P42

102.36 singular,] CER; $\sim_\wedge$ | P42

103.20-21 *Mental Physiology*] H; *rom.* P42

104.22 insentient] WJ/P42,CER; insertient P42 (*error*)

105.2 someone] PP(*em.*) (1112.21); some one P42

105.38-39 Bois-Reymond's] PP(*em.*) (1113.39); Bois' P42,CER

105.39 175-195] PP(*em.*) (1113.40); 174-188 P42,CER

105.40 (Am. ed.)] PP(*em.*) (1113.42); *om.* P42,CER

107.1 everyone] H; every one P42

108.27 anæsthesia] CER; anasthesia P42 (*error*)

109.35 273] H; 237 P42,CER (*error*)

109.37 *sogenannte*] H; *sogennante* P42 (*error*)

112.10 conflict] CER; confliet P42 (*error*)

113.27 [and being]] PP(*em.*) (1171.27); $_\wedge\sim$ $\sim_\wedge$ P42

114.18 immediate–$_\wedge$] CER; $\sim$–, P42

114.32 and the] CER; the and P42 (*error*)

114.38 pp. 122-123] H; p. 123 P42, CER

115.8 *expectation*] CER; *rom.* P42 (*error*)

115.27 so called] H; $\sim$-$\sim$ P42

117.16 attempt] stet P42; attempt we make Mill

117.17 being] stet P42; mental being Mill

117.25 reflection] CER; reflexion P42

117.36 Mill's] CER; Mills' P42 (*error*)

117.36 section] H; chapter P42,CER

119.2 manner$_\wedge$] CER; $\sim$, P42

121.35 Spencer's] H; *om.* P42

121.35 XVII] CER; VII P42 (*error*)

121.38 in *Essays* . . . 244 ff.] H; *om.* P42,CER

122.10 no] P42 (*errata*); *om.* P42 (*text*);CER

122.11,17 free-will] H; $\sim_\wedge\sim$ P42

124.27-28 "force-sense"] H; "$\sim_\wedge\sim$" P42

124.34 downwards] H; downward P42

Notes on the Sense of Dizziness in Deaf-Mutes

The copy-text is P15, untitled note under the heading "Science," *Harvard University Bulletin*, 2 (1881), 173 (McD 1881:2). Reference is made to P24, "Sense of Dizziness in Deaf-Mutes," *Mind*, 6 (July 1881), 412–413.

125.1 An] H; —Professor WILLIAM
JAMES contributes the following
notes on the Sense of Dizziness in
Deaf-mutes: "An P15

125.22 swing$_\wedge$] H; ~, P15
125.23 vertigo),] P24; ~,) P15

THE SENSE OF DIZZINESS IN DEAF-MUTES

The copy-text is P2, "The Sense of Dizziness in Deaf-Mutes," *American Journal of Otology*, 4 (October 1882), 239–254 (McD 1882:3). Reference is made to the reprint in CER, *Collected Essays and Reviews*, edited by R. B. Perry, pp. 220–243 (McD 1920:2).

127.20,21 Baginsky] H; Baginski P2
128.16 whilst] H; while P2
128.27;137.35;139.5 scarlet-fever] H;
~$_\wedge$~ P2
☞128.36 follows:$_\wedge$] CER; ~:— P2
(*similar* 134.29;135.8,14,18,21,25,29,
32;136.1,3;138.7;139.34;140.17;141.13)
128.39 forwards . . . backwards] H;
forward . . . backward P2
130.1 another.$_\wedge$ Löwenfeld[4]] CER;
~.[1] ~$_\wedge$ P2 (*error*)
130.14 forwards] H; forward P2
130.39 *Electrotherapie*] CER;
Electratherapie P2 (*error*)
131.24 centres$_\wedge$] CER; ~, P2 (*error*)
131.27–28 $_\wedge$*Untersuchungen* . . .
Gehirn.$_\wedge$] H; "~ . . . ~." P2

131.36 Crum Brown] H; Crum-Brown
P2
133.26 Breuer] H; Brewer P2
133.30 *Optics*] H; "~" (*rom.*) P2
133.33 farther] H; further P2
134.9 complete—] H; ~,— P2
134.33 604] H; 664 P2,CER
138.4 co-ordination] CER;
coördination P2
138.6 *Harvard . . . Bulletin*] CER;
all rom. P2
141.8–11 Finally$_\wedge$ . . . it!),] CER;
~, . . . ~!)$_\wedge$ P2 (*error*)
141.17 co-operation] CER;
coöperation P2

ON SOME OMISSIONS OF INTROSPECTIVE PSYCHOLOGY

The copy-text is P24, "On Some Omissions of Introspective Psychology," *Mind*, 9 (January 1884), 1–26 (McD 1884:1). Reference is made to PP, *The Principles of Psychology*, the page-line numbers drawn from the edition in the WORKS; the note (*em.*) indicates emendation of the first printing of PP by the present editor to the form shown. The notation WJ/PP indicates a handwritten correction in James's private copy of *Principles*.

☞143.7 -angry—] H; ~,— P24
(*similar* 150.36;158.2,23;160.2;161.38
[*twice*];166.18–19,24;167.13,29,31,32
[*twice*],33)
143.18 but] PP (190.13); *om.* P24
144.19 snowflake] WJ/PP (237.6);
snowflake-crystal P24
144.20 flake] WJ/PP (237.7); crystal
P24
145.40 another] *stet* P24; an adjacent
Spencer

148.8 *naive*] H; *naïve* P24
149.24 hegelian] H; *cap.* P24
149.39 then$_\wedge$] *stet* P24; then,—
Ferrier
149.40 down] Ferrier; *om.* P24
150.15 Everyone] H; Every one P24
155.11 Everyone] PP(*em.*) (244.4);
Every one P24
156.13 someone's] PP(*em.*) (245.6);
some one's P24

159.19 or,] PP (452.1 [*em. to* 'or_∧']);
~_∧ P24

159.20 images_∧] PP (452.2 [*em. to*
'images,']); ~, P24

WHAT IS AN EMOTION?

The copy-text is P24, "What Is an Emotion?" *Mind*, 9 (April 1884), 188–205 (McD 1884:2). Reference is made to PP, *The Principles of Psychology*, the page-line number drawn from the edition in the WORKS, and to the reprint in CER, *Collected Essays and Reviews*, edited by R. B. Perry, pp. 244–275 (McD 1920: 2). The notation WJ/PP indicates a handwritten correction in James's private copy of *Principles*.

☞171.18 key—] H; ~,— P24
(*similar* 171.25;172.4;176.39;180.34,
37;183.38)
173.35 downwards] H; downward P24
173.39 *Society . . . History*] H;
Natural History Society P24,CER
173.40 V [No. 20]] H; XX P24,CER
176.5 everyone] H; every one P24

177.15 to] PP (1073.4);CER; too P24
(*error*)
180.11 evil] WJ/PP (1074.16);
distressing P24,CER
180.23 impossibilities. . . .] H; ~._∧ P24
181.8 *but*] CER; but P24
181.41 1875 . . . –134.] H; 1876 . . . –135.
P24,CER
185.23 III (No. 10)] H; X P24,CER

THE LATEST CURE FOR SEA-SICKNESS

The copy-text is P27a, "The Latest Cure for Sea-Sickness" (Letter to the Editor), *Pall Mall Budget*, October 3, 1884, p. 26 (McD 1884:6).

No emendations

REPORT OF THE COMMITTEE ON HYPNOTISM

The copy-text is P31, "Report of the Committee on Hypnotism," *Proceedings of the American Society for Psychical Research*, 1 (July 1886), 95–102 (McD 1886:1).

190.13;193.2;197.19 anything] H;
any thing P31

196.32 J.] H; W. P31 (*error*)

A SUGGESTION FOR THE PREVENTION OF SEA-SICKNESS

The copy-text is P8, "A Suggestion for the Prevention of Sea-Sickness" (Letter to the Editor), *Boston Medical and Surgical Journal*, 116 (May 19, 1887), 490–491 (McD 1887:7).

198.5 deaf-mutes] H; ~_∧~ P8

Emendations

REACTION-TIME IN THE HYPNOTIC TRANCE

The copy-text is P31, "Reaction-Time in the Hypnotic Trance," *Proceedings of the American Society for Psychical Research*, 1 (December 1887), 246–248 (McD 1887:9).

200.9   *Mind*] H; "Mind" P31
200.10   Stanley Hall] H; ~-~ P31
☞200.11   follows:ₐ] H; ~:– P31
   (*similar* 201.14;203.7)

201.13   810] H; 806 P31
202.36   Professor] H; Prof. P31

THE CONSCIOUSNESS OF LOST LIMBS

The copy-text is P31, "The Consciousness of Lost Limbs," *Proceedings of the American Society for Psychical Research*, 1 (December 1887), 249–258 (McD 1887:10). Reference is made to the reprint in CER, *Collected Essays and Reviews*, edited by R. B. Perry, pp. 285–302 (McD 1920:2).

204.5   *Injuries of Nerves*] H; "Injuries to the Nerves" P31,CER
204.11   these:ₐ] CER; ~:– P31
205.25   deal] CER; dead P31 (*error*)
206.4   thigh amputation] H; ~-~ P31
206.24   forwards] H; forward P31

206.37,38;207.13;214.3,33   amongst] H; among P31
207.40   *des Menschen*] H; *om.* P31,CER
208.10   *Mind*] H; "Mind" P31
208.37   *within*] *stet* P31; in Mitchell

WHAT THE WILL EFFECTS

The copy-text is P37, "What the Will Effects," *Scribner's Magazine*, 3 (February 1888), 240–250 (McD 1888:1). Reference is made to PP, *The Principles of Psychology*, the page-line number drawn from the edition in the WORKS.

216.5   influences–] H; ~,– P37
217.33   What Is an Instinct?] H; The Nature of Instinct, P37
220.39   revery] PP (1132.37); reverie P37

222.24   so called] H; ~- | ~ P37
225.18   re-enforce] H; reinforce P37
231.23   *effort,*] H; ~ₐ P37
232.14   cannot–] H; ~,– P37

RÉPONSE DE M. W. JAMES AUX REMARQUES DE M. RENOUVIER, SUR SA THÉORIE DE LA VOLONTÉ

The copy-text is P9, "Réponse de M. W. James aux remarques de M. Renouvier, sur sa théorie de la volonté," *Critique Philosophique*, n.s. 2 (December 1888), 401–404 (McD 1888:2). Reference is made to the reprint entitled "Réponse aux remarques de M. Renouvier, sur sa théorie de la volonté" in CER, *Collected Essays and Reviews*, edited by R. B. Perry, pp. 303–309 (McD 1920:2).

236.7   parties] CER; partie P9 (*error*)
236.18   dûs] H; dus P9 (*error*)
236.22   touche] CER; touehe P9 (*error*)

237.13   Bowditch] CER; Bourditch P9 (*error*)
238.37   (Mass.) U.S. of] CER; (~ₐ V. S. of. P9 (*error*)

Emendations

"The Psychological Theory of Extension"

The copy-text is P24, " 'The Psychological Theory of Extension,' " *Mind*, 14 (January 1889), 107–109 (McD 1889:1). Reference is made to the reprint in CER, *Collected Essays and Reviews*, edited by R. B. Perry, pp. 310–315 (McD 1920:2).

239.17 any] Robertson; in any P24, CER
240.35 ∧which "are] H; "~ ∧~ P24
240.35 ∧passive∧] *stet* P24; (~) Robertson

240.39 become] Robertson; be P24, CER
242.7 ∧on a "tactile] H; "~ ~ ∧~ P24
242.15 ∧seeking "for] H; "~ ∧~ P24

Report on the Congress of Physiological Psychology at Paris

The copy-text is P24, "The Congress of Physiological Psychology at Paris," *Mind*, 14 (October 1889), 614–615 (McD 1889:5).

243.5 August] H; Aug. P24
243.21 psychologie] H; *cap.* P24
244.30 Salpêtrière] H; Salpétrière P24 (*error*)

245.1 Liégeois] H; Liègeois P24 (*error*)
245.8 individual] H; indvidual P24 (*error*)

The Hidden Self

The copy-text is P37, "The Hidden Self," *Scribner's Magazine*, 7 (March 1890), 361–373 (McD 1890:1). Reference is made to PP, *The Principles of Psychology*, the page-line numbers drawn from the edition in the WORKS; the note (*em.*) indicates emendation of the first printing of PP by the present editor to the form shown.

250.11–12 *L'Automatisme psychologique*] H; "De l'Automatisme Psychologique" P37
250.37 his] H; His P37 (*error*)
251.39 one half] H; ~-~ P37
252.32 not] PP (364.4); *om.* P37 (*error*)
253.25 Witt.] PP(*em.*) (364.32) (~ . . . .); ~ . . . P37
☞255.38 whilst] PP (365.29); while P37 (*also* 256.17;257.4;262.37;263.38;

264.17,19,22 [PP 366.7,36;205.25; 206.25;207.6,8,11])
256.16 upwards] PP (366.6); upward P37
256.37 stupid.' . . .] H; ~.'∧ P37
259.26 towards] PP (202.12); toward P37
259.32 no wise] PP (202.18); nowise P37
262.15 Witt.] PP(*em.*) (205.3) (~.,); ~ . . . P37

Notes on Ansel Bourne

The copy-text is P32, "A Case of Double Consciousness," by Richard Hodgson, *Proceedings of the (English) Society for Psychical Research*, 7 (July 1891), 221–257 (McD [1891:6]). James's contribution appears on pp. 254–255 under the heading "Notes by Professor Wm. James, M.D."

No emendations

Emendations

A PLEA FOR PSYCHOLOGY AS A 'NATURAL SCIENCE'

The copy-text is P28, "A Plea for Psychology as a 'Natural Science,'" *Philosophical Review*, 1 (March 1892), 146–153 (McD 1892:4). Reference is made to the reprint in CER, *Collected Essays and Reviews*, edited by R. B. Perry, pp. 316–327 (McD 1920:2).

271.2–3 *Psychology . . . Course*] H; sg. qts. (rom.) P28
272.4 nature–] H; ~,– P28
274.1–2 *Present . . . Sciences*] H; all rom. P28
274.4–5 *Ceasing . . . philosophy*] stet P28; all rom. Seth
274.11–13 real . . . own] stet P28; all ital. Ladd

274.11–12 being, proceeding] stet P28; being which, although taking its start and direction from the action of the physical elements of the body, proceeds Ladd
275.13,22 brain states] CER; ~-~ P28
276.4 program] H; programme P28

THOUGHT BEFORE LANGUAGE: A DEAF-MUTE'S RECOLLECTIONS

The copy-text is P28, "Thought Before Language: A Deaf-Mute's Recollections," *Philosophical Review*, 1 (November 1892), 613–624 (McD 1892:5).

278.8 Giżycki] H; Gizycki P28
279.16 zurück'?] H; ~?' P28
280.15 for] d'Estrella; om. P28

280.33 and] d'Estrella; aud P28 (*error*)
280.34 After] stet P28; Since d'Estrella

THE ORIGINAL DATUM OF SPACE-CONSCIOUSNESS

The copy-text is P24, "The Original Datum of Space-Consciousness," *Mind*, n.s. 2 (July 1893), 363–365 (McD 1893:1).

294.3 connects?_∧] stet P24; ~?" Ford [*i.e.*, ~?']
294.3 That]_stet P24; that Ford

294.16 Mills'] H; Mill's P24
294.17 'psychic synthesis'] H; _∧~ '~' P24

PROFESSOR WUNDT AND FEELINGS OF INNERVATION

The copy-text is P34, "Professor Wundt and Feelings of Innervation," *Psychological Review*, 1 (January 1894), 70–73 (McD 1894:1).

295.7 von] H; Von P34
296.15 [dem . . . angehörende]] H; parens P34

296.16 [vom . . . herrührenden]] H; parens P34
296.20 Psychology] H; rom. P34

THE PHYSICAL BASIS OF EMOTION

The copy-text is P34, "The Physical Basis of Emotion," *Psychological Review*, 1 (September 1894), 516–529 (McD 1894:2). Reference is made to the re-

427

Emendations

print in CER, *Collected Essays and Reviews*, edited by R. B. Perry, pp. 346–370 (McD 1920:2).

301.5 as ... what] *stet* P34; which Irons

301.23 say] Worcester; say that P34, CER

301.36 n.s., III, 77–97] H; p. 78 P34, CER

301.38 285–298] H; 285 P34,CER

302.15 supposing] Worcester; suppose P34,CER

302.19 fear] Worcester; fears P34,CER

303.16–17 *Die ... Gefühlslebens*] CER; *sg. qts.* (*rom.*) P34

304.14 How] *stet* P34; How then Irons

304.16 If] *stet* P34; Why, if Irons

304.16 can] *stet* P34; can of themselves Irons

304.16 why] *stet* P34; *om.* Irons

304.17 disturbance?" (85).] H; ~ (85.)?" P34

304.31 outwards] H; outward P34

305.8 *Psychology*] CER; *rom.* P34

306.28 presented suddenly] *stet* P34; abruptly presented in certain circumstances Irons

306.30 time] *stet* P34; lapse of time Irons

309.28 credible] *stet* P34; ~, to return to the example mentioned above, Worcester

309.28 *repugnance*] *stet* P34; *rom.* Worcester

309.29 than] *stet* P34; than that Worcester

309.33 *likes*] *stet* P34; *rom.* Worcester

309.34 296–297] H; *Ibid.* P34,CER

309.35 or] Worcester; and P34,CER

312.34 'If] CER; ∧~ P34 (*error*)

312.41 241–266] H; 241 P34,CER

313.20 *ibid.*] H; ibia∧ P34 (*error*)

PERSON AND PERSONALITY

The copy-text is J, *Johnson's Universal Cyclopædia* (New York: A. J. Johnson, 1895), 6, 538–540 (McD 1895:15).

318.19 simplicity] *stet* J; *simplicity* in it Hume

318.19 identity] *stet* J; *ital.* Hume

320.9 Félida] H; Felida J

320.16 are] H; are are J (*error*)

321.19 of] H; on J

CONSCIOUSNESS UNDER NITROUS OXIDE

The copy-text is P34, "Consciousness Under Nitrous Oxide," *Psychological Review*, 5 (March 1898), 194–196 (McD 1898:1).

No emendations

INTRODUCTION TO *The Psychology of Suggestion* BY BORIS SIDIS

The copy-text is S, *The Psychology of Suggestion*, by Boris Sidis (New York: D. Appleton, 1898), pp. v–vii (McD 1898:6).

No emendations

Emendations

INTRODUCTION TO *The Elements of Psychology* BY EDWARD L. THORNDIKE

The copy-text is T, *The Elements of Psychology*, by Edward L. Thorndike (New York: A. G. Seiler, 1905), pp. v–vii (McD 1905:10).

No emendations

ON SOME MENTAL EFFECTS OF THE EARTHQUAKE

The copy-text is P39, "On Some Mental Effects of the Earthquake," *Youth's Companion*, 80 (June 7, 1906), 283–284 (McD 1906:2).

No emendations

Textual Notes

30.36–37 suggestions] In view of the change in PP 985.2 to the singular, the plural 'suggestions' in P21 may be an error, whether of James's or the printer's, caused by association with the plurals 'analogies' and 'particulars'. But the P21 plural makes sufficient sense, and error is not so certain as to require emendation despite the superiority of the PP reading, which could be classed more as a revision than a correction. For what may be a similar example, see PP 'basis' (988.7) for P21 'bases' (34.2).

64.35 loudnesses$_\wedge$] The comma in P21 after 'loudnesses' is ambiguous owing to the breakdown of the semicolon series by the use of a comma after 'intensities'. Syntactically, therefore, it is not clear whether 'loudnesses', 'intensities', and 'good and evil' are each separate elements in a series with luminosities and tints as the first and second elements, or whether the 'intensities' refers to 'loudnesses' or to 'good and evil'. The former would seem to be the intention. Thus to clarify the text the comma has been removed after 'loudnesses' and a semicolon substituted for the comma after 'intensities'. We then have the meaning that there is an evenly graduated order of loudnesses of all intensities.

70.23 0.045″] This figure and that at 70.29 were transferred without change to "The Perception of Space" (P24) and thence to *Principles*. Exner's figures are provided here as a correction.

89.2 expressly] It is possible that this P42 reading is a misprint, corrected in PP to 'expressively', a more likely hypothesis than the reverse. But both adverbs make sense; hence it is probable that in PP James was revising and not correcting. The case is too uncertain to warrant emendation.

Historical Collation

This list comprises the substantive variant readings that differ from the edited text in the authoritative documents noted for each essay and includes for their intrinsic interest the substantive variants (less bibliographical additions and cross-references) in *Collected Essays and Reviews* (CER), edited by R. B. Perry (1920), in which a number of the essays in this volume were reprinted. The reading to the left of the bracket is that of the present edition. The rejected variants in the noted documents follow in chronological order to the right of the bracket. Any collated texts not recorded are to be taken as agreeing with the edition-reading to the left of the bracket; only variation appears to the right. The noting of variant readings is complete for the substantives. In order to save space, no accidental variants are recorded save for some linguistic differences such as doesn't] does not, can't] cannot, or everyone] every one, which are also noted for their intrinsic interest. Differences in quotation marks as opposed to no quotation marks enclosing words are also included as being of a 'semi-substantive' nature. Variants are not repeated in the Historical Collation when the copy-text has been emended since the details may be found in the list of Emendations.

The headnote to the Emendations list may be consulted for general conventions of notation, and the Note on the Editorial Method outlines types of variants that are not recorded. Readings grouped together with multiple page-line references may be concerned with only the particular feature being recorded and not with inessential types of variation as between roman and italic.

BRUTE AND HUMAN INTELLECT

The copy-text is P21, "Brute and Human Intellect," *Journal of Speculative Philosophy*, 12 (July 1878), 236–276 (McD 1878:4). Reference is made to passages directly utilized by PP, *The Principles of Psychology*, the page-line numbers drawn from the edition in the WORKS; for the details of the relationship, see The Text of *Essays in Psychology*. All references to the right of the bracket are to PP; the note (*em.*) indicates emendation of the first printing of PP by the present editor to the form shown in the lemma.

11.14	quite] *om.* 966.18	11.17	ingredients] parts 966.22
11.14	is] is not reasoned, but 966.18	11.22–28	A . . . *reasoned*;] In neither
11.15	enters] there enters 966.19		of these cases could the result be
11.16	not last] fade 966.20		anticipated without full previous

431

acquaintance with the entire phenomenon. It is not a result of reasoning. 966.26–28

11.33–37 who . . . intelligently] such a man would make the right inferences for all these objects 966.33–34

11.39 mediate] would mediate 966.37

12.5 pendulum] pendulum I spoke of above 967.5

12.6 the door] a door 967.6

12.6 is hardly] in the earlier example would hardly be 967.6

12.7 all] all agree in this, that they 967.7

12.7–8 consequent . . . its] conclusion than did the immediate data in their 967.8

12.9–10 antecedent phenomenon] immediate data 967.10–11

12.11 consequent] conclusion 967.12

12.12–34 properties. . . . Each] properties, as we have seen, amongst which the fool, or man with little sagacity, will inevitably go astray. But no matter for this point now. The first thing is to have seen that every possible 967.13–16

12.35 about. Whilst] $\sim$, and that whilst 967.17–18

12.36 the] *om.* 967.18

12.38 couplings] $\sim$, consequences, and implications 967.21–22

13.3 as] *om.* 967.26

13.8 unfamiliar] comparatively unfamiliar 967.31

13.17 of] *om.* 968.2

14.6 concrete] *om.* 968.28

14.13 such . . . notion] these notions 968.35

14.14 the . . . concerns] those which concern 968.36

14.15 and] *om.* 968.38

14.20 light?] *light?* Why cannot anybody reason as well as anybody else? 969.4–5

14.28 whole.$_\wedge$] $\sim$.[14] + *fn.* 969.13,40

15.1 Mr.] Charles 969.25

15.6 point] corner 969.33

15.10 analyze] they analyze 969.34

15.10–31 Knowledge . . . them] It is full of delicately differenced ingredients which their education has little

by little brought to their consciousness, but of which the novice gains no clear idea. [¶] How this power of analysis was brought about we saw in our chapters on Discrimination and Attention. We dissociate the elements of originally vague totals by attending to them or noticing them alternately 969.34–970.2

15.33 practical] practical or instinctive 970.4

15.35 moment] $\sim$, and are instinctively exciting to these several creatures 970.7

15.35 child] infant 970.8

15.37 these] those 970.9

16.12 interests] instinctive impulses, or interests 970.21

16.15 varied] varied instincts, 970.25

16.16 his] *om.* 970.25

16.34 As] Mr. 478.37

17.2–3 As . . . Martineau,] And still more to the point Dr. Martineau, in the passage I have already quoted, writes: 479.8–9

18.11 must . . . left] is a little of 479.22

18.11 mystery.] $\sim$. One might suppose the nerve-processes of the various concomitants to neutralize or inhibit each other more or less and to leave the process of the common term alone distinctly active. 479.22–25

18.12 of its being] that the common term is 479.25–26

18.13 a] such a 479.27

18.14 equivalent . . . interest] that its abstraction must needs ensue 479.27–28

18.15 , at first sight,] *om.* 479.29

18.16 It] For it 479.30

18.19 succeed . . . our] arrest the 479.33

18.29–30 often-repeated] more familiar 480.7

21.5 who] when he 971.1

21.26 revealed] *om.* 971.22

21.26–33 Spencer's . . . immediately—] This will immediately be recognized by those who have read Mill's *Logic* as the ground of Utility in his famous 'four methods of experimental inquiry,' the methods of agreement, of difference, of residues,

and of concomitant variations. Each
of these gives a list of analogous
instances out of the midst of which
a sought-for character may roll and
strike the mind. [¶] Now it is
obvious that any mind in which
association by similarity is highly
developed is a mind which will
spontaneously form lists of instances
like this. Take a present case A,
with a character *m* in it. The mind
may fail at first to notice this
character *m* at all. But if A calls up
C, D, E, and F,— 971.22–32

21.36   of the] of the reader's 971.35

21.38   simultaneous] *om.* 971.37

21.38–39   investigator] $\sim$, and may
lead to the noticing of *m* in an
abstract way 971.37–38

22.1   only . . . out] chief help towards
noticing 971.40–972.1

22.3   reasons] $\sim$, class names,
essences, or middle terms 972.2–3

22.13;35.17–18   Diagram] Figure
972.13;989.22

22.20   one] the one 972.20

22.23   sway.] $\sim$. [¶] Geniuses are, by
common consent, considered to
differ from ordinary minds by an
unusual development of association
by similarity. One of Professor
Bain's best strokes of work is the
exhibition of this truth.[15] It applies
to geniuses in the line of reasoning
as well as in other lines. And as
the genius is to the vulgarian, so the
vulgar human mind is to the
intelligence of a brute. Compared
with men, it is probable that brutes
neither attend to abstract characters,
nor have associations by similarity.
Their thoughts probably pass from
one concrete object to its habitual
concrete successor far more uniformly than is the case with us. In other
words, their associations of ideas are
almost exclusively by contiguity. It
will clear up still farther our understanding of the reasoning process,
if we devote a few pages to | THE
INTELLECTUAL CONTRAST BETWEEN

BRUTE AND MAN + *fn.* 972.24–
973.11,38–39

22.24   try now] first try 973.12

23.2   as scattering] who scatter 973.16

23.18   renew.] $\sim$. It would be a case of
immediate suggestion or of that
'Logic of Recepts' as Mr. Romanes
calls it, of which we spoke above on
p. 954. 973.33–34

23.27   trotted the latter] he trotted
974.6

23.34   boat] his boat 974.13

24.10   then] then always 974.29

24.10   mere . . . interest] peculiar
practical interests 974.29

24.16–18   whether . . . way,] however it
be represented in his mind—it is
represented probably by a 'recept'
(p. 954) or set of practical tendencies,
rather than by a definite concept or
idea— 974.35–38

24.20   the reverse] playing with you
974.40

24.22   objects] objects which 975.2

24.23   We] I 975.4

24.27   overboard . . . dove] over, he
immediately dived 975.7

24.30   things.$_\wedge$] $\sim$.[16] + *fn.* 975.10–47,
976.27–41

24.33   may have been] was probably
976.2

24.35   probably] *om.* 976.5

25.6   us to far] me far to 976.16

25.8   mere] *om.* 976.18

25.11   hardly been] been no 976.20

25.27   sensorium] mind 977.11

25.28   there.$_\wedge$] $\sim$.[18] + *fn.* 977.12,38–42

25.29   not] not be found to 977.12–13

25.30   only] *om.* 977.14

25.38   were] are 977.31

25.38–40   There . . . place.] I believe
that they are so, and that the only
difference between a muddle-head
and a genius is that between
extracting wrong characters and
right ones. In other words, a
muddle-headed person is a genius
spoiled in the making. I think it will
be admitted that all *eminently*
muddle-headed persons have the
temperament of genius. They are
constantly breaking away from the

usual consecutions of concretes. A
common associator by contiguity is
too closely tied to routine to get
muddle-headed. 977.31–37

26.2 all.] ∼. [¶] Professor . . . think."[19]
+ *fn.* 977.20–979.20,30–43

26.3–4 Another . . . animal.] Other
classical *differentiæ* of man besides
that of being the only reasoning
animal, also seem consequences of
his unrivalled powers of similar
association. He has, e.g., been called
'the laughing animal.' 979.21–24

26.4 has] has often 979.24

26.5 certain] *om.* 979.24

26.10 *Language* is certainly] Man is
known again as 'the talking animal';
and language is assuredly 980.1–2

26.39 third] third thing 980.31

27.6 As] It arises as 980.37

27.7 the sign] a *sign* 980.38

27.8 it] this notion 980.39

27.10–11 import— . . . constitution]
several imports and natures 981.1

27.14 have] probably thereupon 981.5

27.14 speaker] general sign-maker, or
speaker 981.5–6

27.16–17 so often repeated] laid down
(p. 478) 981.8

27.29 as] as the idea of 981.20–21

27.29 or] or of 981.21

27.30 they] these 981.22

27.30 -hunt] -hunt idea 981.22

28.20 criterion—] ∼, for 982.20

29.13 error . . . ²thought] his error . . .
his thought 983.9

29.25–26 characteristic] *elementary*
983.21–22

29.31–32 But . . . interests.] If a
character stands out alone, it is
always some obvious sensible quality
like a sound or a smell which is
instinctively exciting and lies in the
line of the animal's propensities;
or it is some obvious sign which
experience has habitually coupled
with a consequence, such as, for the
dog, the sight of his master's hat
on and the master's going out.
983.27–32

29.38 an . . . on] *om.* 982.38

29.39 1877.] ∼). Dr. Romanes, in the

book from which I have already
quoted, seeks to show that the
'consciousness of truth as truth' and
the deliberate intention to predicate
(which are the characteristics of
higher human reasoning) presuppose
a consciousness of ideas as such,
as things distinct from their
objects; and that this consciousness
depends on our having made signs
for them by language. My text seems
to me to include Dr. Romanes's
facts, and formulates them in what
to me is a more elementary way,
though the reader who wishes to
understand the matter better should
go to his clear and patient exposition also. 982.39–41,983.33–38

30.3 we . . . back,] *om.* 984.9

30.6 approbation] selection 984.12

30.8 then] *then,* as has already been
said 984.13

30.9–10 , in . . . *Character,*] *om.* 984.15

30.13 He . . . how] *om.* 984.18

30.21 reasoners] ∼, properly so called
984.25–26

30.30 association] similarity 984.35

31.21–22 should not] is not as liable
to 985.26–27

32.13–14 We . . . how] *om.* 986.21

32.15 were . . . their] may have
identical 986.22

32.25–34 ᴧYou . . . pleasure.ᴧ] *db. qts.*
around all dialogue 986.33–987.2

32.27 doesn't] does not 986.34

32.39 1876] 1879 987.40 (*em.*)

33.11 actions—] ∼, of 987.17

33.16–17 abstraction] abstraction can
work 987.23

33.17–20 words . . . first] *om.* 987.23

33.20 will] will therefore probably
987.24

33.34 the] one and the 987.37

34.2 bases] basis 988.7

34.4 an . . . department] immense
departments 988.8

34.19 mere . . . figure] bare figure with
unduly flexed joints 988.22–23

34.19 suggest all] so suggest 988.23

34.20 can't] cannot 988.24

34.36 final] *physiological* 989.1

34.36–39 theory . . . up] principles

laid down in Chapter XIV are true
989.1–2

34.40 is] must be 989.3–4

35.7 But] *om.* 989.10

35.9 which . . . seems] we found, in
the chapter in question, to be the
basis of similar association. (See
especially pp. 544–547.) It would
seem to be 989.12–14

35.10 localize-] localized$_\Lambda$ 989.15

35.19 at least] *om.* 989.24

35.25–27 We . . . hands.] We can but
bequeath the problem to abler hands
than our own. 989.30–31

35.29 , with . . . conclude] *om.* 989.33

36.5 Spencer's] the 990.10

36.7–8 , both . . . others,] *om.* 990.12

36.10–12 The . . . constitute] In
Chapter XXVIII we shall see what
we may call 990.14–15

36.15 be the probable] possibly be the
990.18

36.17 and . . . law] *om.* 990.20

36.17 do] certainly do 990.20

36.23 of Spencer's] *om.* 990.25

36.31 quality] quality of intellect
990.34

36.36 Spencer's law] the law that
habits are inherited 990.39–991.1

37.8 probably could] may probably
991.13

37.13 placed.$_\Lambda$] ∼.^{25} + *fn.* 991.17,33–42

37.24 condition by] ground on 991.28

37.25 are formed] grow up 991.29

ARE WE AUTOMATA?

The copy-text is P24, "Are We Automata?" *Mind,* 4 (January 1879), 1–22
(McD 1879:5). Reference is made to passages directly utilized by PP, *The Principles of Psychology*, the page-line numbers drawn from the edition in the
WORKS; for the details of the relationship, see The Text of *Essays in Psychology*. All references to the right of the bracket are to PP.

39.39–40.1 Nothing . . . all.] *om.* 138.20

42.13 It . . . which] But this very
vagueness 142.27–28

42.17 Now] *om.* 142.31

42.26 woman's first] *om.* 143.1

42.34 seems] ∼, in short, 143.9–10

43.13 our next] the 143.28

46.27–28 even . . . mentality.] *om.*
273.29

46.29 senses] very senses 273.29

47.3–4 , in a word,] *om.* 274.6

47.7 the attention] Attention 274.10

47.9–10 immortal . . . *Optics*] work on
Optics 274.12

47.15 , as . . . out,]$_\Lambda$ without special
training$_\Lambda$ 274.17

47.16 , until . . . sensation] *om.* 274.18

47.17 overlooked . . . men] ignorant
are most men of this 274.18–19

47.18 not know it.^{6}] never know the
fact.$_\Lambda$ (*no fn.*) 274.20

48.26 The] In like manner, the 274.39

48.38 form] form for us 275.11

48.39 with] with what we call 275.12

48.40 we . . . it] it may yield us 275.13

48.40–49.6 themselves . . . rest.^{7}] mere
sensations like the latter. The mind
chooses to suit itself, and decides
what particular sensation shall be
held more real and valid than all the
rest.$_\Lambda$ (*no fn.*) 275.13–16

49.10–11 be . . . reality] stand for the
objective reality *par excellence*
275.20

49.11 the mind's] *om.* 275.21

49.13 objects] things 275.22

49.14–15 objects and events] things
275.23

49.16,21 An object] A thing 275.25,29

50.8–10 an . . . show] a future chapter
we shall see 276.5

50.12 partial . . . elements] parts 276.7

50.13–14 theoretical or practical] *om.*
276.9

50.17 , as it were,] *om.* 276.12

50.19–23 Association . . . maximum.]
om. 276.14

50.25 that] the 276.16

50.25–26 which . . . spontaneity] of the
mind 276.16

50.27–28 ¹the . . . of] its æsthetic department 276.17

51.1 longing] our longing 276.30

51.10 *Selves*] Characters 276.39–40

51.11 his . . . *Ego*] he 276.40

51.16 very] *om.* 277.4

51.16 character] character itself 277.5

51.17 kind of a] *om.* 277.6

51.35 even] , if we like 277.22–23

51.40 as . . . statue] like sculptors, 277.28

51.40–52.1 the other . . . stone] certain portions of the given stuff 277.28–29

52.2 chaos] monotonous and inexpressive chaos 277.30–31

52.2 Goethe's] My 277.31

52.4 Some . . . exist] How different must be the worlds 277.32–33

52.5 crab . . . -fish.] cuttle-fish, or crab! 277.33

54.15 That . . . be] Consciousness, for example, is only 145.7

54.16–21 retarded . . . of] hesitant. In rapid, automatic, habitual action it sinks to a minimum. Nothing could be more fitting than this, if consciousness have the teleological function we suppose; nothing more meaningless, if not. Habitual actions are certain, and being in no danger of going astray from their end, need no extraneous help. In hesitant action, there seem many alternative possibilities of final 145.8–13

54.23 nerve-track] alternative nerve-tract 145.15

54.30–31 The . . . chain] The phenomena of 'vicarious function'

which we studied in Chapter II seem to form another bit 145.23–24

54.32–35 functions . . . functioning] acts . . . acting 145.25–27

55.2–5 Why . . . ones?] *om.* 145.34

55.8 If . . . taking] Some of the restoration is undoubtedly due to 'inhibitions' passing away. But if the consciousness which goes with the rest of the brain, be there not only in order to take 145.36–39

55.9 able] also 146.1

55.10 inhibit] check 146.1

55.10 ²to] and to 146.2

55.11 the nerve-defect] it 146.2

55.12–13 of the brain] *om.* 146.4

55.18 force.⁸] ~.ₐ At the end of Chapter XXVI I shall return to this again. (*no fn.*) 146.9–10

55.19 by] on 146.11

55.20;56.1,16 efficacity] efficacy 146.12,27;147.3

55.20–21 has . . . noticed] *is a well-known fact* 146.12–13

55.27–28 , in . . . has] and others have 146.20

56.4 a thrill] thrills 146.30

56.5 agony.⁹] ~.ₐ (*no fn.*) 146.31

56.6 this] the 146.32

56.11 would] would now be born to 146.37

56.12,19 very] *om.* 146.38;147.6

56.13 ever] *om.* 146.39

56.19 brain] brain-action 147.6

56.26 more than] quite 147.13

57.1 its] its causal 147.14

57.1 Conscious-] *om.* 147.14

THE SPATIAL QUALE

The copy-text is P21, "The Spatial Quale," *Journal of Speculative Philosophy*, 13 (January 1879), 64–87 (McD 1879:6). Reference is made to passages directly utilized by PP, *The Principles of Psychology*, the page-line references drawn from the edition in the WORKS; for the details of the relationship, see The Text of *Essays in Psychology*. All references to the right of the bracket are to PP. Although the PP text utilizing P21 was immediately derived from P24, "The Perception of Space," *Mind*, 12 (January, April 1887), 1–30, 183–211 (McD 1887:4), only the PP variants are provided.

68.19 Let the objector] If the reader will 781.35
68.27 author] writer 781.39
68.34 Now] But 782.6
69.1 us.⁴] ∼.ᴧ (*no fn.*) 782.13
69.3 state.ᴧ] ∼.¹⁰ + *fn.* 782.15,36–40
69.16–18 Just . . . motion] *The feeling of motion has generally been assumed by physiologists* 810.7–8
69.20 their] the 810.9
69.20 occupancies] occupancies of these positions 810.9–10
69.21 time.ᴧ] ∼.³² + *fn.* 810.11,37–39

69.23 I] we 810.13
70.19 young] *om.* 811.10
70.30 or] or from the 811.21
73.1 seems to be] is 808.24
73.24 a more] the more 807.21
73.25 belly-ache] of a 'bellyache' 807.22
73.25–27 I . . . my . . . I am] one . . . one's . . . one is 807.22–25
73.27 former] former region 807.24–25
75.31–33 Again . . . require] *The local differences require then* 807.26
75.34 But] *om.* 807.27

THE FEELING OF EFFORT

The copy-text is P42, "The Feeling of Effort," *Anniversary Memoirs of the Boston Society of Natural History* (1880), pp. 3–32 (McD 1880:3). Reference is made to passages directly utilized by PP, *The Principles of Psychology*, the page-line numbers drawn from the edition in the WORKS; for the details of the relationship, see The Text of *Essays in Psychology*. All references to the right of the bracket are to PP unless otherwise noted; the note (*em.*) indicates emendation of the first printing of PP by the present editor to the form shown in the lemma. The notation WJ/PP indicates a handwritten correction or revision in James's private copy of *Principles*. Reference is also made to the reprint in CER, *Collected Essays and Reviews*, edited by R. B. Perry, pp. 151–219 (McD 1920:2), which has been collated for substantives only.

84.1 *the*] *om.* CER
86.4–5 Plausibility . . . law:] It is a general principle in Psychology 1107.7
86.5 seems to desert] deserts 1107.7
86.6 any] *om.* 1107.8
86.7–8 in Psychology] *om.* 1107.10
86.8 logical] *om.* 1107.10
86.8 parsimony] parsimony in logic 1107.10
86.11 function] work 1108.1
86.18 The] That 1108.8
86.20 thinks] ends by thinking 1108.10
86.22 in space] of the pole 1108.12
86.23 by movement] *om.* 1108.13
87.22 Now] For 1109.13
87.22 second] *om.* 1109.14
87.23 idea] idea of the movement 1109.14
87.25 ideas] ideas of movement 1109.16

87.25 feelings.⁶] centres.ᴧ (*no fn.*) 1109.17
87.26 specific] with a specific feeling of innervation attached to its discharge 1109.17–18
87.28 they] the feelings of innervation 1109.20–21
87.29 notion . . . end] idea of a movement 1109.22
87.32 "ends"] our kinæsthetic ideas 1109.24–25
87.35,37 (*twice*) end] idea 1109.27,30 (*twice*)
88.6 encumbrance] ∼, and to presume that the peripheral ideas of movement are sufficient mental cues 1109.36–37
89.8 intensity.⁹] ∼.ᴧ 1110.30 (*fn. keyed to* 1108.36 'remote.')
89.9 what] which 1110.31
89.11 altogether?ᴧ] ∼?¹² + *fn.* 1110.33,38–41

437

89.30 result,¹⁰] ~,ʌ (*no fn.*) 1111.19
89.36 Harless] Prof. Harless 1108.38
89.38–39 our . . . movement] these
   images 1108.40
90.7 feelings are afferent] are
   incoming feelings 1111.28
90.10 Except . . . called] There is
   indeed 1111.32
90.17 or . . . example] arm, for
   example, or the left 1111.38–39
90.18–26,37–38 So . . . discharge.¹¹] *An*
   . . . on. 1111.40–1112.7
90.27–29 Is . . . strong.] Since there is
   no direct introspective evidence for
   the feelings of innervation, is there
   any indirect or circumstantial
   evidence? Much is offered; but on
   critical examination it breaks down.
   Let us see what it is. 1113.9–12
90.29 says,¹²] ~,ʌ 1113.12 (*fn. keyed to*
   91.7 [PP 1113.26] 'formerly." ')
91.12 Dr.] But Dr. 1114.3
91.24–46 Dr. . . . make.] *om.* 1114.43
93.23 add.ʌ] ~.¹⁸ + *fn.* 1115.31,33–44,
   1116.37–39
93.31 where] where next 1116.7
93.33 last] *om.* 1116.9
93.34–37 And . . . failure.] *om.* 1116.10
93.38–94.1 examine . . . few] recall our
   1116.12
94.13 (*twice*) shall] *om.* 1116.23
94.25 on.] ~. (See above, pp. 734–736.)
   1116.35–36
95.6 *effects*] *effect* 1117.18 (*em.*)
95.22 very] *om.* 1117.23
95.39 S. 18] pp. 18–21 1117.41
96.31 show.ʌ] ~.²² + *fn.* 1118.40–41,
   1119.26–43
97.27 alone.ʌ] ~.²³ + *fn.* 1120.11,21–45
97.29 ¶ Not] (*no* ¶) It most assuredly
   can, for not 1120.12–13
97.31 function] act WJ/PP 1120.16
97.33 Now] *om.* 1120.17
97.34–37 also . . . to] naturally
   undistinguished as respects
   1120.18–19
98.13 respectively] severally 1121.2
98.15 ¶ Now] (*no* ¶) Similarly 1121.2
98.16 also] *om.* 1121.3
102.17–18 As . . . says:²³] To quote
   Lotze once more:ʌ 1133.18–19 (*fn.*

   keyed to 103.18 [PP 1131.32]
   'thought." ')
102.37 1852,] *om.* 1131.33
102.44 so] such 1131.40
103.14;110.28 oneself] one's self
   1131.28;1167.44
103.15 actions] acts 1131.29
105.15 air.ʌ] ~.¹³ + *fn.* 1112.34–41,
   1113.29–32
105.38 is] after being 1113.39
105.39 195] 188 is, as far as the
   anatomical and physiological
   grounds go, again thrown into doubt
   by Mays: Zeitschrift für Biologie, Bd.
   xx 1113.40–41 ('188' *em. to* '195')
107.21–22 do . . . representation] then
   follows or not 1165.6–7
107.23 of . . . represented] itself 1165.7
107.28 write.ʌ] ~.⁶⁰ + *fn.* 1165.13,
   31–42
107.30 *intention* or *consent*] stable
   state of the idea 1165.14
107.31 upon its completion] *om.*
   1165.15
107.32–34 belonging . . . unconscious]
   depending on executive ganglia
   whose function lies outside the mind
   1165.16–17
108.1 which they prefigure]
   anticipated 1165.12
108.5 remains.³⁰] ~,ʌ (*no fn.*) 1165.26
108.6 associative] associated 1165.26–27
108.13 passive] passive as before 1166.3
108.20 We (*no* ¶)] ¶ Or we 1101.36
108.39 will the] make a muscular
   1166.35
109.31 in] *om.* 1102.32
109.34 533.] ~. Concerning all such
   cases see the remarks made above on
   pp. 840–841. 1102.35–36
110.26 volitional] *om.* 1167.42
110.26 great] great volitional 1167.43
110.36 contractions] attractions CER
   (*error*)
114.8 it."³⁶] ~."ʌ 1171.44 (*text found
   in fn.* 65 [PP 1171.26–41])
114.36–37 Muscular] These 1167.24
115.4 has . . . reality] must make its
   volitional effort in stably representing their reality and consequently
   bringing it about 1167.27–29

438

115.5   our bodily] muscular 1167.29
115.7   engendered . . . bodily] from his muscular 1167.31
115.8   *consenting to*] sustaining 1167.31
115.9   of . . . pumps] required for a painful muscular effort 1167.32
118.38 products] product CER (*error*)
119.15 its] the 1154.29
119.15 follows] is in 1154.30
119.16–19 When . . . motivation.] *om.* 1154.31
119.20–21 is . . . resistance] never speaks of volition with effort in this way 1154.32
119.23–26 law . . . he] physical law must also hold good in the mental sphere. But we *feel*, in all hard cases of volition, as if the line taken, when the rarer and more ideal motives prevail, were the line of greater resistance, and as if the line of coarser motivation were the more pervious and easy one, even at the very moment when we refuse to follow it. He 1154.34–39
119.28 ostracism] social obloquy 1155.1
119.34 motives as sensual] springs of action as propensities 1155.8
119.34 moral] ideals 1155.8
119.36 conscience] ideals 1155.10
119.37 appetite] propensities 1155.11
119.38 ideal] ideals 1155.12
119.39 moral] ideal 1155.13
120.1   sensual impulse] propensities 1155.15

120.1   moral one] ideal impulse 1155.15
120.3–4 sensual force] force of propensity 1155.18
120.4   moral] ideal force 1155.19
120.6   moral force] an ideal motive 1155.20–21
120.8   impulses are] propensity is 1155.22–23
120.8   moral] *om.* 1155.23
120.10 moral] ideal or moral 1155.24–25
120.13–14 S . . . moral$_\Lambda$] P standing for the propensity, I for the ideal impulse, 1155.28–29
120.15–16 M . . . > S.] I *per se* < P. | I + E > P. 1155.30–31
120.17 M, S] I, P 1155.32
120.19 M] I 1155.34
120.30–31 and probabilities,] *om.* 1176.20
120.31 decide] decide the point 1176.20–21
120.33 evidence for] reasons adduced on 1176.23
120.34 question . . . refined] discussion more refined 1176.24
120.35 his . . . is] our . . . be 1176.24–25
120.37 genius[40]] ~$_\Lambda$ (*no fn.*) 1176.26
120.38 him] us 1176.28
121.1   his . . . he] our . . . we 1176.29
121.2   alternatives . . . mind,] alternative views$_\Lambda$ 1176.29–30
121.2   *him*] us; we must so fill our mind with the idea of it that it becomes our settled creed 1176.30–31

THE SENSE OF DIZZINESS IN DEAF-MUTES

The copy-text is P2, "The Sense of Dizziness in Deaf-Mutes," *American Journal of Otology*, 4 (October 1882), 239–254 (McD 1882:3), with reference to unique substantive variants contained in the reprint in CER, *Collected Essays and Reviews*, edited by R. B. Perry, pp. 220–243 (McD 1920:2).

132.3   incline] inclined CER
133.9–10 sea-sickness.[6] As . . . presumption] sea-|seasick.$_\Lambda$ This, it

is true, is negative evidence, and | sumption CER (*error*)
133.31 sufferers'] sufferer's CER

ON SOME OMISSIONS OF INTROSPECTIVE PSYCHOLOGY

The copy-text is P24, "On Some Omissions of Introspective Psychology," *Mind*, 9 (January 1884), 1–26 (McD 1884:1). Reference is made to passages directly utilized by PP, *The Principles of Psychology*, the page-line numbers drawn from the edition in the Works; for the details of the relationship, see The Text of *Essays in Psychology*. All references to the right of the bracket are to PP; the note (*em.*) indicates emendation of the first printing of PP by the present editor to the form shown in the lemma.

143.5,6 (*twice*) feeling] state 190.1,2 (*twice*)

143.11 force.₍₎] ~.⁸ + *fn.* 190.6,33–40

143.14 have . . . may] had . . . might 190.9

143.15–16 Mohr . . . work.¹] Mohr.₍₎ 190.11 (*fn. keyed to* 143.22 [PP 190.17] 'consciousness." ')

143.28 When . . . rapid] As we take, in fact, a 236.15

143.29 the] this 236.16

143.30 different portions] parts 236.17

143.30 Our mental life,] *om.* 236.17

143.30 seems] it seems 236.17

144.2–3 We . . . say] It then appears 236.27–28

144.7 Of . . . hereafter.] *om.* 236.32

144.8 Now . . . seeing] Now it is very difficult, introspectively, to see 236.33

144.34–38 If . . . stream.] The results of this introspective difficulty are baleful. If to hold fast and observe the transitive parts of thought's stream be so hard, then the great blunder to which all schools are liable must be the failure to register them, and the undue emphasizing of the more substantive parts of the stream. 237.20–24

146.17–18 On the contrary,] *om.* 238.16

146.31–33 In . . . ways.] *om.* 238.29

146.38 the] that 238.35

146.39 which . . . namely] of which we said a word in Chapter VII, (see p. 194) 238.35–36

146.40 *dumb*] dumb or anonymous 239.1

153.2 Some . . . always] Ever some tracts are 229.4

153.3–4 , however,] *om.* 229.5

153.4 the discharges] any 229.6

153.5 consequently] *om.* 229.6

153.6 to . . . corresponds] *om.* 229.7

153.9 really] *om.* 229.9

153.10–11 distribution of] *om.* 229.11

153.12 the aurora . . . or] *om.* 229.12

153.13 the brain's] its 229.13

153.14–15 that . . . -grained,] and 229.14

153.22 As] And (to consider shorter periods) just as, 228.30–31

153.32 feel.₍₎] ~.⁹ + *fn.* 229.3,34–40

154.9,10 Counting] leaving 243.4,5

154.21 proposed] proposed to us 243.16

155.31 "What?"] *om.* 244.24

156.28 say] admit 245.22

157.23 reader's] *om.* 246.16

157.24 have] ~, as we shall see in Chapter XVIII, 246.16–17

157.26 Mr. . . . overthrowing] Another is made in the overthrow of 246.19–20

157.28 feelings] subjective feelings 246.21–22

158.12 process.₍₎] ~.¹⁷ + *fn.* 247.5,33–41

159.10–160.3,8–48 Now . . . contempt.] *text found in fn.* 17 451.33–452.51, 453.33–38

159.10 Now] *om.* 451.35

159.31 forth] forth [in Chapter IX] 452.10

159.32 reveals] may reveal 452.12

159.38–39 ¹of . . . strength] *om.* 452.16

160.8 not,] ~, then, 452.19

160.11 past . . . south,] the poles 452.22

160.18 grasps] may grasp 452.28

160.18 universal] *om.* 452.29

160.37 an] *om.* 452.47 (*em.*)

160.38 for granted] as a matter of course 452.47–48

161.7–8 When . . . this] Usually the 253.21

164.4 The . . . is] But the *Object* of your thought is really 265.28

164.12–15 not . . . and] strictly speaking neither Columbus, nor America, nor its discovery. It is nothing short of the entire sentence, 'Columbus-discovered-America-in-1492.' And 265.37–39

164.17 in full] thus 265.40

164.17 short of] but 266.1

WHAT IS AN EMOTION?

The copy-text is P24, "What Is an Emotion?" *Mind*, 9 (April 1884), 188–205 (McD 1884:2). Reference is made to passages directly utilized by PP, *The Principles of Psychology*, the page-line numbers drawn from the edition in the WORKS; for the details of the relationship, see The Text of *Essays in Psychology*. All references to the right of the bracket are to PP unless otherwise noted; the note *(em.)* indicates emendation of the first printing of PP by the present editor to the form shown in the lemma. Reference is made to the reprint in CER, *Collected Essays and Reviews*, edited by R. B. Perry, pp. 244–275 (McD 1920:2), which has been collated for substantives only.

170.8 standard] coarser 1065.27
170.11 thesis] theory 1065.30
170.26 could] should 1066.7
172.28 And the] The 1066.18
173.23 on.¹] ∼.ᴧ *(no fn.)* 1067.12
173.26 characteristic] *om.* 1067.15
174.15 feelings] feeling 1067.35
174.18 impossible] impossible for me 1067.38
174.19 of it] *om.* 1067.39
174.39 changes] changes which 1068.19
176.21–22 But . . . asked] Let me now notice a few objections. The replies will make the theory still more plausible. [¶] *First Objection.* There is no real evidence, it may be said, 1072.2–4
176.26 The . . . there] *Reply.* There 1072.8
177.13 effects.] ∼. [¶] Professor . . . them."¹⁰ 1072.30–1073.2
177.19 effect] effect which 1073.8
177.22 a representation] an anticipation 1073.11
177.26–27 I . . . seemed] In cases of morbid terror the subjects often confess that what possesses them seems 1073.15–16
177.28 the fear of] fear of the 1073.16–17
177.38–39 presented . . . which] vivid feeling of the manifestations, or the idea of them; and the 1073.27–28
177.40 its sum . . . -trade] and sum and substance 1073.29
178.4 ²be] be this: 1077.10
178.5 voluntary] voluntary and cold-blooded 1077.10
178.6 Of course in] Now this (the objection says) is not found to be the

case. An actor can perfectly simulate an emotion and yet be inwardly cold; and we can all pretend to cry and not feel grief; and feign laughter without being amused. [¶] *Reply.* In 1077.12–16
178.8 volitional] voluntary 1077.18
178.9 Still] Few people in pretending to cry can shed real tears, for example. But 1077.18–19
178.9–10 fully . . . test] corroborates rather than disproves the corollary from our theory, upon which the present objection rests 1077.20–21
178.10 Everyone] Every one 1077.21 *(em.)*
178.25 *motions*] *movements* 1077.37
178.26 we] which we 1077.37
178.33–35 The great . . . talked] It is true that we say of certain persons that "they would feel more if they expressed 1081.24–25
179.18 effects] effects later on 1080.34
179.21 relief.] ∼. This . . . strong." 1081.2–11
179.22 emotions] emotional talk and display 1081.12–13
179.24 nerve-] *om.* 1081.14
179.25,35–41 brain.³ | ³This . . . decision.] brain.ᴧ In . . . child. 1081.16–24
179.26–27 The . . . we] One of the chief merits, in fact, of the view which I propose seems to be that we can so easily 1073.35–36
179.34–180.1 will cause] causes 1074.6
180.1 as a consequence] *om.* 1074.7
180.39 with] and yet, as I believe, with 1074.41

180.40–43 Whether . . . field.] *om.*
1074.42
181.28 be] is 1082.1
181.32–33 it . . . affirmed] the reader
will remember that we agreed at the
outset to affirm this 1082.5–6
181.34 agreed . . . "standard"] called
the 'coarser' 1082.7
181.35 sensibilities that] states of
emotional sensibility which 1082.8
181.36–38 had . . . remember,] must
now say a word or two about these
latter feelings, the 'subtler'
emotions, as we then agreed to call
them. [¶] These are 1082.10–13
182.1 fitnesses] fitness CER
182.4–5 tried to distinguish]
distinguished 1082.18
182.6 geometrical] mathematical
1082.19
182.8–9 here . . . there] *om.* 1082.21
182.12 so-called "standard"] 'coarser'
1082.24
182.18,39 "standard"] 'coarser'
1082.30;1085.14

182.18–19 the presence . . . events]
other kinds of objects 1082.31
182.22–29 But . . . rather] In . . . this
is 1082.34–1085.3
182.30 But] *om.* 1085.4
182.30 the intellectual . . . does]
, however, the moral and intellectual
cognitions hardly ever do 1085.4–5
182.33 effects] ∼, even æsthetic ones,
1085.8–9
182.34 emotional . . . thereto] mere
emotional excitability 1085.9
182.35 ¹the] *om.* 1085.10
183.37–184.5 Cognition . . . of] And . . .
by 1086.11–1087.18
184.8 perfectly] *om.* 1087.21
184.10 and . . . centre] affects a cortical
part, and is perceived 1087.22–23
184.11 in . . . way] inwardly 1087.23
184.14 apperceived] perceived 1087.26
184.15 specific] *om.* 1087.27
184.18 is] *om.* 1087.30
184.18 circuit] circuits 1087.30
184.19 topical] local 1087.31

REPORT OF THE COMMITTEE ON HYPNOTISM

The copy-text is P31, "Report of the Committee on Hypnotism," *Proceedings of the American Society for Psychical Research*, 1 (July 1886), 95–102 (McD 1886:1). Reference is made to passages directly utilized by PP, *The Principles of Psychology*, the page-line numbers drawn from the edition in the WORKS; for the details of the relationship, see The Text of *Essays in Psychology*. All references to the right of the bracket are to PP.

192.6 all!³] ∼!ᴧ (*no fn.*) 1207.19
192.23 state.⁴] ∼.ᴧ (*no fn.*) 1207.37
194.14–27 This . . . surrenders] Just so
we may remember a friend's house
in a street by the single character
of its number rather than by its
general look. The trance-subject

would seem, in these instances, to
surrender 975.28–31
194.29,31 general] total 975.32,34
195.19 out altogether. The] off
altogether, and then the 976.35–36
195.19 then] *om.* 976.36

THE CONSCIOUSNESS OF LOST LIMBS

The copy-text is P31, "The Consciousness of Lost Limbs," *Proceedings of the American Society for Psychical Research*, 1 (December 1887), 249–258 (McD 1887:10), with reference to the reprint in CER, *Collected Essays and Reviews*, edited by R. B. Perry, pp. 285–302 (McD 1920:2), which has been collated for substantives only.

212.41 it] *om.* CER

WHAT THE WILL EFFECTS

The copy-text is P37, "What the Will Effects," *Scribner's Magazine*, 3 (February 1888), 240–250 (McD 1888:1). Reference is made to passages directly utilized by PP, *The Principles of Psychology*, the page-line numbers drawn from the edition in the WORKS; for the relationship, see The Text of *Essays in Psychology*. All references to the right of the bracket are to PP; the notation WJ/PP refers to a correction or revision in James's private copy of *Principles*.

218.16 that child] this youngster 1099.17–18

218.17 ¹as] as much 1099.18

218.19 already] *om.* 1099.20

220.18 from] out of 1131.12

220.25 all] *om.* 1132.23

220.27 of us] persons 1132.25

220.28 ourselves] themselves 1132.26

222.30 , as . . . see] *om.* 1135.14

222.31 will prompt] prompts 1135.15

222.38 all.²] ∼.ᴧ (*no fn.*) 1135.22

226.31 pocket] avoid a fight as to begin one, to pocket 1167.6–7

226.32 pay . . . easy] squander it on one's cupidities, 1167.7

226.32–33 in . . .¹of] towards 1167.8

226.38–39 that . . . If] those uncertainties and risks of failure which abound upon our path; if 1167.14–15

226.40 flowers and spring] travels, loves, and joys 1167.15–16

227.5;230.35,36 ideas] objects 1167.21;1175.18 (*twice*)

227.14 "*Hæc* . . . feel.] *om.* WJ/PP 1168.8

227.19 like] *om.* 1168.13

227.27 moral . . . calling] difficult object erelong begins to call 1168.20

227.28 changing] changing the disposition of 1168.21

227.29–30 actions . . . are] action changes, for the new object, once 1168.22–23

227.30–31 mental . . . their] field of his thoughts, infallibly produces its own 1168.23–24

227.31–37 struggle . . . . The] difficulty lies in the gaining possession of that field. Though the spontaneous drift of thought is all the other way, the attention must be kept strained on that one object until at last it *grows*, so as to maintain itself before

the mind with ease. This strain of the attention is the fundamental act of will. And the will's work is in most cases practically ended when the bare presence to our thought of the naturally unwelcome object has been secured. For the 1168.24–31

227.37–38 ideas . . . cerebral] thought and the 1168.32

228.1 that] how 1168.35

228.2 voluntary] volitional 1168.36

228.2 does . . . but] lies exclusively 1168.36

228.3 in] within WJ/PP 1168.36

228.3 world. It] ∼. The whole drama is a mental drama. The whole difficulty is a mental difficulty, a difficulty with an object of our thought. If I may use the word *idea* without suggesting associationist or Herbartian fables, I will say that it 1168.36–1169.1

228.11–13 There . . . some] If the idea be that, or include that, of a 1169.9–10

228.13 we] then we 1169.10

228.14 volition] motor volition 1169.11

228.14–16 The . . . real.] *om.* 1169.11

228.16 Nature] For Nature 1169.11–12

228.17–18 of . . . . Nature] on her own part. She 1169.13

228.18–19 than . . . movements] *om.* 1169.14

230.30–32 The . . . chose.] It certainly appears to us indeterminate, and as if, even with an unchanging object, we might make more or less, as we choose. 1175.13–14

230.37–38 of attention] *om.* 1175.20

231.2 attention] attention or consent 1175.24

231.4 idea . . . or] object, or are they 1175.26

231.5 attention] effort 1175.26

RÉPONSE DE M. W. JAMES AUX REMARQUES DE M. RENOUVIER,
SUR SA THÉORIE DE LA VOLONTÉ

The copy-text is P9, "Réponse de M. W. James aux remarques de M. Renouvier, sur sa théorie de la volonté," *Critique Philosophique*, n.s. 2 (December 1888), 401–404 (McD 1888:2), with reference to the reprint entitled "Réponse aux remarques de M. Renouvier, sur sa théorie de la volonté" in CER, *Collected Essays and Reviews*, edited by R. B. Perry, pp. 303–309 (McD 1920:2), which has been collated for substantives only.

238.4 l'expérience] l'expérience
organisée par une formation interne,

et en partie tracées par l'experience
CER (*error*)

THE HIDDEN SELF

The copy-text is P37, "The Hidden Self," *Scribner's Magazine*, 7 (March 1890), 361–373 (McD 1890:1). Reference is made to passages directly utilized by WB, *The Will to Believe*, and by PP, *The Principles of Psychology*, the page-line numbers for each drawn from the editions in the WORKS; for the details of the relationships, see The Text of *Essays in Psychology*. All references to the right of the bracket are to WB or to PP, as indicated.

[*begin* WB]

247.6 less . . . ignore] more easy to ignore than to attend to 222.6

248.7 unclassed] unclassified 223.11

248.32–33 , standards,] *om.* 223.37

248.36 subscriber . . . MAGAZINE] reader 223.40

249.32 writer] writer of these pages 224.36

249.36 scientifically] certain scientifically 225.1

[*end* WB; *begin* PP]

251.5–7 ²blind . . . color] color-blind, or there is hemianopsia (blindness to one half the field of view), or the field is contracted 200.13–14

251.10 well learned] learned well 200.17

251.12 lately] recently 200.19

251.21 being] becoming 200.29

252.1 you] any person 201.15

252.2 stopped . . . anyone] talked directly with any one," says M. Janet 201.16 (*em. to* 'anyone')

252.3 anyone else] any other person 201.17

252.3 might] may 201.17

252.16 The . . . considering] These hysterical anæsthesias 200.30

252.18 metal,] ~, or 200.32

252.25 question.²] ~.ₐ (*no fn.*) 201.1

252.30–32 One . . . just] But one day when the hysteric anæsthetic named Lucie was already in the hypnotic trance, M. Janet for a certain reason continued to make passes over her for a full half-hour 364.1–4

252.34 another half] half an 364.6

252.35 hitherto] thitherto 364.7

253.4 was] became 364.12

253.18 seemed] seemed to M. Janet to be 364.26

253.19–20 —of . . . facts] *om.* 364.27

253.21 trance] trance and change of personality 364.28

253.23 , best of all,] *om.* 364.30

253.27–28 modification . . . personality.ₐ] individuality.⁵⁶ + *fn.* 364.35,39–40

253.29–30 ⁴the . . . transformed] these subjects turned 364.36–37

253.31 grow] grew 364.38

253.31–32 here . . . this:] hereupon M. Janet spins a theoretic generalization. 364.38–365.1

253.33 sensation] *sensation*, he says, 365.1

254.2–6 effects . . . so] consequences of this law would be great, for all experiences belonging to a sphere

444

of sensibility which afterwards
became anæsthetic, as, for example,
touch, would have been stored away
and remembered in tactile terms,
and would be incontinently
forgotten as 365.10–14

255.29–30 such . . . that] that all sorts
of memories, absent in the ordinary
condition, came back too, and
365.19–20

255.30–31 ²of . . . inexplicable]
otherwise inexplicable things in
their life 365.21–22

255.32 attack] crisis 365.23

255.32 -epilepsy] -∼, for example,
365.23

255.32 ²the] *om.* 365.23

255.33 *la*] the 365.24

255.39–40 her . . . 3] the deeper trance
365.30–31

255.40 crises] crisis 365.31

256.7 recollects] recollected 365.37

256.8–9 , and . . . disappeared] *om.*
365.39

256.10 the case of] M. Janet's subject
365.40

256.10–11 ²the . . . beautifully]
interesting, and shows best 365.40

256.23 than] when 366.13

256.40 1] 1 [as M. Janet calls the
waking woman] 366.31

257.11 since] *om.* 367.1

257.13 second] second or deepest
367.3–4

257.27 Dr. Perrier,] *om.* 367.17

259.15 of the] of a 202.1

259.17 all] *om.* 202.3

259.23 etc.] etc., etc. 202.9

260.3 things] thing 202.28

260.12 could] would 202.38

260.15 of the] in 203.1

260.31 But] *om.* 203.18

260.35 upper] *om.* 203.22

261.2 here] in this spot 203.25

261.12 couldn't] could not 203.35

261.13 Similarly . . . colors] Colors are
similarly perceived by the
sub-conscious self 204.1

261.15 Again,] *om.* 204.3

261.22 them, . . . still—] ∼. More . . .
still, they 204.10

261.34–35 picked . . . those] said she
saw those only 204.22–23

262.14 and] or 205.1

262.15 subject] well-known subject of
the Salpêtrière 205.2–3

262.15 had] *om.* 205.4

262.23 deeper] deepest 205.11

262.37 Janet] J. 205.25

263.11 The] The *writing on the*
205.38–39

263.15 go.ᴧ] ∼.⁷ + *fn.* 206.2,39

263.16 in] *in the so-called* 206.3

263.24 comes over him] possesses the
man 206.11

263.26 was] is 206.13

263.32 orders] orders which 206.19

263.34 execution.ᴧ] ∼.⁸ + *fn.* 206.21,40

264.13 remains] remained 207.2

264.17 3ᴧ] ∼⁹ + *fn.* 207.6,38–39

264.22 being] *om.* 207.10

264.28 obtain] exist 207.17

264.30 hysteric] hysterical 207.19

264.32 all] *om.* 207.21

264.39 self-] sub- 207.28

265.18 Léonie 1] Léonie's normal self
208.9

[*end* PP]

A Plea for Psychology as a 'Natural Science'

The copy-text is P28, "A Plea for Psychology as a 'Natural Science,'" *Philo-sophical Review*, 1 (March 1892), 146–153 (McD 1892:4), with reference to unique substantive variants contained in the reprint in CER, *Collected Essays and Reviews*, edited by R. B. Perry, pp. 316–327 (McD 1920:2).

274.16 thereby a] thereby a | force it   thereby a | CER (*error*)
on their attention, and perpetuate

Word-Division

The following is a list of possible hyphenated compounds divided at the end of the line in the copy-text but which were not confirmed in their forms as printed in the present edition because the copy-text did not derive from an earlier document. If the form of the word could be confirmed somewhere else in the essay it was not included in this list. In a sense, then, the hyphenation or the non-hyphenation of possible compounds in the present list is in the nature of editorial emendation.

10.17	anti-dyspeptic	161.14	rat-trap
11.23	mantle-clock	176.23	wide-spread
24.37	lumber-camp	176.29	heart-swelling
40.19	non-existence	177.24	heart-sinking
52.11	nonentity	198.13	counter-irritating
57.7	self-preservation	209.34	non-feeling
80.13	air-wave	227.22	death-bringing
106.5	non-congenital	232.8	hilltops
106.15	prearrangement	240.27	pre-eminent
133.1	over-excitement	264.30	co-ordinating
145.27	supersensible	326.20	ultra-marginal
149.25	quasi-mechanical	330.6	anti-pedantic
153.39	reinterpret		

The following is a list of words divided at the ends of lines in the present edition but which represents authentic hyphenated compounds as found within the lines of the copy-text. Except for this list, all other hyphenations at the ends of lines in the present edition are the modern printer's and are not hyphenated forms in the copy-text.

12.23	chair-|maker	54.18	nerve-|tracks
13.35	stove-|pipe's	56.16	double-|aspect
18.29	often-|repeated	63.6	non-|spatial
24.25	fish-|basket	71.39;221.25	re-|enforced
27.27	rat-|hunt	73.24	spacious-|sounding
28.18;176.4	self-|consciousness	80.12	end-|organs
35.10	localize-|vibration	81.9	pre-|existent
39.12	rational-|seeming	81.26	non-|spatial
42.6	pre-|occupations	83.6	elle-|même
48.7	ultra-|sensational	108.18	quasi-|accidental
50.20	breaking-|up	108.38	non-|performance
54.4;126.36;138.24;210.19	so-|called	110.10	amusement-|craving

122.30;123.8 -force-|sense	214.21 cut-|off
126.29 co-|ordinations	216.15 natural-|history
132.6 twenty-|three	224.24 sluice-|way
137.21 all-|sufficient	225.24 nerve-|action
142.8 in-|itself	227.2 fever-|fit
150.39 -the-|contrast-	231.13 free-|will
153.17 brain-|redistributions	233.15 snap-|decision
156.27 *-to-|say-*	239.12 Space-|perception
162.12 Green-|after-	242.6 space-|feelings
163.7 -with-|something-	250.34 trance-|conditions
165.3 *-complete-|thought*	259.26 half-|way
165.39 sense-|perception	261.31 post-|hypnotic
167.19 text-|books	265.1;267.5;268.29 sub-|consciousness
169.10 brain-|physiology	278.2;279.2 deaf-|mute's
170.35 hermit-|crab's	286.41 door-|steps
172.19 heart-|beats	291.2 gold-|piece
173.27 mind-|stuff	304.26 feeling-|attitude
174.25 cold-|blooded	312.36 non-|existent
176.15 emotion-|arousing	316.30 air-|current
188.22 sea-|sickness	324.20 prison-|house
193.32 after-|image	329.17 paragraph-|headings
202.27 reaction-|time	336.14 sky-|scrapers
207.6 foot-|moving	337.3 landscape-|painter
210.26 nerve-|ends	338.21 drawing-|rooms
213.6 hand-|or-	

The following are actual or possible hyphenated compounds broken at the end of the line in both the copy-text and the present edition.

1.21 self-|consciousness (i.e., self-consciousness)	208.22 deeper-|lying (i.e., deeper-lying)
20.15 index-|finger (i.e., index-finger)	231.36 sober-|minded (i.e., sober-minded)
162.8 post-|Kantians (i.e., post-Kantians)	271.33 subject-|matter (i.e., subject-matter)
178.24 cold-|bloodedly (i.e., cold-bloodedly)	293.1 space-|determinations (i.e., space-determinations)
202.4 half-|an- (i.e., half-an-)	329.13 text-|book (i.e., text-book)
208.1 brain-|centres (i.e., brain-centres)	332.24 chimney-|breasts (i.e., chimney-breasts)
208.2 *counter-|motive* (i.e., *counter-motive*)	

Index

This index is a name and subject index for the text of *Essays in Psychology* and Appendixes I and II. It is an index of names only for the "Notes," "A Note on the Editorial Method," and "The Text of *Essays in Psychology*."

Names of persons, localities, and institutions, and titles of books are indexed. However, such items are not indexed if no information about them is provided—if they are only a part of the identification of a discussed item or are merely used to indicate its location. This excludes, most of the time, names of editors, translators, and titles of reference books consulted in connection with the present text. Except for those by James himself, articles in periodicals are not indexed.

Throughout these essays James offers introspective evidence or refers to informal studies conducted on students and friends. Furthermore, he comments on his own experimental procedures and mentions various abandoned projects. Observations of this kind are listed in the index under James's name. Otherwise, references to James are not indexed.

The introduction to the present edition is also not indexed.

Absence, 155
"Absolutism and Empiricism" (W. James), 404
Abstraction, 33, 34
Academics, 248–249
Accident, 42, 53, 54, 213–214
Accommodation, 18, 99
Action: and brain, 35, 223; and sensation, 42, 217; and habit, 54; voluntary, 86–87, 105–106, 107; and ideas, 88–90, 101–105, 225; and effort, 110–114; and will, 115; moral, 119–121; and experience, 218–219; and inhibition, 221–222; and consent, 222; and pleasures and pains, 223–225; and attention, 227; and reflexes, 237–238; and knowledge, 304; and suffering, 338. *See also* Movement
Adamük, E., 97, 354
Adjectives, 33
Aeneid (Virgil), 366
Aesthetics: and interest, 15–16, 18, 21–22; and intuition, 31; reasons in, 34;

and faith, 39–40; and selection, 48, 50, 57–58; study of, 168; and emotion, 175
Affect, 300
Afferent currents, 84, 306, 307–308
Affirmation, 124
After-images, 191, 193
Algiers, 265
Allen, Charles Grant Blairfindie, 56, 347
Almy, Francis, 358, 359
Altérations de la personnalité, Les (A. Binet), 321, 377
American Asylum, 125, 128, 141, 358, 360
American character, 337, 338
American Nervousness (G. M. Beard), 360
American School for the Deaf, 358
American Society for Psychical Research, 190, 364, 405
Amnesia, 326
Amputation, 91n. *See also* Lost limbs

Index